Professional ASP.NET Web Services with VB.NET

Russ Basiura
Mike Batongbacal
Brandon Bohling
Mike Clark
Andreas Eide
Robert Eisenberg
Kevin Hoffman
Brian Loesgen
Chris Miller
Matthew Reynolds
Bill Sempf
Srinivasa Sivakumar

with contributions from
Don Lee

Wrox Press Ltd. ®

Professional ASP.NET Web Services with VB.NET

Trademark Acknowledgments

wrox

Published by Wrox Press Ltd,
Arden House, 1102 Warwick Road, Acocks Green,
Birmingham, B27 6BH, UK
Printed in the United States
ISBN 1-86100-775-2

Credits

Authors
Russ Basiura
Mike Batongbacal
Brandon Bohling
Mike Clark
Andreas Eide
Robert Eisenberg
Kevin Hoffman
Brian Loesgen
Chris Miller
Matt Reynolds
Bill Sempf
Srinivasa Sivakumar

Code Conversion
Don Lee

Commissioning Editor
Daniel Kent

Lead Technical Editor
Matthew Cumberlidge

Technical Editor
Douglas Paterson

Managing Editor
Louay Fatoohi

Author Agent
Charlotte Smith

Index
Andrew Criddle
John Collin
Fiona Murray

Technical Reviewers
Kenneth Avellino
Maxime Bombardier
Andreas Christiansen
Robert Eisenberg
Jeannine Gailey
John Godfrey
Mark R Harrison
Mark Horner
Erik Hougaard
Tom Kern
Don Lee
Dianna Leech
Craig McQueen
Frank Miller
Arun Nair
Christophe Nasarre
Johan Normén
Matthew Rabinowitz
Larry Schoeneman
David Schultz
Trevor Scott
Bill Sempf
Keyur Shah
Marc H. Simkin
John Timney
Konstantinos Vlassis

Production Team Leader
Abbie Forletta

Production Assistant
Sarah Hall

Cover
Natalie O'Donnell

Proof Reader
Dev Lunsford

About the Authors

Russ Basiura

Russ is an independent consultant and founder of RJB Technical Consulting, Inc. (http://www.rjbtech.com), a web security firm and a Microsoft Certified Solution Provider and Security Partner located in the US, Russ specializes in the design and development of integration solutions that enable business partners to exchange confidential information and conduct business securely and efficiently across the Internet. Many of his solutions have used Microsoft technologies to integrate authentication and authorization processes between heterogeneous applications seamlessly. Russ can be contacted at russ@rjbtech.com.

Russ would like to say thank you to his wife Darlene and their beautiful children, Rachel, Lauren, and Joseph for all their love and support.

Mike Batongbacal

Mike Batongbacal caught the technology bug in the early 1980's when he started developing software for the original IBM PC. Since then, he's forged a successful career as a technology consultant developing n-tiered systems using Microsoft technologies such as Visual Basic, ASP, COM+, SQL Server, and, most recently, the .NET platform. He has presented at various events and conferences including Microsoft Tech Ed and MSDN Technical Briefings. Mike is currently the E-Business Practice Lead for Magenic Technologies, one of the nation's premiere Microsoft Gold Certified Partners dedicated to solving today's business problems using Microsoft tools and technologies.

I wish to thank God for giving me this opportunity to share my passion for technology with others through this book. Much gratitude goes out to my wife, Norma, as well. I couldn't have accomplished this without her love and encouragement. You've put up with a lot, baby. This book is for you!

To my family and friends, I apologize for my self-imposed exile while I wrote this book. Yes, I'm alive! And I intend to spend time with you all again.

Brandon Bohling

Brandon Bohling is a software engineer for Intel Corporation in Phoenix, Arizona. He has been developing ASP-based web sites since its creation, which is quite different from teaching middle school kids in Ackley, Iowa, which he did in a previous life. Now he has fully embraced the .NET technologies and is devoted to spreading his knowledge. When no one wants to listen to his .NET ramblings, he escapes to the outdoors with his wife and two dogs.

Mike Clark

Mike is currently working in the UK for Lucin as Senior Analyst. Having been responsible for the design and implementation of www.salcentral.com (Web Services brokerage) and www.webservicewatch he has been involved in grass roots Web Service development for over two years. Having been predominantly involved in Microsoft Windows development over the last eigth years his main expertise lies in his ability to quickly adapt his technique to current project requirements and his still enthusiastic approach to all development.

Andreas Eide

Andreas Eide has a Master of Science degree from the Norwegian Institute of Technology in Trondheim. He has been working as a developer and software architect for the past eight years. Andreas is an MCSD, MCT, and is also MSDN Regional Director and a regular speaker at seminars and conferences.

When not writing books and speaking about software, Andreas makes his living as a principal consultant for Objectware. Objectware is a Norwegian consulting company focusing on component-based development using .NET and Java based technologies.

Andreas thanks Maria, Kristine, and Grete for their patience during the time he worked on this book.

You can contact Andreas at andreas.eide@objectware.no.

Robert Eisenberg

Robert Eisenberg is currently an independent consultant specializing in Web Services. In 1999 he was the CEO and cofounder of an e-commerce consulting firm that was acquired by Framfab Inc., the largest Internet Professional Services firm in Europe. Prior to that, as a consultant he was in charge of many production systems for Ocular Science Inc., one of the largest manufacturers of contact lenses in the world. Prior to that he ran a computer consulting firm working with many companies including Pacific Bell, the Federal Reserve Bank, and Cushman & Wakefield. He has written for DevX and spoken on .NET at Microsoft and at local user groups.

Kevin Hoffman

Kevin Hoffman is a software technology junkie who is currently eating and breathing anything and everything that has to do with the .NET Framework. He started programming in BASIC on a Commodore VIC-20 that his grandfather had repaired after being found in the trash, and has been a tech addict ever since, working at everything from nationwide UNIX mainframe support to being a Software Engineer for one of the most popular e-commerce web sites on the Internet. Recently he has found that he loves to write and teach about programming as much as he loves doing it himself.

I would like to dedicate my work for this book to my mother Marie, who has always been a treasured source of infinite love and support. Also I would like to dedicate my work to my brother Kurt and sister-in-law Nina who have both always been encouraging and supportive.

Brian Loesgen

Brian Loesgen is a San Diego-based independent consultant, with extensive experience in advanced enterprise and mobile solutions. Brian utilizes his expertise to translate new, leading-edge technologies into real-world value. He is a co-author of the *Professional XML*, *Professional ASP/XML*, *Professional Windows DNA*, and *Professional ASP.NET Web Services* books from Wrox. In addition, Brian has written technical white papers for Intel, Microsoft, and others. Brian is a frequent speaker at major technical conferences worldwide. Brian is a co-founder of, and currently serves on the Board of Directors of the International .NET Association (ineta.org). He co-leads the San Diego .NET user group, and leads the San Diego Software Industry Council Web Services SIG.

In his spare moments, Brian enjoys outdoor activities such as cycling, hiking in the mountains, kayaking, camping in the desert, or going to the beach with his wife Miriam and children Steven and Melissa.

Brian can be reached at bloesgen@msn.com.

Chris Miller

Christopher L. Miller is a consultant with Crossoft Inc. (www.crossoft.com), where he specializes in intranet development. His current projects include financial and document management intranet applications, as well as an extensible intranet package called Quicktranet (www.quicktranet.com). Serving as the .NET User Group president in Pittsburgh, PA, Christopher is working to bring the awareness and understanding of this revolutionary new platform to light (www.pghdotnet.org).

He began developing with Visual Basic with version 1.0 (the DOS version) in 1991, making the tough conversion from QuickBASIC. Since 1992, VB has been his primary development language (although admittedly, C# is gaining quickly). An ASP developer since 1997, Christopher began making the switch to ASP.NET in early 2000.

With the support of his wife, Stacy, and his cat, Jones (who never cares to visit with him until he's working on a book), Christopher has spent countless hours working toward Microsoft certifications and other technical accomplishments. After several months of seemingly around-the-clock work, he vows to spend more time with his family this fall...with the usual allowances for enjoying some (American) football and hockey.

Matt Reynolds

After working with Wrox Press on a number of projects since 1999, Matthew Reynolds is now an in-house author for Wrox Press writing about and working with virtually all aspects of Microsoft .NET. He's also a regular contributor to Wrox's ASPToday and C#Today, and Web Services Architect. He lives and works in North London and can be reached on matthewr@wrox.com.

Bill Sempf

Bill Sempf is co-author of *Professional VB.Net* from Wrox Press. He is an experienced Internet strategist with a ten-year track record of using technology to help organizations accomplish specific business objectives. A Microsoft Certified Professional, Certified Internet Business Strategist, and member of the International Webmaster's Association, Bill has built nearly one hundred dynamic webs for startups and Fortune 50 companies alike.

Currently, Bill is a Senior Consultant at Paros Business Partners, and owner of Products Of Innovative New Technology. He has written several articles on COM, COM+, and .NET technologies for *TechRepublic*, *Internet.com,* and *Inside Web Development Journal.* Web Services are rapidly becoming a passion of Bill's and he is quite certain they are going to be the Next Big Thing. Bill can be reached at bill@sempf.net.

Thanks to Wrox for keeping these quality books on the shelf, and keeping these quality authors in work. Thanks to all my friends, family and fellow programmers for their support.

To my wife Gabrielle for helping with four projects and a book going on all at once: your love, support and strength go a long way toward keeping me sane. Thank you.

Srinivasa Sivakumar

Srinivasa Sivakumar is a software consultant, developer, and writer. He specializes in web and Mobile technologies using Microsoft solutions. He currently works in Chicago for TransTech, Inc. He also writes technical articles for ASPToday.com, CSharpToday.com, .NET Developer, and so on. In his free time he likes to watch Tamil movies and listen to Tamil sound tracks (especially ones sung by Mr. S.P Balasubramaniyam).

I'd like to dedicate my section of the book to my beloved mother Mrs. Rajam Sathyanarayanan. Mother, thanks a lot for everything that you've done for me and I've no way of paying back the wonderful things that you've given me. And also I'd like to thank my wife Annapoorna, my daughter Sruthi and (-3) month old junior.

Professional
ASP.NET
Web
Services

Table of Contents

Professional
ASP.NET
Web
Services

Introduction

Web Services are being hailed as a leap forward in distributed computing. Web Services evangelists foresee a future where functionality can be programmatically discovered and accessed over the Internet, as and when it is required. Of course, some commentators disagree, seeing Web Services as nothing more than a standardized iteration of older distributed computing systems.

Whether or not we see Web Services as a big step or a small evolution, we must all agree that they are generating a lot of interest. The technologies and standards behind Web Services are being adopted by a wide range of companies in the computing industry. At the forefront of the drive for acceptance of these standards are IBM, Sun Microsystems, and Microsoft.

IBM and Sun have chosen Java as their preferred development platform for Web Services, providing tools and support to Java Web Services developers. Microsoft initially provided tools to allow Visual Basic and Active Server Pages developers to begin creating Web Services. With the latest incarnation of Active Server Pages, ASP.NET, Microsoft has fully embraced Web Services, building Web Service functionality into the system itself.

ASP.NET makes exposing functionality through a Web Service very straightforward. That is not to say, however, that there is little to learn about developing Web Services in ASP.NET. Although Web Services can be seen as an evolution of previous distributed computing standards, they do have new considerations which must be taken into account if we are to harness their full potential.

What Does This Book Cover?

In this book, we aim to give a solid grounding in the technologies that underpin Web Services and the specifics of developing Web Services with ASP.NET.

Introducing Web Services

We start by introducing Web Services. We look at what Web Services are in **Chapter 1** and show how to implement and consume a basic Web Service with ASP.NET in **Chapters 2 and 3**.

Web Services Standards

We then take a closer look at the standards that Web Services rely on to operate. **Chapter 4** examines WSDL (Web Service Description Language), the language that allows Web Services to be accurately described.

Chapter 5 investigates SOAP (Simple Object Access Protocol), which allows clients to communicate with the Web Services they consume. Then, in **Chapter 6**, we look at how we can harness the Extensibility of SOAP to augment its functionality.

Chapter 7 looks at the important Web Services concept of Discovery and shows how we can harness the power of UDDI (Universal Description, Discovery and Integration).

Web Services Techniques

The bulk of the book is taken up with detailed discussions of the various techniques and considerations that will be important in developing Web Services. We open this section with **Chapter 8**, an overview of the design considerations that Web Services introduce.

In **Chapter 9**, we compare synchronous and asynchronous Web Services and show the additional coding required to build asynchronous services.

The concept of a 'stateful' Web Service is considered in **Chapter 10**, along with the architectural questions that this idea raises.

Chapter 11 looks at Transactions and how we can use them in our Web Services.

In **Chapter 12,** we show how caching can increase the performance and scalability of Web Services.

Chapters 13 and 14 consider the topic of security, demonstrating how to build Web Services that authenticate their users, and explaining how SOAP allows secure communications with Web Services.

In **Chapter 15**, we look at some practical uses of Web Services – exposing data from a variety of data sources.

Chapter 16 rounds off the techniques and design considerations section with an analysis of what Web Services could mean for your business.

Case Studies

Chapter 17 is a case study in which Web Services are orchestrated with BizTalk.

We present another case study in **Chapter 18**, this time seeing how we can use Web Services to create a reusable authentication framework.

Our final case study, in **Chapter 19**, examines a system in which processing of a demanding task is distributed to a number of machines, coordinated by a Web Service.

Appendices

In **Appendix A**, we take a peek at one of the biggest current Web Services projects – .NET My Services, in which Microsoft plans to offer a wide range of functionality through Web Services.

Appendix B looks at the Web Service behavior for Internet Explorer 5.5 +, which allows recent versions of Internet Explorer to access Web Services.

Who Is This Book for?

This book is aimed at ASP.NET programmers who want solid information about building Web Services. It does not cover the basics of ASP.NET – we assume readers have read *Professional ASP.NET* or have a similar level of knowledge before they read this book. This allows us to concentrate on providing as much valuable information specific to creating Web Services as possible.

Why VB.NET?

The code samples in this book are all in VB.NET. We have included some C# code in the early chapters that deal with the syntax for defining Web Services, in order to highlight the differences between VB.NET and C#. We decided that including a single language in the book would increase clarity and allow us to fit more material in.

What You Need To Use this Book

To run the samples in this book you need to have the following:

- Windows 2000 or Windows XP.
- ASP.NET.
- Some examples illustrate the use of Visual Studio .NET for some tasks – the ASP.NET code presented does not require Visual Studio .NET.
- Some examples use SQL Server for their database storage.

The complete source code for the samples is available for download from our web site at http://www.wrox.com/Books/Book_Details.asp?isbn=1861007752.

Conventions

We've used a number of different styles of text and layout in this book to help differentiate between different kinds of information. Following are examples of the styles we used and an explanation of what they mean.

Code has several fonts. If it's a word that we're talking about in the text – for example, when discussing a `For...Next` loop, it's in this font.

If it's a block of code that can be typed as a program and run, then it is placed in a gray box:

```
<?xml version 1.0?>
```

Sometimes we'll see code in a mixture of styles, like this:

```
<?xml version 1.0?>
<Invoice>
   <part>
      <name>Widget</name>
      <price>$10.00</price>
   </part>
</invoice>
```

In cases like this, the code with a white background is code we are already familiar with; the line highlighted in gray is a new addition to the code since we last looked at it.

There are occasions in this book that you will type code at a command line; in many cases you can just copy what you see. However, sometimes the line of code may carry onto the next line, due to the width of the page: in this case, we have included a continuation character, '↴', at the end of the line showing that the line should be entered continuously and unbroken, as follows:

```
vbc /out:SimpleLibrary1.dll /t:library SimpleClass1.vb ↴
    /r:System.Runtime.Remoting.dll
```

Advice, hints, and background information come in this type of font.

Important pieces of information come in boxes like this.

Bullets appear indented, with each new bullet marked as follows:

- **Important Words** are in a bold type font.
- Words that appear on the screen, or in menus like File or Window, are in this similar font to the one you would see on a Windows desktop.
- Keys that you press on the keyboard, like *Ctrl* and *Enter*, are in italics.

Customer Support

We always value hearing from our readers, and we want to know what you think about this book: what you liked, what you didn't like, and what you think we can do better next time. You can send us your comments, either by returning the reply card in the back of the book, or by e-mail to feedback@wrox.com. Please be sure to mention the book title in your message.

How To Download the Sample Code for the Book

When you visit the Wrox site, http://www.wrox.com/, simply locate the title through our Search facility, or by using one of the title lists. Click on Download in the Code column, or on Download Code on the book's detail page.

The files that are available for download from our site have been archived using WinZip. When you have saved the attachments to a folder on your hard drive, you need to extract the files using a de-compression program such as WinZip or PKUnzip. When you extract the files, the code is usually extracted into chapter folders. When you start the extraction process, ensure that your software (WinZip, PKUnzip, etc.) is set to use folder names.

Errata

We've made every effort to make sure that there are no errors in the text or in the code. However, no one is perfect and mistakes do occur. If you find an error in one of our books, such as a spelling mistake or a faulty piece of code, we would be very grateful for feedback. By sending in errata you may save another reader hours of frustration, and of course, you will be helping us provide even higher quality information. Simply e-mail the information to support@wrox.com, your information will be checked and if correct, posted to the errata page for that title, or used in subsequent editions of the book.

To find errata on the web site, go to http://www.wrox.com/, and simply locate the title through our Advanced Search or title list. Click on the Book Errata link, which is below the cover graphic on the book's detail page.

E-mail Support

If you wish to directly query a problem in the book with an expert who knows the book in detail then e-mail support@wrox.com, with the title of the book and the last four numbers of the ISBN in the subject field of the e-mail. A typical e-mail should include the following things:

- The **title of the book**, **last four digits of the ISBN**, and **page number** of the problem in the Subject field.
- Your **name**, **contact information**, and the **problem** in the body of the message.

We *won't* send you junk mail. We need the details to save your time and ours. When you send an e-mail message, it will go through the following chain of support:

- Customer Support – Your message is delivered to our customer support staff, who are the first people to read it. They have files on most frequently asked questions and will answer anything general about the book or the web site immediately.
- Editorial – Deeper queries are forwarded to the technical editor responsible for that book. They have experience with the programming language or particular product, and are able to answer detailed technical questions on the subject.
- The Authors – Finally, in the unlikely event that the editor cannot answer your problem, he or she will forward the request to the author. We do try to protect the author from any distractions to their writing; however, we are quite happy to forward specific requests to them. All Wrox authors help with the support on their books. They will e-mail the customer and the editor with their response, and again all readers should benefit.

The Wrox support process can only offer support to issues that are directly pertinent to the content of our published title. Support for questions that fall outside the scope of normal book support, is provided via the community lists of our http://p2p.wrox.com/forum.

p2p.wrox.com

For author and peer discussion, join the P2P mailing lists. Our unique system provides **programmer to programmer**™ contact on mailing lists, forums, and newsgroups, all in addition to our one-to-one e-mail support system. If you post a query to P2P, you can be confident that it is being examined by the many Wrox authors and other industry experts who are present on our mailing lists. At p2p.wrox.com you will find a number of different lists that will help you not only while you read this book, but also as you develop your own applications. Particularly appropriate to this book are the `aspx` and `aspx_professional` lists.

To subscribe to a mailing list just follow these steps:

1. Go to http://p2p.wrox.com/.
2. Choose the appropriate category from the left menu bar.
3. Click on the mailing list you wish to join.
4. Follow the instructions to subscribe and fill in your e-mail address and password.
5. Reply to the confirmation e-mail you receive.
6. Use the subscription manager to join more lists and set your e-mail preferences.

Why This System Offers the Best Support

You can choose to join the mailing lists or you can receive them as a weekly digest. If you don't have the time, or facility, to receive the mailing list, then you can search our online archives. Junk and spam mails are deleted, and your own e-mail address is protected by the unique Lyris system. Queries about joining or leaving lists, and any other general queries about lists, should be sent to listsupport@p2p.wrox.com.

Professional
ASP.NET
Web
Services
ROFESSIONAL ASP.NET
Web Services
ROFESSIONAL ASP.NET
Web Services
ROFESSIONAL ASP.NET
Web Services
ROFESSIONAL ASP.NET
Web Services
ROFESSIONAL ASP.NET
Web Services
ROFESSIONAL ASP.NET
Web Services
ROFESSIONAL ASP.NET
Web Services
ROFESSIONAL ASP.NET
Web Services
ROFESSIONAL ASP.NET
Web Services
ROFESSIONAL ASP.NET
Web Services
ROFESSIONAL ASP.NET
Web Services
ROFESSIONAL ASP.NET
Web Services
ROFESSIONAL ASP.NET
Web Services
ROFESSIONAL ASP.NET
Web Services
ROFESSIONAL ASP.NET
Web Services
ROFESSIONAL ASP.NET
Web Services
ROFESSIONAL ASP.NET
Web Services
ROFESSIONAL ASP.NET
Web Services
ROFESSIONAL ASP.NET
Web Services
ROFESSIONAL ASP.NET
Web Services
ROFESSIONAL ASP.NET
Web Services
ROFESSIONAL ASP.NET
Web Services
ROFESSIONAL ASP.NET
Web Services
ROFESSIONAL ASP.NET

1

Web Services

Have you ever wondered what you could accomplish as a programmer if every business function ever written became available to your new application by simply adding a reference to it? What if all these functions could be discovered and used at run time? What if you could be part of a new multi-billion dollar market? The marketers of the latest 'revolutionary' technology claim that Web Services make all this possible.

Every time there is a shift in the way we build software, there is a lot of hype and confusion. We are already seeing the term "Web Service" being misused by marketing people and put on many products having little or nothing to do with Web Service technologies and protocols.

In this chapter, we will try to cut through the hype and describe exactly what Web Services are and why we need them. We'll also explain how ASP.NET makes it easy for us to build and use Web Services and when it is best to use them.

When going through a shift, it is always useful to look back and learn from history. Two of the major shifts in software development over the last couple of decades have been the development of object-oriented programming and component technology.

Object-oriented programming joined the mainstream in the early 80s. Many saw object-oriented programming as the solution to the software crisis that resulted from the increasing complexity and size of the software being built. Most projects were late and over budget, and the end result was often unreliable. The promise of object-orientation was that by structuring your code into objects that map to other objects in the solution domain, you would get code that was reusable and easily maintainable. Object-oriented programming has improved software quality, but software projects are still often over budget and late.

The 1990s saw the birth of component technology. Visual Basic is now ten years old, but it was revolutionary in many ways. It allows developers to build Windows applications by dragging controls onto a form. In 1995 people were talking about how component technology would make it possible to build applications by assembling components. Component reuse has turned out to be most commercially successful in the building of user interfaces. Component evangelists also talked about a market for reusable business components, but third-party business components as a market has not lived up to its promise. Sites such as www.ComponentSource.com list thousands of GUI and general-purpose components but finding business components is hard, because business logic is often extremely complex and company-specific.

Alongside the evolution of programming models, the Internet grew from a playground for universities and academics to a network reaching out to most corners of the world. The Internet has clearly had a major impact on society and our industry in particular.

In many ways, Web Services can be seen as an extension of the component model to the Internet, as essentially a Web Service is application logic that is accessible over the Internet. Many of the promises of Web Services are the same as those of component technology. Web Services will allow us to assemble applications from pre-built application logic available somewhere on the Internet. Similarly, Web Services will solve many problems we encounter when trying to build reusable application logic and building applications that span the Internet.

Once again, many promote Web Services as the new silver bullet that will revolutionize the way we build software. However, looking back over the last decade or two, we know that there is no such thing as a silver bullet.

In this chapter we will look with objective eyes at the "why", "what", and "how" of Web Services with ASP.NET. Specifically, we will look at:

- Why we need Web Services. What problems do Web Services solve?
- What a Web Service is. What are the standards and technologies behind Web Services?
- How ASP.NET can help you implement Web Services.

This chapter will give you a high-level perspective on the various Web Service standards and how ASP.NET implements them. Later chapters in this book will go into this in much greater detail.

Component-Based Distributed Computing and Web Services

To fully understand the impact of Web Services, you need an understanding of distributed computing. So before we go into the details of Web Services, let's see some background on component-based distributed computing.

Distributed computing is the partitioning of application logic into units that are physically distributed among two or more computers in a network. The idea of distributed computing has been around a long time and numerous communication technologies have been developed to allow the distribution and reuse of application logic.

There are many reasons for distributing application logic:

- Distributed computing makes it possible to link different organizations and organizational units.
- Often the data accessed by the application is on a different machine. The application logic should be close to the data.
- Distributed application logic may be reused in several applications. Pieces of a distributed application may be upgraded without upgrading the whole application.
- By distributing the application logic, the load is spread out to different machines, giving potentially better performance.
- As new needs arise, application logic may be redistributed or reconnected.
- It is easier to scale one layer than it is to scale a whole application. If, for example, the data layer isn't fast enough, more resources can be added to this layer without affecting the entire application.

The Internet has increased the importance and applicability of distributed computing. The simplicity and ubiquity of the Internet makes it a logical choice as the backbone for distributed applications.

The dominant protocols in component-based distributed computing are **CORBA** (Common Object Request Broker Architecture) from the Object Management Group and Microsoft's **DCOM** (Distributed Component Object Model). Although CORBA and DCOM have a lot in common, they differ in the details, making it hard to get the protocols to interoperate.

The following table summarizes some similarities and differences between CORBA, DCOM, and Web Services and introduces a slew of acronyms.

Characteristic	**CORBA**	**DCOM**	**Web Services**
Remote Procedure Call (RPC) mechanism	Internet Inter-ORB Protocol (IIOP)	Distributed Computing Environment Remote Procedure Call (DCE-RPC)	Simple Object Access Protocol (SOAP)
Encoding	Common Data Representation (CDR)	Network Data Representation (NDR)	Extensible Markup Language (XML)
Interface description	Interface Definition Language (IDL)	Interface Definition Language (IDL)	Web Service Description Language (WSDL)
Discovery	Naming service and trading service	Registry	Universal Discovery Description and Integration (UDDI)
Firewall friendly	No	No	Yes
Complexity of protocols	High	High	Low
Cross-platform	Partly	No	Yes

Both CORBA and DCOM allow the invocation of remote objects. CORBA uses a protocol called Internet Inter-ORB Protocol (IIOP); DCOM uses a variation on OSF's (Open Software Foundation) DCE-RPC. The encoding of data in CORBA is based on a format named Common Data Representation (CDR). In DCOM, the encoding of data is based on a similar but incompatible format named Network Data Representation (NDR).

DCOM is often described as 'COM with a longer wire'. In the code, a developer does not need to do anything special to invoke a remote object. The code to call a remote object is the same as the code to invoke a local object. This is known as **location transparency**. This is accomplished by using surrogate objects on both the client and on the server. On the client side the surrogate is called a **proxy**. The proxy has the same interface as the real object. On the server side, there is a surrogate for the client called a **stub**. The stub invokes the real object. CORBA uses the same concept, but the terminology is different. The proxy in CORBA is confusingly called a stub and the stub is called a skeleton.

The figure below shows a high-level view of what happens when a DCOM client calls a method on a DCOM server (the figure is similar in the case of CORBA):

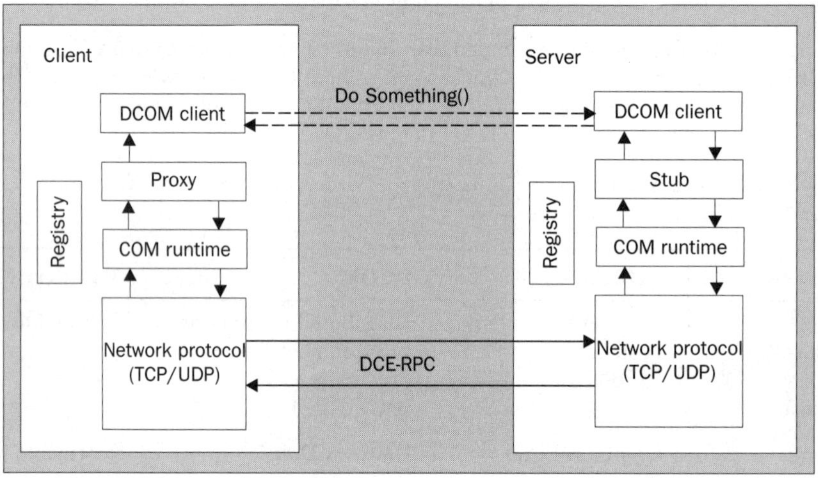

The DCOM client calls the `DoSomething()` method on the remote object. The method is actually a call to the proxy. The proxy encodes the data into the data representation of DCOM and sends the message to the server using a network protocol. On the server side, the stub decodes the data and calls the actual method on the DCOM server. The same happens in reverse when returning the result from the server to the client.

Every object has one or more interfaces and is only callable on an interface. To use an interface, a description of it is needed. As shown in the table, both COM and CORBA use an Interface Definition Language (IDL) to describe the interface. COM and CORBA use different IDLs but they are very similar. The IDL serves as a contract between the server and its clients. IDL is independent of the programming languages used to implement the client and the server.

One thing to note about DCOM is that it is **connection-oriented**. The DCOM client holds on to a connection to the DCOM server. While holding the connection the client may make multiple calls to the DCOM server. The connection-oriented nature of DCOM gives a lot of flexibility; the server may hold state on behalf of the client, it may call back to the client, raise events to notify the client, and so on. However, there are technical issues with this. The client may hold on to the reference and only make calls when, for example, the user hits a button. For large periods of time, the server is idle waiting for requests from the client. What happens if the client crashes and will never use the server again? Alternatively, imagine an Internet scenario where the DCOM or CORBA server is used by thousands of clients. Since each client has a connection to the server, valuable server resources may be reserved for a client that seldom uses the server or even no longer exists.

Although DCOM has ways to deal with these problems, it all adds up to a great deal of complexity, which is one of the problems Web Services attempts to solve. Let's now look closer at some of the benefits of Web Services.

Why Web Services?

Web Services are interesting from several perspectives. From a technological perspective, Web Services try to solve some problems faced when using tightly-coupled technologies such as CORBA and DCOM. These are problems such as getting through firewalls, the complexities of the protocols, and integrating heterogeneous platforms.

Web Services are also interesting from an organizational and economic perspective, as they open up doors for new ways of doing business and dealing with organization issues.

Web Services as a Better Distributed Component Technology

DCOM and CORBA are fine for building enterprise applications with software running on the same platform and in the same closely administered local network. They are not fine, however, for building applications that span platforms, span the Internet, and need to achieve Internet scalability; they were simply not designed for this purpose.

This is where Web Services come in. Web Services represent the next logical step in the evolution of component-based distributed technologies. Some key features are:

- Web Services are loosely coupled to the clients. A client makes a request to a Web Service, the Web Service returns the result and the connection is closed. There is no permanent connection, and none of the complexity mentioned above.
- The Web Service may extend its interface; add new methods and parameters without affecting the clients, as long as it still services the old methods and parameters.
- Web Services are stateless: they do not hold on to state on behalf of the client. This makes it easy to scale up and out to many clients and use a server farm to serve the Web Services. The underlying HTTP protocol used by Web Services is also stateless. It is possible to achieve some state handling with Web Services the same way it is possible on the web today using techniques such as cookies.

Many of the concepts from DCOM and CORBA have their offspring in Web Services. That is not surprising since they try to solve the same problem: how to make calls to remote objects.

- The foundation of Web Services is **SOAP**, the **Simple Object Access Protocol**. SOAP is much simpler to implement than DCOM and CORBA. DCOM is Microsoft-specific, CORBA is used by many other vendors. SOAP is based on open Internet protocols such as HTTP and bridges the gap between Microsoft and the rest.
- For serialization, DCOM and CORBA are based on complex formats. The serialization format for Web Services is based on **XML** and the **XML schema** specification. XML is simple, extensible, and readable, and XML has already reached wide acceptance and adoption.
- Where DCOM and CORBA use IDL to describe interfaces, Web Services use the **Web Service Description Language**, **WSDL**. WSDL is more flexible and is richer than IDL.

The figure below shows a Web Service being consumed by a client. The client may be a web application, another Web Service, an application such as Microsoft Word, and so on.

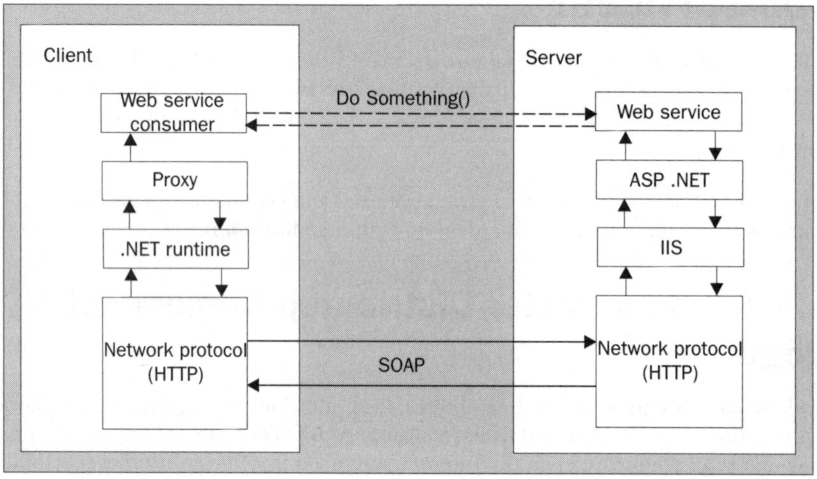

The Web Service consumer calls a method called `DoSomething()` on the Web Service. This is illustrated by the dotted lines. The actual call travels down the layers, over the network as a SOAP message, and up the layers to the Web Service. The Web Service executes, and the response (if any) travels back.

The figure above shows the ASP.NET way of doing Web Services. Web Services are implemented differently on different platforms. The crucial point is that what goes on the wire accords to standards.

The figure above looks similar to the DCOM figure we saw earlier. In both cases the client uses a proxy as a surrogate for the real object. Also note that the DCOM figure is more symmetrical than the Web Service figure.

There is a provider/consumer relationship between the client and the server in the case of Web Services. The server cannot call back to the client. The client does not host a web server. The client may in some cases be another Web Service where there is a web server. Nevertheless, the service being called does not have a reference to the client, and so cannot raise events back to the client. In this respect, tightly-coupled protocols such as DCOM/CORBA are more powerful (but also more expensive) than Web Services.

It is possible to implement two-way notifications from the Web Service back to the client or publish/subscribe functionality, but it must be done manually. The client can implement its own Web Service and pass a reference to this Web Service in the call to the server. The server may store this reference, and then it can call back to the client.

Firewalls – Beating the System Administrator?

Firewalls are put into place for good reasons: to stop intruders from getting into your network and to stop unwanted traffic out from the local network. Such tight security comes at a cost: it can block legitimate traffic. Getting firewalls configured properly to get DCOM and IIOP traffic through can be difficult because of both political and technical reasons. The problem with accessing objects through firewalls is not just a problem when using the Internet. It can also bite you when you are working within the boundaries of an organization.

The only thing that almost always gets through firewalls is HTTP traffic on ports 80 and 443. The designers of the SOAP protocol learned the lessons of DCOM and IIOP and decided to standardize the use of HTTP for object invocation.

> **SOAP uses HTTP as its communication protocol so method calls will be able to pass through firewalls.**

It is still possible to use the firewall to block SOAP traffic. This is possible since the HTTP header of a SOAP message identifies the message as a SOAP message, and an administrator may configure the firewall to stop SOAP traffic by looking at the header. For business-to-business scenarios, the firewall may only allow SOAP traffic from selected ranges of IP addresses.

The 'S' in SOAP Means Simple

Even though DCOM has location transparency and the programs need not contain any special DCOM code, getting a DCOM system up and running and keeping it running is not trivial. Getting through the firewall is one issue; there are other issues as well. The DCOM servers must be registered on the client. When the server is modified, the clients' code must be updated with new proxies. Getting the security settings correct to get all this to work requires a master's degree in distributed computing.

When implementing DCOM and CORBA you need to rely on existing implementations of the DCOM and CORBA infrastructure. It is not practically feasible to implement the protocols yourself. SOAP, however, is much more lightweight, it is simple and relatively low tech. A SOAP server can be implemented using generally available XML parsers and HTTP servers in a matter of days.

A Multi-Everything World

The reality for most businesses is that they have a multitude of platforms from different vendors. They may have a system running on IBM AS/400 for their back-office applications, the CRM system may run on UNIX servers, and the new e-commerce application may run on Windows 2000. As new systems are acquired, the old systems are not replaced. Instead the new systems need to integrate with the old systems, and if you need to integrate with business partners, it is very likely that their system is different from yours.

The problem with DCOM and CORBA is that you are basically stuck with a single vendor. If you are using DCOM you have to use Microsoft Windows to run your servers and clients. Although there are implementations of DCOM on other platforms, they are not widely adopted. Despite the fact that CORBA is a specification implemented by several vendors, interoperability is only achieved in simple cases. Not to speak of integrating DCOM and CORBA...

> **Web Services, however, are based on open standards and can be used on any platform. They have the potential to be an integration technology that will work across platforms and vendors. It is still too early to say if this will be the reality, though.**

If you are running your components in a tightly controlled environment where the platform is the same and the servers are directly connected, CORBA and DCOM are perfectly fine technologies to use. If your web server needs to use components on an application server, using DCOM will be more efficient than using Web Service technologies. The .NET Framework also has a new technology, .NET Remoting, which is to be used in such controlled environments. Remoting is the successor to DCOM on the .NET platform. If you want to know more about Remoting, you can read *Professional C# Web Services* (ISBN 1-86100-499-0) also by Wrox, which covers Web Services with .NET Remoting.

Centralization of Information

When using the Internet you often enter personal information, such as address information, in a large number of different places. Information is scattered all over the web in different applications and different databases. This information is always out of sync. What happens if you move to a new house? The address information is outdated in a large number of places. A related problem is all the different usernames and passwords you need to keep track of.

Another scenario: how many places do you need to enter the telephone numbers of your colleagues and friends? I have some information in my cell phone, some in Microsoft Outlook, and some on my Pocket PC. They store different information, have different formats, and are always out of sync. Web Services can facilitate the centralization of data. Imagine a central registry where you can update your personal information and then all you need to do is allow the e-commerce site access to your central data.

Microsoft has set out to create this central registry in its .NET My Services initiative, although its plans for rolling out the service have been considerably scaled back from initial projections. Rather than a truly centralized global initiative, Microsoft has announced that they will concentrate on implementing .NET My Services on a per-enterprise basis. .NET My Services is built around the already established Passport service, a single sign-on authentication service. Passport already has a large number of users, primarily because the popular Hotmail and MSN services use Passport for all its users.

Based around the Passport user identity, Microsoft has announced a series of personal services. These services are general-purpose services that you can take advantage of in your applications to provide greater personalization and customization. They include:

- .NET Calendar – central calendar and tasks
- .NET Profile – central storage of your name, nickname, special dates and pictures
- .NET Documents – central document storage
- .NET Alerts – central management of notification subscriptions and routing
- .NET Contacts – central address book
- .NET Inbox – central inbox for e-mail, voice mail, etc.

Appendix A covers .NET My Services in detail.

Making Money with Web Services

A new technology is doomed if it does not give new opportunities for the people concerned with making money. From a business person's perspective, Web Services open up new possibilities:

- By centralizing information and services, new payment structures may be used. The user of a Web Service can pay a subscription fee for using the service. One example may be the news feed from Associated Press. Another possibility is 'pay per view'. A provider of a credit verification service, for instance, may charge per request.
- Web Services enable real-time interaction and collaboration. Today, data is typically replicated and used locally. Web Services enable real-time queries to remote data. An example is an e-commerce site selling computer games. The e-commerce site may hook up to a warehouse to get the number of items in stock in real time. This enables the e-commerce site to provide a better service. Nothing is more frustrating than buying something over the Internet just to learn the next day that the product you wanted is out of stock.
- There is a potential for aggregated services. An aggregated service may aggregate different types of services including other Web Services, screen-scraped web sites, access services exposed using proprietary protocols, and so on. A typical example of an aggregated service is a comparative service giving you the best deal on products. Another type of service is one that groups related services. Someone could provide us with a service that can update our address at the post office, find the transportation company to move all our stuff, etc.

In this section, we touched on some of the possibilities exposed by Web Services. Web Services are by no means the only technology that can provide these solutions. Many similar solutions are available today using existing technology. However, Web Services have the momentum and standards to make these kinds of services generally available.

Web Services have the potential to fulfill the promise of component technology by vitalizing the market for reusable business components or services. Since Web Services will be run by the provider of the service, they can do many things that locally installed components cannot do.

What are Web Services?

The term 'Web Service' opens the door to confusion. Is a hosted solution provided through the Internet a Web Service? What about software that is downloaded from the Internet when needed, is that a Web Service?

In this book, we will use the following definition of the term 'Web Service':

> **A Web Service is application logic accessible to programs via standard web protocols in a platform-independent way.**

Let's break up this definition:

- **Application logic** – a Web Service exposes some application logic or code. This code can do calculations, it can do database look-ups, anything a computer program can do.
- **Accessible to programs** – whereas most web sites today are accessed by humans using a web browser, Web Services will be accessed by computer programs.
- **Standard web protocols** – the whole concept of Web Services is based on a set of web standards such as HTTP, XML, SOAP, WSDL, and UDDI. These will be discussed later in this chapter.
- **Platform independent** – Web Services can be implemented on any platform. The standard protocols are not proprietary to a single vendor, and are supported by all major vendors.

A Web Service is accessed by a program. The program may be a web application, a Windows application, or any type of application as indicated in the figure below:

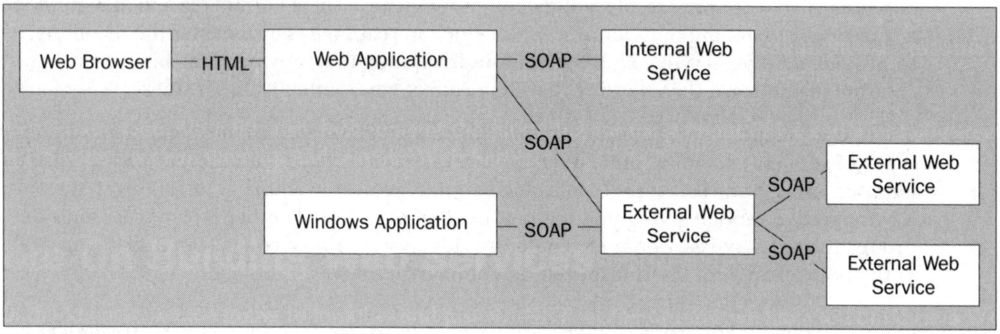

The application may use internal Web Services within the organization or external Web Services provided by partners or as general building block services. A Web Service may also be used by other Web Services.

Leverage Existing Technologies

A key factor to the success of Web Services is that to implement Web Services and Web Service infrastructure you can leverage a lot of what is already in place and working on the Internet. One of the design principles behind SOAP has been to avoid inventing a new technology.

Here is a list of some key infrastructure and technologies that can be reused when implementing Web Services.

- Web servers – web servers are not required to implement a Web Service but a Web Service can be implemented entirely using existing web servers. For instance, without the .NET Framework, you can implement a Web Service using an XML parser and an ASP script running on IIS. The omnipresence of web servers means that Web Services can be installed everywhere.
- Authentication – a Web Service may need to authenticate the client before using the Web Service. The same mechanisms used for web pages may also be used here, including client certificates, basic authentication, digest authentication and NTLM authentication. See Chapter 13 for further details.
- Encryption – Web Services will often send and receive sensitive business data. Sensitive data exchanged with a Web Service requires encryption. Encryption can be done the same way as for regular web traffic. The Secure Sockets Layer protocol (SSL) may also be used with Web Services. See Chapter 14 for further details on encryption.
- Load balancing techniques – since Web Services are stateless, the same load balancing techniques used to load balance web pages may be used to load balance Web Services. Web Services make load balancing a lot easier than using, for instance, the Component Load Balancing features of Application Center 2000.
- Application servers – Web Services need many of the same services as traditional components behind the scenes: transactional services, object pooling, connection pooling, and so on. By hosting the Web Services in a component container (COM+/EJB) you can leverage these services from the application server.

If the Web Services standards had tried to implement new technologies to handle all these things, they would have ended up on the graveyard alongside large-scale efforts such as the Open System Interconnect (OSI) model and CORBA.

The Web Service Stack

The key to the success of Web Services is that they are based on open standards **and** that major vendors such as Microsoft, IBM, and Sun are behind these standards. Still, open standards do not automatically lead to interoperability. First of all, the standards must be implemented by the vendors. Furthermore they must implement the standards in a compatible way.

Telecommunications depend heavily on standards and interoperability. The way this is handled in the telecom industry is by cooperation and interoperability testing. Interoperability events where developers come together are commonplace in the telecom industry.

We are seeing cooperation also in the Web Services space. There seems to be a lot of commitment in the industry to get Web Services to interoperate. There is a group for implementers of SOAP at http://groups.yahoo.com/group/soapbuilders. They have established test suites and interoperability events. Without this commitment to interoperability, Web Services will end up as another technology that failed.

There are several specifications that are used when building Web Services. The figure below shows the 'Web Service stack' as it exists today:

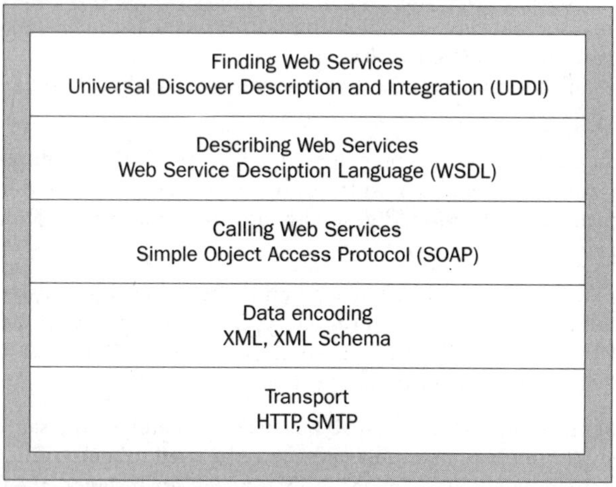

Each layer in the stack will be explained below.

It should be noted that the figure shows a conceptual layering, not a physical layering; WSDL, for instance, is not built on top of SOAP. WSDL is used to describe what the SOAP interface of a Web Service looks like.

Although there is agreement on several of these specifications, most of them are not standardized yet. We will see changes in the specifications as they move forward within the standardization process.

With the pace at which our industry is moving it is impossible to wait for specifications to be blessed as being official before using them. It is most important to standardize the lower-level connectivity protocols as the stack is being built bottom-up:

- Web Services leverage existing standardized transport protocols. The SOAP 1.1 specification opens the door to different transport protocols such as the Simple Mail Transfer Protocol (SMTP) and queues, but only specifies a binding to the HTTP 1.1 protocol.
- Web Services leverage several W3C recommendations including the XML specification and the XML Schema specification. SOAP uses XML as the encoding format. WSDL is built on XML Schema. The XML Schema specification became a W3C recommendation as of May 2001.

- The Simple Object Access Protocol (SOAP) is the heart of the Web Service stack. It is a lightweight protocol for the exchange of information. SOAP is submitted to the W3C and is a W3C note as of May 2000. It is not yet an official standard. There is, however, broad consensus on the specification.
- The Web Service Description Language (WSDL) is used to describe the interface of a Web Service. It serves the same role to Web Services that IDL serves to components. WSDL is submitted to the W3C and is a W3C note as of March 2001.
- In the context of Web Services, UDDI (Universal Description, Discovery and Integration) is a repository. UDDI is a cross-industry effort driven by the major platform and software providers. UDDI is maintained by the UDDI organization and is not yet submitted to a standardization organization but there are already implementations from Microsoft and IBM.

These specifications are used at different times within the Web Service lifecycle, as illustrated by the figure below:

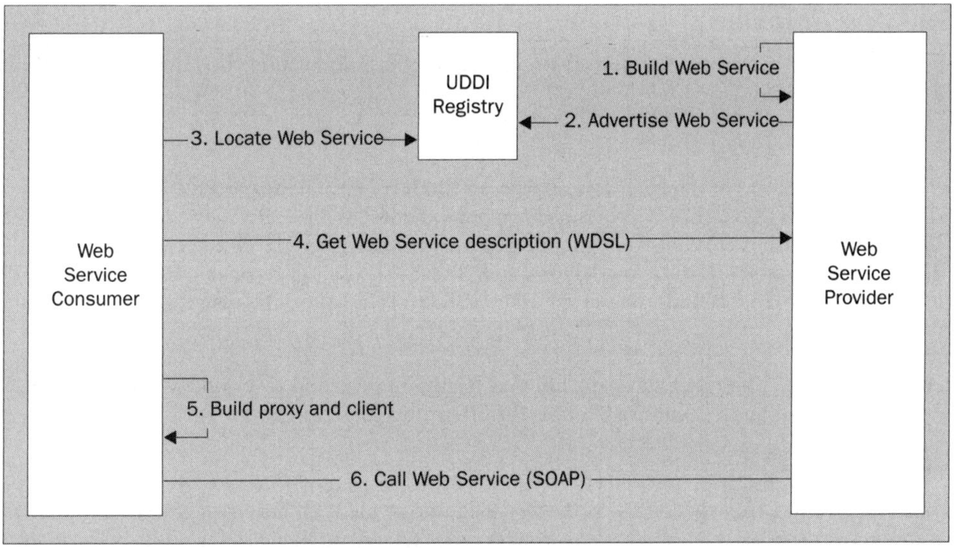

A Web Service provider builds a Web Service using a tool such as ASP.NET. When the service is built, tested and deployed, the service can be published in the UDDI directory where others can find it. A Web Service consumer may consult the UDDI directory to find a Web Service.

The developer of the Web Service consumer needs a description of the interface of the Web Service, similar to the IDL of COM/CORBA. WSDL fills this role for Web Services. The developer of the client application downloads the WSDL description. If .NET is used, a proxy for the Web Service can be built using Visual Studio .NET or a command-line tool.

When the client application executes, it uses the SOAP protocol to call the Web Service.

There are several things to note about this:

- The only 'required' piece in this figure is the call to the Web Service using SOAP. This is Step 6 in the above diagram.
- Publishing your Web Service in UDDI is not a requirement. It is likely that most Web Services will not be published in UDDI.
- You may build a Web Service consumer without the WSDL. All you need is a description of the format of the parameters expected by the Web Service. WSDL makes your life much easier, however. And as you will see, ASP.NET gives WSDL to you for free.

The figure above shows UDDI and WSDL as being used at design and build time. It is also possible to use these at run time. An application may, at run time, find an appropriate Web Service, get the WSDL description, and invoke methods on the Web Service.

The Building Blocks

Web Services use several protocols and standards in going about their business. Descriptions of these follow.

HTTP

The tremendous success of the Internet is based on the Hypertext Transfer Protocol (HTTP) in combination with HTML. HTTP is a request/response protocol typically layered on top of TCP/IP. An HTTP client establishes a TCP connection to a server and sends an HTTP request. The request contains the HTTP method, which may be a GET or a POST. GET is used to retrieve a file such as an HTML page from the server. To submit data in the request a POST is used. The response contains the data returned.

The HTTP protocol is simple and uses plain text for the request and response. Much of the success of the Internet is based on the simplicity of the HTTP protocol.

XML and XML Schema

Extensible Markup Language (XML) is **the** key technology for Web Services. XML has gained a lot of momentum over the last year and so most readers won't need another primer on it. If you want to know more about XML there are many good books to choose from. A good one is *Professional XML 2nd Edition* (ISBN 1-86100-505-9), also from Wrox Press.

XML is actually a series of specifications. For our purpose the most important are:

- The XML specification, including namespaces.
- The XML Schema specification. This specification adds data types to XML.

SOAP, WSDL, and UDDI are all based on XML. SOAP uses XML as the data-encoding format. WSDL uses an XML schema to describe the structure of a Web Service. UDDI uses an XML schema to define the structure of the registry and uses SOAP to specify the communication with the registry.

Calling Web Services

ASP.NET supports three protocols for calling Web Services:

- HTTP-GET
- HTTP-POST
- SOAP

In all cases, HTTP is used and data is submitted in the HTTP request, and returned in the HTTP response as illustrated below:

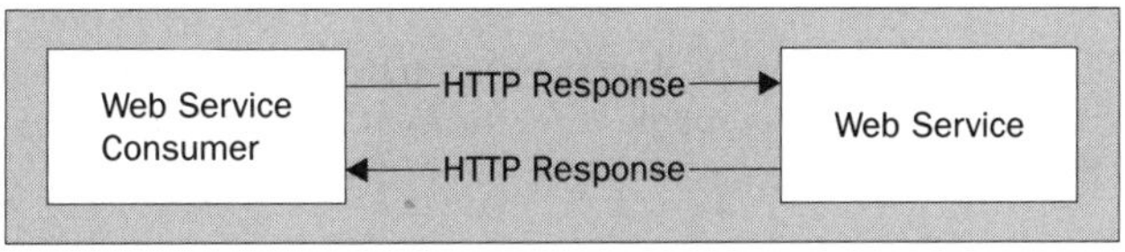

With HTTP-GET and HTTP-POST parameters are passed as name/value pairs. HTTP-GET passes the parameters in the URL. HTTP-POST passes the parameters in an HTTP request message. In both cases, the response is encoded as XML. SOAP uses XML in both the request and the response.

Since the parameters to the Web Service can only be name/value pairs, HTTP-GET and HTTP-POST are more limited than SOAP with regards to the data types that can be passed. They are not as widely supported as SOAP. However, HTTP-GET and HTTP-POST are useful for integrating with existing systems already built using HTTP-GET and HTTP-POST. If the client platform does not have any support for SOAP, it is very easy to create a client that consumes a Web Service based on HTTP-GET and HTTP-POST. HTTP-GET is also used for testing ASP.NET Web Services.

When using ASP.NET, we do not have to choose the protocol. An ASP.NET Web Service can support all protocols at the same time. Chapter 5 will describe these protocols in detail. Here we will look briefly at SOAP, but let us start with a predecessor to SOAP, XML-RPC.

XML-RPC

Dave Winer, one of the authors of the SOAP specification, created XML-RPC. The XML-RPC specification is very simple and is only six printed pages long. The following is from the specification available from UserLand Software, Inc. at http://www.xmlrpc.com:

> **"XML-RPC is a Remote Procedure Calling protocol that works over the Internet. An XML-RPC message is an HTTP-POST request. The body of the request is in XML. A procedure executes on the server and the value it returns is also formatted in XML."**

The XML-RPC specification describes:

- How to encode scalar data types such as integers, strings, Boolean and floating-point numbers.
- How to encode arrays and structs.
- How to handle errors. A binding to HTTP.

XML-RPC has the advantage of being simpler than SOAP and there are many implementations of XML-RPC available. However, all the major vendors have committed to SOAP and as SOAP support becomes available out-of-the-box in tools and platforms, SOAP will be the dominant protocol.

SOAP

SOAP, or the Simple Object Access Protocol, is the essential part of the Web Service protocol stack. The first sentence of the specification available from the W3C site at http://www.w3.org/TR/SOAP/ defines what SOAP is:

> **"SOAP is a lightweight protocol for exchange of information in a decentralized, distributed environment."**

The beauty of SOAP is its simplicity; it does not try to build a completely new infrastructure. As an example, consider the security of Web Services. Security is obviously an important issue, but SOAP does not address it. Instead, it specifies a binding to HTTP and leverages the security mechanisms available with HTTP.

The SOAP specification is 33 pages including references and appendices. It is significantly larger than the XML-RPC protocol, but it is still fairly short and simple.

SOAP is similar to XML-RPC, but note the following differences:

- SOAP can be used as an RPC mechanism but can also be used to exchange XML documents.
- SOAP uses XML namespaces.
- SOAP references the XML Schema specification and allows for encoding of more complex data types and structures than XML-RPC.
- A SOAP message consists of an envelope. The envelope contains the actual message in the body and may optionally contain additional headers. SOAP headers are an extensibility mechanism and are discussed further in Chapter 5.

> **The SOAP 1.1 specification does not mandate the use of HTTP as the transport protocol. Other transports such as mail and message queues can be used. The only binding that is specified in the specification is HTTP. Throughout this book we will assume HTTP when discussing Web Services.**

Describing Web Services

To call Web Services you invoke methods on the service. To do this you need to know what methods it supports, what parameters the Web Service takes, and what it returns.

When building applications, you typically read Help files. Lately, I have also become addicted to IntelliSense, in the same way that I can no longer live without a spell checker. IntelliSense relies on the ability to resolve method calls at code time.

To use a Web Service, you need a description of that service. You could read a Word document or a Help file documenting the interface and implement according to this document. If you use late binding techniques you can call the Web Service without any programmatic description or IntelliSense.

To be able to use early binding and IntelliSense, the Web Service description must be read by a tool. A Word document or a Help file is not very useful to tools. A structured standardized description format is needed. Structured descriptions can be consumed by tools and used to generate proxy code. When you have a proxy, you can use early binding to the proxy and get full support for IntelliSense.

DCOM and CORBA use IDL to describe the interfaces of components. IDL is not suited for Web Services because Web Services need an XML-based description. Enter WSDL.

WSDL

Ariba, IBM, and Microsoft have submitted the Web Service Description Language (WSDL) to the W3C. WSDL replaces earlier specifications such as NASSL from IBM and SCL/SDL from Microsoft. From the specification (http://www.w3.org/TR/wsdl):

> **"WSDL (...) defines an XML grammar for describing network services as collections of communication endpoints capable of exchanging messages."**

The WSDL document is a schema describing a Web Service:

- The WSDL document describes the methods the Web Service understands, including the parameters and the response. The data types of the parameters are defined. This makes it possible for tools such as Visual Studio .NET to generate a strongly-typed proxy.
- The WSDL document describes the protocols supported by the Web Service (SOAP, HTTP-GET, and HTTP-POST).
- The WSDL document specifies the address of the Web Service.

As developers using ASP.NET, we normally do not need to concern ourselves with WSDL. When we develop a Web Service, ASP.NET automatically generates WSDL for us. To do this, ASP.NET uses a feature of the .NET Framework called Reflection. Reflection is a mechanism by which metadata about code can be examined at run time. The WSDL file for an ASP.NET Web Service is generated on the fly by the ASP.NET runtime.

It is possible to build Web Service applications without WSDL. However, WSDL makes it much easier to consume a Web Service.

WSDL is described in detail in Chapter 4.

Finding and Publishing Web Services

We have seen that SOAP is used to call Web Services and that WSDL can be used to describe the interfaces of Web Services. The next question is: how do we find Web Services to use in our application?

In many cases someone will tell us or we will find it manually. If we want to use the shipping service of the Magic Shipping Company we may call them or go to their web site and find a reference to their Web Service.

This is similar to the early days of the web. To find a web site you needed to know its address. Then some bright guys set out to create a directory of web sites. They called it Yahoo! and made a lot of money.

We are now seeing Web Service directories emerging. Two such directories are XMethods, http://www.xmethods.com, and Salcentral, http://www.salcentral.com. We can browse their directory, search for a Web Service, or add our own Web Service to their directory.

UDDI

Universal Description, Discovery, and Integration (UDDI) is a cross-industry initiative to create a global registry of Web Services. UDDI is actually (at least) three things:

- A central registry of Web Services.
- Specifications of the structure of the registry, and specifications of the APIs to access the registry.
- An organization, http://www.uddi.org.

The specifications are maintained by the UDDI organization. They have not yet been submitted to a standardization organization, but that is the said intention.

As a Web Service developer, you can publish your Web Services to the UDDI registry and search for other Web Services in it. The central registry is operated by several companies. Currently Microsoft and IBM host UDDI registries. These registries are synchronized, so if you publish your Web Service in the IBM directory it will also be available in Microsoft's directory.

To publish or find information in UDDI you can use a web browser and browse to one of the directories. You can also publish and find information programmatically using SOAP. The UDDI API specification describes the SOAP messages to be used when accessing a UDDI registry. By exposing the UDDI directory through SOAP you can find Web Services at run time in your application.

UDDI is covered in more detail in Chapter 7.

How to Implement Web Services with ASP.NET

We have discussed why you need Web Services and what they are, so how do you implement them?

As we know, Web Services are based on SOAP, and SOAP is independent of how the services are implemented. To the Web Service provider, however, the manner in which the Web Service is implemented does matter.

There are many ways to implement Web Services. All vendors of developer tools are or will be providing Web Service tools. IBM has a Web Services Toolkit, the Apache SOAP project has a toolkit, and there are many others.

Even if you are committed to a Microsoft platform, there are several ways to implement SOAP-based Web Services, including:

- Hand-code (yuck!) your Web Service by formatting the SOAP XML yourself.
- Use the SOAP Toolkit, downloadable from http://msdn.microsoft.com. The SOAP Toolkit allows existing COM components to be exposed as Web Services. If you must deploy your Web Service on a server where the .NET Framework is not installed, the SOAP Toolkit is a good choice.
- Use ATL Server. ATL Server is part of Visual Studio .NET. An ATL Server implementation is similar to an ISAPI extension. It is implemented in C++ and provides the best performance. You do not need the .NET Framework to deploy a Web Service developed with ATL Server.
- Use .NET Remoting. .NET Remoting allows classes inheriting from a base class called `MarshalByRefObject` to be exposed as Web Services using SOAP. .NET Remoting in addition allows you to configure your code to be exposed using other more efficient formats and protocols than XML and HTTP. You may, for instance, use binary encoding of data over a raw TCP channel.
- Use ASP.NET.

So just from Microsoft there are at least four implementations of SOAP, and two from the .NET Framework! If you want to know more about ATL Server and .NET Remoting, read *Professional C# Web Services* (ISBN 1-86100-439-7) also from Wrox Press.

It is my opinion that the .NET Framework is the superior platform for building, deploying, and consuming Web Services. Other platforms and tools have Web Services bolted on top of them. The .NET Framework is built from the ground up to support XML and Web Services.

In this book, we are focusing on ASP.NET and the use of ASP.NET to implement Web Services. The figure below shows where ASP.NET fits within the .NET Framework architecture:

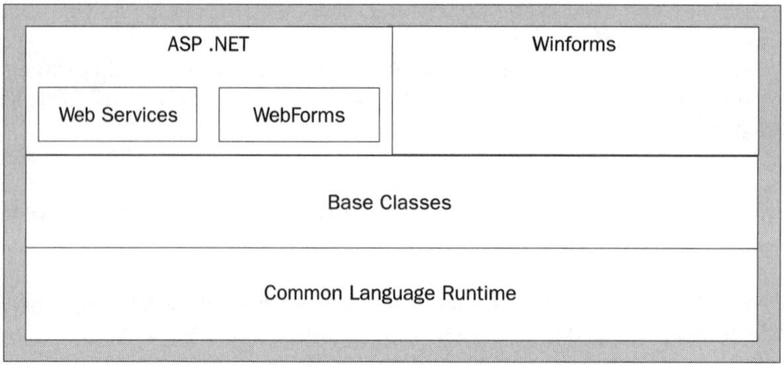

So why should you use ASP.NET to implement Web Services? Well, partly because ASP.NET is the easiest way to write a Web Service. The next chapter will show you how you can create a Web Service with ASP.NET, by using Notepad or by using Visual Studio .NET.

Basically all you do is create an `.asmx` file, add a directive to the top of the file, and add an attribute to the methods you want to expose as a Web Service. To deploy the Web Service, simply copy the file to a web directory on a server with IIS and ASP.NET installed. If you do things this way, ASP.NET gives you:

- A Web Service accessible to SOAP, HTTP-POST, and HTTP-GET. ASP.NET handles all the details of the protocols.
- A WSDL description of your Web Service. Writing the WSDL yourself is not trivial.
- Test pages we can use to test our service.

By using ASP.NET to build our Web Service we can also take advantage of the ASP.NET infrastructure, for instance:

- ASP.NET has extensive support for caching data at the server side. Web Services can use ASP.NET caching to cache the result of a Web Service call. This is covered in Chapter 12.
- You can leverage the security support in ASP.NET to secure your Web Services. This is covered in Chapters 13 and 14.
- You can build HTTP modules to do things such as billing, custom authentication, and so on.

The ASP.NET Web Service infrastructure also has some extensibility points of its own:

- You can manipulate the SOAP messages at a low level using the SOAP Extension. This is covered in Chapter 6.
- ASP.NET has support for using custom SOAP headers. This is also covered in Chapter 6.

The rest of this book will focus on showing you how you can use ASP.NET to create efficient Web Services that take advantage of the .NET Framework and how you can use Web Services efficiently in your applications.

Summary

This chapter introduced you to Web Services. We looked at:

- Why you need them
- What they are
- How you can implement them using ASP.NET

Web Services are a natural extension to distributed component technology. They bring the idea of reusable components to the Internet and allow you to assemble applications from reusable Web Services.

Web Services are built on a foundation of standardized web specifications, namely XML, SOAP, WSDL, and UDDI. Some of these specifications are not yet officially standardized, but there seems to be broad consensus within the industry on these initiatives.

In the next chapter we will start developing some of the theory behind Web Services we looked at here, by actually building a Web Service of our own.

Professional
ASP.NET
Web
Services
Web Services
ROFESSIONAL ASP.NET
Web Services
ROFESSIONAL ASP.NET
Web Services
ROFESSIONAL ASP.NET
Web Services
ROFESSIONAL ASP.NET
Web Services
ROFESSIONAL ASP.NET
Web Services
ROFESSIONAL ASP.NET
Web Services
ROFESSIONAL ASP.NET
Web Services
ROFESSIONAL ASP.NET
Web Services
ROFESSIONAL ASP.NET
Web Services
ROFESSIONAL ASP.NET
Web Services
ROFESSIONAL ASP.NET
Web Services
ROFESSIONAL ASP.NET
Web Services
ROFESSIONAL ASP.NET
Web Services
ROFESSIONAL ASP.NET
Web Services
ROFESSIONAL ASP.NET
Web Services
ROFESSIONAL ASP.NET
Web Services
ROFESSIONAL ASP.NET
Web Services
ROFESSIONAL ASP.NET
Web Services
ROFESSIONAL ASP.NET
Web Services
ROFESSIONAL ASP.NET
Web Services
ROFESSIONAL ASP.NET
Web Services
ROFESSIONAL ASP.NET
Web Services
ROFESSIONAL ASP.NET

2

Building ASP.NET Web Services

The first chapter explained what Web Services are and why you need them. In this chapter we will take our first look at how you actually build Web Services with ASP.NET.

We will discuss the various options we have when building Web Services. Examples will be shown primarily in VB.NET, but we will also look at some C# syntax for building Web Services. We will use the built-in test support in ASP.NET to test these services. The next chapter will show you how you can use the Web Services from an ASP.NET client application.

As this is an introductory chapter, the examples will be kept simple.

More specifically, we will look at:

- The minimum requirements needed for building a Web Service with ASP.NET.
- How to build a Web Service using a text editor such as Notepad.
- How to use Visual Studio .NET to build Web Services.
- The attributes and properties we can use to control the Web Service behavior.

Building a Web Service Using Notepad

Visual Studio .NET has excellent support for building Web Services. Nevertheless, it is very easy to build Web Services without the support of VS.NET. In fact, to build Web Services we really only need:

- A text editor.
- A .NET compiler, such as the C# or VB.NET compilers.

There are many reasons why you may want to build a Web Service without VS.NET. It may be too expensive or you may prefer a different text editor or development environment. Many developers prefer the simplicity that a text editor affords, and many large-scale projects also use makefiles to control the build process.

In the upcoming section we will use Notepad, the world's most available text editor, to build a Web Service. In Windows XP, Notepad also has an option to enable line numbers, so there is one less reason to use a different text editor. Before we dig into the details of Web Services, let's look at the example that we will use in this chapter and the next to illustrate the main concepts of ASP.NET Web Services.

The Application Settings Example

In this chapter and the next we will use an example that exposes the application settings of a web application as a Web Service. In ASP.NET, application settings may be stored in two places, in the `Application` object and in the `web.config` file.

If you have used classic ASP, you probably know the `Application` object already. It is a dictionary where you can store key/value pairs, and is typically used to store application-wide settings. One common use of the `Application` object is to cache application data that changes infrequently. In classic ASP, many people also use the `Application` object to store configuration settings such as a database connection string.

In ASP.NET we will typically store application configuration settings in the `web.config` file. This file is placed in the web application's root directory and can be used to configure many aspects of the web application. The `web.config` file contains several sections, including sections for authentication, security, error handling, and Web Services. We'll see several examples of configuration settings affecting Web Services later in this chapter.

For the purposes of this opening explanation, we'll look at one of the `Web.config` setting sections now; a section in which you can define your own application settings, the `appSettings` section. Here is a database connection string in the `appSettings` section:

```
<configuration>
  <appSettings>
    <add key="ConnectString" value="user id=sa; password=;database=pubs;
                                    server=localhost" />
  </appSettings>
</configuration>
```

The name of the key, `ConnectString`, is an arbitrary name we are using for the purposes of this example. We could use whatever name we want.

Here is a simple VB.NET class that allows us to write strings to the `Application` object, retrieve strings from the `Application` object, and retrieve strings from the `appSettings` section of the `web.config` file. The class is available with the download package for this book in the `AppService.vb` file in the `Ch2-3` folder:

```
Imports System.Configuration
Imports System.Web

Public Class AppService

  Public Sub SetAppState(ByVal key As String, ByVal value As String)
    Dim Application As HttpApplicationState
    Application = HttpContext.Current.Application

    Application.Lock()
    Application(key) = value
    Application.UnLock()
  End Sub

  Public Function GetAppState(ByVal key As String) As String
    Dim Application As HttpApplicationState
    Application = HttpContext.Current.Application

    If Application(key) Is Nothing Then
      Return Nothing
    ElseIf TypeOf Application(key) Is String Then
      Return Application(key)
    Else
      Return Nothing
    End If
  End Function

  Public Function GetAppSettings(ByVal key As String) As String
    Return ConfigurationSettings.AppSettings(key)
  End Function

End Class
```

The `SetAppState` function writes a string value to the `Application` object and associates it with the given key:

```
Public Sub SetAppState(ByVal key As String, ByVal value As String)
  Dim Application As HttpApplicationState
  Application = HttpContext.Current.Application

  Application.Lock()
  Application(key) = value
  Application.UnLock()
End Sub
```

It uses the Application property of the HttpContext class. The context is always available from ASP.NET code. Later in this chapter we will see another way of getting at the Application object.

To be on the safe side, the function synchronizes access to the Application object by calling Lock before writing to the Application object and UnLock after writing. This is necessary since many threads may access the function at the same time.

The GetAppState function retrieves the value of a key:

```
Public Function GetAppState(ByVal key As String) As String
  Dim Application As HttpApplicationState
  Application = HttpContext.Current.Application

  If Application(key) Is Nothing Then
    Return Nothing
  ElseIf TypeOf Application(key) Is String Then
    Return Application(key)
  Else
    Return Nothing
  End If
End Function
```

It checks whether the value stored is really a string before returning it, since we are only dealing with strings in this service, not other objects that may be stored in the Application object.

The last function in the class, GetAppSettings, retrieves an application setting from the web.config file.

```
Public Function GetAppSettings(ByVal key As String) As String
  Return ConfigurationSettings.AppSettings(key)
End Function
```

The function uses the AppSettings property of the ConfigurationSettings class in the .NET Framework to get this value. This property is a dictionary of all key/value pairs in the web.config file. Note that the AppSettings property is read-only. To modify the application settings we have to edit the web.config file.

The class we have just built is a regular class, and is not yet exposed as a Web Service. As it stands it can be used from .aspx or code-behind files within an ASP.NET web application. The next section will look at how we can expose this class to the world outside the ASP.NET web application: we are of course going to expose it as a Web Service.

Why would we want to expose this class as a Web Service? One reason might be to integrate classic ASP pages and ASP.NET pages. If you have an ASP application you may want to develop new pages in ASP.NET to take advantage of all the new features of ASP.NET. ASP and ASP.NET pages can coexist in the same web application. However, the Application object of ASP.NET is separate from the Application object of ASP. The "Application Settings" Web Service can be used from ASP to get at the ASP.NET application state and configuration. This allows us to modify application settings such as database connection strings in one place. We will see an example of an ASP page accessing the Web Service later in this chapter.

The Application Settings service can also be used if you want to expose the application settings to other applications such as other web applications, Windows applications, and so on.

If you want to expose application settings as a Web Service, you should secure your Web Service so that only authorized clients can access it. Chapters 13 and 14 describe security with Web Services in detail.

Exposing Application Settings As a Web Service

To expose our class as a Web Service with ASP.NET we have to do the following:

- Place our class in a file with an `.asmx` extension.
- Add a `WebService` directive to the top of the page.
- Add a `WebMethod` attribute to the methods we want to expose to the world.

We have other options as well when we want to expose a class as an ASP.NET Web Service, but these are the minimum requirements. The other options will be shown later.

The `.asmx` file is the entry point into the Web Service. The code for the Web Service can either be in the `.asmx` file or in a code-behind file as we'll see later.

The `.asmx` extension is used for ASP.NET Web Services in the same way that the `.aspx` extension is used for ASP.NET web pages. The code in the `.asmx` file can be any .NET language. Let us first look at how we can expose our class as a Web Service with all the code in a single file.

VB.NET

Here is the VB.NET code that we need to expose the class as a Web Service. You can find this in the `AppServiceVB.asmx` file in the code download for this chapter. The changes to the original code are highlighted:

```
<%@ WebService language="VB" class="AppService" %>

Imports System.Configuration
Imports System.Web
Imports System.Web.Services

Public Class AppService

  <WebMethod> Public Sub SetAppState(ByVal key As String, ByVal value As String)
    Dim Application As HttpApplicationState
    Application = HttpContext.Current.Application

    Application.Lock()
    Application(key) = value
    Application.UnLock()
  End Sub

  <WebMethod> Public Function GetAppState(ByVal key As String) As String
    Dim Application As HttpApplicationState
    Application = HttpContext.Current.Application

    If Application(key) Is Nothing Then
```

```
      Return Nothing
    ElseIf TypeOf Application(key) Is String Then
      Return Application(key)
    Else
      Return Nothing
    End If
  End Function

  <WebMethod> Public Function GetAppSettings(ByVal key As String) As String
    Return ConfigurationSettings.AppSettings(key)
  End Function

End Class
```

As you can see, we don't have to write any program logic ourselves to expose a Web Service. We simply add the `WebService` directive and decorate all our methods with a `WebMethod` attribute.

The `WebService` directive names the class as one to be exposed as a Web Service. We also specify that the language used in the `.asmx` file is VB.NET so that ASP.NET knows which compiler to invoke when compiling the file. We don't, however, have to specify what the language is since VB.NET is the default language for ASP.NET Web Service development. The default compiler for ASP.NET is specified in the machine-wide configuration file. The location of this file is:

`%SystemRoot%\Microsoft.NET\Framework\`*`<version>`*`\CONFIG\machine.config`

You can, however, override the default language in the local `web.config` file if you want to:

```
<configuration>
  <system.web>
    <compilation defaultLanguage="C#" />
  </system.web>
</configuration>
```

This sets the default language to C# for all ASP.NET files in the application. Other applications will still use the compiler specified in the machine-wide configuration file.

> **The `.asmx` file may contain several classes, but only one class can be exposed as a Web Service.**

The `WebMethod` attribute is part of the `System.Web.Services` namespace, which we have referenced at the beginning of the file. In VB.NET this is done by an `Imports` statement. It is not really necessary to reference the namespace, as we could also have fully qualified the attribute:

```
<System.Web.Services.WebMethod> Public Sub SetAppState(ByVal key As String, _
                                                      ByVal value As String)
```

Referencing the namespace is a good idea, however. It makes the code more readable.

> **The Web Service class and all methods you want to expose in the Web Service must be declared as public.**

If we add the `WebMethod` attribute to a private function, we won't get an error. The function will simply be missing from the Web Service and we won't be able to call it.

C#

Here is the C# code for exposing the code as a Web Service. You will notice that it is very similar to the VB.NET other than the syntactical differences:

```
<%@ WebService Language="C#" class="AppService" %>

using System.Configuration;
using System.Web;
using System.Web.Services;

public class AppService
{
  [WebMethod]
  public void SetAppState(string key, string value)
  {
    HttpApplicationState Application;
    Application = HttpContext.Current.Application;

    Application.Lock();
    Application[key] = value;
    Application.UnLock();
  }

  [WebMethod]
  public string GetAppState(string key)
  {
    HttpApplicationState Application;
    Application = HttpContext.Current.Application;

    if (Application[key] == null)
      return null;
    else if (Application[key] is System.String)
      return Application[key].ToString();
    else
      return null;
  }

  [WebMethod]
  public string GetAppSettings(string key)
  {
    return ConfigurationSettings.AppSettings[key];
  }
}
```

Deploying the Web Service

Deploying a Web Service is very simple. ASP.NET Web Services have the same easy deployment model as ASP and ASP.NET web pages. All we have to do is place the .asmx file in the directory of a web application.

Changing the Web Service is just as easy. We just change the source file and hit save, as in classic ASP.

If we do not have a web application, we can create one using the Internet Information Services (IIS) administration tool. We simply create a virtual directory and point this virtual directory to the folder in which we put our .asmx file.

For the Application Settings example, we will assume that we have created a virtual directory on our machine at the location http://localhost/PWS/Ch2-3/, or indeed simply dropped the parent PWS folder of the code download into the wwwroot directory and created a web application in IIS.

Testing the Web Service

So just by creating an .asmx file and adding a few attributes, we have created a Web Service. But wait; there's more! In addition to exposing the method as a Web Service with SOAP serialization, ASP.NET also gives us:

- Test pages we can use to test our Web Service.
- A structured description of the Web Service in the form of a Web Service Description Language (WSDL) file.

We don't have to write a test client just to test that our Web Service is functioning. We simply point our browser at the .asmx file:

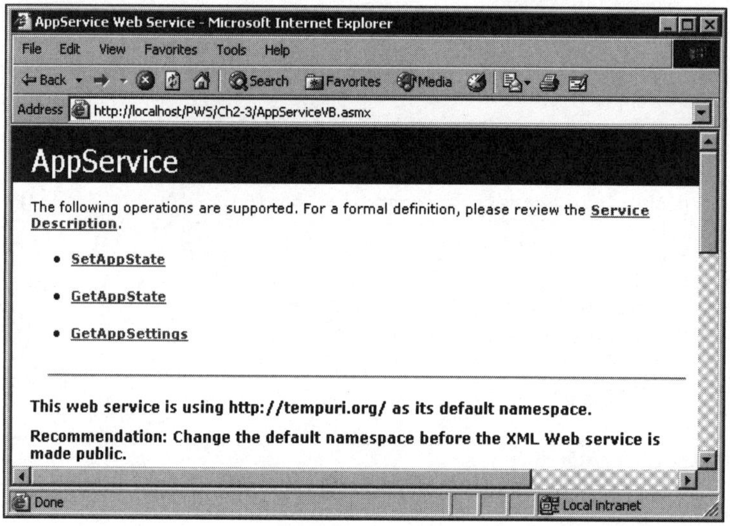

There is a note at the bottom saying that the namespace is http://tempuri.org and that this should be changed. To change the namespace we simply add a `WebService` directive to the Web Service class:

```
<%@ WebService language="VB" class="AppService" %>

Imports System.Configuration
Imports System.Web
Imports System.Web.Services

<WebService(Namespace="http://www.wrox.com/")> Public Class AppService
...
```

The `WebService` directive is described later in this chapter.

The generated page has a link to the service description. Here is a screenshot of some of the WSDL document that is generated if we click the Service Description link in the test page:

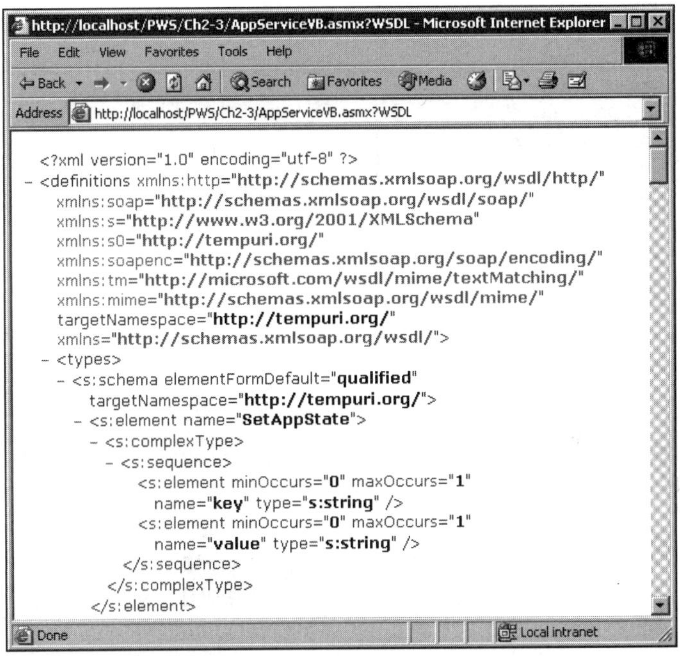

WSDL is thoroughly described in Chapter 4.

The generated test page also allows us to test the individual methods of the Web Service. If we click on the GetAppSettings link, a test page where we can test this method appears. This test page has input fields for the input parameters of the Web Service:

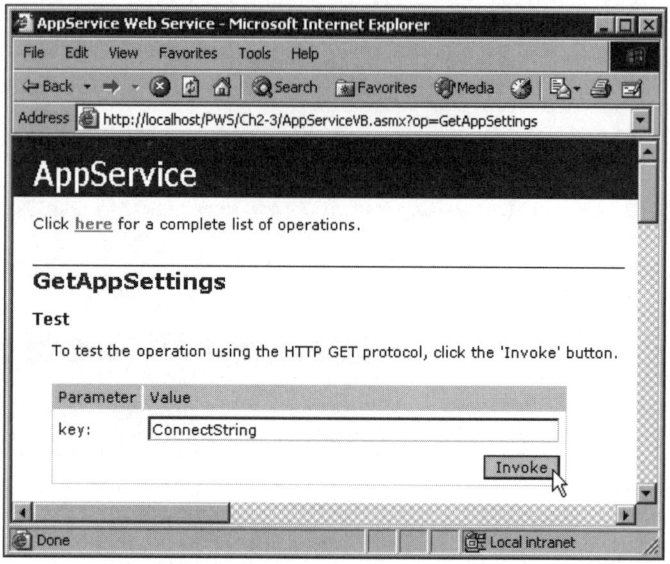

We can now enter a value for the field (ConnectString in this case) and click Invoke. This invokes the Web Service method with the parameter we have specified and returns the XML result:

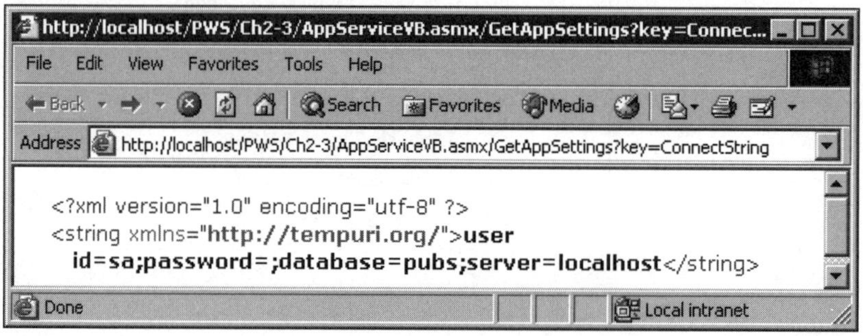

As was mentioned in Chapter 1, ASP.NET supports three protocols for calling Web Services: SOAP, HTTP-GET, and HTTP-POST. The test page uses HTTP-GET. With HTTP-GET, parameters are passed in the URL, as can be seen in the screenshot above. HTTP-GET returns the response as XML, in this case a single string.

The test pages make it easy for us to test our Web Services as we don't have to write a test client just to see if our methods are functioning.

With HTTP-GET and HTTP-POST, parameters are passed as name/value pairs. HTTP-GET passes the parameters in the URL, whereas HTTP-POST passes the parameters in the HTTP Request message. With SOAP, parameters are passed in an XML string. SOAP thus allows complex structures to be passed into the Web Service.

> **If our Web Service takes complex parameters, we cannot use HTTP-GET or HTTP-POST and ASP.NET will not be able to render test pages. We can only test methods that take simple name/value parameters.**

The test pages are rendered by ASP.NET on the fly, and as such they never exist as a file on your disk. The file that does the rendering is:

```
%SystemRoot%\Microsoft.NET\Framework\<version>\CONFIG\↵
DefaultWsdlHelpGenerator.aspx
```

It may be that we want to modify the look or behavior of this page. If so, we simply copy the `DefaultWsdlHelpGenerator.aspx` file to our Web Service directory, modify and rename it, and then change the `web.config` file to point to our new rendering page (for your convenience we have already added a customized rendering page to the code download package, `MyWsdlHelpGenerator.aspx`):

```
<configuration>
  <system.web>
    <webServices>
      <wsdlHelpGenerator href="MyWsdlHelpGenerator.aspx"/>
    </webServices>
  </system.web>
</configuration>
```

The Help file generator uses HTTP-GET to test the Web Service. You can modify the generator to use HTTP-POST instead. The first lines of the Help generator `.aspx` file look like this:

```
<html>
  <script language="C#" runat="server">

  // set this to true if you want to see a POST test form
  // instead of a GET test form
  bool showPost = true; // false is default
```

The `showPost` variable is set to `false` by default in the machine-wide `DefaultWsdlHelpGenerator.aspx` file. If you set this variable to `true`, as we have in our implementation, the test pages will use HTTP-POST instead of HTTP-GET.

Using the Web Service from Classic ASP

One motivation for building this Web Service might be to synchronize application values between ASP and ASP.NET applications. Here is an example that calls our Web Service from the `global.asa` file of an ASP application to get the connection string from an ASP.NET `web.config` file:

```
<SCRIPT LANGUAGE="VBScript" RUNAT="Server">
Option Explicit

Sub Application_OnStart()
  Application("ConnectString") = GetAppSettings("ConnectString")
End Sub
```

The `Application_OnStart` event is fired when the ASP application starts. It calls the `GetAppSettings` method and stores the result in the ASP `Application` object.

```
Function GetAppSettings(key)

  Dim url, xmlhttp, dom, node

  'Call Web Service using HTTP-GET
  url = "http://localhost/PWS/Ch2-3/AppServiceVB.asmx/"
  url = url & "GetAppSettings?key=" & key

  Set xmlhttp = Server.CreateObject("Microsoft.XMLHTTP")
  Call xmlhttp.Open("GET", url, False)
  Call xmlhttp.send

  'Parse result
  Set dom = Server.CreateObject("Microsoft.XMLDOM")
  dom.Load(xmlhttp.responseBody)
  Set node = dom.SelectSingleNode("//string")

  If Not node Is Nothing Then
    GetAppSettings = node.text
  End If

End Function

</SCRIPT>
```

The `GetAppSettings` method uses the `XMLHTTP` object to issue a HTTP-GET to the Web Service. The `XMLDOM` object is used to search the result for the return value.

If you want to run this code you may need to change the URL in the `GetAppSettings` function to match where you have installed the AppService Web Service.

In the download for this chapter there is a file that allows you to test the Web Service from classic ASP. The file is `TestAppService.asp`. This test file writes out the value of `Application("ConnectString")` as set in `global.asa`. The test file also allows you to exercise the AppService Web Service directly from the ASP page. The screenshot below shows the test page in the browser after we have entered the application setting to be retrieved and clicked the button:

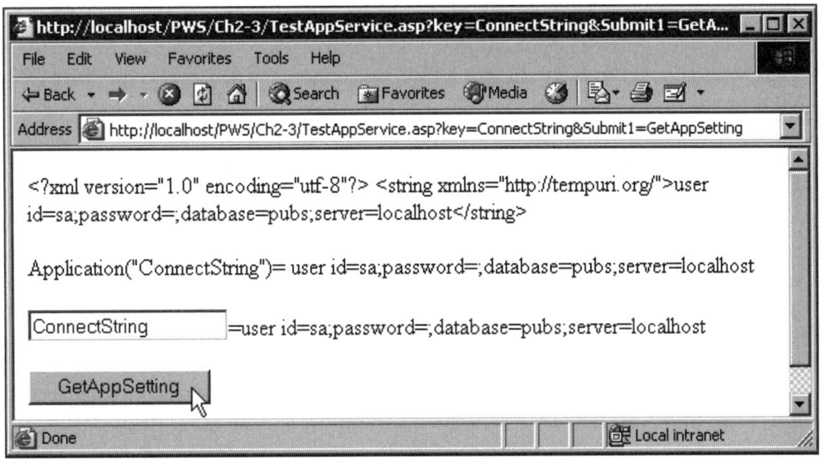

This example illustrates one of the advantages of the HTTP-GET and HTTP-POST protocols. If you don't have any special SOAP tool support, it is much easier to format a request using these protocols than to obey the rules of SOAP. To use SOAP you must format a valid SOAP XML string and set the appropriate HTTP headers.

Note that if the connection string is changed in the `web.config` file, the ASP application must be restarted for the changes to be updated in the ASP `Application` object (of course, with .NET, this is no longer required).

Using a Separate Assembly

In our first example we placed the code for the Web Service directly into the `.asmx` file. The `.asmx` file is compiled to Intermediate Language (IL) code the first time anyone makes a request to the service.

We can also place the Web Service class in a separate code-behind file and have it compiled to a separate assembly. You then need two files:

- One `.asmx` file with the `WebService` directive
- One file containing the Web Service class, with the methods decorated with the `WebMethod` attribute.

The `.asmx` file contains a single line, the `WebService` directive:

```
<%@ WebService class="AppService, AppServiceVBcodebehindassembly%>
```

The `class` property names the class and, optionally, the assembly.

To create the assembly, you must compile the Web Service class. If you use VB.NET, move the class to a separate file and name it; we've named ours `AppServiceVBcodebehind.vb`, which you can find in the `CodeBehind` folder of the code download for this chapter. To compile the VB.NET class, use the following command:

```
vbc /out:bin/AppServiceVBcodebehindassembly.dll /t:library↵
/r:System.dll,System.web.services.dll,System.web.dll AppServiceVBcodebehind.vb
```

We must reference the assembly files used in our Web Service class, in this case `System.dll`, `System.web.dll`, and `System.web.services.dll`. The compiled assembly, `AppServiceAssembly.dll`, contains the IL code. It must be placed in the `bin` directory of the web application. We have provided a `.bat` file which will run this command for you.

In the `WebService` directive above we named the assembly. We could have also just named the class, which would mean that ASP.NET will search all assemblies in the `bin` directory for the class.

Why Use a Separate Assembly?

What are the advantages and disadvantages of using a separate assembly? The answer is: it depends.

If you have your code in a separate assembly it may also be used as a normal assembly from within the web application and from other applications:

- We can use the class directly within our web application without incurring the overhead of SOAP and HTTP calls. Thus the same class may be used both internally within the application and externally as a Web Service.
- We can also use all the other features of an assembly such as versioning.

If we do use a separate assembly, we must manually invoke the compiler when we modify the class file. This makes deployment a bit harder, as we can't simply edit and save. On the other hand, it can be better to detect programming errors at compile time instead of having the first user hitting the service detect the error. The user of a Web Service is typically another program. If the calling program does not report errors properly, it may be hard to figure out what has caused the error.

If we have the source code in the `.asmx` file we are also deploying the source code. We may not want to expose the source code to everyone who has access to the server where our Web Service is hosted. The compiled IL code is harder to read, modify, and tamper with than uncompiled C# or VB.NET code.

Building a Web Service with Visual Studio .NET

The previous section showed how we can create a Web Service with ASP.NET simply by using a text editor and the compilers that ship with the .NET Framework.

We can also use the support of Visual Studio .NET to create Web Services.

Building and Running a HelloWorld Example

To demonstrate how to build a Web Service with Visual Studio .NET, we are going to use the simplest example of all, the HelloWorld example. In fact, when we create a Web Service project with Visual Studio .NET, it automatically creates a HelloWorld example as a starting point.

To follow this example, start up Visual Studio .NET and create a new VB.NET ASP.NET Web Service Project.

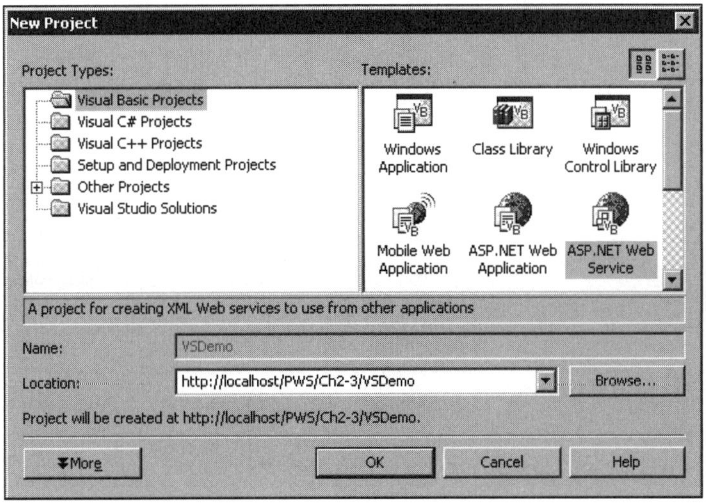

In the dialog that appears, you can name the project. Let's name it VSDemo. You also specify the location of the project. VS.NET automatically creates a virtual directory in IIS named VSDemo at this location.

When we click OK, VS.NET gives us a number of files. The screenshot on the right shows the Solution Explorer with the files created by VS.NET.

One of the files is named `Service1.asmx` and contains the actual Web Service code. The name of the Web Service class is also `Service1`. In the real world, we wouldn't want all our services to be named `Service1`, so the first thing we need to do is come up with a better name. Since we are building a HelloWorld example, let's name the Web Service `Hello`.

When we rename the .asmx file, VS.NET does not propagate the changes to the code. Instead of manually going through the code and changing the name, it is often easier to just delete the Service1.asmx file and add a new Web Service file with a more meaningful name. We can add a new Web Service file by selecting File | Add New Item.

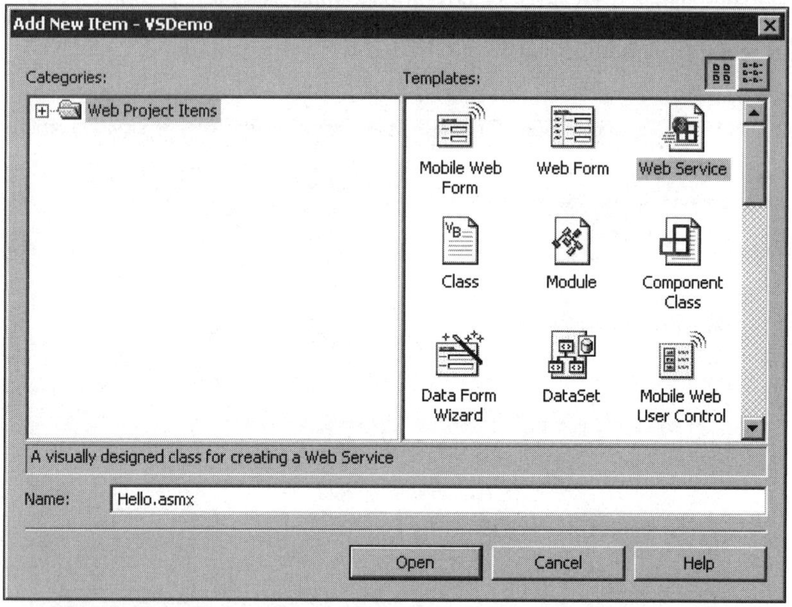

Let's take a look at the code generated by VS.NET for the HelloWorld example in the code-behind, Hello.asmx.vb:

```
Imports System.Web.Services

<WebService(Namespace := "http://tempuri.org/")> _
Public Class Hello
  Inherits System.Web.Services.WebService

#Region " Web Services Designer Generated Code "

  Public Sub New()
    MyBase.New()

    'This call is required by the Web Services Designer.
    InitializeComponent()

    'Add your own initialization code after the InitializeComponent() call

  End Sub
```

```
    'Required by the Web Services Designer
    Private components As System.ComponentModel.IContainer

    'NOTE: The following procedure is required by the Web Services Designer
    'It can be modified using the Web Services Designer.
    'Do not modify it using the code editor.
    <System.Diagnostics.DebuggerStepThrough()> Private Sub InitializeComponent()
      components = New System.ComponentModel.Container()
    End Sub

    Protected Overloads Overrides Sub Dispose(ByVal disposing As Boolean)
      'CODEGEN: This procedure is required by the Web Services Designer
      'Do not modify it using the code editor.
      If disposing Then
        If Not (components Is Nothing) Then
          components.Dispose()
        End If
      End If
        MyBase.Dispose(disposing)
    End Sub

  #End Region

    ' WEB SERVICE EXAMPLE
    ' The HelloWorld() example service returns the string Hello World.
    ' To build, uncomment the following lines then save and build the project.
    ' To test this web service, ensure that the .asmx file is the start page
    ' and press F5.
    '
    '<WebMethod()> Public Function HelloWorld() As String
    '  HelloWorld = "Hello World"
    ' End Function

  End Class
```

The code contains a HelloWorld example, which is commented out when you first add the new file. You can see that the code is similar to the code we created earlier.

Visual Studio .NET also adds some code so that you can work with the visual designer. Using the designer you can drag components from the toolbox into your Web Service. These may be components such as timer components, event log components, and so on.

To run the Web Service, simply uncomment the HelloWorld example and set the `Hello.asmx` file as the start page for the project by right-clicking on it in Solution Explorer and selecting **Set As Start Page**. Then hit *F5* or select **Start** in the **Debug** drop-down menu. VS.NET will compile your code and run it. ASP.NET renders the test page as we saw before:

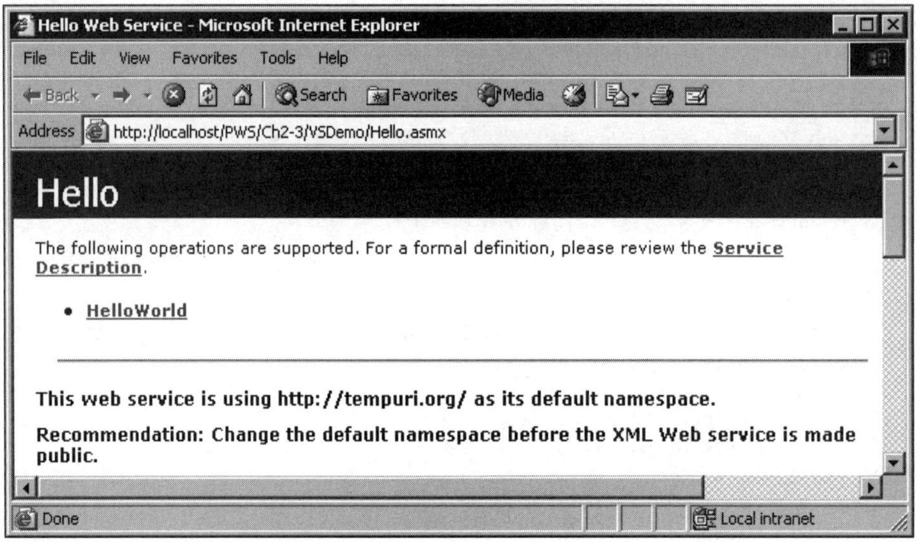

Selecting HelloWorld will bring up a test page where you can invoke the `HelloWorld` function.

The code generated for a new Web Service is copied from a template. You can modify the template for new Web Services.

The VB.NET template is stored in the file:

```
..\Program Files\Microsoft Visual Studio ↴
.NET\Vb7\VBWizards\DesignerTemplates\1033\NewWebServiceCode.vb
```

The C# template is stored in the file:

```
..\Program Files\Microsoft Visual Studio ↴
.NET\VC#\DesignerTemplates\1033\NewWebServiceCode.cs
```

Generating the skeleton for the Web Service is easy. Now the hard work starts, making the Web Service do something useful. This is up to you!

The Anatomy of a VS.NET-Generated Web Service

When we create a new Web Service project with VS.NET, quite a number of files are generated. There are actually more files than meet the eye at first. If we select Show All Files in the Solution Explorer we will see some additional files:

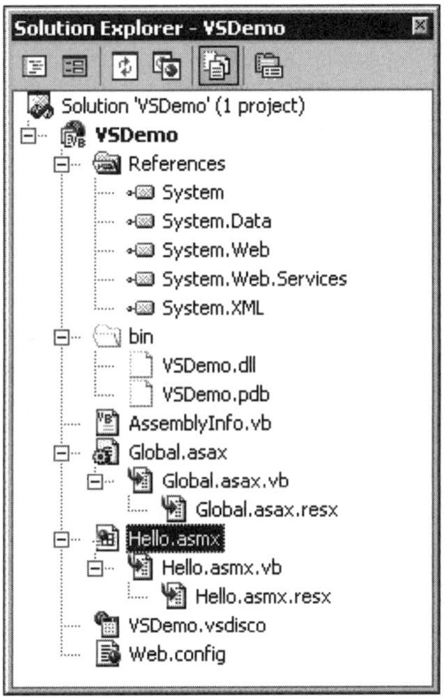

File/Folder	Description
`References`	The references are not files, but references to assemblies used by the Web Service. They are stored in the VS.NET project file.
`bin`	The `bin` folder contains the assemblies for our Web Service. You can view the `VSDemo.dll` using the IL disassembler.
`AssemblyInfo.vb`	The `AssemblyInfo.vb` file contains information such as title, description, and version that is added to the assembly.

`Global.asax`
`Global.asax.vb`
`Global.asax.resx`
	The `Global.asax` file can be used for Web Services the same way it is used for web applications. You can add code to the events available in the `Global.asax` file.

`Hello.asmx`	The `Hello.asmx` file contains the `WebService` directive.
`Hello.asmx.vb`	The `Hello.asmx.vb` file contains the code-behind for the Web Service.

Table continued on following page

File/Folder	Description
`Hello.asmx.resx`	A file consisting of XML entries for the resources added in the designer. It is normally empty.
`VSDemo.vsdisco`	The Web Service discovery file. See Chapter 7 for more information about Disco.
`Web.config`	The configuration file for the Web Service.

The `Hello.asmx` file contains a single line, the Web Service directive (to open this file from Visual Studio .NET, right-click on the file and select **Open With...**, then select the **Source Code (Text) Editor**):

```
<%@ WebService Language="vb" Codebehind="Hello.asmx.vb" Class="VSDemo.Hello" %>
```

This is the same directive we saw earlier. Note the `Codebehind` attribute. This attribute is not used by ASP.NET. It is used by Visual Studio to associate a code-behind file with the `.asmx` file.

> **Visual Studio .NET uses code-behind for Web Services. If you don't want to use code-behind in VS.NET, remove the `Codebehind` attribute from the `.asmx` file and delete the code-behind file.**

Why Use Visual Studio .NET?

So if it is so easy to create Web Services with a simple text editor such as Notepad, why should we use Visual Studio .NET? The answer is simple: VS.NET is a fantastic tool.

VS.NET gives us an integrated development environment where we can develop, debug, test and deploy the Web Service. We also get IntelliSense, which completes the code for us.

As we have seen, VS.NET also does some of the plumbing for us; it creates files and a virtual directory in IIS where we can develop and test our Web Service.

More On Building Web Services

In this section, we are going to look beyond just VS.NET, at the options we have to configure a Web Service using the various directives and attributes that are available with ASP.NET. We will look at:

- The `WebService` directive
- The `WebService` attribute
- The `WebMethod` attribute
- The `WebService` class

WebService Directive

The `WebService` directive is placed on the first line of an `.asmx` file. It specifies the class to expose as a Web Service.

```
<%@ WebService Language="vb" Codebehind="Hello.asmx.vb" Class="VSDemo.Hello" %>
```

The directive is required for ASP.NET Web Services. If the class for the Web Service is in a code-behind file, this line will be the only line in the `.asmx` file.

The directive may use the following attributes:

- `Language`
- `Codebehind`
- `Class`

Language

The `Language` attribute is optional. It specifies the language to use to compile the Web Service. Any .NET compiler installed on the system may be specified. By default the installed compilers are C#, VB.NET, and JScript.NET. These are specified using the values `VB`, `C#`, or `JS`.
The default language is VB.NET as specified in the `machine.config` file, unless it is overridden in the `web.config` file for a particular application.

Codebehind

The `Codebehind` attribute is optional. It is used by Visual Studio .NET to locate the code-behind file for the `.asmx` file so that when you click on the `.asmx` file to view its code it can open the code-behind file. The attribute is only used in Visual Studio .NET; it has no effect when the Web Service is executing.

Class

The `Class` attribute specifies the class to expose as a Web Service. If the class is within a namespace, the namespace is specified, as in the following example. In this example, the namespace is `VSDemo` and the class is `Hello`:

```
<%@ WebService class="VSDemo.Hello"%>
```

If the class is not within a namespace, we specify the class directly:

```
<%@ WebService class="Hello"%>
```

The `Class` attribute may optionally also specify the assembly where the class exists:

```
<%@ WebService class="VSDemo.Hello,VSDemo"%>
```

If the assembly is not specified, ASP.NET searches all assemblies in the `bin` directory for the `Hello` class.

WebService Attribute

The `WebService` attribute is used to add additional information about a Web Service, such as a description of the Web Service. The attribute is implemented by the `System.Web.Services.WebServiceAttribute` class and may use any of the following properties:

- `Description`
- `Name`
- `Namespace`

The attribute is added to the Web Service class as follows:

```
Imports System.Web.Services

<WebService(Description := "This is a simple test service", _
            Name := "Hello Universe", _
            Namespace := "http://www.wrox.com/services")> _
Public Class Hello
  Inherits System.Web.Services.WebService
  Public Sub New()
    MyBase.New()
    ...
```

This attribute is not required to build Web Services. The attribute and its properties are added to the metadata of the Web Service. The metadata is stored in the assembly along with the compiled code.

Now, let's go on to see what each property does.

Description

The `Description` property is used to add a description to the Web Service:

```
<WebService(Description := "This is a simple test service")> _
Public Class Hello
  Inherits System.Web.Services.WebService
```

ASP.NET uses the description when rendering test pages, as you can see in the screenshot below:

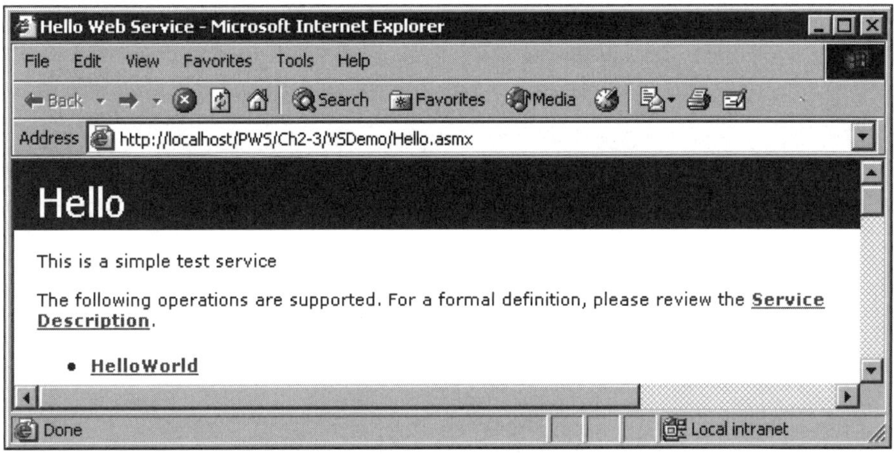

When ASP.NET creates the WSDL file it also includes the description in the <documentation> element of the WSDL service description, which we can view by clicking the Service Description link on the test page:

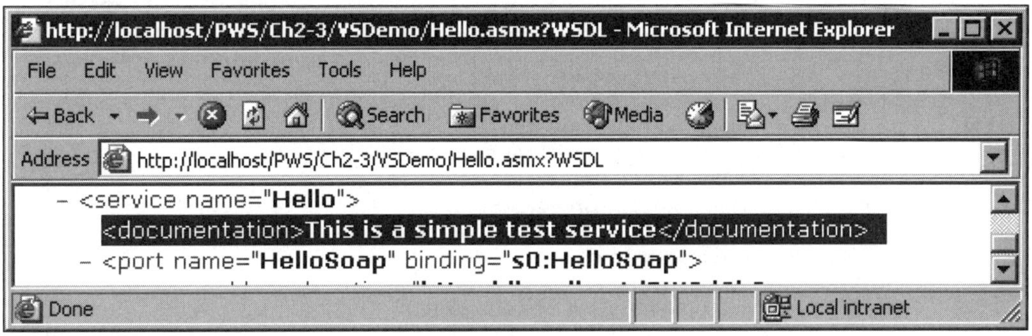

Name

By default, the name of the Web Service is the same as the name of the class. The Name property is used to give the Web Service a different name from that of the class. We'll discuss why in a moment, but here is how you use the property:

```
<WebService(Name := "Hello Universe")> _
Public Class Hello
  Inherits System.Web.Services.WebService
```

The value specified becomes the name of the Web Service. Here is the test page:

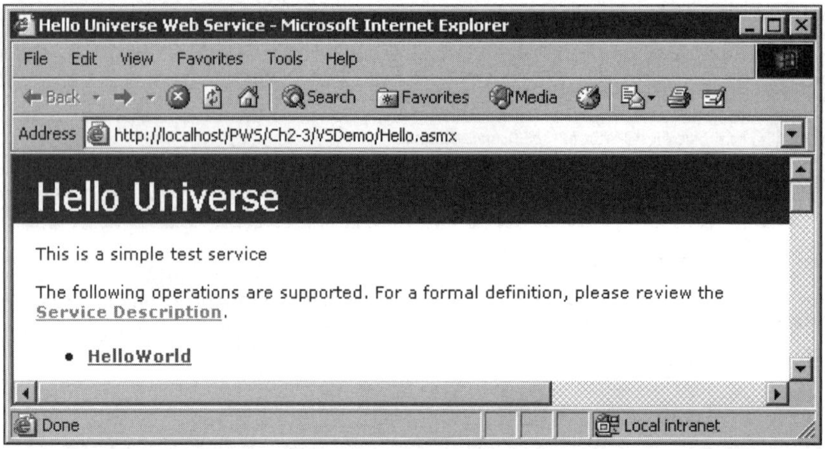

The new name is also exposed to the outside world through the WSDL:

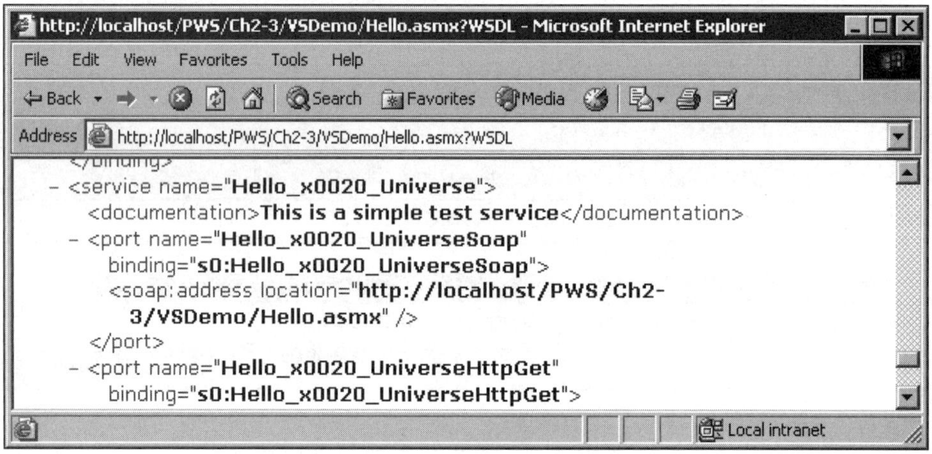

Why would we want to give the Web Service a different name? It may be a matter of taste: we can use a name that is different from the internal name of the class. If we use an internal naming convention for classes, for instance, we may not want to use the convention when exposing the class as a Web Service.

We may also give the Web Service a name that we are not allowed to use for our class. This may for instance be a name that is reserved in the language. Say we are building a trade application and we want a Web Service with the name "Imports". We are not allowed to use this as the name of a VB.NET class since `Imports` is a key word in VB.NET. However, by using the `Name` property we can give the Web Service the name "Imports".

Namespace

All the generated test pages we have seen up to now have had a message on them underneath the link for the name of the method we are exposing:

This web service is using http://tempuri.org/ as its default namespace.
Recommendation: Change the default namespace before the XML Web Service is made public.

The pages also explain how you change the namespace. You do that by setting the `Namespace` property of the `WebService` attribute as follows:

```
<WebService(Namespace := "http://www.wrox.com/services")> _
Public Class Hello
  Inherits System.Web.Services.WebService
```

The namespace uniquely identifies your Web Service methods and allows two different Web Services to have methods with the same name.

When you set the `Namespace` property the warning disappears:

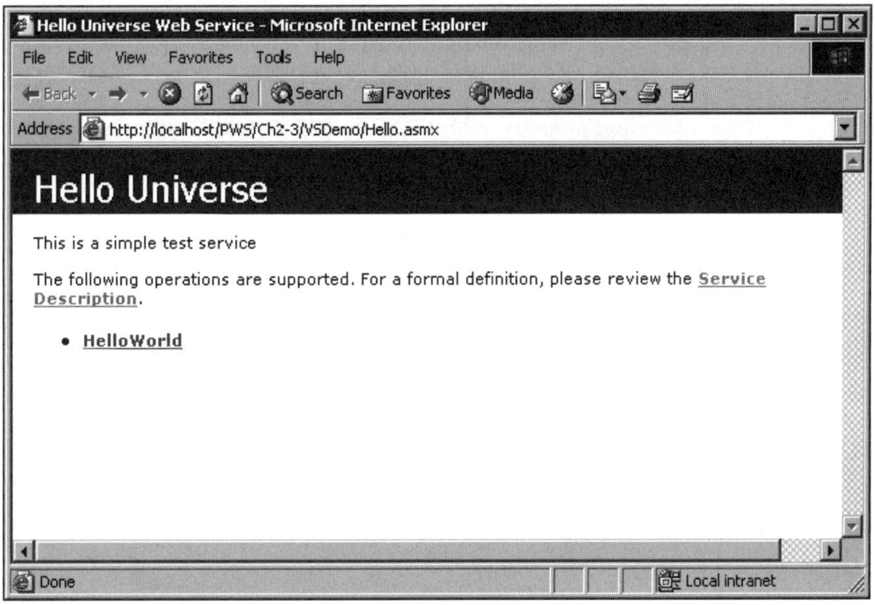

The namespace is also used in the WSDL:

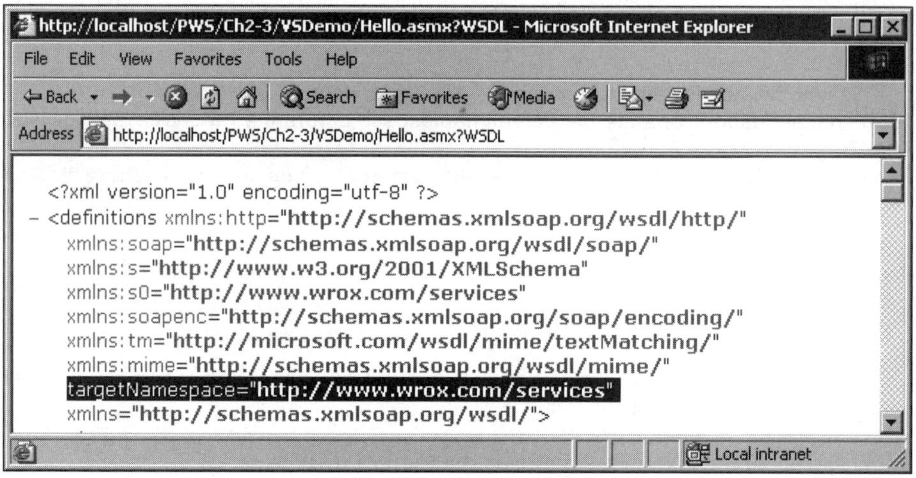

The namespace is a URI or a Universal Resource Identifier. This may be a URL, but it need not be. It need not point to a valid HTTP address. It should be unique so we should use a name that we control. It is a good idea to use your company's domain name as a starting point.

If we don't specify the `Namespace` property, ASP.NET uses http://tempuri.org/. This name should only be used during development and should be changed before we go live with our Web Service.

WebMethod Attribute

We have now seen the `WebService` directive and the `WebService` attribute. They apply to the Web Service as a whole.

The `WebMethod` attribute is added to each individual method we want to expose as a Web Service.

The attribute is implemented by the `System.Web.Services.WebMethodAttribute` class and it supports a number of properties that control the behavior of the methods.

The following properties are available:

- `CacheDuration`
- `Description`
- `EnableSession`
- `MessageName`
- `TransactionOption`
- `BufferResponse`

Here we will describe each of the properties with simple examples. The examples can be found in the `Properties.asmx` file in the WebMethodExamples VS.NET project in the code download. Caching with Web Services is described in more detail in Chapter 12. Session state and Web Services are covered in detail in Chapter 10. Transaction handling and Web Services is covered in Chapter 11.

CacheDuration

ASP.NET has built-in support for caching the data on the server. Web Services can use the caching support of ASP.NET to cache the result of a web method.

Caching makes sense when the data returned from the Web Service does not change often and many clients call the service with the same parameters to get the same result. Good examples of this are Web Services for news feeds, currency services returning the currency conversion rate, stock quotes, and so on.

Caching the result of a web method does not make sense when the results are highly dynamic. For example, if a currency service actually takes in the amount to convert, it does not make much sense to cache the result as each request will most likely be different.

The `CacheDuration` property is used to enable caching of the web method result:

```
<WebMethod(CacheDuration:=10, _
Description:="Returns current time, format 'hh:mm:ss'")> _
Public Function GetTime() As String

  GetTime = DateTime.Now().ToString("T")

End Function
```

The duration is specified in seconds. The example above sets the cache to expire after 10 seconds. The default value is 0, which means that caching is disabled.

If the web method takes parameters, the parameters are used as keys for the cache. The result will be cached for each combination of the parameters. Here is an extension of the `GetTime` function above that takes the format string as a parameter:

```
<WebMethod(CacheDuration:=10, _
Description:="Returns the current time using the specified format string")> _
Public Function GetTime(ByVal format As String) As String

  GetTime = DateTime.Now().ToString(format)

End Function
```

The result will be different for each format string. If the format string is 'd' the time will be returned in the format `M/d/yyyy`, if the format string is 'g', the time will be returned in the format `M/d/yyyy HH:mm`, and so on. If the web method is called within 10 seconds with the same format string, the result will be fetched from the cache.

> **Using the `CacheDuration` property, results from the Web Service are cached on the server on which the Web Service is running. You should also consider adding caching on the client calling the Web Service.**

If the client is an ASP.NET page, we can use the ASP.NET cache to cache the result of the Web Service on the clientside.

Description

The `Description` property of the `WebMethod` attribute is used to describe the web method in the same way that the description property of the `WebService` attribute is used to describe a Web Service.

We've already seen it, but here is the `GetTime` method with the `Description` property highlighted:

```
<WebMethod(CacheDuration:=10, _
Description:="Returns current time, format 'hh:mm:ss'")> _
Public Function GetTime() As String

  GetTime = DateTime.Now().ToString("T")

End Function
```

The description is added to the test pages:

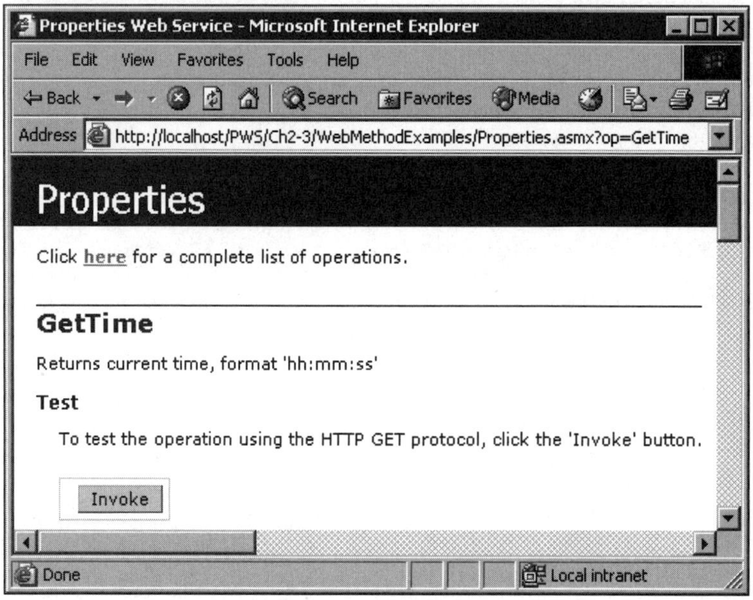

and to the <documentation> element in the WSDL:

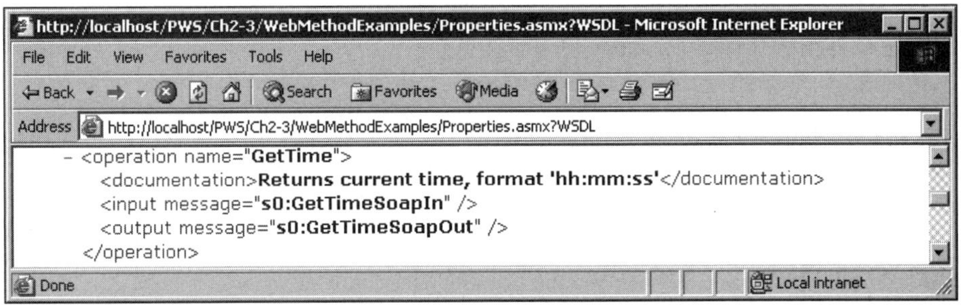

Adding a textual description to your Web Service and to the methods is good practice. It makes your Web Service more user-friendly.

EnableSession

The best practice for ASP web applications has been to disable session state. This best practice applies to Web Services as well. By default, Web Services do not support session state. Most Web Services should be designed to be stateless to achieve Internet scalability, as session state consumes memory for each client on the server.

There are cases, however, where we might want to enable session state for Web Services. We can enable session state for individual methods. To enable session state for a Web Service method we use the EnableSession property of the WebMethod attribute. Here is an example of a function that counts the number of times it is called for each user.

```
<WebMethod(EnableSession:=True, _
Description:="Counts usage of method")> _
Public Function UserCount() As String
  Dim Session As System.Web.SessionState.HttpSessionState

  Session = System.Web.HttpContext.Current.Session

  Session("UsageCount") = Session("UsageCount") + 1
  Return Session("UsageCount")

End Function
```

Session state is enabled by setting the EnableSession property to True. The Session object is used within the function to keep a usage count for each user.

Session state handling is not specified in the SOAP specification. As is often the case with Web Services, you must rely on the support of the underlying infrastructure. ASP.NET relies on HTTP cookies to support session state. The session cookie stores a session ID and ASP.NET uses the session ID to associate the client with the session state on the server.

> **Session handling is not specified in the SOAP specification, so different SOAP implementations may handle session state differently.**

When you test the `UserCount` function from a browser using the ASP.NET test pages, you get the expected behavior. Each time you refresh the browser, the count increases:

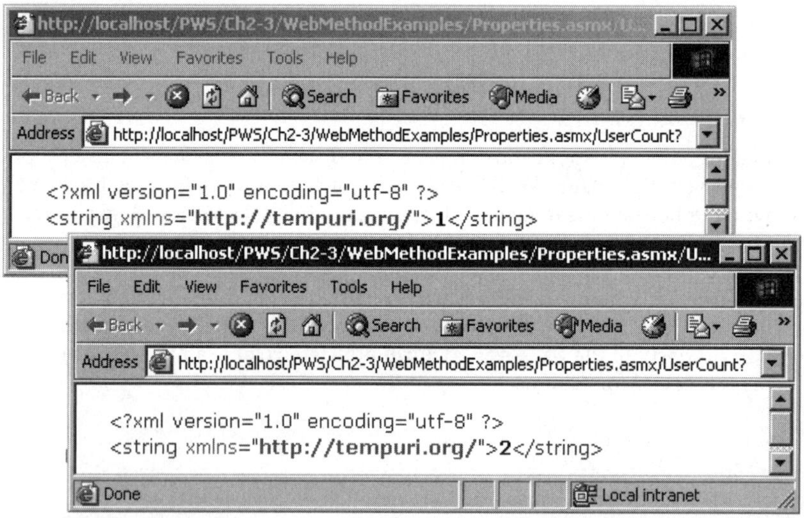

If you open a new browser instance, you will see the count start from 1 again. Note that if you open several browser instances from a test page, they will share cookies. You need to open a brand new browser instance from, for instance, the **Start** menu.

Chapter 3 will show you how to generate a proxy for the Web Service. If you call the Web Service through the generated proxy you need to supply the proxy with what is called a "cookie container". The cookie container is used to host the cookies. The proxy object has a `CookieContainer` property for this purpose.

In the download available with this chapter is a Windows Forms application that can be used to test the session state handling. The form for this application is available in the `TestAppVB` folder. You can either open up the VS.NET project or start the application directly.

The class contains a private `CookieContainer` object. This class is defined in the `System.Net` namespace:

```
Public Class Form1
  Inherits System.Windows.Forms.Form

  Private Shared MyCookieContainer As New System.Net.CookieContainer()
```

We make the variable shared so that each time the callback is called, the same object will be used. If the `MyCookieContainer` variable is not declared as shared, we will get a new `CookieContainer` object each time we click the button.

Here is an example of a button callback function in the Windows Forms application. This function calls the `UserCount` web method and displays a message box:

```
Private Sub Button5_Click(ByVal sender As Object, ByVal e As System.EventArgs) _
                          Handles Button5.Click

    Dim service As WebMethodExamples.Properties
    Dim message As String

    service = New WebMethodExamples.Properties()
    service.CookieContainer = MyCookieContainer

    message = "Calling UserCount() returns "
    message = message & service.UserCount()
    MessageBox.Show(message, "WebMethodExamples")

End Sub
```

We create the Web Service proxy and set the `CookieContainer` property of the proxy to our shared cookie container object. When we then call the Web Service, the session cookie will be sent to the service and we are able to use session state.

If we press the button three times we see that the count is 3.

The Web Service client may be a web application. In this case we have three parties involved:

- The user(s) of the web application
- The web application
- The Web Service

The web application needs to store the cookie container in an appropriate place. If each user of the web application needs a separate session, we can store the `MyCookieContainer` object in the `Session` object of the web application. Note that the session state of the web application is different from the session state of the Web Service.

If we need a session for the web application, we can store the `MyCookieContainer` object in the `Application` object of the web application.

Chapter 10 has more information on session handling in Web Services.

MessageName

When we expose a method, the name of the Web Service method is by default the same as the name of the method in our class. There are cases when we want to give the web method a different name from the class method.

One example is with overloaded methods. In our `CacheDuration` samples we saw two different methods for returning the time:

```
<WebMethod(CacheDuration:=10, _
Description:="Returns current time, format 'hh:mm:ss'")> _
Public Function GetTime() As String

  GetTime = DateTime.Now().ToString("T")

End Function

<WebMethod(CacheDuration:=10, _
Description:="Returns the current time using the specified format string")> _
Public Function GetTime(ByVal format As String) As String

  GetTime = DateTime.Now().ToString(format)

End Function
```

Since C# and VB.NET allow overloaded methods, this code compiles just fine. However, if we try to use the Web Service we will get an error. We can see this if we browse to the test page:

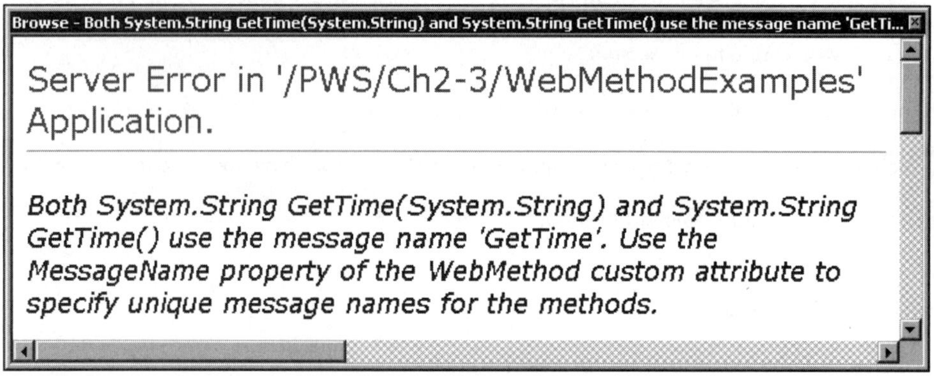

We need to supply unique names for each web method. One way to do this is to rename one method. Another way is to use the `MessageName` property to give the second web method a new name:

```
<WebMethod(CacheDuration:=10, _
Description:="Returns the current time using the specified format string", _
MessageName:="GetTimeFormat")> _
Public Function GetTime(ByVal format As String) As String

  GetTime = DateTime.Now().ToString(format)

End Function
```

The web method is now named `GetTimeFormat`. When the method is called, the SOAP message will identify the message as `GetTimeFormat`. The WSDL will now contain two messages, one `GetTime` message and one `GetTimeFormat` message. It will also show two `GetTime` operations:

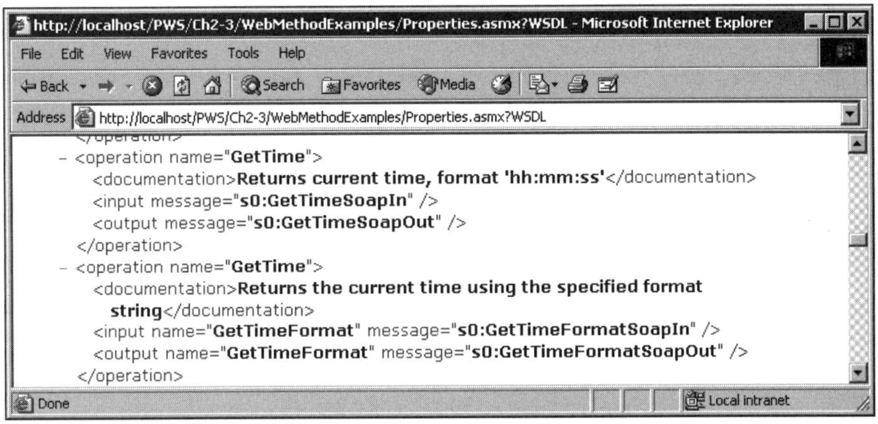

When we build a proxy as shown in the next chapter, we will again get two `GetTime` functions, each with a different signature.

TransactionOption

ASP.NET is integrated with the transactional services of COM+. We can set ASP.NET pages to be transactional. We don't need to build COM+ components and register them in Component Services. We simply mark our ASP.NET page with a transaction attribute, and all code within that page will be in the same transaction.

ASP.NET Web Services support the same model. We can mark our web method as transactional. All code within that method will be executed in the same transaction. Note that with ASP.NET we can specify transactional support on a method level. This contrasts with COM+ components where transactional support has to be declared at the class level.

To set transaction support for a web method, we use the `TransactionOption` property of the `WebMethod` attribute as in the following example, which is part of the `Pubs.asmx` Web Service from the WebMethodExamples project in the code download:

```
Imports System.Web.Services
Imports System.EnterpriseServices

Public Class Pubs
  Inherits System.Web.Services.WebService

  <WebMethod(TransactionOption:=TransactionOption.Required)> _
  Public Function UpdatePublisher(ByVal name As String, _
                              ByVal blowup As Boolean) As Integer
    Dim conn As String
    Dim sql As String

    conn = "server=localhost;uid=sa;pwd=;database=pubs"
```

```
      sql = "update publishers set pub_name='" + name + "' where pub_id=0736"

      Dim connection As New System.Data.SqlClient.SqlConnection(conn)
      Dim command As New System.Data.SqlClient.SqlCommand(sql, connection)

      connection.Open()
      UpdatePublisher = command.ExecuteNonQuery()

      If blowup Then
        Err.Raise(vbObjectError, "You killed me!")
      End If

    End Function

  End Class
```

The transactional services live in the `System.EnterpriseServices` namespace. So we need to set a reference to the `System.EnterpriseServices` assembly found in `System.EnterpriseServices.dll`.

The method updates a specific row in the **Publishers** table in the **Pubs** database, a demo database that comes with SQL Server 2000. The method takes two parameters. The first is the name of the publisher. The second is a Boolean that is used to simulate errors. If this is set to `True`, the web method will raise an error. When an error is raised, all database updates executed will be rolled back. The method returns the number of rows updated.

If you are familiar with MTS or COM+, you may ask why we don't call `SetComplete` and `SetAbort`. This is because COM+ has a feature called "AutoComplete" that is turned on for Web Services. If a method returns without an error, this is considered as a `SetComplete`. If the method raises an error, this is considered a `SetAbort`.

`System.EnterpriseServices.TransactionOption` is an enumeration with the following possible values:

- `Disabled`
- `NotSupported`
- `Required`
- `RequiresNew`
- `Supported`

A web method will always be the root of a transaction, so the only value that makes sense for a Web Service is `Required`. `RequiresNew` will have the same effect: turning on transactional support.

> **A Web Service cannot participate in an ongoing transaction. It will always start a new transaction. The Web Service and the client cannot share transaction context.**

If a transacted Web Service calls COM+ transacted objects, these objects are able to participate in the transaction of the Web Service. If a transacted Web Service calls another transacted Web Service, they will not be part of the same transactions. Transactions are covered in more detail in Chapter 11.

BufferResponse

The `BufferResponse` property allows you to control when data returned from the Web Service is sent to the client. By default, the `BufferResponse` property is set to `True`. This means that the entire result is serialized before it is sent to the client. By setting this property to `False`, ASP.NET will start returning output as it is serialized.

```
<WebMethod(BufferResponse:=False, _
Description:="Long running method")> _
Public Function GetLargeResultset() As String
  GetLargeResultset = GetXML()
End Function
```

> **Setting `BufferResponse` to `False` only makes sense when the Web Service returns a large amount of data.**

The Web Service method will always complete execution before anything is returned. Buffering on/off relates to the serialization that takes place after the method has executed. With buffering turned off, the first part of the result is serialized and sent. Then the next part of the result is serialized and sent, and so on.

Deriving from the WebService Class

There is one more option for implementing Web Services that we have not yet discussed. A Web Service class may inherit from a class in the `System.Web.Services` namespace, the `WebService` class. You may have seen this already, since the code emitted by Visual Studio .NET inherits from this class:

```
Public Class Service1
  Inherits System.Web.Services

  <WebMethod> _
  Public Function HelloWorld() As String
    HelloWorld = "Hello World"
  End Function
End Class
```

Inheriting from the `WebService` class is mainly a convenience; it does not add any functionality to our Web Service. The convenience is that the `WebService` class provides direct access to the `Web.HTTPContext` object of the current request. We saw earlier in this chapter that to get at the `Application` object we had to write the following code:

```
Dim Application As HttpApplicationState
Application = HttpContext.Current.Application
```

By inheriting from the WebService class we can access the Application object directly. The code above becomes unnecessary, so we can write:

```
Public Class Service1
  Inherits System.Web.Services

  <WebMethod> _
  Public Function SetAppState(ByVal key As String, ByVal value As String)
    Application.Lock()
    Application(key) = value
    Application.UnLock()
  End Function
End Class
```

The WebService class adds the following properties:

Property	Description
Application	The Application object holding the application state of the Web Service.
Context	The Web.HTTPContext object of the current request.
Server	The HTTPServerUtility object of the current request. This is similar to the Server object found in ASP. It contains, for instance, the CreateObject function.
Session	The Session object holding the session state of the Web Service. See the description of the EnableSession property earlier.
User	The User object is used to get access to security information such as whether the user is authenticated and the name of the authenticated user. See Chapter 13 for more information about security.

Since the .NET Framework only supports single inheritance, inheriting from WebService means that our class cannot inherit from other classes. This is really the only reason not to inherit from WebService.

An interesting point with inheriting from WebService is that WebService is derived from the System.MarshalByRefObject class. This class is the base class for .NET Remoting.

This allows our class to be remoted using Remoting as well. Remoting is a Microsoft proprietary technology available in the .NET Framework. It allows objects to be passed by reference between machines and application domains. .NET Remoting is somewhat similar to DCOM but is much more flexible. We can configure how data should be serialized, if it should use binary, XML, or other formats, and how data should be transported: using TCP, HTTP, and so on.

By inheriting from `WebService` (and indirectly from `MarshalByRefObject`) we have several options for our class:

- The class can be used directly within an application, without going through serialization at all.
- The class can be exposed as an ASP.NET Web Service.
- We can configure the class to use .NET Remoting and, for example, we could use a binary formatter over TCP.

If you want to know more about .NET Remoting, you can read *Professional C# Web Services* (ISBN 1-86100-439-7) also by Wrox Press.

Summary

This chapter has showed how we can create basic Web Services using ASP.NET. We can create a Web Service using any text editor or we can use Visual Studio .NET.

An ASP.NET Web Service exists in an `.asmx` file. The code for the service can be in the same file or in a code-behind file.

By adding a directive and a few attributes to our code, a .NET class is exposed as a Web Service. ASP.NET gives us:

- Support for HTTP-GET, HTTP-POST, and SOAP.
- Test pages we can use to test the Web Service.
- A description of the Web Service in the form of a WSDL file.

The following table summarizes the main options we have when building ASP.NET Web Services:

Option	Mandatory	Description
`WebService` directive	Yes	Added as first line in an `.asmx` file.
`WebService` attribute	No	Added to the class. Used to set the namespace, add a description, and give the Web Service a name other than the name of the class.
`WebMethod` attribute	Yes	Add to public methods you want to expose. May also add attributes to specify caching, enable session state, enable transactions, and so on.
Inherit from `WebService` class	No	Gives direct access to intrinsic objects such as the `Application` object.

So now that we have seen how we can create Web Services using ASP.NET, let us see how we can turn around and consume Web Services from ASP.NET.

PROFESSIONAL
ASP.NET
WEB
SERVICES

3

Using a Proxy To Consume a Web Service

In this chapter, we will take the value of Web Services to the next level by incorporating Web Service functionality into other applications. Sure, the built-in features of the .NET Framework make creating and even testing Web Services relatively painless, but do we really want to require our Web Service consumers to use the browser-based testing interface to retrieve data? Of course not! This would essentially make Web Services useless. On the other hand, we don't want each consumer to expend time and resources developing proprietary code to interface with our Web Service and enforce data types.

As you may already know (or have guessed), there's a great middle ground where developers can implement Web Service logic within their applications without building the code from scratch. In .NET, the tool that makes this possible is the **proxy class**. The proxy class enables us to reference a remote Web Service and use its functionality within our application, as if the data it returns were generated locally.

We'll continue the use of our AppService Web Service from Chapter 2 and walk through several proxy scenarios, each of which demonstrates the use of Web Service functions within a separate program.

By the end of this chapter, you will have learned:

- The definition and role of proxies
- How to create proxies from the command prompt and Visual Studio .NET
- The difference between synchronous and asynchronous proxies
- How to modify the base settings of a proxy

The Role of the Proxy

Before we jump headlong into creating a proxy, let's discuss an analogy that helps illustrate the need and use of a proxy.

The Telephone Illustration

When you place a phone call, you have a single intent: to speak with an individual or group at the endpoint, regardless of their location. Your only responsibility is to provide the phone with enough information to know how to reach the other party: the phone number. Once the call is placed, your phone converts your voice into a series of waves that jumps from tower to tower, and perhaps even from base station to satellite, ultimately reaching the call recipient.

The wonder of it all is that your voice arrives not only audible, but distinguishable. A friend who worked for a local telephone system once told me, "If you only knew what they did to your voice to disassemble and reassemble it, you'd be amazed it even sounds similar." While that may be true, as soon as we finish dialing our phones, we are concerned with speaking to the other person, not how our voice is traveling there.

The same holds true for the Web Service proxy. Our application is presented with an interface that looks just like the original (although, admittedly, the telephone doesn't precisely look like the original person, often it can "listen" and "talk" just like they can). The program calls the method(s) exposed by this proxy interface as much as required without regard to where or how the request is communicated. All the work of transforming and transmitting this request is done by the proxy – just like the telephone circuitry and antennae do for our voice.

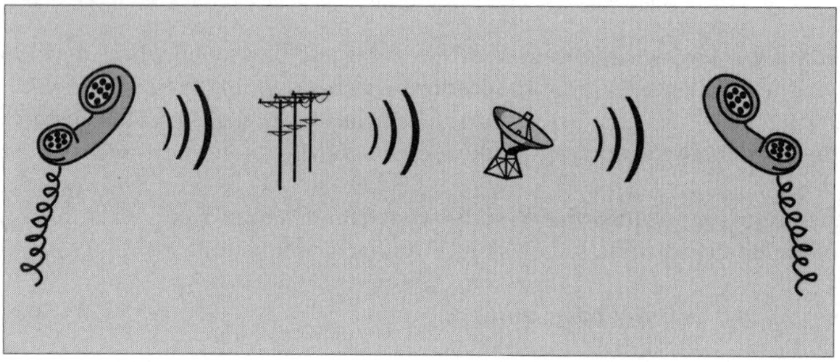

Proxies Everywhere

In fact, the function of **proxying** has its origins far earlier than .NET Web Services. Although certainly not the first case of proxying, web proxy software, like Microsoft's Internet Security and Acceleration (ISA) Server (and previous Proxy Server), provides a single point for web requests. Each computer on the network that requests Internet resources actually sends its request to the proxy server, whose job it is to formulate a new request to the actual Internet destination. We don't have to use a different version of the browser to use a web proxy server; we simply tell it where to make its requests, and the proxy's role becomes **transparent**.

If you have built applications based on COM, especially using Visual Basic 5.0 or 6.0, you've made extensive use of proxies, perhaps without realizing it. In COM, the `IDispatch` interface enabled a similar method to automate compatible classes. All COM object-to-object communication is handled behind the scenes; when developing a COM-based Visual Basic application, as far as we're concerned, we're simply calling methods within our application, when, in reality, we're using proxies.

Proxies, a Long-Time Friend

Step back from the Web Service mindset for a moment. If we were creating a standalone application that contained all the logic required to retrieve the values from the site configuration (like our Web Services from the previous chapter), we would still follow a particular design pattern. To keep our program modular, we'd create separate functions for `GetAppState`, `SetAppState`, and `GetAppSettings` that each performed its own data updates and queries. From our application, we'd call each method to retrieve any needed values and use them, letting the functions themselves perform the work of parsing the data accordingly.

Using the same application structure, Web Services can become just as integral to our applications. Instead of the logic within the methods doing simple file I/O, or other local machine or network functions, the same black-boxed functions can call Web Service methods anywhere. Our application neither knows nor cares where the data comes from, nor the logic behind it.

Creating a Proxy Class

The tools provided with the .NET Framework (and Visual Studio .NET) make building a proxy to our Web Service rather simple. When we build the proxy class, the tools use the WSDL that defines our Web Service to generate the appropriate methods, with related data types intact.

> **WSDL (Web Services Description Language) defines the communication requirements of a Web Service, including function names and parameter types. For more details on WSDL, see Chapter 4.**

With the proxy built, the consumer simply calls the web method from it, and the proxy, in turn, performs the actual request of the Web Service. This request may, of course, have its endpoint anywhere from the local network to another continent via the Internet. When we reference the Web Service in the consumer application, it appears to be part of the consumer application itself, like a normal internal function call.

Let's take a look at a diagram that illustrates the process:

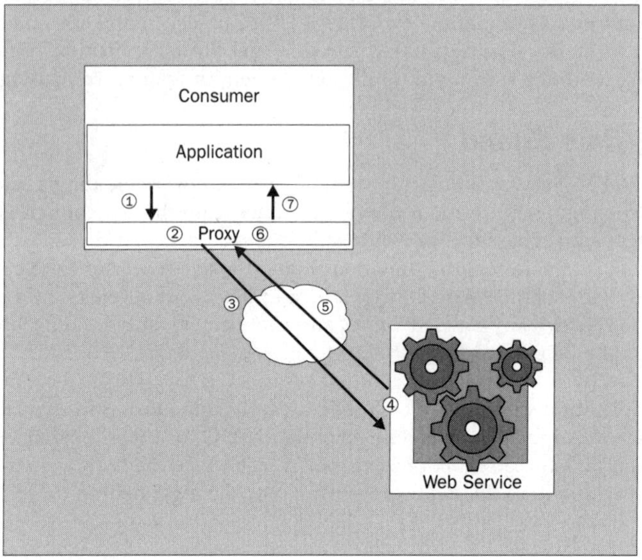

The procedure works as follows:

1. Your application executes a function in the proxy code, passing any appropriate parameters to it, unaware that the proxy is going to call a Web Service.

2. The proxy receives this call and formulates the request that will be sent to the Web Service, using the parameters the consumer has specified. The difference between synchronous and asynchronous calls ends here in the process (we'll discuss each later in this chapter).

3. This function call is sent from the proxy to the Web Service. This call can be within the confines of the same machine, across a Local Area Network (LAN), or across the Internet. The method of calling remains the same.

4. The Web Service uses the parameters provided by the proxy to execute its web-callable function and build the result in XML.

5. The resulting data from the Web Service is returned to the proxy at the consumer.

6. The proxy parses the XML returned from the Web Service to retrieve the individual values generated. These values may be as simple as integers and strings, or they may define more complex data types.

7. Your application receives the expected values from the proxy function, completely unaware that they resulted from a Web Service call.

We'll take a look at how to do this in the following example.

Using WSDL.EXE to Create the Proxy Class

You'll remember from Chapter 2 that our Web Service is located at http://localhost/PWS/Ch2-3/AppServiceVB.asmx. The command-line tool for generating proxies, `wsdl.exe`, needs to know the interfaces provided by our Web Service (the WSDL that describes it), so we'll ask the Web Service to provide that information for us. Simply enough, ASP.NET can automatically generate the self-describing WSDL for the Web Service by adding ?WSDL to its URL: http://localhost/PWS/Ch2-3/AppServiceVB.asmx?WSDL.

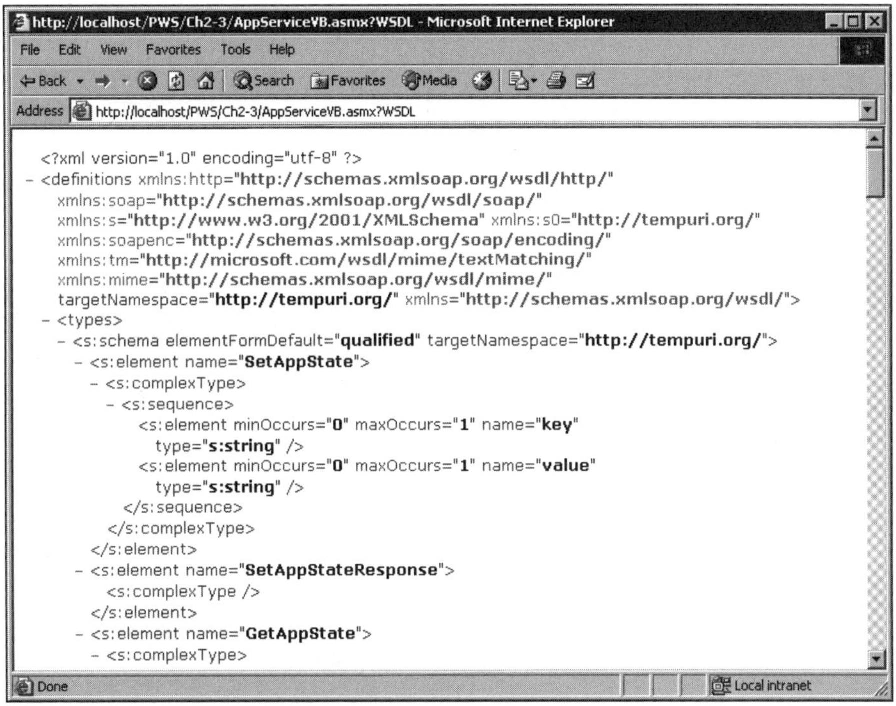

Using this same information, `wsdl.exe` will create our proxy class. Called from the command prompt, `wsdl.exe` requires this syntax (see the following table for a breakdown of potential parameters):

```
wsdl.exe <parameters> <URL or path>
```

Parameter	Description
`<URL or path>`	A URL or path to a WSDL contract, an XSD schema or `.discomap` document. We will talk about these later.
`/nologo`	Suppresses the banner.

Table continued on following page

Parameter	Description
`/language:<language>`	The language to use for the generated proxy class. Choose from 'CS', 'VB', 'JS', or provide a fully-qualified name for a class implementing `System.CodeDom.Compiler.CodeDomProvider`. The default is 'CS' (C#). Short form is `/l:`.
`/server`	Generate an abstract class for a Web Service implementation based on the contracts. The default is to generate client proxy classes.
`/namespace:<namespace>`	The namespace for the generated proxy or template. The default namespace is the global namespace. Short form is `/n:`.
`/out:<fileName>`	The filename for the generated proxy code. The default name is derived from the service name. Short form is `/o:`.
`/protocol:<protocol>`	Override the default protocol to implement. Choose from `SOAP`, `HttpGet`, `HttpPost`, or custom protocol as specified in the configuration file.

`/username:<username>`
`/password:<password>`
`/domain:<domain>`
	The credentials to use when connecting to a server that requires authentication. Short forms are `/u:`, `/p:`, and `/d:`.

`/proxy:<URL>`	The URL of the proxy server to use for HTTP requests. The default is to use the system proxy setting.

`/proxyusername:<username>`
`/proxypassword:<password>`
`/proxydomain:<domain>`
	The credentials to use when connecting to a proxy server that requires authentication. Short forms are `/pu:`, `/pp:`, and `/pd:`.

`/appsettingurlkey:<key>`	The configuration key to use in the code generation to read the default value for the URL property. The default is to not read from the config file. Short form is `/urlkey:`.
`/appsettingbaseurl:<baseURL>`	The base URL to use when calculating the URL fragment. The `appsettingurlkey` option must also be specified. The URL fragment is the result of calculating the relative URL from the `appsettingbaseurl` to the URL in the WSDL document. Short form is `/baseurl:`.

Another great feature of the `wsdl.exe` tool is its ability to generate proxy class code in your language of choice. VS.NET also provides this flexibility.

> **Which language should you use? In .NET, it's truly a matter of preference. If you have a strong background in Visual Basic, it's quite possible that VB.NET will be your choice. Those of you with more familiarity with C-based languages like C++ or Java will probably be more comfortable with C# or even MC++ (Managed C++). The reality is that, since there are so few differences between the .NET languages in terms of features and performance, you are free to select the one that you simply enjoy the most.**

Before we attempt to build our proxy, we need to be certain that we have configured our system to know where specific programs are located (these being `wsdl.exe`, `vbc.exe`, and `csc.exe`, which we'll use below). By designating the location of these files, proxy building and compilation becomes much simpler, saving us the headache of typing the full paths to each file at the command prompt.

Environment variables provide a central location to maintain values like this path information. To add the paths to our programs, right-click on My Computer (on the desktop) and select Properties. Select the Advanced tab at the top of the window, and click on the Environment Variables button. In the window that displays, scroll to the Path value in the System variables pane. Click the Edit button, and append this string to the end of the value, where `%systemroot%` points to the root directory of your version of Windows (for example `c:\WINNT`), and replacing the `XXX` with the actual number of your version of the .NET Framework (don't forget the trailing semi colon, which separates one path from another):

```
;%systemroot%\Microsoft.NET\Framework\v1.0.3XXX
```

and

```
;C:\Program Files\Microsoft.NET\FrameworkSDK\Bin
```

Click OK to close each window to apply the changes to the path.

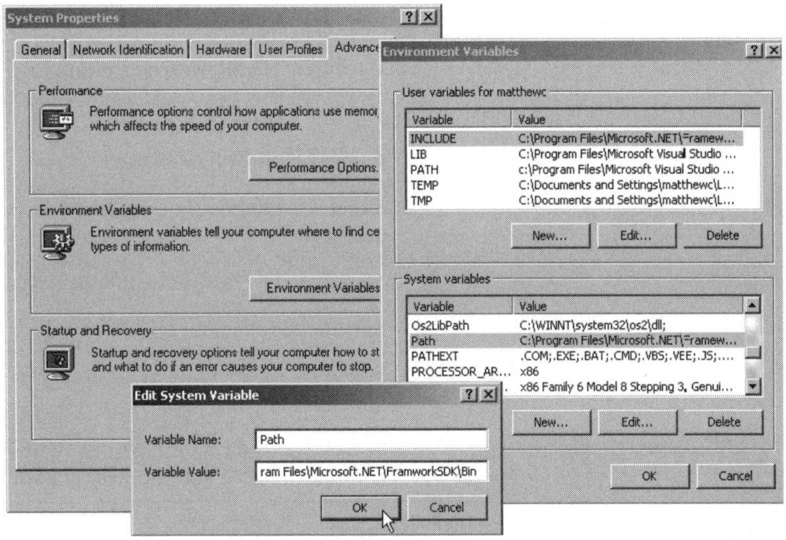

Open a command prompt, navigate to the directory in which your `AppServiceVB.asmx` file resides, and execute this statement:

```
wsdl /l:vb /o:AppServiceProxy.vb ↵
http://localhost/PWS/Ch2-3/AppServiceVB.asmx?WSDL /n:AppSettings
```

You should see something like the following:

```
Microsoft (R) Web Services Description Language Utility
[Microsoft (R) .NET Framework, Version 1.0.3705.0]
Copyright (C) Microsoft Corp. 1998-2001. All rights reserved.

Writing file 'AppServiceProxy.vb'.
```

Once the VB.NET file is created, we need to compile it to a DLL, a new .NET DLL, that will be used by other programs for the proxy. Execute this command from the same location:

```
vbc /out:AppServiceProxy.dll /t:library ↵
/r:system.dll,system.xml.dll,system.web.services.dll, AppServiceProxy.vb
```

You should see something like these results after executing this:

```
Microsoft (R) Visual Basic .NET Compiler Version 7.00.9466
for Microsoft (R) .NET Framework version 1.00.3705
Copyright (C) Microsoft Corporation 1987-2001. All rights reserved.
```

This is a table of all of the available parameters for the compile commands (both `vbc` and `csc`):

Parameter	Description
`/out:<outfile>`	Specifies the output file name.
`/t[arget]:winexe`	Creates a Windows application.
`/t[arget]:exe`	Creates a console application (default).
`/t[arget]:library`	Creates a library assembly.
`/t[arget]:module`	Creates a module that can be added to an assembly.
`/main:<class>`	Specifies the class that contains `Main`.
`/baseaddress:<addr>`	Specifies the default DLL base address (hex).
`<filespec>`	Specifies a source file to compile. The `filespec` may contain wildcards.
`/recurse:<filespec>`	Searches sub directories for all matching files to compile. The `filespec` may contain wildcards.

Parameter	Description
/r[eference]:<str>	References an external assembly.
/imports:<namespace>,...	Imports a namespace from a referenced assembly.
/nostdlib[+/-]	Does not add standard reference libraries.
/res[ource]:<file>[,<name>[,<public|private>[,<locale>[<desc>[,<mime>]]]]]	Adds a file internally to the assembly.
/linkres[ource]:<file>[,<name>]	Creates a link to a managed resource.
/win32icon:<iconfile>	Specifies an icon file (.ico).
/win32resource:<resfile>	Specifies Win32 resource file (.res).
/keyfile:<file>	Specifies key file for the assembly.
/keycontainer:<str>	Specifies key container name for the assembly.
/version:<#.#.#.#>	Specifies the assembly version.
/rootnamespace:<str>	Specifies the root namespace for all declarations.
/removeintchecks[+/-]	Removes integer checks.
/cls[+/-]	Verifies common language specification compliance.
/d[efine]:<str=val>,...	Defines conditional compilation symbol(s).
/debug[+/-]	Emits debugging information.
/optionexplicit[+/-]	Requires explicit declaration of variables.
/optionstrict[+/-]	Enforces strict language semantics.
/optioncompare:text	Specifies text-style string comparisons.
/optioncompare:binary	Specifies binary-style string comparisons (default).
/optimize[+/-]	Enables optimizations.
/nologo	Does not display compiler copyright banner.
/? or /help	Displays usage message.
@<responsefile>	Inserts command-line settings from a text file.
/bugreport:<file>	Creates bug report file.
/time	Displays elapsed compilation time.
/verbose	Displays verbose messages.

Referencing the DLL

So now we have a proxy class that we have compiled into a library assembly. The .NET Framework expects to find the DLL in the /bin directory of this particular site. Navigate to the directory you're using as the application root (if you're following the steps that we suggested earlier in the book, this will be C:\PWS\Ch2-3), create a folder there called bin, and copy the newly created AppServiceProxy.dll over from the original test directory.

Now that we have a proxy class, and we've moved it to the correct location, we're ready to make use of our AppSettings Web Service from within an ASP.NET page. We'll call the page AppSettingsInfoVB.aspx, and use it to call the web-callable function GetAppSettings in AppService.asmx. By using a proxy, our reference to the function's namespace will appear as if it were a function residing within the same page.

Create the AppSettingsInfoVB.aspx file in your test directory (or use the one we have provided in the code download for this chapter), and enter the following code:

```
<%@ Page Language="VB" Debug="true"%>
<%@ Import namespace="AppSettings" %>

<script language="VB" runat="server">
Private Sub GetSetting(ByVal sender As System.Object, _
                       ByVal e As System.EventArgs)
  Dim ws As New AppSettings.AppService()
  lblValue.Text = ws.GetAppSettings(txtSetting.Text)
End Sub
</script>

<html>
  <body>
    <form id="Form1" method="post" runat="server">
      <strong>Enter the Application Setting to retrieve:</strong><br />
      <asp:TextBox id="txtSetting" runat="server"></asp:TextBox><br />
      <asp:Button id="Button1"
                  runat="server"
                  Text="Submit"
                  OnClick="GetSetting"></asp:Button><br />
      <br />
      <% If (IsPostBack) then %>
        <strong>Value retrieved:</strong><br />
        <asp:Label id="lblValue"
                   runat="server"
                   Width="100%"
                   Height="23px"></asp:Label>
      <% End If %>
    </form>
  </body>
</html>
```

By setting the reference (importing the namespace):

```
<%@ Import namespace="AppSettings" %>
```

...the page looks in the /bin directory for the DLL that corresponds with this namespace, AppServiceProxy.dll.

Save the file and open the URL in your browser: http://localhost/PWS/Ch2-3/AppSettingsInfoVB.aspx. Note that it may take a few seconds for the page to appear, since it is compiled the first time it is accessed. Once this has taken place, the .aspx page will execute in the browser:

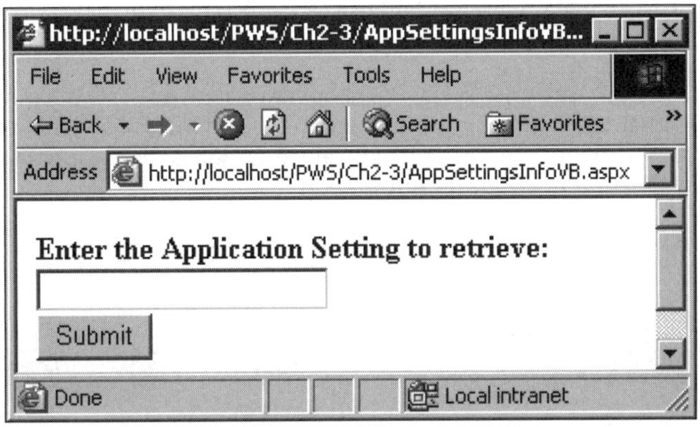

We enter the setting name connectstring and press the Submit button.

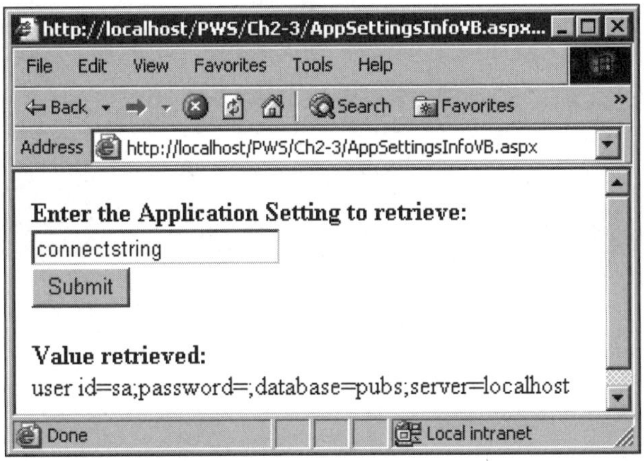

This simple web form has used the proxy class we created to access the Web Service, simply by calling a function on the page.

Building Proxies with Visual Studio .NET

While the command line tools provide all the proxying features we need, the visually appealing interface of Visual Studio .NET makes building a proxy even easier. In Visual Basic 5.0 and 6.0, to ensure early binding took place, we would set a reference in our project to a given COM object. This also helped us with IntelliSense, giving us hints of what properties and methods were available for a given object. Of course, setting a reference in those earlier Visual Basic days was, in fact, building a proxy to another COM object.

In the case of Web Services, we're not really doing anything new. Let's walk through the process of building the proxy within the VS.NET environment. We'll start off with a Windows Application, which we'll create in the `Ch2-3` directory of the code download for this and the previous chapter. Click New Project | Visual Basic Projects | Windows Application:

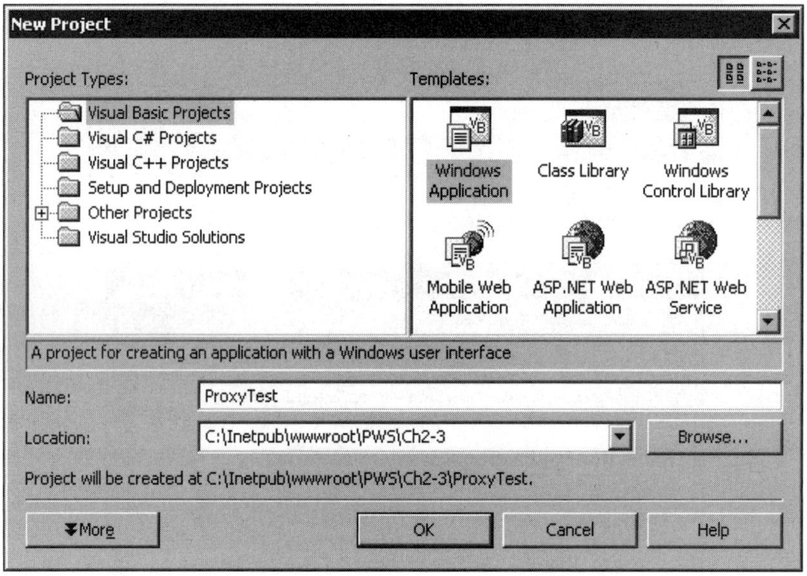

To access a Web Service natively (by building a proxy that becomes part of the solution), select Project | Add Web Reference:

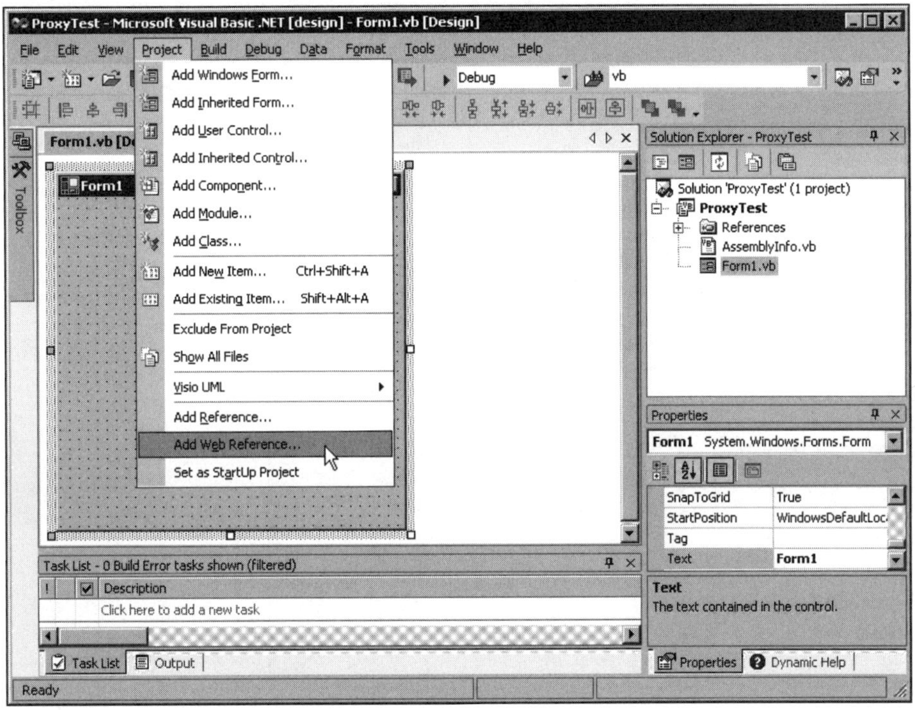

Making this selection invokes a nice, informative dialog box, complete with UDDI login information:

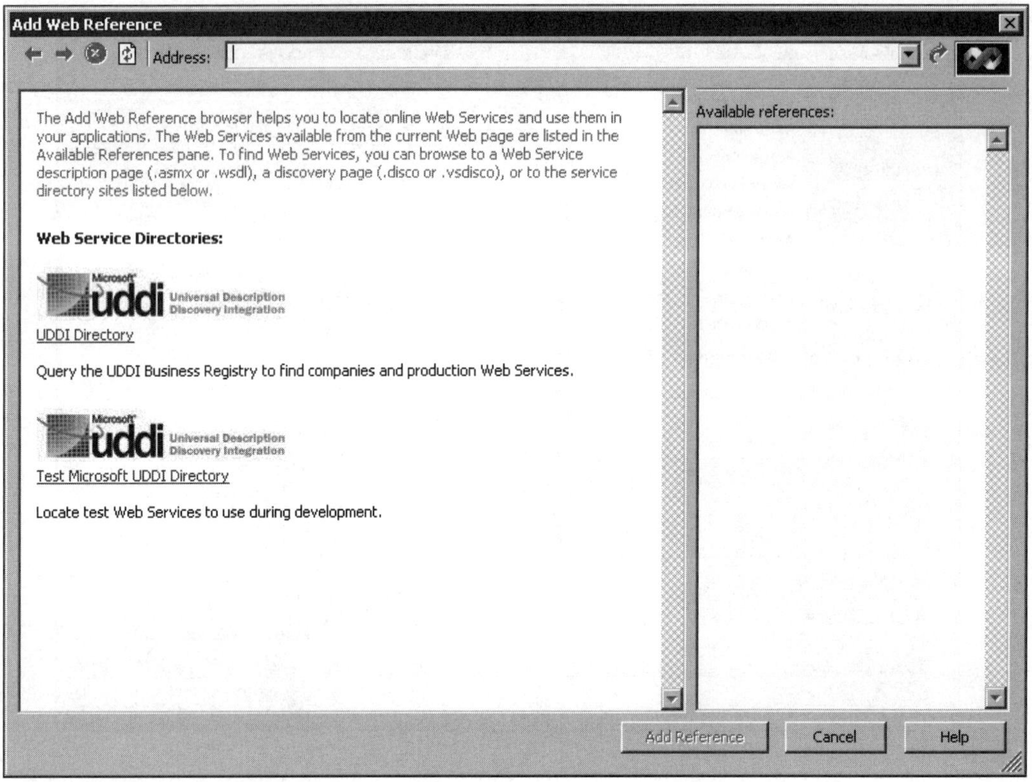

For our purposes, we need to type the following into the Address bar at the top of the page:

http://localhost/PWS/Ch2-3/AppServiceVB.asmx?WSDL

Once Visual Studio .NET retrieves the Web Service information, we click Add Reference.

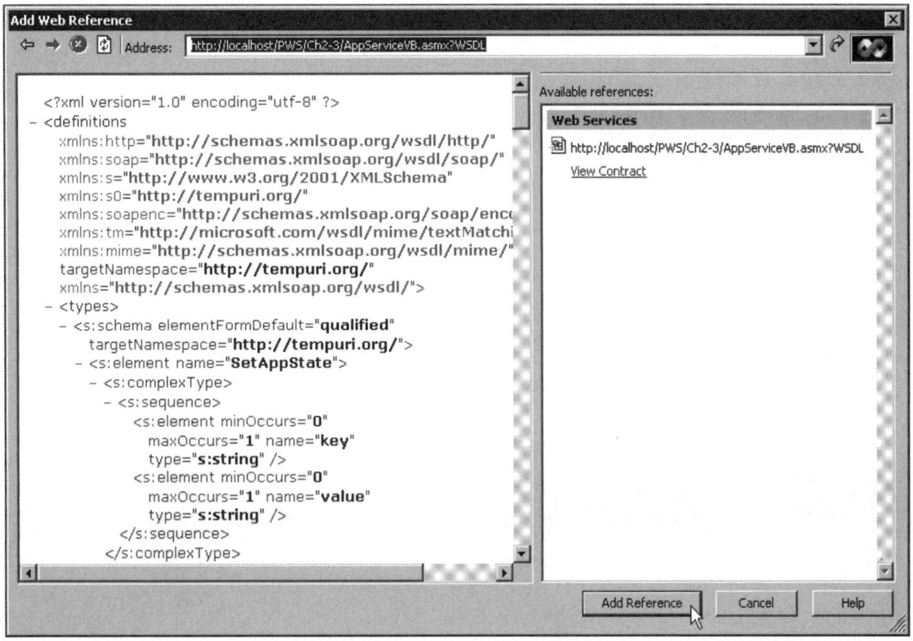

The proxy class is generated and placed in the Solution Explorer. To view the newly-created proxy class, select the Class View of Solution Explorer. Expand the tree down to localhost and you'll see the class created to access the Web Service, `AppService`.

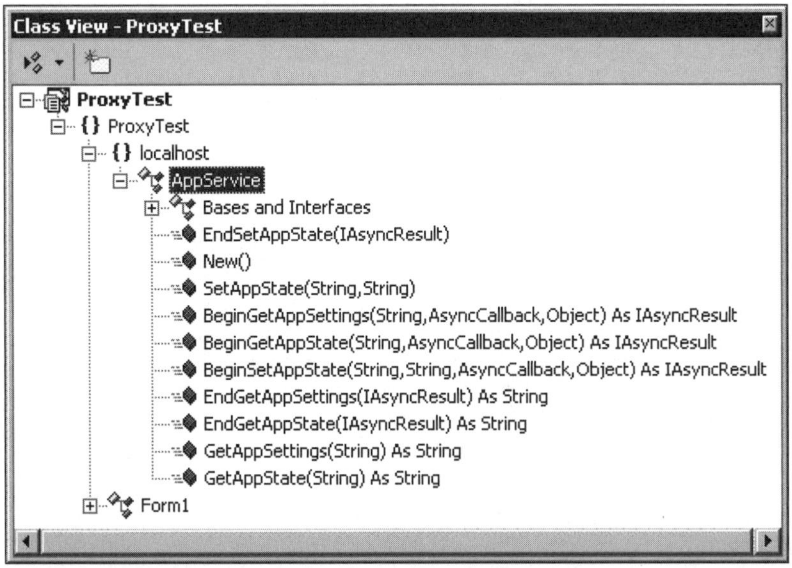

Double-click AppService to view the proxy code that was created. All this was done with a few mouse clicks! A quick examination of the proxy class code shows us the interfaces created for us:

```
Imports System
Imports System.ComponentModel
Imports System.Diagnostics
Imports System.Web.Services
Imports System.Web.Services.Protocols
Imports System.Xml.Serialization

'
'This source code was auto-generated by Microsoft.VSDesigner, Version 1.0.3705.0.
'
Namespace localhost

  '<remarks/>
  <System.Diagnostics.DebuggerStepThroughAttribute(),  _
   System.ComponentModel.DesignerCategoryAttribute("code"),  _
   System.Web.Services.WebServiceBindingAttribute(Name:="AppServiceSoap", _
   [Namespace]:="http://tempuri.org/")>  _
  Public Class AppService
    Inherits System.Web.Services.Protocols.SoapHttpClientProtocol

    '<remarks/>
    Public Sub New()
      MyBase.New
      Me.Url = "http://localhost/PWS/Ch2-3/AppServiceVB.asmx"
    End Sub

    '<remarks/>
    <System.Web.Services.Protocols.SoapDocumentMethodAttribute( _
     "http://tempuri.org/SetAppState", RequestNamespace:="http://tempuri.org/", _
     ResponseNamespace:="http://tempuri.org/", _
     Use:=System.Web.Services.Description.SoapBindingUse.Literal, _
     ParameterStyle:=System.Web.Services.Protocols.SoapParameterStyle.Wrapped)> _
    Public Sub SetAppState(ByVal key As String, ByVal value As String)
      Me.Invoke("SetAppState", New Object() {key, value})
    End Sub

    '<remarks/>
    Public Function BeginSetAppState(ByVal key As String, _
                                     ByVal value As String, _
                                     ByVal callback As System.AsyncCallback, _
                                     ByVal asyncState As Object) _
                                     As System.IAsyncResult
      Return Me.BeginInvoke("SetAppState", New Object() {key, value}, _
                            callback, asyncState)
    End Function

    '<remarks/>
    Public Sub EndSetAppState(ByVal asyncResult As System.IAsyncResult)
      Me.EndInvoke(asyncResult)
    End Sub
```

```
    '<remarks/>
    <System.Web.Services.Protocols.SoapDocumentMethodAttribute( _
     "http://tempuri.org/GetAppState", RequestNamespace:="http://tempuri.org/", _
     ResponseNamespace:="http://tempuri.org/", _
     Use:=System.Web.Services.Description.SoapBindingUse.Literal, _
     ParameterStyle:=System.Web.Services.Protocols.SoapParameterStyle.Wrapped)> _
    Public Function GetAppState(ByVal key As String) As String
      Dim results() As Object = Me.Invoke("GetAppState", New Object() {key})
      Return CType(results(0),String)
    End Function

    '<remarks/>
    Public Function BeginGetAppState(ByVal key As String, _
                                     ByVal callback As System.AsyncCallback, _
                                     ByVal asyncState As Object) _
                                     As System.IAsyncResult
      Return Me.BeginInvoke("GetAppState", New Object() {key}, _
                            callback, asyncState)
    End Function

    '<remarks/>
    Public Function EndGetAppState(ByVal asyncResult As System.IAsyncResult) _
                                   As String
      Dim results() As Object = Me.EndInvoke(asyncResult)
      Return CType(results(0),String)
    End Function

    '<remarks/>
    <System.Web.Services.Protocols.SoapDocumentMethodAttribute( _
     "http://tempuri.org/GetAppSettings", _
     RequestNamespace:="http://tempuri.org/", _
     ResponseNamespace:="http://tempuri.org/", _
     Use:=System.Web.Services.Description.SoapBindingUse.Literal, _
     ParameterStyle:=System.Web.Services.Protocols.SoapParameterStyle.Wrapped)> _
    Public Function GetAppSettings(ByVal key As String) As String
      Dim results() As Object = Me.Invoke("GetAppSettings", New Object() {key})
      Return CType(results(0),String)
    End Function

    '<remarks/>
    Public Function BeginGetAppSettings(ByVal key As String, _
                                        ByVal callback As System.AsyncCallback, _
                                        ByVal asyncState As Object) _
                                        As System.IAsyncResult
      Return Me.BeginInvoke("GetAppSettings", New Object() {key}, _
                            callback, asyncState)
    End Function

    '<remarks/>
    Public Function EndGetAppSettings(ByVal asyncResult As System.IAsyncResult) _
                                      As String
      Dim results() As Object = Me.EndInvoke(asyncResult)
      Return CType(results(0),String)
    End Function
  End Class
End Namespace
```

Functional Divisions of Proxies

Earlier in this chapter, we discussed why we need proxies and then provided details of the proxy model. When we develop applications that use proxies, there are two pieces of each proxy to distinguish: the transparent proxy and the real proxy.

Transparent Proxies

Following our phone illustration, the **transparent proxy** is analogous to the mouthpiece and earpiece of the phone. These pieces of the whole telephone conversation process do a small percentage of the work, but their role is vital, as they are the only pieces of the puzzle that are tangible. After all, the entire voice send-and-receive may be successful, but a malfunctioning earpiece will impair your attempts to carry on a conversation.

In .NET, the transparent proxy is the local interface generated by `wsdl.exe` (or through Visual Studio .NET). As we've said, these proxies appear just like the object they represent, including parameters and parameter types. The benefit of the transparent proxy to us as the developer is that methodology need not change. We first prototype our application without the Web Service (using a local function as a placeholder), then later we add the Web Service reference, accessing the remote functionality through the transparent proxy, replacing the local function.

Real Proxies

The portion of the proxy that performs the actual work of interacting with the Web Service is the **real proxy**. The part of your phone that corresponds to the real proxy is the circuitry that sends your voice over the air or wire. In .NET, real proxies expose a single method, called `Invoke`, to the Transparent proxy. We'll look at the code built for the proxies below, when we alter the base functionality of a proxy. Remember that the part of the proxy doing most of the work is the "real" one. Using our previous proxy diagram, let's take a look at the two pieces of the proxy.

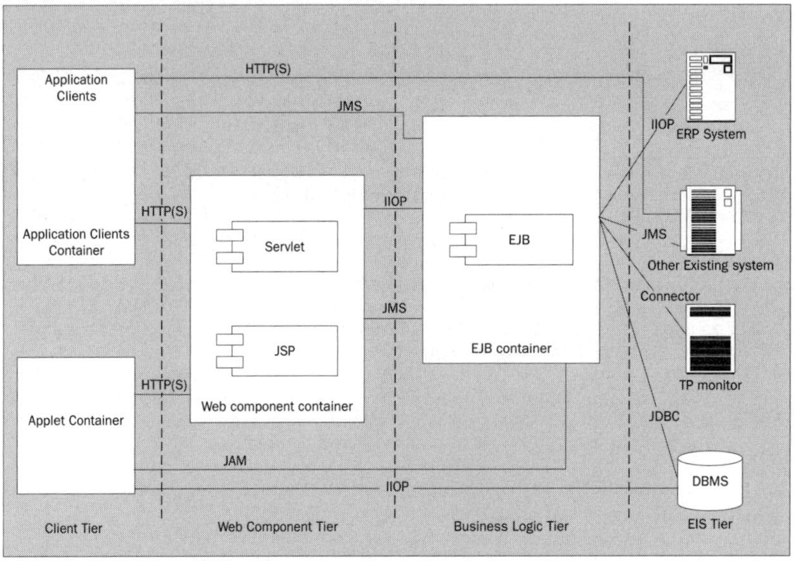

Synchronous Versus Asynchronous

Our previous use of a Web Service proxy from the web form illustrated a synchronous call. That is, the application was forced to wait for a result from the Web Service before it could continue processing anything else. Think of synchronous calls as code in which everything is processed single-file and any bottleneck slows the process down. Asynchronous processing simply issues the remote command and continues to proceed. Synchronous remote calls are generally easier to develop, and they guarantee that the invoking process knows when the remote operation is complete. Asynchronous remote calls, while slightly more involved, are generally more efficient all around.

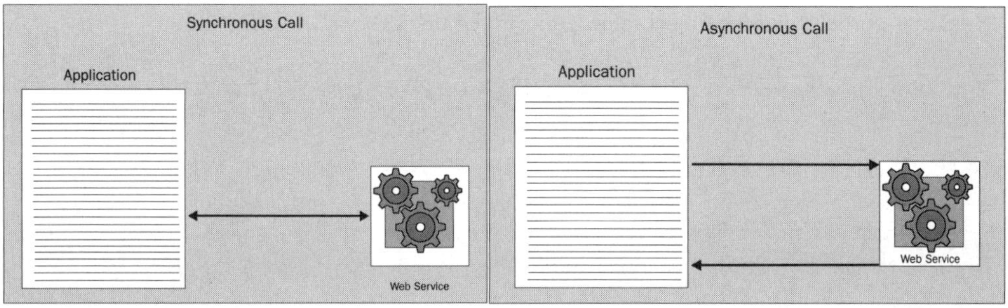

The tools that create the proxy class provide capabilities to call the Web Service both synchronously and asynchronously. Accessing a Web Service asynchronously allows your application to continue executing its calling thread without halting until a response is received. Generally, this provides significant performance gains on the client. The endpoint (the Web Service itself) is completely unaware whether it is called synchronously or asynchronously, which relieves us from specifically designing a Web Service to handle the call types differently.

Even though synchronous calls can be time-limited (with the `Timeout` property of the proxy class, which we'll discuss later in the chapter), our application must still wait for the call to time out before continuing on. In truth, as Web Services become more and more available, asynchronous usage *may* be the most practical method of invoking them, as the guarantees of network uptime and bandwidth diminish for each hop those request packets must make along the way. Remember that, unlike on a LAN, there is no way to limit the time a call may require when routed over the Internet.

Convenient enough to remember, the proxy class contains two methods, `Begin`*`MethodName`* and `End`*`MethodName`*, to enable asynchronous access. This two-step process begins by initiating the `Begin`*`MethodName`* method, which returns an object of type `System.Web.Services.Protocols.WebClientAsyncResult`. This object enables us to query the status of our Web Service request, and to manage multiple calls to the same Web Service. The asynchronous code generated by Visual Studio .NET for our `AppService` Web Service proxy is the following:

```
Public Function BeginGetAppState(ByVal key As String, _
                                 ByVal callback As System.AsyncCallback, _
                                 ByVal asyncState As Object) _
```

```
                                  As System.IAsyncResult
    Return Me.BeginInvoke("GetAppState", New Object() {key}, callback, asyncState)
  End Function

  Public Function EndGetAppState(ByVal asyncResult As System.IAsyncResult) _
                                As String
    Dim results() As Object = Me.EndInvoke(asyncResult)
    Return CType(results(0),String)
  End Function
```

The simplest method of waiting for an asynchronous call to complete is to periodically check the `IsCompleted` property of the object returned from the `Begin`*`MethodName`* method:

```
Dim ar As New IAsyncResult = AppSettings.BeginGetAppSettings(key, delay, _
                                                            callback, asyncstate)

While ar.IsCompleted = False

  ' Perform other tasks
End While
```

The `IAsyncResult` interface also provides a series of `WaitHandle` methods that allow us to manage various calls to the Web Service and present a way to wait for the completion of an asynchronous call.

We could even simply call the `EndGetAppSettings` method. Essentially, this creates a synchronous call condition, as control will not return to the program until the Web Service completes.

The fourth option for waiting on the asynchronous operation is, as we'll use in our Windows Forms example below, passing the `BeginGetAppSettings` method the address to a `Public` method so that it may return the results to our program when it completes. This allows our form application to continue doing whatever it needs to do while the Web Service is being called, executed, and returns information.

In our next example we'll make a quick modification to the Web Service that defines a second parameter to the `GetAppSettings` method of `AppService`, one that we can use to specify a delay in milliseconds. This added parameter will help us test asynchronous remote calls and watch them return values independently.

```
<WebMethod()> Public Function GetAppSettings(ByVal key As String, _
                                        ByVal delay As Integer) As String
  Try
    System.Threading.Thread.Sleep(delay)
    Return ConfigurationSettings.AppSettings(key)
  Catch
    Return "Timed Out."
  End Try
End Function
```

This modified version of the AppService Web Service is in a file called AppServiceVBMod.asmx in the code download. To test the use of asynchronous calls, we'll build a simple Windows Form that has a few textboxes and a button to start the calling process. You can find this in the AsyncTestVB folder of the code download. When the button is pressed, each call is issued, passing the address of the callback function that will process the return value.

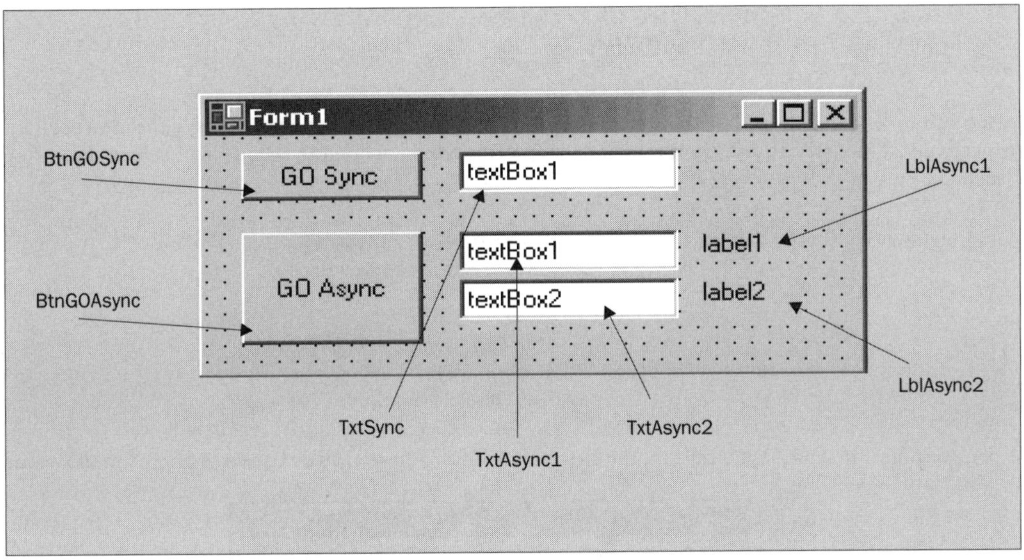

Let's take a quick look at the code within the GO Async button click handler to make each Web Service call:

```
Private Sub BtnGOAsync_Click(ByVal sender As System.Object, _
                             ByVal e As System.EventArgs) _
                             Handles BtnGOAsync.Click
  Dim objService As New localhost.AppService()

  ' First async call
  Dim adrCallBack1 As New System.AsyncCallback(AddressOf AppServiceCallback1)
  TxtAsync1.Text = "" : LblAsync1.Text = ""
  objService.BeginGetAppSettings("connectstring", 2500, _
                                 adrCallBack1, objService)

  ' Second async call
  Dim adrCallBack2 As New System.AsyncCallback(AddressOf AppServiceCallback2)
  TxtAsync2.Text = "" : LblAsync2.Text = ""
  objService.BeginGetAppSettings("connectstring", 5000, _
                                 adrCallBack2, objService)
End Sub

Public Sub AppServiceCallback1(ByVal resAr As IAsyncResult)
  Dim objService As localhost.AppService
  Dim objDetails As String
  objService = resAr.AsyncState
  TxtAsync1.Text = objService.EndGetAppSettings(resAr)
```

```
    LblAsync1.Text = Now.ToLongTimeString.ToString()
  End Sub

  Public Sub AppServiceCallback2(ByVal resAr As IAsyncResult)
    Dim objService As localhost.AppService
    Dim objDetails As String
    objService = resAr.AsyncState
    TxtAsync2.Text = objService.EndGetAppSettings(resAr)
    LblAsync2.Text = Now.ToLongTimeString.ToString()
  End Sub
```

In the call to `BeginGetAppSettings`, we're passing 2500 and 5000 to the two asynchronous calls, respectively. The first call will then return data in 2.5 seconds, while the second will return data after 5 seconds.

```
objService.BeginGetAppSettings("connectstring", 2500, _
                              adrCallBack1, objService)

 ...

objService.BeginGetAppSettings("connectstring", 5000, _
                              adrCallBack2, objService)
```

When we press the **GO Async** button, the first results return to `AppServiceCallback1` in 2.5 seconds:

After another 2.5 seconds, the second results return to `AppServiceCallback2`:

By declaring variables of type `System.AsyncCallback` and passing it the address of the method `AppServiceCallback1` and `AppServiceCallback2` (using `AddressOf`), the proxy knows exactly what to do when it is completed. `BeginGetAppSettings` accepts the standard parameters we've defined, the `key` and the `delay` in milliseconds, as well as the address of the callback method and an instance of the object we're accessing (`AppService`). If you're reasonably familiar with asynchronous callbacks, you will recognize logic implemented here. If we were creating a synchronous call, the code in `AppServiceCallback1` would most likely be placed inline within the button's `Click` event. The instance of `AppService`, `objService`, is retrieved from the `IAsyncResult` variable `resAr.AsyncState`. That's it!

Modifying Default Proxy Settings

The generated proxy class provides some healthy features, but undoubtedly there is room for making adjustments to the way the proxy executes. Since the proxy class inherits from several classes, there are a number of properties and methods available. We'll discuss the following of these properties and how to use each:

- Changing the URL
- Timeout
- Proxy Server
- Encoding
- User Agent
- Redirection

Changing the URL

The location of the Web Service is defined by the WSDL that describes it. There are circumstances that may warrant changing the URL, such as relocation of the Web Service. This may happen, for example, if the organization providing the service is acquired by another company; in this case, you may be required to change the URL to the Web Service.

It's important to know that the URL can be modified at run time, which makes the proxy class very flexible. Some uses of changing the `Url` property are:

- Implementing round-robin logic to balance the load
- Attempting a different URL after a `Timeout` or other error occurs

The `Url` property is implemented in the proxy like this:

```
Me.Url = "http://localhost/PWS/Ch2-3/AppServiceVB.asmx"
```

Let's take a look at a simple method of providing round-robin Web Service access. You can find this example in the AsyncTestVB-2 folder of the code download. Without creating mammoth algorithms, we'll use the current second to determine which URL we choose in our proxy class. While it may not be foolproof, handling various URLs based on the time gives a statistically even spread.

Our proxy constructor remains the same, but we'll add in a Case-type structure to set the Url appropriately:

```
Public Sub New()
  MyBase.New()
  Dim Seconds As Integer = System.Math.IEEERemainder(DateTime.Now.Second, 3)
  If Seconds = 0 Then
    Me.Url = "http://localhost/PWS/Ch2-3/CopyUrls/AppServiceVB1.asmx"
  ElseIf Seconds = 1 Then
    Me.Url = "http://localhost/PWS/Ch2-3/CopyUrls/AppServiceVB2.asmx"
  Else
    Me.Url = "http://localhost/PWS/Ch2-3/CopyUrls/AppServiceVB3.asmx"
  End If
End Sub
```

Depending on the current second, we'll select one of three URLs, which we have all specified as being in the CopyUrls folder in the code download. Using the IEEERemainder function, it's easy to do, giving us an even distribution.

Timeout

It's very important to be prepared if the Web Service refuses to answer, or if any kind of network communication problem arises. After all, without some such mechanism, our program will wait patiently indefinitely (while our users most certainly will not!). Unlike the prospect of handling an excessive delay elsewhere in the program, with regard to synchronous Web Service access, it's best to handle the timeout condition within the proxy. Still using the new GetAppSettings method that includes a delay parameter, this short code snippet illustrates the handling of a client-side timeout condition. You can find this code in the AsyncTestVB-3 folder of the code download.

First, we add the Timeout property to the constructor of our AppService. By setting it to one millisecond, it is almost certain that our Web Service will not respond in time, generating an exception caused by the timeout.

```
Public Class AppService
  Inherits System.Web.Services.Protocols.SoapHttpClientProtocol

  Public Sub New()
    MyBase.New()
    Me.Timeout = 1     ' one millisecond, definitely not enough time!
    Me.Url = "http://localhost/PWS/Ch2-3/AppServiceVBMod.asmx"
  End Sub
```

Then we modify the `GetAppSettings` method by adding "`Try...Catch`" logic to handle the impending timeout:

```
<System.Diagnostics.DebuggerStepThroughAttribute(), _
System.Web.Services.Protocols.SoapDocumentMethodAttribute( _
"http://tempuri.org/GetAppSettings", _
RequestNamespace:="http://tempuri.org", ResponseNamespace:="http://tempuri.org, _
Use:=System.Web.Services.Description.SoapBindingUse.Literal, _
ParameterStyle:=System.Web.Services.Protocols.SoapParameterStyle.Wrapped)> _
Public Function GetAppSettings(ByVal key As String, _
                              ByVal delay As Integer) As String
  Try
    Dim results() As Object = Me.Invoke("GetAppSettings", New Object() _
                                        {key, delay})
    Return CType(results(0), String)
  Catch
    Return CType("Timed out.", String)
  End Try
End Function
```

When the call to the `GetAppSettings` Web Service fails, the `Catch` clause will execute, returning the string "Timed Out.".

> **Regardless of the method you use to proxy to Web Services, you should provide ample logic to catch timeouts and other communication errors.**

An even more robust example of combining the `Url` and `Timeout` properties is attempting to access various URLs, one after another, if the previous one times out. For this example, which you can find in `AsyncTestVB-4`, we'll create a routine called `GenerateUrl`, whose job it is to return the URL to attempt, based on the number of attempts. Using a counter integer called `Attempts`, we'll track how many times we've attempted to connect to a Web Service.

We've added the integer declaration and ensured our `Timeout` will cause our call to expire as before:

```
Public Class AppService
  Inherits System.Web.Services.Protocols.SoapHttpClientProtocol
  Dim Attempts As Integer = 0

  Public Sub New()
    MyBase.New()
    Me.Timeout = 50
    Me.Url = "http://localhost/PWS/Ch2-3/AppServiceVBMod.asmx"
  End Sub
```

Within the `GetAppSettings` function, we build our logic to handle timeout conditions and select alternative URLs appropriately. We know that the URLs provided by `GenerateUrl` are nonexistent, so using VS.NET, we can step through the entire application, watching the `Catch` of each timeout condition.

```
...
Public Function GetAppSettings(ByVal key As String, ByVal delay As Integer) _
                              As String
  Try
    Dim results() As Object = Me.Invoke("GetAppSettings", New Object() _
                                        {key, delay})
    Return CType(results(0), String)
  Catch
    Attempts += 1
    If Attempts < 3 Then
      Me.Url = GenerateUrl(Attempts)
      Return GetAppSettings(key, delay)
    Else
      Return CType("Timed out.", String)
    End If
  End Try
End Function

Private Function GenerateUrl(ByVal Attempts As Integer) As String
  Select Case Attempts
    Case 1
      Return "http://localhost/PWS/Ch2-3/AppServiceVB2.asmx"
    Case 2
      Return "http://localhost/PWS/Ch2-3/AppServiceVB3.asmx"
    Case Else
      Return "http://localhost/PWS/Ch2-3/AppServiceVB4.asmx"
  End Select
End Function
```

Proxy Server

When we first introduced the idea of proxying, we mentioned Microsoft's Internet Security and Acceleration (ISA) Server, which accepts Internet requests from computers on a LAN/WAN and sends them out to the Internet on their behalf. This software is called a **Web Proxy**, not to be confused with a Web Service Proxy.

> **Web Proxy Servers provide a single access point to the Internet, acting similar to a router. Some implementations also provide encryption, caching, and other advanced features that boost Internet access performance for a network.**

If your consumer resides on a network that accesses the Internet via a Web Proxy Server, you'll need to ensure that your proxy class can reach the Internet. The proxy class is intelligent enough to check Internet Explorer's web proxy settings on the consumer's computer, which it then uses to set its own web proxy details. If, for some reason, you need to change the Web Proxy server settings from Internet Explorer's defaults, you can use the `Proxy` property.

The value of this property is set with an object of type `WebProxy`.

```
Dim proxyObject As New WebProxy("http://proxy.domain.com:80", True)
Me.Proxy = proxyObject
```

Encoding

Not all platforms use the same text encoding standards. Should you need to change the encoding type of your message to match that of the Web Service, the `RequestEncoding` property of the proxy, coming from the inherited `WebClientProtocol` class, allows you to do just that. If you change the `RequestEncoding` value, which defaults to `Nothing`, the `ContentType` of the request will be changed accordingly.

The short example below shows how to change your encoding to UTF-8:

```
Me.RequestEncoding = System.Text.Encoding.UTF8
```

User Agent

Web Servers identify certain information about the browsers that access them by interpreting the User Agent string. Part of the HTTP standards of communication, the User Agent most often lists the browser type and the platform of the computer making the request. It is the duty of the browser to generate this information. The Web Server can make some informed judgments based on these details, such as the type of data or HTML with which to respond. Some organizations customize the User Agent string to include other details, including user-specific information.

The `UserAgent` property defines what User Agent string will be passed in the HTTP protocol headers of the Web Service request. This defaults to **MS Web Services Client Protocol *x***, where ***x*** is the version of the common language runtime.

A Web Service may use the User Agent string to determine the type of consumer, whether as part of some versioning scheme, or even as a form of identification. Just as the browser can provide user-specific information in the User Agent sent to the Web Server, our proxy classes can provide unique details to the Web Services they call.

```
Me.UserAgent = "AppServiceProxy v1.2"
```

Redirection

Another part of the HTTP protocol is the use of redirection. As part of a response, the Web Service may issue a redirection (no different from `Response.Redirect`, since each uses HTTP), to a different URL. The following illustrates the details sent from the Web Server that instruct a browser (or Web Service proxy class) to seek a new URL, in this case, `http://newlocation/file.aspx`.

```
HTTP/1.0 302 Found
Server: Microsoft-IIS/5.0
Date: Sun, 23 Jun 2002 13:35:22 GMT

Location: http://newlocation/file.aspx
Content-Type: text/html
Content-Length: 734
```

The `AllowAutoRedirect` property, by default, is set to `False` to prevent such redirection within a proxy class. When set to `True`, the proxy will follow redirection to another URL provided in the HTTP response. Why permit redirection? Maintenance is reduced, in the case of a change in the Web Service URL. If the Web Service provider is kind enough to introduce the redirection message, your proxy will be able to locate the new Web Service seamlessly (albeit with an extra round-trip to the server).

```
Me.AllowAutoRedirection = True
```

Summary

The Web Service proxy class greatly enables the integration of Web Service functionality into our everyday applications. Abilities to interpret WSDL and generate the appropriate source code for calling any Web Service make implementing Web Service logic within our applications very natural. Life without the simple ability to generate these proxies would mean that every developer would have his/her own methods of accessing Web Services and enforcing type constraints, not to mention a fairly steep learning curve. Instead of investing significant development time at the beginning of each project simply connecting to a Web Service, our focus goes directly to the functionality we are seeking to provide with our application.

Proxies aren't just limited to the role of accessing Web Services. The same features apply to all proxy utilizations, such as web proxy servers and COM. The functional divisions of a proxy, transparent and real, also apply. While the transparent proxy provides our application with an interface like the actual Web Service, the real proxy performs all the work of communication. Since the idea of proxying isn't new, we are not venturing into a world of new methodologies; rather, we are taking this paradigm to the world of web-based applications. This is the basis for the publicity that Web Services are receiving throughout the industry.

We've seen the two primary ways to build a proxy class: using `wsdl.exe` at the command prompt, and setting a Web Reference from within Visual Studio .NET. Each technique created a proxy class in the language we specified, complete with the facility to call the Web Service both synchronously and asynchronously.

While the generated proxy class is fully featured, we can make modifications to its code to override some of its defaults. For synchronous operation, we can force a timeout if we wait too long for a Web Service to respond. We can change the URL where the Web Service resides, and with a little extra code, we can produce a round-robin Web Service call strategy to offset the load to a particular Web Service.

Understanding why we need proxies and how to make effective use of them is very important, since most practical use of Web Services is carried out with their help. Excitement and adrenaline may not be the hallmark of the proxy class, but certainly the fact that most of the proxy work is done for us (and very efficiently) is reason to rejoice.

In this chapter we have covered the following subjects:

- The definition and role of proxies
- Using `WSDL.exe` from a command prompt to create a proxy class
- Using Visual Studio .NET to create a proxy class
- The difference between synchronous and asynchronous proxies
- How to modify the base settings of a proxy

PROFESSIONAL
ASP.NET
WEB
SERVICES

4

Web Service Description Language

This chapter contains two sections: the first describes the basic usage of the Web Service Description Language (WSDL) with ASP.NET, Visual Studio .NET, and how to expose COM objects with WSDL files with the SOAP Toolkit 2.0. The second section contains a look at the structure of a WSDL file.

In the first section we will cover the functional steps necessary to generate WSDL files and in the second section we will look more closely at a breakdown of the meaning of the different elements in a WSDL file. The second section will also look at some of the more advanced topics in WSDL. Here are some of the main points that will be covered in this chapter:

- How to use the SOAP Toolkit 2.0 to create WSDL files to expose COM objects.
- How to access WSDL documents in .NET with Visual Studio .NET.
- A sample ASP.NET Web Service and the web method attributes used to configure a Web Service.
- A detailed view of a WSDL document and its components.
- A brief description of how WSDL is extended for SOAP, HTTP GET/POST, and MIME.
- An example of the flexibility of WSDL using a screen scrape example that shows how WSDL files can be used with standard HTML forms.

By the end of this chapter, you will have a solid understanding of what WSDL is; you will know how to create WSDL files in the SOAP Toolkit 2.0 to expose COM objects as Web Services; and you will know how to access WSDL files in Visual Studio .NET. If you have not already taken the time to learn about WSDL, you'll see that WSDL offers a lot of potential, which is well worth getting to grips with.

As far as some of the more complicated aspects of WSDL are concerned, this chapter will not provide every detail, or complete explanations of the WSDL specifications, as the specifications are too new, transient, vast, and extensible to provide absolute definitions. What this chapter will do is present an accurate introductory discussion of the language, which will leave you with a working knowledge and insight into its essence and implementation.

What Is WSDL?

Web Service Description Language (WSDL) is an XML-based language used to describe Web Services or network endpoints. A WSDL contract describes the messaging between a Web Service and a client, the location of a Web Service, and the protocols available to communicate with a Web Service.

WSDL works in conjunction with SOAP and UDDI to enable Web Services to interact with other Web Services, applications, and devices across the Internet. Essentially, UDDI provides a central registry for published Web Services; WSDL describes the Web Service; and SOAP provides transport information for the Web Service. WSDL describes a Web Service or network endpoint to the extent that it can be accessed by other services over the network without any human intervention. Essentially a WSDL document describes a Web Service very much like a type library describes a COM object.

The combination of SOAP and UDDI provides the ability to discover, publish, and send messages between a client and a Web Service. Without WSDL, this messaging interface would have to be created manually. For example, after locating a stock quote service, it would be necessary to understand the method map information, parameters, and the protocols supported by the service and then hand-craft the SOAP request and response messages. If each time a new service has to be accessed, human intervention is required, the move towards Web Services would certainly be inhibited. The power of WSDL is that it is truly platform and object model agnostic. It is an XML grammar that provides an interface to Web Services across all platforms.

Here is a scenario of how an application would locate a freight calculation service via UDDI and would then analyze the WSDL and create a Proxy file from it, enabling the application to access the freight calculation service:

- Search a UDDI directory for a service that provides the functionality you need; that is, a freight calculation service.
- Once the service is located, request the WSDL contract and extract the location or URI, the method map information, and the protocols supported.
- Create a Proxy file that provides this information, along with the SOAP request, and response messages so that the remote service or application can be accessed.

WSDL is a W3C submitted specification (at the time of writing it is not yet a W3C standard) supported by a number of industry leaders, including Microsoft and IBM. WSDL is based on a combination of the Software Definition Language (SDL) from Microsoft and the Network Accessible Services Specification Language (NASSL) from IBM. IBM turned over development of NASSL to Apache so that there could be a standard way to create WSDL documents in the Java world. More information on the Apache SOAP and WSDL implementation can be found at http://xml.apache.org/soap/index.html. The Apache Software Foundation handles a number of open-source development initiatives. They will work to make this available to the Java world so that WSDL should be available ubiquitously.

It is necessary that WSDL is made available across platforms for it to fulfill its promise of platform and object model agnostic Web Services interacting with each other across the Internet. That said, this is an ASP.NET Web Service book, so we will cover using WSDL documents with Microsoft technologies here.

Why Is It Necessary To Understand WSDL?

One question many of you are probably asking is, if WSDL files can be created by tools on all of the major platforms, why should I take the time to understand them? WSDL documents are new enough that learning how they work under the hood is probably wise, as the bullets below explain. As Web Services become more prevalent, it will become more apparent how often it is necessary to understand and/or to tweak WSDL documents.

- The promise of complete automation in creating WSDL files is very compelling. However, Web Service standards are very new, and only time will tell precisely how they are able to automatically create the proper SOAP request and response messages based on a WSDL contract. Tweaking may be necessary to fix small bugs between platforms or versions, or it may be necessary to optimize the SOAP request and response messages. It is very common that tools create standard code that is not optimized to specific environments and situations. There are also so many standards, including the WSDL, SOAP, and UDDI schemas, that it seems there will be times when different vendors will support different versions of these standards.
- As Web Services become more ubiquitous, it will become beneficial to be able to examine a WSDL document for a specific Web Service and to be able to understand it. Understanding WSDL gives us a way to read the functionality of a Web Service across the Web, as we become more reliant on using the functionality of Web Services in our own applications.
- In some cases it may be appropriate to create WSDL files first, so that a method contract is available before coding starts. This is similar to what is done with COM components, when IDL interfaces with method contracts are laid out before the programming begins.
- It is always helpful to understand how things work under the hood. Not only for tinkering, as mentioned above, but, in general, developers who have a solid grasp of the underpinning technologies are better able to write code that takes advantage of the technology.
- There is an `Import` statement feature supported in WSDL documents. The fact that this is in the standard means that there is some thought that WSDL documents will be created from source libraries and not on the fly for every Web Service created. One possible option is to define all the methods and data types ahead of time. This would let us create the functionality and store it in WSDL library files that could be mapped to specific protocol information later. This point will become clearer when we walk through the different sections of the WSDL documents later.
- The WSDL document was created manually for the screen scrape example at the end of this chapter. It is possible that there are other rare occasions when creating WSDL documents manually will be necessary, although having to modify them is more likely than having to create them.

How To Create WSDL Files in .NET and COM

First we will cover how to create WSDL files to work with COM objects, using the SOAP Toolkit 2.0, and then move on to WSDL file usage with ASP.NET and Visual Studio .NET. There is more material to cover on creating WSDL files with the SOAP Toolkit 2.0, because WSDL files are automatically created with .NET.

Creating WSDL files with the SOAP Toolkit 2.0 involves using the toolkit to create a Web Service Meta Language (WSML) file that is used to map a COM object to a WSDL file. That said, it is not difficult to use the SOAP Toolkit 2.0 as it provides an easy-to-use interface. If you do not have any need to expose COM objects, skip to the *How to Create WSDL files in .NET* section.

WSDL Documents and COM Objects

This section relies on the SOAP Toolkit 2.0, which can be downloaded from Microsoft at http://msdn.microsoft.com/downloads/default.asp?URL=/code/sample.asp?url=/msdn-files/027/001/580/msdncompositedoc.xml. At the time of going to press, the SOAP 3.0 Toolkit is in early beta, and should be available in late 2002, but we have decided to go with the 2.0 version for the purposes of this discussion. In order to use the SOAP Toolkit 2.0, you must have Visual Basic 6.0 or Visual Studio installed. In order to use WSDLGEN (the graphical component of the SOAP Toolkit 2.0 used below) to expose the COM object you create as a Web Service, you must have Windows 2000 or NT installed. There is a utility called `wsdlstb.exe` that can be used instead of WSDLGEN. It can be accessed from the command line or from within scripts. We will not cover the `wsdlstb.exe` utility in this chapter, as it is not directly relevant to the topic in hand.

The SOAP Toolkit 2.0 is WSDL 1.1 compliant. WSDL and WSML files that were created with the SOAP Toolkit 1.0 are not compatible and must be recreated with the SOAP Toolkit 2.0. The SOAP Toolkit 2.0 is supported by Microsoft technical support, whereas the 1.0 version is not.

The service names and other components in the SOAP Toolkit 2.0 are case-sensitive. Be precise and consistent with respect to the case used when naming files.

Using the SOAP Toolkit 2.0

You don't need to use the SOAP Toolkit 2.0 to expose COM objects as Web Services. However, it is a neat utility that does almost all the work for you. Therefore, unless you really like to or have reason to create WSDL, WSML, and SOAP listener files by hand, it is a good idea to use the SOAP Toolkit 2.0.

In order to expose COM objects as Web Services, Microsoft has built specific utilities into the SOAP Toolkit 2.0. The process basically works by selecting a COM object and a WSDL file. A Web Service Meta Language File (WSML) and an ASP or ISAPI SOAP listener file is then created for the selected COM object. The WSML file maps the COM methods to the WSDL file, and the ASP, ISAPI listener file, or SOAP server file provides an interface to be called from the outside world.

Let's fill out this basic process by actually creating a COM object and exposing it as a Web Service. Over the next few steps we will create the following files:

- Script File – a VBScript file that we can use to access the COM exposed Web Service we will be creating.

- DLL file – a Visual Basic 6 COM object that will have one method to multiply numbers and one to add numbers. We will use the SOAP Toolkit 2.0 to expose this COM object as a Web Service.
- WSDL File – generated by the SOAP Toolkit 2.0.
- WSML File – generated by the SOAP Toolkit 2.0. WSML files are specific to the SOAP Toolkit 2.0 implementation and provide an interface between COM objects and WSDL files.
- ASP File – we will use the SOAP Toolkit 2.0 to create an ASP SOAP Server file.

After creating these files, we will place all of them, with the exception of the script, in a virtual directory and run the script file. Running the script file will execute the Web Service. It is important to create the virtual directory ahead of time when using the SOAP Toolkit 2.0 because the file locations and names are placed in the WSDL, WSML, and ASP files created below.

Now we can create the Arithmetic COM object, which contains one method for adding numbers and one for multiplying numbers. The code is shown below. If you prefer, you can download the `ArithmeticCOMProject.dll` file from the source for this chapter and register it with the `regsvr32` tool. Type regsvr32 ArithmeticCOMProject.dll from the command prompt to do this.

The WSML file generated by the WSDL/WSML Generator contains the dispatch IDs of the methods corresponding to each operation. If you use Visual Basic to create the DLL, dispatch IDs are based on the order of methods in the DLL. If you change the order of methods in the DLL, the dispatch IDs will reflect the change. In this case the WSML file must be updated accordingly.

In order to create the necessary files follow the steps below. If you want to download the files instead of creating them, skip to the download files section directly below.

To create the COM object in Visual Basic:

- Create a directory named /PWS/Ch4/ArithmeticCOM/ in the root directory of the web server. Go into Internet Information Server and mark this directory as a virtual directory.
- Create a new Visual Basic ActiveX DLL project.
- Change the project name to ArithmeticCOMProject.
- Change the class name to ArithmeticCOM.
- In the class, enter the code below:

```
Public Function multiplyNumbers(ByVal NumberOne As Double, _
                                ByVal NumberTwo As Double) As Double
  multiplyNumbers = NumberOne * NumberTwo
End Function


Public Function addNumbers(ByVal NumberOne As Double, _
                           ByVal NumberTwo As Double) As Double
  addNumbers = NumberOne + NumberTwo
End Function
```

- Save the project.
- Choose Make ArithmeticCOMProject.dll from the file menu.

If you prefer to use the code download for this chapter follow the steps below.

Here is a list of the files that need to be downloaded:

- `ClientArithmeticCOM.vbs` – This is a VBScript file that will be used to access the COM exposed Web Service we will download and register.
- `ArithmeticCOMProject.dll` – This is the COM object that uses the SOAP Toolkit 2.0 to enable itself to be exposed as a COM object.
- `ArithmeticCOM.wsdl` – This is the WSDL file that was generated by the SOAP Toolkit 2.0.
- `ArithmeticCOM.wsml` – This is the WSML file that was generated by the SOAP Toolkit 2.0.
- `ArithmeticCOM.asp` – This is the ASP SOAP Server file that was generated by the SOAP Toolkit 2.0.

Here are the steps necessary to download and install the sample files.

- Download the source code for this book from www.wrox.com.
- Create a directory named PWS/Ch4/ArithmeticCOM in the root directory of the web server. Go into Internet Information Server and mark this directory as a virtual directory.
- Copy all of the files, with the exception of the script file, into this directory.
- Register the DLL file by typing regsvr32 c:\inetpub\wwwroot\PWS\Ch4\ArithmeticCOM\ArithmeticCOMProject.dll from the command prompt. A dialog box stating successful registration should be displayed.
- Copy the script file into any other directory on your system.

NOTE: If you create a different directory structure than recommended above, you will need to manually modify the WSDL file.

> **The COM object has to be registered for the SOAP Toolkit 2.0 utilities to be able to work with it.**

Now it is time to create the files necessary to expose the COM object as a Web Service. If you downloaded the files, you do not need to do this, but it would still be worth looking through the screens to see how to use the SOAP Toolkit 2.0.

To use the Wizard, select the WSDL Generator from the SOAP Toolkit 2.0. You will see that the Welcome to the SOAP Toolkit 2.0 Wizard screen is displayed:

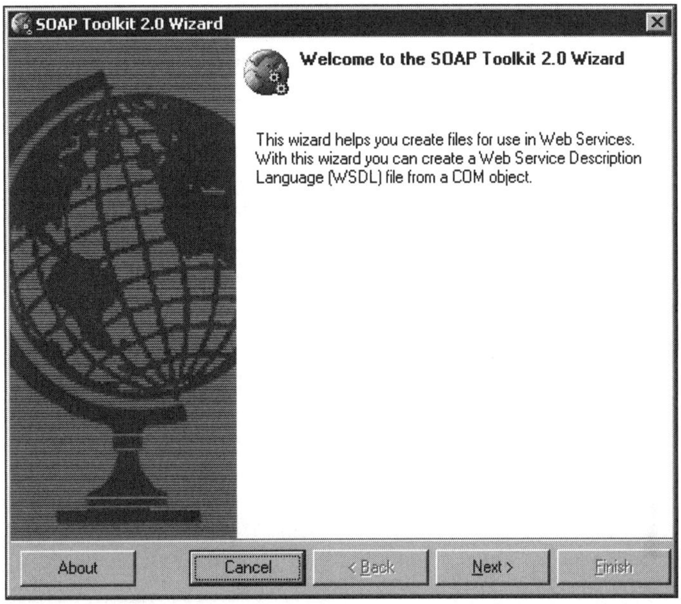

Click Next to begin the configuration. We provide a name for the service and a path to our COM object on this next screen:

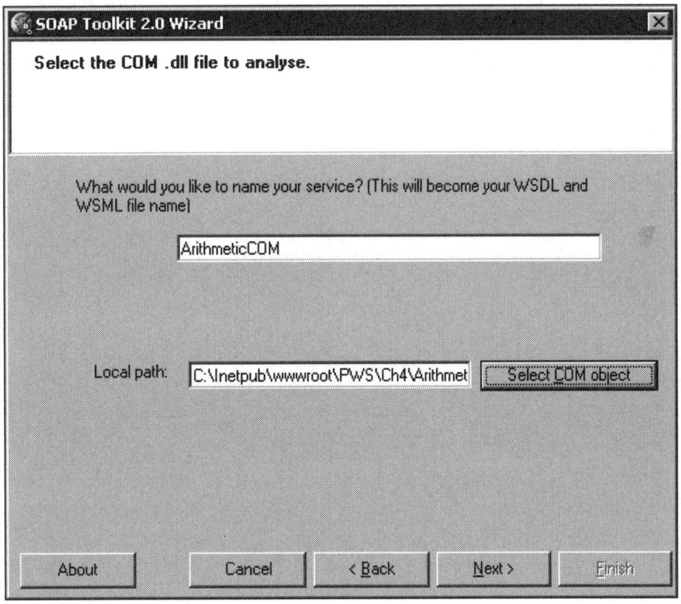

Name the WSDL and WSML files ArithmeticCOM, and in the Local path box, insert the path to the DLL on your system, and click Next.

Here, we select the services we would like to expose:

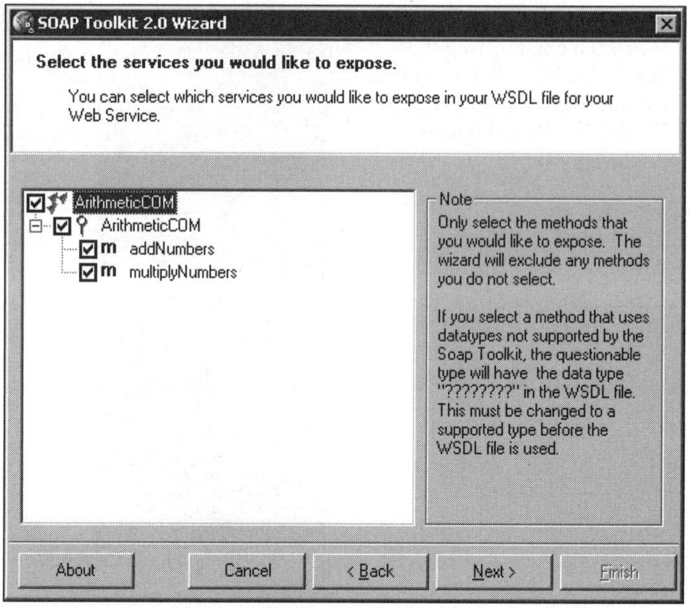

We need to select both the addNumbers and multiplyNumbers methods, as we want to expose both of them. On the following screen, we provide the SOAP listener URI, listener type, and XSD Schema Namespace:

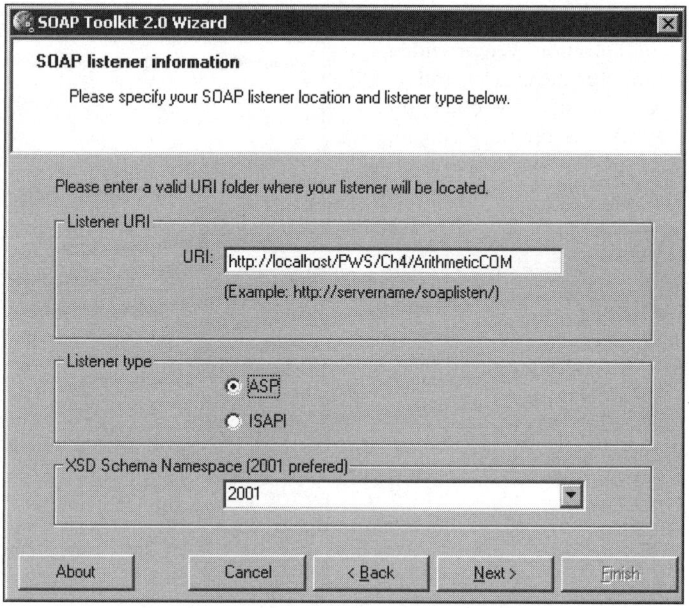

The Listener URI section requires the URI of the virtual folder you created earlier. This should be http://localhost/PWS/Ch4/ArithmeticCOM. Select ASP for the Listener type, and 2001 for the XSD Schema Namespace. Older schemas can be used if necessary for backwards compatibility.

Our final task here is to choose the WSDL file character set and the destination of where the WSDL, WSML, and SOAP Server ASP files are to be stored:

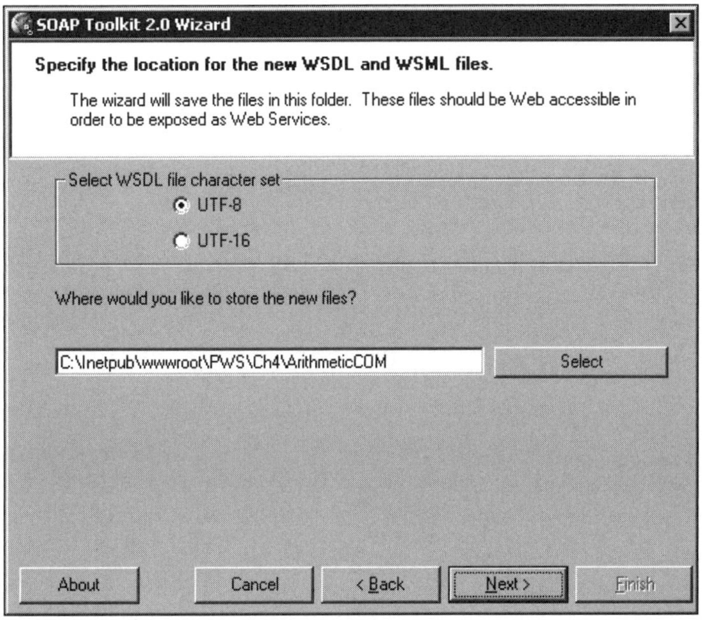

Where would you like to store the new files? Select the directory created above for the virtual root. Click Next and then Finish to complete the Wizard.

We are done creating our WSDL, WSML, and SOAP server files. Now let's take a look at them.

The SOAPServer or Listener File

We created an ASP listener file by choosing the ASP option as the listener type on the SOAP listener information screen. Although ISAPI provides better performance, ASP is easier to modify. Choose the appropriate listener type, based on your requirements.

The code for the SOAP listener was generated by the WSDL Generator utility. This ASP file serves as the network endpoint. It is similar in function to the Proxy files that we create for .NET Web Services. It handles the SOAP communication on the wire, between the Web Service and the application, device, or service calling the endpoint.

The code is displayed here:

```
<%@ LANGUAGE=VBScript %>
<%
Option Explicit
On Error Resume Next
Response.ContentType = "text/xml"
Dim SoapServer
If Not Application("ArithmeticCOMInitialized") Then
```

```
    Application.Lock
    If Not Application("ArithmeticCOMInitialized") Then
      Dim WSDLFilePath
      Dim WSMLFilePath
      WSDLFilePath = Server.MapPath("ArithmeticCOM.wsdl")
      WSMLFilePath = Server.MapPath("ArithmeticCOM.wsml")
      Set SoapServer = Server.CreateObject("MSSOAP.SoapServer")
      If Err Then SendFault "Cannot create SoapServer object. " & Err.Description
      SoapServer.Init WSDLFilePath, WSMLFilePath
      If Err Then SendFault "SoapServer.Init failed. " & Err.Description
      Set Application("ArithmeticCOMServer") = SoapServer
      Application("ArithmeticCOMInitialized") = True
    End If
    Application.UnLock
  End If
  Set SoapServer = Application("ArithmeticCOMServer")
  SoapServer.SoapInvoke Request, Response, ""
  If Err Then SendFault "SoapServer.SoapInvoke failed. " & Err.Description
  Sub SendFault(ByVal LogMessage)
    Dim Serializer
    On Error Resume Next
    ' "URI Query" logging must be enabled for AppendToLog to work
    Response.AppendToLog " SOAP ERROR: " & LogMessage
    Set Serializer = Server.CreateObject("MSSOAP.SoapSerializer")
    If Err Then
      Response.AppendToLog "Could not create SoapSerializer object. " & _
                                                           Err.Description
      Response.Status = "500 Internal Server Error"
    Else
      Serializer.Init Response
      If Err Then
        Response.AppendToLog "SoapSerializer.Init failed. " & Err.Description
        Response.Status = "500 Internal Server Error"
      Else
        Serializer.startEnvelope
        Serializer.startBody
        Serializer.startFault "Server", "The request could not be processed due " _
                                   & "to a problem in the server. Please contact " _
                                   & "the system admistrator. " & LogMessage
        Serializer.endFault
        Serializer.endBody
        Serializer.endEnvelope
        If Err Then
          Response.AppendToLog "SoapSerializer failed. " & Err.Description
          Response.Status = "500 Internal Server Error"
        End If
      End If
    End If
    Response.End
  End Sub
  %>
```

Looking through the code, the first key point is the `SoapServer` object, which is invoked with the paths of the WSDL and WSML files. It is then set to the name of our application `ArithmeticCOM` with the word `Server` appended. The second significant creation is that of the XML `Serializer` object, created to handle the SOAP messaging for the different sections of a SOAP message. Most of the rest of the code is error handling.

The WSML File

This file acts as a bridge between the COM object and the WSDL file and is specific to the SOAP Toolkit 2.0. It maps the methods in the COM object to the WSDL file. When we went through the WSDL Generator utility above, we selected both of our methods, and thus both of them were mapped. The code is as follows:

```
<?xml version='1.0' encoding='UTF-8' ?>
 <!-- Generated 07/01/02 by Microsoft SOAP Toolkit WSDL File Generator, Version
1.02.813.0 -->
<servicemapping name='ArithmeticCOM'>
  <service name='ArithmeticCOM'>
    <using PROGID='ArithmeticCOMProject.ArithmeticCOM' cachable='0'
           ID='ArithmeticCOMObject' />
    <port name='ArithmeticCOMSoapPort'>
      <operation name='multiplyNumbers'>
        <execute uses='ArithmeticCOMObject' method='multiplyNumbers' •
                 dispID='1610809344'>
          <parameter callIndex='1' name='NumberOne' elementName='NumberOne' />
          <parameter callIndex='2' name='NumberTwo' elementName='NumberTwo' />
          <parameter callIndex='-1' name='retval' elementName='Result' />
        </execute>
      </operation>
      <operation name='addNumbers'>
        <execute uses='ArithmeticCOMObject' method='addNumbers'
                 dispID='1610809345'>
          <parameter callIndex='1' name='NumberOne' elementName='NumberOne' />
          <parameter callIndex='2' name='NumberTwo' elementName='NumberTwo' />
          <parameter callIndex='-1' name='retval' elementName='Result' />
        </execute>
      </operation>
    </port>
  </service>
</servicemapping>
```

Unlike WSDL files that are rather long and somewhat complicated, WSML files are fairly simple. The root level of a WSML file is the `<servicemapping>` element. The `<servicemapping>` element contains the mapping to the `<service>` element in the WSDL file.

The `<service>` element, in turn, can have one or more `<using>` and `<port>` elements. Furthermore, each `<port>` element can have one or more `<operation>` elements.

The <port> element contains the mapping of the methods and their associated properties in the COM object to the <portType> element in the WSDL file. The <portType> element in the WSDL file groups the operations based on the protocols or binding to be used on the wire. For practical purposes, this groups the messages under a SOAP port that is mapped to a location in the <service> element. The <operation> element contains the names of the methods. <execute> uses elements that provide specific information to access the methods. The <parameter> element contains the parameter names and properties. A callIndex value of -1 signifies that this is the return value.

The PROGID attribute contains the fully-qualified class name. This is the only place that the project name is referenced in any of the files.

The Boolean cacheable attribute specifies whether the object stays in memory as long as the soapServer object is in memory. When it is set to 0, the object is not cacheable.

The final point to note here is that the ID attribute contains the ID that refers to the COM object.

The WSDL file

The WSDL file itself (displayed below) is typical of a WSDL file generated with the SOAP Toolkit 2.0. The major difference between this WSDL file and the one generated with ASP.NET is the <message> section. In .NET, the parameters of the message are defined in the <definition> section and referenced in the <message> section. In the SOAP Toolkit 2.0 version, the message is defined in the <message> section:

```
<?xml version='1.0' encoding='UTF-8' ?>
 <!-- Generated 07/01/02 by Microsoft SOAP Toolkit WSDL File Generator, Version
1.02.813.0 -->
<definitions name ='ArithmeticCOM' targetNamespace = 'http://tempuri.org/wsdl/'
             xmlns:wsdlns='http://tempuri.org/wsdl/'
             xmlns:typens='http://tempuri.org/type'
             xmlns:soap='http://schemas.xmlsoap.org/wsdl/soap/'
             xmlns:xsd='http://www.w3.org/2001/XMLSchema'
             xmlns:stk='http://schemas.microsoft.com/soap-toolkit/wsdl-extension'
             xmlns='http://schemas.xmlsoap.org/wsdl/'>
  <types>
    <schema targetNamespace='http://tempuri.org/type'
      xmlns='http://www.w3.org/2001/XMLSchema'
      xmlns:SOAP-ENC='http://schemas.xmlsoap.org/soap/encoding/'
      xmlns:wsdl='http://schemas.xmlsoap.org/wsdl/'
      elementFormDefault='qualified'>
    </schema>
  </types>
  <message name='ArithmeticCOM.multiplyNumbers'>
    <part name='NumberOne' type='xsd:double'/>
    <part name='NumberTwo' type='xsd:double'/>
  </message>
  <message name='ArithmeticCOM.multiplyNumbersResponse'>
    <part name='Result' type='xsd:double'/>
  </message>
  <message name='ArithmeticCOM.addNumbers'>
    <part name='NumberOne' type='xsd:double'/>
    <part name='NumberTwo' type='xsd:double'/>
```

```
  </message>
  <message name='ArithmeticCOM.addNumbersResponse'>

    <part name='Result' type='xsd:double'/>
  </message>
  <portType name='ArithmeticCOMSoapPort'>
    <operation name='multiplyNumbers' parameterOrder='NumberOne NumberTwo'>
      <input message='wsdlns:ArithmeticCOM.multiplyNumbers' />
      <output message='wsdlns:ArithmeticCOM.multiplyNumbersResponse' />
    </operation>
    <operation name='addNumbers' parameterOrder='NumberOne NumberTwo'>
      <input message='wsdlns:ArithmeticCOM.addNumbers' />
      <output message='wsdlns:ArithmeticCOM.addNumbersResponse' />
    </operation>
  </portType>
  <binding name='ArithmeticCOMSoapBinding' type='wsdlns:ArithmeticCOMSoapPort' >
    <stk:binding preferredEncoding='UTF-8'/>
    <soap:binding style='rpc' transport='http://schemas.xmlsoap.org/soap/http' />
    <operation name='multiplyNumbers' >
      <soap:operation
           soapAction='http://tempuri.org/action/ArithmeticCOM.multiplyNumbers' />
      <input>
        <soap:body use='encoded' namespace='http://tempuri.org/message/'
              encodingStyle='http://schemas.xmlsoap.org/soap/encoding/' />
      </input>
      <output>
        <soap:body use='encoded' namespace='http://tempuri.org/message/'
                   encodingStyle='http://schemas.xmlsoap.org/soap/encoding/' />
      </output>
    </operation>
    <operation name='addNumbers' >
      <soap:operation
             soapAction='http://tempuri.org/action/ArithmeticCOM.addNumbers' />
      <input>
        <soap:body use='encoded' namespace='http://tempuri.org/message/'
                   encodingStyle='http://schemas.xmlsoap.org/soap/encoding/' />
      </input>
      <output>
        <soap:body use='encoded' namespace='http://tempuri.org/message/'
                   encodingStyle='http://schemas.xmlsoap.org/soap/encoding/' />
      </output>
    </operation>
  </binding>
  <service name='ArithmeticCOM' >
    <port name='ArithmeticCOMSoapPort' binding='wsdlns:ArithmeticCOMSoapBinding' >
      <soap:address
          location='http://localhost/PWS/Ch4/ArithmeticCOM/ArithmeticCOM.ASP' />
    </port>
  </service>
</definitions>
```

The sections of the WSDL file will be covered extensively later in the chapter.

Client Script file

In our example, we are going to use a VBScript file to access the Web Service. Create this script file in Notepad and name it `arithmeticVB6Client.vbs`:

```
Option Explicit

Dim soapclient
set soapclient = CreateObject("MSSOAP.SoapClient")
On Error Resume Next
Call
soapclient.mssoapinit("http://localhost/PWS/Ch4/ArithmeticCOM/ArithmeticCOM.wsdl",
"ArithmeticCOM", "ArithmeticCOMSoapPort")
if err <> 0 then
  wscript.echo "initialization failed " + err.description
  wscript.echo 1111
end if

wscript.echo  soapclient.multiplyNumbers(2, 3)
wscript.echo  soapclient.addNumbers(2, 3)
```

The first thing the script does is to create the `soapClient` object. The `mssoapinit` method is then called with the following parameters:

- The Web Server location. This is the URI of the SOAP listener we entered on the SOAP listener screen above, with the name of the WSDL file appended. This reflects a network endpoint or port.
- The name of our class or service (not the project name but the class name) is used to name the service in the WSDL and WSML file.
- The SOAP Port name. By default this is the service name with the `SoapPort` appended to it.

Now for the fun part, let's run the application. Shell to the command prompt, navigate to the directory where you have your client script file, and type this command:

```
cscript arithmeticVB6Client.vbs
```

Two numbers (6 and 5) should be displayed, demonstrating the responses from the two web methods we have exposed.

There is a lot of functionality in the SOAP Toolkit 2.0 that is useful when we have specific requirements. However, when we just want to expose a COM object, it would be nice to be able to simply add a reference to our project. This is similar to what happens in .NET, where we can create Proxy files by adding a reference in Visual Studio .NET or use the `wsdl.exe` utility when we have more specific requirements.

Microsoft has an FAQ document on the SOAP Toolkit 2.0 that provides some good pointers on installation on client machines and other useful information. It can be found at http://msdn.microsoft.com/library/default.asp?url=/library/en-us/dnsoap/html/soap_faq.asp?frame=true.

WSDL Documents and .NET

For our .NET example, we also have a Web Service that exposes two methods: one to multiply numbers and one to add numbers. It is the same as the COM object we created above. The major difference is that we use the `WebService` and `WebMethod` attributes to set the name, description, and namespace URI of the Web Service.

Let's take a look at the `Arithmetic` class in the ASP.NET Web Service that we are going to use as the basis of the WSDL document detailed throughout the next few sections of this chapter. Remember the WSDL document created with Visual Studio .NET is slightly different from the WSDL document we generated with the SOAP Toolkit 2.0. The main differences are the `<types>` and `<message>` elements – we will elaborate further when explaining these elements.

The `Arithmetic` Web Service contains two methods: `multiplyNumbers` and `addNumbers`. They both take two parameters and return the results as one parameter. Part of the reason we included two methods is because there are places in the WSDL file where having two methods better demonstrates what elements are at the method level and what elements are at the Web Service level. The `WebService` and `WebMethod` attribute lines have been highlighted in the code below (see Chapter 2 for a more detailed explanation of the `WebService` and `WebMethod` attributes). The `WebService` attribute has had its `Namespace` and `Description` properties changed from the default Visual Studio .NET values. The `WebMethod Description` attribute has been set for both methods in our Web Service.

All of the changes are cosmetic and simply provide documentation elements in the WSDL file. The one change that is more than cosmetic is the `WebService Namespace` change. This changes the default ASP.NET Web Service namespace from `http://tempuri.org` to a domain name in our system. In this case that would be `http://www.wrox.com/`. The code shown below is the `arithmetic.asmx.vb` code-behind file in the download specified for this chapter.

In order to create the files necessary, follow these steps. If you want to download the files instead of creating them, skip to the download files section directly below.

To create the Web Service in VB.NET:

- Create a new VB.NET project in Visual Studio .NET, and select the ASP.NET Web Service template.
- Name the Web Service Arithmetic, and place it in http://localhost/PWS/Ch4/.
- Change the name of the `Service1.asmx` class to `arithmetic.asmx` in the Solution Explorer.
- Press *F7* to change to the code view.
- Replace the code in the code window with the code from below:

```
Imports System.Web.Services

<WebService(Namespace:="http://www.wrox.com/", _
Description:="Class with one method to add numbers and one to subtract numbers", _
Name:="Arithmetic")> _
Public Class Service1
```

```
    Inherits System.Web.Services.WebService

  #Region " Web Services Designer Generated Code "

    Public Sub New()
      MyBase.New()

      'This call is required by the Web Services Designer.
      InitializeComponent()

    End Sub

    'Required by the Web Services Designer
    Private components As System.ComponentModel.Container

    <System.Diagnostics.DebuggerStepThrough()> Private Sub InitializeComponent()
      components = New System.ComponentModel.Container()
    End Sub

    Protected Overloads Overrides Sub Dispose(ByVal disposing As Boolean)

    End Sub

  #End Region

    <WebMethod(Description:="Method that mulitiplies two numbers")> _
    Public Function multiplyNumbers(ByVal mnum1 As Integer, _
                                    ByVal mnum2 As Integer) As Integer
      multiplyNumbers = mnum1 * mnum2
    End Function

    <WebMethod(Description:="Method that adds two numbers")> _
    Public Function addNumbers(ByVal mnum1 As Integer, _
                               ByVal mnum2 As Integer) As Integer
      addNumbers = mnum1 + mnum2
    End Function

  End Class
```

Alternatively, you can just use the Arithmetic VS.NET project included in the code download for this chapter.

How To Create WSDL files in .NET

ASP.NET programmers do not generally have to create or modify WSDL documents by hand. There are three ways to generate WSDL documents in ASP.NET. The first way is to request the Web Service in a browser and append ?WSDL to the file name when we type in the URL. The second way is to click on the Service Description link on the Web Service Help Page (the page that is displayed when we browse to the `.asmx` file). This also appends the ?WSDL to the Web Service name in the requested URL. The third way is to create the WSDL documents manually or through `Import` statements and other advanced features that will be described in detail later in this chapter.

The Web Service Help Page was explained in Chapter 2. Here we will focus on the aspects that relate to WSDL and SOAP. When we access the Web Service Help page for our `Arithmetic` Web Service, there are three links: Service Description, multiplyNumbers and addNumbers.

- Service Description – clicking on this link brings up the WSDL document for the `Arithmetic` service. Notice that we did not have to add a reference through Visual Studio .NET, nor did we use the `wsdl.exe` tool. That is because the preceding two items are used to create Proxy files and not WSDL files. It is easy to confuse WSDL files with Proxy files when dealing with .NET Web Services, because WSDL documents are displayed when referencing Web Services in Visual Studio .NET and the command line tool is called `wsdl.exe` and not `Proxy.exe`.
- multiplyNumbers – clicking on this link brings up a screen that enables you to input the two method parameters. It also contains the SOAP and HTTP GET request and response message data for the method. This is a very good place to go and view the SOAP that is sent across the wire and to trace it to its origins in the WSDL files.
- addNumbers – clicking on this link brings up a screen that enables you to input the two method parameters and also contains the SOAP and HTTP GET request and response message data for the method. Again, this is a good place to view the SOAP that is sent across the wire and to trace it to its origins in the WSDL files.

Here is a collapsed version of the WSDL document that appears after clicking on the Service Description link:

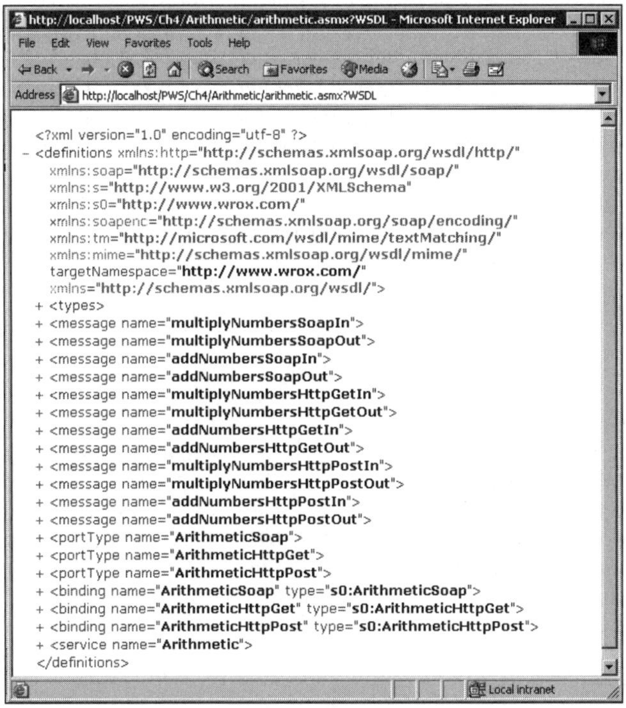


```
  <?xml version="1.0" encoding="utf-8" ?>
- <definitions xmlns:http="http://schemas.xmlsoap.org/wsdl/http/"
    xmlns:soap="http://schemas.xmlsoap.org/wsdl/soap/"
    xmlns:s="http://www.w3.org/2001/XMLSchema"
    xmlns:s0="http://www.wrox.com/"
    xmlns:soapenc="http://schemas.xmlsoap.org/soap/encoding/"
    xmlns:tm="http://microsoft.com/wsdl/mime/textMatching/"
    xmlns:mime="http://schemas.xmlsoap.org/wsdl/mime/"
    targetNamespace="http://www.wrox.com/"
    xmlns="http://schemas.xmlsoap.org/wsdl/">
  + <types>
  + <message name="multiplyNumbersSoapIn">
  + <message name="multiplyNumbersSoapOut">
  + <message name="addNumbersSoapIn">
  + <message name="addNumbersSoapOut">
  + <message name="multiplyNumbersHttpGetIn">
  + <message name="multiplyNumbersHttpGetOut">
  + <message name="addNumbersHttpGetIn">
  + <message name="addNumbersHttpGetOut">
  + <message name="multiplyNumbersHttpPostIn">
  + <message name="multiplyNumbersHttpPostOut">
  + <message name="addNumbersHttpPostIn">
  + <message name="addNumbersHttpPostOut">
  + <portType name="ArithmeticSoap">
  + <portType name="ArithmeticHttpGet">
  + <portType name="ArithmeticHttpPost">
  + <binding name="ArithmeticSoap" type="s0:ArithmeticSoap">
  + <binding name="ArithmeticHttpGet" type="s0:ArithmeticHttpGet">
  + <binding name="ArithmeticHttpPost" type="s0:ArithmeticHttpPost">
  + <service name="Arithmetic">
  </definitions>
```

An Advanced Look At WSDL

Now that we know how to create and access WSDL files with the SOAP Toolkit 2.0 and with ASP.NET, it is time to look into some of the details, structure, and inner workings of WSDL documents.

WSDL provides a way of describing Web Services in enough detail that they can be accessed by endpoints across the network. WSDL documents consist of five main elements that combine to describe a Web Service. The first three of these are abstract and define the messaging. The last two are concrete and define the protocol and address information.

> *The WSDL 1.1 specification classifies messaging-related items as abstract, and protocol and location related items as concrete. Not all programmers agree with this, but I will use their terminology.*

The three abstract elements, the `<types>`, `<message>`, and `<portType>` elements, combine to define the interface of the Web Service. They define the methods, parameters, and the properties of a Web Service. The two concrete elements, the `<binding>` element and the `<port>` element, combine to provide the protocol (SOAP over HTTP) and address information (URI of the service) of a Web Service. Separating the message definition elements from the location and protocol information provides the flexibility to reuse a common set of messages and data types with different protocols. This architecture increases the likelihood of more advanced protocols being utilized thus decreasing the legacy burden. It also provides the flexibility to define a set of messages and protocols that represent business logic once, and to reuse the same set of business logic multiple times with varying protocols.

The WSDL 1.1 specification comes with SOAP, HTTP GET/POST, and MIME extensions layered on top of the base specification. The base specification is referred to as the core definition framework. ASP.NET primarily supports the HTTP GET/POST operations for applications that accept parameters from either the FORM GET or POST mechanism. Unlike the WSDL 1.1 specification, ASP.NET does not support the MIME extension. There is nothing prohibiting the specification from being extended to support other protocols, however, as it is designed so that other protocols can be added and bound to the core specification without affecting it.

Since WSDL is most commonly implemented utilizing SOAP over HTTP and since that is the default in ASP.NET, this chapter will focus on WSDL in relation to SOAP and HTTP. SOAP is really dominant and there seems to be no real competitor to it at this point. Microsoft seems to be more interested in supporting raw SOAP over TCP, a transfer protocol known as Direct Internet Message Encapsulation (DIME), and building work abounds to the HTTP request response structure, than they are in supporting MIME.

The way that WSDL works is that it defines a core service definition framework that defines the five major elements of a WSDL document. This framework is currently extended by three binding specifications: SOAP, HTTP, and MIME. The abstract elements are largely defined within the WSDL core service definition framework. The concrete ones, especially the `<binding>` element, largely constitute a structure that is made available for a binding extension. The WSDL document we will go through in this section utilizes the SOAP binding extension. Elements that use the SOAP binding extension as we go through the document will be pointed out. We will also include a brief section on HTTP GET/POST binding following this section. We won't cover MIME because it is not supported by ASP.NET.

The WSDL, the SOAP binding extension, the HTTP binding extension, and the MIME binding extension schemas are also included in the WSDL 1.1 specification, which is available at http://msdn.microsoft.com/library/default.asp?url=/library/en-us/dnwebsrv/html/wsdl.asp.

Here is an overview of the five main elements of a WSDL document:

- **Types** – embedded XML schema where the data types are defined. Other type systems can be used through extensibility.
- **Messages** – provides details of the messages and the message parameters.
- **PortType** – groups messages in input/output message fashion and provides a bridge to concrete protocols and addressing.
- **Binding** – provides protocol information for the `<portType>` element or the operations.
- **Service** – provides URI address information for a service.

> **When searching for a Web Service across the Internet, it is a good idea to look it up in a UDDI registry. This will ensure that you use the correct WSDL document for the service. We point this out because if a custom WSDL document is created and the Web Service is queried, that is, Arithmetic.ASMX?WSDL is passed in, the default WSDL document will be automatically created by ASP.NET. It is not very useful to get the wrong service contract or WSDL document. The UDDI registry is the standard now so it should be used.**

Sample WSDL Document

Here is the WSDL document that was generated by ASP.NET for the `Arithmetic` class above. You can view it in your browser if you request the `arithmetic.asmx` service and append ?WSDL to the URL. We will go over it section-by-section below. We have included the whole file here, so that you can review it first and reference it throughout the chapter whenever you would like to see the whole file unobstructed. The parts of the file that reference HTTP POST and HTTP GET have been removed for clarity. WSDL documents are busy enough and can be difficult to follow, so removing the parts of the document that contain the extra protocols makes it easier to follow.

> **This WSDL document was automatically generated by ASP.NET. WSDL documents generated by other tools may vary slightly, as we saw above with the WSDL document created with the SOAP Toolkit 2.0, but the principles are the same.**

```
<?xml version="1.0" encoding="utf-8" ?>
  <definitions xmlns:http="http://schemas.xmlsoap.org/wsdl/http/"
               xmlns:soap="http://schemas.xmlsoap.org/wsdl/soap/"
               xmlns:s="http://www.w3.org/2001/XMLSchema"
               xmlns:s0="http://www.wrox.com/"
               xmlns:soapenc="http://schemas.xmlsoap.org/soap/encoding/"
               xmlns:tm="http://microsoft.com/wsdl/mime/textMatching/"
               xmlns:mime="http://schemas.xmlsoap.org/wsdl/mime/"
               targetNamespace="http://www.wrox.com/"
               xmlns="http://schemas.xmlsoap.org/wsdl/">
    <types>
```

```
    <s:schema elementFormDefault="qualified"
              targetNamespace="http://www.wrox.com/">
      <s:element name="multiplyNumbers">
        <s:complexType>
          <s:sequence>
            <s:element minOccurs="1"
                       maxOccurs="1"
                       name="mnum1"
                       type="s:int" />
            <s:element minOccurs="1"
                       maxOccurs="1"
                       name="mnum2"
                       type="s:int" />
          </s:sequence>
        </s:complexType>
      </s:element>
      <s:element name="multiplyNumbersResponse">
        <s:complexType>
          <s:sequence>
            <s:element minOccurs="1"
                       maxOccurs="1"
                       name="multiplyNumbersResult"
                       type="s:int" />
          </s:sequence>
        </s:complexType>
      </s:element>
      <s:element name="addNumbers">
        <s:complexType>
          <s:sequence>
            <s:element minOccurs="1"
                       maxOccurs="1"
                       name="mnum1"
                       type="s:int" />
            <s:element minOccurs="1"
                       maxOccurs="1"
                       name="mnum2"
                       type="s:int" />
          </s:sequence>
        </s:complexType>
      </s:element>
      <s:element name="addNumbersResponse">
        <s:complexType>
          <s:sequence>
            <s:element minOccurs="1"
                       maxOccurs="1"
                       name="addNumbersResult"
                       type="s:int" />
          </s:sequence>
        </s:complexType>
      </s:element>
      <s:element name="int"
                 type="s:int" />
    </s:schema>
  </types>
  <message name="multiplyNumbersSoapIn">
    <part name="parameters" element="s0:multiplyNumbers" />
  </message>
  <message name="multiplyNumbersSoapOut">
    <part name="parameters" element="s0:multiplyNumbersResponse" />
  </message>
```

```
    <message name="addNumbersSoapIn">
      <part name="parameters" element="s0:addNumbers" />
    </message>
    <message name="addNumbersSoapOut">
      <part name="parameters" element="s0:addNumbersResponse" />
    </message>
    <portType name="ArithmeticSoap">
      <operation name="multiplyNumbers">
        <documentation>Method that multiplies two numbers</documentation>
        <input message="s0:multiplyNumbersSoapIn" />
        <output message="s0:multiplyNumbersSoapOut" />
      </operation>
      <operation name="addNumbers">
        <documentation>Method that adds two numbers</documentation>
        <input message="s0:addNumbersSoapIn" />
        <output message="s0:addNumbersSoapOut" />
      </operation>
    </portType>
    <binding name="ArithmeticSoap" type="s0:ArithmeticSoap">
      <soap:binding transport="http://schemas.xmlsoap.org/soap/http"
                    style="document" />
      <operation name="multiplyNumbers">
        <soap:operation soapAction="http://www.wrox.com/multiplyNumbers"
                        style="document" />
        <input>
          <soap:body use="literal" />
        </input>
        <output>
          <soap:body use="literal" />
        </output>
      </operation>
      <operation name="addNumbers">
        <soap:operation soapAction="http://www.wrox.com/addNumbers"
                        style="document" />
        <input>
          <soap:body use="literal" />
        </input>
        <output>
          <soap:body use="literal" />
        </output>
      </operation>
    </binding>
    <service name="Arithmetic">
      <documentation>Class with one method to add numbers and one
                     to subtract numbers</documentation>
      <port name="ArithmeticSoap" binding="s0:ArithmeticSoap">
        <soap:address
             location="http://localhost/PWS/Ch4/Arithmetic/arithmetic.asmx" />
      </port>
    </service>
  </definitions>
```

Section-By-Section In Detail

We will now go through each section of the file in detail, beginning with the `<definitions>` section.

Definitions Section

The <definitions> element is the root element of a WSDL document. It is where most of the namespaces are defined. Other namespaces that are specific to a section may be specified in that section instead. They will remain in scope for the duration of the section they are defined in. Namespaces are used to uniquely identify elements in an XML document by using a Uniform Resource Identifier (URI), thus avoiding naming conflicts. They can also work with XML Schemas to ensure that the elements, attribute names, and characteristics are valid, as database tables would be prefixed to reference the correct field name, and the data structure would validate the characteristics of the fields being used.

All WSDL elements belong to the WSDL namespace, which is defined as:
`http://schemas.xmlsoap.org/wsdl/`.

The table below lists the namespaces that appear in a WSDL document. The Prefix column identifies the prefix used to reference the namespace throughout the document. For example, the first row contains "s:" for the URI http://www.w3.org/2001/XMLSchema. This means that all elements that are part of the XMLSchema namespace are prefixed with "s:". The prefixes are shorthand convention for working with XML documents.

Prefix	Corresponding URI	Description
s:	http://www.w3.org/2001/XMLSchema	XMLSchema namespace. The default typing system in WSDL documents.
tm:	http://microsoft.com/wsdl/mime/textMatching/	Microsoft-only text matching the schema namespace.
soap:	http://schemas/xmlsoap.org/wsdl/soap/	WSDL namespace for WSDL SOAP binding.
Soapenc:	http://schemas.xmlsoap.org/soap/encoding/	Encoding namespace as defined by SOAP 1.1.
s0:	http://www.wrox.com/	Namespace of the sample Web Service.
no prefix	http://schemas.xmlsoap.org/wsdl/	WSDL namespace for WSDL framework. Because there is no prefix, this is the default namespace for the document.

Prefix	Corresponding URI	Description
`targetNamespace:`	`http://www.wrox.com/`	The namespace of the XML data that is described or validated by this module. It lets us define the namespace of the schema we are creating, independently of other namespace declarations being used.

> **The URI we have used for the namespace of the sample Web Service is http://www.wrox.com/ and not http://tempuri.org, which is the default. This is because we changed the Web Service attribute name in our class, as detailed in the *How To Create WSDL files in .NET* section above.**

The `<definitions>` element contains support for the following attributes:

- `Name` – to name the document
- `Definitions` – to define the namespaces
- `targetNamespace` – to define the `targetNamespace`

Here are the parts of the WSDL document that relate to this section. You can see the `definitions` and `targetNamespace` attributes being defined:

```
<?xml version="1.0" encoding="utf-8" ?>
  <definitions xmlns:http="http://schemas.xmlsoap.org/wsdl/http/"
               xmlns:soap="http://schemas.xmlsoap.org/wsdl/soap/"
               xmlns:s="http://www.w3.org/2001/XMLSchema"
               xmlns:s0="http://www.wrox.com/"
               xmlns:soapenc="http://schemas.xmlsoap.org/soap/encoding/"
               xmlns:tm="http://microsoft.com/wsdl/mime/textMatching/"
               xmlns:mime="http://schemas.xmlsoap.org/wsdl/mime/"
               targetNamespace="http://www.wrox.com/"
               xmlns="http://schemas.xmlsoap.org/wsdl/">
```

Types Section

The `<types>` section of a WSDL document is where the data types are defined. The `<types>` element is actually an embedded XML Schema, and all XML Schema data types are valid. Other type systems can be added through extensibility if required. As the specification states, XSD is the current preferred choice, but it is unreasonable to expect that one type system will be able to express all types in the present and in the future. It is also possible to define complex types, such as defining a customer by using standard XML Schema syntax as follows:

```
<types>
  <schema targetNamespace="someNamespace" xmlns:typens="someNamespace">
    <xsd:complexType name="CUSTOMER">
      <xsd:sequence>
```

```
            <xsd:element customer="companyName type="xsd:string"/>
            <xsd:element customer="firstName type="xsd:string"/>
            <xsd:element customer="lastName type="xsd:string"/>
            <xsd:element customer="salesRank type="xsd:int"/>
          </xsd:sequence>
        </xsd:complexType>
      </schema>
    </types>
```

In our example, a complex type is used to define the messages. It describes the method name, its parameters, the minimum and maximum occurrences attribute for each parameter, and the data types for each parameter. The names of these complex types are referred to in the <message> element. Complex types can also support more complicated items, including purchase orders, which would have a header and line item components. If you are not familiar with XML Schemas, you should read *Professional XML Schemas* (ISBN 1-86100-547-4) also from Wrox Press, or see the XML Schema specification at http://www.w3.org/2001/XMLSchema.

In essence, the `types` section is defining the parameters for the <message> element, which is used to define the SOAP payload.

To return to our WSDL file, both methods from our `Arithmetic` class contain two elements:

- One for the input message
- One for the output message

The input message has the same name as the method, and the output message has the word "`Response`" appended to the message name. Both the input and output message have their parameters defined using a complex type:

```
<types>
  <s:schema elementFormDefault="qualified"
          targetNamespace="http://www.wrox.com/">
    <s:element name="multiplyNumbers">
      <s:complexType>
        <s:sequence>
          <s:element minOccurs="1"
                     maxOccurs="1"
                     name="mnum1"
                     type="s:int" />
          <s:element minOccurs="1"
                     maxOccurs="1"
                     name="mnum2"
                     type="s:int" />
        </s:sequence>
      </s:complexType>
    </s:element>
    <s:element name="multiplyNumbersResponse">
      <s:complexType>
        <s:sequence>
          <s:element minOccurs="1"
                     maxOccurs="1"
                     name="multiplyNumbersResult"
```

```
                        type="s:int" />
            </s:sequence>
          </s:complexType>
        </s:element>
        <s:element name="addNumbers">
          <s:complexType>
            <s:sequence>
              <s:element minOccurs="1"
                         maxOccurs="1"
                         name="mnum1"
                         type="s:int" />
              <s:element minOccurs="1"
                         maxOccurs="1"
                         name="mnum2"
                         type="s:int" />
            </s:sequence>
          </s:complexType>
        </s:element>
        <s:element name="addNumbersResponse">
          <s:complexType>
            <s:sequence>
              <s:element minOccurs="1"
                         maxOccurs="1"
                         name="addNumbersResult"
                         type="s:int" />
            </s:sequence>
          </s:complexType>
        </s:element>
        <s:element name="int"
                   type="s:int" />
      </s:schema>
    </types>
```

This is another example of how flexible complex types are. Here, we use one to define the request and response methods and their parameters. In the WSDL file created with the SOAP Toolkit 2.0, the `<types>` element is limited to a few namespace elements. In the ASP.NET version that we are now looking at, it is used to detail the messages and their parameters.

When we get on to talking about the `<message>` section below, you will see the `<message>` elements from both the WSDL document created by the SOAP Toolkit and that created by ASP.NET. The two `<message>` elements are drastically different, and indeed it is a very common occurrence for the `<message>` section of WSDL documents to vary widely. Some use the `<types>` element to define the methods and parameters and refer to this in the `<message>` element, while others define the methods and parameters in the `<message>` element directly.

Message Section

The `<message>` element contains the methods and their parameters. It contains a definition of the data being communicated. Our ASP.NET implementation defines the methods and their properties in the `<types>` element and refers to these definitions in the `<message>` element. On the other hand, the SOAP Toolkit 2.0 defines both the methods and their parameters solely in the `<message>` element. As stated above, both implementations will be shown here.

The <message> element in our sample WSDL file contains three parts:

- <message name> – the <message name> element contains the combination of the method name plus SoapIn for the calling message and SoapOut for the results message. It is this name that is used as the operation name below. SoapIn and SoapOut are appended because these messages are being defined as bound to SOAP. If we were using HttpGet, they would have HttpGetIn and HttpGetOut appended to the name.
- <part name> – the <part name> attribute is set to parameters referring to the fact that the parameters for this message were set above in the <types> element.
- <part element> – the <part element> attribute references the complex types by name defined in the schema above for each input and output message.

The <part type> element is not used in the ASP.NET WSDL document, but is used and explained in the SOAP Toolkit version of the WSDL document below.

We have four messages in this section: two request messages and two response messages. We have a request and response message for our multiplyNumbers method, and a request and response message for our addNumbers method. This corresponds to the four messages defined above in the <types> element.

ASP.NET Implementation

```
<message name="multiplyNumbersSoapIn">
  <part name="parameters" element="s0:multiplyNumbers" />
</message>
<message name="multiplyNumbersSoapOut">
  <part name="parameters" element="s0:multiplyNumbersResponse" />
</message>
<message name="addNumbersSoapIn">
  <part name="parameters" element="s0:addNumbers" />
</message>
<message name="addNumbersSoapOut">
  <part name="parameters" element="s0:addNumbersResponse" />
</message>
```

Let's assume we have a method named addCustomers. The WSDL below demonstrates how the customer complex type created above would be used:

```
<message name="addCustomers">
  <part name="addCustomers" type="s0:addCustomers" />
```

SOAP 2.0 Implementation

Here is a description of the <message> element contained in the WSDL document created with the SOAP Toolkit 2.0:

- The <message name> element here refers to the request and response operations of the methods defined in our WSDL file, just as it does in the ASP.NET version above.

- The <part name> attribute defines the parameters and the data types of the messages. It contains one row for each parameter; thus it contains two rows for each request method and one row for each response methods. The request methods each contain two parameters, and the response methods each contain one parameter.
- The <part type> attribute contains the data type information of the parameter. In the ASP.NET version of the <message> element, the data type information was defined in the <types> element. Both of these methods work. If you are handcrafting WSDL documents, it is a design choice you must make. If you are using a tool, it will make the decision for you.

```
<message name='abc.multiplyNumbers'>
  <part name='NumberOne' type='xsd:double'/>
  <part name='NumberTwo' type='xsd:double'/>
</message>
<message name='abc.multiplyNumbersResponse'>
  <part name='Result' type='xsd:double'/>
</message>
<message name='abc.addNumbers'>
  <part name='NumberOne' type='xsd:double'/>
  <part name='NumberTwo' type='xsd:double'/>
</message>
<message name='abc.addNumbersResponse'>
  <part name='Result' type='xsd:double'/>
</message>
```

PortType Section

So far we have built a schema that describes the parameters of the messages and have used that schema in our message section. Now we are going to define operations based on the messages we created, and group the operations in a portType. Unlike the <message> element above, which contained independent elements for the input and output messages, these operations are tied together in a request-response grouping. The operation name is the name of the method and the portType is a collection of operations. The <portType> element is referred to in the <binding> element, to bind a set of operations to a protocol. The operations are mapped to the SOAP operation calls contained within the <binding> element. In essence, the portType is bound to a protocol and the operations are mapped to the SOAP methods, providing the linkage between the abstract and concrete portions of a WSDL document.

There are four types of operations: one-way, request-response, solicit-response, and notification. The current WSDL specification defines only bindings for the one-way and request-response operation types. The other two can have bindings defined via binding extensions. The latter two are simply the inverse of the first two; the only difference is whether the endpoint in question is on the receiving or sending end of the initial message. HTTP is a two-way protocol, so the one-way operations will work only with MIME (which is not supported by ASP.NET) or with another custom extension.

Here is a description of the parts in the portType section:

- <portType name> – the name of the service with SOAP added. The <portType name> is used to bind the <portType> element to the protocol information contained in the <binding> element.

- <operation name> – there is one operation for each of our methods, and the method names are used to name the operations.
- <documentation> – the documentation comes from the WebMethod documentation attribute as used in our sample Arithmetic class earlier.
- <input> and <output message> – the input and output messages correspond to the messages above. Just as above, we have four messages: one input for each method and one output for each method.
- <fault> element – we are not using this in our WSDL document. It is used to specify the error message returned for all non-protocol errors.

```
<portType name="ArithmeticSoap">
  <operation name="multiplyNumbers">
    <documentation>Method that multiplies two numbers</documentation>
    <input message="s0:multiplyNumbersSoapIn" />
    <output message="s0:multiplyNumbersSoapOut" />
  </operation>
  <operation name="addNumbers">
    <documentation>Method that adds two numbers</documentation>
    <input message="s0:addNumbersSoapIn" />
    <output message="s0:addNumbersSoapOut" />
  </operation>
</portType>
```

Binding Section

The binding section contains several features, which we'll run through here:

- <binding name> – the <binding name> is the service name with Soap appended to it. It is used to connect the binding (protocol information) with the port (location information). The <binding name> is connected to the <port name> binding attribute in the <service> section below.
- <binding name type> – the <binding name type> is used to link the <binding> section to the <portType> section, referenced above.
- <soap:binding> – the <soap:binding> element is an extension to the WSDL core definition framework. It contains two attributes:

  style – there are two valid binding name styles: document and rpc. The rpc (or remote procedure call) style is used to specify that methods and method parameters will be contained in the SOAP envelope in the request and response messages. The document style is used to specify that XML documents will be transmitted in the SOAP envelope. For example, the request message may contain a purchase order and the response message may contain a purchase order receipt.

  transport – this refers to the SOAP HTTP schema and sets the binding to SOAP over HTTP.
- <operation name> – <operation name> is described in the <portType> section. Here it is set to soapAction.

- <soap:operation> – this is another extension to the WSDL core definition framework. The <soap:operation> element is used to set the document style and the handler information for this operation. The document style defaults from the <soap:binding> element above and can be set for this specific operation here. The handler information contains the name and location of the method.
- <input> and <output name> – the <input> element and the <output> element each contain three child elements: <soap:body>, <soap:header>, and <soap:headerFault>. In our example we are using only the <soap:body> child element. The other two elements and the attributes not being used here can be seen in the *SOAP Binding Extension* section later. The use attribute can be set to encoded or literal. When set to literal, the parts are sent as is. When set to encoded, each message part is looked up through a URI. See Chapter 5 for more details.

```
<binding name="ArithmeticSoap" type="s0:ArithmeticSoap">
  <soap:binding transport="http://schemas.xmlsoap.org/soap/http"
              style="document" />
  <operation name="multiplyNumbers">
    <soap:operation soapAction="http://www.wrox.com/multiplyNumbers"
                    style="document" />
    <input>
      <soap:body use="literal" />
    </input>
    <output>
      <soap:body use="literal" />
    </output>
  </operation>
  <operation name="addNumbers">
    <soap:operation soapAction="http://www.wrox.com/addNumbers"
                    style="document" />
    <input>
      <soap:body use="literal" />
    </input>
    <output>
      <soap:body use="literal" />
    </output>
  </operation>
</binding>
```

Service Section

The <service> section contains a collection of ports or endpoints. A port provides address information or a URI. In our case we only have one port because we have removed the non-SOAP protocols from the document. The original ASP.NET-generated file contains three ports: one for SOAP, one for HTTP GET, and one for HTTP POST.

The service attribute provides a unique name among all ports defined in the WSDL document. Here the SOAP address of our Arithmetic class is combined with the protocol information from our binding section:

```
<service name="Arithmetic">
  <documentation>Class with one method to add numbers and one
               to subtract numbers</documentation>
```

```
    <port name="ArithmeticSoap" binding="s0:ArithmeticSoap">
      <soap:address
           location="http://localhost/PWS/Ch4/Arithmetic/arithmetic.asmx" />
    </port>
  </service>
```

Here's a breakdown of the attributes and elements involved:

- <documentation> – the documentation comes from the WebService Description attribute we used in our sample Arithmetic class earlier.
- <port name> – provides a unique name among all ports in the class by appending the protocol name, in our case SOAP, to the service name.
- <port name binding> – used to connect the port (URI) with the protocol in the <binding> section. This is the same as the <binding name> in the <binding> section.
- <soap:address> – the URI of the service or the network endpoint.

SOAP Message Examples

Here we will examine the SOAP messages as they would appear in three different scenarios based on the WSDL document we went through above. The elements used to determine the shape of the SOAP message are the <soap:binding style>, <soap body use>, <soap:body encodingStyle="*uri*">, and <soap:body namespace="*uri*">. Each different SOAP message contains elements as set out in the tables below which identify the settings for that scenario.

Name	Value
SOAP Binding Style	rpc
SOAP Body Use	literal
SOAP Body encoding style URI	None
SOAP Body namespace URI	None

Notice that the <soap:body> element's child element is the method name multiplyNumbers. This is because the Binding Style is set to **rpc**:

```
POST /arithmetic/arithmetic.asmx HTTP/1.1
Host: localhost
Content-Type: text/xml; charset=utf-8
Content-Length: length
SOAPAction: "http://www.wrox.com/multiplyNumbers"

<?xml version="1.0" encoding="utf-8"?>
<soap:Envelope xmlns:xsi="http://www.w3.org/2001/XMLSchema-instance"
               xmlns:xsd="http://www.w3.org/2001/XMLSchema"
               xmlns:soap="http://schemas.xmlsoap.org/soap/envelope/">
  <soap:Body>
    <multiplyNumbers>
      <mnum1>int</mnum1>
```

```
      <mnum2>int</mnum2>
    </multiplyNumbers>
  </soap:Body>
</soap:Envelope>
HTTP/1.1 200 OK
Content-Type: text/xml; charset=utf-8
Content-Length: length
```

Name	Value
SOAP Binding style	document
SOAP Body Use	literal
SOAP Body Encoding Style URI	None
SOAP Body Namespace URI	None

Notice that the <soap:body> element's child element is the method parameters and not the method itself. This is because the Binding Style here is set to **document,** and when set to document the data is sent directly:

```
POST /arithmetic/arithmetic.asmx HTTP/1.1
Host: localhost
Content-Type: text/xml; charset=utf-8
Content-Length: length
SOAPAction: "http://www.wrox.com/multiplyNumbers"

<?xml version="1.0" encoding="utf-8"?>
<soap:Envelope xmlns:xsi="http://www.w3.org/2001/XMLSchema-instance"
               xmlns:xsd="http://www.w3.org/2001/XMLSchema"
               xmlns:soap="http://schemas.xmlsoap.org/soap/envelope/">
  <soap:Body>
    <mnum1>int</mnum1>
    <mnum2>int</mnum2>
  </soap:Body>
</soap:Envelope>
HTTP/1.1 200 OK
Content-Type: text/xml; charset=utf-8
Content-Length: length
```

Name	Value
SOAP Binding style	rpc
SOAP Body Use	encoded
SOAP Body Encoding Style URI	http://schemas.xmlsoap.org/soap/↵ envelope/
SOAP Body Namespace URI	http://www.wrox.com/

This time we set the SOAP Body Use attribute as **encoded** and thus have to provide the encoding and namespace URIs:

```
POST /arithmetic/arithmetic.asmx HTTP/1.1
Host: localhost
Content-Type: text/xml; charset=utf-8
Content-Length: length
SOAPAction: "http://www.wrox.com/multiplyNumbers"

<?xml version="1.0" encoding="utf-8"?>
<soap:Envelope xmlns:xsi="http://www.w3.org/2001/XMLSchema-instance"
               xmlns:xsd="http://www.w3.org/2001/XMLSchema"
               xmlns:soap="http://schemas.xmlsoap.org/soap/envelope/">
  <soap:Body>
    <multiplyNumbers xmlns="http://www.wrox.com/">
      <mnum1>int</mnum1>
      <mnum2>int</mnum2>
    </multiplyNumbers>
  </soap:Body>
</soap:Envelope>
HTTP/1.1 200 OK
Content-Type: text/xml; charset=utf-8
Content-Length: length
```

SOAP Binding Extensions

We pointed out SOAP 1.1 binding extensions we used as we went through our sample WSDL file above. Here is a summary of all the SOAP binding extensions to WSDL 1.1 (highlighted in the code).

```
<definitions .... >
  <binding .... >
    <soap:binding style="rpc|document" transport="uri">
    <operation .... >
      <soap:operation soapAction="uri" style="rpc|document">
      <input>
        <soap:body parts="nmtokens" use="literal|encoded"
                   encodingStyle="uri-list" namespace="uri"/>
        <soap:header message="qname" part="nmtoken" use="literal|encoded"
                     encodingStyle="uri-list" namespace="uri"/>
          <soap:headerfault message="qname" part="nmtoken"
                            use="literal|encoded" encodingStyle="uri-list"
                            namespace="uri"/>
        <soap:header>

      </input>
      <output>
        <soap:body parts="nmtokens" use="literal|encoded"
                   encodingStyle="uri-list" namespace="uri" />
        <soap:header message="qname" part="nmtoken"
                     use="literal|encoded"encodingStyle="uri-list"
                     namespace="uri"/>
        <soap:headerfault message="qname" part="nmtoken" use="literal|encoded"
                          encodingStyle="uri-list" namespace="uri"/>
        <soap:header>
```

```
        </output>
        <fault>*
          <soap:fault name="nmtoken" use="literal|encoded"
                      encodingStyle="uri-list" namespace="uri">
        </fault>
      </operation>
    </binding>

    <port .... >
        <soap:address location="uri"/>
    </port>
  </definitions>
```

As you can see, most of the <binding> elements and the address elements of the <service> element are SOAP binding extensions. In essence, WSDL defines a binding framework around the <operation> element, and the SOAP binding extension adds all of the functionality. This is consistent with the WSDL mantra of supporting unlimited binding extensions.

HTTP Binding Implementation

In this section, we will take a brief look at implementing our service with HTTP.

The <message> element for HTTP GET is similar to the SOAP Toolkit 2.0 implementation, where the parameters of the methods are defined by using the part name and type, rather than by using the <types> element, as is done in the ASP.NET implementation. The response, or in this case, the Out message, is set to body, because HTTP GET returns values as URLs:

```
<message name="multiplyNumbersHttpGetIn">
  <part name="mnum1" type="s:string" />
  <part name="mnum2" type="s:string" />
</message>
<message name="multiplyNumbersHttpGetOut">
  <part name="Body" element="s0:int" />
</message>
<message name="addNumbersHttpGetIn">
  <part name="anum1" type="s:string" />
  <part name="anum2" type="s:string" />
</message>
<message name="addNumbersHttpGetOut">
  <part name="Body" element="s0:int" />
</message>
```

The <portType> element is pretty much identical to the SOAP ones we looked at above. The only difference is that the message names now have HttpGet appended to them:

```
<portType name="ArithmeticHttpGet">
  <operation name="multiplyNumbers">
    <documentation>Method that multiplies two numbers</documentation>
    <input message="s0:multiplyNumbersHttpGetIn" />
    <output message="s0:multiplyNumbersHttpGetOut" />
  </operation>
  <operation name="addNumbers">
```

```
      <documentation>Method that adds two numbers</documentation>
      <input message="s0:addNumbersHttpGetIn" />
      <output message="s0:addNumbersHttpGetOut" />
    </operation>
  </portType>
```

Now we have reached the actual HTTP binding extension:

```
  <binding name="ArithmeticHttpGet" type="s0:ArithmeticHttpGet">
    <http:binding verb="GET" />
    <operation name="multiplyNumbers">
      <http:operation location="/multiplyNumbers" />
      <input>
        <http:urlEncoded />
      </input>
      <output>
        <mime:mimeXml part="Body" />
      </output>
    </operation>
    <operation name="addNumbers">
      <http:operation location="/addNumbers" />
      <input>
        <http:urlEncoded />
      </input>
      <output>
        <mime:mimeXml part="Body" />
      </output>
    </operation>
  </binding>
```

Let's look at some aspects of this section:

- <binding name> – common options are GET or POST, but other options are possible. Note that HTTP verbs are case-sensitive.
- <operation location="*URI*"> – this is the relative URI of the operation. It combines with the http:address in the <service> element to form the full URI. This element must contain a relative URI.
- <input> and <output> elements – in general, the input and output are urlEncoded. urlEncoded transmits the parameters as follows: mnum1=string&mnum2=string. The other option is urlReplacement, which will perform a lookup on the message parts by searching the relative URI of the operation for a set of search patterns. For each match, the value of the corresponding message part is substituted.

There is only one binding extension for both the GET and POST implementations. They are both pretty much the same. HTTP POST transmits data over the wire as name/value pairs, and HTTP GET transmits data over the wire in the query string.

The <service> element is very straightforward. The <http:address location> attribute provides the name of the service that is mentioned above. This is the first part of the URI, which is then combined with the operation location URI, above, to specify the address. The rest of the element is identical to the <service> element in the ASP.NET WSDL document:

```
<service name="Arithmetic">
  <documentation>Class with one method to add numbers and
               one to subtract numbers</documentation>
  <port name="ArithmeticHttpGet" binding="s0:ArithmeticHttpGet">
    <http:address
          location="http://localhost/PWS/Ch4/arithmetic/arithmetic.asmx" />
  </port>
</service>
```

The HTTP binding extension is much simpler than the SOAP binding extension. It is utilized to support HTTP GET and POST method calls in WSDL. The Web Service Help page also contains a sample HTTP POST and GET message for a Web Service.

If you bring up a WSDL file in ASP.NET through the Web Service Help page, you can see the HTTP GET and POST elements. We did not cover these in detail because SOAP is the most common way to work with Web Services in ASP.NET.

HTTP Message Examples

Here is an example of HTTP GET and POST request and response messages using the `urlEncoded` method of transmission. The `multiplyNumbers` method is being used with `3` and `6` as the parameters.

```
GET /PWS/Ch4/arithmetic/arithmetic.asmx/multiplyNumbers?mnum1=3&mnum2=6 HTTP/1.1
<int xmlns=http://www.wrox.com/>18</int>
```

```
POST /PWS/Ch4/arithmetic/arithmetic.asmx/multiplyNumbers HTTP/1.1
3=string&6=string
<int xmlns=http://www.wrox.com/>18</int>
```

HTTP Binding Extension

Here are the actual HTTP binding extensions:

```
<definitions .... >
  <binding .... >
    <http:binding verb="nmtoken"/>
    <operation .... >
      <http:operation location="uri"/>
      <input .... >
        <-- mime elements -->
      </input>
      <output .... >
        <-- mime elements -->

      </output>
    </operation>
  </binding>
  <port .... >
    <http:address location="uri"/>
  </port>
</definitions>
```

The only part of this we have not covered is that the request and response messages can be sent as MIME elements. This permits the sending of graphical content.

WSDL Screen Scrape Example

Screen scraping has been around since before the PC, and it is still a very common mechanism used to extract data from mainframe systems. It is also very common on the web, which is not such a good thing. As Web Services become more common, screen scraping should become a technique of the past. At present, there are still many HTML pages that do not express themselves as Web Services, and thus, the best way to extract data from them is to programmatically read the HTML form.

One new item that makes screen scraping a little better is the support of regular expression matching in .NET. This means that if the overall structure of the page is changed, but the specific data being searched for is not, the program will not break. Creating a WSDL document also makes it a little easier to support screen scraping where the methods and properties can be stored in a WSDL document. Even if you do not have a use for screen scraping, the example below provides a neat way to use and learn about WSDL.

The following section covers the creation of a WSDL file in a screen scraping example that searches a web page and returns the title of that web page. Since the WSDL for ASP.NET Web Services is auto-generated, we will write our own WSDL file that uses a simple web page as the service. One of the important things to keep in mind is that if you create and use proxies for these WSDL files, the methods in the services will return a structure that has the various text matches as member variables, with the names defined in the WSDL file.

Hello World

In this example of WSDL authoring, we will write a WSDL file that reads a web page's title and returns it as a result. This will provide a very basic example of how screen scraping works with WSDL. We'll begin with a brief overview of the WSDL document, and then walk through creating the WSDL and accessing the service.

The WSDL Document for the HelloWorld Application

Here is the source for the WSDL file, `HelloWorld.wsdl`:

```
<?xml version="1.0" encoding="utf-8" ?>
<definitions xmlns:s="http://www.w3.org/2001/XMLSchema"
             xmlns:http="http://schemas.xmlsoap.org/wsdl/http/"
             xmlns:mime="http://schemas.xmlsoap.org/wsdl/mime/"

             xmlns:tm="http://microsoft.com/wsdl/mime/textMatching/"
             xmlns:soap="http://schemas.xmlsoap.org/wsdl/soap/"
             xmlns:soapenc="http://schemas.xmlsoap.org/soap/encoding/"
             xmlns:s0="http://tempuri.org/"
                   targetNamespace="http://tempuri.org/"
             xmlns="http://schemas.xmlsoap.org/wsdl/">
  <types>
    <s:schema targetNamespace="http://tempuri.org/"
```

```
              attributeFormDefault="qualified"
              elementFormDefault="qualified">
      <s:element name="TestHeaders">
        <s:complexType derivedBy="restriction"/>
      </s:element>
      <s:element name="TestHeadersResult">
        <s:complexType derivedBy="restriction">
          <s:all>
            <s:element name="result" type="s:string" nullable="true"/>
          </s:all>
        </s:complexType>
      </s:element>
      <s:element name="string" type="s:string" nullable="true"/>
  </s:schema>
 </types>
  <message name="TestHeadersHttpGetIn"/>
  <message name="TestHeadersHttpGetOut">
    <part name="Body" element="s0:string"/>
  </message>
  <portType name="TestItHttpGet">
    <operation name="TestHeaders">
      <input message="s0:TestHeadersHttpGetIn"/>
      <output message="s0:TestHeadersHttpGetOut"/>
    </operation>
  </portType>
  <binding name="TestItHttpGet" type="s0:TestItHttpGet">
    <http:binding verb="GET"/>
    <operation name="TestHeaders">
      <http:operation location="/MatchServer.html"/>
      <input>
        <http:urlEncoded/>
      </input>
      <output>
        <text xmlns="http://microsoft.com/wsdl/mime/textMatching/">
          <match name='Title' pattern='TITLE&gt;(.*?)&lt;'/>
         </text>
      </output>
    </operation>
  </binding>
  <service name="TestIt">
    <port name="TestItHttpGet" binding="s0:TestItHttpGet">
      <http:address location="http://localhost/PWS/Ch4/HelloWorld" />
    </port>
  </service>
</definitions>
```

The `types` section is basic because we have no parameters and only one result. Similarly, our `message` and `port` definitions are basic due to the lack of complexity of our service. One of the important things to notice in the `message`, `port`, and `binding` definitions is that we only use HTTP GET as our method of making requests. Since we are querying a simple web page, we cannot send SOAP as a request, and because we are sending no parameters to the service, it is irrelevant whether we use HTTP POST or HTTP GET.

The binding section of our WSDL file is where things get interesting. Instead of simply telling it to send back SOAP for the output, we will use Microsoft's text matching element, which uses a schema separate from the other binding schemas. The pattern attribute of the match element uses a regular expression to select the title of a page. One of the interesting things about using text matching is that all of the items you match have a specific name that is specified in the match element, but not in the type definition. Finally, the service definition is pretty simple because the service only has one port.

Creating the HelloWorld Application

The HelloWorld screen scrape application will consist of a WSDL document, a Proxy file, an HTML page, and an .aspx page that will have a code-behind file.

The WSDL document is quite large, so we assume that you will use the file from the code download rather than typing it in yourself. The other functions are small, so we will input them manually.

To create the application in VB.NET:

- Create a new VB.NET project in Visual Studio .NET, and select the ASP.NET Web Application template. Name the application HelloWorld, and place it in the http://localhost/PWS/Ch4/ location.
- Place the HelloWorld.WSDL document from the code download into the directory you created above.
- From the Project menu in Visual Studio .NET, choose Add Existing Item, select All Files (*.*) from the File of type dropdown, and select the HelloWorld.WSDL file.
- The HelloWorld WSDL file should now appear in the Solution Explorer. Double-click on it to view the file:

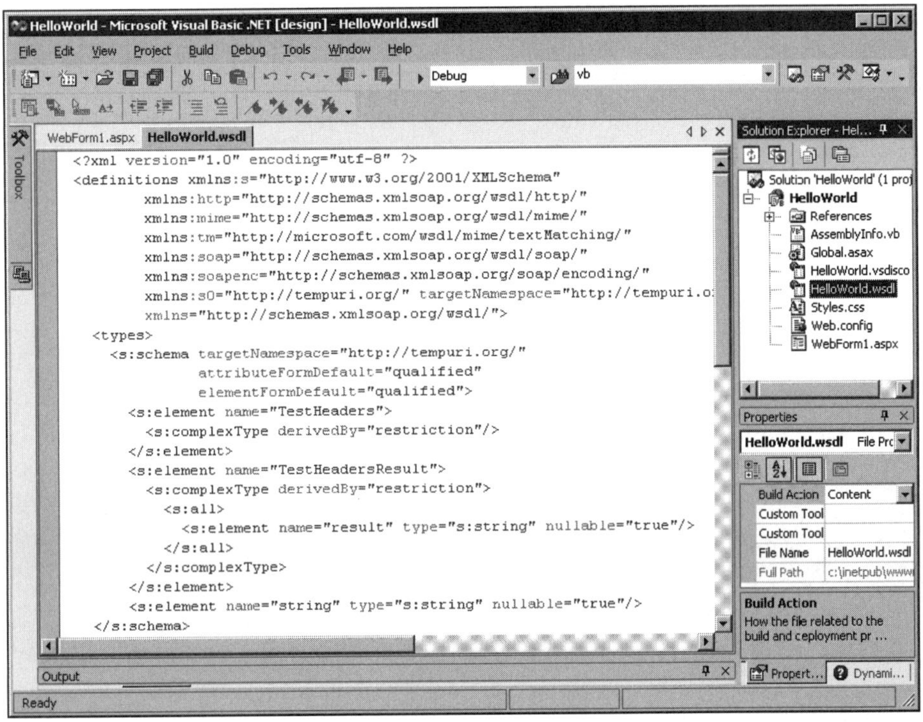

- Now it is time to create the proxy file, which is done by referencing the WSDL document we just added to the project. Right-click the Project name in the Explorer menu and choose Add Web Reference.
- In the address type the location of the WSDL document. The location should be http://localhost/PWS/Ch4/HelloWorld/HelloWorld.wsdl. Hit *Enter*, and then click on the Add Reference button in the lower right-hand corner, which will become highlighted.
- Notice that below References in the Explorer menu we now have a Web Reference item. Right-click the localhost reference directly below the Web Reference item, and change the name to HelloRef.
- Save the `MatchServer.html` document from the code download in the same directory as the other files. Then choose Add Existing Item and add the `MatchServer.html` page to our project. This is the page that contains HelloWorld in the title.

We have now built the Proxy file that you can see below, or you can view it at its location on your hard drive, at `C:\Inetpub\wwwroot\PWS\Ch4\HelloWorld\Web References\HelloRef\Reference.vb`:

```
'------------------------------------------------------------------------------
' <autogenerated>
'     This code was generated by a tool.
'     Runtime Version: 1.0.3705.0
'
```

```
'     Changes to this file may cause incorrect behavior and will be lost if
'     the code is regenerated.
' </autogenerated>
'------------------------------------------------------------------------------

Option Strict Off
Option Explicit On

Imports System
Imports System.ComponentModel
Imports System.Diagnostics
Imports System.Web.Services
Imports System.Web.Services.Protocols
Imports System.Xml.Serialization

'
'This source code was auto-generated by Microsoft.VSDesigner, Version 1.0.3705.0.
'
Namespace HelloRef

  '<remarks/>
  <System.Diagnostics.DebuggerStepThroughAttribute(),  _
  System.ComponentModel.DesignerCategoryAttribute("code")>  _
  Public Class TestIt
    Inherits System.Web.Services.Protocols.HttpGetClientProtocol

    '<remarks/>
    Public Sub New()
      MyBase.New
      Me.Url = "http://localhost/PWS/Ch4/HelloWorld"
    End Sub

    '<remarks/>
    <System.Web.Services.Protocols.HttpMethodAttribute(GetType( _
    System.Web.Services.Protocols.TextReturnReader), _
    GetType(System.Web.Services.Protocols.UrlParameterWriter))>  _
    Public Function TestHeaders() As TestHeadersMatches
      Return CType(Me.Invoke("TestHeaders", (Me.Url + "/MatchServer.html"), _
                             New Object(-1) {}),TestHeadersMatches)
    End Function

    '<remarks/>
    Public Function BeginTestHeaders(ByVal callback As System.AsyncCallback, _
                                     ByVal asyncState As Object) _
                                     As System.IAsyncResult
      Return Me.BeginInvoke("TestHeaders", (Me.Url + "/MatchServer.html"), _
                            New Object(-1) {}, callback, asyncState)
    End Function

    '<remarks/>
    Public Function EndTestHeaders(ByVal asyncResult As System.IAsyncResult) _
                                   As TestHeadersMatches
      Return CType(Me.EndInvoke(asyncResult),TestHeadersMatches)
    End Function
```

```
    End Class

    Public Class TestHeadersMatches

      <System.Web.Services.Protocols.MatchAttribute("TITLE>(.*?)<")> _
      Public Title As String
    End Class
  End Namespace
```

Now let's add the functions.

- From the **Project** Menu, choose **Add Web Form...** and name it **Hello.aspx**.
- Push *F7* to access the code-behind for that ASP.NET page, and add the following `CallService` function:

```
Public Class Hello
  Inherits System.Web.UI.Page

...

  Private Sub Page_Load(ByVal sender As System.Object, _
                        ByVal e As System.EventArgs) Handles MyBase.Load
    'Put user code to initialize the page here
  End Sub

  Public Sub CallService()
    Dim matcher As HelloRef.TestIt
    matcher = New HelloRef.TestIt()

    Dim matches As HelloRef.TestHeadersMatches
    matches = matcher.TestHeaders()
    Response.Output.WriteLine(matches.Title)
  End Sub

End Class
```

Next, in the HTML part of the `.aspx` page, you need to add a simple call to the `CallService` function. You can use the following source for your HTML:

```
<%@ Page language="VB" Codebehind="Hello.aspx.vb" AutoEventWireup="false"
         Inherits="HelloWorld.Hello" %>
<html>
  <body>
    <%
      CallService()
    %>
  </body>
</html>
```

Once you have saved the project, enter *Control-Shift-B* to build it. Right-click on the `Hello.aspx` page in Explorer and choose **View in Browser**.

Summary

In this chapter, we looked at:

- The SOAP Toolkit 2.0
- WSDL documents and .NET
- A WSDL document in detail
- A screen scraping example

The first goal of this chapter was to explain what WSDL is and why it is important. We discussed that SOAP and UDDI are not enough to create a truly automated Web Service world. This is a world where every Web Service consumed would have to be understood and have handcrafted SOAP coded on it.

The second goal of this chapter was to examine how to work with WSDL documents, which is why we covered the SOAP Toolkit 2.0 as well as WSDL documents and .NET. In the near future, a lot of us will be interfacing our Web Services to COM objects. After all, there are quite a few COM objects out there.

Web Services, WSDL, SOAP, and UDDI are still very new, so it is hard to know how they will be implemented in large-scale projects in the future, but we now understand enough WSDL that we can work with the tools to customize it when necessary.

Professional
ASP.NET
Web
Services

5

Standard Wire Formats and Data Types

There has been a lot of discussion on the Internet lately about Web Services and how they will revolutionize the way in which applications and web sites will communicate. Theoretically, the concept of Web Services will allow a client running on virtually any operating system to communicate seamlessly with a Web Service running on a web server hosted by an entirely different OS with an entirely different set of core technologies. A client can, theoretically, query a server for what Web Services are available, and then obtain all relevant information required in order to access any of those services.

At a high level, this all seems quite wonderful, but how exactly does it all happen? With all of the hype surrounding .NET and Web Services, you probably haven't managed to escape the term **SOAP** (Simple Object Access Protocol). SOAP is the "wire format" that enables all of this fantastic, language-agnostic communication to take place for Web Services.

This chapter will give you an introduction to several of the most common wire formats, as well as discussing what wire formats and protocols are. This chapter will then round out its discussion of wire formats with a detailed overview of SOAP and how it relates to Web Services. We hope that once you have finished reading this chapter, you will have been able to take away the following knowledge:

- What a wire format is
- What some of the most common wire formats are and how they may or may not be related to SOAP
- What SOAP is, what SOAP messages look like, and how they're used in Web Services
- Why SOAP is used for Web Services
- Using simple and complex data types with SOAP

What is a Wire Format?

A **Wire Format** is the form (you can think of it as a *shape* if that helps) data takes when transmitted across the network "wire". The term "wire" is used in quotes because it could just as easily be a cellular connection, a wireless LAN connection, or a satellite link.

One distinction that many people find confusing is the difference between the wire format and the transport. Whereas the wire format is the form or shape of the data, the transport is the method by which that data is transferred from place to place.

Consider the analogy of a transport truck on a highway. Its cargo can take many shapes and forms, but the truck itself is still the *transport*, and as such is responsible for taking its payload from its origination point to its destination.

There are many ways to represent data, and all of them have their own specific benefits and disadvantages. Storing data in raw binary format might have the advantage of a compressed structure and a smaller storage requirement, but it might make things more difficult for the receiver of the binary data. XML data has a larger storage requirement, but allows for a greater ease of use and flexibility on the part of the receiver.

Wire Formats

This next section of the chapter will give a brief overview of some of the more common ways in which data is sent across the "wire" for Internet and/or distributed applications. The overview of wire formats will conclude with a detailed discussion of SOAP as a wire format.

HTTP GET

The HTTP GET protocol is an industry standard protocol that uses the HTTP (HyperText Transfer Protocol) verb "GET" for retrieving data from web servers. HTTP GET makes a request of a web server that consists of a series of HTTP request headers that define things like the client browser and more. Parameters to the request are sent UUencoded (the process that converts a space into the "%20" character).

Next to SOAP, HTTP GET and HTTP POST are the most commonly used transport protocols for Web Services in the .NET Framework. The limitation of the HTTP GET and POST protocols is that they have limited support for complex data types.

Because your web browser (such as IE or Netscape) typically hides all of the underlying HTTP details from you and serves up nicely formatted and colored pages, you are insulated from a lot of what is going on with the HTTP GET protocol. The following screenshot illustrates some of what is going on in an HTTP GET request.

```
Command Prompt                                                    _ □ ×
GET /iishelp/iis/misc/default.asp HTTP/1.1
Accept:*/*
Accept-language:en-us
Connection:Keep-Alive
Host:localhost
User-Agent:Mozilla/4.0 (compatible; MSIE 5.5; Windows NT 5.0)
Accept-Encoding: gzip, deflate

HTTP/1.1 200 OK
Server: Microsoft-IIS/5.0
Date: Fri, 12 Feb 2002 12:32:15 GMT
Connection: Keep-Alive
Content-Length: 1614
Content-Type: text/html
Set-Cookie: ASPSESSIONIDQQQGQOBK=PNFBABFDNPIDOFJBNLEAAHCD; path=/
Cache-control: private

<!DOCTYPE HTML PUBLIC "-//W3C//DTD HTML 3.2//EN">

<html dir=ltr><head><title>Microsoft Internet Information Services 5.0 Docu
mentation</title>

<META NAME="ROBOTS" CONTENT="NOINDEX">
<META HTTP-EQUIV="Content-Type" content="text/html; charset=Windows-1252">
```

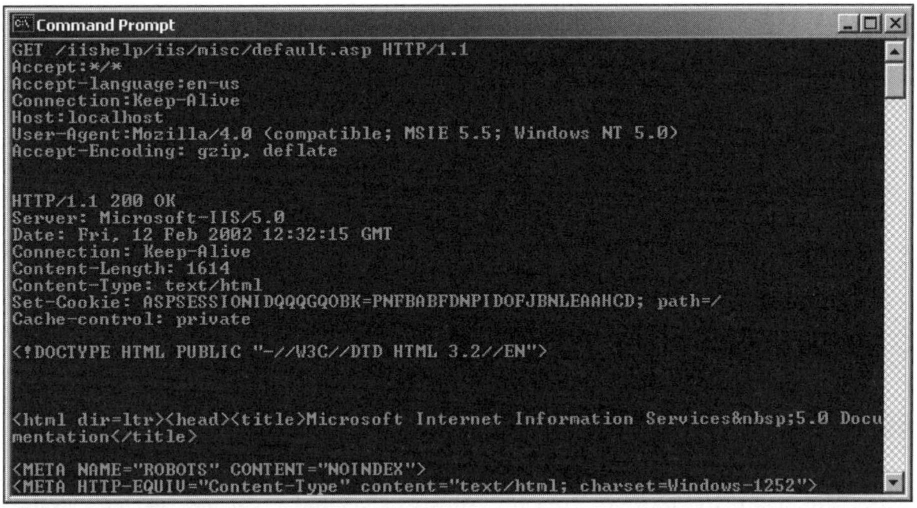

What we've done is opened up a command prompt in Windows 2000 and typed "telnet localhost 80",
which opens up a raw ASCII TCP/IP connection to our web server. We turned local echo on (by
pulling up the telnet command prompt (hit *Ctrl-]*), and typing the appropriate echo on command) so you
could see what was happening, and issued the following request:

GET /iishelp/iis/misc/default.asp HTTP/1.1

This, followed by the HTTP headers you see in the screenshot and a blank line (you have to hit *Enter*
twice from the telnet prompt to indicate to the server that you're done sending your request), will issue a
HTTP GET request against the web server for that filename, using the HTTP v1.1 protocol. You can see
that the server issued a response with the standard response code of "200 OK" (I'm sure you're familiar
with the dreaded "404", which indicates a file not found error). It then sent some header information
including the server type and version number, as well as the server date, content length, and a request
to set an ASP Session cookie. Once the headers were done, the HTML output began streaming to the
console. Every time you request a web page (or request a Web Service) via the HTTP GET protocol,
this is the interaction that is occurring at a low level.

HTTP POST

HTTP POST is the second half of the standard HTTP GET/POST verbs. HTTP POST parameters are
UUencoded, but sent to the web server directly in the HTTP request message itself. This protocol is
used to transmit information to the web server, such as posting a new message on a forum, clicking
"OK" on a search form, and so on.

In terms of Web Services, this protocol also suffers from the inability to carry complex data types to a
Web Service. Complex data types are serializations of complex object graphs such as a `DataSet` or
your own object. HTTP POST by itself is limited to primitive string types. However, as we'll see later,
when SOAP messages are carried on top of this protocol (HTTP is used as the SOAP *transport*) this
limitation can be overcome.

BXXP/BEEP

BXXP was an XML-based framework for building application protocols that was used as a starting point for the IETF's **BEEP** (Blocks Extensible Exchange Protocol) working group. BEEP can now be found residing on the web site http://www.beepcore.org.

BEEP supports distributed applications that work in peer-to-peer environments as well as client/server and server-to-server environments. It allows for the carriage of arbitrary MIME (Multipurpose Internet Mail Extensions) payloads including XML and supports a standard layer for session management. BEEP is the brainchild of Dr. Marshall Rose and is a relatively new Internet protocol that is in the middle of the standardization process. There is currently no native .NET Framework support for BEEP applications, but there is strong Java and Tcl support for the BEEPcore library available on the BEEPcore.org web site.

ebXML

Electronic Business XML (ebXML) is an XML dialect sponsored by UN/CEFACT and OASIS designed to replace traditional EDI (Electronic Data Interchange) methodologies with a stronger, more extensible way of allowing businesses to communicate electronically and automatically. The goals of this protocol are to provide a system for reliable messaging and error handling, message routing, security, auditing, platform independence, and recovery from interrupted messages and transactions.

ebXML is a modular suite of specifications that enables businesses to conduct business over the Internet. Anyone who has worked for an Internet-visible business that has needed to exchange information with other business partners knows the challenge present in communicating information and processes between businesses. The ebXML protocol provides for not only the exchange of business information, but messages and business processes as well.

The inner workings of the protocol are far too complex to explain in any detail in this chapter, but there is plenty of information available at the web site for the effort, www.ebXml.org.

GIOP/IIOP

CORBA (Common Object Request Broker Architecture) has a General Purpose Inter-ORB Protocol (**GIOP**) that is a general purpose wire protocol for use in CORBA-based distributed application architectures. There is a TCP/IP specialized version of this protocol available called the Internet Inter-ORB Protocol (**IIOP**). Both of these protocols use a binary structure for transferring remote method invocation information between distributed systems.

XML-RPC

The XML-RPC protocol is probably the wire format that most closely resembles SOAP in goal and nature. XML-RPC is a protocol that uses HTTP as the transport and XML as the encoding format. The goal of XML-RPC is to allow remote method invocations and responses between two peers across a "wire". Again, "wire" should be taken as an abstract and not limited to physically connected devices.

Without getting into too much detail on the inner workings of XML-RPC, let's take a look at how it might be used. What we're going to do is take a look at the HTTP conversation that might take place if a client application is attempting to look up the full name that belongs to a specific customer's ID number.

Here is the text that is sent to the server:

```
POST /RPC2 HTTP/1.0
User-Agent: MyApp 1.0 (Windows NT 5.0)
Host: customerlookup.somecompany.com
Content-Type: text/xml
Content-length: 250

<?xml version="1.0"?>
<methodCall>
  <methodName>contactmanager.LookupCustomer</methodName>
  <params>
    <param>
      <value>
        <i4>1852</i4>
      </value>
    </param>
  </params>
</methodCall>
```

As we can see, the immediate benefit is that the payload carried by this HTTP POST request is human-readable XML. It should be fairly obvious that we're trying to invoke the `LookupCustomer` method in the `contactmanager` object, and pass it the argument `1852`. Assuming the function call on the remote machine completed properly, an XML-RPC response might look like the following:

```
<methodResponse>
  <params>
    <param>
      <value>
        <string>John Doe</string>
      </value>
    </param>
  </params>
</methodResponse>
```

This response is typically received with the HTTP result code of "200 OK".

This looks like a pretty robust implementation, but we should mention that XML-RPC only supports a few core data types, such as:

- 4-byte Signed Integer (represented by the `<i4>` or `<int>` tag)
- Boolean values (represented by the `<boolean>` tag)
- Strings (represented by the `<string>` tag)
- Double-precision, signed floating point numbers (`<double>`)
- ISO 8601 International standard dates for example, 20020717T12:12:21 (`<dateTime.iso8601>`)
- Base-64 encoded binary data (represented by the `<base64>` tag)

While the XML-RPC specification (found at www.xmlrpc.com/spec) allows for the extension of these types by supporting arrays and structures (VB user-defined types or C `structs`), those arrays and structures can only have the above-listed basic types as members. This limitation makes this protocol very impractical for transmitting complex types like ADO.NET datasets, complex or jagged arrays, recordsets, and so on.

XMLP

XMLP (The XML Protocol) is a rapidly progressing W3C standard. The requirements for this protocol can be found at www.w3c.org/TR/xmlp-reqs, while the working group on the protocol can be found at www.w3.org/2000/xp/Group/.

This is an extremely robust protocol whose main goal is to allow two or more peers to communicate in a distributed environment with XML as the data-encoding format. It sports a layered architecture on top of an extensible and simple messaging format. This extensible and simple messaging format might look extremely familiar to those who are familiar with SOAP. In fact, the progression from SOAP to XMLP is enough to have many people saying that SOAP will eventually be superseded by XMLP.

An XMLP Application is a consumer of services provided by the XMLP Layer. The XMLP Layer provides services or operations that transfer packages of XMLP Blocks between peer XMLP Applications with zero or more XMLP Intermediaries. An XMLP Intermediary is an XMLP Receiver and an XMLP Sender that processes XMLP Blocks and forwards the XMLP Message on to the next Receiver in the line toward the message's ultimate Receiver or destination.

Obviously, there are a lot of intricate inner workings involved in the XML Protocol. To make things a bit simpler, we have included a diagram of an XMLP Envelope, which are the basic units of data transferred in XMLP Messages. This diagram is from the W3C requirements specification:

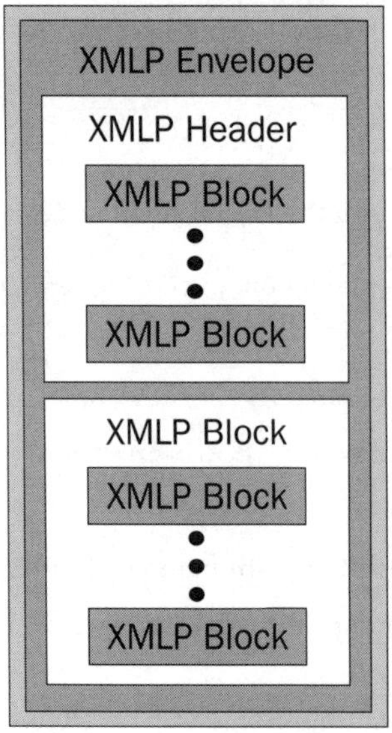

SOAP

SOAP (Simple Object Access Protocol) is a protocol that allows not only for remote method invocations in distributed environments, but it also allows for the transfer of rich and complex data types as well as the messaging of arbitrary payloads. We'll discuss SOAP in detail in the next section of this chapter. SOAP support is built into the .NET Framework, and it is a key part of the .NET Framework's implementation of Web Services.

An Introduction to SOAP

SOAP is a fairly new protocol being developed as an industry standard. With all of the hype surrounding the .NET Framework, Microsoft, and SOAP, many people think that SOAP is just another Microsoft acronym. While there has been significant support from Microsoft on the SOAP initiative, the protocol itself is designed to be vendor- and platform-independent. SOAP began its life as a request for standardization some time before the .NET betas began to surface. In fact, many Microsoft teams were internally using other technologies when they decided to adopt SOAP in the middle of the process of building what we now know as .NET.

The goal of SOAP is to allow for a standardized method of exchanging textual information between clients and applications running on the Internet. It provides for a standard method of encoding data into a portable format, but (in version 1.1) makes no distinction about how that data is to be transported from application to application. The original 1.0 specification of SOAP required that SOAP messages be transmitted using only the HTTP protocol. This has since changed with the acceptance of the 1.1 standard, allowing SOAP messages to be sent using other transports such as FTP and SMTP.

Why SOAP?

The main benefit of SOAP is that it is an incredibly lightweight protocol. That is, it doesn't require an enormous amount of work on the part of either the sender or the recipient to communicate using the protocol. In fact, because SOAP uses conformant XML as its data encoding format, any system capable of parsing XML should be capable of communicating via SOAP.

It's all well and good for us to say how wonderful SOAP is, but to many programmers (myself included), 'seeing is believing'. Before getting into the detail of *what* SOAP is and how you can build SOAP messages (the basic unit of communication in SOAP), let's take a look at some of the communication problems that SOAP attempts to resolve.

Consider the example of a client application (this could be a Windows application or a web site) that needs to get at data maintained by the web site of a business partner. Let's say that the Northwind Company (we all should be thoroughly sick of them by now) has a business partner that requires access to their customer list for marketing purposes.

How is this partner supposed to access this information? If the web site is worth anything, its database is tucked securely away behind a firewall, so accessing it directly is out of the question. We could try and hit an HTML-formatted page containing customer information and try and "scrape" the useful information off of the web page, but that would be considered a cheap hack at best. The real solution is to provide a way for the partner to obtain the actual customer list using HTTP so the business partner doesn't have to worry about firewalls or NT authentication (after all, the partner could be running Netscape or IE on a system that isn't supported by NT authentication).

The two business partners get together and decide that they'll exchange customer data in the form of an XML-persisted ADO recordset. What they decide on next is to create an ASP page that only that one business partner can use that will simply place onto the Response stream the XML persisted from the recordset.

Let's take a look at how this all works. The first thing we'll look at is a hypothetical marketing application written in VB6 that the Northwind partner uses to make annoying phone calls. You can find this sample application in the `XMLHTTP_VB6` directory in the code download for this chapter. Its associated ASP page is called `Northcustomers.asp`, and can also be found in that directory. We'll start with a screenshot of the VB6 application that "pulls" the information from a fictitious Northwind web site.

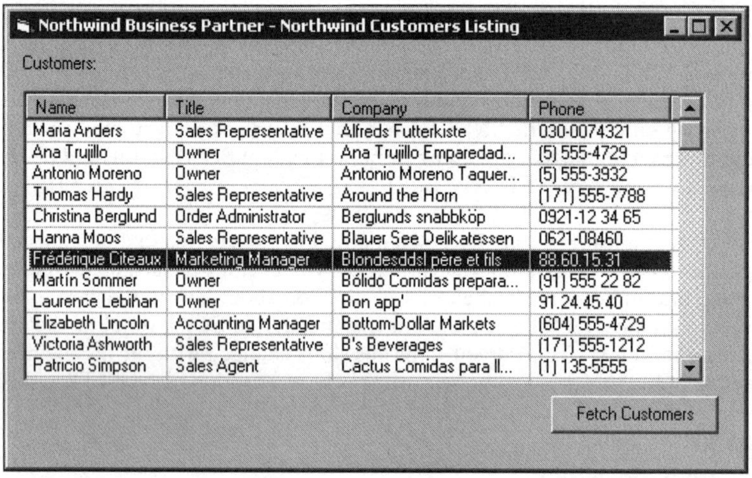

Nothing too complicated here. We're looking at a `ListView` control with a couple of column headers and a "Fetch Customers" button. Let's take a look at the code we execute in response to clicking that button.

```
Public oRS As ADODB.Recordset

Private Sub Command1_Click()
  Dim oStream As New ADODB.Stream
  Dim oReq As MSXML.XMLHTTPRequest
  Dim strXML As String
  Dim newItem As ListItem

  Set oReq = New MSXML.XMLHTTPRequest

  oReq.Open "POST", "http://localhost/PWS/Ch5/XMLHTTP_VB6/Northcustomers.asp", _
            False
  oReq.send ""

  strXML = oReq.responseText
  Set oRS.ActiveConnection = Nothing
  oRS.CursorLocation = adUseClient
  oStream.Open
```

```
    oStream.WriteText strXML, adWriteChar
    oStream.Position = 0
    oRS.Open oStream
    If oRS.State = adStateClosed then
      Do While Not oRS.EOF
        Set newItem = ListView1.ListItems.Add(, , oRS("ContactName").Value, 0, 0)
          newItem.ListSubItems.Add , , oRS("ContactTitle").Value, 0, ""
          newItem.ListSubItems.Add , , oRS("CompanyName").Value, 0, ""
          newItem.ListSubItems.Add , , oRS("Phone").Value, 0, ""
        oRS.MoveNext
      Loop
    End If
  End Sub
```

For those of you not familiar with the `XMLHTTPRequest` object, it's a component found in Microsoft XML version 2.0 and above that allows your VB6 application or component to communicate at a low level with an HTTP server. In our case, as you can see above, we're attempting to open the file `http://localhost/PWS/CH5/XMLHTTP_VB6/Northcustomers.asp`. The assumption is that the response from this ASP page will be a stream of text containing a recordset serialized in XML format. We open the recordset based on this stream and then proceed to populate the `ListView` control. So far the code looks pretty simple, tight, and is accomplishing a lot of good things... So why is this a problem? You'll find out shortly.

Now let's look at the source code for the `Northcustomers.ASP` page:

```
<%@ LANGUAGE=VBScript %>

<%
  Dim oRS
  Dim oConn

  Set oRS = Server.CreateObject("ADODB.RecordSet")
  Set oConn = Server.CreateObject("ADODB.Connection")
  oConn.ConnectionString = "Driver={SQl Server};Server=localhost;" & _
                           "Database=Northwind; UID=sa; PWD=;"

  oConn.Open

  oRS.Open "SELECT * FROM Customers", oConn

  oRS.Save Response, 1
  oRS.Close
%>
```

It still looks pretty simple. We're just creating a recordset and saving it to the `Response` stream. Because our ASP page doesn't know the constant value for `adPersistXML`, we use the real value for it (`1`).

So we just showed that in an extremely small number of lines of code, we can use XML documents over the HTTP transport to communicate directly from a web server to any number of clients, including a Windows application. Sounds pretty cool!

Now for the bad news. How could we extend this sample to be able to transfer an instance of an object? How would we modify the above example to use the same ASP page to service multiple methods with complex arguments? How would we pass an array of arbitrary length to a method call hosted by our ASP page? If something were to go wrong on the server, how would the client learn about it? Now it sounds a bit more complicated, doesn't it?

While this one small solution may work for a very narrow scope, it isn't viable for anything real-world that requires scalability or extensibility. This is where SOAP comes to the rescue. SOAP is a protocol that allows you to pass messages and complex data back and forth between disparate systems in a distributed architecture enabling remote method invocation.

SOAP provides for the encoding of complex data, messaging, remote method invocation, and error communication in a standardized format readable by any XML parser.

The SOAP Format

Now that we've taken a brief look at some of the hardships people face when attempting to interface disparate systems without the benefit of SOAP, let's take a look at what's inside SOAP and how it works. The following is a diagram of a **SOAP Message**. The Message is a combination of an Envelope, Header, and Body. We'll discuss each portion of the Message in some detail.

SOAP Message Format

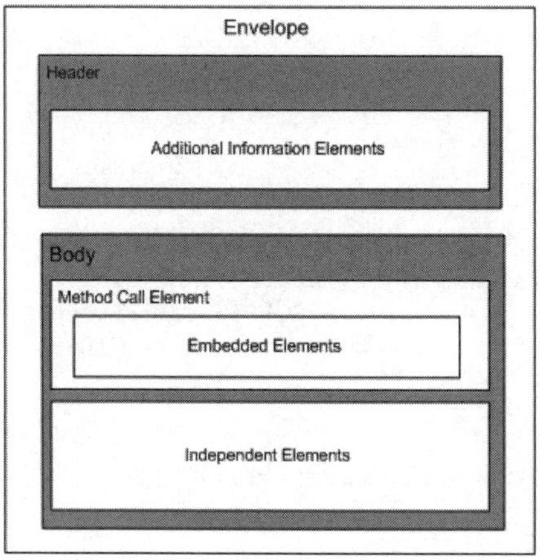

Every SOAP Message is an XML document. This XML document has a single root (or document) element that is a SOAP Envelope. Within the envelope is where the rest of the data relevant to the message is stored.

Keep in mind that unlike some other *routed* messaging and distributed access protocols (such as RMI, CORBA's protocol), SOAP provides no means for encoding source and destination information into the Envelope. The Envelope is simply a neat and tidy package containing information; it is up to the individual consumer of SOAP at the time to decide where and how that information is to be transmitted. In the case of the focus of this book, ASP.NET Web Services, the Web Services infrastructure determines how and where to send the SOAP Messages.

The SOAP Envelope

As we said, the Envelope is the top-most or root element in the XML document that represents a SOAP Message. Beneath the envelope, there is an **optional** Header element, and a **required** Body element. Let's take a look at an empty SOAP Message to see what the XML looks like:

```
<SOAP-Env:Envelope>
  <SOAP-Env:Header>
  </SOAP-Env:Header>

  <SOAP-Env:Body>
  </SOAP-Env:Body>
</SOAP-Env:Envelope>
```

We've left out the namespace definitions and the XML header here to keep things simple. However, it is important to notice that the Envelope, Body, and Header elements are all namespace-qualified to the `SOAP-ENV` namespace. It is actually a requirement to qualify the namespace and unlike some other XML protocols, we cannot leave these in the default namespace.

According to the Envelope's schema, you are allowed to include your own custom attributes on the Envelope itself, but those must be namespace-qualified. In addition, you can add your own elements to the Envelope so long as those are also namespace-qualified and occur **after** the Body element in the document. This flexibility allows you to create your own SOAP handlers to tune your XML Web Services implementation to your individual needs. Here's an example of a SOAP Envelope that has a custom attribute in place:

```
<SOAP-Env:Envelope xmlns:SOAP-ENV="http://schemas.xmlsoap.org/soap/envelope/"
                   xmlns:CUSTOM="urn:schemas-mycustom-com:custom"
                         CUSTOM:somevalue="2150">

  <!-- Header and body Tags -->
</SOAP-Env:Envelope>
```

The SOAP Header

SOAP allows you to place a payload header in the top of your SOAP Envelope. This allows you to provide further detailed information describing the payload being carried by the SOAP Body. This is where naming conventions get slightly confused.

The schema for the optional SOAP Header Element (`SOAP-Env:Header`) allows for an unlimited number of child elements to be placed within the header. Each one of these child elements represents an instance of Microsoft's `SoapHeader` class. So, the confusion is in that the SOAP specification refers to *the* SOAP Header as the `Header` element, while Microsoft's `SoapHeader` class considers *a* SOAP Header to be a child element within the `Header` element.

What this allows for is for Web Service clients to place extra data into the header of the message so that every single method call on that service doesn't have to accept that data as an argument. For example, you could use the header information to supply credentials to the Web Service. Rather than requiring every single method call on the Web Service to ask for a username and password, you could simply stuff that information into the SOAP Header.

For example, a SOAP Envelope sent from a client using the custom header might look like this:

```
<SOAP-Env:Envelope>
  <SOAP-Env:Header>
    <Custom-App:Credentials xmlns:Custom-App="urn:schemas-myapp-com:Credentials">
      <Username>Administrator</Username>
      <Password>328309xka4ja8x9241a;xj2</Password>
    </Custom-App:Credentials>
  </SOAP-Env:Header>

  <!-- Body of SOAP Message here -->

</SOAP-Env:Envelope>
```

To make your Web Service aware of the custom header (remember, this is Microsoft's definition of a Header, which is a child element of the `SOAP-Env:Header` element), all you have to do is create a class that derives from the `SoapHeader` class and modify your Web Service to indicate that the header is being used.

The `SoapHeader` class that you create is really nothing more than a data container that knows how to be serialized in and out of the `SOAP-Env:Header` element in a SOAP Message. Let's take a look at how to use a custom SOAP Header in the real world (well, almost). We'll expand on the SOAP Envelope we showed earlier with the Username and Password information contained in it.

The first thing we'll do is create a Web Service. To do this, we'll just open up Visual Studio .NET and create a new VB.NET Web Service project called `SOAPHeader`. Rename the `Service1.asmx` file to `HeaderService.asmx`. Make sure that you also modify the `.asmx` file to point to the appropriate class name. Before we actually get into writing the Web Service, we need to define the derived class for our custom SOAP Header (put this in `AuthHeader.vb`, a simple class file added to our project):

```
Imports System
Imports System.Web.Services.Protocols

Namespace SOAPHeader

  Public Class AuthHeader
    Inherits System.Web.Services.Protocols.SoapHeader
    Public UserName As String
    Public Password As String
  End Class
End Namespace
```

Now that we have this defined and part of our Web Service project in Visual Studio .NET, let's take a look at the source listing for `HeaderService.asmx.vb`. We've cut out the IDE-generated code to keep things easier to read:

```
Imports System
Imports System.Collections
Imports System.ComponentModel
Imports System.Data
Imports System.Diagnostics
```

```
Imports System.Web
Imports System.Web.Services
Imports System.Web.Services.Protocols

Namespace SOAPHeader
  Public Class HeaderService
    Inherits System.Web.Services.WebService

    Public Sub New()
      MyBase.New()
      InitializeComponent()
    End Sub
```

Below, we declare a public instance of the custom `SoapHeader` class that we just defined above in the `AuthHeader.vb` file:

```
    Public myHeaderVariable As AuthHeader
```

In the code below, we use the `<WebMethod>` custom code attribute here to indicate that this method will be exposed publicly via our Web Service. Also, we use the `SoapHeaderAttribute` custom code attribute to indicate the name of the variable that contains the `SoapHeader` class that this method is expecting. Within this method, we can be assured that our `SoapHeader` class instance will have its properties set according to the information found in the `SOAP-Env:Header` element in the request issued to the Web Service.

```
    <WebMethod(), SoapHeader("myHeaderVariable")> _
    Public Function HelloWorld() As String
      Return "Hello, " + myHeaderVariable.UserName
    End Function

  End Class
End Namespace
```

The code above defines the standard "Hello World" sample application, but with a twist. Instead of greeting generically, it returns the name of the user found in the SOAP Header passed from the client application. The ability to pass custom information, serialized as a standard XML element, is an invaluable tool in securing, customizing, and extending Web Services to perform the tasks that you want in the way you want them performed.

Let's take a look at the code for the client application that will consume this Web Service. To create this client application, we created a VB.NET Console Application from within Visual Studio .NET and called it `SOAPHeaderClient`. Then we simply added a **Web Reference** (right-click the project, click Add Web Reference) to our `HeaderService` Web Service. With this accomplished, we were able to enter the following into our `Class1.vb` file:

```
Imports System

Public Module Class1

  Sub Main(ByVal args As String())
```

By default, when we added the Web Reference to the project, it added it in the "localhost" namespace (defaults to the site name from which the reference was obtained in reverse, therefore a reference from Microsoft.com would be in the Com.Microsoft namespace). The code listed overleaf instantiates a new proxy object as well as an instance of the custom SOAP Header class. Note that when we obtained the Web Reference and Visual Studio .NET created the proxy object for us, it also gave us a copy of the AuthHeader class in the localhost namespace.

```
    Dim proxy As New localhost.HeaderService()
    Dim myHeader As New localhost.AuthHeader()
```

The next two lines of code populate the <UserName> and <Password> elements in the <AuthHeader> element that will be in our SOAP Header.

```
    myHeader.UserName = "Admin"
    myHeader.Password = "Administrator"
```

Before we make the actual request of the Web Service, we need to set the value of the AuthHeaderValue property (this was created by the proxy class generation code to provide a property of type AuthHeader for the proxy class) to our instance of AuthHeader (myHeader).

```
    proxy.AuthHeaderValue = myHeader
    Console.WriteLine(proxy.HelloWorld())
    proxy.Dispose()
    Console.ReadLine()
  End Sub
End Module
```

Now that we've seen how to write an ASP.NET Web Service that expects a custom SOAP Header, and we've seen how to write a client that consumes such a Web Service, let's see what the output of the client looks like when we put everything together and run it:

What we've seen here is an incredibly simple example that allowed us to supply some simple text information in the SOAP Header when communicating between our Console Application client and our Web Service. The true benefit of the ability to add arbitrary SOAP Headers when communicating with a Web Service comes into play when you need to secure communications between the client and the server, allowing you to encrypt data and store it in a SOAP Header as well as store complex, serialized objects in the header. Please see Chapter 14 for more information on using SOAP for security.

SOAP Body

The body of a SOAP Envelope is where the meat of the remote method calls is placed. The SOAP Body is where the method call information and its related arguments are encoded, it is where the response to a method call is placed, and it is where error information can be stored. In addition to storing these three main types of elements, the body can also contain things called **independent elements**, which are used in encoding data (we'll discuss that in the next section on *Encoding Data Types*).

Call Body

When the SOAP Body is used to *send* a remote method call, that method call and its arguments are serialized directly into the <SOAP-ENV:Body> element. The outer element of the function call serialization is an element with the same name as the function being called. Each argument to that function is then serialized as a child element. Let's consider a standard function prototype that looks something like this:

```
Function Sum(OperandA As Integer, OperandB As Integer) As Integer
End Function
```

It's a fairly standard function that just adds two integers and returns an integer containing the sum of the two values. Let's take a look at how the SOAP Body might look containing a serialized method call for the above prototype if we invoke the method in an attempt to add 2 and 2:

```
<SOAP-ENV:Envelope xmlns:xsi="http://www.w3c.org/1999/XMLSchema/instance"
                   xmlns:SOAP-ENV="http://schemas.xmlsoap.org/soap/envelope/">
  <SOAP-ENV:Body xmlns:adder="urn:schemas-mysite-com:adder">
    <adder:Sum>
      <OperandA xsi:type="int">2</OperandA>
      <OperandB xsi:type="int">2</OperandB>
    </adder:sum>
  </SOAP-ENV:Body>
</SOAP-ENV:Envelope>
```

It is possible to transmit complex data types as method arguments, but we will cover that in the section on *Encoding Data Types.*

> **The method element is always the first child element of the Body element, and is always namespace-qualified. The method arguments, however, do not need to be namespace-qualified as it is assumed they are part of the same namespace as the method element.**

Response Body

Again, it is worth reminding you that SOAP makes no provisions for *transport*, and is on its own simply a protocol for data being encoded onto the wire. It is up to the supporting infrastructure (in our case XML Web Services) to provide the means by which the SOAP Messages are transmitted between systems.

Once a SOAP Message containing a call body (a method element and serialized arguments in the body) has been sent, it is reasonable for us to expect that we will receive another SOAP Message in response, one containing a `Body` element that somehow contains the results of our remote method call. In the case of SOAP over HTTP, a message containing the response body will be sent as text in response to an HTTP POST of the message containing the call body.

By convention, *not* by requirements in the specification, the response body's first child element is an element of the same name as the method name with a suffix of "`Response`" appended. Following our example above, the response to a method call for the `Sum` method would be an element named `SumResponse`, also namespace-qualified. As the child element of the method response element, the `return` element is used to contain the method's return value. If the method call had parameters defined as `[out]` or `[in,out]` (COM definition, VB programmers would consider these `ByRef` parameters) those parameters would be contained as embedded elements within the method response element.

Let's take a look at a sample response envelope from the above function call (keep in mind that these are sample envelopes and may contain slightly more or less detail than something automatically generated for you by the .NET Framework, depending on the circumstances):

```
<SOAP-ENV:Envelope xmlns:xsi="http://www.w3c.orc/1999/XMLSchema/instance"
                   xmlns:SOAP-ENV="http://schemas.xmlsoap.org/soap/envelope/">
  <SOAP-ENV:Body xmlns:adder="urn:schemas-mysite-com:adder">
    <adder:SumResponse>
      <return>4</return>
    </adder:SumResponse>
  </SOAP-ENV:Body>
</SOAP-ENV:Envelope>
```

Again, just as with the call body, the method response element is namespace-qualified, and is the first child of the `Body` element (we'll see later an example of more than one child element in the Body). Also, the `return` element does not need to be namespace-qualified.

> **By convention, the method response element is named the same as the method with the "`Response`" suffix. This response element is the first child of the `Body` element and must be namespace-qualified.**

Fault Body

If your infrastructure tries to send a SOAP Message, and there is a network failure, then you should receive the appropriate network error message. In the case of sending a SOAP Message over HTTP, you should receive a timeout or similar error. However, if when processing your SOAP Message, some error occurs, then you might be likely to receive a SOAP Message in response whose `Body` element contains the `Fault` element.

Thankfully, when you are using the XML Web Services infrastructure provided by the .NET Framework, the interpretation of SOAP Faults is done automatically for you. If the system sees a SOAP Message containing a `Fault` in response, then a new exception is thrown on the client end containing the details of the `Fault` element. This allows a function call on a server to throw an exception that can be trapped, extracted, and interpreted in a user-friendly manner on the client.

The Fault element can contain a lot of information, but in general the Fault element contains a faultcode element, a faultstring element, and an optional detail element, which can be used to store additional information about the error that occurred. We won't go into too much detail on the operations of the Fault element, as most of the work is being done for you. However, it is helpful to know what kind of information is being transferred when errors occur. Let's take a look at a sample Fault body that might have occurred with some problem with our Sum method:

```
<SOAP-ENV:Envelope xmlns:SOAP-ENV="http://schemas.xmlsoap.org/soap/envelope/">
  <SOAP-ENV:Body>
    <SOAP-ENV:Fault>
      <faultcode>SOAP-ENV:Server</faultcode>
      <faultstring>Error</faultstring>
      <detail>
        <!-- additional method-specific detail information -->
      </detail>
    </SOAP-ENV:Fault>
  </SOAP-ENV:Body>
</SOAP-ENV:Envelope>
```

When an error occurs on the other end of a SOAP Message exchange (such as a client call to a Web Service) then that error is returned as an instance of the SoapException class. This class has properties and methods that relate very closely to its SOAP XML format shown above. It contains a property that allows access to the detail element, the Message (faultstring), and so on.

For your reference, the following is a list of the possible values for the <faultcode> element, all of which should be namespace-qualified as part of the SOAP-ENV namespace.

Value	Description
VersionMismatch	Indicates that there was a bad or mismatched namespace in the conversation. Namespaces are used to version SOAP Envelopes, therefore a namespace mismatch is considered a version mismatch.
MustUnderstand	A mustUnderstand attribute in the SOAP Header indicates that some custom value in the header must be recognized. This error occurs when the custom information is not recognized.
DataEncodingUnknown	This fault indicates that the encoding format used in the body was not a format known to the message decoder.
Client	Covers the broad range of client-side SOAP faults.
Server	Covers the broad range of server-side SOAP faults.

Before we move on to encoding data types, let's take a look at what it looks like when we throw an exception from inside a Web Service and capture it on the client. As we discussed above, this is made possible by the SOAP Fault in the body of the Envelope. Under the hood, when we throw an exception within a Web Service, it is then wrapped up by a new SoapException instance, which as we just learned can be stuffed into a SOAP Envelope and sent back to the client.

The first thing we'll do is create a simple Web Service (you can find the full code for this in the `SOAPFault` directory). We'll skip some of the details and just show the `WebMethod` for our service that is going to throw this exception in the `ErrorService.asmx.vb` file:

```
<WebMethod()> _
Public Function HelloWorld() As String
  Throw New Exception("This is a really big error!")
  Return "Hello World"
End Function
```

As you can see, it's pretty straightforward. The first thing we do once we get into this method is throw an `Exception`. One really big benefit here is that we're not doing *anything* that is at all related to XML, SOAP, HTTP, TCP/IP, or anything else for that matter, we're simply throwing an `Exception`. The Web Services infrastructure sees this, wraps it in a `SoapException` (which we know is responsible for building the SOAP Fault) and then sends it on back to the client.

Let's take a look at the client method call that invokes this Web Service. Again, we'll skip some of the mundane details of setting this up and jump right to the method call. The full code for the client can be found in the `ErrorServiceClient` directory in the code download for this chapter:

```
Sub Main(ByVal args As String())
  Dim proxy As New localhost.ErrorService()
  Try
    Console.WriteLine(proxy.HelloWorld())
  Catch e As Exception
    Console.WriteLine("An error occurred in accessing the Web Service in: {0}", _
                      e.Source)
    Console.WriteLine()
    Console.WriteLine(e.Message)
  Finally
    Console.ReadLine()
  End Try
End Sub
```

Again, pay special attention to the fact that we're trapping a standard exception, just like we would trap any other exception generated by any other kind of code in the .NET Framework. Think back to the beginning of the chapter when we discussed how to "roll our own" XML-over-HTTP implementation of client-server communications. Can you imagine trying to hand-code into that implementation the ability to pass exceptions back and forth automatically? I didn't think so. Because `SoapException` derives from `Exception`, we can catch `SoapExceptions` just like any other thrown exception. Here's a screenshot of the output when we execute our client application:

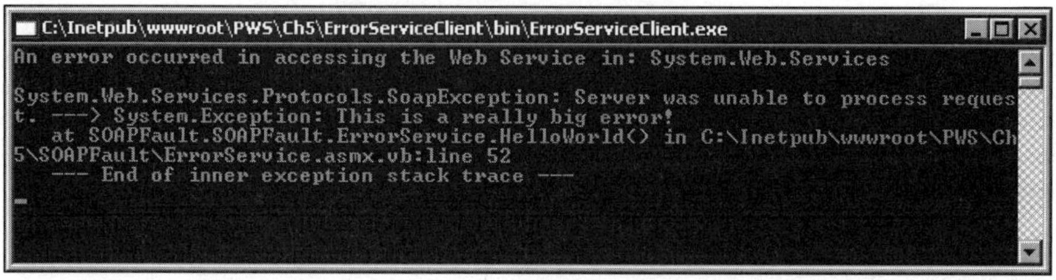

We can see pretty clearly that the outermost exception is a `SoapException` that has wrapped in it the text and information from the `Exception` we threw on the server.

> **When exceptions are thrown during a SOAP conversation, those exceptions are passed as `SoapException` instances, which can be serialized directly into the `Body` element of a SOAP Message.**

Encoding Data Types

In our discussion of various other wire formats at the beginning of this chapter, we mentioned that a limitation some of the other formats have is a limited ability to encode data types. For example, the XML-RPC protocol only supports a few basic data types. SOAP is far more flexible, allowing a greater range of data types. In general, a good rule of thumb to follow is that if a particular data type can be represented with an XML Schema (XSD), then it can be serialized or encoded into a SOAP Message.

Default Data Types

The SOAP specification indicates that there are a number of data types already built into the specification that can be considered *default.* These data types are the same data types that are considered *built-in* data types from the XML Schema specification, *Part 2: Data Types.* Some of these data types are listed below:

Data Type	Description
`string`	Simple character strings
`boolean`	Represents `True` or `False` values
`decimal`	Arbitrary precision numbers
`float`	Single-precision, 32-bit floating point numbers
`double`	Double-precision, 64-bit floating point numbers
`duration`	Represents a duration of time
`dateTime`	Represents a specific instant in time
`time`	Represents an instant in time that occurs daily
`date`	Represents a single calendar date

There are two main types of data that can be encoded into a SOAP Message, **simple types** and **compound types**. A simple type is a type that represents a value that has no named parts. The simple types are those that are defined as the built-in types in the XSD specification. A compound type is defined to be an aggregate of relations to other values. In other words, a compound type contains, in some form, a set of simple types that are related and distinguished in some way. Arrays and Structs are examples of compound types.

Compound types are aggregates of related simple types that can be arrays or structures of simple or compound types.

Single and Multiple Reference Values

Before we go on to talk about encoding complex data, and how the .NET Framework provides serialization support for the SOAP Message format, there is one other facet to storing information in a SOAP Message that we should take a look at.

Those of us who were forced to endure formal programming training early on in our careers may remember the first discussions on how data is stored in variables. Those of us with C training probably remember the lengthy discussions about how a variable is really just a symbol that represents a memory location, and so on. This would lead to a discussion about pointers to data and actual data.

We have a similar ability when encoding data in SOAP. Let's say, for example, that we want to call a function with two string arguments:

```
result = StringFunction("Hello World", "Goodbye World")
```

It looks pretty straightforward. We know from our previous exposure to the SOAP Envelope that this method call might be encoded as follows:

```
<SOAP-ENV:Envelope xmlns:SOAP-ENV="http://schemas.xmlsoap.org/soap/envelope/">
  <SOAP-ENV:Body>
    <stringroutines:StringFunction
           xmlns:stringroutines="urn:schemas-mysite-com:stringroutines">
      <String1>Hello World</String1>
      <String2>Goodbye World</String2>
    </stringroutines:StringFunction>
  </SOAP-ENV:Body>
</SOAP-ENV:Envelope>
```

This method of placing the values for the arguments *embedded* within the structure is called **single-reference**. This means that there is one and only one reference to the literal string `Hello World` and one and only one reference to the literal string `Goodbye World`. You can think of them as being similar to constants, or in terms of Visual Basic, being passed as `ByVal` arguments.

However, what happens if we want two arguments to refer to the same exact string? In other words, two arguments will both be passed a *reference* to the actual string. C programmers can consider this analogous to passing a pointer to a value as an argument, and VB programmers can continue with the `ByRef` analogy. Let's say our client code is changed to look like this:

```
Dim HelloAndGoodbye As String = "Hello World, Goodbye World"
result = StringFunction(HelloAndGoodbye, HelloAndGoodbye)
```

The great thing here is that you can be assured that the plumbing underneath the .NET Framework will appropriately handle this, and realize that you're actually passing a *reference* to the value and not the value itself. This is accomplished in the XML world with the `href` attribute. The parameter data is moved out of the method element and becomes an **independent element** with an **id** attribute. Let's take a look at the SOAP that would be appropriate for our new method call:

```
<SOAP-ENV:Envelope xmlns:SOAP-ENV="http://schemas.xmlsoap.org/soap/envelope/">
  <SOAP-ENV:Body xmlns:stringroutines="urn:schemas-mysite-com:stringroutines">
    <stringroutines:StringFunction
      <String1 href="#thestring"/>
      <String2 href="#thestring"/>
    </stringroutines:StringFunction>
    <stringroutines:String1 id="thestring" xsi:type="string">
      Hello World, Goodbye World
    </stringroutines:String1>
  </SOAP-ENV:Body>
</SOAP-ENV:Envelope>
```

Now what we have is the string we passed to the method being contained in an *independent element* outside the scope of the method element (though it is part of the same namespace, by requirement). Then we look and see that the embedded elements `String1` and `String2` now simply contain `href` attributes pointing to the same element. This provides us with the facility of maintaining reference even when the value is returned. For example, if the method on the server modifies the value in the `String1` argument, that value will be carried across in the independent element, also reflecting itself in the `String2` argument, which is what you would expect when passing data by reference.

Complex Data Types

So far in this section on SOAP, we've seen the benefit of its very simple and extensible architecture, and you've been told that you can encode virtually any data type into a SOAP Message so long as the type can be represented by an XML Schema. Let's put that to the test and try and encode some complex pieces of data.

Two of the most common types of complex data that people will be serializing in and out of SOAP messages are object instances and datasets, which are an extremely useful source of portable, disconnected, serializable data.

For our first example, we're going to look at putting SOAP to the e-commerce test by creating a class that represents a customer's order. Not only does this class have its own set of properties, but it also maintains an `ArrayList` of Order Items, which are actually instances of the `OrderItem` class. This is where SOAP's XML nature becomes really beneficial.

Let's take a look at our `Order` class (you can find all of the code for this sample in the `SOAPObject` directory in the code download for this chapter, which contains all of the code needed for this Console Application):

```
Imports System
Imports System.Collections

Namespace Wrox.ASPWebServices.SOAPObject
```

The key to being able to take this object and serialize it into the body of a SOAP Envelope is the `Serializable` attribute. Unless this attribute is here (or the object implements the `ISerializable` interface), the SOAP formatter will not serialize it for us.

```
<Serializable()> _
Public Class Order : Inherits Object
```

Here are our private member variables, all strings except for the `ArrayList` containing the instances of `OrderItem` classes:

```
  Private _OrderID As String
  Private _CustomerID As String
  Private _FirstName As String
  Private _LastName As String
  Private _EmailAddress As String
  Private _OrderItems As ArrayList

  Public Sub New()
    _OrderItems = New ArrayList()
  End Sub

  Public Sub New(ByVal OrderID As String)
    _OrderItems = New ArrayList()
    _OrderID = OrderID
  End Sub
```

Just to round the class out, we've added a utility function to speed up the process of adding new order items to an instance of the `Order` class.

```
  Public Sub AddItem(ByVal Quantity As Integer, _
                     ByVal Price As Double, _
                     ByVal SKU As String)
    Dim Itm As New OrderItem(_OrderID, Quantity, Price, SKU)
    _OrderItems.Add(Itm)
  End Sub

  ...

 End Class
End Namespace
```

For clarity and ease of reading, we've cut out all of the property definitions and a few of the methods. The full source code is available with the download. However, our purpose here is to show how complex classes can be serialized into a SOAP Envelope, not to demonstrate our nifty `Order` class.

The `OrderItem` class is pretty straightforward. It has a constructor that allows it to take an `OrderID`, a `Quantity`, a `Price`, and an `SKU` ("Stock Keeping Unit", a simple unique inventory tag for a given item) at instantiation time and it contains some private member variables and some straightforward properties for those members. Again, you can find all of this source code available for download from the Wrox web site.

Without trying to create a Web Service that accepts as method arguments an object of type `Order`, what we'll do is create a Console application in VB.NET that uses the `SoapFormatter` to create a SOAP serialization of this object for us and store that on disk so we can look at the underlying XML. Here is the source code to that Console application, `Class1.vb` in the code download:

```
Imports System
Imports System.IO
Imports System.Runtime.Serialization.Formatters.Soap

Namespace Wrox.ASPWebServices.SOAPObject
  Public Module Class1

    Sub Main(ByVal args As String())
```

The code below instantiates us a nice new `Order` object. We set up some dummy information about the customer requesting the order, as well as call the `AddItem` method a few times to add some merchandise (and complexity) to the order.

```
      Dim NewOrder As New Order("ORDER1")

      NewOrder.CustomerID = "JDOE"
      NewOrder.FirstName = "John"
      NewOrder.LastName = "Doe"
      NewOrder.EmailAddress = "jdoe@somewhere.over.there.com"
      NewOrder.AddItem(8, 12.99F, "BOX12")
      NewOrder.AddItem(12, 15.99F, "ITEM1")
      NewOrder.AddItem(9, 6.99F, "ITEM5")
```

The `SoapFormatter` class is used throughout the .NET Framework and the Web Services system for SOAP serialization and related tasks. We're going to use it here to serialize our object onto a stream, which is actually a file on disk.

```
      Dim sf As New SoapFormatter()
      Dim fs As New FileStream("SOAPorder.soap", FileMode.Create, _
                               FileAccess.ReadWrite)
      sf.Serialize(fs, NewOrder)
      fs.Close()
```

Because we're the type of people that don't believe it until we see it, we've added some code below that will attempt to instantiate a new `Order` object. This time, however, instead of building it by hand, we're building it by de-serializing it from our SOAP-formatted disk file. We write out to the console a couple of properties to verify that the data is indeed identical.

```
      Dim fs2 As New FileStream("SOAPorder.soap", FileMode.Open, _
                                FileAccess.Read)
      Dim DSOrder As Order
      DSOrder = CType(sf.Deserialize(fs2), Order)
      Console.WriteLine("Deserialized Order for {0} {1} Contains {2} Items.", _
                        DSOrder.FirstName, DSOrder.LastName, DSOrder.Items.Count)
      Console.ReadLine()
    End Sub
  End Module
End Namespace
```

The end result of running this program is just a simple regurgitation of some of the data we placed into the `Order` instance to begin with. However, the good stuff is sitting in a disk file called `SOAPorder.soap` (in the `SOAPObject\bin\debug` directory beneath the directory you installed the code samples (`C:\Inetpub\wwwroot\PWS\Ch5\SoapObject\` for example)), the contents of which we have displayed below:

```
<SOAP-ENV:Envelope xmlns:xsi="http://www.w3.org/2001/XMLSchema-instance"
                   xmlns:xsd="http://www.w3.org/2001/XMLSchema"
                   xmlns:SOAP-ENC="http://schemas.xmlsoap.org/soap/encoding/"
                   xmlns:SOAP-ENV="http://schemas.xmlsoap.org/soap/envelope/"
                   xmlns:clr="http://schemas.microsoft.com/soap/encoding/clr/1.0"
 SOAP-ENV:encodingStyle="http://schemas.xmlsoap.org/soap/encoding/">
```

As we said in our samples earlier, we were leaving out some details that the .NET Framework supplies for you, such as the various namespace declarations above in the Envelope tag. You can see that it is providing namespace qualifiers for encoding, the envelope itself, and even a namespace for the Common Language Runtime to indicate CLR-native data types.

```
  <SOAP-ENV:Body>
    <a1:Order id="ref-1"
xmlns:a1="http://schemas.microsoft.com/clr/nsassem/SOAPObject.Wrox.ASPWebServices.
SOAPObject/SOAPObject%2C%20Version%3D1.0.914.30356%2C%20Culture%3Dneutral%2C%20Pub
licKeyToken%3Dnull">
      <_OrderID id="ref-3">ORDER1</_OrderID>
      <_CustomerID id="ref-4">JDOE</_CustomerID>
      <_FirstName id="ref-5">John</_FirstName>
      <_LastName id="ref-6">Doe</_LastName>
      <_EmailAddress id="ref-7">jdoe@somewhere.over.there.com</_EmailAddress>
      <_OrderItems href="#ref-8"/>
    </a1:Order>
```

In the `a1:Order` element above, we see that all of the private member variables have been given IDs in order to distinguish them from other members. Also, make special note of the `href` attribute in the `_OrderItems` element. It is pointing at another independent element (shown immediately below) with an ID of `ref-8`. That next element below is an `ArrayList` element. SOAP allows for only certain kinds of compound types, including arrays and structs. The SOAP Formatter has done a lot of work for us by reducing the `ArrayList` into a set of related structures (multi-level XML elements). Note that the `_items` element in the structure below points at yet another element with an ID of `ref-9`.

```
    <a2:ArrayList id="ref-8"
            xmlns:a2="http://schemas.microsoft.com/clr/ns/System.Collections">
      <_items href="#ref-9"/>
      <_size>3</_size>
      <_version>3</_version>
    </a2:ArrayList>
```

In the section below, the `ArrayList _items` element has been reduced to a simple SOAP array (indicated by the `SOAP-ENC` namespace). Because each of the `OrderItem` elements is actually an instance of a class on its own, each of the items in this list has *also* been further referenced out into a structure. Again, keep in mind that every compound type in SOAP must be represented by an aggregate of related simple types in either array or structure form.

```
    <SOAP-ENC:Array id="ref-9" SOAP-ENC:arrayType="xsd:anyType[16]">
      <item href="#ref-10"/>
      <item href="#ref-11"/>
      <item href="#ref-12"/>
    </SOAP-ENC:Array>
```

The XML below has created independent elements for the serialization of each `OrderItem` instance, turning that instance into a structure usable within SOAP. Note the lengthy namespace of this item pointing to a CLR-specific item. It contains the version, culture and public key token for the assembly containing the data type.

```
    <a1:OrderItem id="ref-10"
xmlns:a1="http://schemas.microsoft.com/clr/nsassem/SOAPObject.Wrox.ASPWebServices.
SOAPObject/SOAPObject%2C%20Version%3D1.0.914.30356%2C%20Culture%3Dneutral%2C%20Pub
licKeyToken%3Dnull">
      <_OrderID href="#ref-3"/>
      <_Quantity>8</_Quantity>
      <_Price>12.989999771118164</_Price>
      <_SKU id="ref-13">BOX12</_SKU>
    </a1:OrderItem>
    <a1:OrderItem id="ref-11"
xmlns:a1="http://schemas.microsoft.com/clr/nsassem/SOAPObject.Wrox.ASPWebServices.
SOAPObject/SOAPObject%2C%20Version%3D1.0.914.30356%2C%20Culture%3Dneutral%2C%20Pub
licKeyToken%3Dnull">
      <_OrderID href="#ref-3"/>
      <_Quantity>12</_Quantity>
      <_Price>15.989999771118164</_Price>
      <_SKU id="ref-14">ITEM1</_SKU>
    </a1:OrderItem>
    <a1:OrderItem id="ref-12"
xmlns:a1="http://schemas.microsoft.com/clr/nsassem/SOAPObject.Wrox.ASPWebServices.
SOAPObject/SOAPObject%2C%20Version%3D1.0.914.30356%2C%20Culture%3Dneutral%2C%20Pub
licKeyToken%3Dnull">
      <_OrderID href="#ref-3"/>
      <_Quantity>9</_Quantity>
      <_Price>6.9899997711181641</_Price>
      <_SKU id="ref-15">ITEM5</_SKU>
    </a1:OrderItem>
  </SOAP-ENV:Body>
</SOAP-ENV:Envelope>
```

So now that we've seen how to use the SOAP Formatter to serialize an object instance in SOAP standard format rather than simple XML, let's take a look at using some object instance passing using Web Services.

For our example, we're going to write a Web Service that takes a complex structure (doesn't rely on method invocations for being de-serialized properly at the other end of the wire) as an argument and builds a dataset based on the data in the structure. This `DataSet` is then sent back to the client as a return value from the Web Service. Just to make sure that the data has been preserved throughout the entire conversation, we then bind the resulting `DataSet` to a `DataGrid` in a Windows Forms application.

Let's start with the code for our Web Service (you can find this code in the `SOAPComplex` directory in the download for this chapter). The code listing below is the listing for the code-behind class for our Web Service (`ComplexService.asmx.vb`):

```
Imports System
Imports System.Collections
Imports System.ComponentModel
Imports System.Data
Imports System.Diagnostics
Imports System.Web
Imports System.Web.Services

Namespace Wrox.ASPWebServices.SOAPComplex
```

The structure below is the structure that defines an "Order". Earlier on in the chapter we saw a class that maintained a similar structure. One thing to keep in mind is that Web Services is an architecture best suited for messaging conversations. If you are truly looking for pure RPC over HTTP or TCP where you can expect to remotely invoke instances of remote objects, then the Remoting infrastructure is your best bet. For Web Services, the architecture works best when presented with pure data that can be marshaled by *value*. We've used strings here for everything just to make the sample as easy as possible, but to match Northwind we should've made `OrderID` an `Integer`.

```
  Public Structure OrderStruct
    Dim OrderID As String
    Dim CustomerID As String
    Dim FirstName As String
    Dim LastName As String
    Dim EmailAddress As String
    Dim OrderItems As OrderItemStruct()
  End Structure

  Public Structure OrderItemStruct
    Dim OrderID As String
    Dim Quantity As Integer
    Dim Price As Double
    Dim SKU As String
  End Structure

  Public Class ComplexService
    Inherits System.Web.Services.WebService
```

In order to get closer to the point (and avoid boring you to tears) we've cut out some of the housecleaning code that Visual Studio .NET puts into the empty Web Service class for us. As we can see, the `WebMethod` below takes a filled-in `OrderStruct` as an argument and returns a populated DataSet that contains the information previously contained in the `OrderStruct`.

```
    <WebMethod()> _
    Public Function BuildOrderDS(ByVal CustomerOrder As OrderStruct) As DataSet

      Dim DS As New DataSet()
      Dim Orders As New DataTable("Orders")
      Orders.Columns.Add(New DataColumn("OrderID", GetType(String)))
      Orders.Columns.Add(New DataColumn("CustomerID", GetType(String)))
      Orders.Columns.Add(New DataColumn("EmailAddress", GetType(String)))
      Orders.Columns.Add(New DataColumn("FirstName", GetType(String)))
      Orders.Columns.Add(New DataColumn("LastName", GetType(String)))
      DS.Tables.Add(Orders)
```

```
      Dim OrderItems As New DataTable("OrderItems")
      OrderItems.Columns.Add(New DataColumn("OrderID", GetType(String)))
      OrderItems.Columns.Add(New DataColumn("Price", GetType(Double)))
      OrderItems.Columns.Add(New DataColumn("Quantity", GetType(Integer)))
      OrderItems.Columns.Add(New DataColumn("SKU", GetType(String)))
      DS.Tables.Add(OrderItems)

      Dim ParentOrderID As DataColumn
      Dim ChildOrderID As DataColumn

      ParentOrderID = Orders.Columns("OrderID")
      ChildOrderID = OrderItems.Columns("OrderID")
      DS.Relations.Add(New DataRelation("OrderItems", ParentOrderID, _
                                        ChildOrderID, True))

      Dim Order As DataRow
      Order = Orders.NewRow()
      Order("CustomerID") = CustomerOrder.CustomerID
      Order("FirstName") = CustomerOrder.FirstName
      Order("LastName") = CustomerOrder.LastName
      Order("EmailAddress") = CustomerOrder.EmailAddress
      Order("OrderID") = CustomerOrder.OrderID
      Orders.Rows.Add(Order)

      Dim Item As OrderItemStruct

      For Each Item In CustomerOrder.OrderItems
        Dim ItemRow As DataRow
        ItemRow = OrderItems.NewRow()

        ItemRow("OrderID") = Item.OrderID
        ItemRow("Quantity") = Item.Quantity
        ItemRow("Price") = Item.Price
        ItemRow("SKU") = Item.SKU
        OrderItems.Rows.Add(ItemRow)
      Next
        Return DS
    End Function
  End Class
End Namespace
```

With all of this code entered, we should then be able to build our Web Service and compile the appropriate DLL into the `bin` directory. Before we look at writing the client application, let's take a look at a sample of the SOAP involved here. Microsoft was kind enough to present us with sample SOAP message conversations when we view the `.asmx` page in our browser. If we browse over to our Web Service's page (http://localhost/PWS/Ch5/SOAPComplex/ComplexService.asmx) we'll see that it has generated some sample SOAP to illustrate a potential request/response pair for us (after we've invoked the method once):

```
POST /PWS/Ch5/SOAPComplex/ComplexService.asmx HTTP/1.1
Host: localhost
Content-Type: text/xml; charset=utf-8
Content-Length: length
```

```
SOAPAction: "http://tempuri.org/BuildOrderDS"

<?xml version="1.0" encoding="utf-8"?>
<soap:Envelope xmlns:xsi="http://www.w3.org/2001/XMLSchema-instance"
               xmlns:xsd="http://www.w3.org/2001/XMLSchema"
               xmlns:soap="http://schemas.xmlsoap.org/soap/envelope/">
  <soap:Body>
    <BuildOrderDS xmlns="http://tempuri.org/">
      <CustomerOrder>
        <OrderID>string</OrderID>
        <CustomerID>string</CustomerID>
        <FirstName>string</FirstName>
        <LastName>string</LastName>
        <EmailAddress>string</EmailAddress>
        <OrderItems>
          <OrderItemStruct>
            <OrderID>string</OrderID>
            <Quantity>int</Quantity>
            <Price>double</Price>
            <SKU>string</SKU>
          </OrderItemStruct>
          <OrderItemStruct>
            <OrderID>string</OrderID>
            <Quantity>int</Quantity>
            <Price>double</Price>
            <SKU>string</SKU>
          </OrderItemStruct>
        </OrderItems>
      </CustomerOrder>
    </BuildOrderDS>
  </soap:Body>
</soap:Envelope>
```

We see that in the sample SOAP Envelope above, the structure of the potential envelope is laid out for us, including two sample order items illustrating the parent-child relationship that our structure conveys. In the example response below, we see that we're receiving a complex type defined by an XML Schema. There is an element placeholder for the schema as well as for the associated data.

```
HTTP/1.1 200 OK
Content-Type: text/xml; charset=utf-8
Content-Length: length

<?xml version="1.0" encoding="utf-8"?>
<soap:Envelope xmlns:xsi="http://www.w3.org/2001/XMLSchema-instance"
               xmlns:xsd="http://www.w3.org/2001/XMLSchema"
               xmlns:soap="http://schemas.xmlsoap.org/soap/envelope/">
  <soap:Body>
    <BuildOrderDSResponse xmlns="http://tempuri.org/">
      <BuildOrderDSResult>
        <xsd:schema>schema</xsd:schema>xml</BuildOrderDSResult>
    </BuildOrderDSResponse>
  </soap:Body>
</soap:Envelope>
```

This web page allows people developing XML Web Services outside the realm of the .NET Framework to examine the format of the SOAP Envelope responses and requests and use this information to build a consumer for this Web Service on another platform such as Unix, or suchlike.

Now let's take a look at our Visual Studio .NET VB.NET Windows Forms consumer for this Web Service (a project in the code download called `SOAPComplexClient`). We've created a Windows Forms application and placed a `DataGrid` onto the main form. From there, we've added a button with some text ("Build Order DS") that will populate an `OrderStruct`, send it to the Web Service, and then bind our `DataGrid` to the resulting `DataSet`.

To do all of this, the first thing we do after setting up our form is to add a Web Reference to our recently created `ComplexService`. After we've done this, we should notice that nested within the `localhost` namespace, in addition to seeing the proxy class for our Web Service, there is also a copy of the `OrderStruct` and `OrderItemStruct` structures. This is because Visual Studio .NET automatically downloads any pertinent data types when importing information from a Web Service.

Here is the code that is executed in response to our button's click event:

```
Private Sub Button1_Click(ByVal sender As System.Object, _
                          ByVal e As System.EventArgs) Handles Button1.Click
  Dim myDS As DataSet
```

This next section of code is just some simple structure population. We populate the fields of the `OrderStruct` instance, and then we create an array of `OrderItemStruct` items and place that in the `OrderItems` field of the `OrderStruct` instance. This gets the data complete and ready to send to the Web Service.

```
  Dim myOrder As New localhost.OrderStruct()

  myOrder.OrderID = "ORDER1"
  myOrder.CustomerID = "JDOE"
  myOrder.EmailAddress = "jdoe@somewhere.out.there.com"
  myOrder.LastName = "Doe"
  myOrder.FirstName = "John"
  ReDim myOrder.OrderItems(1)
  myOrder.OrderItems(0) = New localhost.OrderItemStruct()
  myOrder.OrderItems(1) = New localhost.OrderItemStruct()
  myOrder.OrderItems(0) = New localhost.OrderItemStruct()
  myOrder.OrderItems(0).OrderID = "ORDER1"
  myOrder.OrderItems(0).Price = 12.99F
  myOrder.OrderItems(0).Quantity = 15
  myOrder.OrderItems(0).SKU = "ITEM1"
```

The next few remarkably simple lines of code are the ones responsible for actually calling the Web Service and sending the data. We set the result of the `BuildOrderDS` method to be stored in the `myDS` `DataSet` variable, which we then immediately bind to our `DataGrid`.

```
  Dim proxy As New localhost.ComplexService()
  myDS = proxy.BuildOrderDS(myOrder)
  DataGrid1.DataSource = myDS.Tables("Orders")
```

```
        DataGrid1.Refresh()
    End Sub
End Class
```

There's actually an enormous amount of work going on here. First, the `BuildOrderDS` method is being serialized into the `Body` element of a SOAP Envelope. Then, the `myOrder` instance is serialized into the SOAP Message. After that, the Web Services infrastructure takes over and places the entire envelope into an HTTP POST to the `/localhost/PWS/Ch5/SOAPComplex/ComplexService.asmx` file. Then, it waits for a response. This response is then taken in the form of an HTTP 200 OK response; the body of the HTTP response is a new SOAP Envelope, which is then opened. Once opened, the `DataSet` schema is loaded into a new `DataSet` instance to reconstitute the data structure. Then, the XML from the response envelope is loaded into the `DataSet` for you. Now, aren't you glad all of this is being done for you automatically when all you've had to do is enter the following line of code?

```
myDS = proxy.BuildOrderDS(myOrder)
```

Let's take a look at the `DataGrid` after it has been bound to the `DataSet` we received from our Web Service, and we've drilled down through the `OrderItems` relation to examine the child data:

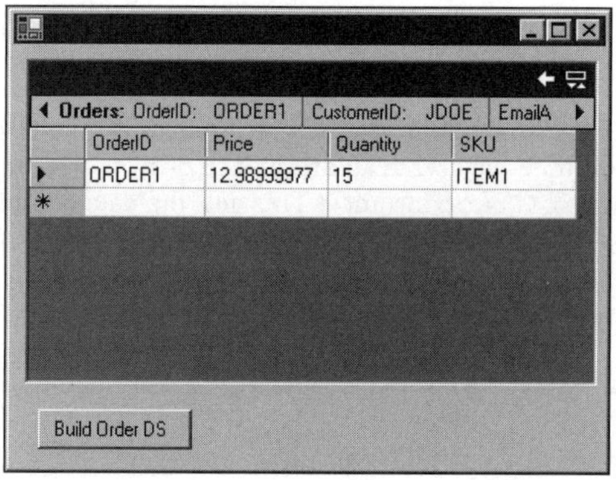

Summary

This chapter's focus has been on wire formats, with the SOAP protocol being the main attraction. SOAP is an incredibly extensible, powerful, and lightweight protocol that allows for a great many possibilities when used in combination with XML Web Services. Throughout the chapter we showed various examples of other wire formats, as well as samples of SOAP in action. Hopefully you will be able to take away with you the following knowledge after having read this chapter:

- What a wire format is
- What some of the most common wire formats are and how they may or may not be related to SOAP
- What SOAP is, what SOAP messages look like, and how they're used in Web Services
- Why SOAP is used for Web Services
- Using simple and complex data types with SOAP

PROFESSIONAL
ASP.NET
WEB
SERVICES

6

Custom SOAP Techniques

ASP.NET makes it very easy to create and use Web Services, as we saw in Chapter 2, where we saw how we can create a Web Service by just adding a few attributes to our code. Chapter 3 showed how we can easily use a Web Service by creating a proxy from the WSDL file. Chapters 4 and 5 described WSDL and SOAP. ASP.NET handles the mapping of our code to WSDL and SOAP automatically.

An additional feature of the ASP.NET architecture is that it is extensible, and allows us to customize the behavior of ASP.NET Web Services. Why would we want to customize the behavior of ASP.NET Web Services? Well, in most cases we don't need to. The standard behavior will often be just fine. We can concentrate on the logic of our Web Service and leave the SOAP formatting to ASP.NET.

However, there are cases when we need to modify the behavior of ASP.NET. Firstly, we may need to extend our ASP.NET Web Service with functionality not provided out-of-the-box. We may want to encrypt the XML in the SOAP message before it is sent to the recipient. Or we may want to compress the SOAP message. In these cases we need to access the XML in the SOAP message before it is sent over the wire. We will look at how we can do this.

Another case is if we have problems interoperating with other SOAP implementations. We may need to tweak the XML in the SOAP message so it can be understood by other SOAP implementations. But isn't SOAP a standard? Yes, but a standard does not guarantee interoperability. The SOAP specification opens the door to various ways of encoding SOAP messages. This is understandable, since SOAP addresses several needs. It is early days for SOAP, and the level of support for the various options in the SOAP specification varies among tools.

In this chapter we will look at ways in which we can get under the hood of ASP.NET Web Services. More specifically we will look at:

- SOAP Extensions, a framework for getting at the SOAP message before and after it is sent over the wire. We will build a SOAP extension that writes SOAP messages to the event log.
- How we can customize the XML format of SOAP messages using the `XmlSerializer`.
- How complex data types such as datasets, XML data, and binary data can be used with Web Services.

Let us start by looking at SOAP Extensions.

SOAP Extensions

SOAP Extensions is an extensibility mechanism available with ASP.NET. A SOAP Extension is added to a Web Service simply by adding an attribute to a web method (in addition to the `WebMethod` attribute).

The canonical example of SOAP Extensions is the tracer extension. This extension writes the contents of SOAP messages to a file. This extension is very useful when debugging Web Services. Later in this chapter we will customize the SOAP message. When doing this it is very useful to see the actual XML sent over the wire. The code for the tracer extension is available with the downloadable code for this chapter in the folder `PWS\Ch6\TraceExtension`.

The file `SimpleMath_VB.asmx` in the `Ch6` folder contains an example of adding the trace extension to a Web Service.

```
<%@ WebService Language="VB" class="SimpleMath" %>

Imports System.Web.Services

Public Class SimpleMath

  <WebMethod, _
  TraceExtension(Filename:="c:\temp\SimpleMath.txt")> _
  Public Function Add(a As Integer, b As Integer) As Integer
    Return a+b
  End Function

  <WebMethod, _
  TraceExtension(Filename:="c:\temp\SimpleMath.txt")> _
  Public Function Div(a As Integer, b As Integer) As Integer
    Return a/b
  End Function

End Class
```

The Web Service in this example is a very simple math service with just two methods. The trace extension is added to each method by using the `TraceExtension` attribute. This attribute has a `Filename` property specifying the name of the trace file.

To test the Web Service and the tracer extension you can use the `SimpleMathClientVB.exe` test application that ships with the code download. This is a simple Windows Forms application.

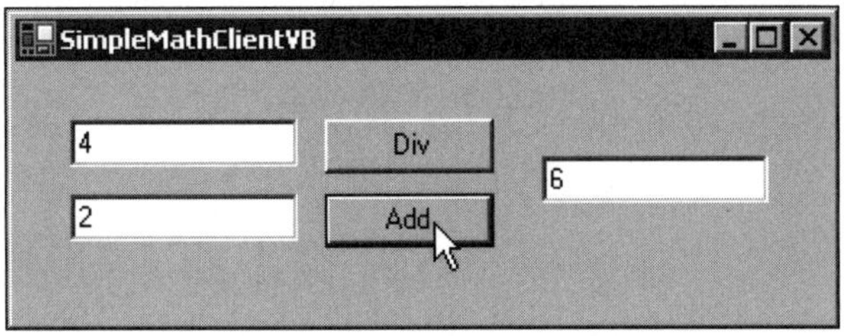

When we execute this program, it calls the Web Service. When the Web Service is called, the trace extension writes the contents of the SOAP messages to the `c:\temp\SimpleMath.txt` file. Here is what the trace file looks like after calling the `Add` method (we've formatted it so it is easier to read):

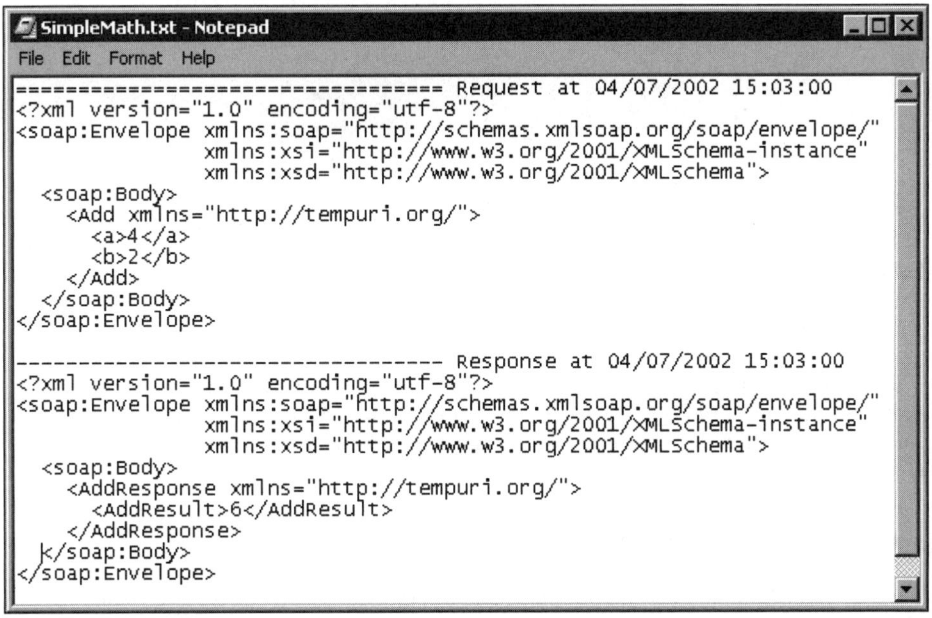

```
================================== Request at 04/07/2002 15:03:00
<?xml version="1.0" encoding="utf-8"?>
<soap:Envelope xmlns:soap="http://schemas.xmlsoap.org/soap/envelope/"
               xmlns:xsi="http://www.w3.org/2001/XMLSchema-instance"
               xmlns:xsd="http://www.w3.org/2001/XMLSchema">
  <soap:Body>
    <Add xmlns="http://tempuri.org/">
      <a>4</a>
      <b>2</b>
    </Add>
  </soap:Body>
</soap:Envelope>

---------------------------------- Response at 04/07/2002 15:03:00
<?xml version="1.0" encoding="utf-8"?>
<soap:Envelope xmlns:soap="http://schemas.xmlsoap.org/soap/envelope/"
               xmlns:xsi="http://www.w3.org/2001/XMLSchema-instance"
               xmlns:xsd="http://www.w3.org/2001/XMLSchema">
  <soap:Body>
    <AddResponse xmlns="http://tempuri.org/">
      <AddResult>6</AddResult>
    </AddResponse>
  </soap:Body>
</soap:Envelope>
```

You cannot use the ASP.NET-generated test pages to test SOAP extensions. The SOAP extensions only apply when you use the SOAP protocol, not the HTTP GET and HTTP POST protocols. The test pages use the HTTP protocols.

This can be confusing at first. We must build a client using the SOAP protocol for the extension to take effect.

How Do SOAP Extensions Work?

The process of converting objects to XML is known as **serialization**, and the process of reconstructing the objects from XML is know as **deserialization**. The module that does the conversion is the **Xml Serializer**.

The figure below illustrates the process.

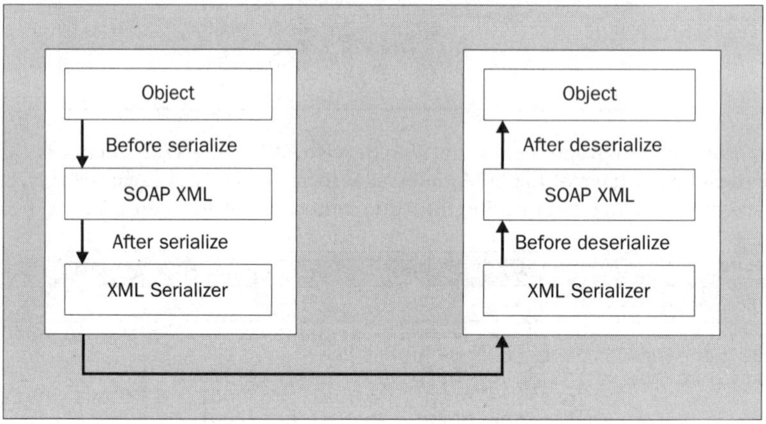

SOAP Extensions allow us to get access to the data before and after the objects are converted to and from XML. On outgoing requests and responses, this means we have access to the SOAP stream before and after it is serialized and sent down the wire to the recipient. On incoming requests and responses, this means that we have access to the SOAP stream before and after it is deserialized.

The tracer extension does not do anything with the SOAP messages. It simply peeks into the message after serialization and before deserialization and writes the SOAP XML to disk. SOAP Extensions may also alter the contents of SOAP messages. In Chapter 14 we will see an example that uses SOAP Extensions to encrypt the contents of a SOAP message after serialization and decrypt the contents of the message before deserialization.

Using SOAP Extensions

SOAP Extensions can be used on both the client and the server. To add an extension to the server side of a Web Service we need to do two things:

- Add SOAP Extension attributes to the methods where we want the extension applied.
- Copy the extension assembly to the `bin` directory of the Web Service.

Below is the simple math service, `SimpleMath_VB.asmx`, we saw earlier. We use the `TraceExtension` attribute on each method we want to trace:

```
<%@ WebService Language="VB" class="SimpleMath" %>

Imports System.Web.Services
```

```
Public Class SimpleMath

  <WebMethod, _
  TraceExtension.TraceExtension(Filename:="c:\temp\SimpleMath.txt")> _
  Public Function Add(a As Integer, b As Integer) As Integer
    Return a+b
  End Function

  <WebMethod, _
  TraceExtension.TraceExtension(Filename:="c:\temp\SimpleMath.txt")> _
  Public Function Div(a As Integer, b As Integer) As Integer
    Return a/b
  End Function

End Class
```

When adding attributes to our code, we are actually using a shorthand notation. In the code download you will find a project called `TraceExtension`. The attribute referenced above is implemented in this extension with a class named `TraceExtensionAttribute`. We can shorten the name of the attribute by omitting the word `Attribute` at the end. This means that the following is equivalent to the code above.

```
<WebMethod, _
TraceExtension.TraceExtensionAttribute(Filename:="c:\temp\SimpleMath.txt")> _
Public Function Add(a As Integer, b As Integer) As Integer
  Return a+b
End Function
```

The example above used the extension on the server side in the Web Service method. Extensions may also be used on the client side. In the case of encryption they *must* be used on both the client side and the server side; it does not make a lot of sense to encrypt on one side without decrypting on the other side.

To add SOAP Extensions on the client side we need to modify the generated proxy and add attributes to the methods in the proxy. Here is a snippet of the proxy code from the `SimpleMathClientVB` project, showing what we need to add:

```
<System.Web.Services.Protocols.SoapDocumentMethodAttribute( _
"http://tempuri.org/Div", _
RequestNamespace:="http://tempuri.org/", _
ResponseNamespace:="http://tempuri.org/", _
Use:=System.Web.Services.Description.SoapBindingUse.Literal, _
ParameterStyle:=System.Web.Services.Protocols.SoapParameterStyle.Wrapped), _
TraceExtension.TraceExtension(Filename:="c:\temp\SimpleMathClient.txt")> _
Public Function Div(ByVal a As Integer, ByVal b As Integer) As Integer
  Dim results() As Object = Me.Invoke("Div", New Object() {a, b})
  Return CType(results(0),Integer)
End Function
```

The highlighted line is added to the proxy. In the code download we need to add this in the file:

```
SimpleMathClientVB\Web References\localhost\Reference.vb
```

To run the code you must also copy the assembly of the `TraceExtension` to the client side, into the `bin` folder of `SimpleMathClientVB`, and add a reference to the assembly to the client project.

> **If you regenerate the proxy, the changes you have made will be lost, and you must add the attributes again.**

Using the trace extension on the client side allows us to trace the contents of SOAP messages exchanged with Web Services we use.

Creating a SoapLog Extension

We have just seen that we can use the trace extension to write the contents of SOAP messages to a file. In this section we will look at how we can implement our own SOAP extensions.

We will develop a new SOAP Extension called `SoapLogVB`. This extension will write SOAP messages to the event log. SOAP faults will be logged as errors in the event log. You may find the `SoapLogVB` extension useful in your own projects. The principles described can also be used to implement other extensions.

If you want to jump ahead and see the extension in action you can run the `SoapLogClientVB.exe` program available with the download. This client is identical to the `SimpleMathClient.exe` we saw earlier, except it uses a Web Service with the `SoapLogVB` extension applied (in `SimpleMath2_VB.asmx`). Execute the program and call the `Add` and `Div` methods. To see the result of the extension, bring up the event viewer. The event viewer is available under Start | Program Files | Administrative Tools.

The screenshot below shows what the event log looks like after the `SoapLogVB` extension has written information to it. The screenshot shows eight messages in the event log:

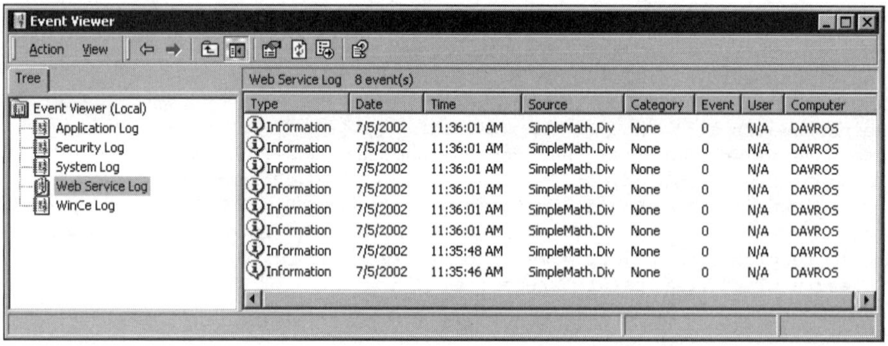

Using the log, we can view the contents of the SOAP messages by right-clicking on an event and selecting Properties. The Description field shows the XML contained in the SOAP message.

> **Just before releasing the .NET Framework, Microsoft changed the default security policy of ASP.NET applications. They now run in the context of the low privilege ASPNET account. This account does not have access to create event sources in the event log. You must either give the ASPNET proper privileges or change the default setting in `machine.config`. See the `ReadMe.txt` file in the code download for this chapter for instructions on how to do this.**

The `SoapLogVB` extension implements two properties:

- A `Name` property used as source name in the event log. Above the source name is `SimpleMath.Div`. The default name is `SoapLog`.
- A `Level` property setting the logging level. The level may be 0 (no logging), 1 (only errors), 2 (messages and errors), and 3 (messages, errors, and additional information). The default is 1.

Let us look at the code for the `SoapLog` extension.

The SoapLog Code

SOAP Extensions are implemented by creating an assembly with classes deriving from two abstract classes in the .NET Framework. These classes are the `SoapExtensionAttribute` class and the `SoapExtension` class. We must implement some methods defined in these classes. The SOAP Extensions live in the `System.Web.Services.Protocols` namespace.

Here is an overview of the classes we will implement and their base classes:

Implemented class	Base class	Description
`SoapLogVBAttribute`	`SoapExtension Attribute`	Implements the attribute we add to methods.
`SoapLogVB`	`SoapExtension`	Contains the code to perform the work of the extension.

Most of the work of a SOAP Extension is done in a method named `ProcessMessage` defined in the `SoapLogVB` class.

Here is the entire code for the `SoapLogVB` extension. The next section will discuss the code. The code is available in `SoapLogVB` folder in the code download.

```
Imports System
Imports System.Diagnostics
Imports System.Web.Services.Protocols
Imports System.IO
```

```
<AttributeUsage(AttributeTargets.Method)> _
Public Class SoapLogVBAttribute
  Inherits System.Web.Services.Protocols.SoapExtensionAttribute

  Private m_Priority As Integer
  Private m_Name As String = "SoapLog"
  Private m_Level As Integer = 1

  Public Overrides Property Priority() As Integer
    Get
      Return m_Priority
    End Get
    Set(ByVal Value As Integer)
      m_Priority = Value
    End Set
  End Property

  Public Property Name() As String
    Get
      Return m_Name
    End Get
    Set(ByVal Value As String)
      m_Name = Value
    End Set
  End Property

  Public Property Level() As Integer
    Get
      Return m_Level
    End Get
    Set(ByVal Value As Integer)
      m_Level = Value
    End Set
  End Property

  Public Overrides ReadOnly Property ExtensionType() As Type
    Get
      Return GetType(SoapLogVB)
    End Get
  End Property
End Class

Public Class SoapLogVB
  Inherits System.Web.Services.Protocols.SoapExtension

  Private m_OldStream As Stream
  Private m_NewStream As Stream
  Private m_Name As String = "SoapLog"
  Private m_Level As Integer = 1

  Public Overloads Overrides Function GetInitializer( _
     ByVal methodInfo As System.Web.Services.Protocols.LogicalMethodInfo, _
     ByVal attribute As System.Web.Services.Protocols.SoapExtensionAttribute) _
     As Object
```

```
      Return CType(attribute, SoapLogVBAttribute)
    End Function

    Public Overloads Overrides Function GetInitializer(ByVal obj As Type) _
                                                        As Object
      Return obj
    End Function

    Public Overrides Sub Initialize(ByVal initializer As Object)
      If TypeOf initializer Is SoapLogVBAttribute Then
        m_Name = (CType(initializer, SoapLogVBAttribute)).Name
        m_Level = (CType(initializer, SoapLogVBAttribute)).Level
      End If
    End Sub

    Public Overrides Sub ProcessMessage( _
      ByVal message As System.Web.Services.Protocols.SoapMessage)

      Select Case message.Stage
        Case System.Web.Services.Protocols.SoapMessageStage.BeforeSerialize
          If (m_Level > 2) Then
            WriteToLog(message.Stage.ToString(), EventLogEntryType.Information)
          End If
        Case System.Web.Services.Protocols.SoapMessageStage.AfterSerialize
          LogOutputMessage(message)
        Case System.Web.Services.Protocols.SoapMessageStage.BeforeDeserialize
          LogInputMessage(message)
        Case System.Web.Services.Protocols.SoapMessageStage.AfterDeserialize
          If (m_Level > 2) Then
            WriteToLog(message.Stage.ToString(), EventLogEntryType.Information)
          End If
      End Select
    End Sub

    Public Overrides Function ChainStream(ByVal theStream As Stream) As Stream
      m_OldStream = theStream
      m_NewStream = New MemoryStream()
      Return m_NewStream
    End Function

    Private Sub CopyStream(ByVal fromstream As Stream, ByVal tostream As Stream)
      Dim reader As New StreamReader(fromstream)
      Dim writer As New StreamWriter(tostream)

      writer.WriteLine(reader.ReadToEnd())
      writer.Flush()
    End Sub

    Private Sub LogInputMessage(ByVal message As SoapMessage)
      CopyStream(m_OldStream, m_NewStream)
      message.Stream.Seek(0, SeekOrigin.Begin)
      LogMessage(message, m_NewStream)
      message.Stream.Seek(0, SeekOrigin.Begin)
    End Sub
```

```
    Private Sub LogOutputMessage(ByVal message As SoapMessage)
      message.Stream.Seek(0, SeekOrigin.Begin)
      LogMessage(message, m_NewStream)
      message.Stream.Seek(0, SeekOrigin.Begin)
      CopyStream(m_NewStream, m_OldStream)
    End Sub

    Private Sub LogMessage(ByVal message As SoapMessage, ByVal theStream As Stream)
      Dim eventMessage As String
      Dim reader As TextReader

      reader = New StreamReader(theStream)
      eventMessage = reader.ReadToEnd()
      If (m_Level > 2) Then
        eventMessage = message.Stage.ToString() + "\n" + eventMessage
      End If

      If (eventMessage.IndexOf("<soap:Fault>") > 0) Then
        'The SOAP body contains a fault
        If (m_Level > 0) Then
          WriteToLog(eventMessage, EventLogEntryType.Error)
        End If
      Else
        ' The SOAP body contains a message
        If (m_Level > 1) Then
          WriteToLog(eventMessage, EventLogEntryType.Information)
        End If
      End If
    End Sub

    Private Sub WriteToLog(ByVal message As String, _
                           ByVal type As EventLogEntryType)
      Dim log As EventLog
      If (Not EventLog.SourceExists(m_Name)) Then
        EventLog.CreateEventSource(m_Name, "Web Service Log")
      End If

      log = New EventLog()
      log.Source = m_Name

      log.WriteEntry(message, type)
    End Sub
  End Class
```

Dissecting the SoapLogVB Code

The following UML sequence diagram shows the sequence in which the different methods are called on both the client and the server when the client calls the `Div` method on the service.

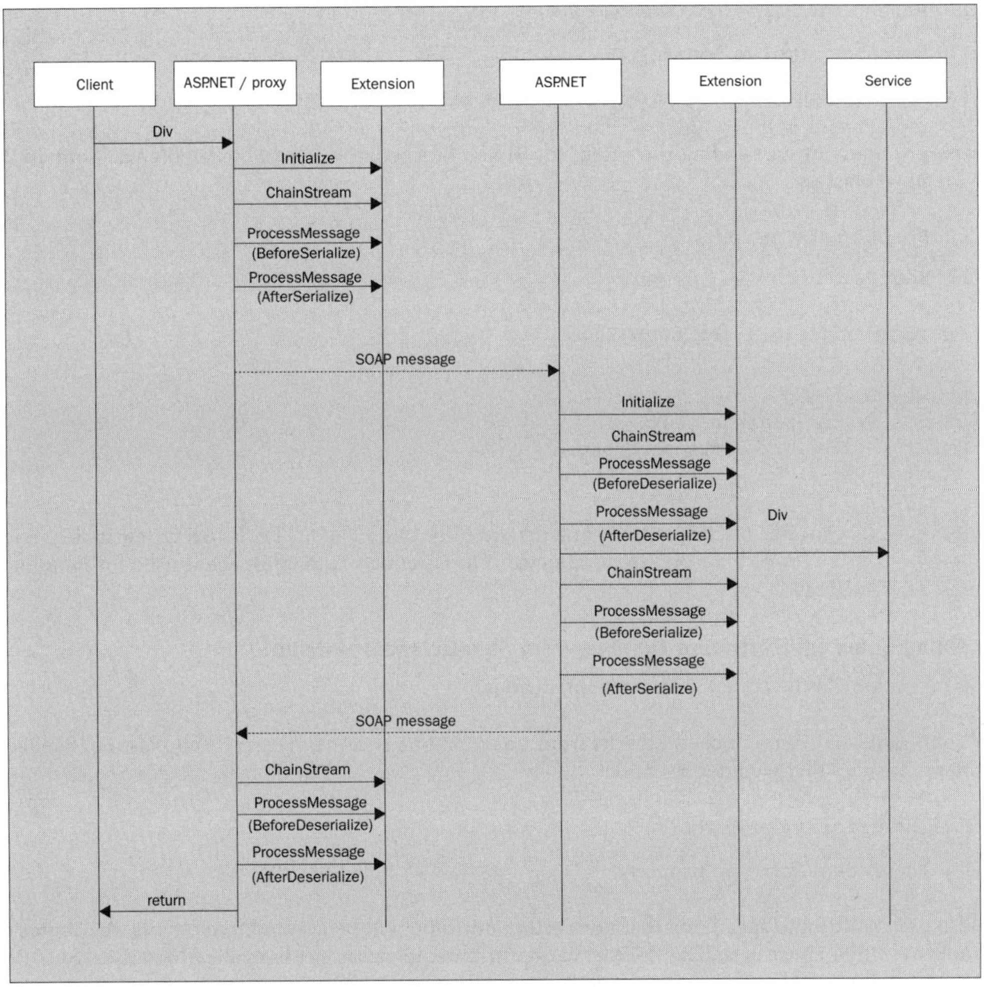

The SoapLogVB extension is implemented as a VB.NET class library. If you want to create the extension yourself, do the following:

- Create a new VB.NET Class Library project named SoapLogVB.
- Rename the Class1.vb file to SoapLog.vb.
- Rename Class1 to SoapLogVB.
- Add a reference to System.Web.Services.dll.

We are now ready to start coding the extension. When finished, the SoapLog.vb file will contain the following two classes:

- SoapLogVBAttribute
- SoapLogVB

The SoapLog.vb file uses some namespaces:

```
Imports System
Imports System.Diagnostics
Imports System.Web.Services.Protocols
Imports System.IO
```

The System.Diagnostics namespace contains the EventLog class. The SOAP Extensions live in the System.Web.Services.Protocols namespace. The System.IO namespace is used for handling streams, as we will see later.

Implementing SoapLogVBAttribute Deriving from SoapExtensionAttribute

Let us take a look at the code for our custom attribute:

The SoapLogVBAttribute class inherits from SoapExtensionAttribute. This class contains two abstract properties that we must override:

- The Priority property
- The ExtensionType property

We also use an attribute specifying that our custom attribute will be applied to methods. Attributes may also apply to other constructs. The WebService attribute, for instance, is applied to classes. SOAP Extension attributes always apply to methods.

```
<AttributeUsage(AttributeTargets.Method)> _
Public Class SoapLogVBAttribute
  Inherits System.Web.Services.Protocols.SoapExtensionAttribute
```

The SoapExtensionAttribute base class has an abstract property Priority that we must override. This property is used to set the priority of extensions if several extensions are applied to the same Web Service method. If we use both an encryption and a compression extension, we should set the priority so that the compression extension is applied before the encryption extension, otherwise the compression will be very inefficient.

```
Private m_Priority As Integer
Private m_Name As String = "SoapLog"
Private m_Level As Integer = 1

Public Overrides Property Priority() As Integer
  Get
    Return m_Priority
  End Get
  Set(ByVal Value As Integer)
    m_Priority = Value
  End Set
End Property
```

We add two new properties: `Name` and `Level`, and they are stored in private variables.

```
Public Property Name() As String
  Get
    Return m_Name
  End Get
  Set(ByVal Value As String)
    m_Name = Value
  End Set
End Property

Public Property Level() As Integer
  Get
    Return m_Level
  End Get
  Set(ByVal Value As Integer)
    m_Level = Value
  End Set
End Property
```

Finally, we specify what class implements the extension using the `ExtensionType` property. This property returns the type of the `SoapLog` class. The `ExtensionType` property is the link between the attribute and the `SoapLog` class.

```
    Public Overrides ReadOnly Property ExtensionType() As Type
      Get
        Return GetType(SoapLogVB)
      End Get
    End Property
  End Class
```

Implementing SoapLogVB Deriving from SoapExtension

The bulk of the code is in the SoapLogVB class. This class inherits from the SoapExtension class and overrides the following functions:

- GetInitializer
- Initialize
- ProcessMessage
- ChainStream

The private variables m_OldStream and m_NewStream are used to store stream references in the ChainStream function discussed later.

```
Public Class SoapLogVB
  Inherits System.Web.Services.Protocols.SoapExtension

  Private m_OldStream As Stream
  Private m_NewStream As Stream
  Private m_Name As String = "SoapLog"
  Private m_Level As Integer = 1
```

The GetInitializer and Initialize functions are used to handle properties in the attribute. The GetInitializer method is called with the attribute as parameter the first time a web method is accessed. The parameter is of type SoapExtensionAttribute. We cast it to the subclass SoapLogAttribute.

```
  Public Overloads Overrides Function GetInitializer( _
      ByVal methodInfo As System.Web.Services.Protocols.LogicalMethodInfo, _
      ByVal attribute As System.Web.Services.Protocols.SoapExtensionAttribute) _
      As Object
    Return CType(attribute, SoapLogVBAttribute)
  End Function
```

GetInitializer returns a SoapLogAttribute object. This object is cached. Each time a web method is invoked, the Initialize method is called with this cached object.

```
  Public Overloads Overrides Function GetInitializer(ByVal obj As Type) As Object
    Return obj
  End Function
```

The SoapLogAttribute object contains the actual properties. The Initialize method pulls out the properties from the SoapLogAttribute and stores them locally so that they can be used later.

```
  Public Overrides Sub Initialize(ByVal initializer As Object)
    If TypeOf initializer Is SoapLogVBAttribute Then
      m_Name = (CType(initializer, SoapLogVBAttribute)).Name
      m_Level = (CType(initializer, SoapLogVBAttribute)).Level
    End If
  End Sub
```

The workhorse of the extension is the `ProcessMessage` method. The SOAP Extension framework calls this method at various stages of the serialization process. The following stages are defined:

- **BeforeSerialize** – this is before the SOAP request or response is serialized into XML.
- **AfterSerialize** – this is after the SOAP request or response is serialized to XML and sent over the wire.
- **BeforeDeserialize** – this is before the SOAP request or response is deserialized from XML.
- **AfterDeserialize** – this is after the SOAP request or response is deserialized from XML.

The `SoapLog` extension only deals with the `AfterSerialize` and `BeforeDeserialize` stages because we are only interested in the XML that is available at these stages. `ProcessMessage` calls private functions to write the contents of a message to the event log. If the logging level is greater than two we also write the name of the stage to the event log. This is useful for examining the sequence in which the stages are called.

```
Public Overrides Sub ProcessMessage( _
  ByVal message As System.Web.Services.Protocols.SoapMessage)
  Select Case message.Stage
    Case System.Web.Services.Protocols.SoapMessageStage.BeforeSerialize
      If (m_Level > 2) Then
        WriteToLog(message.Stage.ToString(), EventLogEntryType.Information)
      End If
    Case System.Web.Services.Protocols.SoapMessageStage.AfterSerialize
      LogOutputMessage(message)
    Case System.Web.Services.Protocols.SoapMessageStage.BeforeDeserialize
      LogInputMessage(message)
    Case System.Web.Services.Protocols.SoapMessageStage.AfterDeserialize
      If (m_Level > 2) Then
        WriteToLog(message.Stage.ToString(), EventLogEntryType.Information)
      End If
  End Select
End Sub
```

The XML in the SOAP message is contained in a stream. The stream has a pointer pointing to the current position in the stream. When we read from a stream we move the pointer. This means that if the log extension reads a stream that is about to be deserialized, it will move the pointer and the pointer must be set back after the extension has read the stream. We need to control the stream that the extension reads from and writes to.

The `ChainStream` function is used to help chain together streams. `ChainStream` is called before serialization or deserialization takes place. A reference to the original stream is saved and a new memory stream is created and returned to the next extension in the chain. This happens for each extension in the chain.

```
Public Overrides Function ChainStream(ByVal theStream As Stream) As Stream
  m_OldStream = theStream
  m_NewStream = New MemoryStream()
  Return m_NewStream
End Function
```

The CopyStream function is a private helper function. It copies the contents of one stream to another stream. Note that after this function is executed, the position pointer for both streams will be at the end of the streams.

```
Private Sub CopyStream(ByVal fromstream As Stream, ByVal tostream As Stream)
  Dim reader As New StreamReader(fromstream)
  Dim writer As New StreamWriter(tostream)

  writer.WriteLine(reader.ReadToEnd())
  writer.Flush()
End Sub
```

When deserializing, the input stream contains the XML to deserialize and the pointer is at the beginning of the stream. The LogInputMessage method copies the input stream into the memory stream buffer, and logs the contents of the stream. It sets the pointer to the beginning of the memory stream buffer so that the next extension can get access to the stream.

```
Private Sub LogInputMessage(ByVal message As SoapMessage)
  CopyStream(m_OldStream, m_NewStream)
  message.Stream.Seek(0, SeekOrigin.Begin)
  LogMessage(message, m_NewStream)
  message.Stream.Seek(0, SeekOrigin.Begin)
End Sub
```

When serializing, the serializer writes to the memory stream created in ChainStream. When the LogOutputMessage function is called after serializing, the pointer is at the end of the stream. The LogOutputMessage function sets the pointer to the beginning of the stream so that the extension can log the contents of the stream. Before returning, the content of the memory stream is copied to the outgoing stream and the pointer is then back at the end of both streams.

```
Private Sub LogOutputMessage(ByVal message As SoapMessage)
  message.Stream.Seek(0, SeekOrigin.Begin)
  LogMessage(message, m_NewStream)
  message.Stream.Seek(0, SeekOrigin.Begin)
  CopyStream(m_NewStream, m_OldStream)
End Sub
```

The private LogMessage helper function logs the contents of a SOAP message to the event log. This function is called from the LogInputMessage and LogOutputMessage functions. It reads the stream and writes the contents of the stream to the event log. The function also checks if the SOAP message contains a fault. In that case, the message is logged in the event log as an error.

The LogMessage function uses the private m_Level field to control if only errors should be written to the event log. This happens if the level is greater than 0. If the log level is greater than 1, all messages are written to the event log. If the level is greater than 2 we also append the name of the stage to the event log message.

```
Private Sub LogMessage(ByVal message As SoapMessage, _
                       ByVal theStream As Stream)
  Dim eventMessage As String
```

```
    Dim reader As TextReader

    reader = New StreamReader(theStream)
    eventMessage = reader.ReadToEnd()

    If (m_Level > 2) Then
      eventMessage = message.Stage.ToString() + "\n" + eventMessage
    End If

    If (eventMessage.IndexOf("<soap:Fault>") > 0) Then
      'The SOAP body containts a fault
      If (m_Level > 0) Then
        WriteToLog(eventMessage, EventLogEntryType.Error)
      End If
    Else
      ' The SOAP body contains a message
      If (m_Level > 1) Then
        WriteToLog(eventMessage, EventLogEntryType.Information)
      End If
    End If
  End Sub
```

The actual writing to the event log is handled in the private function `WriteToLog`. The function uses the `EventLog` class to create a new 'Web Service Log' if it does not already exist. The source of the message in the event log is then set to the name specified in the `m_Name` field.

```
  Private Sub WriteToLog(ByVal message As String, _
                         ByVal type As EventLogEntryType)

    Dim log As EventLog

    If (Not EventLog.SourceExists(m_Name)) Then
      EventLog.CreateEventSource(m_Name, "Web Service Log")
    End If

    log = New EventLog()
    log.Source = m_Name

    log.WriteEntry(message, type)
  End Sub
End Class
```

Using the SoapLogVB Extension

If we compile the `SoapLogVB` extension, we get an assembly. To use the extension we can copy the compiled DLL from the `bin` directory of our extension to the `bin` directory of the Web Service. We can then use the extension by adding an attribute to the code of a Web Service, or by adding the `soapExtensionTypes` element to the `web.config` or `app.config` file.

Here we add the `SoapLogVB` extension to the `SimpleMath` service. The example is available as `SimpleMath2_VB.asmx` in the code download.

```
<%@ WebService Language="VB" class="SimpleMath" %>

Imports System.Web.Services

Public Class SimpleMath

  <WebMethod, _
  SoapLogVB.SoapLogVB(Name:="SimpleMath.Add",Level:=3)> _
  Public Function Add(a As Integer, b As Integer) As Integer
    return a+b
  End Function

  <WebMethod, _
  SoapLogVB.SoapLogVB(Name:="SimpleMath.Div",Level:=3)> _
  Public Function Div(a As Integer, b As Integer) As Integer
    return a/b
  End Function

End Class
```

To test the extension we need to build a client using the service. When we call the service, messages should appear in the event log. The `SoapLogClientVB.exe` test client available with the code download can be used to test the Web Service.

Here is a screenshot of the event log after calling first 'Div' and then 'Add':

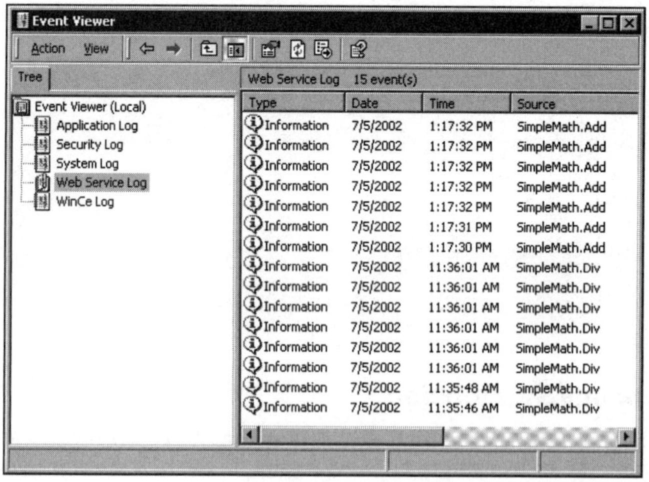

The `SoapLogVB` extension is a useful tool when developing Web Services. It can also be used when running the Web Service to monitor the SOAP messages transmitted.

Shaping the SOAP Message

Web Services are based on the SOAP and WSDL specifications. These specifications open the door to various ways of encoding the XML in the SOAP messages.

The SOAP specification itself specifies the overall structure of the SOAP message, as we saw in Chapter 5. The SOAP message may contain a header, it must contain a body, and the body must be formatted as XML. However, the SOAP specification does not say what the XML within the body should look like. We may put any valid XML in the body and it will be a valid SOAP message.

The SOAP specification is available at http://www.w3.org/TR/SOAP/. Section 5 of the SOAP specification contains the bulk of the specification and describes how data types such as integers, strings, arrays, and structures *can* be encoded. Note the emphasis on 'can'. The specification does not mandate the use of the encoding rules specified in section 5.

Section 7 of the SOAP specification specifies how SOAP can be used for RPC. The section specifies that the method invocation is modeled as a structure named after the method name. Once again, following section 7 is optional.

There are two principal styles of SOAP. **Document style SOAP** views the data exchanged as documents. Your Web Service may receive and/or return an XML document. The XML document is carried in the body of the SOAP message. The document may, for example, be an invoice as illustrated in the figure below.

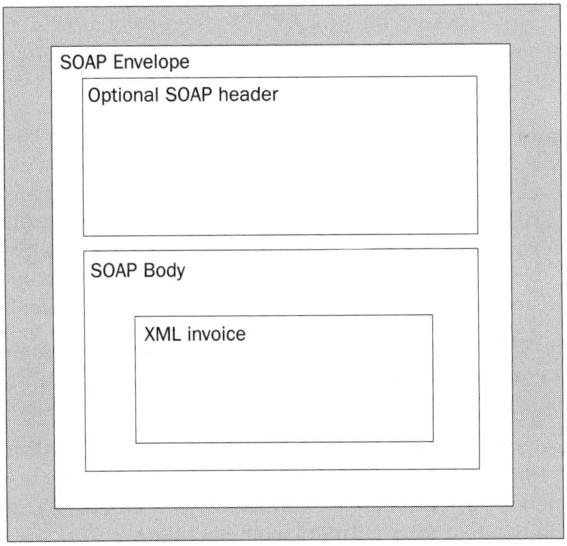

RPC style SOAP views the data exchange as method calls on remote objects. The remote object may for instance be a Java object, a COM component, or a .NET object. In RPC style SOAP, the outermost element in the request will be named after the method and there will be an element for each parameter on that method. In the response, the outermost element will be named after the method with the string 'Response' appended as illustrated in the figure below.

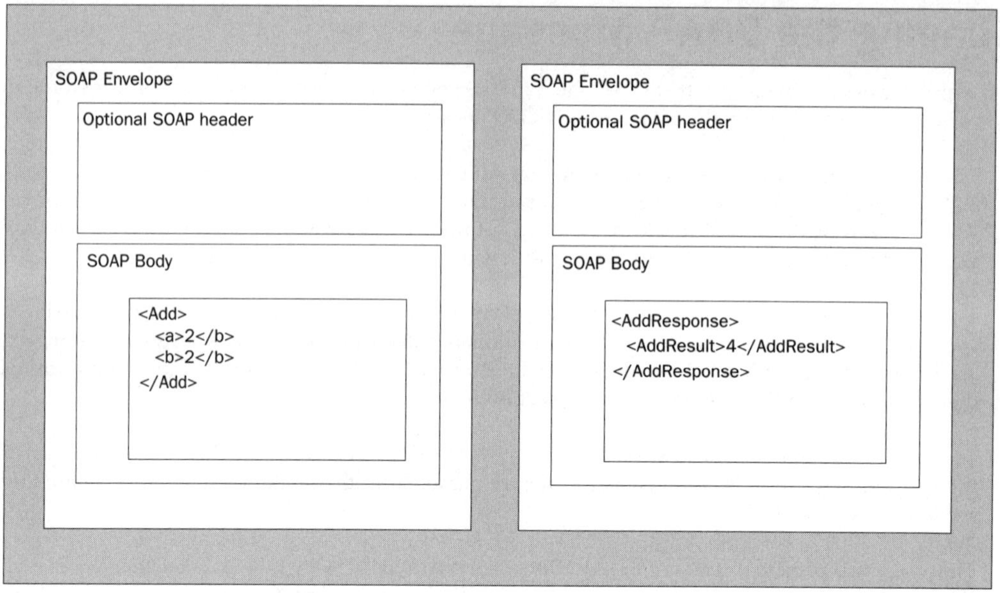

When we create Web Services, ASP.NET handles the details of the XML in the SOAP message received and returned automatically. It does this through a process called serialization. We discussed serialization earlier in this chapter. Serialization is the process of converting objects to XML. The process of reconstructing the objects from XML is known as deserialization. The module that does the conversion is the `XmlSerializer`.

Using ASP.NET we can influence the way the `XmlSerializer` works. There are several reasons we may want to control the shape of the XML:

- We need the XML returned from our Web Service to conform to a predefined schema. If we are returning an invoice, we may have agreed on the XML schema with our partner. Internally we may have an object representing the invoice and we want to map the object to the XML schema. In this case we need to instruct the `XmlSerializer` on how it should do the serialization.
- We receive an XML document from a partner. The XML document is formed according to a schema and we want to map the document to an internal object. In this case we need to instruct the `XmlSerializer` how it should do the deserialization.
- We need to use a Web Service implemented using another SOAP tool, for example a Java-based toolkit. Ideally, this should be transparent, but in the real world there will be differences in the implementations especially in the early days of SOAP. We may need to tweak the XML in the SOAP message to work around incompatibilities.

ASP.NET allows us control over the shaping of the XML in the SOAP message. There are two ways we can shape the SOAP message:

- Specify the overall encoding of the message, that is, should it be document style or RPC style? Classes in the `System.Web.Services` namespace handle the overall encoding.
- Control how data types such as integers, structures, and arrays are serialized and deserialized using the `XmlSerializer` and other classes in the `System.Xml.Serialization` namespace.

These mechanisms may be used together or separately to shape the XML the way we want it. The figure below illustrates the process:

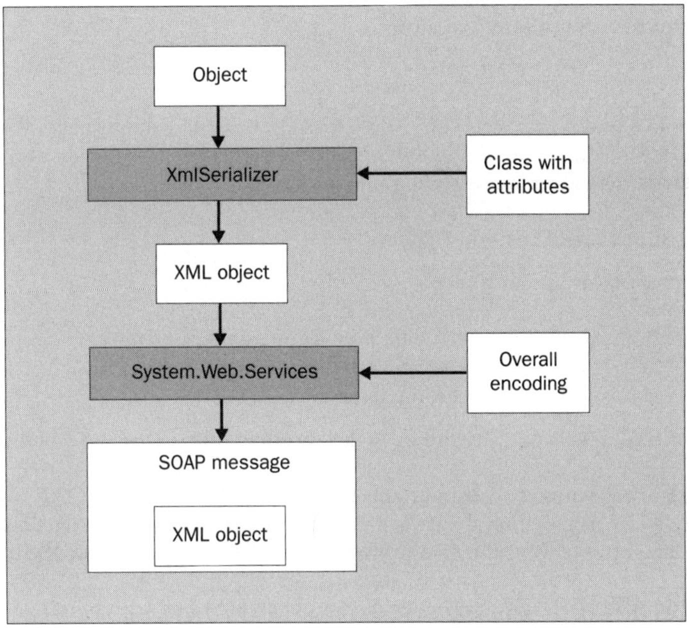

The `XmlSerializer` serializes the object into an XML representation. To do this, it uses the class definition. The class definition contains the name of classes and fields and may also be annotated with attributes, as we will see later.

The result from the `XmlSerializer` is then wrapped in a SOAP message (with envelope, header, and body) by classes in the `System.Web.Services` namespace. The overall encoding can be specified using attributes on the Web Service, as we will see in the next section.

Overall Encoding of the Message

As we touched on above, there are two main ways in which the overall SOAP message may be encoded:

- The messages may be constructed according to Section 7 of the SOAP specification. This is known as **RPC style** SOAP. RPC style SOAP is suited for exposing object methods. The SOAP Toolkit for COM components and .NET Remoting uses RPC style SOAP by default.
- The messages may be constructed according to an XML schema document definition in a WSDL file. This is known as **document style** SOAP. ASP.NET uses document style SOAP by default.

ASP.NET has two attributes we can use to control the overall encoding of all methods in a Web Service:

- The `SoapDocumentService` attribute.
- The `SoapRpcService` attribute.

These attributes live in the `System.Web.Services.Protocols` namespace. When applied to a Web Service, they affect the encoding of all methods in the Web Service. We may also apply attributes to individual methods. The attributes affecting methods are:

- The `SoapDocumentMethod` attribute.
- The `SoapRpcMethod` attribute.

In addition there are two ways in which data may be encoded:

- **Literal** – data is encoded according to an XML schema.
- **Encoded** – data is encoded according to the encoding rules in Section 5 of the SOAP specification.

RPC style SOAP always uses encoded parameters. With document style SOAP we can choose between literal and encoded. Normally literal data is used with document style SOAP. This is logical for exchanging documents; we want the data in the document to conform to an XML schema.

The default for an ASP.NET Web Service is document style SOAP with literal parameters. If we want to specify a different overall encoding we do so by adding one of the attributes above. Here is a sample that sets the overall encoding of all methods in the Web Service to RPC style SOAP. The sample is available in the code download as `SimpleMathRPC_VB.asmx`.

```
<%@ WebService Language="VB" class="SimpleMath" %>

Imports System.Web.Services
Imports System.Web.Services.Protocols

<SoapRpcService()> _
Public Class SimpleMath

  <WebMethod> _
  Public Function Add(a As Integer, b As Integer) As Integer
    return a+b
  End Function
```

```
    <WebMethod> _
    Public Function Div(a As Integer, b As Integer) As Integer
      return a/b
    End Function

  End Class
```

> **If you have problems calling .NET Web Services from other SOAP implementations, setting the encoding style to RPC in some cases fixes the problems.**

To view the result of applying this parameter we need to call it using the SOAP protocol. The ASP.NET-generated test pages do not use SOAP when calling the Web Service but they show a sample SOAP request and response.

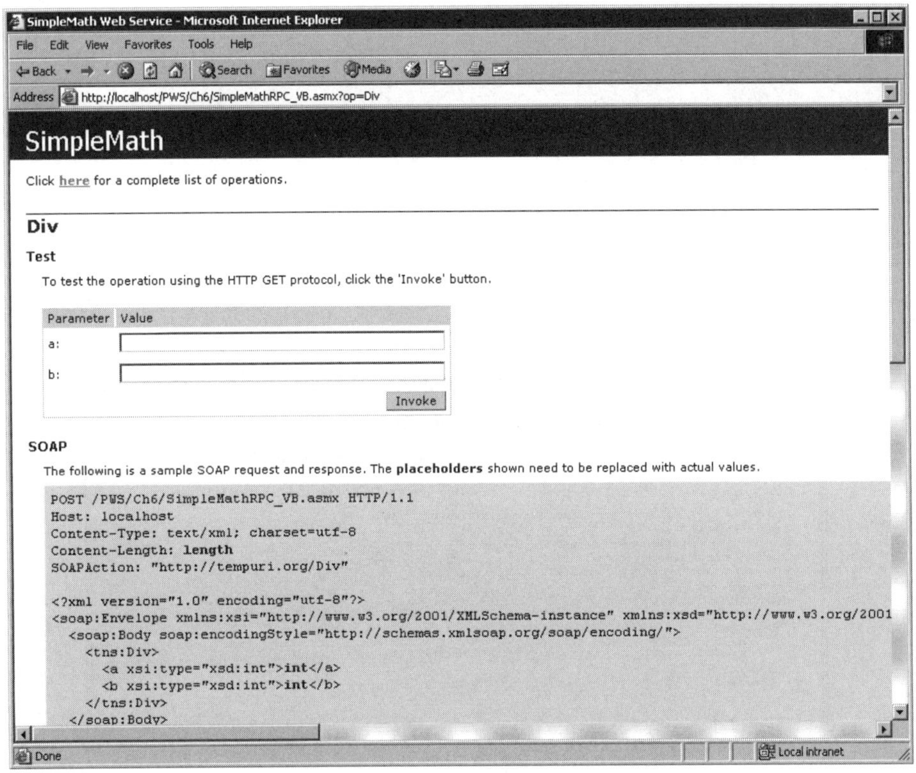

By default, the request and response appear wrapped in a `Div` or `DivResponse` element, respectively. In addition, document style SOAP allows us to specify **bare** parameters. We do this using the `ParameterStyle` property on the `SoapDocumentService` or the `SoapDocumentMethod` attribute. With bare parameters, the request and response data is directly under the `Body` element.

Here is how we can specify bare parameters. The example is available as `SimpleMathDocumentBare_VB.asmx` in the code download.

```
<%@ WebService Language="VB" class="SimpleMath" %>

Imports System.Web.Services
Imports System.Web.Services.Protocols

Public Class SimpleMath

  <WebMethod, _
  SoapDocumentMethod(ParameterStyle:=SoapParameterStyle.Bare)> _
  Public Function Add(a As Integer, b As Integer) As Integer
    return a+b
  End Function

  <WebMethod, _
  SoapDocumentMethod(ParameterStyle:=SoapParameterStyle.Bare)> _
  Public Function Div(a As Integer, b As Integer) As Integer
    return a/b
  End Function

End Class
```

The `SoapParameterStyle` enumerator lives in the `System.Web.Services.Protocols` namespace. Here is what the SOAP looks like:

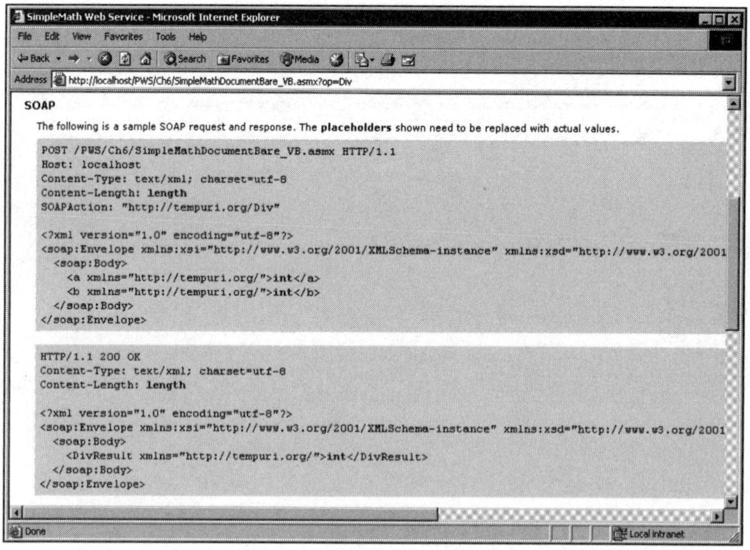

As we can see, there are no longer any elements wrapping the request and the response.

Using the XmlSerializer

The .NET Framework has built-in XML support. Objects can be serialized to XML and objects may be reconstructed from XML automatically. If you try to accomplish this using, for example, Visual Basic 6, you need to write code yourself to serialize objects to XML and to reconstruct objects from XML.

The `System.XML.Serialization` namespace contains a number of classes that can be used when serializing and deserializing objects. Many of the classes in this namespace allow us to control the format of the XML.

The `XmlSerializer` is used by ASP.NET Web Services. ASP.NET uses the `XmlSerializer` to serialize objects to XML and then adds the SOAP envelope, header and body around the output from the `XmlSerializer`.

The `XmlSerializer` and its attributes can also be used on their own. Before we dive into Web Services, let us start by looking at the `XmlSerializer` class. This class can serialize objects into XML and it can reconstruct the objects from XML. The serializer relies on the reflection support in the .NET Framework. Reflection is a mechanism by which code can be inspected at run time.

Serializing and deserializing objects is useful for different purposes, for instance:

- XML serialization can be used to store objects to a file, in a database, and so on. We could for instance have an object representing a user's preferences in an application. On application startup we read an XML file and construct an object representing the preferences. When changes are made to the preferences, the XML file is regenerated.
- Serialized objects can be transported over the network. A Web Service is a good example of the `XmlSerializer` in action.

As an example of XML serialization we will use a class representing `Titles` with `Authors`. The structure is loosely based on the structure of the `pubs` database that ships with SQL Server 2000. The example is available in the code download as `PWS\Ch6\PublicationsVB\Publications1VB.vb`.

```
Imports System

Namespace Publications1

  Public Class Author

    Public firstname As String
    Public lastname As String
  End Class

  Public Class Title

    Public title_id As String
    Public title As String
    Public pubdate As DateTime
    Public price As Double
    Public authors As Author()
```

```
    Public Sub CreateDummy()

      title_id = "BU7832"
      title = "Straight Talk About Computers"
      price = 19.99
      pubdate = New DateTime(1992, 6, 9)

      ReDim authors(2)

      authors(0) = New Author()
      authors(0).firstname = "Dean"
      authors(0).lastname = "Straight"

      authors(1) = New Author()
      authors(1).firstname = "Dean2"
      authors(1).lastname = "Straight2"
    End Sub
  End Class
End Namespace
```

The `Title` class contains a number of fields and an array of `Author` objects. The `CreateDummy` method initializes the object with some dummy data.

If we have an object of this class we can easily get an XML representation using the `XmlSerializer`. The code download contains a Windows Forms application, `PublicationClientVB.exe`, which you can use to test the serialization. When we click on the **Publications1** button, the serialized XML is written to a text field.

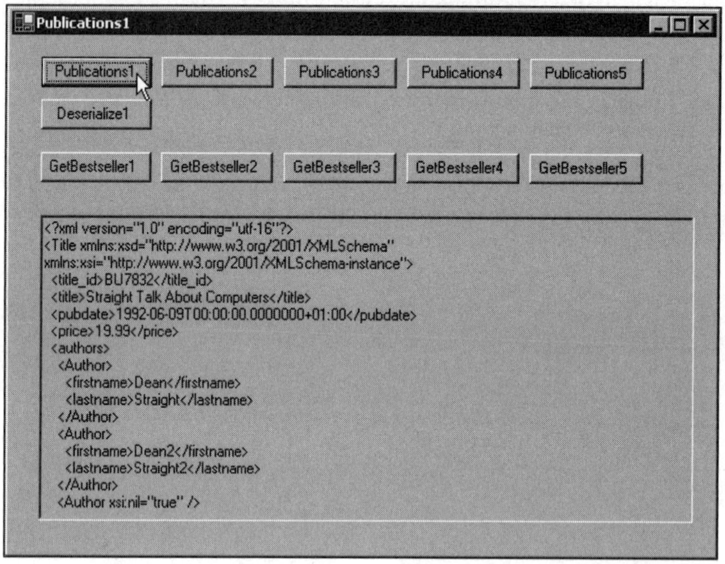

Here is the code for the Publications1 button callback:

```
Imports System.Xml.Serialization
Imports PublicationsVB

...

  Private Sub button1_Click(ByVal sender As System.Object, _
                            ByVal e As System.EventArgs) Handles button1.Click
    Dim serializer As New XmlSerializer(GetType(Publications1.Title))

    Dim writer As New System.IO.StringWriter()
    Dim theTitle As New Publications1.Title()

    ' Create object
    theTitle.CreateDummy()

    ' Serialize object to XML
    serializer.Serialize(writer, theTitle)

    ' Show button text in form caption
    Me.Text = CType(sender, Button).Text

    ' Show XML in text box
    textBox1.Text = writer.ToString()
  End Sub
```

First we create an instance of the `XmlSerializer`. The constructor takes the type of the object to serialize as a parameter. It uses the type information to construct the XML.

The `Serialize` method does the actual serialization. It can serialize to a stream or to a `TextWriter` object. A `TextWriter` is an object for character output. Here we serialize to a `StringWriter`. `StringWriter` is a subclass of `TextWriter`.

Finally, we show the name of the button in the title of the form, and show the serialized XML in the textbox.

We can also recreate the object from the XML. If you use the test application, you can first serialize the object into XML (click Publications1), then click Deserialize1. Here is the code for the Deserialize1 button callback:

```
  Private Sub button2_Click(ByVal sender As System.Object, _
                            ByVal e As System.EventArgs) Handles button2.Click
    ' We only deserialize if the text box contains correct data
    If (Me.Text = "Publications1") Then
      Dim serializer As New XmlSerializer(GetType(Publications1.Title))

      ' Get text from text box
      Dim reader As New System.IO.StringReader(textBox1.Text)

      ' Reconstruct the object
      Dim theTitle As Publications1.Title
      theTitle = CType(serializer.Deserialize(reader), Publications1.Title)
```

```
        ' Show the title
        Me.Text = CType(sender, Button).Text

        textBox1.Text = "Deserialize: theTitle.title=" + theTitle.title
      End If

    End Sub
```

The code first checks if the previous click was on Publications1 (remember that the callback writes the name of the button to the caption of the form). If so, we can deserialize. The code is otherwise very similar to the code for serialization, except we call the `Deserialize` method on the `XmlSerializer`.

The callback shows the title of the publication in the textbox:

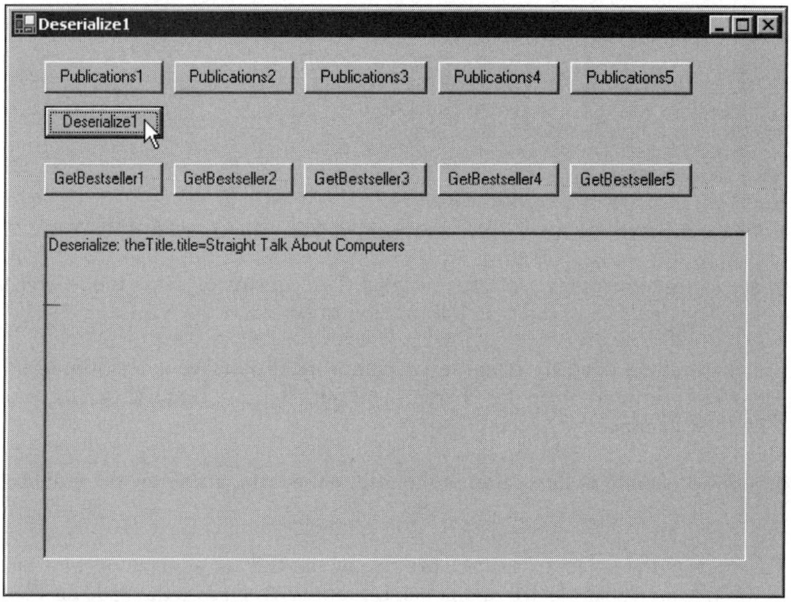

A few lines of code are all that is needed to get the XML representation of an object. As we can see, XML serialization is a very powerful mechanism.

Using Attributes to Shape the XML

The format of the XML in the previous section is automatically generated based on the layout of the objects. The elements are named after the fields and all fields become elements.

What if we want the XML to look different? What if we don't want `title_id` to be an element, but instead to be an attribute of the root `<Title>` element? And what if we want the XML attribute to be named `Id`, instead of being named `title_id` after the field?

The answer to all these questions is 'use attributes'. We annotate our class with attributes. The `XmlSerializer` reads the annotated class definition and uses that when generating the XML representation of the object as illustrated in the figure below:

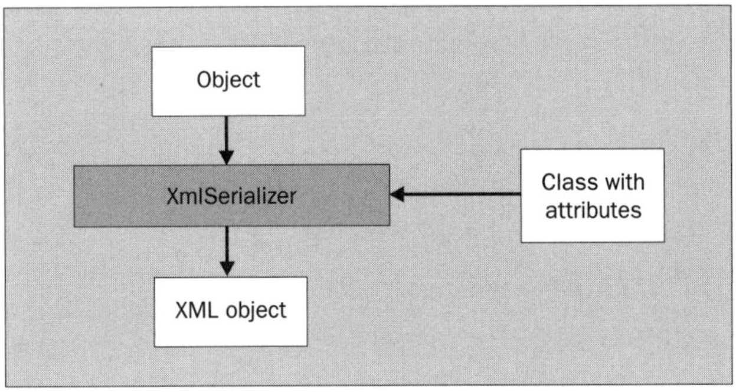

Why would we want to rename the fields in the first place? It may be a matter of taste; we can use a different name from the internal name of the field. If we use a naming convention for our code, we may not want to use the convention when exposing the XML.

We may also give the fields a name that we are not allowed to use in our code. This may, for instance, be a name that is reserved in the language. Say we are building a biology application and we want to specify the class of a species as an element named `Class`. We are not allowed to use this as the name of a VB.NET field since `Class` is a reserved word in VB.NET. By using attributes we can give the XML element the name `Class`.

The `System.XML.Serialization` namespace contains a number of classes implementing attributes that can be used to shape the XML. To make `title_id` an XML attribute, simply add the `XmlAttribute` attribute to the `title_id` field (the code for this is in `Publications2VB.vb`).

```
Imports System
Imports System.Xml.Serialization

Namespace Publications2

  Public Class Author

    Public firstname As String
    Public lastname As String
  End Class

  Public Class Title

    <XmlAttribute("Id")> _
    Public title_id As String
    Public title As String
    Public pubdate As DateTime
    Public price As Double
    Public authors As Author()
    ...
```

The Publications2 callback in the test application uses this class definition:

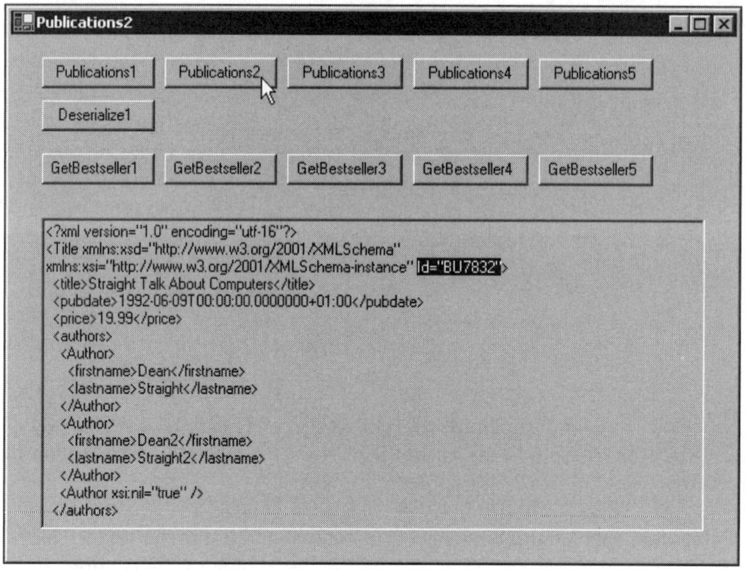

By adding the `XmlAttribute` attribute we have now named the `title_id` field in the class `Id` and it is an attribute of the enclosing `Title` element instead of being a nested element.

> **The name of the class implementing `XmlAttribute` is `XmlAttributeAttribute`. As with all attributes in the .NET Framework we can write a shorthand notation omitting the last `Attribute` word.**

XML Attributes and SOAP Attributes

Above we used the `XmlAttribute` attribute. The `System.Xml.Serialization` namespace contains a large number of attributes that can be used to control the shape of the XML. There are two sets of attributes, one where the attributes are named Xml*XXX*Attribute and another where the attributes are named Soap*XXX*Attribute.

Which attributes are used depends on how the parameters are encoded. As discussed in the section *Overall Encoding of the Message*, there are two types of serialization: literal and encoded. Literal serialization is based on an XML schema, and encoded serialization is based on the serialization rules in Section 5 of the SOAP specification.

The Xml*XXX*Attribute attributes apply when we use literal style parameters. The Soap*XXX*Attribute attributes apply when we use encoded style parameters.

This means that the `Xml`*XXX*`Attribute` attributes apply in the following cases:

- It is the default for ASP.NET Web Services.
- When we use the `XmlSerializer` by itself.
- When we use the HTTP GET or HTTP POST protocols.
- When we use the `SoapDocumentService` or `SoapDocumentMethod` attribute with the `Use` property set to `Literal`.

The `Soap`*XXX*`Attribute` attributes apply in the following cases:

- When we use the `SoapRpcService` or `SoapRpcMethod` attribute.
- When we use the `SoapDocumentService` or `SoapDocumentMethod` attribute with the `Use` property set to `Encoded`.

A method may have both the `Soap`*XXX* and the `Xml`*XXX* attributes applied at the same time. Which one is used depends on the type of serialization being performed.

The table below lists most of the available attributes.

XML Attribute	SOAP attribute	Description
`XmlAttributeAttribute`	`SoapAttributeAttribute`	Used to make fields into XML attributes instead of elements.
`XmlElementAttribute`	`SoapElementAttribute`	Used to name the XML elements. Can also be used with arrays to list array elements without being nested under a common element.
`XmlArrayAttribute`		Used to name arrays.
`XmlIgnoreAttribute`	`SoapIgnoreAttribute`	Used to prevent fields from being serialized.
`XmlIncludeAttribute`	`SoapIncludeAttribute`	Used with derived classes.
`XmlRootAttribute`		Used to name the top-level element.
`XmlTextAttribute`		Used to serialize fields directly in the XML text without elements.
`XmlEnumAttribute`	`SoapEnumAttribute`	Used to give the members of an enumeration a name different from the name used in the enumeration.
`XmlTypeAttribute`	`SoapTypeAttribute`	Used to control the name of types in the WSDL file.

Most of the attributes contain a number of properties. Some properties are common to most attributes, such as the `Namespace` property and the `Datatype` property. The space here does not permit a complete description of all attributes and properties. For a complete reference, see *ASP.NET Namespace Reference with VB.NET* (ISBN 1-861007-45-0) also from Wrox Press.

Let's use a simple Web Service returning the `Title` structure above as an example for testing the attributes. The Web Service is available in the file `PublicationService1_VB.asmx` in the code download.

```
<%@ WebService Language="VB" class="PublicationService" %>

Imports System.Web.Services
Imports PublicationsVB.Publications1

Public Class PublicationService
  <WebMethod, _
  TraceExtension.TraceExtension(Filename:="C:\temp\PublicationService1.txt")> _
  Public Function GetBestseller() As Title
    Dim theTitle As New Title()
    theTitle.CreateDummy()
    return theTitle
  End Function
End Class
```

The Web Service uses the `CreateDummy` function to initialize the object with dummy data and returns the object. We also apply the trace extension so we can see the full SOAP message.

If we invoke the `GetBestseller` method using the ASP.NET generated test pages we will see the result of the `XmlSerializer` without the SOAP wrapping:

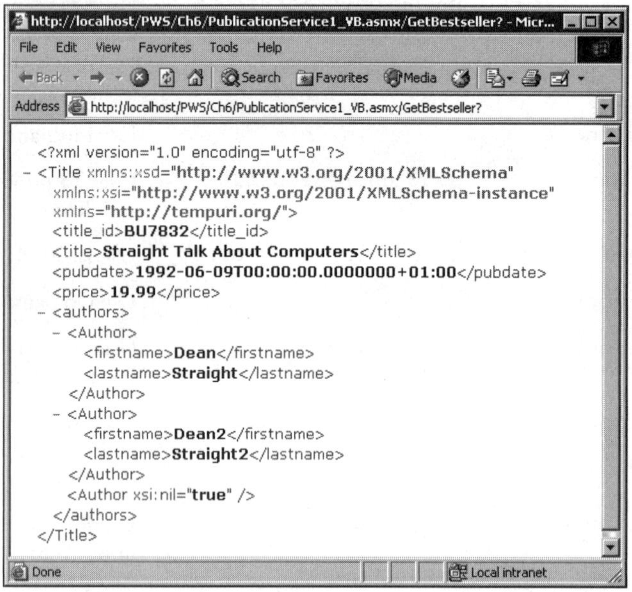

To see the SOAP wrapping we must call the Web Service using the SOAP protocol, not HTTP GET. To do this you can use the supplied `PublicationClientVB.exe` test application and click **GetBestseller1**. Because the Web Service uses the trace extension, the file `c:\temp\PublicationService1.txt` will contain the SOAP messages:

PublicationService1.txt - Notepad

File Edit Format Help

```
=================================== Request at 05/07/2002 16:19:32
<?xml version="1.0" encoding="utf-8"?>
<soap:Envelope xmlns:soap="http://schemas.xmlsoap.org/soap/envelope/"
               xmlns:xsi="http://www.w3.org/2001/XMLSchema-instance"
               xmlns:xsd="http://www.w3.org/2001/XMLSchema">
  <soap:Body>
    <GetBestseller xmlns="http://tempuri.org/" />
  </soap:Body>
</soap:Envelope>

----------------------------------- Response at 05/07/2002 16:19:33
<?xml version="1.0" encoding="utf-8"?>
<soap:Envelope xmlns:soap="http://schemas.xmlsoap.org/soap/envelope/"
               xmlns:xsi="http://www.w3.org/2001/XMLSchema-instance"
               xmlns:xsd="http://www.w3.org/2001/XMLSchema">
  <soap:Body>
    <GetBestsellerResponse xmlns="http://tempuri.org/">
      <GetBestsellerResult>
        <title_id>BU7832</title_id>
        <title>Straight Talk About Computers</title>
        <pubdate>1992-06-09T00:00:00.0000000+01:00</pubdate>
        <price>19.99</price>
        <authors>
          <Author>
            <firstname>Dean</firstname>
            <lastname>Straight</lastname>
          </Author>
          <Author>
            <firstname>Dean2</firstname>
            <lastname>Straight2</lastname>
          </Author>
          <Author xsi:nil="true" />
        </authors>
      </GetBestsellerResult>
    </GetBestsellerResponse>
  </soap:Body>
</soap:Envelope>
```

This is similar to the XML we got from the `XmlSerializer` class, the difference being that the result is wrapped in a SOAP message and the root element is `<GetBestsellerResponse>`.

> **When shaping the XML, the log extension and the tracer extension described earlier in this chapter are very useful. They allow us to see the format of the serialized XML.**

The following sections show the most commonly used attributes and how they can be used to shape the XML returned from a Web Service.

Shaping Classes

When we used the `XmlSerializer`, the root element was named `Title` after the class. When we returned the data from a web method, the root element was named `GetBestsellerResult` after the method.

Using the `XmlRoot` attribute we can control the name of the root element. Here is an example of using the `XmlRoot` attribute to name the root element explicitly. The root element is given the name `TitleRoot`. The full code is in `Publications3VB.vb`.

```
Imports System
Imports System.Xml.Serialization

Namespace Publications3

  Public Class Author

    Public firstname As String
    Public lastname As String
  End Class

  <XmlRoot("TitleRoot")> _
  Public Class Title

    <XmlAttributeAttribute("Id")> _
    Public title_id As String

    <XmlElement(ElementName:="Name")> _
    Public title As String
  ...
```

This gives the following SOAP, which is obtained by clicking **GetBestseller3** in the test client:

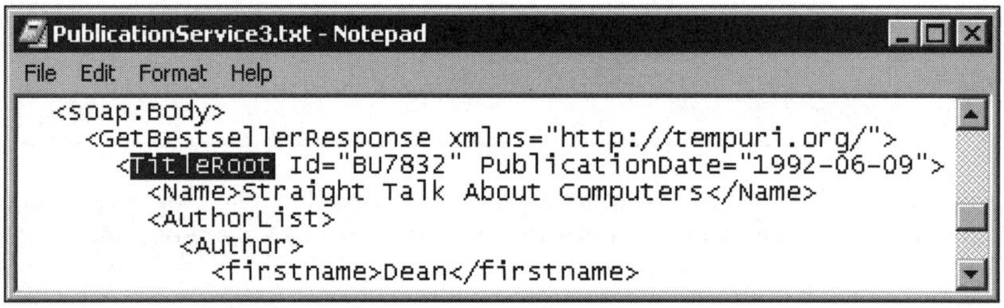

Shaping Fields and Properties

By default, fields and properties become elements in the XML. Using the `XmlElement` attribute, the elements can be given a name other than the field name. Using the `XmlAttribute` attribute, fields can be serialized as XML attributes instead of XML elements.

Here is some code for controlling the shape of the serialized fields (from `Publications3VB.vb`):

```
  <XmlRoot("TitleRoot")> _
  Public Class Title

    <XmlAttributeAttribute("Id")> _
    Public title_id As String

    <XmlElement(ElementName:="Name")> _
    Public title As String
```

```
    <XmlAttributeAttribute(AttributeName:="PublicationDate", DataType:="date")> _
    Public pubdate As DateTime
  ...
```

The code performs the following modifications to the XML:

- The `title_id` field is serialized as an attribute with the name `Id`. It becomes an attribute of the enclosing `TitleRoot` element.
- The `title` field is serialized as an element with the name `Name`.
- The `pubdate` field is serialized as an attribute named `PublicationDate` with data type `date`. It becomes an attribute of the enclosing `TitleRoot` element.

Here is a snippet of the returned SOAP message showing these attributes in action:

The default behavior of a field is to be represented as an element named after the field.

Ignoring Fields

By default, all public fields of our class are serialized. If there are public fields we don't want to serialize, we can use the `XmlIgnore` attribute.

Why would we want to ignore fields? If we exchange documents with partners, it may be that our class contains fields we don't want included in the XML. The field may contain confidential information or information that for other reasons is not relevant to our business partners. We could make the field private. But if our class is also used by an internal application, we may want that application to see the field, so we can't make it private.

Another case is if the field is calculated based on other fields in the class. In this case it does not necessarily make sense to have the field represented in the serialized XML.

The `Publications3VB.vb` file ignores the price field.

```
<XmlRoot("TitleRoot")> _
Public Class Title

  <XmlAttributeAttribute("Id")> _
  Public title_id As String

  <XmlElement(ElementName:="Name")> _
  Public title As String
```

```
    <XmlAttributeAttribute(AttributeName:="PublicationDate", _
                           DataType:="date")> _
    Public pubdate As DateTime

    <XmlIgnore()> _
    Public price As Double
...
```

This causes the serializer to skip the price field.

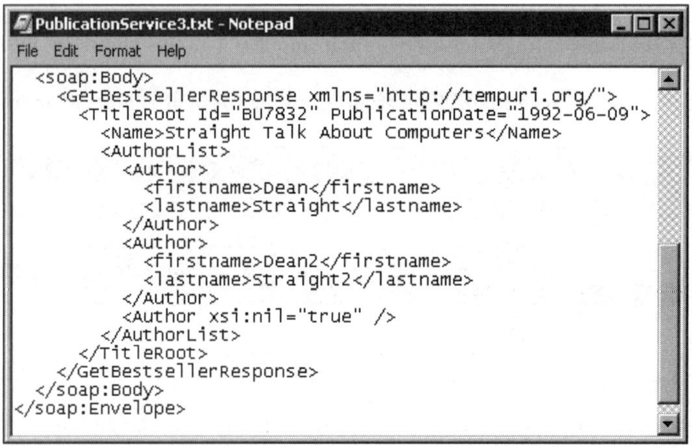

Shaping Arrays

The default behavior of arrays is to create a root element for the array. This element is given the name of the array and all items in the array are nested inside this element.

There are several attributes we can use to shape the array, including the XmlArray attribute and the XmlElement attribute.

Renaming the Array

We saw above that all the elements of the authors array were contained in a root element named after the array. We can use the XmlArray attribute to rename the array.

```
<XmlRoot("TitleRoot")> _
Public Class Title

    <XmlAttributeAttribute("Id")> _
    Public title_id As String

    <XmlElement(ElementName:="Name")> _
    Public title As String

    <XmlAttributeAttribute(AttributeName:="PublicationDate", _
                           DataType:="date")> _
```

```
    Public pubdate As DateTime

    <XmlIgnore()> _
    Public price As Double

    <XmlArray(ElementName:="AuthorList")> _
    Public authors As Author()
  ...
```

This results in the array being named `AuthorList` instead of `authors`.

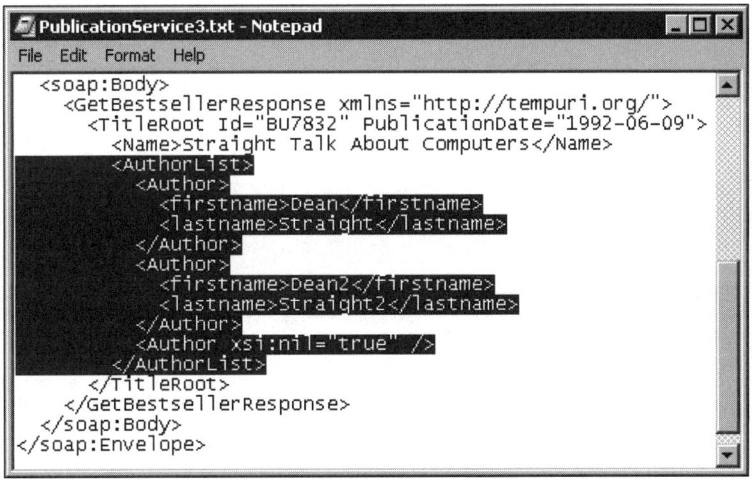
PublicationService3.txt - Notepad

File Edit Format Help

```
  <soap:Body>
    <GetBestsellerResponse xmlns="http://tempuri.org/">
      <TitleRoot Id="BU7832" PublicationDate="1992-06-09">
        <Name>Straight Talk About Computers</Name>
        <AuthorList>
          <Author>
            <firstname>Dean</firstname>
            <lastname>Straight</lastname>
          </Author>
          <Author>
            <firstname>Dean2</firstname>
            <lastname>Straight2</lastname>
          </Author>
          <Author xsi:nil="true" />
        </AuthorList>
      </TitleRoot>
    </GetBestsellerResponse>
  </soap:Body>
</soap:Envelope>
```

Empty Arrays

By default, if the array is empty, it appears in the XML with an `xsi:nil="true"` attribute. This is equivalent to `Nothing` in Visual Basic.

```
  <AuthorList xsi:nil="true" />
```

If we don't want this XML element generated for empty arrays we can set the `IsNullable` property of the `XmlArray` attribute to `False`. Here is a snippet from `Publications4VB.vb`:

```
...
<XmlRoot("TitleRoot")> _
Public Class Title

  <XmlAttributeAttribute("Id")> _
  Public title_id As String

  <XmlElement(ElementName:="Name")> _
  Public title As String

  <XmlAttributeAttribute(AttributeName:="PublicationDate", DataType:="date")> _
```

```
    Public pubdate As DateTime

    <XmlIgnore()> _
    Public price As Double

    <XmlArray(ElementName:="AuthorList", IsNullable:=False)> _
    Public authors As Author()

    Public Sub CreateDummy()

      title_id = "BU7832"
      title = "Straight Talk About Computers"
      price = 19.99
      pubdate = New DateTime(1992, 6, 9)

    End Sub
...
```

Note in the code above that the `CreateDummy` method does not create the array of authors. We get an empty array. If you use the test application and click GetBestseller4 you will see that there is no reference to the authors array.

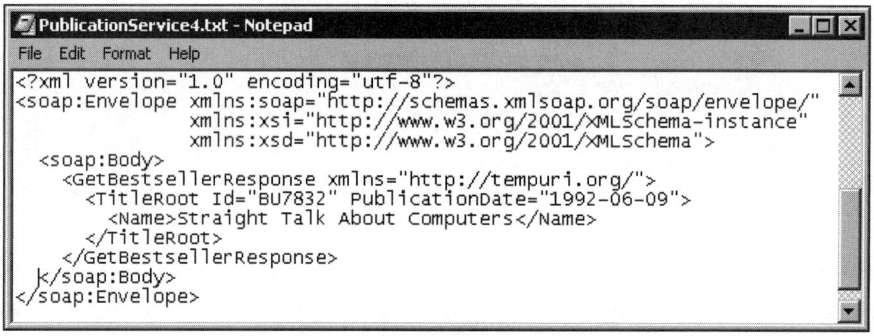

Removing the Root Array Element

We can remove the root array element and have the array elements listed directly under the root of the class. We do this by using the `XmlElement` attribute on the `authors` array. We can also set the name of the array elements. Here is an example (from `Publications5VB.vb`) that names the array elements `Writer`.

```
<XmlRoot("TitleRoot")> _
Public Class Title

  <XmlAttributeAttribute("Id")> _
  Public title_id As String

  <XmlElement(ElementName:="Name")> _
  Public title As String
```

```
    <XmlElement(ElementName:="Title")> _
    Public type As TitleType

    <XmlAttributeAttribute(AttributeName:="PublicationDate", _
                           DataType:="date")> _
    Public pubdate As DateTime

    <XmlIgnore()> _
    Public price As Double

    <XmlElement(ElementName:="Writer")> _
    Public authors As Author()
```

When serialized, the XML looks like this:

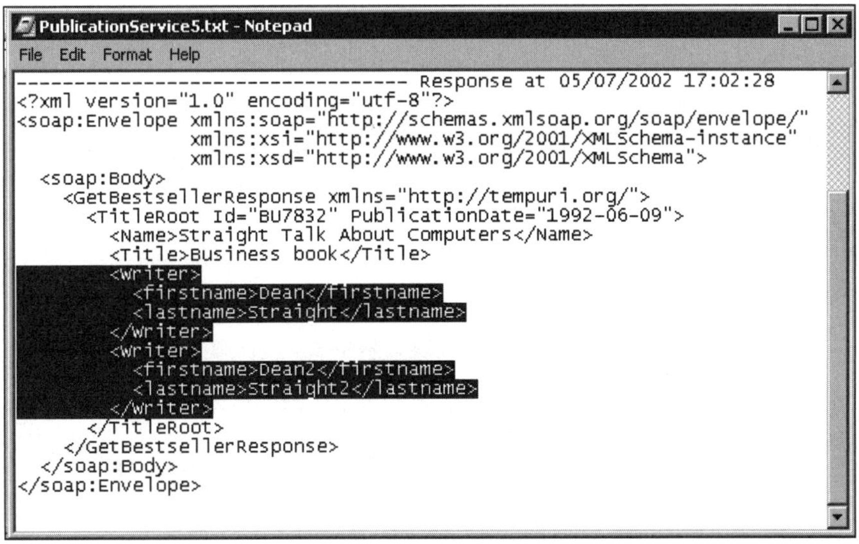

```
PublicationService5.txt - Notepad
File Edit Format Help
---------------------------------- Response at 05/07/2002 17:02:28
<?xml version="1.0" encoding="utf-8"?>
<soap:Envelope xmlns:soap="http://schemas.xmlsoap.org/soap/envelope/"
               xmlns:xsi="http://www.w3.org/2001/XMLSchema-instance"
               xmlns:xsd="http://www.w3.org/2001/XMLSchema">
  <soap:Body>
    <GetBestsellerResponse xmlns="http://tempuri.org/">
      <TitleRoot Id="BU7832" PublicationDate="1992-06-09">
        <Name>Straight Talk About Computers</Name>
        <Title>Business book</Title>
        <Writer>
          <firstname>Dean</firstname>
          <lastname>Straight</lastname>
        </Writer>
        <Writer>
          <firstname>Dean2</firstname>
          <lastname>Straight2</lastname>
        </Writer>
      </TitleRoot>
    </GetBestsellerResponse>
  </soap:Body>
</soap:Envelope>
```

Note that there is no enclosing element for the array.

Shaping Enumerations

By default, enumeration values are serialized as the name of the enumeration member. We can use the `XmlEnum` attribute to give the enumeration member a different name when it is serialized. We'll expand our title class with an enumerator for the type of title.

The `XmlEnum` attribute specifies the value to use when serializing the enumeration. Here is our class expanded with a new field for the type of title (`Publications5VB.vb`). We also use the `XmlElement` attribute to name the element.

```
Imports System
Imports System.Xml.Serialization

Namespace Publications5
```

```
Public Class Author
  Public firstname As String
  Public lastname As String
End Class

Public Enum TitleType
  <XmlEnum(Name:="Business book")> _
  business
  <XmlEnum(Name:="Modern cooking")> _
  mod_cook
  <XmlEnum(Name:="Other")> _
  other
End Enum

<XmlRoot("TitleRoot")> _
Public Class Title

  <XmlAttributeAttribute("Id")> _
  Public title_id As String

  <XmlElement(ElementName:="Name")> _
  Public title As String

  <XmlElement(ElementName:="Title")> _
  Public type As TitleType
```

When serialized with a `Title` object with the `type` field set to `business` we get:

```
--------------------------------- Response at 05/07/2002 17:02:28
<?xml version="1.0" encoding="utf-8"?>
<soap:Envelope xmlns:soap="http://schemas.xmlsoap.org/soap/envelope/"
               xmlns:xsi="http://www.w3.org/2001/XMLSchema-instance"
               xmlns:xsd="http://www.w3.org/2001/XMLSchema">
  <soap:Body>
    <GetBestsellerResponse xmlns="http://tempuri.org/">
      <TitleRoot Id="BU7832" PublicationDate="1992-06-09">
        <Name>Straight Talk About Computers</Name>
        <Title>Business book</Title>
        <Writer>
          <firstname>Dean</firstname>
          <lastname>Straight</lastname>
        </Writer>
        <Writer>
          <firstname>Dean2</firstname>
          <lastname>Straight2</lastname>
        </Writer>
      </TitleRoot>
    </GetBestsellerResponse>
  </soap:Body>
</soap:Envelope>
```

Passing Complex Data Types

The examples we have seen so far have all used simple data types, arrays, and structures. This section will show how we can pass more complex data types to and from a Web Service. Specifically, we will look at how we can pass:

- A `DataSet`
- An XML string
- Binary data

The `XmlSerializer` is able to serialize and deserialize these complex types. By passing complex data types we can do interesting things. For example: by returning a `DataSet` from a Web Service, we can use data binding and bind user interface elements to the `DataSet`. By passing binary data we can transfer images from a Web Service.

In this section we will use a Visual Studio .NET project that is available with the code download. The project is `\PWS\Ch6\DataTypesVB\DataTypesVB.sln`. You should create an application in IIS for http://localhost/PWS/Ch6/DataTypesVB.

Let us start with looking at how datasets can be used with Web Services.

Passing DataSets

The `DataSet` is part of the ADO.NET architecture. A `DataSet` may be described as a disconnected ADO `Recordset` on steroids. It can contain a single table in a similar way to a `Recordset`. It can also contain several tables and the relationships between tables. In that respect it is sort of a mini-database in memory. We may look at the data in the `DataSet` as relational data or as XML data. When serialized and transported, the `DataSet` is represented as XML. Note that although datasets are similar to recordsets in functionality, there is no explicit relationship between the ADO.NET `DataSet` and the ADO `Recordset`.

Datasets are powerful. We can bind user interface elements such as a data grid to a `DataSet`. A `DataSet` also keeps track of changes made to it so that we can have changes updated in the database.

What's more, datasets can be passed to and from a Web Service. Imagine a news service returning a set of news. On the client, we may simply bind the `DataSet` to a grid, set up the grid format, and have the `DataSet` displayed without writing any display code.

Returning a DataSet

As an example of a Web Service returning a `DataSet` we will use a service that returns a `DataSet` with rows from the `titles` table in the `pubs` database. The following Web Service was created using Visual Studio .NET. The file is available as `DataSetService.asmx.vb` in the code download. The highlighted code is the code we have added manually for our Web Service. Some of the code generated by VS.NET has been removed for brevity.

```
Imports System.Web.Services
Imports System.Data
Imports System.Data.SqlClient
```

```
<WebService(Namespace := "http://tempuri.org/")> _
Public Class DataSetService
  Inherits System.Web.Services.WebService

  ' private variable used for retrieving data from SQL server
  Private sqlAdapter As SqlDataAdapter

  Public Sub New()
    MyBase.New()

  ...

    ' declare Command builder
    Dim builder As SqlCommandBuilder

    ' select statement
    Dim sql As String = "SELECT * FROM titles"

    ' connect string to database. You may need to modify this
    Dim connstr As String = _
                      "user id=sa;password=;database=pubs;server=localhost"

    ' create data adapter
    sqlAdapter = New SqlDataAdapter(sql, connstr)

    ' generate insert, update, and delete statements automatically
    builder = New SqlCommandBuilder(sqlAdapter)
  End Sub

  ...
```

We import the `System.Data` and the `System.Data.SqlClient` namespaces. In the constructor we create a `SqlDataAdapter` that we will use to query the database. We also use the `SqlCommandBuilder` to create SQL commands for updating the database.

Now we create our first web method:

```
  <WebMethod()> _
  Public Function GetTitles() As DataSet
    Dim ds As New DataSet()
    ' queries the data base and fills the data set
    sqlAdapter.Fill(ds, "Titles")
    Return ds
  End Function
```

The `GetTitles` method returns a `DataSet`. No special code is needed to return a `DataSet`. The `XmlSerializer` is able to serialize a `DataSet` into XML.

If we test the `GetTitles` function using the test pages generated by ASP.NET, we will see the XML representation of a `DataSet`. The XML contains both a description of the data (the schema), and the actual data, some of which you can see in the screenshot below:

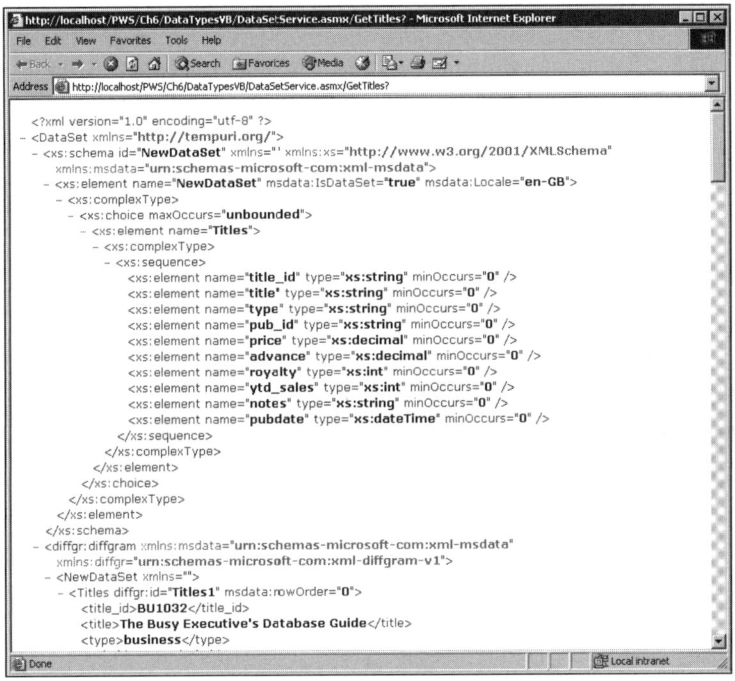

Updating Data Using a DataSet

We can also pass a `DataSet` back to a Web Service. When the data is retrieved from the Web Service it is disconnected from the database. We can work with it locally and then after some time we can send it back to the Web Service and have the data source updated. The `DataSet` keeps track of what has changed since it was retrieved from the data source.

Here is another web method we can use to update a `DataSet`:

```
<WebMethod()> _
Public Sub UpdateTitles(ds As DataSet)

  ' we call update if there are changes made
  ' to the data set
  If (ds.HasChanges()) Then
    sqlAdapter.Update(ds, "Titles")
  End If
End Sub
```

The `UpdateTitles` method checks whether there are any changes made to the `DataSet` and calls `Update` on the `sqlAdapter` to update the database.

Using DataSets on the Client

To test the `UpdateTitles` method we cannot use the ASP.NET test pages. The ASP.NET test pages use HTTP GET/POST and can only handle simple name/value parameters. Instead we build a simple Windows Forms application with a `DataGrid` control and some buttons as shown below (this is `DataSetClientVB` in the code download):

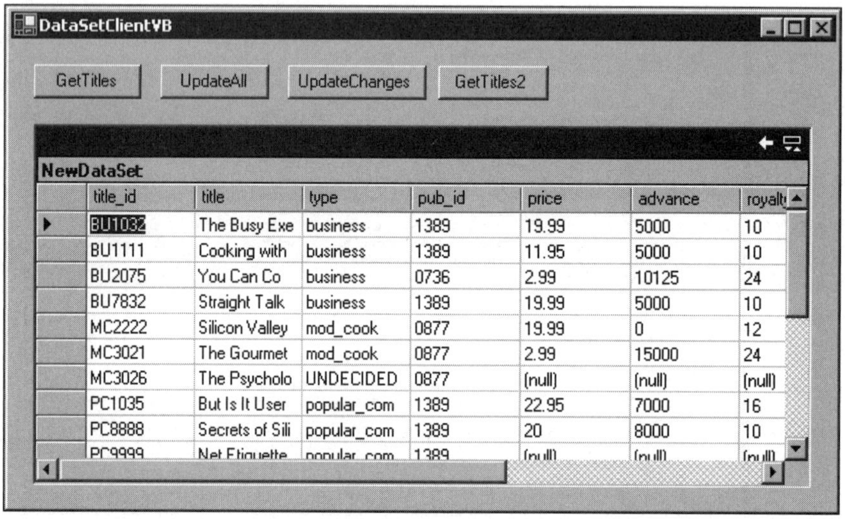

If you want to build this application yourself you can perform the following steps:

- Create a new Windows application by selecting File | New | Project... from Visual Studio .NET.
- Add a `DataGrid` from the toolbox.
- Add the buttons from the toolbox as shown in the screenshot above.
- Add a Web Reference by selecting Project | Add Web Reference... from the menu and browsing to http://localhost/PWS/Ch6/DataTypesVB/DataSetService.asmx.

The callback code for the GetTitles button is simple:

```
Private Sub button1_Click(ByVal sender As System.Object, _
                          ByVal e As System.EventArgs) _
                          Handles button1.Click
  'Declare variables
  Dim service As localhost.DataSetService
  Dim ds As DataSet

  'Create web service proxy
  service = New localhost.DataSetService()
```

```
    'Call web service
    ds = service.GetTitles()

    'Display result
    dataGrid1.DataSource = ds
End Sub
```

The callback code for the UpdateAll button is almost as simple:

```
Private Sub button2_Click(ByVal sender As System.Object, _
                          ByVal e As System.EventArgs) Handles button2.Click
    'Declare variables
    Dim service As localhost.DataSetService
    Dim ds As DataSet

    'Get data set from grid
    ds = CType(dataGrid1.DataSource, DataSet)

    'Create web service proxy
    service = New localhost.DataSetService()

    'Call web service
    service.UpdateTitles(ds)

    'Mark changes as updated
    ds.AcceptChanges()
End Sub
```

The only special thing here is the call to `AcceptChanges`. The `DataSet` keeps track of the changes made to it. After we have successfully updated the database we call `AcceptChanges` on the `DataSet`. This commits all the marked changes so that they will not be marked as changes the next time we call the Web Service.

These two callback functions are all that is needed to be able to change the data in the application. This shows the power of returning datasets from Web Services. Data binding to controls can be used in Windows applications and in Web applications.

Reducing the Amount of Data Sent

When updating the `Titles` table, a `DataSet` is sent back with all the data in the `Titles` table that was originally retrieved from the database *in addition* to the changes made to the `DataSet`. Even if we changed just a single row in the `DataSet`, it will contain a lot of data. This can be inefficient for large datasets.

The `DataSet` has functionality we can use to send only the changes back to the service. The `GetChanges` method returns a `DataSet` with only the changed data. This function is used in the callback for the UpdateChanges button:

```
Private Sub button3_Click(ByVal sender As System.Object, _
                          ByVal e As System.EventArgs) Handles button3.Click
    'Declare variables
    Dim service As localhost.DataSetService
```

```
        Dim ds As DataSet

        'Get data set from grid
        ds = CType(dataGrid1.DataSource, DataSet)

        'Create web service proxy
        service = New localhost.DataSetService()

        'Call web service with changes
        service.UpdateTitles(ds.GetChanges())

        'Mark changes as updated
        ds.AcceptChanges()
    End Sub
```

When calling `GetChanges`, a `DataSet` with only the changes is returned. This reduced `DataSet` is transmitted back to the service and can be used to update the database.

We call the `AcceptChanges` method here as well. This commits all the marked changes so that they will not be retrieved the next time we call `GetChanges`.

Strongly Typing the DataSet

The `DataSet` can be bound to controls such as a `DataGrid`. We can also navigate the `DataSet`. When we navigate the `DataSet`, we name the tables and the columns we want to retrieve. Since the client application does not know the structure of the `DataSet` in advance, late binding has to be used.

To get early binding with strong typing of tables and columns we can create a **typed `DataSet`**. A typed `DataSet` is a class deriving from `DataSet`. It has all the functionality of a `DataSet`, in addition to new accessors giving us early binding and IntelliSense.

Creating a typed `DataSet` with Visual Studio .NET is very easy. To add a typed `DataSet` to the Web Service, create a new `DataSet` item:

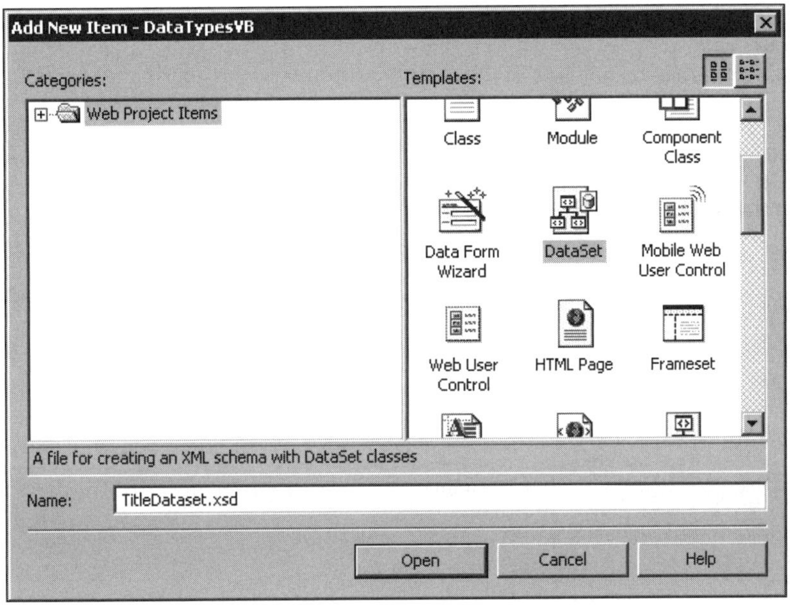

Give the `DataSet` a meaningful name. We'll name it `TitleDataset`. VS.NET creates an XML schema file, `TitleDataset.xsd`.

Now, to bind the file to a table in the database, use the Server Explorer and navigate to the `titles` table. Then drag the table onto the design surface of the XSD file.

When we build the Web Service, a typed `DataSet` is created in the `TitleDataset.vb` file. This file contains a class named `TitleDataset` that derives from `System.Data.DataSet`. The code for the typed `DataSet` is almost 600 lines, so we won't show it here.

To use the typed `DataSet` in our Web Service is a piece of cake. We simply replace `DataSet` with `TitleDataset`:

```
<WebMethod()> _
Public Function GetTitles2() As TitleDataset
  Dim ds As New TitleDataset()
  sqlAdapter.Fill(ds, "Titles")
  Return ds
End Function
```

To get IntelliSense on the client side, we must update our proxy code. The proxy code is the code added to our client when we add the web reference. If we don't update the proxy code, the client will still work since all the functionality of the DataSet is preserved by our derived typed DataSet.

> **When we change the interface of the Web Service we need to regenerate the proxy. In Visual Studio .NET this is done by right-clicking on the web reference and selecting Update Web Reference.**

After updating the client proxy, we can also navigate the DataSet using strongly-typed accessors. Here is the callback for the GetTitles2 button:

```
Private Sub button4_Click(ByVal sender As System.Object, _
                          ByVal e As System.EventArgs) Handles button4.Click
  'Declare variables
  Dim service As localhost.DataSetService
  Dim ds As localhost.TitleDataset

  'Create web service proxy
  service = New localhost.DataSetService()

  'Call web service
  ds = service.GetTitles2()

  'Display result
  dataGrid1.DataSource = ds

  'Iterate through result
  Dim row As localhost.TitleDataset.titlesRow
  For Each row In ds.titles.Rows
    If (row.title_id = "BU1032") Then
      MessageBox.Show(row.title)
    End If
  Next
End Sub
```

In addition to displaying the DataSet in the grid, we iterate through the DataSet and display the title of one selected book:

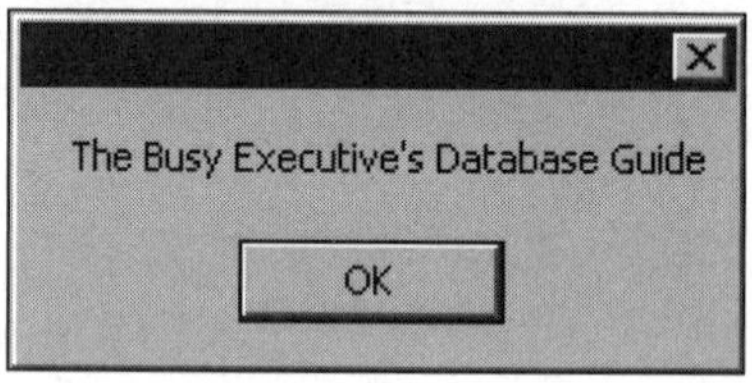

By using a typed `DataSet` we get the advantage of IntelliSense in Visual Studio .NET. We also get strong typing and compile-time checking of access to columns. It is much better to detect typing errors at compile time than at run time.

XML Strings

In some cases we might have an XML string that we want to return from a Web Service. This may be, for instance, an XML string returned from a legacy COM component.

Many different ways have been used in the past to send data between the tiers in an n-tier application, including variant arrays, disconnected ADO Recordsets, and objects. Lately many have started using XML as the data carrier technology in their COM-based architecture.

If a business COM component returning an XML string is to be exposed as a Web Service using ASP.NET, how can the XML be returned from the Web Service? From ASP.NET we can access the COM component by using COM Interop.

The next question is, how can the XML string be returned from the Web Service? Here we will look at the following ways of returning the XML string:

- Returning the raw XML string as a parameter.
- Strongly typing the XML by creating a schema.

Returning the XML String

We are using an XML string in the format we got from our `XmlSerializer` example earlier. The file is available in the code download as `\PWS\Ch6\titles.xml`.

```
<?xml version="1.0" encoding="utf-8"?>
<Title xmlns:xsd="http://www.w3.org/2001/XMLSchema"
       xmlns:xsi="http://www.w3.org/2001/XMLSchema-instance"
       xmlns="http://tempuri.org/">
  <title_id>BU7832</title_id>
  <title>Straight Talk About Computers</title>
  <pubdate>1992-06-09T00:00:00.0000000+02:00</pubdate>
  <price>19.99</price>
  <Author>
    <firstname>Dean</firstname>
    <lastname>Straight</lastname>
  </Author>
  <Author>
    <firstname>Dean2</firstname>
    <lastname>Straight2</lastname>
  </Author>
</Title>
```

Returning this from a Web Service as a string is simple. We simply declare the return type from our web method to be a string. The following example is available in the code download as `XmlService.asmx.vb`.

```
Imports System.Web.Services
Imports System.Xml.Serialization

<WebService(Namespace := "http://tempuri.org/")> _
Public Class XmlService
  Inherits System.Web.Services.WebService

...

  <WebMethod()> _
  Public Function GetXMLString() As String

    Return ReadXmlFile()
  End Function

  <WebMethod()> _
  Public Function GetXmlTitles() As Title

    Dim serializer As XmlSerializer
    Dim reader As System.IO.StringReader
    Dim str As String

    serializer = New XmlSerializer(GetType(Title))

    Str = ReadXmlFile()

    reader = New System.IO.StringReader(Str)

    Return CType(serializer.Deserialize(reader), Title)
  End Function

  Private Function ReadXmlFile() As String

    Dim reader As System.IO.StreamReader
    reader = New System.IO.StreamReader( _
        "C:\inetpub\wwwroot\PWS\Ch6\titles.xml")

    Return reader.ReadToEnd()

  End Function
End Class
```

There are two issues with returning the raw string:

- The SOAP message does not actually contain XML. It contains an XML-encoded string.
- The WSDL does not indicate the schema of the returned XML. We need to communicate the schema to the consumers of our Web Service some other way.

To see the first point, we can look at the XML that is sent over the wire:

```
<?xml version="1.0" encoding="utf-8"?>
<soap:Envelope xmlns:soap="http://schemas.xmlsoap.org/soap/envelope/"
xmlns:xsi="http://www.w3.org/2001/XMLSchema-instance"
xmlns:xsd="http://www.w3.org/2001/XMLSchema">
  <soap:Body>
  <GetXMLStringResponse xmlns="http://tempuri.org/">
    <GetXMLStringResult>&lt;?xml version="1.0" encoding="utf-16"?&gt;
&lt;Title xmlns:xsi="http://www.w3.org/2001/XMLSchema-instance"
     xmlns:xsd="http://www.w3.org/2001/XMLSchema"&gt;
  &lt;title_id&gt;BU7832&lt;/title_id&gt;
  &lt;title&gt;Straight Talk About Computers&lt;/title&gt;
... stuff removed
&lt;/Title&gt;
</GetXMLStringResult>
  </GetXMLStringResponse>
  </soap:Body>
</soap:Envelope>
```

As we can see, the XML angle brackets are escaped using `<` and `>`. If we look at the WSDL we see that the schema only defines the return type as a string:

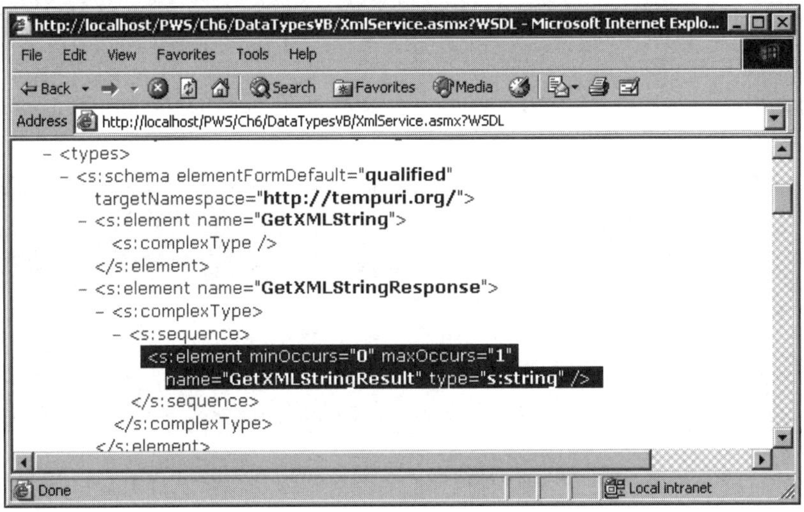

The consumer is able to reconstruct the XML from this string, but it is clearly not an optimal way to send the XML. Nevertheless, returning the XML as a string is simple and all SOAP implementations should be able to handle a string.

Returning Strongly-Typed Data Structures

We may instead create an XML schema for our XML structure and use the schema in our code. We could write the schema by hand, and in our simple case this should be quite feasible.

The .NET Framework provides a tool that makes this job much easier. The XML Schemas/Datatype Support utility (`xsd.exe`) is able to generate schemas from XML files, generate classes from schemas, generate typed datasets from schemas, and more.

To return strongly-typed data structures we will do the following:

- Create an XML schema, `titles.xsd`, from the `titles.xml` file.
- Create a VB.NET class file, `titles.vb`, from the `titles.xsd` file.
- Use the `XmlSerializer` class in our Web Service to return the structure.

To start off, we need a sample of our XML structure in an XML file. We use the `titles.xml` that is available with the code download. We run the `xsd.exe` utility on this file:

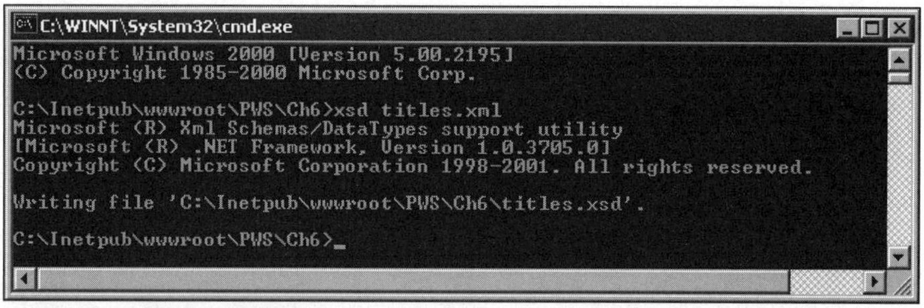

This generates an XML schema definition for the XML. We then run the `xsd.exe` tool again, this time on the `XSD` file we just generated:

This generates a VB.NET file with classes representing our structure. Here is the code generated:

```
'------------------------------------------------------------------------------
' <autogenerated>
'     This code was generated by a tool.
'     Runtime Version: 1.0.3705.0
'
'     Changes to this file may cause incorrect behavior and will be lost if
'     the code is regenerated.
' </autogenerated>
'------------------------------------------------------------------------------
```

```
Option Strict Off
Option Explicit On

Imports System.Xml.Serialization

'
'This source code was auto-generated by xsd, Version=1.0.3705.0.
'

'<remarks/>
<System.Xml.Serialization.XmlTypeAttribute([Namespace]:="http://tempuri.org/"), _
 System.Xml.Serialization.XmlRootAttribute([Namespace]:="http://tempuri.org/", _
 IsNullable:=false)> _
Public Class Title

  '<remarks/>
  Public title_id As String

  '<remarks/>
  Public title As String

  '<remarks/>
  Public pubdate As String

  '<remarks/>
  Public price As String

  '<remarks/>
  <System.Xml.Serialization.XmlElementAttribute("Author")> _
  Public Author() As TitleAuthor
End Class

'<remarks/>
<System.Xml.Serialization.XmlTypeAttribute([Namespace]:="http://tempuri.org/")> _
Public Class TitleAuthor

  '<remarks/>
  Public firstname As String

  '<remarks/>
  Public lastname As String
End Class

'<remarks/>
<System.Xml.Serialization.XmlTypeAttribute([Namespace]:="http://tempuri.org/"), _
 System.Xml.Serialization.XmlRootAttribute("NewDataSet", _
[Namespace]:="http://tempuri.org/", IsNullable:=false)> _
Public Class NewDataSet

  '<remarks/>
  <System.Xml.Serialization.XmlElementAttribute("Title")> _
  Public Items() As Title
End Class
```

As we can see, the classes have attributes applied to them so that the `XmlSerializer` can map between objects and XML.

Here is a Web Service method that returns an object of the generated type `Title`. The method is available in the `XmlService.asmx.vb` file in the code download:

```
<WebMethod()> _
<WebMethod()> _
Public Function GetXmlTitles() As Title

  Dim serializer As XmlSerializer
  Dim reader As System.IO.StringReader
  Dim thetitle As Title
  Dim str As String

  serializer = New XmlSerializer(GetType(Title))
  str = ReadXmlFile()

  reader = New StringReader(str)

  If True Then
    Try
      Dim obj As Object
      obj = serializer.Deserialize(reader)

      thetitle = CType(obj, Title)
    Catch err As Exception

    End Try
      Return thetitle
  End If

End Function
```

As we can see, no explicit code is required to map from XML to the class. This is all handled by the `XmlSerializer` using the attributed class.

Our WSDL file now contains a description of the structure we are returning:

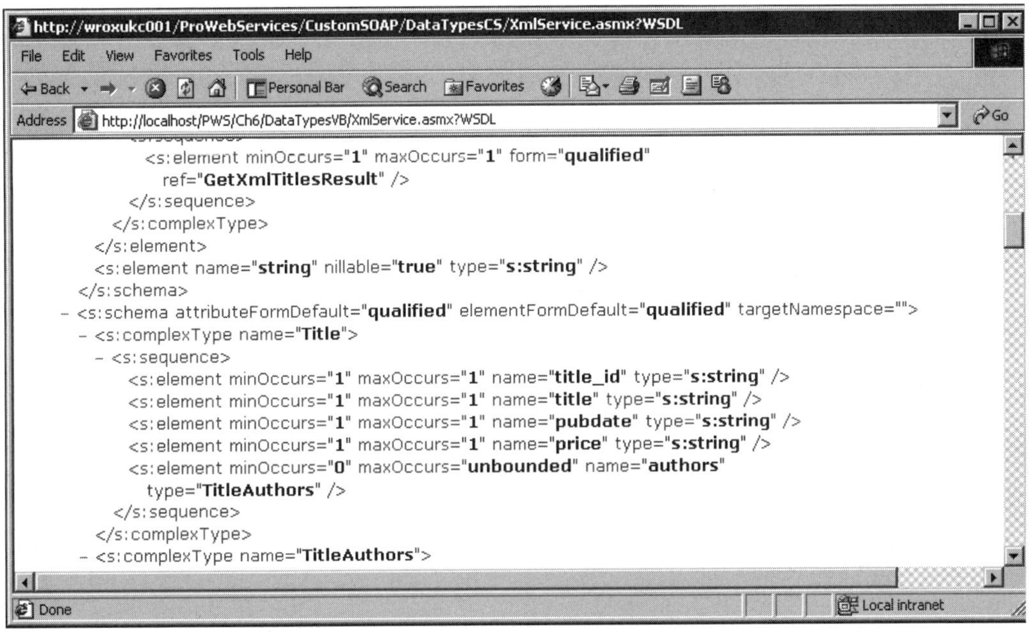

When generating proxy code from this WSDL file, we will get strongly-typed access to the structure in the XML string. This makes the work of programming the client application much easier. If we return the raw XML string it has to be parsed. Using a strongly-typed proxy we can access the fields in the XML string directly. The WSDL file also serves as documentation for the data returned by the Web Service.

Using the `xsd.exe` tool, we can also create a typed `DataSet` by typing:

```
xsd titles.xsd /dataset /language:vb
```

By generating a `DataSet` we get all the flexibility of the `DataSet` that we saw in the previous section, for instance binding user interface elements to the `DataSet`.

Binary Data

We may pass binary data to and from a Web Service. Passing binary data can be used for a variety of purposes: for passing word documents, PDF files, images, and so on. A simple way to pass binary data is to send it as an array of bytes.

The code download contains a simple example that returns an image on the hard disk. The Web Service is available in `DataTypesVB\BinaryService.asmx.vb`.

```
<WebMethod()> _
Public Function GetImage(ByVal filename As String) As Byte()

   ' Declare variables
```

```
    Dim myBitmap As System.Drawing.Bitmap
    Dim stream As System.IO.MemoryStream

    ' Create memory stream to
    stream = New System.IO.MemoryStream()

    Try
      ' Create Bitmap from file
      myBitmap = New System.Drawing.Bitmap(filename)

      ' Save image as JPEG to stream
      myBitmap.Save(stream, System.Drawing.Imaging.ImageFormat.Jpeg)

      ' Return array representation
      Return stream.ToArray()
    Catch err As Exception
      ' If file does not exist, we return an empty array
      Return Nothing

    End Try
  End Function
```

We need to make sure that we have set a reference to the `System.Drawing.dll` assembly using Project | Add Reference.

The `Bitmap` class in the `System.Drawing` namespace does all the hard work in this method. Calling `Save` on a `Bitmap` object serializes the data into a memory stream. The memory stream has a method named `ToArray` that writes the entire stream contents to a byte array.

To test this function we create a simple Windows Forms application that takes a filename as a parameter and displays the image. The test application is available in the directory `BinaryClientVB` in the code download.

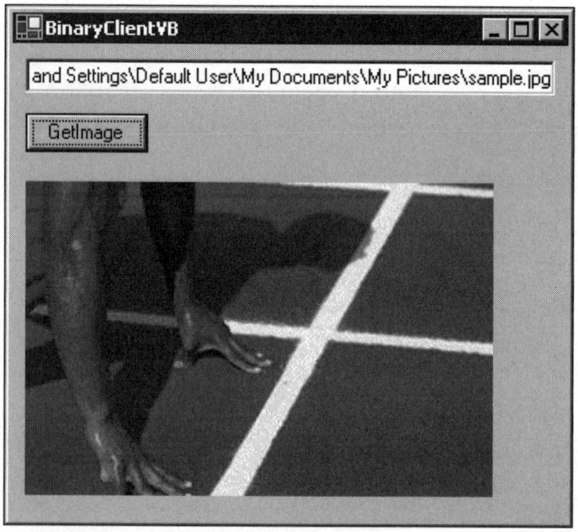

The code for the GetImage button callback is simple:

```
Private Sub button1_Click(ByVal sender As System.Object, _
                          ByVal e As System.EventArgs) Handles button1.Click
  'Declare variables
  Dim service As localhost.BinaryService
  Dim bytes As Byte()
  Dim stream As System.IO.MemoryStream
  Dim Image As Bitmap

  ' Create web service proxy
  service = New localhost.BinaryService()

  ' Call web service
  bytes = service.GetImage(textBox1.Text)

  'Create image from array
  If (Not bytes Is Nothing) Then
    stream = New System.IO.MemoryStream(bytes)
    Image = New Bitmap(stream)

    'Display image
    pictureBox1.Image = Image

  Else
    MessageBox.Show("No image returned")
  End If
End Sub
```

The `GetImage` method returns a byte array. A `MemoryStream` is created from the byte array. Then we create a `Bitmap` object and give it the stream in the constructor. To display the image we use a `PictureBox` control.

The SOAP message returned contains the byte array. Here is a snippet of the SOAP message:

```
<?xml version="1.0" encoding="utf-8"?>
<soap:Envelope xmlns:soap="http://schemas.xmlsoap.org/soap/envelope/"
xmlns:xsi="http://www.w3.org/2001/XMLSchema-instance"
xmlns:xsd="http://www.w3.org/2001/XMLSchema">
  <soap:Body>
  <GetImageResponse xmlns="http://tempuri.org/">
<GetImageResult>/9j/4AAQSkZJRgABAgAAZABkAAD//gASQWRvYmUgSW1hZ2VSZWFkef/sABFEdWNreQ
ABAAQAAAAuAAD/7gAOQWRvYmUAZMAAAAAB/9sAQwAKBwcHBwcKBwcKDg
... removed lots
kICQ4QDAoKDBATDw8QD//2Q==</GetImageResult>
  </GetImageResponse>
  </soap:Body>
</soap:Envelope>
```

Summary

This chapter described various ways by which we can get more control over the XML passed to and from Web Services. The techniques covered are pretty advanced, and in many cases we can create excellent Web Services without them.

There are cases when we need to get under the hood and extend and customize the functionality provided by ASP.NET:

- When we need to modify the XML in the SOAP messages before it is sent and after it is received.
- When we need to sort out interoperability problems with other SOAP implementations.

With this in mind we looked at:

- SOAP Extensions as a powerful mechanism by which we can get access to the SOAP stream before and after it is serialized. We wrote an extension that writes SOAP messages to the Event Log. SOAP Extensions can also be used to modify the SOAP message. This can be used for compression, encryption, and so on. Chapter 14 covers encryption using SOAP extensions.
- Ways in which we can shape the XML used in the SOAP message. The `XmlSerializer` class is used under the hood of ASP.NET Web Services. Using attributes we can, for instance, specify that a field should be serialized as an XML attribute instead of as an XML element.
- How we can pass complex data types such as datasets, XML strings, and binary data.

PROFESSIONAL
ASP.NET
WEB
SERVICES

7

Web Service Discovery

Let me guess. You've just completed the greatest Web Service in the civilized world, put it on a computer that's attached to the Internet, and you're wondering why no one's using it. You sit back and all of a sudden it dawns on you, instead of being a developer you've now got something else to consider. You need to market your Web Service.

With the onset of Web Service technology and ASP.NET, our industry role is changing; it's all very well developing that Web Service, but if no one uses it you might as well have developed a component DLL instead. Discovery can help you advertise (this is a dirty word in some quarters, but we'd better get used to it with Web Services) your functionality by giving you some unique tools and standards to allow you to tell people that you exist.

Component development up until now has been a process of allowing people to download a utility and if they like it, carry on using it. You can use that technique with Web Services by simply telling people where your WSDL file is. However, this chapter explains that there is much, much more to discovery than simply giving someone your WSDL file. Discovery can be used to save you enormous amounts of time by keeping your own libraries of past work, or by telling millions of developers about that new Web Service you've got rather than the few thousand that actually visit a single ASP.NET web site.

As developers we must consider the following. Instead of thinking I'm a VB.NET or C# programmer, I am now a developer that creates functionality for EVERY operating system. By adopting ASP.NET you can expand the number of platforms where your functionality can be used by thousands, overnight.

This chapter will enlighten you about how you can utilize Web Service discovery to tell the world about what you're doing and hopefully put you and your Web Services ahead of the game.

Web Service Discovery is the process of locating and interrogating Web Service definitions, which is a preliminary step for accessing a Web Service. It is through this discovery process that Web Service clients learn that a Web Service exists, what its capabilities are, and how to properly interact with it. There are several methods of promoting your Web Service to the outside world with the tools in ASP.NET, although most have a common result: the creation of a predefined XML-formatted file that can be read to advise interested parties of where your Web Services are.

> **The term "Web Service Discovery" is often referred to as simply DISCO.**

DISCO first of all came into conception as a file that simply wrapped together XML Web Services that a Web Service developer wanted others to use. It has now become apparent that Microsoft will be using this open standard as their de facto standard for discovering Web Services from within ASP.NET. Fundamentally speaking it's here to stay.

The term DISCO, although now often associated with ASP.NET technology, is designed as an open standard making it freely available for all to use. However, currently it has not been submitted to W3C along with other well-known Web Services standards such as SOAP and WSDL. As an open standard it is not specifically designed for ASP.NET but can be incorporated within a client or search engine that chooses to understand how DISCO files are constructed. DISCO has currently had no significant adoption from the industry outside of ASP.NET and for the moment seems to be remaining solely within the ASP.NET technology suite of applications.

In this chapter we'll cover the basics of promoting your Web Services as well as some advanced ideas about how you can make sure that your Web Service is used by others without reproducing work you or other development teams have done previously.

Here's what we'll cover in this chapter:

- How to use discovery to advertise Web Services
- Solving some of those intrinsic problems about component and resource sharing between teams
- Realizing that discovery is an essential part of programming even for the sole developer

Essential Changes to Your Version of VS.NET

Many of the examples used within this chapter describe the display of a file with the suffix `.vsdisco` – this file is automatically generated every time a user attempts to view it. However, this automatic generation has been turned off in the final release version of .NET so it's essential that you make the following changes to use the examples explained within this chapter. Please follow these steps to ensure your version of VS.NET is set up correctly:

- First of all you need to locate a file called `machine.config`. This file contains setup information for your VS.NET applications. It will reside in the `CONFIG` subdirectory of the root directory where the runtime is installed, for example

```
C:\WINNT\Microsoft.NET\Framework\v1.0.3705\CONFIG\machine.config
```

You may need to change the above to the version of the framework you are running, as an example the first production release of VS.NET came out with framework version v1.0.3705.

- Now edit the `machine.config` file using a simple editor such as Notepad, then search for `vsdisco` within your file. You will now be presented with code similar to the following:

```
<httpHandlers>
  <!--<add verb="*" path="*.vsdisco"
  type="System.Web.Services.Discovery.DiscoveryRequestHandler,
  System.Web.Services, Version=1.0.3300.0, Culture=neutral,
  PublicKeyToken=b03f5f7f11d50a3a" validate="false"/>-->
</httpHandlers>
```

Note that the line containing the `vsdisco` entry you just searched for has been commented out, (see the comment tags `<!--` and `-->` above). You must uncomment this line by removing the comment tags.

- Now either restart IIS or reboot your server for the changes to take effect.

Why Do We Need Discovery?

Discovering Web Services is an important part of Web Service development. However, it is currently too often ignored. Without discovery, you would simply end up developing a Web Service that could not be found by others.

Web Service discovery is broken up into two distinct types:

- Web Services developed for private or internal use within an organization or limited group
- Web Services developed for public or external use on the Internet

The idea behind Web Service discovery is to allow your functionality (whichever of the above types you select) to be used by others. Therefore, for the first time, component promotion is being seen as part of the entire development process, not as some additional service you perform at the end of a development cycle.

To explain a little of how discovery can benefit you, let's discuss a number of scenarios where Web Service discovery really comes into its own:

Scenario 1

Working inside a development team can be interesting but often exasperating. Not mentioning any names, the worst I came across was one contract where our manager approached us and asked us why we were developing a utility to work out whether a zip code was correctly formatted. Anyway, after much deliberation the manager decided to walk around each team in turn, and subsequently found eight teams all either having done or doing exactly the same utility to check for a correctly formatted zip code.

Everyone who's worked in large corporate teams realizes that this isn't unusual; in fact, some would even say it was the norm.

By producing a central library, which contains DISCO-formatted files that can be shared by all the development teams, these teams can develop Web Services and immediately make them available for others to use. This library then forms the central repository for Web Services within an organization meaning common components can be reused very easily, therefore significantly reducing development overlap.

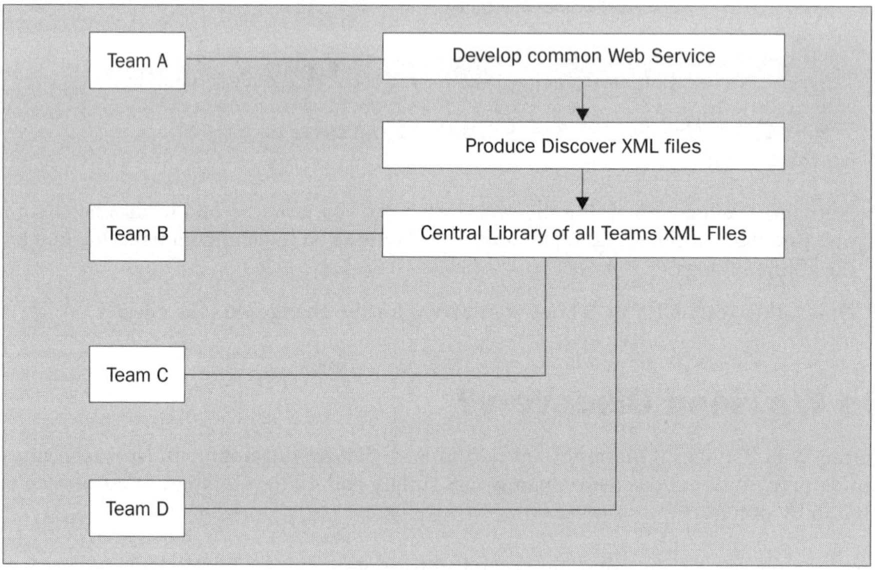

Scenario 2

Releasing products used to mean producing EXEs or packages that needed to be installed on other companies' computers. This technique often leads to confusing installation problems and techniques along with compatibility concerns.

Using discovery, however, you can now release many Web Services from different ASP.NET projects and even different operating systems using one single DISCO XML file. This allows you to promote your system as a package of functionality rather than as individual Web Services.

The Three Main Discovery XML Files

When a Web Service is created, you create a suite of additional discovery XML files that contain information to help other clients find out what Web Services you have available. Let's go through our first example to help describe the three main files that are common to Web Service discovery:

- `.disco`
- `.vsdisco`
- `.map`

The .disco File

For our first example, we need to create an ASP.NET Web Service project called `Discovery1`. It does not matter which language you choose as the creation of these XML files is the same for each, however during the examples in this chapter we will predominantly be using VB.NET.

- After opening a VS.NET session, select File | New | Project.
- Then create an ASP.NET Web Service project called Discovery1.

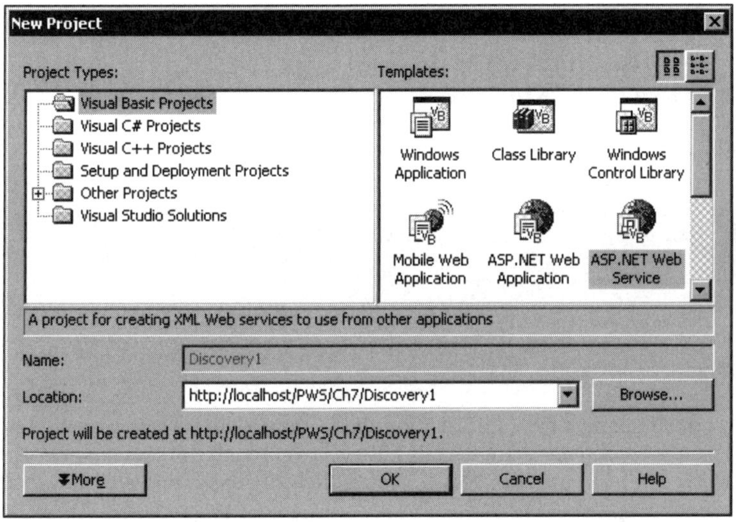

After the project has been created, select View, then Solution Explorer to see the following window displayed:

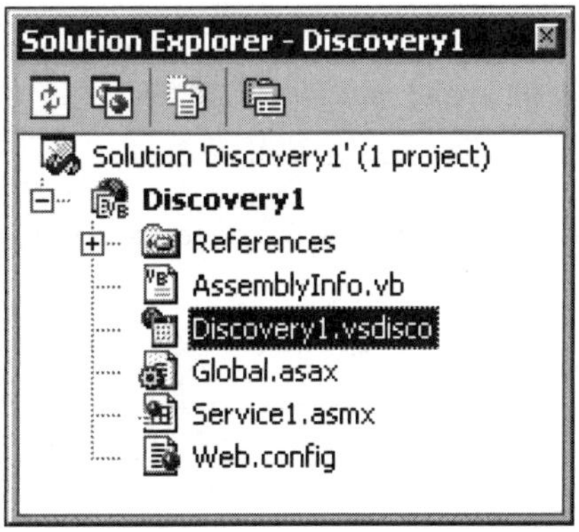

You may already be familiar with some of these automatically generated files but let us explain further the associated discovery files contained within this project:

The first area we're interested in is the `Service1.asmx` file. This VS.NET project dynamically generates the `.disco` XML file when you browse a specific Web Service (`.asmx`) and suffix it with `?disco`. To display the `.disco` file, follow these steps:

- Select the Debug menu
- Select the Start menu option
- Wait for Internet Explorer to be displayed
- Type on the address line the following URL and hit enter: http://localhost/PWS/Ch7/Discovery1/Service1.asmx?disco

The `.disco` file will be displayed and will look like this:

```
<?xml version="1.0" encoding="utf-8" ?>
<discovery xmlns:xsd=http://www.w3.org/2001/XMLSchema
           xmlns:xsi=http://www.w3.org/2001/XMLSchema-instance
           xmlns="http://schemas.xmlsoap.org/disco"/>
  <contractRef ref="http://localhost/PWS/Ch7/Discovery1/Service1.asmx?wsdl"
               docRef=" http://localhost/PWS/Ch7/Discovery1/Service1.asmx"
               xmlns="http://schemas.xmlsoap.org/disco/scl/" />
</discovery>
```

The above `.disco` file contains the information that is most relevant when promoting your Web Service. The description of the structure of this file is covered later in this chapter. You may have noticed that we have not yet actually created any publicly available methods within the `.asmx` Web Service file for anyone to run.

Therefore, before we continue, let's actually create a method within our Web Service to see how it affects our `.disco` file. To do this:

- Click on the `Service1.asmx` file
- Press the right mouse button and select View Code
- Uncomment the example `HelloWorld` web method

Now let's view the `.disco` file again by starting the project and using the `?disco` suffix:

```
<?xml version="1.0" encoding="utf-8" ?>
<discovery xmlns:xsd=http://www.w3.org/2001/XMLSchema
           xmlns:xsi=http://www.w3.org/2001/XMLSchema-instance
           xmlns="http://schemas.xmlsoap.org/disco"/>
  <contractRef ref=" http://localhost/PWS/Ch7/Discovery1/Service1.asmx?wsdl"
               docRef=" http://localhost/PWS/Ch7/Discovery1/Service1.asmx"
               xmlns="http://schemas.xmlsoap.org/disco/scl/" />
  <soap address="http://localhost/PWS/Ch7/Discovery1/Service1.asmx"
        xmlns:q1="http://tempuri.org/"
        binding="q1:Service1Soap"
        xmlns="http://schemas.xmlsoap.org/disco/soap/" />
</discovery>
```

A new element has been added to the `.disco` file: the `<soap>` element reproduces a portion of the binding information found within a WSDL schema. It does this to allow a Web Service client to locate a service using lightweight information. Therefore, rather than having to load the WSDL schema file every time it needs to find the relevant information, it uses this summary information within the `.disco` file to identify the contents of a specific WSDL file.

This `<soap>` element is actually optional information – it does not have to be included for the `.disco` file to be used within a discovery process. The information it contains identifies the binding information. Binding information is directly correlated to the transport that is acceptable for a Web Service, so if you are after a Web Service (you know its HTTP location) but you specifically want the SOAP transport, only then will the `<soap>` element advise you whether it's available.

Structure of the .disco File

Discovery is performed by the creation of an XML file with a `.disco` extension. It is not compulsory to create a discovery file for each Web Service. In some cases you may not wish to supply the `.disco` file, because (for example) your Web Service is going to be consumed by another non-ASP.NET client that does not understand the `.disco` file format. In this case you can simply supply the location of the WSDL schema instead.

The DISCO standard is based around a strictly defined XML-structured file that is freely available for Web Service clients to read to ascertain what Web Services are available. In the case of ASP.NET, this file is created at run time by the ASP.NET runtime when you browse to the `.asmx` file for a specific Web Service project. During creation, the file is cached within the ASP.NET runtime. Subsequent calls are therefore faster.

As previously mentioned it is not a mandatory requirement that a `.disco` file is created along with the Web Service. In fact, we can create our own `.disco` file, independently of the `.asmx` file, that can be placed on another Internet server (such as IIS) to point towards our Web Service (more about this later in the *Creating Your Own .disco File* section). This advanced customization can be used to create a series of linking DISCO files that promote packages of functionality combining multiple Web Services. Even though we have this flexibility to create our own custom `.disco` files away from the original project it does not mean that our project's `.disco` file is suppressed. In fact these files are always created.

This XML `.disco` file uses XML attributes and elements to supply a Web Service client with information as to the location of Web Services that may be available on our server.

An example of an XML-structured `.disco` file is shown below. The following file contains all the elements and attributes that are supported by the DISCO standard:

```
<?xml version="1.0" encoding="utf-8"?>
<discovery xmlns:xsd=http://www.w3.org/2001/XMLSchema
           xmlns:xsi=http://www.w3.org/2001/XMLSchema-instance
           xmlns="http://schemas.xmlsoap.org/disco/">
  <contractRef ref="http://localhost/PWS/Ch7/discovery1/service1.asmx?wsdl"
               docRef="http://localhost/PWS/Ch7/discovery1/service1.asmx"
               xmlns="http://schemas.xmlsoap.org/disco/scl/" />
  <soap address="http://localhost/PWS/Ch7/discovery1/service1.asmx"
        xmlns:q1="http://tempuri.org/"
        binding="q1:Service1Soap"
        xmlns="http://schemas.xmlsoap.org/disco/soap/" />
  <schemaRef ref="http://localhost/PWS/Ch7/discovery1/xmlfile1.xml"
```

```
               xmlns="http://schemas.xmlsoap.org/disco/schema/" />
  <discoveryRef ref="http://localhost/PWS/Ch7/discovery1/service1.asmx?disco"
                xmlns="http://schemas.xmlsoap.org/disco/" />
</discovery>
```

The above DISCO file contains links to WSDL files (<contractRef>) that describe the methods and arguments that a specific Web Service has available for a remote Web Service client to consume. In addition there are other elements: <soap>, <schemaRef>, and <discoverRef> which will be covered later within this chapter.

As previously mentioned there is one .disco file for every ASP.NET Web Service .asmx file. However, .disco files can in fact point to other .disco files (see the <discoveryRef> element) to allow for multiple Web Service promotion.

The previous .disco file shows the five main constituent parts:

- Header (discovery element)
- Contract (contractRef element)
- Discovery (discoveryRef element)
- Schema (schemaRef element)
- Soap Binding (soap element)

Please note that URL locations defined within any .disco element are either specific or relative. If the location is relative, paths are always relative to the location of the .disco file.

In the following sections, we'll describe the attributes and structure for each of these elements, and we'll give an indication as to how they can be used in some real-world scenarios.

discovery Element

This section is mandatory and defines the XML header along with all relevant namespaces. It contains the mandatory discovery namespace, http://schemas.xmlsoap.org/disco/. For those not familiar with XML constructs, this simply states that this file conforms to the XML DISCO standard. It does not in this case point towards a specific Internet file that contains that standard definition, though it should be noted that often this is the case with other XML standard definitions. In addition, two other namespaces are mentioned within this element, which again signify standards to which this particular XML-formatted file conforms.

This brings up an interesting thought about namespaces, because this namespace defines the DISCO namespace. The elements within this XML-structured file only exist because that namespace standard definition states that they should exist. For example, the DISCO namespace states that there can be zero or more <discoveryRef> elements within a .disco file.

This leads us to the point about customization: we can in fact extend the DISCO format by creating our own DISCO format. For example http://www.anycompany.org/myformat.xsd may actually define an additional standard which extends a basic DISCO standard. See the following file:

```
<disco:discovery xmlns:disco="http://www.anycompany.org/myformat.xsd" >
  <contractRef ref=""
               docRef=""?
               xmlns="http://schemas.xmlsoap.org/disco/scl/"? > *
  <webserviceDescription ref=""
                         xmlns="http://www.anycompany.org/wsdesc/"? > *
  <discoveryRef ref=""
                xmlns="http://schemas.xmlsoap.org/disco/"? > *
  <schemaRef ref=""
             xmlns="http://schemas.xmlsoap.org/disco/schema/"? > *
  <soap ref=""
        binding=""
        xmlns="http://schemas.xmlsoap.org/disco/soap/"? > *
</disco:discovery>
```

This advanced option is a little out of context for this chapter, however, one interesting point to note is that the above definition describes the current `.disco` XML standard but also significantly adds a new element to the standard called the `<webserviceDescription>` element. This ability to extend the schema definition allows you to add additional definition files, information, documentation, and so on to the original DISCO standard in order to suit your own potentially unique requirements. An example of this would be a development team that required a version or release number attached to each `.disco` file, which changed every time a Web Service changed that was pointed to by this `.disco` file.

contractRef Element

The `<contractRef>` element defines the location of the WSDL schema, but in addition can also include the URL location of some help or another Web Service description document.

Here is an example of the `<contractRef>` element:

```
<contractRef ref="http://localhost/PWS/Ch7/Discovery1/Service1.asmx?wsdl"
             docRef="http://localhost/PWS/Ch7/Discovery1/Service1.asmx"
             xmlns="http://schemas.xmlsoap.org/disco/scl/" />
```

This element contains the location information for the WSDL schema file within the `ref` XML attribute.

```
ref="http://localhost/PWS/Ch7/Discovery1/Service1.asmx?wsdl"
```

The WSDL schema file describes the Web Service methods, arguments, and the Web Service's server location. Please note that appending the `?wsdl` parameter to the end of the `.asmx` file location will always display the WSDL schema file, which describes the Web Service using an XML definition.

The `<contractRef>` element also contains the optional `docRef` attribute, which identifies the location of an associated page, which can contain any HTML browser-readable text:

```
docRef="http://localhost/PWS/Ch7/Discovery1/Service1.asmx"
```

This text could contain any of (but is not limited to) the following subjects:

- Help
- Testing tools (for example an ASP.NET .asmx file)
- Service level agreement
- Company information

By default, the docRef attribute link is automatically generated for ASP.NET and points to the .asmx file. This page allows us to test a Web Service using a web browser front end, which is built by ASP.NET, as we have seen in previous chapters.

> **We can specify multiple contractRef elements within one .disco file, however, Visual Studio .NET automatically limits this functionality to one contractRef element per generated .asmx?disco file.**

It's worth noting that the DISCO standard specifies that only WSDL schema files can be identified using this element, making the WSDL file type **the only currently supported** use of the contractRef element. This support is identified by the use of the http://schemas.xmlsoap.org/disco/scl/ namespace (the DISCO standard). However, we can also use other namespace definitions, allowing us to extend the use of the DISCO standard. To do this we would need to define (using an XML definition) a new namespace, for example http://www.newnamespace.com/yournamespace.xml, and then change the namespace name within this element to match the new definition being used. That namespace then needs to be defined using an XML definitions file to describe a new file type that can be used within this element.

discoveryRef Element

The <discoveryRef> element allows us to further extend the abilities of our .disco file. We can use this mechanism to point to other .disco files either on other servers or within our own localhost. It's worth noting that the linking of .disco files is primarily to allow automated search engines, such as www.salcentral.com, to browse through Web Services using a tree-like structure, discovering Web Services and using this information to populate their search database.

The following diagram shows how multiple `.disco` files can create a peer-to-peer structure for the discovery of Web Services:

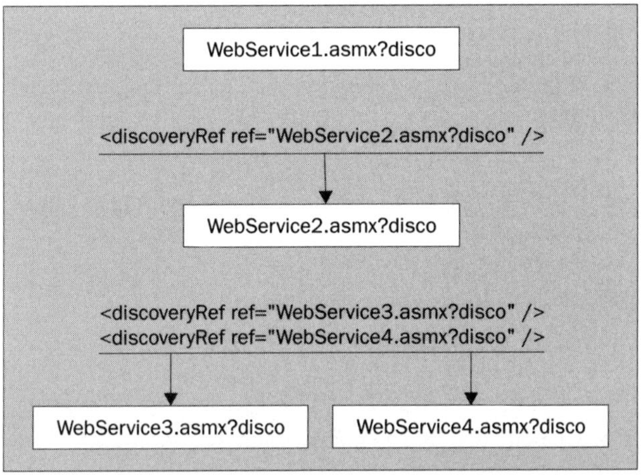

Although this element is available within the `.disco` file, there is currently no method of adding it to a definition for an `.asmx` file. However, as the `.vsdisco` format shares the same structure as the `.disco` file, this extremely powerful element can be utilized successfully, as we will see later.

schemaRef Element

The `<schemaRef>` element allows us to attach an XML schema definition to the `.disco` file. This allows extra information to be encapsulated within the `.disco` file to describe data types being transferred within the Web Service:

```
<schemaRef ref="http://localhost/PWS/Ch7/discovery1/xmlfile1.xml" />
```

An example of when this would be used is when we have created a Web Service which creates its own data type using an XML parser, or by simply concatenating string elements together in a preordained fashion. The Web Service in these cases would not know about the structure, but we must still be able to relay this information to the calling client. In that case we would create an additional `.xsd` XML definition file and simply attach it to our `.disco` file using this `<schemaRef>` element.

soapRef Binding Element

The `<soapRef>` element reproduces a portion of the binding information found within a WSDL schema. It does this to allow a Web Service client to locate a service using lightweight information, so that rather than having to load the WSDL schema file every time it needs to find the relevant information, it uses this summary information to identify the contents of a specific WSDL file.

The .vsdisco File

The .vsdisco file contains multiple .disco files and is dynamically generated when browsed to, similar to how the .disco file works.

It conforms to the exact same standards as defined in the .disco file, but instead of being generated by the information found within a single .asmx file it is generated from all the .asmx files found within the current project.

The .vsdisco file and .disco file perform similar tasks, however, they can be simply differentiated as follows:

The VS.NET .disco file:

- Points to one WSDL Web Service
- Is dynamically created by the ASP.NET runtime
- Contains additional elements such as <soap> and <schemaRef>

The VS.NET .vsdisco file:

- Points to more than one .disco file
- Can be used to package together many Web Services
- Is dynamically created by the VS.NET runtime
- Points to all Web Services contained within a VS.NET Web Service project

Before we display the .vsdisco file, we first need to create a new Web Service .asmx file. To accomplish this just follow these steps:

- Click on the project name Discovery1 in Solution Explorer.
- Right-click your mouse
- Select Add | Add Web Service...
- Press the Open button to use the default name, which should be Service2.asmx.

Within the Solution Explorer window, you will see the file suffixed with .vsdisco:

- Highlight the .vsdisco file within your Solution Explorer window
- Right-click your mouse and choose the View in Browser menu option

The .vsdisco file will now be generated. This may take some time, but please note that subsequent calls are usually quicker. It's only when you change a file within the project that it takes a while to generate.

Looking at the file, you should be able to see some remarkable resemblances to the `.disco` file displayed previously. This is because, first of all, the `.vsdisco` file conforms to the DISCO standard, and the namespace of `http://schemas.xmlsoap.org/disco` is being used in its header. Secondly, it contains information on all the Web Services contained within this project.

Now it may become apparent why we added a new Web Service to this project: this was to see how it reflects the information within this `.vsdisco` file by adding a new `<contractRef>` element line.

Your `.vsdisco` file, when browsed to, should now contain the following:

```
<?xml version="1.0" encoding="utf-8" ?>
<discovery xmlns:xsd="http://http://www.w3.org/2001/XMLSchema"
           xmlns:xsi="http://www.w3.org/2001/XMLSchema-instance"
           xmlns="http://schemas.xmlsoap.org/disco/" >
  <contractRef ref="http://localhost/PWS/Ch7/Discovery1/Service1.asmx?wsdl"
               docRef="http://localhost/PWS/Ch7/Discovery1/Service1.asmx"
               xmlns="http://schemas.xmlsoap.org/disco/scl/" />
  <contractRef ref="http://localhost/PWS/Ch7/Discovery1/Service2.asmx?wsdl"
               docRef="http://localhost/PWS/Ch7/Discovery1/Service2.asmx"
               xmlns="http://schemas.xmlsoap.org/disco/scl/" />
</discovery>
```

You must browse to the file by typing the following location into your browser address field. Do not simply load the file into VS.NET by double-clicking your mouse on it: http://localhost/PWS/Ch7/Discovery1/Discovery.vsdisco

Looking at the above file you will see that the `<contractRef>` elements describe the `Service1.asmx` and `Service2.asmx` Web Services. However, neither have an associated `<soap>` element. This is because this information is not meant to be included within these `.vsdisco` files as it is already covered within each Web Service's associated `.disco` file. This omission is a feature of ASP.NET.

Linking to Remote Web Services Using a .vsdisco File

Previously we discussed how we can link discovery files from outside sources using the `<discoveryRef>` element. What we'll see now is how we can attach multiple Web Service projects together using this method.

For this example, you will need to add a new Web Service project to your existing project:

- Select File | Add Project | New Project
- Select to create a ASP.NET Web Service project
- Type in Discovery2 as the project name
- Press the OK button to create project

Now we need to add a reference to this new Web Service (`Discovery2`) into our current Web Service project (`Discovery1`). To do this, follow these steps:

- Right-click on the new `Service1.asmx` in the **Discovery2** project and select **Set as Start Page**
- Build the solution
- Select the **References** folder of project **Discovery1**
- Right-click your mouse button
- Select **Add Web Reference**
- Type in the following and hit enter: **http://localhost/PWS/Ch7/Discovery2/Service1.asmx**
- Click the **Add Reference** button

Your project should now look as follows:

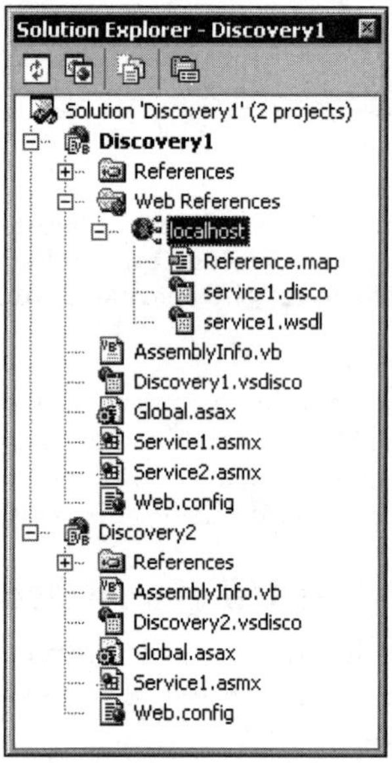

What we want to do now is make the `Discovery1.vsdisco` file link to the new **Discovery2** project. We can do this by double-clicking the mouse on the `Discovery1.vsdisco` file, which will display the following:

```
<?xml version="1.0" encoding="utf-8" ?>
<dynamicDiscovery xmlns="urn:schemas-dynamicdiscovery:disco.2000-03-17">
  <exclude path="_vti_cnf" />
  <exclude path="_vti_pvt" />
  <exclude path="_vti_log" />
  <exclude path="_vti_script" />
  <exclude path="_vti_txt" />
  <exclude path="Web References" />
</dynamicDiscovery>
```

This is unlike the browsed version of the `.vsdisco` file we've seen previously, and in fact the information contained within this file is used dynamically to create the `.vsdisco` file when viewed in a browser.

Notice the above line that states `<exclude path="Web References" />`. This indicates that when creating the `.vsdisco` file, ASP.NET should not include any Web Services contained within the `Web References` directory (and others listed above). This is in fact where our newly imported `Discovery2/Service1` Web Service resides.

> **All paths contained within the `.vsdisco` file are relative to the `.vsdisco` file location.**

We can use the ability to include Web Services within our `.vsdisco` file by simply removing the `<exclude path="Web References" />` element, thus allowing the `.vsdisco` file to generate itself using any Web Services it now finds in the `Web References` folder, in addition to the other folders it's allowed to scan.

Once you've removed that element and saved the file, right-click on the `Discovery1.vsdisco` file and click View in Browser:

```
<?xml version="1.0" encoding="utf-8" ?>
<discovery xmlns:xsd="http://www.w3.org/2001/XMLSchema"
           xmlns:xsi="http://www.w3.org/2001/XMLSchema-instance"
           xmlns="http://schemas.xmlsoap.org/disco/">
  <contractRef ref="http://localhost/PWS/Ch7/Discovery1/Service1.asmx?wsdl"
               docRef="http://localhost/PWS/Ch7/Discovery1/Service1.asmx"
               xmlns="http://schemas.xmlsoap.org/disco/scl/" />
  <contractRef ref="http://localhost/PWS/Ch7/Discovery1/Service2.asmx?wsdl"
               docRef="http://localhost/PWS/Ch7/Discovery1/Service2.asmx"
               xmlns="http://schemas.xmlsoap.org/disco/scl/" />
  <discoveryRef
         ref="http://localhost/PWS/Ch7/Discovery1/old/Discovery1.vsdisco" />
  <discoveryRef
           ref="http://localhost/PWS/Ch7/Discovery1/Web References/↵
                localhost/service1.disco" />
</discovery>
```

Now a new element has appeared:

```
<discoveryRef
    ref="http://localhost/PWS/Ch7/Discovery1/Web References/↵
         localhost/Service1.disco" />
```

This element was dynamically created because the system recognized our need to include Web Services in the Web References directory. What actually happens during generation of the .vsdisco file is that it searches the current root of your project and all subdirectories within the project for files with the suffix .disco and then places them as <discoveryRef> element links.

> **When ASP.NET is generating the .vsdisco file it searches for other .disco files.**

The .vsdisco file automatically generates and searches for these files because it has the .vsdisco extension and because it contains the following basic XML construct:

```
<?xml version="1.0" ?>
<dynamicDiscovery xmlns="urn:schemas-dynamicdiscovery:disco.2000-03-17">
  . . . optional excludes goes here . . .
</dynamicDiscovery>
```

We can in fact create this file at any level and not necessarily within an ASP.NET Web Service project. To make sure that all .disco files are discovered on your entire web server, simply place this file at a root level on a web server that has had the server version of ASP.NET installed. When browsed to it will then generate all the .disco files it finds in all subdirectories.

> **.disco files generated by using the command .asmx?disco in a URL are not recognized by dynamic discovery using the .vsdisco file. It can only discover files that actually exist and are not dynamically generated by the ASP.NET runtime.**

Add Web Reference

Within VS.NET, we can consume someone else's Web Service by adding it directly into our VS.NET project. This is done using the Add Web Reference menu option from within Visual Studio .NET. Once added to our project, we may call that Web Service as part of the general functionality of our application.

Adding a Single Web Service to Your Project

Let's create a client project using the following steps, to which we will add a web reference:

- Select File | Add Project | New Project | Windows Application.
- Type in DiscoveryClient for your project name, then press the OK button. You should now have the following files and projects in your Solution Explorer window:

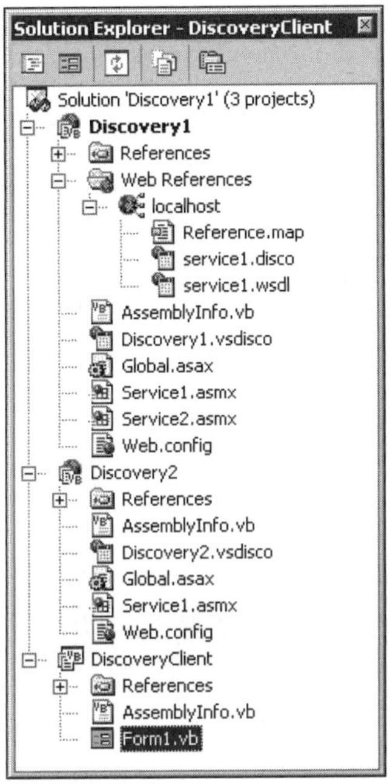

- Right-click on the References folder in your new DiscoveryClient project.
- Select Add Web Reference.
- Type in the following address and hit *Enter*: http://localhost/PWS/Ch7/Discovery1/Service1.asmx.

You will now see the following screen. This screen allows us to view the details of the Web Service we want to add into our project, and in the case of .asmx files also allows us to test the Web Service before we use it:

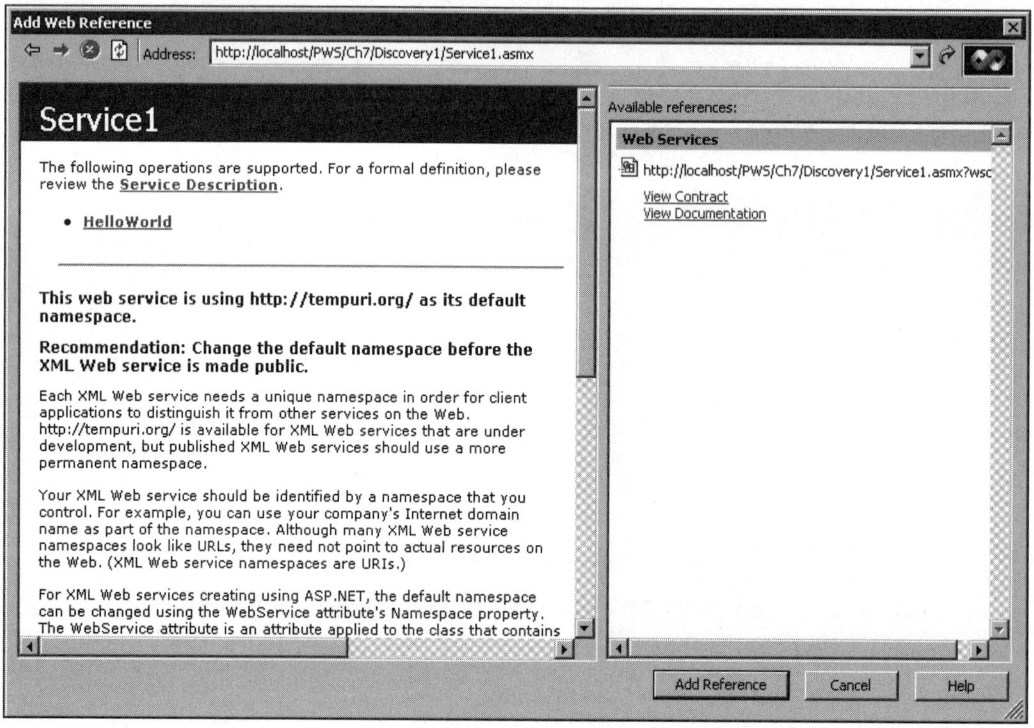

The Add Reference button will have become enabled. We can therefore click on it to add our Web Service directly into our new client project. However, before you do, let's consider the following. The question is how does the Add Reference button know that we have identified a Web Service?

It can all be revealed by looking at the source for our .asmx file. To view the source for the .asmx file, click on the Service1 page on the left within the above screen, then right-click your mouse, now choose View Source. Notepad will now load and you will be able to see the following link in the HTML header:

```
<link rel="alternate" type="text/xml" href="Service1.asmx?disco"/>
```

This simple link identifies to the Add Web Reference browser that there is an associated .disco file for this page, so when it loads, your .asmx file also looks for the location of the above tag. If found, the Add Web Reference browser also reads and interprets the associated .disco file. Then, if a <contractRef> link exists (or even multiple <contractRef> elements), it automatically enables the Add Reference button.

This in-built facility is actually a designated use for the .disco file. However, for the moment only two ASP.NET Search Directories support it, UDDI and www.salcentral.com (more about these later).

The Add Web Reference address field will accept any of the following file types and at the same time enable the Add Reference button to allow us to add Web Service(s) into our project:

- `.disco` (Discovery file)
- `.vsdisco` (dynamic Discovery file)
- `.wsdl` (Web Service Description Language file)
- `.asmx`

Adding Multiple Web Services to Your Project

In a previous part of this chapter (section on *Linking to Remote Web Services Using a .vsdisco File*) we created a `.vsdisco` file which included links to two local Web Services using the `<contractRef>` element and a remote Web Service using the `<discoveryRef>` element.

What we'll do now is see how it can actually be used to help in the discovery of Web Services. For this example, we will need to display the Add Web Reference screen for the client project we just created and then type in the name of the following dynamic discovery file from our first project:

```
http://localhost/PWS/Ch7/Discovery1/Discovery1.vsdisco
```

Once loaded, the following screen will be displayed:

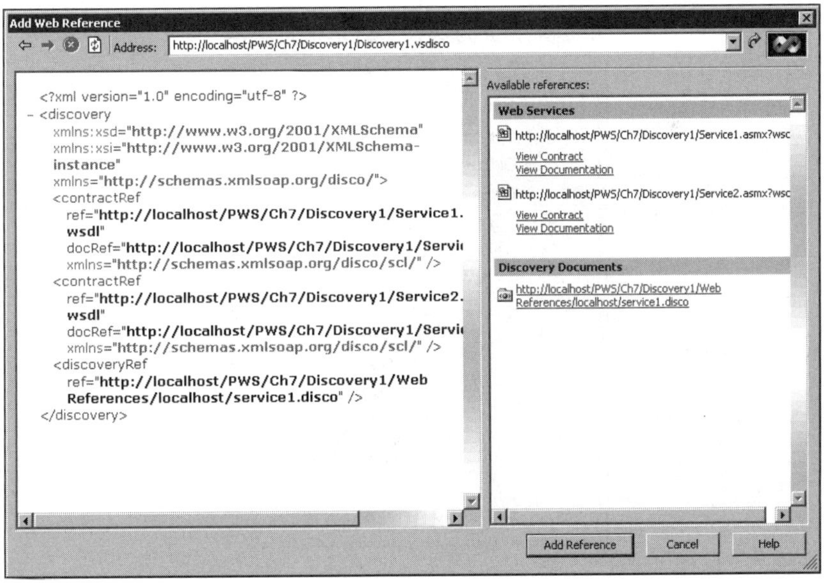

For ASP.NET a single `.disco` file is always associated with a single `.asmx` file. However, the DISCO standard allows for multiple `.disco` files pointing toward the same Web Service, allowing for greater customization.

The important bit that interests us is in the window (headed Available references) on the right, which contains the Web Service links:

Icon	Description
	This link denotes that it is a link to the WSDL definition of a Web Service and when the Add Reference button is pressed, it will be added into your project and will be able to be consumed.
	This link denotes that a sublist of Web Services exist and by selecting this link you can browse to further Web Services. If you press the Add Reference button while this is displayed, then the Web Services this links to (that are currently not displayed) are ignored.

If you click the Add Reference button then the Web References folder now contains (under localhost1) links to two Web Services, which reflects the two Web Services contained within the `Discovery1` project. You should see something similar to the following screen:

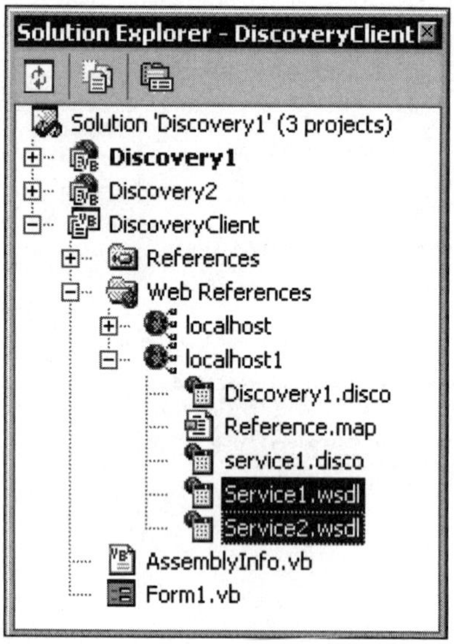

Look at the new files that have been copied into your project. It's apparent that the two Web Services have now been attached to this client by importing copies of the relevant `.wsdl` files. However, in addition to these files it has also imported two `.disco` files. All files within the Web References folder are copies of the original WSDL files and can be changed accordingly. You can experiment by changing the local WSDL and later replacing your changed copies with the originals by clicking your mouse on localhost1 (or the server name) and selecting Update Web Reference.

The .map File

A DISCO `.map` file is an XML document published by a Web Service that contains the original links to its resources, for example links to `.wsdl` and `.disco` files that describe the Web Service. These links are used to associate this linked remote file name with the name of a local file contained within the current project.

The `.map` file is created by the client at the time you add a web reference. We can view it by simply double-clicking our mouse on the file called `Reference.map` within the Web References folder. On creation, the `.map` file is *always* named `Reference.map`.

After loading the `Reference.map` file you will now see the following displayed. The values contained within the following file are based upon the assumption that you have carried out all previous steps in this chapter:

```
<?xml version="1.0" encoding="utf-8"?>
<DiscoveryClientResultsFile xmlns:xsd="http://www.w3.org/2001/XMLSchema"
                            xmlns:xsi="http://www.w3.org/2001/XMLSchema-instance">
  <Results>
    <DiscoveryClientResult
              referenceType="System.Web.Services.Discovery.ContractReference"
              url="http://localhost/PWS/Ch7/Discovery1/Service1.asmx?wsdl"
              filename="Service1.wsdl" />
    <DiscoveryClientResult
              referenceType="System.Web.Services.Discovery.ContractReference"
              url="http://localhost/PWS/Ch7/Discovery1/Service2.asmx?wsdl"
              filename="Service2.wsdl" />
    <DiscoveryClientResult
        referenceType="System.Web.Services.Discovery.DiscoveryDocumentReference"
        url="http://localhost/PWS/Ch7/Discovery1/Discovery1.vsdisco"
        filename="Discovery1.disco" />
    <DiscoveryClientResult
        referenceType="System.Web.Services.Discovery.DiscoveryDocumentReference"
        url="http://localhost/PWS/Ch7/Discovery1/↵
        Web References/localhost/service1.disco" filename="service1.disco" />
  </Results>
</DiscoveryClientResultsFile>
```

The `Reference.map` file is regenerated every time you use the Update Web Reference feature of VS.NET. Using the previous screenshot, Update Web Reference can be run by selecting the host name (in our case "localhost1") and right-clicking your mouse button. This feature refreshes all files contained underneath the host name.

As far as finding uses for the .map file, it is most helpful in allowing you to see where the copies of the original file are located. For example, if for some reason the Update Web Reference feature was not working, you could load each of the files listed within the .map file and make sure that each could be viewed within your browser. This would effectively check that the connection was valid for each file.

DiscoveryClientResult Element

The <DiscoveryClientResult> element within the .map file can be repeated as many times as there are relevant links to the referenced Web Service. Each element is broken down into three attributes:

Attribute Name	Description
referenceType	Refers to a string constant value that is a recognized and valid name in the System.Web.Services.Discovery namespace. The only three valid entries are currently: ❑ System.Web.Services.Discovery.DiscoveryDocumentReference (indicates element points to a .disco file) ❑ System.Web.Services.Discovery.ContractReference (indicates element points to a .wsdl schema file) ❑ System.Web.Services.Discovery.SchemaReference (indicates element points to an .xsd schema file)
url	Points to the remote URL location of the specified file.
filename	Points to the name of the file that was created **locally** when the Web Service was added to the current project.

The <DiscoveryClientResult> element is populated by the information contained in the .disco file it finds (if any) when adding a remote WSDL schema into the current VS.NET client project. If no .disco file is found, then only the ContractReference is created inside the DISCO .map file.

Creating Your Own .disco File

It seems that because the .disco file is created by VS.NET it is created to a predefined limited structure. Therefore, even though the DISCO standard allows for considerable flexibility, VS.NET itself actually restricts this flexibility when automatically generating the .disco file. An example of this restriction is that the .asmx?disco file only ever creates one <contractRef> element for every .disco file, whereas the DISCO standard allows for multiple <contractRef> elements.

This leads us nicely to how we can get around these restrictions by manually creating additional .disco files that point towards the Web Services we wish to promote.

Create a new XML file within your project following these steps:

- ❑ Right-click on the Discovery1 project
- ❑ Select Add | Add New Item

- Select the **XML File** template
- Change the file name to `XMLFile1.disco`
- Enter the following XML elements into your new XML file:

```
<?xml version="1.0" encoding="utf-8"?>
<discovery xmlns="http://schemas.xmlsoap.org/disco/">
  <contractRef
    ref="http://localhost/PWS/Ch7/Discovery1/Service2.asmx?wsdl"
    docRef="http://localhost/PWS/Ch7/Discovery1/Service2.asmx"
    xmlns="http://schemas.xmlsoap.org/disco/scl/" />
</discovery>
```

The above example exactly copies the `.disco` file that would have been produced if we had simply browsed to the file using the following browser HTTP command:

http://localhost/PWS/Ch7/Discovery1/Service2.asmx?disco

However, we've now created a local file that can be edited locally and has the same discovery features as an automatically generated `.disco` file. Before we see how this looks inside the **Add Web Reference** browser, and as this is a little tedious simply reproducing the same file, let's elaborate on the file structure a little and see how we can use this technique to link `.disco` files together.

Let's embellish this `.disco` file by adding a `<discoveryRef>` element. This element allows us to link from one DISCO file to another, simulating peer-to-peer discovery of Web Services.

The diagram below describes how peer-to-peer discovery can work within DISCO, by linking together multiple `.vsdisco` and `.wsdl` files.

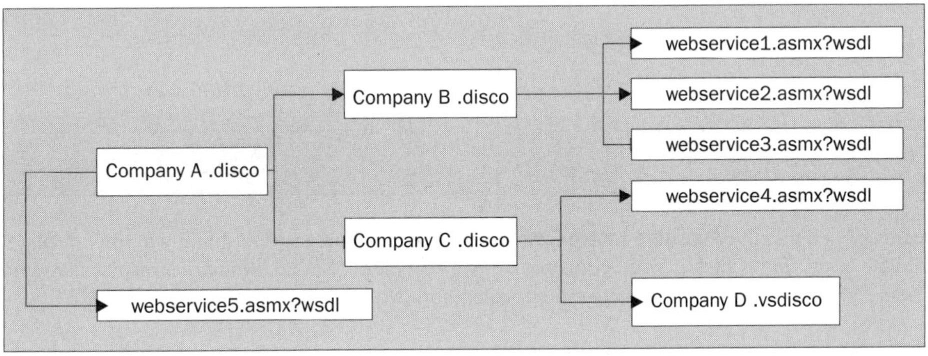

Enter the following discoveryRef element line in your XMLFile1.disco file inside the <discovery> tags:

```
<discoveryRef
    ref="http://localhost/PWS/Ch7/Discovery1/Discovery1.vsdisco" />
```

The new element location points towards an existing valid .vsdisco file. To see how this affects the discovery process, we simply need to use the **Add a Web Reference** menu option again (for this example we'll use the previously created DiscoveryClient project). However, this time type the location of your newly altered XMLFile1.disco file in the **Address** field:

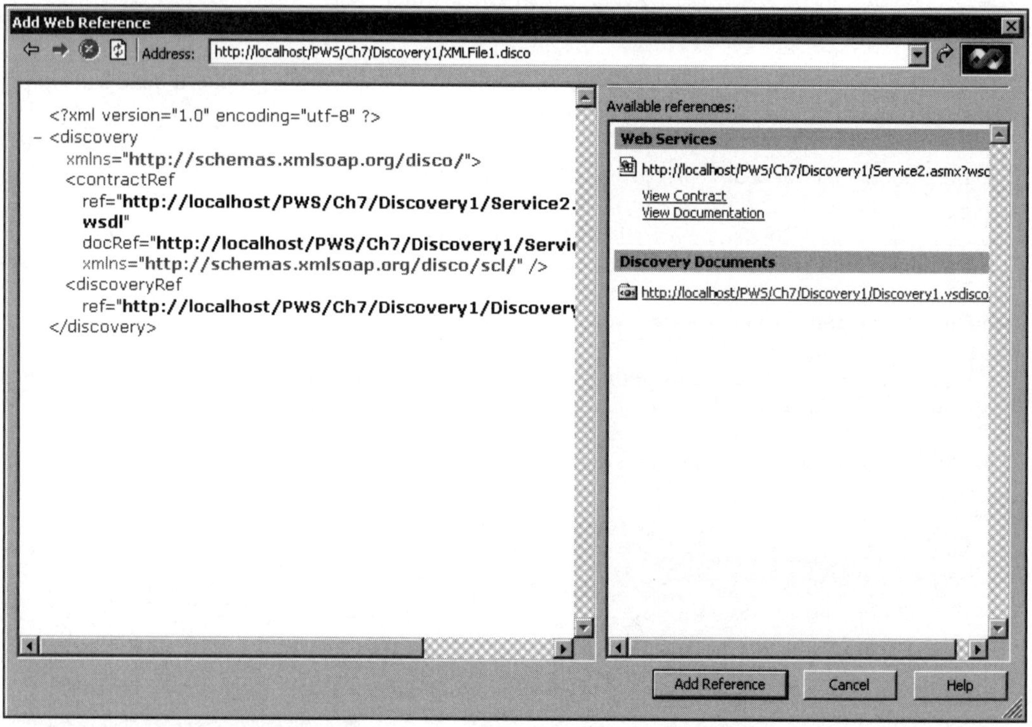

You can now see that the **Available references** window of the browser (right-hand window) displays the Service2.asmx file (which is your <contractRef> element), but additionally it displays the linked .vsdisco file (which is the <discoveryRef> element), which is the extra line we added.

We can now simply add the web reference to our project, as we have done previously, or we can click on the **Linked reference groups** and navigate to another .disco file.

At first glance it is not obvious, but the repercussions of this type of linking ability are astonishing, as it provides the ability to connect together vast numbers of Web Services, in a similar manner to how you would link web pages together. The future of this type of ability is to create a Napster-style series of Web Services that allow a user to browse from Web Service to Web Service, similar to how you browse between HTML pages today.

In addition, in the above example we have linked a `.vsdisco` file instead of a `.disco` file. Clicking on it will display the following screen:

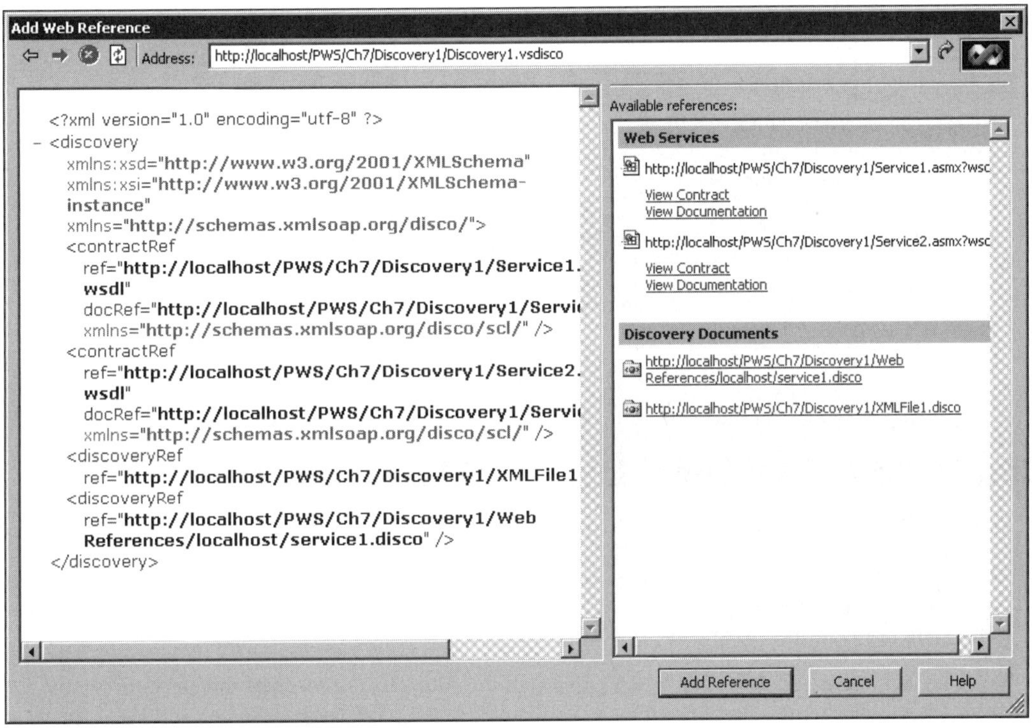

We've already displayed this screen before (see *Adding Multiple Web Services to your Project*), however, it's actually now changed. Because we previously discussed how the `.vsdisco` file dynamically updated its own entries, you will see that the file we've just added, `XMLFile1.disco`, has also now been added to the `.vsdisco` list. This link in fact allows us to navigate back to the file that displayed this page.

Using `.disco` customization in real-world situations can add significant and advanced features to how we roll out our applications. For example, say we created three Web Services all in separate projects and we require promotion of all of these Web Services together as a package. Normally there would be no option other than to give our customer three XML files (`.wsdl` or `.disco`). However, by creating a `.disco` file with multiple `<contractRef>` elements and giving this `.disco` file to our customer, who can subsequently browse to it from within their ASP.NET application, we can roll out our application using one single file.

> **The location of a created `.disco` file is not important as long as it can be accessed remotely by your customer.**

Using this technique we could set up multiple `.disco` files for each specific software package we wish to promote, each package containing links to multiple WSDL schemas. We may also mix Web Services in these `.disco` packages, allowing us to easily reuse common components.

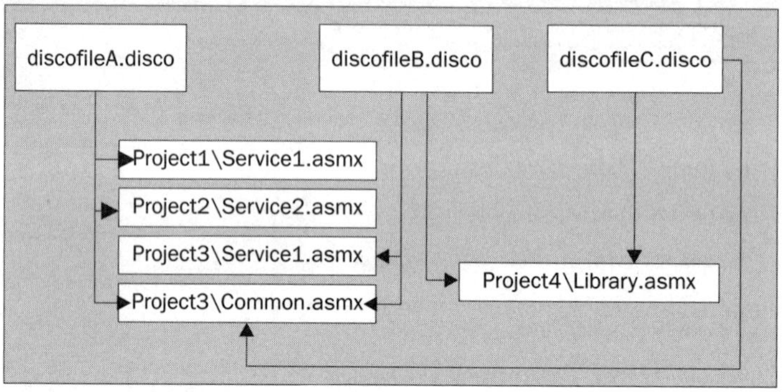

Create Your Own Local Library of Web Services

One significant benefit of Web Service discovery is in the area of keeping track of your own Web Services.

It's apparent that even as individuals we do not reuse work as well as we could. Therefore, what we'll do now is describe a simple way to create and administer our own list of Web Services to allow us to easily reuse them in our own subsequent projects in ASP.NET.

You may have noticed that every time you viewed the Add Web Reference screen (in previous examples in this chapter), the first thing that's displayed is a UDDI search screen similar to the following one (this screen may change in subsequent versions of Visual Studio .NET):

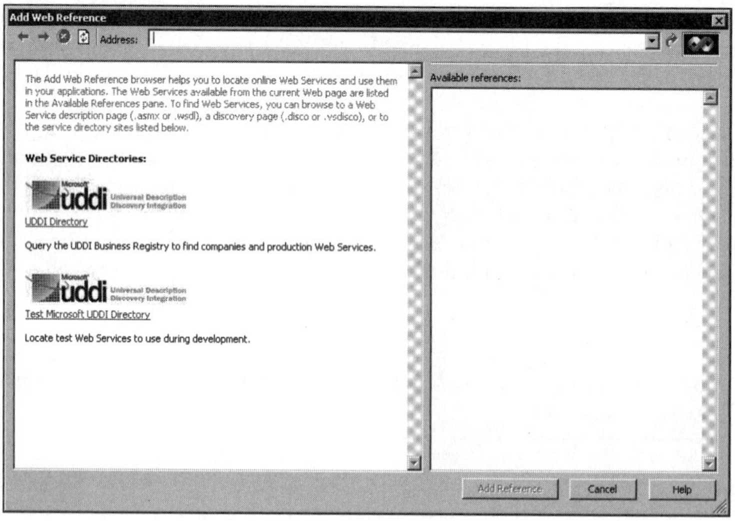

When we display this screen, what is not generally apparent but becomes evident after inspection is that the left hand screen is actually a simple HTML file situated on your local hard drive. To get a better feel for how the browser operates:

- Click your mouse anywhere on the left-hand window (on the text area not the UDDI logo's)
- Right-click your mouse and select Properties

You will now see that the home page is actually the following link:

file://C:\Program%20Files\Microsoft%20Visual%20Studio%20.NET\Common7\Packages\1033\HelpWatermark.htm

This is actually the location of the default page for your Add Web Reference browser. This location will change depending on your original installation path for VS.NET.

You can change the default `HelpWatermark.htm` yourself using either Notepad or any simple HTML editor; just treat it as you would any other HTML file. This ability to customize our home page can allow us to use advanced features such as adding additional search engines that support the `.disco` standard (see www.whatwebservice.com) or create a custom-built Web Services library that is specific to your own requirement, such as contact information or a list of commonly used Web Services. A minus point of this type of feature is that you need to roll it out to each developer.

This ability to keep track of our own Web Services allows us to more easily share Web Service development between projects or even individuals within the same company, but instead of linking together XML files we can use HTML files with much more descriptive and relevant information.

UDDI is a platform-independent database, which contains information on the location and category of businesses and Web Services. This allows us to more easily find business partners or suppliers and also locate and consume Web Services.

Sharing Web Services within a department would mean simply linking from the `HelpWatermark.htm` to a simple HTML file, which contains a list of descriptions and links to each WSDL schema. If a developer wanted to use a Web Service, they would simply decide by reading the text and then browse to the relevant WSDL schema, which immediately activates the Add Reference button at the bottom of the browser window. In addition, some development teams may even use this feature to omit the UDDI link to discourage the use of third-party Web Services.

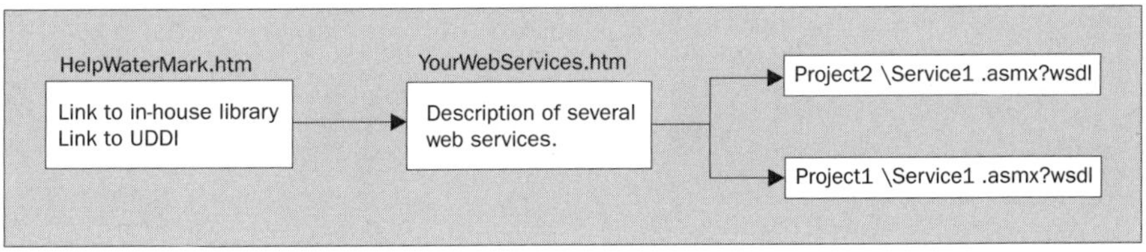

Creating a HTML Library of Web Services

Simply linking to `.vsdisco` files is a little uninspiring and tells us very little about the Web Service we are viewing. Therefore, let's add a specialist HTML file that acts as a library for our own Web Services.

Create the following HTML file (called `disco.htm`) and place it in the root of your `localhost` server:

```
<html>
<head>
<meta http-equiv="Content-Language" content="en-gb">
<meta http-equiv="Content-Type" content="text/html; charset=windows-1252">
<meta name="GENERATOR" content="Microsoft FrontPage 4.0">
<meta name="ProgId" content="FrontPage.Editor.Document">
<title>New Page 1</title>
</head>
<body>
  <h1>My Local Web Services</h1>
  <p>Very simple method that passes back the words "hello world".<br>
  <a href="http://localhost/PWS/Ch7/Discovery1/Service1.asmx">
    HelloWorld
  </a>
  (Service1.asmx)</p>
  <p>Another simple method that passes back the words "hello world".<br>
  <a href="http://localhost/PWS/Ch7/Discovery1/Service2.asmx">
    HelloWorld
  </a>
  (Service2.asmx)</p>
</body>
</html>
```

The above HTML file contains two links, one to the `Discovery1\Service1.asmx` file and the other to the `Discovery1\Service2.asmx` file, the files we created in our previous examples.

Now edit your `HelpWaterMark.htm` file using Notepad (it will probably be in `c:\Program Files\Microsoft Visual Studio .NET\Common7\Packages\1033\`) and add the following link:

```
<a href="http://localhost/disco.htm">Web Services on Local Server</a>
```

This was the link behind the **Web References on Local Server** link and why we had to create a `default.vsdisco` file last time.

That's all the changes we require. Now within our client ASP.NET project, click on the Web Services on Local Server link to select it. You will see the following screen displayed:

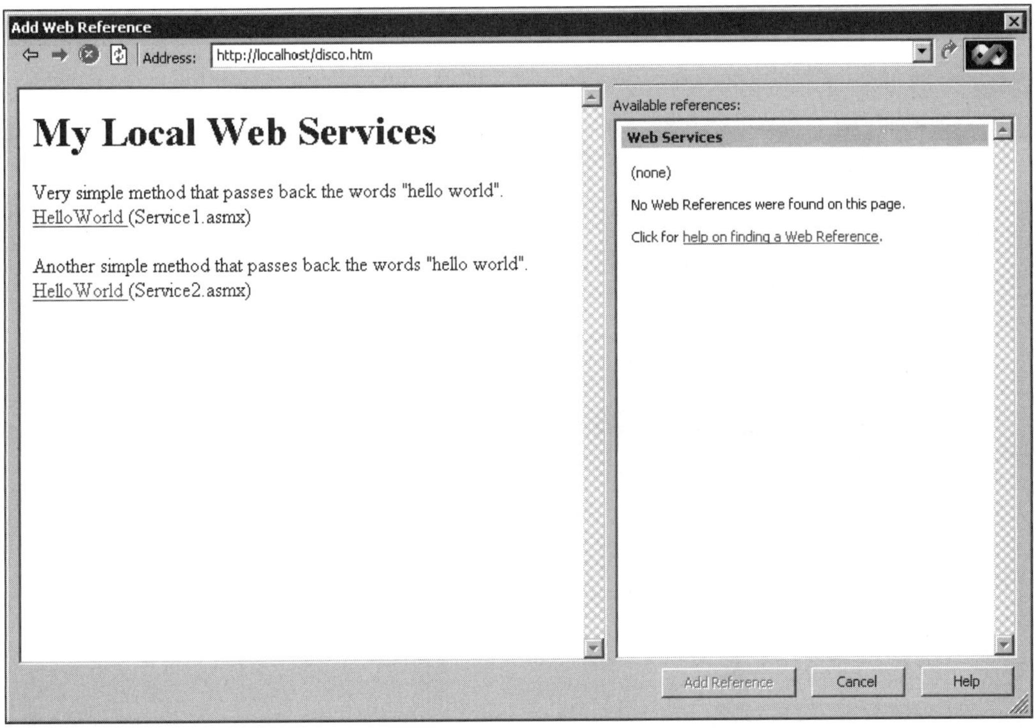

Simply click on the link for each Web Service to view the WSDL schema for each Web Service. When you've selected the `.wsdl` file the Add Reference button will immediately become active and you will be able to add it to your project. Using this method of updating the HTML file we've created we can keep developer notes, keep track of all our common Web Services, and allow them to be reused within any project we develop.Though this has a certain amount of overhead in maintenance, it has the advantage of saving time and money throughout the project as developers can now easily understand and reuse additional Web Services.

Specialist Search Engines

We've covered previously in this chapter how we can use DISCO technology to link pages together and attach `.disco` files to an HTML page using the `<link>` tag on an HTML file. What we'll do now is see what we can accomplish by using the technology commercially available over the Internet and how third-party search engines (outside of UDDI) can allow us to search for Web Services. SalCentral is a company that has placed this technology into their Web Services search engine to allow developers to dynamically consume Web Services from companies around the world.

SalCentral is a search engine that supports the DISCO standard. To see how it works, within the Address field of the Add Web Reference browser type the following link:

http://www.salcentral.com/dotnet.asp

This is the opening page for the SalCentral search engine; you will now see the following screen:

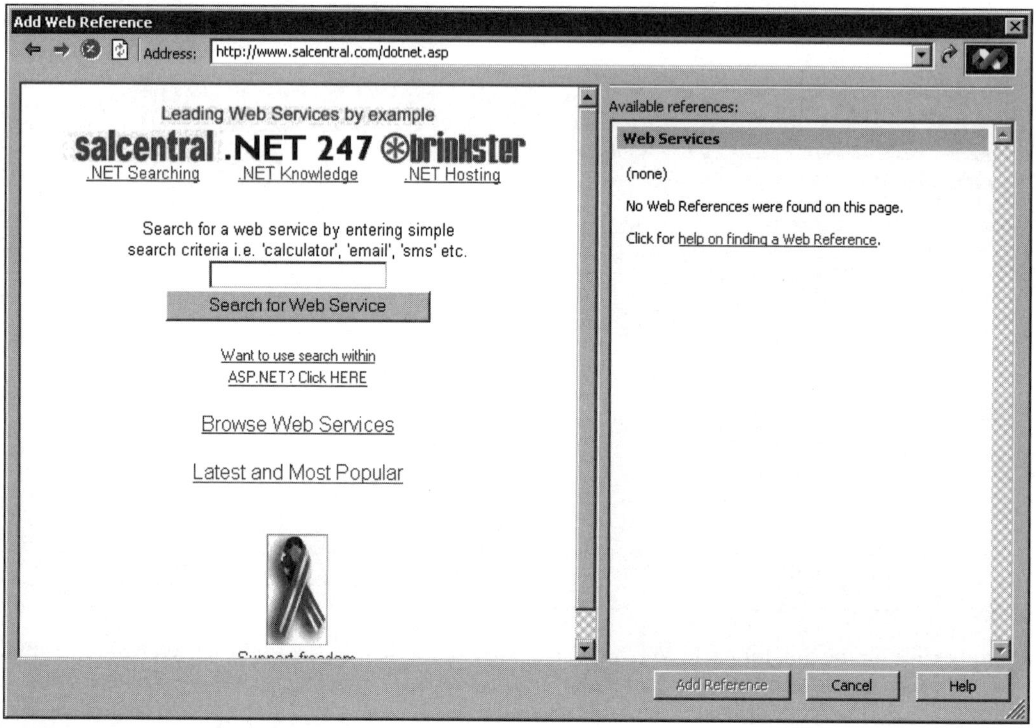

This screen has been specifically designed by SalCentral to allow simple search techniques, similar to how a web site search engine works. As you use this search engine, you will notice that the Add Reference button remains disabled.

For this example, we'll skip the selection process (everyone by now should know how to use a search engine). What we'll do is type in the end location of a screen that will be shown once we navigate down to a specific Web Service:

http://sal006.salnetwork.com:83/lucin/SMSMessaging/addserv.htm?WSURL=http://www.soap engine.com/lucin/soapenginex/smsx.asmx?wsdl

This screen shows you the result of searching for an SMS Text messaging Web Service within SalCentral:

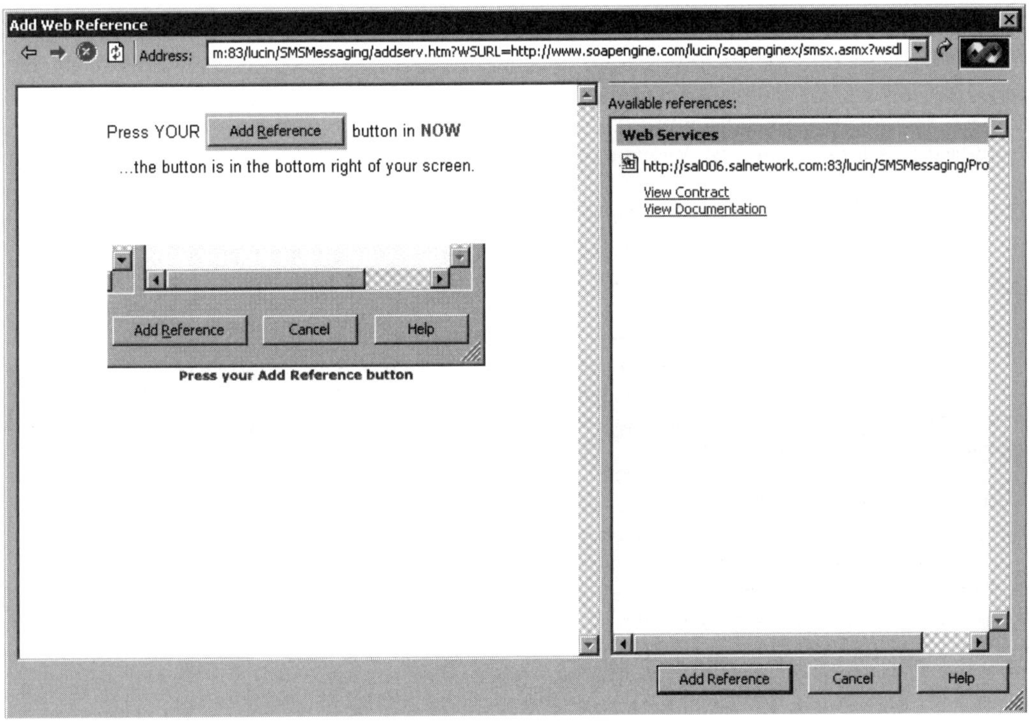

As you can see the **Add Reference** button has now been enabled. To see why, follow these steps:

- Select the left hand browser page, try not to click on a graphic
- Press your right mouse button and select **View Source**

You will now be able to see that the searching mechanism is simply displaying the `<link>` tag that we described earlier that attaches a `.disco` file to the current HTML page. This mechanism is then read by the **Add Web Reference** browser and the **Add Reference** button is then enabled:

```
<link rel="alternate" type="text/xml"
     href="http://sal006.salnetwork.com:83/soapengine/SMSMessaging/disco.xml"/>
```

It's a simple mechanism which is used very effectively to search for Web Services and to allow us to pull them into our ASP.NET project.

What's actually happening here is that the search engine is creating the `disco.xml` files and `.htm` files prior to when we view the page, using a specialist HTML file creation tool and SQL Server as the database. This simple technique means that HTML links are dynamically created from the Web Services contained within the search engine's database.

Please note that to continue and use this service you need to register for credits at
http://www.webservicebuy.com

Promoting Your Web Services

You can also enter your Web Services onto a specialist search engine. These search engines simply ask for basic information about your Web Service and then promote your Web Services using newsletters and general search techniques. An example of such a search engine is:

http://www.salcentral.com/salnet/add.asp

UDDI

We could not cover discovering Web Services without mentioning UDDI (Universal Description, Discovery, and Integration). UDDI is a significant departure from general Microsoft technologies as it offers a platform-independent database, which contains information on the location and category of businesses and Web Services. This allows us to find business partners or suppliers more easily and also locate and consume Web Services.

Why have UDDI? Well, one reason for backing UDDI is that if you have a central repository that all organizations can collaborate in populating, it acts in a similar way to how a phone book operates, in that we can find and locate organizations either in our area or in a specific category that we are interested in. Currently we can trawl through vast quantities of Internet pages looking for that specific supplier, which is more akin to sticking a pin in a map than a selection using categorized information. It seems sensible to search for, say, a specific supplier (supplier of tape backups) in our area (Washington); the UDDI registry helps us to accomplish this.

The UDDI Web Service

When we search, update or add a Web Service to UDDI it is always done through a Web Service. There are currently three ways of interacting with UDDI:

- Sending SOAP request messages and receiving SOAP responses
  This is certainly the most complex, and means that you require a significant understanding about firstly the SOAP message but also how the UDDI registry is structured.
- Using the UDDI SDK for ASP.NET
  This SDK hides the creation of SOAP messages from the developer by wrapping them within an object-based interface. A VS.NET version is available at the following location:
  http://uddi.microsoft.com/developer/default.aspx.
- Using the UDDI SDK for Windows 95, 98 and NT
  Same as above but for a different operating system. A COM version is available at the following location
  http://uddi.microsoft.com/developer/default.aspx.

Who Controls UDDI?

The UDDI registry is not solely run by Microsoft. IBM and Ariba are also controlling repositories for UDDI. This means that if we post information with one, then it's replicated on all databases held by those companies. Each of the independent repositories have the same interface to give any outside organization or individual the opportunity to post information to UDDI using the **UDDI Publish** Web Service and search UDDI using the **UDDI Inquire** Web Service:

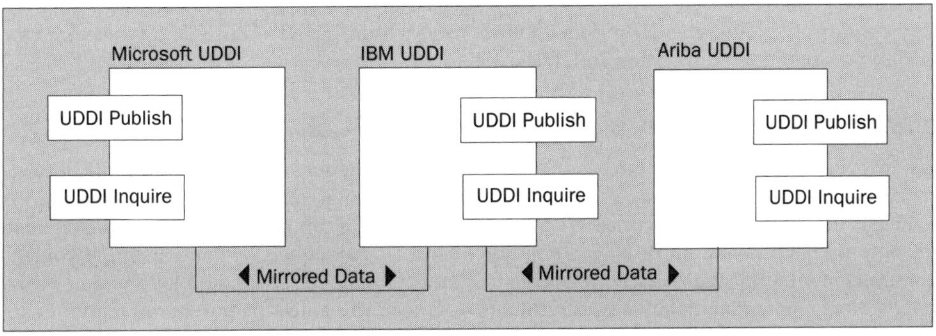

The following are the Web Service server end-points for each of the three holding organizations; these end-points are purely for UDDI inquiries only. The publishing end-points will be alternative server locations and usually require HTTPS secure transmissions:

- Microsoft inquiry server
  `http://uddi.microsoft.com/inquire`
- IBM inquiry server
  `http://www-3.ibm.com/services/uddi/inquiryapi`
- Ariba inquiry server
  `http://uddi.ariba.com/UDDIProcessor.aw/ad/process`

In simple terms, if you want to inquire about an entry in the UDDI register, you send the correct SOAP message to any one of the above Internet locations. Each one will process the request and send back a valid SOAP response (or fault) message.

The UDDI Web Service Definition

The UDDI Web Service has a SOAP interface, which can be used to send messages to a SOAP server to search or edit the UDDI registry. It also has a WSDL schema definition that defines this Web Service.

The UDDI WSDL Schema definition is split into two distinct files:

- Searching (locating businesses and Web Services)
  `http://www.uddi.org/wsdl/inquire_v1.wsdl`
- Publishing (adding, updating and removing businesses and Web Services)
  `http://www.uddi.org/wsdl/publish_v1.wsdl`

It should be noted that the above WSDL schema specifications as at the time of publishing this book were not supported from within VS.NET by browsing to the schemas using the above-mentioned Add Web Reference *menu option. However, it's expected that a developer can use the ASP.NET UDDI SDK to interact with the UDDI database.*

Both of these files contain a link to the following XML data type definition file:
`http://www.uddi.org/schema/2001/uddi_v1.xsd`

This file contains the data type definitions that are used within UDDI – valid data types that can be used when sending/receiving information in UDDI.

Understanding the Structure of the UDDI WSDL Schemas

On first inspection the XML structure defined in the WSDL schema looks vague and difficult to understand, but learning a few simple concepts will allow you to greatly improve your understanding of the technical side of how UDDI works. With this knowledge you can change the method of sending information to UDDI, for example by sending down your SOAP request by constructing it yourself and using a simple communication TCP/IP package to connect to UDDI. This could help you in situations where you have a potential memory constraint and you need to reduce the number of components loaded.

First, each of the two functionality files, Searching (locating businesses and Web Services) and Publishing (adding, updating, and removing businesses and Web Services) contains the Web Service methods and arguments that are available for us to use.

The following XML extract is from the Searching file (`http://www.uddi.org/wsdl/inquire_v1.wsdl`) and outlines the definition for the methods to use if you wish to **Find Business** within UDDI:

```
<operation name="find_business">
  <soap:operation soapAction="" style="document" />
  <input message="tns:find_business">
    <soap:body use="literal" parts="body" namespace="urn:uddi-org:api" />
  </input>
  <output message="tns:businessDetail">
    <soap:body use="literal" parts="body" namespace="urn:uddi-org:api" />
  </output>
  <fault name="error" message="tns:dispositionReport">
    <soap:fault name="error" use="literal" />
  </fault>
</operation>
```

Without going into SOAP message construction (this is covered elsewhere within this book), we'll use the following diagram to explain what the above XML extract shows us:

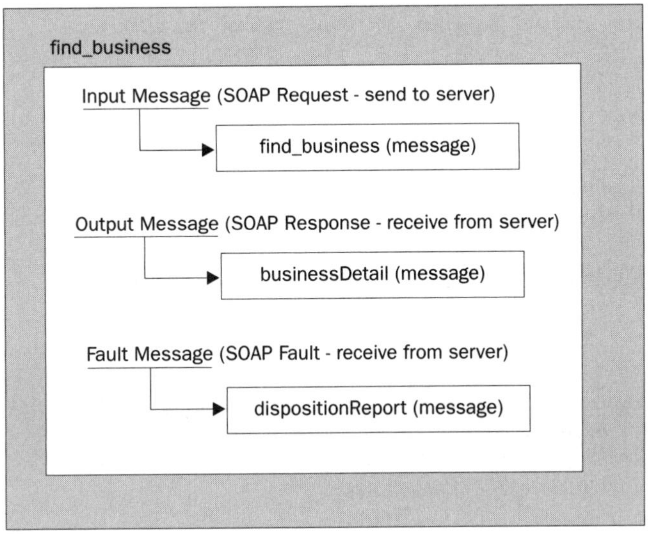

In the XML extract it refers to the `find_business` and the `businessDetail` messages. If you perform a text search within that *same* WSDL schema, you will see the following two sections (they will not necessarily be situated together):

`find_business` message:

```
<message name="find_business">
  <part name="body" element="uddi:find_business" />
</message>
```

`businessDetail` message:

```
<message name="businessDetail">
  <part name="body" element="uddi:business_Detail" />
</message>
```

So far, the above definitions have already described how the basic SOAP message will look. However, often in the above `<part name>` element, you will see a recognized data type (`string`, `boolean` or such like). This time it used the data type definition `find_business` and `business_Detail`. These definitions are unique to UDDI and they contain an XML structure that defines the arguments we should send within the SOAP request message. They also define the expected XML construct to receive back from UDDI. These data type definitions can be found in the UDDI XML data type definition file located at http://www.uddi.org/schema/2001/uddi_v1.xsd.

Below is an example of how the SOAP message would look if you were to construct it yourself:

```
<?xml version='1.0' encoding='UTF-8'?>
<Envelope xmlns='http://schemas.xmlsoap.org/soap/envelope/'>
  <find_business generic="1.0" maxrows=30 xmlns="urn:uddi-org:api">
    <name>Microsoft</name>
  </find_business>
</Envelope>
```

That's it, just send this SOAP message to the Inquiry (`http://uddi.microsoft.com/inquire`) UDDI server, and the returned result will be the `businessDetail` XML structure.

Searching the UDDI Register Using the ASP.NET SDK

There seems to be an SDK for everything these days, and UDDI is no exception. The UDDI SDK gives you as a developer a common and simple interface to interact with UDDI, without the requirement of understanding SOAP. The SDK allows you to remove, update, search and add entries into the UDDI registry. To access this component you must first download and install the UDDI SDK. You will find the ASP.NET version available at:

http://uddi.microsoft.com/developer/default.aspx

Once installed you need to add a reference to the DLL. The easiest way to accomplish this is to use the Add Reference menu option to browse to the file `Microsoft.UDDI.SDK.dll` situated in the directory where you installed the SDK.

Once this is done you will be able to use the following code to access UDDI from within VS.NET. Simply create a new client project and type in the following code:

```
 Imports Microsoft.Uddi
 Imports Microsoft.Uddi.Business
 Imports Microsoft.Uddi.Service
 Imports Microsoft.Uddi.Binding
 Imports Microsoft.Uddi.ServiceType
 Imports Microsoft.Uddi.Api

Module modMain

  Sub Main()
    Dim oUDDI As New FindBusiness()
    Dim oBusinessList As BusinessList

    Inquire.Url = "http://test.uddi.microsoft.com/inquire"
    oUDDI.Name = "Microsoft"
    oBusinessList = oUDDI.Send()
    MsgBox(oBusinessList.BusinessInfos.Count)
  End Sub

End Module
```

The above code actually does the same as the SOAP construct we created earlier, but this time the SOAP messages have been shielded from us and are all created and sent by the SDK.

Note that to send a `publish` message you need to substitute the line below:

```
Inquire.Url = "http://test.uddi.microsoft.com/inquire"
```

...for:

```
Inquire.Url = "http://test.uddi.microsoft.com/publish"
```

This reflects the two Web Service end-points we discussed earlier, one for Search and one for Publish.

The Publish Web Service uses NT Basic authentication to gain access to its Web Service, so by using the following code, which also sets up your login details for UDDI, you can obtain login details by registering at `http://uddi.microsoft.com`:

```
Publish.Url = "https://test.uddi.microsoft.com/publish"
Publish.User = "PassportSignInName"
Publish.Password = "PassportPassword"
```

Disco.exe

Included within VS.NET is the `disco.exe` tool. This tool dynamically scans an `.asmx` or `.disco` file and creates files locally on your computer that correspond to all the Web Services it locates. This tool can be used to locate Web Services on a server, which can then be used to feed into a search engine or local (work offline) repository. This can be helpful if you want to give developers access to information about what Web Services are available without actually giving them access to the Internet.

It creates any combination of the following files while it scans the source location:

- WSDL Schema
- XSD Schema definition
- DISCO file
- DISCO.MAP file

Looking at the above it's apparent that we've seen these files together before and looking at our previously created projects we can recognize them as all being part of the Web References group (underneath `localhost`).

Note the `.map` file output using `disco.exe` is called `results.discomap`. However, it contains exactly the same information as the `reference.map`.

Now what's so special about this application? Well, it scans all files and **all links** when creating output. Let's point it at our project we created earlier, where we linked multiple files together. Just type in the following command at a command prompt, making sure that the `disco.exe` is on the current DOS search path:

```
disco http://localhost/PWS/Ch7/Discovery1/Discovery1.vsdisco
```

You will now see something like the following output:

```
Microsoft (R) Web Services Discovery Utility
[Microsoft (R) .NET Framework, Version 1.0.3705.0]
Copyright (C) Microsoft Corporation 1998-2001. All rights reserved.

Disco found documents at the following URLs:
http://localhost/PWS/Ch7/Discovery1/XMLFile1.disco
http://localhost/PWS/Ch7/Discovery1/Service1.asmx?wsdl
http://localhost/PWS/Ch7/Discovery1/Service2.asmx?wsdl
http://localhost/PWS/Ch7/Discovery1/Discovery1.vsdisco

The following files hold the content found at the corresponding URLs:
  .\XMLFile1.disco <- http://localhost/PWS/Ch7/Discovery1/XMLFile1.disco
  .\Service1.wsdl <- http://localhost/PWS/Ch7/Discovery1/Service1.asmx?wsdl
  .\Service2.wsdl <- http://localhost/PWS/Ch7/Discovery1/Service2.asmx?wsdl
  .\Discovery1.disco <- http://localhost/PWS/Ch7/Discovery1/Discovery1.vsdisco
The file .\results.discomap holds links to each of these files.
```

The first section simply identifies the files it finds, but as it navigates through the `.vsdisco` file it also identifies the links to the other `.disco` files and `.wsdl` files it finds.

The second part of this output signifies the local files it creates in relation to the files it has found.

Using this mechanism and architecture of linking `.vsdisco` files to a central `default.vsdisco` file, you can in fact allow `disco.exe` to discover every Web Service and therefore every application you have written in ASP.NET on a specific server. In team environments this can in fact lead to significant benefits by allowing you to create these local files and feed them into a specialist search engine of your own.

What Does the Future Hold for Discovery?

The DISCO standard in itself is not reliant on whether it's industry-recognized or not. It carries considerable momentum by just being used within the ASP.NET technology.

With the pick-up in interest in ASP.NET fully expected over the next few years we should expect a significant increase in the number of Web Services, which will then make sure that other companies will have to utilize and understand this DISCO technology. Otherwise they will simply omit this potentially huge untapped library of Web Services.

Using other developers' Web Services is not alien to us, as we've been using third-party components or DLLs for years now. However, by combining the ease of use and time saving benefits of components, with the ability to release functionality globally using Internet technology, this medium will have a tremendous impact as the years progress. Reliability and consistency of service will of course be an issue. Nevertheless, as we progress, developers' attitudes will change and the thought of using someone else's SMS text messaging or weather forecasting Web Service will be considered the norm throughout the industry.

Search engines currently search Internet web pages! OK, that's not exactly groundbreaking news, but the DISCO standard has been designed to allow for the discovery of Web Services in exactly the same way, by linking together vast tree-like structures of XML files instead of just web pages. This will allow us to discover Web Services using general searching abilities, but I also expect to see small islands of Web Services emerging, which dedicate themselves to promoting Web Services related to a specific part of the industry, for example hospitals or banks.

Using Web Service discovery for your own benefit is also going to be an extremely important area of development, as even though we all say we like to reuse components, often, we can't be bothered to get that old code off the other disk drive and make sure it works first. If it was compiled as a Web Service and easy to discover on your own internal network, you would just use it immediately.

Because of DISCO's peer-to-peer-like architecture, it also works well at being able to feed database search facilities in the same manner that web sites feed search engines such as Google and Lycos. This would then allow developers to search for Web Services in the same manner as they do web pages. This is not as far-fetched as one might first imagine. In fact, www.salcentral.com already uses a technique of searching through XML files to populate its database with information on the whereabouts of Web Services.

Summary

In this chapter we have seen how the discovery of Web Services is not yet something that we all do at the end of a development cycle. It is crucial to have a fundamental understanding in place that will allow us to utilize this powerful portion of ASP.NET technology as it takes off.

Points to remember and topics covered in this chapter:

- DISCO allows you to promote and advertise your Web Services.
- You can use DISCO to remind you of Web Services you have developed in the past.
- You can link discovery files together forming a peer-to-peer linking of files, similar to how HTML files link together on the Internet.
- UDDI and specialist search engines (for instance, www.salcentral.com) can help you promote your Web Services.
- You can create a library of Web Services along with descriptions and additional information not contained within the DISCO standard.
- `.vsdisco` files link to multiple Web Services.
- `.disco` files link to single Web Services.
- The **Add Web Reference** menu option allows you to add Web Services directly into your project.
- You can adapt the standard by adding XML files or different types to supplement the standard and tailor it for your own needs.
- `.vsdisco` files are generated dynamically at run time by browsing to a `.vsdisco` file.
- `.disco` files are generated dynamically at run time by browsing to `.asmx?disco`.
- You can use the `Disco.exe` utility to create your own off-line search engine.

PROFESSIONAL
ASP.NET
WEB
SERVICES

8

Design Criteria

Web Services have the possibility to change the way business is done on the web. As EDI did for document transfer in the mid-eighties, and HTTP did for information viewing in the mid-nineties, Web Services promise to allow cross-company logic interchange regardless of system. The cross-platform nature of SOAP allows IT managers and application developers to build business logic that spans installed systems with little overhead or increase on upfront cost. This alone may mean that Web Services will make a significant change in the way business gets done in distributed systems.

Notice the use of "may mean", "promises" and "possibility" in the above paragraph. This is because Web Services are not a panacea. There are things that Web Services don't do well, but these things are massively compensated for by the things that Web Services can do well. We saw this with DHTML – its promise was compromised by minor differences between the platform-specific implementations of JavaScript and the DOM, causing massive headaches for programmers and architects that continue to this day.

Could this happen to Web Services? Sure. We keep it from happening by understanding systems and n-tier application development. This chapter will introduce you to the design criteria of Web Services: how, when, and where to use them, how to architect for them when you use them, and how to integrate them with existing logic. Once the subject has been introduced, the following chapters will fill in the details.

So before diving in, let's look at the topics we'll be covering:

- When a Web Service does and doesn't fit into a design
- Fitting Web Services into your design methodology
- Design considerations such as error handling and security
- Performance considerations

When a Web Service Fits in a Design

As with any new technology, the ability to use it correctly is paramount. As mentioned above, DHTML became a hammer for many who saw a nail, and many of us have spent countless hours rewriting intranets for Internet Explorer 5 from IE4-specific code. Let's take a look at where Web Services fit into your architecture or the design of your application.

There are three principal situations in which to use Web Services – Internets, Extranets, and Intranets. That is perhaps a little vague, but it is a good way to look at things. First, Web Services are useful for connecting to information on the Internet that is blocked off by a local or remote firewall, or both. Second, Web Services allow you to expose specific portions of your business logic to customers or partners via your extranet. Third, Web Services make an acceptable distributed architecture to share logic between disparate systems in the same room, building or organization. So here we have three types of common communication – external to customers, external to partners, and internal. Let's look at each in turn.

Consuming the Resources of the Internet

Key to the usefulness of Web Services is their ability to transfer complex data structures through corporate firewalls without compromising already existent security. Web Services travel through the same transport layer as web sites, so the hole through which they fly is already well defined.

Firewalls are designed to prohibit unauthorized traffic between computers within its control and computers outside its control. When computers communicate with the Internet through the firewall, traffic for specific functions travels on designated ports. These ports allow the firewall to restrict traffic to designated protocols, since it can assume that the computers within its control will react in expected ways to that traffic.

Traffic for the World Wide Web travels via HTTP on port 80, or 443 if encrypted. In order for a computer to surf the web, the firewall between it and the Internet must allow port 80 and 443 traffic. These are the ports, and the protocol, that Web Services use. Therefore, all of this functionality flows conveniently through your corporate firewall, without compromising the security of the rest of the system. Other distributed network architectures like DCOM, CORBA, and RMI use custom ports for their information transfers, often encountering firewall-enforced roadblocks.

This is useful in several ways, but the primary benefit is to be able to consume logic from providers that would normally require FTP of preprocessed information. For example, Weather.Com (The Weather Channel) provides a service to ISPs where a large file of weather data, containing data for all of the Midwest of America for example, is FTP-ed to the client site in a preset directory several times a day. Then the client software parses through the text file, looking for the weather data for its specific needs. Often when the end user views the information it is several hours old.

With Web Services, Weather.Com could expose the logic that gathers the data for that text file to the Internet. The client could call the service with its username, password, and zip code if needed. Then the Web Service would return, on demand, the current weather information for that location. The Web Service call can be built directly into the consuming object, treating the logic as though it was resident on the local system. The logic, however, remains safely behind Weather.Com's firewall, being served by its web server.

Selling Business Services

The ubiquitous nature of Web Services provides a prime platform for potential profit. There are an almost unlimited number of processes and pieces of data that can be exposed in the form of a Web Service. Any application that is developed, or any database that is stored, probably is of enough use to someone out there that they will pay twenty cents every time they use it. This is an undeniably marketable concept.

.NET My Services

A fine example of this is Microsoft's .NET My Services, a user-centric architecture and set of XML Web Services. You can read much more about .NET My Services in Appendix A, or at the .NET Services site at http://www.microsoft.com/netservices/userexperiences.asp. These services will make it easier to integrate an average user's information "silos", thus providing a more integrated experience with technology. Microsoft's example is remembering a phone number. Imagine what an average user has to do to make this happen. Often, it must be typed into Outlook with a keyboard, written into a Palm with Graffiti, and punched into a cell phone with a number pad.

With .NET My Services, each of these devices could use a centralized data store, communicating with this database using Web Services as needed. The API is saleable, the services are saleable, and the storage is saleable. This could be a very successful project.

Any organization with information for sale can make fantastic use of Web Services. Weather.com again serves as a good example. I had to integrate their massive text files into a site several years ago, and it took four days of programming to get what I wanted. Then, of course, they added a field and I had to edit my component – three times. We eventually dropped the service. That won't happen with Web Services because all of the logic is inherent to the method call.

Brokerages

Another great business model, and one already being exploited by Lucin, which runs SalCentral, is a Web Services brokerage service (you can find SalCentral at http://www.salcentral.com). They have their own authentication scheme whereby you register your Web Service, and SalCentral will make sure users are authorized to use your service, charge them on your behalf, and take a small brokerage fee.

Exposing Business Logic To Partners

The ability to expose existing business logic to clients, customers or partners becomes a powerful tool. With few security concerns, well-designed Web Services have the power to leverage existing business logic – in-house tools, mind you – and transfer the power of their use to select business partners in a secure fashion.

Currently, if an organization wants to share information with a partner they often use Electronic Data Interchange, passing documents in established formats through message handlers like Gentran or BizTalk. If they want to share business logic, they get a leased line or Virtual Private Network to the partner and write an application. The classic ways to share business logic and information among partners are so fraught with security and technical troubles, however, that few use them. In today's technological environment there should be a better way, and now there is.

Web Services give businesses another potential path. Since the protocol is a standard, similar to HTML for the web or SMTP for e-mail, organizations have a common platform upon which to build these pathways. Additionally, because the standards are open, implementation costs are within the reach of even the smaller companies.

Interop Internally Between Systems

One IT staff, two systems – Unix and NT. Need I say more? Web Services are supported by scores of system vendors already. Although the overhead of using a Web Service for an application function call is rather high, it's better than a batch job. A surprising number of platforms support Web Services intrinsically, including IBM, Microsoft and Sun – the ones you will find in most enterprises.

Of course, any language that will handle XML and HTTP will handle Web Services, but it helps to have a protocol pipeline for SOAP. Of course, .NET has Web Services built in, but what about that **other** platform? For Visual Studio 6, Microsoft provides the SOAP Toolkit, now in version 2. You can learn more about the SOAP Toolkit at http://msdn.microsoft.com/webservices. The fun really starts, though, when you have to interop with a Delphi program, or that Linux box around the corner.

A fantastic example of the SOAP protocol simplified is the SOAP::lite modules. Available for both Perl and COM, this simple API allows a developer to integrate Web Services into any platform that speaks Perl, or any Windows language that speaks COM. Let's look at a quick example. In order to actually do this, you'll need to install ActiveState's Perl 5.6 for Windows, and add the SOAP::lite libraries. Instructions for SOAP::lite can be found on http://www.soaplite.com, and the free ActiveState download can be found at http://aspn.activestate.com/ASPN/Downloads/ActivePerl.

For example, set up a simple service on your .NET development server, just the basic HelloWorld is fine:

```
<%@ WebService Language="VB" Class="HelloWorld" %>

Imports System
Imports System.Web.Services
  Public Class HelloWorld
    Inherits System.Web.Services.WebService

    <WebMethod()> _
    Public Function SayHelloWorld() As String
      Return "Hello World"
    End Function 'SayHelloWorld
  End Class 'HelloWorld
```

Build a simple `.cgi` file on your web server, and slip in this code:

```
use SOAP::Lite;

print SOAP::Lite
  -> service('http://localhost/sd/service1.asmx?wsdl')
  -> SayHelloWorld();
```

How easy was that? We'll spare you the example with a Perl server and a .NET client, it's just as simple. We can see from this simple example that complex logic written in .NET can be run on your Linux web server with practically no coding at all for the web developer.

Interoperability with other platforms is similar. IBM WebSphere, the most common Java/EJB development tool, has Web Service interaction similar to .NET, as does Delphi 6 and the latest version of Fujitsu COBOL (the mainframe version too!). If your company is working on many platforms, Web Services will benefit interoperability greatly.

When NOT To Use Web Services

On the other hand, there are times when it doesn't pay to use Web Services. First, there are some overhead and performance considerations. Second, there are few existing security models. Third, there are better ways to solve some of the problems that Web Services can solve. Web Services aren't here to replace things so much as add a new dimension to interoperability. This is a very fine line, but if it seems that Web Services are missing something intrinsic to be useful, then you are probably trying to use them inappropriately.

Rest assured, this is a great standard, and it is well implemented by .NET, but Web Services won't solve every development task you have on your plate. We talked above about what they do well; now let's look at what they don't do so well.

Internal To an Application, Use DLLs

All of the hype surrounding Web Services has caused an explosion in the number of developers that use SOAP just because the Toolkit or .NET is installed on the server. Aside from the tenet to "keep it simple", there are two primary reasons not to do this.

Firstly, method calls to Web Services are a lot slower than normal method calls. The information in the call, encoded into a SOAP header, has to be parsed to and from text on the client and server side. Although .NET is better with string handling, Microsoft languages are still significantly slower at handling strings than they are at handling binary. Keeping the method call in .NET and away from Web Services speeds up the process significantly. For instance, there have been a lot of applications floating around that use Web Services when a normal DLL would do. If you are writing an application, and have a DLL that supports, say, communications between your application, don't expose those methods as Web Services just because you can. The network hit, the performance crunch, and the complexity aren't worth the interoperability benefits.

Secondly, as we'll discuss below in the *Performance Considerations* section, Web Services don't handle stateful environments well. In a Windows Forms application, where you may handle events or properties, a DLL will give you better performance and is smarter design. Just like maintaining state with COM+ in n-tier applications, maintaining state with Web Services is bad news. It reduces scalability, significantly impacts performance, and eats bandwidth.

Communicating .NET To .NET? Use Remoting

Sometimes, even if you are writing a distributed application – say in Windows Forms – and there are no state issues, you should reconsider your use of Web Services. When writing COM to COM, DCOM was the best solution. When writing .NET to .NET, try Remoting. Learn more about Remoting on the MSDN library by reading the .NET Remoting Overview, or see Chapter 20 of "*Professional VB.NET 2nd Edition*" (Wrox Press, ISBN 1-86100-716-7) .

Remoting provides a feature-rich API for an application distributed across AppDomains, processes or machines. Essentially, it allows the passing of objects from one system to another, so that remote method calls are performed as though the logic was on the calling system:

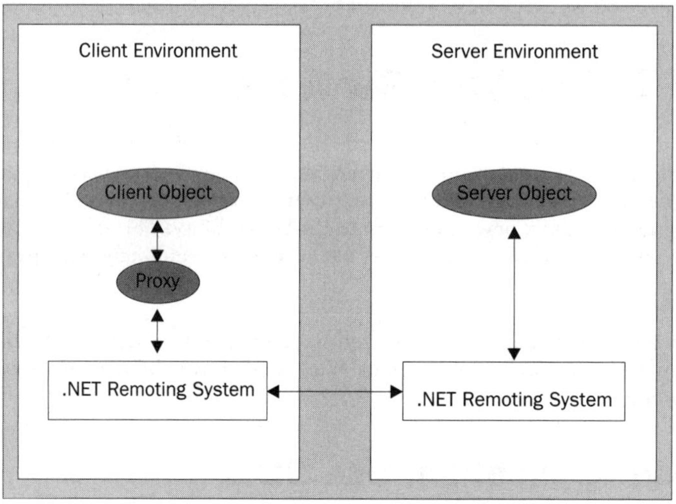

Although Remoting does allow for SOAP calls like the ones Web Services provide, use of the TCP channel speeds up the process to almost five times as fast. Remoting is designed for communications at the DLL level, and should be used that way. What we're trying to prevent is working through the ASP.NET layer with business logic, then back down to the component layer. If you can use Remoting to communicate directly, business layer to business layer, do.

Sometimes, It's Best Not To Distribute

There are times when it would be best not to expose anything to the Internet. If you are running a security installation for the government, you may want to reconsider exposing **any** logic to the outside. Making yourself a target for crackers and thieves may not be worth the benefits of having the services exposed. Balance the needs of the client against the risks and resources available to secure the service.

For instance, we all know about the break-ins at various company and agency web sites over the years. These crimes largely occur because the attacker has a point of entry – mainly the web page. Giving an attacker an obvious door is going to provoke attack in today's computing environment. Web Services will give attackers another door. Sooner or later, with enough tries, some of them will be broken.

If the business process that is being exposed by the Web Service cannot, under any circumstances, be compromised, then don't expose it.

Fitting Into an Existing Design Methodology

So you've decided to use a Web Service. How do you add it to your corporate methodology? How do you diagram a Web Service? How does this fit into your existing design? Fortunately, it's pretty easy. There are two design camps we must discuss in the arena of Web Services.

- Using the service in a new web or Win32 application
- Creating a Web Service

Using a service in an application is a straightforward proposition from the design perspective. To an architect, a Web Service is just another method, enabled by generating another object. In the case of a Web Service the object is a proxy, but it works just like any other DLL, and it looks like one in the design. The most important considerations are in the global view of the network map.

Developing a Web Service, while fairly simple from an architecture perspective, is a daunting task from a design perspective. An architect must consider the ins and outs of distributed method calls as seen above, but a designer has a whole host of considerations. We will look at actual design issues shortly, but will focus here on the architectural viewpoint.

Architectural Considerations

Web Services expose a layer of business logic through a method call. So do DLLs. In fact, as we have learned, the proxy is just a DLL acting as a proxy. From an architectural perspective, that's all there is to it. For the .NET developer, Web Services are just another method call. In reality, though, the network layer is the Internet itself, via whatever network protocol the client and server are using at the moment.

The magic of Web Services is in the WSDL file, which if everything goes well, we'll never see. This file, auto-generated by a call to the originating system if we need it, describes the entire class of methods available in the service along with their parameters (you can view the WSDL file at any time by adding `?wsdl` to the end of a ASMX file name in a URL). The various utilities .NET uses to make a Web Service proxy read this file to generate a DLL that works just like the other compiled .NET Framework components you use in your project. The cross-platform comes in because any language that handles WSDL can generate that file for a specific service, so the business end of your DLL file is truly platform-agnostic.

The Method Call

At the architectural level, a Web Service looks like a method call. Our design should reflect that by showing a Web Service running in the business layer just as if it were a normal business object. The proxy format of the WSDL file on the .NET Framework ensures that essentially it is just another business object.

In this sample sequence diagram of a simple login scheme, we see a Web Service fronting an application, as if we were designing the service as the user interface. When designing a service, this is essentially what we are doing. We are allowing an application to access our application as if it were the user:

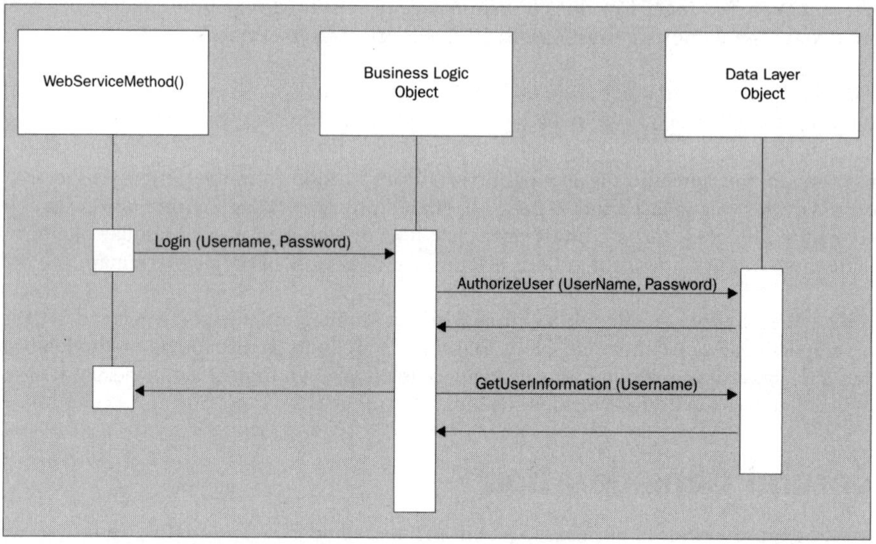

In the case of using a service as part of another application, we must take into account the likely asynchronous nature of the method call – the diagram below represents this scenario. Note the change in arrow type of the login method, since a .NET application can potentially be using the above service for login:

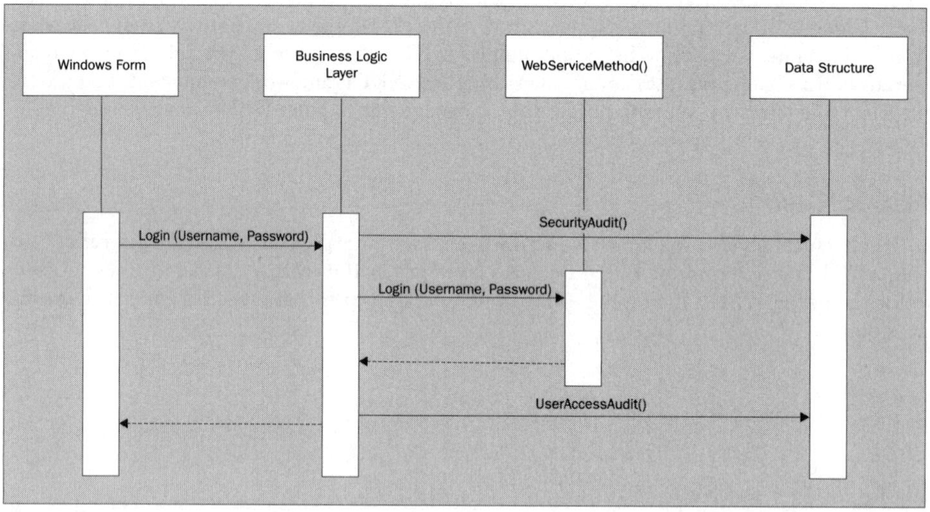

If you are working for an organization with very strict documentation guidelines, some analysis of the WSDL file may be necessary. Since the WSDL description offers all of the information about the service, it makes a service practically self-documenting. Take a look at Chapter 4 for a more in-depth coverage of WSDL.

Designing At the Enterprise Level

At the enterprise level, you'll find that Web Services make for more paperwork. Since we are actually using logic outside of the norm, we can draw a flow diagram that shows the breakdown of the network calls. This diagram lays out the design of network traffic though the .NET portions of the application, as well as the HTTP calls passing SOAP from system to system. This is remarkably important from both a functionality and network perspective.

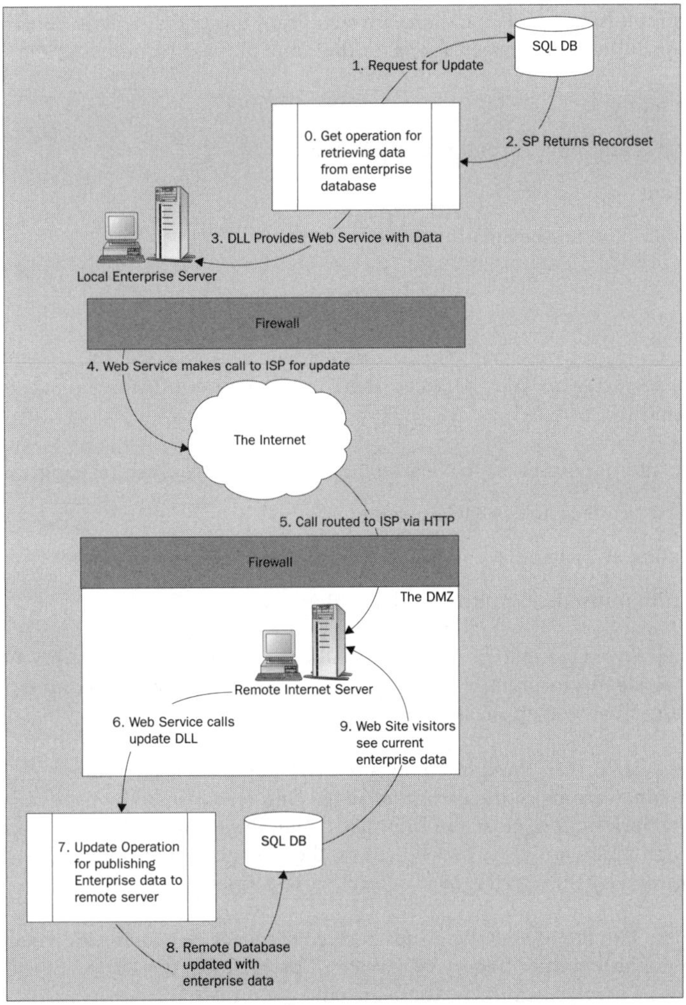

This is a diagram that we'll see again in Chapter 11, in a transactional service example. We show a Web Service that updates a database on a remote server. In the transaction diagram, this would essentially appear the same as a normal database update, but in this diagram we show the SOAP call sliding through the corporate firewalls on both sides. Since the traffic moved on Port 80 or 443 at those points, the firewalls don't require changes to the security profiles.

Once again, a company with a more strict documentation standard may not be pleased to discover that business logic is extending beyond the firewall, so more explanation may be in order. For many projects, however, a basic diagram like the one shown above will do the job.

Design Considerations

Now that we have fitted Web Services into our architecture, how do we fit it into our design? The individual techniques for these considerations are significant topics that will be covered in later chapters. However, we'll look at the design implications for the some of these techniques here, including:

- Error Handling
- Synchronous and Asynchronous connections
- Transactions
- Interoperation with other platforms
- Security

Error Handling

In designing error handling for Web Services, there are a number of situations we must be able to handle. These include:

- Handling internal errors, to make sure the service doesn't crash or hang
- Passing error codes back to the consumer
- Documenting error handling so that a consumer can effectively use it
- Dealing with transmission or network problems

In handling internal errors, good `Try ... Catch` blocks are essential for Quality Of Service reasons. Since these services are just essentially ASP.NET pages with a new interface, most of the error handling one would do in a normal web application still applies.

What of reporting those errors, though? In an ASP.NET page, we would simply display a user-friendly message to the screen, warning of the error and suggesting responses. The user can choose to ignore the error and press the back button, close the browser, e-mail the webmaster, and so on. In the case of a Web Service, though, there are very few choices on the part of the consumer. The client either deals with the error returned by the service, or it doesn't work properly.

To that end, services like the MSDN Favorites Service carefully document the error codes that can be returned by each method in their battery of services. For instance, the `Logon()` method that is used by licensees to access the service can throw these errors:

Number	Description
1002	Invalid licensee key.
1005	Invalid user name.
1006	User not authenticated.

Network problems will turn out to be a significant source of errors in Web Services. In fact, the Microsoft implementation of SOAP doesn't allow Web Services to participate in transactions, as we'll see in a later section. As far as handling these problems with ASP.NET Web Services, the best bet is probably to design around them. A few key things to remember in this respect are:

- Make sure you have the same redundancies you would have in an important web site
- Don't maintain state
- If you need to resend what may be redundant information, do so
- If you need an acknowledgement that something has been handled, require it
- If you need to pass acknowledgement that something has been handled, supply it

Keep in mind how asynchronous technologies like FTP and e-mail have kept working through various network trials and tribulations. FTP maintains reasonable timeout limits. E-mail tries for several hours to get a message through, and then expects a response from the receiving server. When we are in doubt as to how to design around network problems, our best bet is to look at how these protocols have been so successful.

Synchronous vs. Asynchronous

Synchronous communication is connected communication – where the calling application waits for a response from the method called before going on. COM+ and Windows Scripting Host use this type of communication. Asynchronous communication is disconnected communication. MSMQ and BizTalk use asynchronous communication, but, of course, the largest user of asynchronous communication is the Internet itself. Synchronous and Asynchronous communications in an application are important in design considerations and also apply to other considerations like error handling and transactions.

Web Services provide a loosely-coupled model that causes some trouble in enterprise applications. Transactions, as we'll see later, are one of these problem issues – synchronization is another. When your method call has no knowledge of the underlying network layer, you can't always tie up an entire component until the service method has returned.

The best way to deal with the synchronous issue is to design around it. Knowing that the service is loosely coupled should lead a developer to only use an asynchronous call. Microsoft does, however, provide some functionality to assist with synchronous services.

The `System.EnterpriseServices` namespace provides much of the functionality found in COM+. Currently, this includes features such as Just-In-Time activation, loosely-coupled events, pooling and synchronization. To enable synchronization on a serviced component providing a Web Service, you'll need to inherit from `System.EnterpriseServices.ServicedComponent`. Transactional services, Just-In-Time readiness and other COM+ services will not work without synchronous communication.

Another solution is to make use of the naturally asynchronous nature of Web Services. IIS will handle that for you, as `.asmx` pages are by definition asynchronous. For more detail on this topic, please see Chapter 9.

Transactions

Transactional processing is an important part of distributed systems. Since different parts of the program change different parts of the data, transactions are needed to ensure that everything gets done by the end of the method. Since Web Services are loosely-coupled by design, they have no knowledge of the underlying network layer. This makes acknowledgement of transactional coupling very difficult.

There are a few different situations where Web Services could participate in transactions.

- As the creator of a transaction, as in a Web Service that credits and debits an account
- As the participator in a transaction, as a Web Service that is called by another Web Service
- As the participator in a transaction called by a .NET object

We'll look at several different transactional situations in Chapter 11, but let's look at some high-level issues here.

There are two perspectives on transactions as part of Web Services: as the provider, and as the consumer. As the provider, .NET provides a number of technologies, not least of which is COM+, to help maintain the option for distributed transactions.

When providing a Web Service, transactional design considerations are fairly obvious. When you are providing a service that makes a batch transaction, you should provide rollback in case of failure. Normally, this is a service provided by COM+, and that is an option still available in .NET. Despite what many think, .NET is not a replacement for COM+, it is a replacement for COM. Also, .NET provides the same roll-your-own transactions that you found in COM, inheriting from the `System.EnterpriseServices` namespace.

As the consumer, however, distributed transaction coordination is a difficult task. Since the SOAP protocol is loosely-coupled, we have no knowledge of the failure of a service at the network level. Of course, the service can provide an error we can handle at the consumer level, but if the remote machine dies in the middle, there is no response returned to us. Therefore, our application can hang forever waiting for the data to return, except in the case of a timeout or 404 Not Found from the web server.

If we are using COM+ on the consumer side, major problems will occur. Firstly, Web Services don't play well when called in transactions by other services or objects. Secondly, we must consider failures in Web Services in our error handling, as discussed above, so the consumer can properly handle them in the transactional system using the service. If you are consuming a Web Service as part of an enterprise system that requires distributed transactions, you should consider .NET Remoting instead, which provides this feature.

Interoperation with Other Platforms

The whole point of Web Services is cross-platform interoperability. To this end, you'll need to know what Microsoft-only features to avoid in making sure your services are interoperable. When working in a COM/.NET world, you'll be very surprised with the simplicity of Web Services using the SOAP Toolkit 2.0.

Although Web Services by definition are based in interoperability, there are a few specifics that are helpful in more advanced usage. Microsoft provides advanced features for Web Services in .NET that you won't really find on other platforms. These must be considered when designing with Web Services. For instance, the issue of advanced data types is a significant problem. If you send, for instance, a `DataSet` with Web Services from .NET, the client will get – from its perspective – a poorly formed XML file, if not using a .NET server.

So, the general consensus is to stick to the basic data types when working with fully cross-platform Web Services. These consist of the built-in data types found in the XML Specification, as shown in the diagram below:

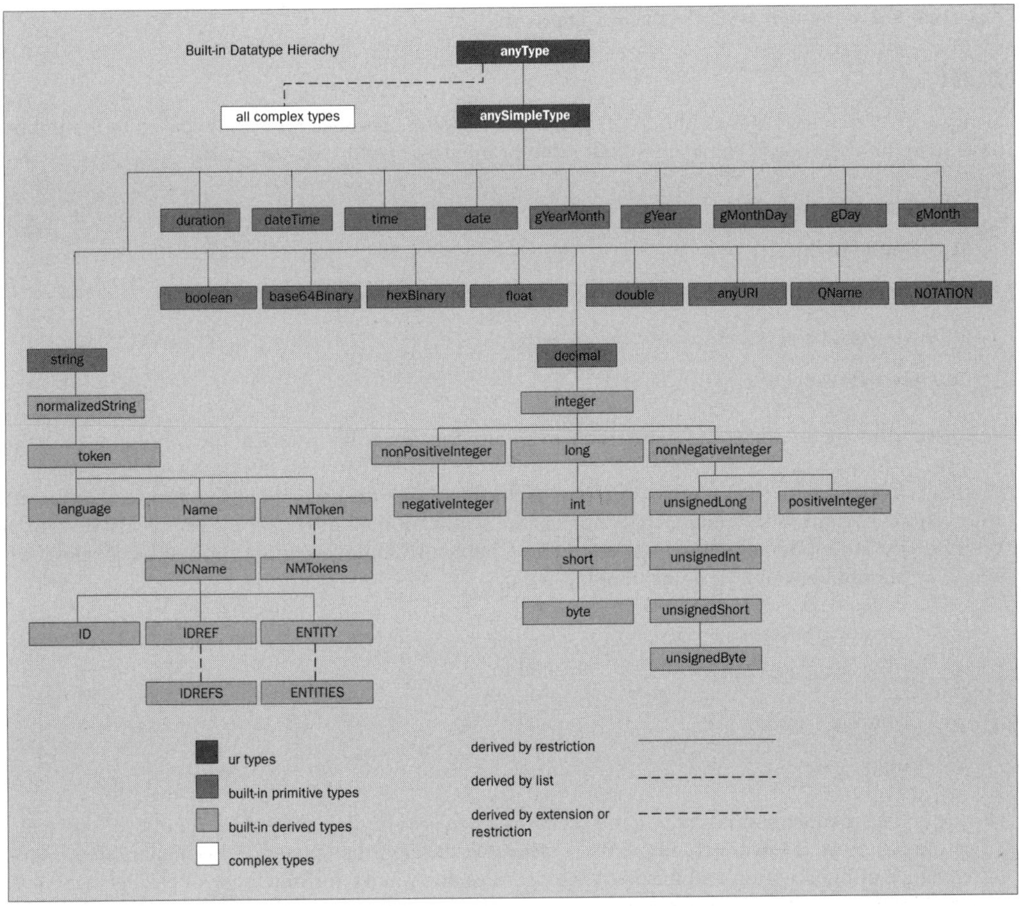

This diagram is more than we really need to know, but it is useful information. Essentially, we are looking at:

- `dateTime`
- `Boolean`
- `string`

- `int`
- `decimal`
- `hex`
- `float`
- `Base64`

One of the more significant uses of Web Services will be interoperability from .NET to COM, and Microsoft has provided a very significant tool (the SOAP Toolkit, now in Version 2.0), which will provide a simpler COM/.NET interop than wrapping each component in formal interop code. We discussed the implementation details in Chapter 4.

Security

Security of Web Services is as important as that of web sites. Because they are exposed to the public, we have to be on the lookout for many of the same problems as we do for our sites:

- Compromised data
- Denial of Service
- Unauthorized use
- Network level issues
- User Privacy

Fortunately, as we are using the same software we use for those sites many of the solutions are the same.

Web Services combine the security problems of the Web with the security problems of a distributed application. This provides quite a challenge for the application architect. While the security within a Web Service is well documented and covered in Chapter 13, there are other tools at our disposal of which we should be well aware, including:

- Operating System security
- Secure Sockets Layer
- Database security
- Policy

Classic NT Authentication is a very good scenario when security is a must on a Windows 2000 web site. Since the password is never actually sent via clear text through the network – even encrypted – there is little chance of interception and misuse. Web Services don't make for much use of NT Security in their external interface, but controlling access internally using access control lists is a must. Remember that when we give the world access to a Web Service, we are letting them run a program on our web server. Controlling what that program has access to is a must when considering overall security.

In the Favorites Service, the MSDN team decided to pass the logon and password of the licensee directly to the services' logon sequence, using Secure Sockets Layer, or port 443 of the web server. SSL makes use of Public / Private Key pairs to ensure that clear text like SOAP sent through the Internet is not available for viewing. Since it is an integral part of IIS, it is fairly easy to use in your service, but hard to set up administratively. Check the MSDN library and IIS documentation for more details there.

In the *Methodology* section above, we discussed how a database server should be placed in the network for optimum control. This applies in the security scenario, too. The database should never have a publicly accessible address. Having a Web Service exposed will certainly draw database crackers, and if we don't have a publicly available database, they don't have anything to crack. Let your Web Service be the gateway to the database.

Finally, as in any good security implementation, policy is our best weapon. Follow the same security procedures that any good administrator follows when designing and maintaining a network or secure facility.

Centrally control passwords. Since your users don't usually have to worry about remembering passwords, make them complex and change them regularly. Remember to watch your log files.

Keeping a vigilant eye for crackers is probably the best defense against problems. The ingenuity of those who want to break into your systems is without end – don't expect to be able to plan around everything, or design out all security flaws – it won't happen. Do, however, follow the basic procedures and keep a sharp eye out for trouble.

Performance Considerations

Finally, we need to consider the performance of a loosely-coupled protocol like SOAP in a tightly-coupled world like .NET. Since Web Services are handled as an XML stream, there are significant performance considerations to even using them. As a general rule of thumb, a method call to a service on the same box runs around five times slower than a call to a .NET object with the same code. Not only are you depending on IIS to broker the transaction, you are forcing XML parsing on both sides of the transaction.

Of course, one of the largest performance considerations is the Internet itself. Since we are dependent on so many different points of presence for the connectivity, performance can never be guaranteed. We only have control on the server itself – just as when developing web applications in general.

So there are two things we can do to improve the performance on the service side: use caching and not use state. Caching allows us to keep useful information around for when we might need it again. State in a web application is dangerous to begin with but some new tools provided by .NET provide an interesting new look at state and its potential.

State

Although state should be avoided in most web applications, Microsoft has provided two "stateless" ways to provide state in .NET. Many of us have built data-driven state tools that use GUIDs to track user existence, then store the GUID in a cookie, or keep it alive in the URL as a `QueryString` variable. As part of .NET, Microsoft has done this for us, providing both implementations of state as part of the familiar `Request` and `Response` objects. These implementations are also available to Web Services.

The problem with state in COM was that it required Windows 2000 to track some secret number and store it in the database for its own private use. As most of us know, that simply didn't work – if you were to load balance your server, it fell apart. Even just using it with a single server added massive overhead. Now, this value assigned to a user is in the open, available to the cookies collection, or merged into the URL.

A Real Performance Hit

Even though this ends the well-known problems that ASP Version 3 has with web farms and load balancing, there is still a significant performance hit. On every page, .NET objects must make behind the scenes calls to generate or parse the `SessionID`, a 120 bit unique code. Then database entries must be made to allow .NET namespace access to this session information. Despite the fact that the .NET Framework does significantly speed up this operation, it still doubles the response time from IIS for an average page.

Another option is to use the cookie-based state option, which is even slower – though more invisible to the user. Since the application has to make a second call to the client and request the cookies file, we have network lag added to the parsing and metadata manipulation.

What it is important to remember is that state is still to be used only when necessary – like within a shopping cart application, for example. Fortunately, it is turned off by default, so a change has to be made in the `web.config` to even turn it on. On the other hand, the new state objects are good enough that when we do need to use them, we can use the built-in tools, rather than rolling our own.

Caching

On the other side of the performance coin is Caching, which provides a window of time in which a value in the response of a Web Service method should be held in a memory cache. Caching is used by many technologies in this networked world. For example, Internet Explorer holds your last 14 days of web sites in a cache, so if you re-request one, it only needs to check for updates before displaying. In the world of Web Services, this feature can significantly reduce server processing time.

For instance, say you are running a weather service. You can set the web method to hold on to the results for 60 seconds, so if it is requested again for that zip code you won't have to reprocess from the database. Alternatively, you could proactively look up the alerts and cache those results, knowing that this will be the next request.

`CacheDuration` is set to 0 as a default, and is a property of the `WebMethodAttribute` class. The `WebMethodAttribute` class is inherited by most Web Services and also provides descriptions, sessions and buffer information. You can read more about the `WebMethodAttribute` in Chapter 2.

Summary

Web Services have the potential to change the Internet and Enterprise application development in one fell swoop. Just as HTML did in the mid-nineties, SOAP provides a much-needed solution to a massive problem – this time, the problem is to share logic like we share data. If they are carefully designed and effectively implemented, Web Services will change the way we do business with clients, partners, and internally.

To this end, we covered the following very important design topics:

- When a Web Service does and doesn't fit into a design
- Fitting Web Services into your design methodology
- Design considerations including:
  - Error handling
  - Synchronous calls versus asynchronous
  - Transactions
  - Interoperability
- Performance Considerations

Through the rest of the book, we'll discuss this design and implementation in high detail, culminating in ideas for using Web Services in your business. You'll find details on some of the topics covered above, and Chapters 7 and 13 on *Discovery* and *Authentication*. Putting it all together, you have the opportunity to seriously improve your enterprise architecture, dramatically increase customer service, and significantly increase shareholder value.

PROFESSIONAL
ASP.NET
WEB
SERVICES

9

Asynchronous Programming

To wait or not to wait; that is the question! Whether or not to implement asynchronous processing is one of the fundamental issues that a developer must answer when invoking function calls across process boundaries. Given that the option to invoke an asynchronous call is available, the programmer has to weigh the relative ease of coding synchronous calls with its inherent drawback – when a synchronous call is made, the calling thread is blocked and has to wait until the function completes. In many instances, this is an acceptable shortcoming, as in the case when a program's logic flow should not continue until data is retrieved from a database. Asynchronous processing, on the other hand, allows more parallelism. A thread that initiates an asynchronous call is not blocked and can therefore do almost any computation while the method is in transit. The case for asynchronous processing becomes very compelling in the enterprise computing space where systems need to handle hundreds of thousands of function call requests and synchronicity may become a barrier to scalability.

Web Services support both synchronous and asynchronous communication between the client application and the server hosting the service. Since both are supported, the developer is challenged with deciding which type of process to initiate in their application. In this chapter, we're going to dive into the subject of synchronous and asynchronous programming as it pertains to ASP.NET Web Services. We'll explore the mechanics of invoking Web Services via an asynchronous mechanism. We'll also look into the .NET Framework and how it provides the infrastructure for asynchronous processing.

So, the topics for this chapter are:

- Synchronous versus asynchronous invocations
- Asynchronous design patterns in .NET
- How to invoke Web Services asynchronously
- What to consider when developing asynchronous Web Service calls

Synchronous Versus Asynchronous Invocations

As we learned in Chapter 2, the .NET Framework shields the programmer from the complexities of generating a remote procedure call (RPC) to a Web Service hosted on another server. As far as we are concerned, they are simply making a method call to another component. The mechanism for invoking the method call looks the same whether the server component is within the application's assembly or many miles away running on another machine.

Despite their similarities on the surface, the underlying plumbing used to invoke a Web Service is very different from an in-process function call. In the case of a Web Service, the function call is packaged into a SOAP message and marshaled across the Internet via the HTTP protocol. Because of the inherent nature of the Internet, performance of the RPC call to the Web Service can vary greatly from one call to the next. The design choices you make when developing your Web Service client application can make a big difference in how your users will perceive application availability and performance.

In this section, we'll compare the merits and shortcomings of both the synchronous and asynchronous approaches to calling Web Services. We'll also learn how to actually develop client applications that make use of the asynchronous mechanisms built into the .NET Framework. This will set the stage for a deeper discussion of asynchronous processing in the subsequent sections.

The Case for Synchronous Processing

Synchronous operations consist of component or function calls that operate in lockstep. A synchronous call blocks a process until the operation completes. Only then will the next line of execution be invoked. There are many examples in life that model this pattern of behavior. The cafeteria line at your local restaurant, for example, behaves in a synchronous fashion. Customers are serviced one at a time. While they are in line, they are blocked from conducting other activities, and they wait until all their food choices are served before they can continue with their lunch break. Of course, after waiting for a very long time they might give up and leave. Here's a diagram illustrating the concept of synchronous processes:

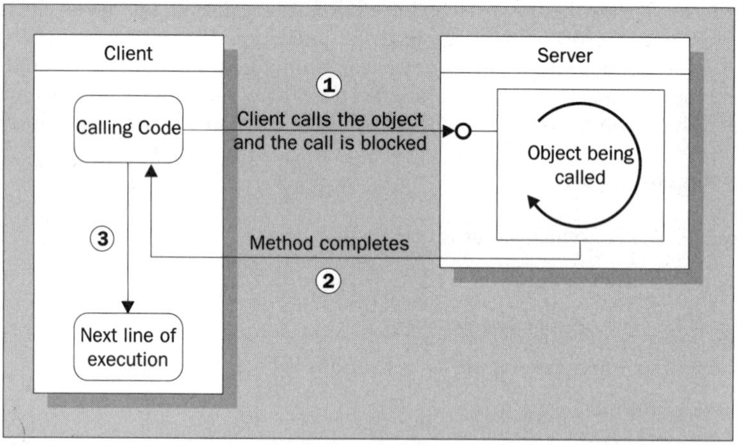

As you can see, the procedure for making synchronous calls is straightforward:

1. The client obtains an interface pointer to the server object and calls a method through that pointer
2. The client waits until the server either completes the method call, or if there is no response for a given period of time the client raises an error
3. Only after the method call returns is the client free to continue with its processing

It is this simplicity that makes synchronous processes a compelling choice. Most of the time, the performance achieved from method calls is acceptable and does not warrant the extra overhead required for concurrent processing. In fact, most of the function calls in the .NET Framework are synchronous to minimize problems that can arise from asynchronous message processing. Likewise, the method calls you will be implementing will be done in a synchronous fashion in most cases.

Asynchronous message passing, on the other hand, is more difficult to code and introduces several problems. What happens if the method call is not delivered to the server object successfully? The calling process does not wait for delivery of the message, and thus never hears about the error. The operating system has to provide the infrastructure for reporting such errors, or worse, the programmer may have to write special code to handle such cases. Another related problem is how will the calling application discover the completion of the called function? The application will either have to create a polling mechanism, event trigger, or callback method in order to be later notified of the operation.

Because synchronous messaging is so easy to implement, you may be tempted to take the simple route and always use a synchronous mechanism when invoking a Web Service from your client code. Consider your choice carefully because this decision will have an impact on how your client application will perform. When implemented properly, using asynchronous communication may improve system usage and avoid delays on the client side while waiting for the Web Service results.

When Asynchronous Processing Is Better

When method calls are invoked across process and machine boundaries via an RPC mechanism, it's often a likely candidate for asynchronous processing. This is definitely true in the case of Web Services where the remote procedure call is sent via HTTP and must deal with issues such as bandwidth constraints and network latency.

What makes asynchronous method invocations a good choice for communicating with Web Services? An asynchronous operation will not block the calling thread, which only initiates the operation. The calling application must then discover completion of the call by polling, by software interrupt, or by waiting explicitly for completion later. An asynchronous operation will need to return a call or transaction ID if the calling application needs to be later notified about the operation. At notification time, this ID would be placed in some global location or passed as an argument to a handle or wait call. Here is a diagram illustrating the concept of an asynchronous process:

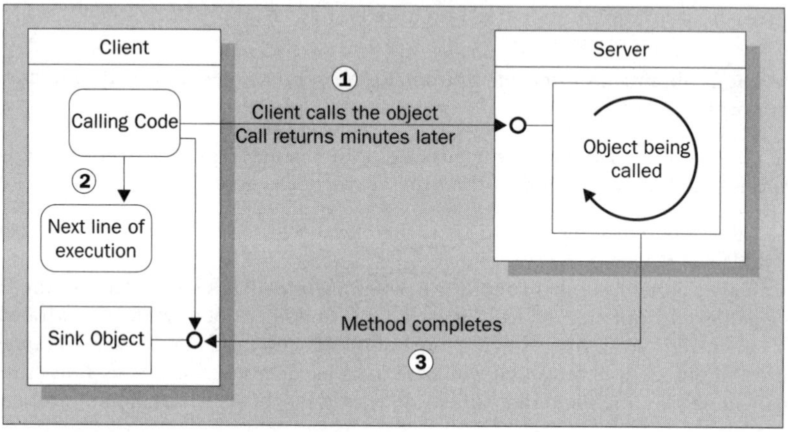

The procedure for making an asynchronous call is not as simple as its synchronous counterpart:

1. The client obtains an interface pointer to the server object and calls the method asynchronously. The client includes a function pointer to a sink object for message callback.

2. The call returns immediately and the calling thread is free to execute the next line of code.

3. When the method is finished processing the request, the server notifies the client through the callback routine in the sink object.

Even with advancements implemented in the .NET Framework, successfully developing asynchronous programming logic is not trivial. You need to examine the requirements of your application carefully to determine whether or not the code you're writing can even benefit from asynchronous events. Here are some general guidelines to consider when making your decision:

- Consider asynchronous processing if the calling thread controls a Windows user interface. In this case, the calling thread can't afford to be blocked during a remote method call because the UI will freeze.

- Asynchronous processing may help with scalability if the Web Services client is an ASP.NET application or another ASP.NET Web Service. In this scenario, a blocked synchronous call in the code can stall the ASP.NET worker thread, which can force other applications' requests to queue and, therefore, impact scalability. Using asynchronous communication instead could at least free up the threads that ASP.NET isn't using for the Web Service calls. Asynchronous server processing is discussed in detail towards the end of this chapter.

- If there is a possibility that the remote procedure call to the Web Service may take a while to complete, asynchronous processing may be beneficial. In this case the client application can do other work on the thread before it needs the results from the remote procedure call.

- The client application may need to make concurrent calls to one or more remote services. In this case, using an asynchronous remote procedure call is much better than spinning off multiple threads to do the same work. For example, if an application needs to make concurrent synchronous calls to three different Web Services, it cannot do so with one thread. It has to spin off at least two threads and make a remote call in each thread. However, if the client uses an asynchronous remote call, it can make all three calls on one thread and then wait for all of them.

A Sample Web Service

Now that we've discussed the pros and cons of both the synchronous and asynchronous programming methodologies, let's write some code to illustrate the concepts. We'll begin by creating an ASP.NET Web Service that our client application can invoke. We'll then create two separate applications, with one calling the Web Service synchronously, and the other asynchronously, so that we can compare the techniques of each approach.

For the purposes of our discussion, we will be making use of an ASP.NET Web Service that returns a stock quote. The Web Service, named `StockService`, accepts a ticker symbol parameter that will return a string representing the value of the stock. In order to properly demonstrate asynchronous programming, the Web Service we will be invoking will also have the ability to simulate a long-running process. For that purpose, the `StockService` example accepts another parameter that represents the number of seconds the service will wait before returning the stock value back to the calling application. Below is a screenshot of the `StockService.asmx` page displaying the `GetStockQuote` method.

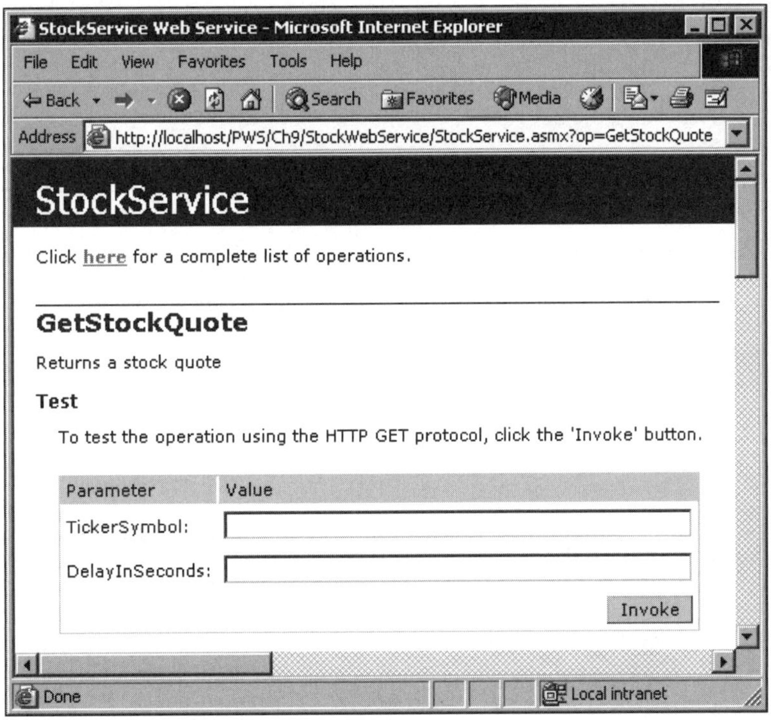

The `TickerSymbol` parameter will accept a string value representing a stock symbol or a company name. The `DelayInSeconds` parameter will accept an integer value representing the number of seconds the Web Service will wait before returning the stock's value. Below is the code for the `StockService` Web Service written in VB.NET. Bear in mind that this Web Service is simply a simulation for illustrative purposes only and obviously doesn't return accurate stock values. The algorithm that a production Web Service would use to return a stock's actual value will be much more complex than this example.

StockService.asmx

```
<%@ WebService Language="vb" Class="StockWebService.StockService" %>

Imports System
Imports System.Collections
Imports System.ComponentModel
Imports System.Data
Imports System.Diagnostics
Imports System.Web
Imports System.Web.Services
Imports System.Threading

Namespace StockWebService

  Public Class StockService
    Inherits System.Web.Services.WebService

    <WebMethod(Description:="Returns a stock quote")> _
    Public Function GetStockQuote(ByVal TickerSymbol As String, _
                                  ByVal DelayInSeconds As Integer) As String

      'Create a delay to simulate a long-running process
      If DelayInSeconds > 0 Then
        'Have the thread sleep based on the DelayInSeconds parameter
        'Note: The constant "1000" is to convert seconds to milliseconds
        System.Threading.Thread.Sleep(DelayInSeconds * 1000)
      End If

      'Retrieve the stock quote based on the TickerSymbol parameter
      'NOTE: Stock values are for simulation purposes only

      Dim Quote As String
      Select Case TickerSymbol.ToUpper()
        Case "MSFT"
          Quote = "67"
        Case "SUNW"
          Quote = "36 31/32"
        Case "IBM"
          Quote = "80"
        Case "ORCL"
          Quote = "25 1/32"
        Case "CSCO"
          Quote = "51"
        Case Else
```

```
          Quote = "Unknown"
        End Select

      'Return value of Quote to calling application
      Return Quote
    End Function
  End Class
End Namespace
```

The Web Service has one method, `GetStockQuote`. `GetStockQuote` accepts the two parameters we previously discussed: `TickerSymbol` and `DelayInSeconds`.

```
<WebMethod(Description:="Returns a stock quote")> _
  Public Function GetStockQuote(ByVal TickerSymbol As String, _
                                ByVal DelayInSeconds As Integer) As String
```

The `GetStockQuote` method returns a string which represents the value of the requested stock. The method will return a string value of `Unknown` if the stock's value is not known.

Additionally, this method has the functionality to delay the delivery of the return message to simulate a long server-side process. The code accomplishes this by retrieving a handle to the current thread and causes the thread to sleep for the duration specified in the `DelayInSeconds` parameter:

```
'Have the thread sleep based on the DelayInSeconds parameter
'Note: The constant "1000" is to convert seconds to milliseconds
System.Threading.Thread.Sleep(DelayInSeconds * 1000)
```

Here is the output of the `GetStockQuote` method when invoked from the test page provided by ASP.NET:

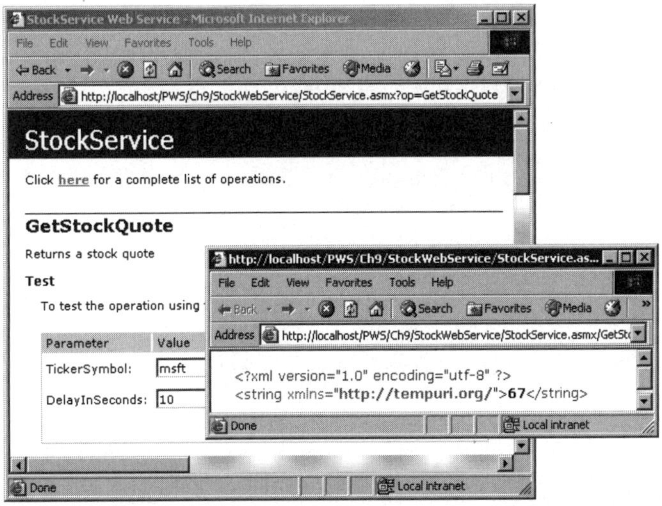

You will notice in our sample Web Service that there is nothing specific in the implementation of `StockService` that provides asynchronous functionality. It's actually the calling application that will decide if a particular call should be asynchronous. This is in keeping with one of the tenets of the .NET Framework, which is that it's not necessary for a called object to do additional programming to support asynchronous behavior by its clients. In fact, the called object doesn't even have to be an ASP.NET Web Service. It could be a Web Service developed on another platform and we would still be able to invoke an asynchronous call from a client running on the .NET Framework.

Using the Sample Web Service

Now let's have some fun by invoking this Web Service from a client application, both synchronously and asynchronously. The client will be developed as a console application using Visual Studio .NET. As you learned in Chapter 3, we'll first need to create a SOAP proxy to serve as a wrapper class for the `StockService` Web Service. You can generate the proxy class using the `WSDL.exe` utility, which comes with the .NET SDK, or simply add a web reference to the Web Service in the Visual Studio .NET development environment.

The generated VB.NET proxy class contains both synchronous and asynchronous versions of the `GetStockQuote` method. The asynchronous version consists of two methods, a `BeginGetStockQuote` and an `EndGetStockQuote` method. The `BeginGetStockQuote` method is used to initiate the call to the Web Service, while the `EndGetStockQuote` method retrieves the results. We'll take a closer look at this proxy class in the *Asynchronous Programming in .NET* section of this chapter.

A Sample Synchronous Method Call

The code for calling a Web Service synchronously should be relatively familiar by now, since many of the examples in this book have been synchronous remote procedure calls to Web Services. This example will be no different. Here's the code for the console application, `SyncStockClient`, which uses the `StockService` Web Service:

```
Imports System
Imports System.Runtime.Remoting.Messaging

Namespace SyncStockClientVB

  Class SyncStockClient

    Shared Sub Main(ByVal args As String())

      Dim ReturnValue As String

      'Create the web service instance via the proxy class
      Dim objStockService As New localhost.StockService()

      'Make sure there are at least two items in args[] array
      'NOTE: the args[] array contains command line arguments
      If (args.GetUpperBound(0) >= 1) Then
        'Invoke the synchronous call to the web service
        'This thread is blocked until method call returns with the return value
```

```
        'NOTE: System.Convert.ToInt32 converts the string argument to integer
        ReturnValue = objStockService.GetStockQuote(args(0), _
                                                   System.Convert.ToInt32(args(1)))

        'Display the results to the user
        Console.WriteLine("Stock quote for " + args(0) + " is " + ReturnValue)
      Else
        'User did not enter the right number of parameters
        Console.WriteLine("You need to input 2 parameters. Try again.")
      End If

      Console.ReadLine()

    End Sub

  End Class

End Namespace
```

The output of this project, `SyncStockClient.exe` in the `bin` folder, is designed to be used at the command prompt. This application accepts two command-line parameters that will then be passed to the `GetStockQuote` method call of the `StockService` Web Service. Here's the line of code that invokes the Web Service method:

```
ReturnValue = objStockService.GetStockQuote(args(0), _
                                           System.Convert.ToInt32(args(1)))
```

When the application starts, the command line is parsed by the `GetCommandLineArgs` method and the command line entries are then stored in the `args` array. When the user starts the application correctly, `args(0)` will contain the `StockSymbol` parameter and `args(1)` will contain the `DelayInSeconds` parameter. Below is the output for `SyncStockClient.exe`:

In this example, the user starts the `SyncStockClient.exe` application, requesting the stock quote for Microsoft (MSFT) and setting a server-side delay of five seconds:

```
SyncStockClient msft 5
```

Since the Web Service call, in this example, is synchronous, the application has no choice but to wait for the processing to conclude before running the next line of execution, which then prints the outcome of the method call:

Stock quote for msft is 67

Let's now look at a similar application that calls `StockService` asynchronously.

A Sample Asynchronous Method Call

This next example will also be a console-based application written in Visual Basic .NET. It's identical in functionality to `SyncStockClient.exe` with the exception that the `GetStockQuote` method will be invoked asynchronously. Here's the VB.NET code for the console application, `AsyncStockClient.exe`, that uses the `StockService` Web Service:

```
Imports System
Imports System.Runtime.Remoting.Messaging

Namespace AsyncStockClient

  Class AsyncStockClient
    Shared Sub Main(ByVal args As String())

      Dim ReturnValue As String
      Dim AsyncResult As IAsyncResult

      'Create the web service instance via the proxy class
      Dim objStockService As New localhost.StockService()

      'Make sure there are at least two items in args[] array
      'NOTE: the args[] array contains command line arguments
      If (args.GetUpperBound(0) >= 1) Then

        'Invoke the asynchronous call to the web service
        'NOTE: System.Convert.ToInt32 converts the string argument to integer
        AsyncResult = objStockService.BeginGetStockQuote(args(0), )
                          System.Convert.ToInt32(args(1)), Nothing, Nothing)

        'Method call returns right away!
        'This thread is free to do more processing
        'Check for method completion in the while loop
        Console.Write("I'm not blocked. I can do more processing")
        While AsyncResult.IsCompleted = False
          Console.Write(".")
        End While
        Console.WriteLine("Method call has returned!")

        'Retrieve return value from the web service
        ReturnValue = objStockService.EndGetStockQuote(AsyncResult)

        'Display the results to the user
        Console.WriteLine("Stock quote for " + args(0) + " is " + ReturnValue)
        Console.ReadLine()

      Else

        'User did not enter the right number of parameters
```

```
        Console.WriteLine("You need to input 2 parameters. Try again.")
        Console.ReadLine()
      End If
    End Sub
  End Class
End namespace
```

The call to `BeginGetStockQuote` starts the asynchronous communication process, sending out the method request and then returning immediately. The return value of this method call is not the actual stock quote, yet, as was the case in the synchronous version. Instead, it's an object of type `AsyncResult`, which is part of the `System.Runtime.Remoting.Messaging` namespace. The `AsyncResult` object will be used later to poll for completion and to fetch the results of the method call:

```
'Invoke the asynchronous call to the web service
'NOTE: System.Convert.ToInt32 converts the string argument to integer
AsyncResult = objStockService.BeginGetStockQuote(args(0), )
                  System.Convert.ToInt32(args(1)), Nothing, Nothing)
```

The parameter list of the `BeginGetStockQuote` begins with the parameters of the synchronous method – `StockSymbol` and `DelayInSeconds`. The method has two additional parameters used in providing a callback mechanism for the asynchronous process. Since we won't be using a callback mechanism in this example, the code simply passes `Nothing` to the last two parameters (we'll be covering the callback mechanism in a later example in this chapter).

Once the Web Service method has been invoked asynchronously, the calling thread needs a way to find out when the operation has completed. The `IAsyncResult` interface contains a property for just this purpose, called `IsCompleted`, which will return the Boolean value `True` when the Web Service is finished processing the request. In the code, outlined below, we call the `AsyncResult.IsCompleted` method periodically to check for method call completion.

```
'Method call returns right away!
'This thread is free to do more processing
'Check for method completion in the while loop
Console.Write("I'm not blocked. I can do more processing")
While AsyncResult.IsCompleted = False
  Console.Write(".")
End While
Console.WriteLine("Method call has returned!")
```

To retrieve the results of the operation, we call the `EndGetStockQuote` method provided by the Web Service's proxy class:

```
'Retrieve return value from the web service
ReturnValue = objStockService.EndGetStockQuote(AsyncResult)
```

The method accepts one parameter of type `IAsyncResult`. In this case, we pass the `AsyncResult` object that we originally received from the `BeginGetStockQuote` method. This is how the .NET infrastructure is able to determine which result to give back to our code, since the client may have invoked any number of requests at the same time.

Note that we need to wait for the `AsyncResult.IsCompleted` to return `True` before invoking the `EndGetStockQuote` method. If we call the `EndGetStockQuote` method before the operation is finished, it will block until the operation does in fact complete. Below is the output for `AsyncStockClient.exe`:

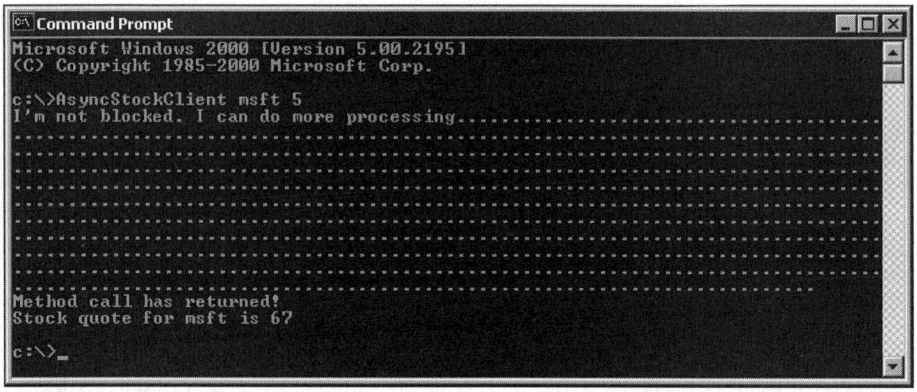

In this example, the user starts the `AsyncStockClient` application, requesting the stock quote for Microsoft (MSFT) and setting a server-side delay of 5 seconds:

```
AsyncStockClient msft 5
```

Since the Web Service call in this example is asynchronous, the method call returns immediately and the calling thread is free to do more processing. In this case, the calling thread writes to the console to demonstrate that it's able to do more work:

```
I'm not blocked. I can do more processing............................................
```

At the same time, the client application is polling to check if the method call has returned. Upon completion of the call request, the client then prints the outcome of the method call:

```
Method call has returned!
Stock quote for msft is 67
```

Asynchronous Programming in .NET

We've now gotten our feet wet with a relatively simple example of an asynchronous method call to a Web Service. Let's dig deeper into the plumbing of the .NET Framework to find out how the common language runtime provides the infrastructure for asynchronous programming.

Until the .NET Framework, coding against an asynchronous model had always been a daunting task: one had to be intimately familiar with the complexities of multi-threaded programming in order to create an asynchronous process. For programmers, synchronous method calls are a no-brainer: a single thread initiates a task, and then does nothing until the task completes. Providing a mechanism to free up the main thread, however, required more complex programming involving spawning worker threads to initiate the function call, thread synchronization, and providing a callback mechanism to alert the main thread that the function call has completed. Thankfully, the .NET Framework provides an infrastructure to address many of these issues.

The .NET Runtime Provides the Plumbing

Having programmed in Visual Basic for most of my professional career, I used to be envious of my C++ counterparts and their seemingly magical ability to create multi-threaded applications that did any number of parallel tasks, which is a requirement for asynchronous processing. Sure, I was able to mimic asynchronous behavior in VB using out-of-process servers and the use of the dreaded timer control. It worked, but it just wasn't elegant. And the application definitely didn't scale.

Life became easier with the advent of VB 6 and its ability to use apartment-model threading. In addition, the programmer's arsenal of tools increased with Windows 2000 providing more ways to make asynchronous calls using COM+ events, and COM asynchronous interfaces.

Although it's still a non-trivial undertaking, the .NET Framework makes programming asynchronous processes much easier than before. .NET has asynchronous code built in, and asynchronous programming is a feature supported by many areas of the .NET Framework, including I/O operations, networking, messaging, message queues, `Async` delegates, ASP.NET Web Forms and, of course, Web Services.

A Common Design Pattern

In order to provide a consistent framework for modeling asynchronous processes, the .NET Framework provides an important common design pattern as a core guiding concept. The basic ideas behind this pattern are as follows:

- The .NET Framework will provide services needed for supporting the asynchronous programming model.
- It is the client code that decides if a particular call should be asynchronous.
- It is not necessary for a called object to do additional programming to support asynchronous behavior by its clients. The common language runtime infrastructure should be able to handle the difference between the caller and called object views.
- The called object can choose to explicitly support asynchronous behavior, either because it can implement it more efficiently than a general architecture, or it wants to support only asynchronous behavior by its callers. However, it is recommended that such called objects follow the asynchronous design pattern for exposing asynchronous operations.
- The common language runtime provides type safety. For `Async` delegates, which are explained in the next section, the compiler generates type-safe method signatures for the `BeginInvoke` and `EndInvoke` method calls.

Because all the .NET languages make use of the common language runtime, the programmer is not constrained to using a specific programming language to provide asynchronous processing within the .NET Framework. The examples demonstrating asynchronous processing provided in this chapter could have easily been written in C# as well as VB.NET.

Let's now examine one of the key concepts in the .NET Framework that makes asynchronous programming possible: the .NET delegate classes.

An Introduction To Delegates

As previously mentioned, one of the requirements of asynchronous programming is that there needs to be a way for a calling thread to find out when an operation has completed processing. The example outlined earlier provided this functionality through a polling mechanism. Another technique is to provide a sink object with a callback method to allow the called object to inform the client that processing is complete.

In the C/C++ languages, the address of a function, known as a function pointer, is used to provide the callback functionality. VB6 had a similar technique using the `AddressOf` operator, although its use was limited to returning the address of procedures in a BAS module. The problem with function pointers is that they are just memory addresses. Memory addresses don't contain any additional information about the function they are referring to, such as the number of parameters expected, the types of the parameters, and the return value type. Also, because function pointers cannot be differentiated from other pointer types, you can essentially point them to anything. In other words, function pointers are not type-safe, and this is often the source of many errors in C++ programs.

The .NET Framework provides the same callback functionality that a C++ function pointer provides through the mechanism of **delegates**. Unlike the function pointer, however, delegates are type-safe. Since one of the goals of the .NET Framework is to be type-safe, all types in the .NET Framework are self-describing, including delegates. A delegate can, therefore, be thought of as a type-safe, self-describing function pointer object.

Using Delegates

.NET delegate classes behave as containers. A delegate contains the information about a single method and is used to provide a communication mechanism between the server object and the client application. Here's a sample delegate declaration in VB.NET:

```
Public Delegate Function MyDelegate(ByVal ParameterValue As String) As Integer
```

When a delegate is created in code, the compiler creates a class that, in addition to a method called `Invoke`, which is used to initiate a synchronous connection to the methods referred to by the delegate, also creates methods called `BeginInvoke` and `EndInvoke`.

BeginInvoke

`BeginInvoke` starts execution of your asynchronous operation on a different thread from the calling method and accepts the parameters specified in the delegate, plus a few others:

- An `AsyncCallback` delegate, which allows you to pass a callback method to be called as soon as the asynchronous method is done.
- An `AsyncState` object representing some context information for the callback.

The return value of the `BeginInvoke` method is a reference to an object that implements the `IAsyncResult` interface. The `IAsyncResult` object returned from the delegate's `BeginInvoke` method can be cast to an `AsyncResult` object. The `AsyncResult` object has the `AsyncDelegate` property that is the delegate object on which the asynchronous call was invoked.

EndInvoke

`EndInvoke` is used to harvest the results of the method call. The `AsyncResult` object returned by `BeginInvoke` is passed to `EndInvoke` as a parameter to provide access to the remoting infrastructure that was used to make the asynchronous call. It returns the value (and output/reference parameters) that the asynchronously invoked method returned. `EndInvoke` will also block the calling thread, if called early, until the asynchronously executing method returns, and then returns the results to you.

Using Asynchronous Calls in .NET

The .NET Framework's scheme for asynchronous processing is relatively simple, but powerful. The beauty of the design is that any method can be called in this manner. All that needs to be done is to define an appropriate delegate and call that delegate's `BeginInvoke` and `EndInvoke` methods to communicate asynchronously. You don't have to write complex code that spawns threads, nor do you have to worry about how parameters are passed or how results are returned. The .NET infrastructure takes care of the heavy lifting for you.

Invoking Web Services Asynchronously

Invoking Web Services asynchronously from within a .NET client application follows the same design pattern used by the .NET Framework for invoking asynchronous processes. The design pattern dictates that, for each synchronous method implemented, there should be two asynchronous methods: a `Begin` and an `End` asynchronous method. The `Begin` method takes input from the client and kicks off the asynchronous operation. The `End` method supplies the results of the asynchronous operation back to the client.

In addition to accepting the input parameters required by the asynchronous operation, the `Begin` method also takes an `AsyncCallback` delegate to be called when the asynchronous operation is completed. The `AsyncCallback` delegate will serve as a pointer to a function that the client application will implement to retrieve the results from the method call. The return value of the `Begin` method is a wait-able object that implements the `IAsyncResult` interface used by the client to determine the status of the asynchronous operation. The client application will then use the `End` method to obtain the results of the asynchronous operation by supplying the `AsyncResult` object.

When calling the `Begin` method to kick-off an asynchronous call, there are two options available to the client for initiating the operation:

- Supply the `AsyncCallback` delegate when beginning the asynchronous operation. This will provide a mechanism for the server to notify the client application that the method call has completed.
- Don't supply the `AsyncCallback` delegate when beginning the asynchronous operation. The callback delegate is not required if the client application chooses to poll for completion instead, or if the return value of the function being called is not needed.

The client application also has a number of options available for completing asynchronous operations:

- Poll the returned `IAsyncResult.IsCompleted` property periodically for completion. Note that this does add processing overhead due to the constant polling.
- Attempt to complete the operation prematurely by calling the `End` method, which blocks the calling thread until the operation completes.
- Wait on the `IAsyncResult` object. The difference between this and the previous option is that the client can use timeouts to wake up periodically.
- Wait for the callback to occur and complete the operation inside the `AsyncCallback` routine.

The asynchronous programming example we studied earlier did not use a callback mechanism, but simply polled the `IAsyncResult.IsCompleted` property to check for method completion. Before we dive into our next example, which makes use of the callback mechanism, let's take another look at the Web Services proxy class to fully understand how Web Services are invoked asynchronously.

A Closer Look At the Web Services Proxy Class

The Web Services proxy class, built by the `WSDL.exe` tool, provides a wrapper around the .NET remoting functionality required by our client application to communicate with a remote Web Service. The proxy class for the `StockService` Web Service, which we built earlier, inherits from the `SoapHttpClientProtocol` class. The `SoapHttpClientProtocol` class is ideal for asynchronous calling and, therefore, has the `BeginInvoke` and `EndInvoke` methods built into its structure. Below is the code for the proxy class, `Reference.vb`:

```
...

Imports System
Imports System.ComponentModel
Imports System.Diagnostics
Imports System.Web.Services
Imports System.Web.Services.Protocols
Imports System.Xml.Serialization

'
'This source code was auto-generated by Microsoft.VSDesigner, Version 1.0.3705.0.
'
Namespace localhost

  '<remarks/>
```

```
    <System.Diagnostics.DebuggerStepThroughAttribute(), _
    System.ComponentModel.DesignerCategoryAttribute("code"), _
    System.Web.Services.WebServiceBindingAttribute(Name:="StockServiceSoap",
    [Namespace]:="http://tempuri.org/")> _
    Public Class StockService
      Inherits System.Web.Services.Protocols.SoapHttpClientProtocol

      '<remarks/>
      Public Sub New()
        MyBase.New
        Me.Url = "http://localhost/PWS/Ch9/StockWebService/StockService.asmx"
      End Sub

      '<remarks/>
      <System.Web.Services.Protocols.SoapDocumentMethodAttribute( _
      "http://tempuri.org/GetStockQuote", _
      RequestNamespace:="http://tempuri.org/", _
      ResponseNamespace:="http://tempuri.org/", _
      Use:=System.Web.Services.Description.SoapBindingUse.Literal, _
      ParameterStyle:=System.Web.Services.Protocols.SoapParameterStyle.Wrapped)> _
      Public Function GetStockQuote(ByVal TickerSymbol As String, _
                              ByVal DelayInSeconds As Integer) As String
        Dim results() As Object = Me.Invoke("GetStockQuote", New Object() _
                                  {TickerSymbol, DelayInSeconds})
        Return CType(results(0),String)
      End Function

      '<remarks/>
      Public Function BeginGetStockQuote(ByVal TickerSymbol As String, _
                                   ByVal DelayInSeconds As Integer, _
                                   ByVal callback As System.AsyncCallback, _
                                   ByVal asyncState As Object) _
                                   As System.IAsyncResult
        Return Me.BeginInvoke("GetStockQuote", New Object() _
                      {TickerSymbol, DelayInSeconds}, callback, asyncState)
      End Function

      '<remarks/>
      Public Function EndGetStockQuote(ByVal asyncResult As System.IAsyncResult) _
                                 As String
        Dim results() As Object = Me.EndInvoke(asyncResult)
        Return CType(results(0),String)
      End Function
    End Class
  End Namespace
```

The Web Service proxy class encapsulates the mechanism for calling a Web Service asynchronously. When the proxy class is auto generated by Visual Studio .NET, there are three methods created for each public Web Service method in the Web Service. The table below describes these three methods:

Method Name in Proxy Class	Description
<NameOfWebServiceMethod>	Invokes a Web Service method synchronously (for `StockService`, the method name is `GetStockQuote`).
`Begin`*<NameOfWebServiceMethod>*	Begins an asynchronous call to a Web Service method (for `StockService`, the method name is `BeginGetStockQuote`).
`End`*<NameOfWebServiceMethod>*	Ends an asynchronous call to a Web Service method, getting the return value(s) for the Web Service method (for `StockService`, the method name is `EndGetStockQuote`).

The `Begin`*<NameOfWebServiceMethod>* method in the proxy class is simply a wrapper around the `BeginInvoke` method call that we discussed earlier. The same is true for the `End`*<NameOfWebServiceMethod>* in the case of the `EndInvoke` method.

An Asynchronous Method Call Using a Callback

Now that we've covered the mechanics of asynchronous processing from within the .NET Framework, we should have enough information to develop another sample application that will make use of a more sophisticated asynchronous mechanism, the use of a callback delegate.

This next example will be a Windows Forms-based application written in VB.NET. The application will have code to invoke our `StockService` Web Service in both a synchronous and an asynchronous fashion:

```
 Imports System
 Imports System.Drawing
 Imports System.Collections
 Imports System.ComponentModel
 Imports System.Windows.Forms
 Imports System.Data
 Imports System.Runtime.Remoting.Messaging

Namespace StockServiceClient

  Public Class frmMain
    Inherits System.Windows.Forms.Form

...

    Shared Sub Main()
      Application.Run(New frmMain())
    End Sub

    'Create an instance of the web service via the proxy class
    Dim objWebService As New localhost.StockService()

    Private Sub btnCallAsync_Click(ByVal sender As System.Object, _
                                   ByVal e As System.EventArgs) _
                                   Handles btnCallAsync.Click
      'Create an instance of a CallBack delegate and
      'point the object to our callback function
      Dim AsyncCallback As New AsyncCallback(AddressOf MyCallBack)
```

```
    'Call the web service asynchronously
    'Display a message box to notify a successful call
    Dim AsyncResult As IAsyncResult
    AsyncResult = objWebService.BeginGetStockQuote(txtSymbol.Text, _
                        System.Convert.ToInt32(txtDelay.Text), _
                        AsyncCallback, Nothing)
    MessageBox.Show("The asynchronous was invoked successfully.", _
                "Asynchronous Call")
  End Sub

  Private Sub btnCallSync_Click(ByVal sender As System.Object, _
                        ByVal e As System.EventArgs) _
                        Handles btnCallSync.Click
    Dim ReturnValue As String

    'Display hourglass to show system is busy
    Me.Cursor = System.Windows.Forms.Cursors.WaitCursor

    'Call the web service synchronously and wait for a response
    ReturnValue = objWebService.GetStockQuote(txtSymbol.Text, _
                              System.Convert.ToInt32(txtDelay.Text))

    'Display stock quote to user
    lblQuote.Text = "Stock Quote = " + ReturnValue

    'Return cursor to default pointer
    Me.Cursor = System.Windows.Forms.Cursors.Default
  End Sub

  Private Sub MyCallBack(ByVal AsyncResult As System.IAsyncResult)
    Dim ReturnValue As String
    'End asynchronous call and retrieve the return value
    'Display a message box to notify a successful return
    ReturnValue = objWebService.EndGetStockQuote(AsyncResult)
    MessageBox.Show("Asynchronous response has returned with the value.", _
                "Asynchronous Call")
    lblQuote.Text = "Stock Quote = " + ReturnValue
  End Sub

  Protected Overrides Sub Finalize()
    MyBase.Finalize()
  End Sub
 End Class
End Namespace
```

This Windows application consists of one form containing two textboxes to provide a way for the user to input the parameters required by the `StockService` Web Service: `TickerSymbol` and `DelayInSeconds`. The form also includes two buttons: one to invoke `StockService` synchronously, and the other for asynchronous operation. Here's a screenshot of the sample application:

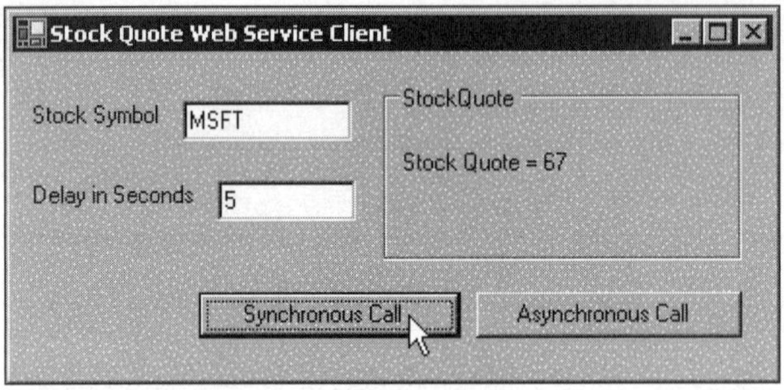

The code for synchronous invocation is essentially the same as the previous example. We will therefore skip this section of the code and jump right into the asynchronous implementation code.

The event handler for the Asynchronous Call button contains the code that initiates the asynchronous call. The code begins with the creation of the `AsyncCallback` delegate object. This will serve as the pointer to the callback function named `MyCallBack`:

```
'Create an instance of a CallBack delegate and
'point the object to our callback function
Dim AsyncCallback As New AsyncCallback(AddressOf MyCallBack)
```

As we saw earlier in our sample of an asynchronous method call, the call to `BeginGetStockQuote` starts the asynchronous communication process, sending out the method request, and then returning immediately. The return value of this method call is not the actual stock quote, yet, as was the case in the synchronous version. Instead, it's an object of type `AsyncResult`, which is part of the `System.Runtime.Remoting.Messaging` namespace. The `AsyncResult` object will be used later to fetch the results of the method call:

```
Dim AsyncResult As IAsyncResult
AsyncResult = objWebService.BeginGetStockQuote(txtSymbol.Text, _
                        System.Convert.ToInt32(txtDelay.Text), _
                        AsyncCallback, Nothing)
```

The parameter list of the `BeginGetStockQuote` method begins with the parameters required by `StockService` – `TickerSymbol` and `DelayInSeconds`. The method has two additional parameters used in providing a callback mechanism for the asynchronous process:

Additional BeginInvoke Parameters	Description
`Callback`	The delegate to call when the asynchronous invoke is complete. If callback is a null reference, the delegate is not called (in this example, we are passing the `AsyncCallback` object which references the `MyCallBack` function).
`asyncState`	The `asyncState` parameter can be used to pass information about the context of the asynchronous call to the delegate. If the parameter is a null reference, the object is not used (in this example, we are not making use of this functionality).

Once the Web Service method has been invoked asynchronously, the call, of course, returns straight away. This is demonstrated by the fact that the Windows Forms application is not blocked and is responsive to user interaction. In this example, the client will not be doing any polling to check for completion. Since the callback delegate was provided to the marshaling infrastructure in the `BeginGetStockQuote` method, the calling thread will be notified that the method is finished through the callback function outlined below:

```
Private Sub MyCallBack(ByVal AsyncResult As System.IAsyncResult)
```

To retrieve the results of the operation, we call the `EndGetStockQuote` method provided by the Web Service's proxy class from within the callback function:

```
Dim ReturnValue As String
'End asynchronous call and retrieve the return value
'Display a message box to notify a successful return
ReturnValue = objWebService.EndGetStockQuote(AsyncResult)
```

The method accepts one parameter of type `IAsyncResult`. In this case, we pass the `AsyncResult` object that we originally received from the `BeginGetStockQuote` method. This is how the .NET infrastructure is able to determine which result to give back to our code, since the client may have invoked any number of requests at the same time.

Design Considerations

This section will cover additional topics about synchronous and asynchronous processing that you may wish to consider when developing your server-side Web Service or client application.

Handling Timeouts

If you decide to use the synchronous Web Service invocation model in your client application, you have to consider how your application will behave if the Web Service is not performing optimally. For example, the communications pipe your client is using may be bandwidth constrained, or the Web Service could become saturated with client requests, causing server response times to degrade significantly.

In cases like these, you may decide to implement a timeout period to prevent the client application from having to wait indefinitely for a Web Service call to complete. The proxy class that is auto-generated by Visual Studio .NET contains additional methods and properties beyond the methods used in our Web Service examples. One of these is the `Timeout` property.

The `Timeout` property is part of the `WebClientProtocol` base class from which our proxy class is derived. The property indicates the time a Web Service client waits for a synchronous Web Service request to complete (in milliseconds). The default value for the property is `-1`, which represents infinity. This indicates that the default behavior of the Web Service client is to wait indefinitely for the remote procedure call to complete. Here's a bit of sample code setting the timeout value to 15 seconds:

```
'Set timeout value to 15 seconds
objWebService.Timeout = 15000
```

Note that even when a Web Service client has the `Timeout` property set to infinity with a value of `-1`, the server hosting the Web Service may still cause the request to time out on the server side. In this case, an exception would be raised to the client application.

Providing a Cancel Method

When using the asynchronous process model in your client application, you have to consider how your application will behave if the callback mechanism doesn't return within an acceptable timeframe. You may decide to abort the call in your code and continue with other processing. The problem with this approach is that it doesn't necessarily free up the resources on the server. Providing a `Cancel` method that stops the server-side processing gracefully can solve this issue.

Sadly, the `IAsyncResult` interface does not provide a `Cancel` method. This is because it's difficult to provide a universal mechanism for stopping all processes elegantly. In many implementations there can be no guarantee that the server will be able to cancel the `BeginInvoke` call on the Web Service proxy class.

Because a `Cancel` methodology will vary from implementation to implementation, exposing and implementing a `Cancel` method is up to the implementer of the proxy class that exposes `BeginInvoke` and `EndInvoke`.

Note that the .NET Framework imposes certain design guidelines on how to implement a `Cancel` method. Here are the things to consider:

- By definition, a `Cancel` method is a request to cancel processing of the `BeginInvoke` method after a desired timeout period has expired.
- The client can only make a `Cancel` request; the server may choose not to honor it.
- The client should not assume that the server has stopped processing the request completely after it receives notification that the method has been canceled. In other words, the client is recommended not to destroy server resources such as file objects, as the server may still be actively using them.
- Our custom `IsCanceled` property will be set to `True` if the call was canceled and the `IsCompleted` property will be set to `True` after the server has completed processing of the call. It is illegal for the server to use any client-supplied resources outside of the agreed-upon sharing semantics after it sets the `IsCompleted` property to `True`. So it is safe for the client to destroy the server resources after the `IsCompleted` property returns `True`.

Asynchronous Server Processing

Our discussion has centered around the asynchronous process originating from the calling application. In this scenario, only the client benefits from the asynchronous mechanism. The process running the Web Services code may still be running synchronously. The scenario that we've been discussing is illustrated here:

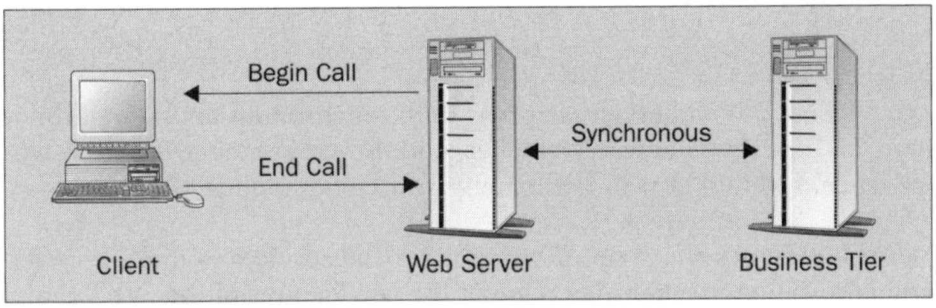

In this scenario, the client gets a call object from the proxy manager and uses it to make the asynchronous call to the server. The called object turns around and makes synchronous calls on the server to the business tier. Because the Web Service thread is blocked during the synchronous call, scalability may be hampered.

If you want the server to asynchronously process requests, you must do a little more work. There are two more modes of operation to consider when using asynchronous interfaces. The second mode is the exact opposite. The client makes a synchronous call to the proxy. The proxy then turns around and makes a call to the server. That call is processed asynchronously:

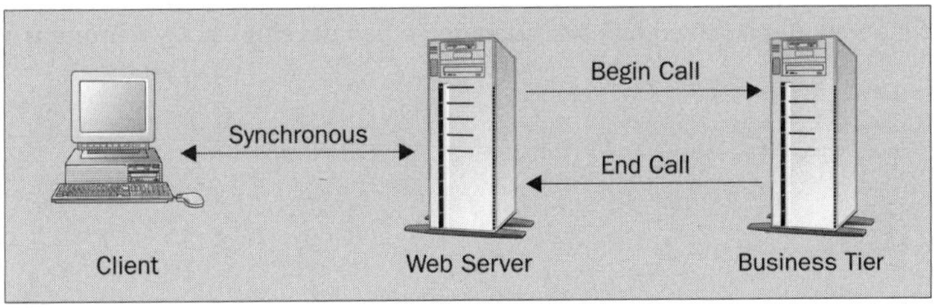

In the third mode, the client makes an asynchronous call, and that call is processed asynchronously, just as the client wanted:

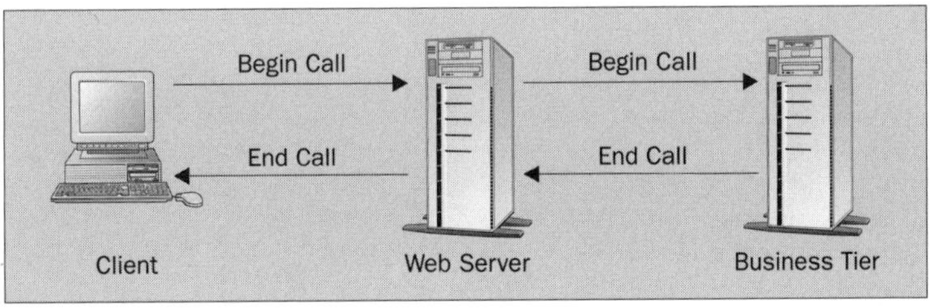

The Web Services themselves, running on a web server, can be designed to be synchronous or asynchronous. Synchronous design allows the ASP.NET thread of execution to run until it's complete, but if a long-running process is invoked server-side, other requests will be blocked. This can stall the ASP.NET worker thread forcing other applications' requests to queue, ultimately resulting in scalability and performance issues. Designing the server-side Web Service to run asynchronously will allow ASP.NET to manage threads of execution more effectively.

Summary

As we've learned, ASP.NET Web Services support both synchronous and asynchronous client invocations. There are benefits to both approaches, and the programmer has to weigh the pros and cons of each approach when deciding how to implement their client application.

The .NET Framework provides a rich set of base classes and services to make it easier to develop asynchronous communication mechanisms. One of the key features of the .NET Framework that makes asynchronous programming possible are the .NET delegate classes. Delegates are type-safe, self-describing function pointers.

Invoking Web Services asynchronously from within a .NET client application follows the same design pattern used by the .NET Framework for invoking asynchronous processes. The Web Service proxy class encapsulates the mechanism for calling a Web Service asynchronously. In this chapter we have discussed the following:

- How to invoke Web Services both synchronously and asynchronously
- How to design an asynchronous application in .NET
- What factors should be taken into consideration when developing asynchronous Web Service calls

PROFESSIONAL
ASP.NET
WEB
SERVICES

10

Managing State

Before Microsoft Transaction Server (MTS) had changed the landscape of object-oriented component development, and web-based applications became the favored system deployment style, we programmers took stateful programming for granted. Back then, we didn't have to write special routines to have our application remember its state from one method call to the next. The objects we instantiated had actions *and* data associated with them. And these objects 'remembered' what condition the data was in from one method call to the next. It just worked, plain and simple.

Then came the Internet. The World Wide Web became the catalyst for a revolution in enterprise application design. And, yes, in many ways, the browser-based application paradigm was a great leap forward because never before had applications had such broad reach. In some ways, though, developing these web-based systems felt like a step backwards. This is definitely true in the case of application state management. Whereas before the system took care of state, with web development we have to explicitly write code to make sure the server remembers application or session state from one HTTP request to the next.

Thankfully, Microsoft has felt our pain. ASP.NET brings with it new features and elements for managing state, both at the application level and at the user session level. In this chapter, we'll explore the topic of managing state in ASP.NET, and its relevance in the development of .NET Web Services. We'll discuss the scalability and performance impact that enabling state has on Web Services, and why, in most instances, it may be better to turn the feature off. When session state is required, however, the ASP.NET environment proves to be a powerful and easy-to-use platform for developing stateful Web Services.

The topics we'll be covering for this chapter are:

- State management in ASP.NET
- Implementing a stateful Web Service
- The `Application` object in ASP.NET
- The `Session` object
- Session state configuration

State Overview

State can be defined as the ability of an object, variable, or other container to remember the values assigned to it over time. Consider the real-life example of a waiter working at a very busy restaurant. This waiter needs to have the ability to manage state because he has the unenviable task of remembering not only the food specials for the day, but also the orders of each customer seated at his tables. You might say that the food specials are "application-level" state variables. They don't vary from one customer to the next and will remain in his memory for the length of his shift. Food orders, on the other hand, can be thought of as user state or "session-level" variables. Each customer will have their own unique request and our waiter will have to remember all of them. He can discard the information from his memory, however, once the customer leaves. We'll explore the concepts of application-level and session-level variables in ASP.NET in the next section, *State Management in ASP.NET*. For now, let's discuss why state management is an important concept when building Internet-based applications such as Web Services.

> **State can be defined as the ability of an object, variable, or other container to remember the values assigned to it over time.**

In the two-tiered client/server world, managing state was pretty straightforward. Take, for example, the implementation of user connections in this client/server scenario. More often than not, a user connection with a back-end server or database is established from the beginning when a client application is executed. This connection is normally maintained until the client application terminates. It was usually better to implement systems in this fashion because establishing these connections was typically expensive and time-consuming.

Since the server maintained one connection per client in the two-tiered system scenario, this model provided a simple mechanism for tracking user sessions. The back-end server would use this one-to-one association between users and connections to track and manage user resources that were being held on the server. When the server picks up a new connection, it knows that a new user has begun using the system. Once the client connection goes away, the user's session with the server ends and corresponding server-side resources are de-allocated.

Distributed web-based applications, on the other hand, must behave differently. In fact, this basic concept of user connections is what makes web-based applications fundamentally different from typical client/server applications. The reason web applications can't use the "one connection per user" model for tracking user sessions is related to the web's underlying protocols. HTTP is truly a stateless protocol. In other words, the HTTP server doesn't remember anything about previous HTTP requests. If a user sends an HTTP request and then sends another one a few minutes later, the HTTP server behaves as if it's the user's first request. The reason HTTP was designed to behave in this manner is that web applications will typically service thousands of concurrent users, and having one connection per user is not a strategy that would allow the system to scale to the required numbers.

For many developers, understanding and handling the stateless nature of Internet applications is one of the more difficult concepts to grasp, especially when transitioning from the client/server, COM-based world to a web-based world. Unlike your standard COM-based applications, where state is supported by the underlying wire protocol, the web developer must provide the mechanism for maintaining state in their application. Because the HTTP protocol itself cannot maintain state, the programmer must use other means to store information that they want the application to remember between requests. Web application developers are required to implement higher-level session management, developing in an environment in which the browser and the server must agree on a mechanism for identifying users on a connection-by-connection basis.

Microsoft had provided just such an infrastructure for managing state in ASP, making use of features such as cookies, query strings, hidden form fields, and application- and session-level storage to provide the mechanisms necessary to maintain user state from one HTTP request to the next. ASP.NET has similar capabilities, further extending the application and session state model and adding the caching model to make it easier to manage state across a web farm. Web Services that are implemented using the .NET Framework make use of the ASP.NET infrastructure and, therefore, have access to the same state management features as other ASP.NET applications. Let's begin by taking a closer look at the design pattern around state management in ASP.NET. We'll then take a look at how Web Services are able to maintain state in ASP.NET.

State Management in ASP.NET

When developing systems that make use of the web, programmers are often faced with the challenge of creating a coherent application in an environment that uses separate and independent ASP and HTML pages. IIS and ASP have typically provided state management facilities to assist the programmer in developing these applications. ASP.NET is, of course, no different. The ASP.NET object model maintains the same design pattern for state management as the previous version. ASP.NET maintains the following core functionalities for state management:

- Provides a mechanism for maintaining a user's identity during an HTTP session through the use of cookies, query string, and so on.
- Provides a way to store state associated with an identity through the use of the ASP `Session` and `Application` intrinsic objects.

The ASP.NET `Application` object and `Session` object are key technologies that we will be using in our Web Service applications to manage state. The **`Application`** object provides a mechanism for storing data that is accessible to all code running within the web application. The **`Session`** object, on the other hand, allows data to be stored on a per client session basis. These `Application` and `Session` objects are built into the ASP.NET object model.

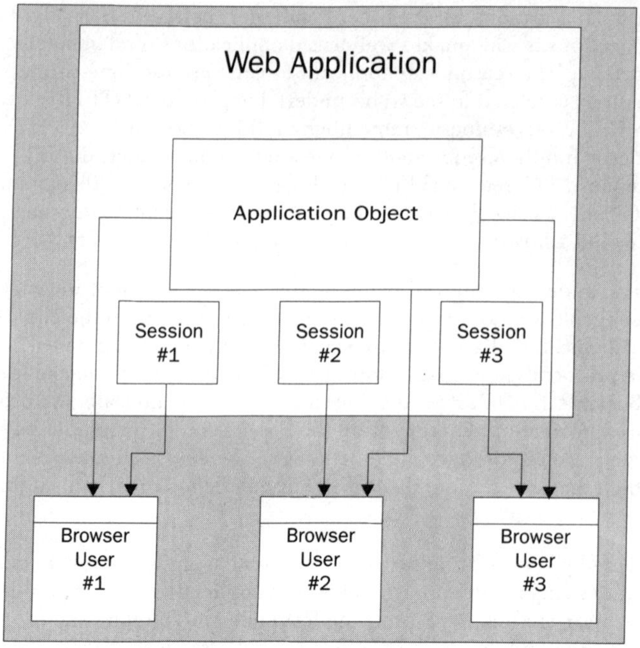

The diagram above illustrates the relationship between the `Application` and `Session` objects. Users of the web application have access to the same `Application` object. Changes made to the `Application` object values will be visible and accessible to other users of the system. `Session` objects, on the other hand, are unique to each user. Only the `Session` object assigned to a user is visible to that user. Other `Session` objects are inaccessible.

The Application Object

You can picture the `Application` object as a global container for information available to all pages or modules of your ASP.NET application. You can store both variables and object references in the `Application` object. The `Application` object is instantiated when the first page of your application is requested. During its lifetime, you can add, update, and delete application-scope values from the `Application` object. The values stay available until the Web Service is shut down. Microsoft has taken an evolutionary approach in furthering the application state management model of ASP.NET. This new version provides the following application state support:

- An easy-to-use state facility that is code-compatible with earlier versions of ASP. It works with all .NET-supported languages such as VB.NET and C#. And it's consistent with other .NET Framework APIs.
- An application state dictionary that is available to all request handlers invoked within an application. Unlike IIS and earlier versions of ASP, which restrict access to application state only to pages, all `IHttpHandler` and `IHttpModule` instances can store and retrieve global variables within the dictionary.

- Whenever data is shared globally and is given access to multiple threads of execution, a data-management facility is required to avoid data contention. ASP.NET provides a simple and intuitive synchronization mechanism that enables developers to easily coordinate concurrent access to global variables stored in the application state.
- Application state values that are accessible only from code running within the context of the originating application. Other applications running on the system cannot access or modify the values.

ASP.NET Application Definition

In order to use the `Application` object effectively, we need to first have an understanding of what constitutes an ASP.NET application. ASP.NET Web Services, and ASP.NET web applications in general, are comprised of all the files, pages, handlers, modules, and code that reside in a given IIS virtual directory, and its subdirectories. For example, the `StockService` application that we developed in the previous chapter is published in a virtual directory named `/StockWebService` on a web server. The directory structure for this application might look something like this:

```
\StockWebService
  \bin\
  \StockService.asmx
  \Global.asax
```

In this example, the `StockService.asmx` and `Global.asax` files, along with any modules stored in the `\bin` directory constitute an ASP.NET Web Service application. Application state objects are shared across all these files and so an `Application` object referenced in one module will be accessible in any other module in the `\StockWebService` directory for the lifetime of the application.

How To Use the Application Object

The syntax for using the `Application` object is pretty straightforward. Programmatically, the `Application` object is nothing more than memory in the shape of a dictionary or collection of key-value pairs. Here's an example of an `Application` object instance being referenced using VB.NET:

```
'VB.NET code running from within an *.aspx, *.asmx, or Global.asax file
Application("DatabaseName") = "Datastore"
```

For compatibility with earlier versions of ASP, these `Application` object variables can also be accessed via an actual **`Contents`** property of the `Application` object (most programmers no longer use the `Contents` property. The preferred method is to use the previously described syntax.) The `Contents` property is a collection of `Application` object values. The collection exposes all variable items that have been added to the `Application` object collection directly in code. Here's an example of its use:

```
'VB.NET code running from within an *.aspx, *.asmx, or Global.asax file
Application.Contents("DatabaseName") = "Datastore"
```

The Session Object

A **session** is defined as the period of time that a unique user interacts with a particular web application. ASP.NET developers who wish to retain data for a unique user session can use the intrinsic feature known as the `Session` object. ASP developers have historically known that IIS session state is a great feature, but one that was somewhat limited. Developers were, therefore, hesitant to make use of it for web applications that went beyond an intranet or required multiple web servers. That is, until ASP.NET came along. Some of these limitations included:

- `Session` objects ran in-process. ASP session state existed in the same process that hosted the ASP runtime. Therefore, the actions that affected the process also affected session state. For example, when the ASP process failed or was recycled, the session state was also invariably lost.
- Session state depended on the use of cookies. This, of course, required client browsers to enable cookie support. Browsers that couldn't accept HTTP cookies, or disabled the feature, couldn't take advantage of session state.
- Session management was limited to one server. As HTTP requests for a given session moved from server to server in a given web farm, the corresponding session state did not follow them. The reason for this is that ASP session state is machine-specific. Each IIS server provided its own session state, and unless the same server handled all HTTP requests for a given user, the session state was inaccessible.

New ASP.NET Session State Features

Microsoft took these well-known limitations into consideration when they designed the state model for ASP.NET. ASP.NET session state overcomes all of the previously mentioned shortcomings associated with classic ASP session state. For example:

- `Session` objects are process-independent – ASP.NET session state can be configured to run in a separate process from the ASP.NET host process. If session state is in a separate process, the ASP.NET process can come and go while the session state process remains available. Of course, you can still use session state in a process similar to classic ASP, too.
- ASP.NET provides support for server farm configurations – by moving to an out-of-process model, ASP.NET also solves the server farm problem. The new out-of-process model allows all servers in the farm to share a session state process that may be hosted on a separate machine. You can implement this by changing the ASP.NET configuration to point to a common State Server (a server that manages session state).
- Session objects are cookie-independent – although solutions to the problem of cookieless state management do exist for classic ASP, they're not trivial to implement. ASP.NET, on the other hand, reduces the complexities of cookieless session state to a simple configuration setting.

Let's now look at each of these features in more detail, including how to configure session state in your application for maximum performance.

Identifying a Session

Unlike application state where objects are not tied to a specific session, successfully implementing session state requires more than just a storage facility on the web server. As stated earlier, due to the nature of the HTTP protocol, a mechanism for identifying users across connections is also required in order to be able to associate a server-side `Session` object with a given user. Because HTTP is a stateless protocol, building web applications that need to maintain some cross-request state information, such as shopping carts, user status, and so on, can be extremely challenging without additional infrastructure help.

ASP.NET imparts that help by providing an infrastructure that assigns a unique ID for each user of the web application. Each active ASP.NET session is identified and tracked using a 128-bit Session ID string containing URL-legal ASCII characters. Session ID values, known as GUIDs (Globally Unique Identifiers) are generated using an algorithm that ensures uniqueness so that sessions do not collide.

These generated Session IDs are communicated across client-server requests and serve as a token for client identification. The token is used to identify session values stored on the server. Depending on how the web application is configured, the Session ID is passed from client to server either by means of an HTTP cookie or a modified URL. With ASP.NET, if the client supports cookies, a cookie can identify the client session; otherwise the modified URL can identify that particular session.

Web Service applications will also need to coordinate with their clients when managing session state. The client application accessing the Web Service will also need to support the use of cookies in order to store the Session ID locally.

How To Use the Session Object

Just as the `Application` object is designed to be a collection of key-value pairs, the `Session` object contains a `Contents` collection that exposes all variable items that have been added to the session state collection directly in code. Here's an example of a `Session` object instance being referenced using VB.NET:

```
'VB.NET code running from within an *.aspx, *.asmx, or Global.asax file
Session("UserName") = "John Smith"
```

For compatibility with earlier versions of ASP, the `Session` object variables can also be accessed via the actual **`Contents`** property of the `Session` object (most programmers no longer use the `Contents` property. The preferred method is to use the previously described syntax). The `Contents` property is a collection of `Session` object values. Here's an example:

```
'VB.NET code running from within an *.aspx, *.asmx, or Global.asax file
Session.Contents("UserName") = "John Smith"
```

Storage Options for Session State

Remember when we first started developing web applications in ASP? One of the first tips we learned was to be afraid of session-level variables. "Stay away from them if you want your application to scale," we were told. Yes, previous versions of the `Session` object did not scale, because storage for the `Session` object was limited to an in-process mechanism on a single server only. If a developer wanted to store session state in a centralized database for use in a web farm, he had to implement a custom solution. ASP did not have a built-in session state solution for web farm scenarios.

With ASP.NET, the developer now has a choice. ASP.NET provides a simple and easy-to-use session state storage model that you can use to store arbitrary data and objects across multiple web requests. One of the ways it accomplishes this is through the use of an in-memory cache of object references that live within the IIS process. This, by the way, is the default configuration. It is identical to the way session state is stored in previous versions of ASP.

The second option available to the developer is to make use of a new ASP.NET feature called the **StateServer**. StateServer is a Windows service that runs in a separate process from IIS that can run either on the same machine as the web server or on a different server altogether. When this mode is chosen, instead of keeping `Session` objects in the same process as IIS, the .NET state server simply stores chunks of binary data, either in memory or in a SQL Server database. ASP.NET worker processes are then able to take advantage of this simple storage service by serializing and saving all objects within a client's session collection at the end of each web request. When the client revisits the server, the relevant ASP.NET worker process retrieves these objects from the state server as binary streams, deserializes them into live instances, and places them back into a new `Session` collection object exposed to the request handler. Note that since the StateServer is running on a separate process from IIS, it will have an associated performance penalty. You will need to weigh the performance hit with the advantages this feature provides.

Lastly, an application can also store session state data into a SQL Server database. This was possible in previous versions, but what makes it different in ASP.NET is that the infrastructure takes care of the steps necessary to make use of SQL Server. ASP.NET worker processes take care of serializing the data and then store the serialized session data into a temporary SQL Server table. The ASP.NET worker process accesses the temporary table by a combination of stored procedures in the database and the managed data access components for SQL Server. Because SQL Server is a tried and tested platform for data storage, this option is typically the preferred method for session state management in most commercial environments.

The session state storage options that were just outlined provide a clean separation between the storage of the session data and the application's use of it. Because of this separation of storage and implementation, ASP.NET can support several powerful scenarios that were unavailable with earlier versions of ASP. These include:

- Recovery from application crashes is possible because the memory used for session state is not within the ASP.NET worker process. Because all state is stored separately from an individual worker process, it is not lost if the process crashes due to an access violation, or is forcibly restarted by the IIS Admin Service in the event of a deadlock or memory leak.
- Periodic state-code purges. Because all state is stored separately from running user code, it is not lost during the regular preventive restarts of each worker process after a given interval. ASP.NET performs preventive restarts every 20 minutes or 5000 requests to help prevent problems resulting from memory leaks, handle leaks, cache irregularities, and the like. This automatic purging process can dramatically improve the perceived availability and reliability of an application.
- Partitioning an application across multiple worker processes. Because all state is stored separately from worker processes, you can cleanly partition an application across multiple processes. Such partitioning can dramatically improve both the availability and the scalability of an application on multiple-processor machines. Moreover, because it associates each worker process with a single computer, ASP.NET is able to eliminate cross-processor lock contention, one of the major scalability bottlenecks in earlier versions of ASP.

- Partitioning an application across multiple web farm computers. Because all state is stored separately from worker processes, you can partition an application across multiple worker processes running on multiple computers. The model for communicating state between a worker process and a state service running on different computers is almost the same as that for processes and servers running on the same computer.

Session State Configuration Option

Session state settings in ASP.NET are configured through the ASP.NET XML configuration file `web.config`. You configure your state management options in the `<sessionState>` section of your `web.config` file as follows:

```
<sessionState
  mode="Inproc"
  stateConnectionString="tcpip=127.0.0.1:42424"
  sqlConnectionString="data source=127.0.0.1;user id=sa;password="
  cookieless="false"
  timeout="20"
/>
```

There are two types of configuration files: a machine-level configuration file and an application-level configuration file, `machine.config` and `web.config` respectively. The two are identical, except that the machine configuration file applies settings to all applications, while the application configuration file is confined at the application level.

Application-level configuration files are optional, in that if an application's `web.config` file is missing, the `machine.config` settings are used instead. Default ASP.NET session state settings can be made at the machine level and overridden for a particular application in its own `web.config` file.

Let's look at the various configuration settings that you can make in the `sessionState` section of the configuration file.

mode Setting

The `mode` setting specifies where and how you would like to store your state information. The options are `Inproc`, `StateServer`, `SqlServer`, or `Off`. ASP.NET supports two modes of storage: in process and out-of-process. "In-process" means that the `Session` object will store state in the same process that is running the web application. There are also two options for out-of-process session state management: memory-based (using ASP.NET's **StateServer** functionality), and SQL Server-based (using Microsoft SQL Server). The following table describes each option for the `mode` setting:

Option	Description
`InProc`	Default setting – session state is stored locally on this server (ASP style).
`StateServer`	Session state is stored in a StateServer process located remotely or potentially locally.
`SqlServer`	Session state is stored in a SQL Server database.
`Off`	Session state is disabled.

stateConnectionString Setting

The stateConnectionString setting only comes into play if you specify the StateServer option in the mode setting. In the out-of-process mode StateServer, it names the server that is running the required Windows service: ASPState. This server is specified by its IP address and could be the same machine that is hosting the web application. Here's how the setting is specified:

```
stateConnectionString="tcpip=127.0.0.1:42424"
```

The example above sets the IP address for the connection to "127.0.0.1" using IP Port "42424".

sqlConnectionString Setting

Similar to the stateConnectionString, the sqlConnectionString setting only comes into play if you specify the SqlServer option in the mode setting. The sqlConnectionString setting contains the database connection string that names the database used for storing state. Here's how the setting is specified:

```
sqlConnectionString="data source=127.0.0.1;user id=sa;password="
```

cookieless Setting

The cookieless option for ASP.NET is configured with a simple Boolean setting (true or false). Here's how the setting is specified:

```
cookieless="false"
```

timeout Setting

This option controls the length of time a session is considered valid. The session timeout, which is specified in minutes, is a sliding value. This means that on each request, the timeout period is reset to the current time plus the timeout value. Here's an example of how the setting is specified:

```
timeout="30"
```

If the setting is not explicitly stated, the default timeout value will be 20 minutes.

State Management Considerations

After going through a high-level overview of the new state management features in ASP.NET, it is clear, as a developer, that we will have a number of options that we need to consider as well as compatibility issues with previous versions of ASP that we may have to deal with. Here are some state management considerations that we will need to keep in mind.

Performance

When developing a web application, we need to consider the performance implications of the state management options that you choose. Each option (whether we decide to use the in-process mode or the SQL Server mode) has its advantages and disadvantages. As far as performance goes, nothing comes for free, of course. In many cases, the in-process mode will continue to be the best performer, followed by StateServer and then SQL Server. You should perform your own tests with your application to ensure that the option you select will meet your performance goals.

COM-Based Components

One thing to keep in mind is that if you rely on storing references to your legacy COM components in the `Session` or `Application` object, you cannot use the new state storage mechanisms (StateServer or SQL Server) within your application. You will need to use the in-process mode. This is due, in part, for the need of an object to be self-serializable in .NET terms, something that COM components obviously cannot do. New, managed components you create, on the other hand, can do this relatively easily and thus can use the new state storage models.

Legacy ASP and ASP .NET Interoperability

Another important thing to consider is that although your application can contain both ASP and ASP.NET pages, you cannot share state variables stored in the intrinsic `Session` or `Application` objects. The `Session` object in ASP.NET is not the same as the `Session` object in legacy ASP. You either need to duplicate this information in both systems or come up with a custom solution until your application is fully migrated. The bottom line is that if you have made little use of the `Session` and `Application` objects in your legacy code, then you should be in good shape. If, on the other hand, you use these objects extensively, you will need to proceed with caution and perhaps come up with a custom short-term solution to sharing your state.

Managing State in Web Services

We've just taken a high-level overview of state management in ASP.NET. We actually have more to cover regarding best practices in the implementation of `Application` and `Session` objects, and we'll make sure to cover that later in this chapter. In the meantime, we have enough background in ASP.NET state management to dive into implementation specifics with Web Services.

ASP.NET does a great job of providing an infrastructure for managing state at both the application and session level. Let's now take a look at how these features are implemented in your Web Services development projects. Actually, in many cases, you may not need to manage state in your Web Service. In fact, state management functionalities in Web Services are optional and are disabled by default. It is often best to design your Web Service using a stateless model, similar to the approach in developing components that run in the COM+ environment. This design approach provides the best way to scale the application to enterprise-level performance.

That being said, there will, of course, be instances where implementing an application that keeps track of state is required. Perhaps you will be developing a financial Web Service that allows multiple types of transactions over a single session. Since the .NET runtime environment treats Web Services as a type of ASP.NET web application, ASP.NET Web Services have access to the same state management functionalities as other ASP.NET applications, particularly the `Session` and `Application` objects.

In order to enable state management in a Web Service, the class implementing the Web Service must derive from the `WebService` class, which is part of the `System.Web.Services` namespace. The `WebService` class contains many of the common ASP.NET objects, including the `Session` and `Application` objects. A class deriving from `WebService` automatically has access to the `Application` object. Session state, on the other hand, requires an extra step. Data stored in the `Session` object is only available when the `EnableSession` property of the `WebMethod` attribute is set to `True` from a class deriving from `WebService`.

Let's go through the steps necessary to enable state in an ASP.NET Web Service:

- Include a Web Service declaration in your ASMX file.

```
<%@ WebService Language="VB" Class="SampleService" %>
```

- Add a reference to the `System.Web.Services` namespace.

```
Imports System.Web.Services
```

- All ASP.NET Web Services require the previous steps. The next step is to derive the class implementing the Web Service from the `System.Web.Services.WebService` base class. This is normally an optional step but is required to enable state in your Web Service.

```
Public Class StateSample
 Inherits System.Web.Services.WebService
```

After implementing the previous steps, the Web Service is ready to make use of the `Application` object. Here are the steps to create `Application` object variables and retrieve the saved values:

- Implement a Web Service method.

```
<WebMethod(Description:="Number of times service is accessed.")> _
Public Function GetServiceUsage() As Integer
```

- Store state in the `Application` object, specifying a name for the state for later retrieval.

```
Application("appServiceUsage") = 1
```

- Access the state variable stored in the `Application` object.

```
Application("appServiceUsage") = _
        System.Convert.Int32(Application("appServiceUsage")) + 1
```

If storing state at the application level is all that you require, then you're set to access and update `Application` object values. Session state, on the other hand, is not yet enabled. Access to the `Session` object is enabled for each function in your Web Service. Here are the steps to access and store state specific to a particular client session:

- Declare a Web Service method, setting the `EnableSession` property of the `WebMethod` attribute to `True`.

```
<WebMethod(EnableSession:=True)> _
Public Function GetSessionServiceUsage() As Integer
```

- Store state in the `Session` object, specifying a name for later retrieval.

```
Session("myServiceUsage") = 1
```

- Access the state variable stored in the `Session` object.

```
Session("myServiceUsage") = _
        System.Convert.Int32(Session("myServiceUsage")) + 1
```

That's all there is to it! ASP.NET makes it very easy to implement state management in your Web Service application. Let's take a closer look at the various pieces that enable state management in your ASP.NET Web Service. We'll then create a simple example of a state-enabled Web Service to put into practice all that we've gone over so far.

Deriving from the WebService Class

As stated previously, state management is optional and turned off by default in ASP.NET Web Services. If you would like to enable this feature, the class implementing your Web Service must derive from the `WebService` class to gain access to the common ASP.NET objects such as `Application`, `Session`, `User`, and `Context`.

The `Application` and `Session` properties provide access to storing and receiving state across the lifetime of the web application or a particular session. The `User` property contains the identity of the caller, if authentication is turned on for the Web Service. Using the `User` property is one way a Web Service can determine whether the user is authorized to call the Web Service. The `Context` property provides access to all HTTP-specific information about the Web Service client's request. Here's a table of the frequently used members of the `WebService` class:

Class Member	Description
`Application`	Gets the `Application` object for the current HTTP request.
`Context`	Gets the ASP.NET `HttpContext` for the current request, which encapsulates all HTTP-specific context used by the HTTP server to process web requests.
`Server`	Provides a handle to the `HttpServerUtility` (which contains helper methods for processing web requests) for the current request.
`Session`	Gets the `Session` object instance for the current request.
`User`	Gets the ASP.NET server `User` object. This can be used to authenticate whether a user is authorized to execute the request.

Here's a code snippet that demonstrates a class that derives from `WebService`. This code example looks up the authenticated username and returns that name.

```
<%@ WebService Language="VB" Class="Util" %>
Imports System.Web.Services

Public Class Util
  Inherits System.Web.Services.WebService

  <WebMethod(Description := "Obtains the User Name")> _
  Public Function GetUserName() As String
    Return User.Identity.Name
  End Function
End Class
```

The EnableSession Property

Because session state management can have a significant impact on system performance, access to the Session object is enabled only at the method level. Web Service methods that do not require access to the Session object can disable access to it to improve performance.

In order to store session state in the ASP.NET HttpSessionState object, the Web Service must inherit from WebService and a WebMethodAttribute applied to the Web Service method, setting the EnableSession property to True. The default value for the EnableSession property is False.

Let's Create a State-Enabled Web Service

Now that we've discussed the intricacies of enabling state management in an ASP.NET Web Service application, let's get down to business and write some code to illustrate the concepts we just covered. We'll begin by creating an ASP.NET Web Service that makes use of the Application and Session objects. We'll then create a Windows Forms client to consume the Web Service and demonstrate the use of a state-enabled web application.

This first application we will be developing is a simple implementation of the Application and Session objects, but it will hopefully illustrate for you the steps you will need to go through when developing more sophisticated state-enabled Web Services.

The service we will be developing is called StatefulService and contains one .asmx file named StatefulService.asmx. Below is a screenshot of the Web Service as seen from the Internet Explorer browser:

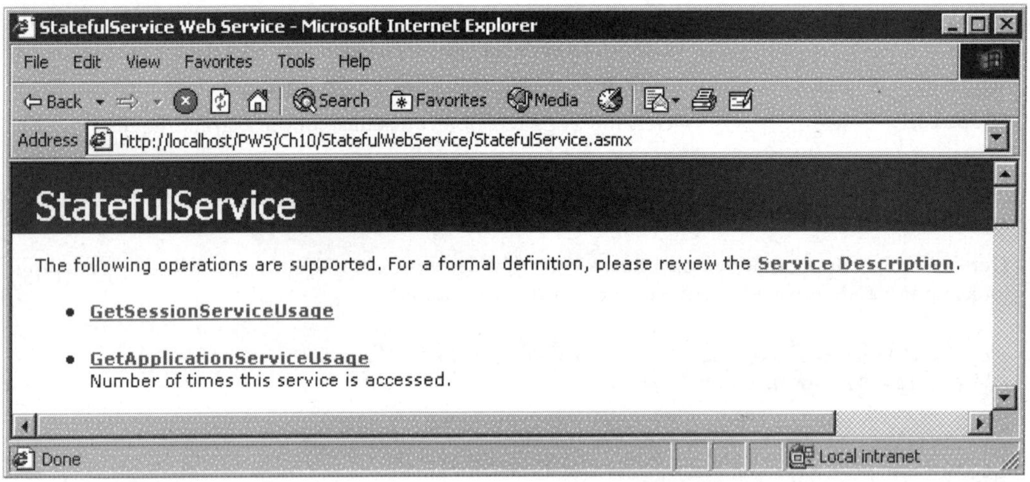

The StatefulService application exposes two methods. Here's a description of what each method does:

Method Name	Description
GetSessionServiceUsage	This method serves as a hit counter for a specific client session. It will return an integer value denoting the number of times a specific session has invoked this method. If three clients were to invoke this method consecutively, each caller will receive the same result of 1 the first time they call the method.
GetApplicationServiceUsage	This method serves as a hit counter for every time the method is called regardless of the client invoking the Web Service method. It will return an integer value denoting the total number of times the method has been called. For instance, if three clients were to invoke this method consecutively, the last client will receive a return value of 3.

Code for StatefulService

```
<%@ WebService Language="vb" Class="StatefulWebService.StatefulService" %>

Imports System
Imports System.Web
Imports System.Web.Services

Namespace StatefulWebService

  Public Class StatefulService

    Inherits System.Web.Services.WebService

    <WebMethod(Description:="Number of times this service is accessed.")> _
    Public Function GetApplicationServiceUsage() As Integer

      'If the Web Service method hasn't been accessed yet
      'Then initialize the application variable to 1
      If Application("ServiceUsage") Is Nothing Then
        Application("ServiceUsage") = 1
      Else
        'Increment the usage count
        Application("ServiceUsage") = CInt(Application("ServiceUsage")) + 1
      End If
      Return CInt(Application("ServiceUsage"))

    End Function

    <WebMethod(EnableSession:=True)> _
    Public Function GetSessionServiceUsage() As Integer

      'If the Web Service method hasn't been accessed yet
```

```
        'Then initialize the session variable to 1
        If Session("myServiceUsage") Is Nothing Then
          Session("myServiceUsage") = 1
        Else
          'Increment the usage count
          Session("myServiceUsage") = CInt(Session("myServiceUsage")) + 1
        End If
        Return CInt(Session("myServiceUsage"))

      End Function
    End Class
  End NameSpace
```

This `Application` object is used in the method `GetApplicationServiceUsage`. First, the code checks to see if the specific object instance with the key value `ServiceUsage` already exists. If it does not yet exist, then it initializes the value to 1:

```
        If Application("ServiceUsage") Is Nothing Then
          Application("ServiceUsage") = 1
```

If the object instance already exists then it simply increments the value by 1:

```
        Else
          'Increment the usage count
          Application("ServiceUsage") = CInt(Application("ServiceUsage")) + 1
```

This `Session` object is used in the `GetSessionServiceUsage` method. The logic is identical to the previous method in that the code first checks to see if the `Session` object instance already exists. If it does not yet exist, then it initializes the value to 1:

```
        If Session("myServiceUsage") Is Nothing Then
          Session("myServiceUsage") = 1
```

If the object instance already exists then it simply increments the value by 1:

```
        Else
          'Increment the usage count
          Session("myServiceUsage") = CInt(Session("myServiceUsage")) + 1
```

Developing a Client for a State-Enabled Service

Let's now complete the circle and develop a client application that will invoke the Web Service application that we just coded. The client will be developed as a Windows Forms application using Visual Studio .NET. Here's a screenshot of the client application:

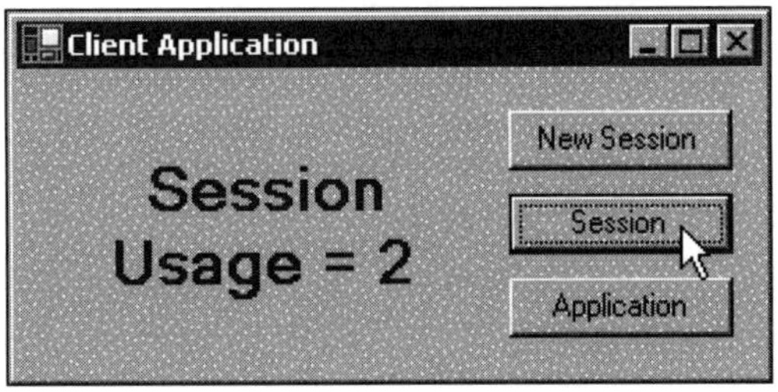

Our Windows application will have three features represented by the command buttons shown above. The first button allows the user to create a brand new user session. The second button invokes the `GetSessionServiceUsage` method from the Web Service which increments a session-level object. The third button invokes the `GetApplicationServiceUsage` method which increments an application-level object. A label is used to display the output of all three functions.

Code for Client Application

```
Imports System.Net

Public Class frmClient

  Inherits System.Windows.Forms.Form

...

  Dim objService As New localhost.StatefulService()

  Private Sub frmClient_Load(ByVal sender As System.Object, _
                             ByVal e As System.EventArgs) Handles MyBase.Load

    Dim objCookie As New CookieContainer()
    objService.CookieContainer = objCookie

  End Sub

  Private Sub Button1_Click(ByVal sender As System.Object, _
                            ByVal e As System.EventArgs) Handles Button1.Click

    objService = Nothing
    objService = New localhost.StatefulService()

    Dim objCookie As New CookieContainer()
    objService.CookieContainer = objCookie

    lblDisplay.Text = "New Session Started."
```

```
    End Sub

    Private Sub Button2_Click(ByVal sender As System.Object, _
                             ByVal e As System.EventArgs) Handles Button2.Click

      Dim iUsage As Integer

      lblDisplay.Text = ""
      iUsage = objService.GetSessionServiceUsage
      lblDisplay.Text = "Session Usage = " & iUsage

    End Sub

    Private Sub Button3_Click(ByVal sender As System.Object, _
                             ByVal e As System.EventArgs) Handles Button3.Click

      Dim iUsage As Integer

      lblDisplay.Text = ""
      iUsage = objService.GetApplicationServiceUsage()
      lblDisplay.Text = "Application Usage = " & iUsage

    End Sub

  End Class
```

The code for the client application is pretty straightforward. It's a standard Web Service client that I'm sure you've seen numerous times by the time you've reached this chapter. What's noteworthy, however, is how the client application does its part to help the server manage user sessions.

Using Cookies on the Client

Remember that we've determined that, due to the nature of the HTTP protocol, a mechanism for identifying users across connections is required in order to be able to associate a server-side `Session` object with a given user. A partnership has to be forged between the client and the server to agree on a moniker for identifying a specific user session.

In this particular example, the moniker used is in the form of an HTTP cookie. In order for our client application to make use of cookies, we must first import the `System.Net` namespace as shown in this code:

```
Imports System.Net
```

The next step is to create a cookie that the Web Services application can use to keep track of a user session. In this application, we create a `Cookie` object and assign it to the Web Service proxy class' cookie container:

```
Dim objCookie As New CookieContainer()
objService.CookieContainer = objCookie
```

This code is invoked when the application first starts in the `Form_Load` event as well as when the user clicks the NewSession button to begin a new user session. A user session is represented by the instance of the Web Service proxy class. De-allocating this class from memory terminates the user session. The following code ends one session and begins another:

```
Dim objService As New localhost.StatefulService()
```

Below is a screenshot demonstrating multiple instances of our client application running on the same machine:

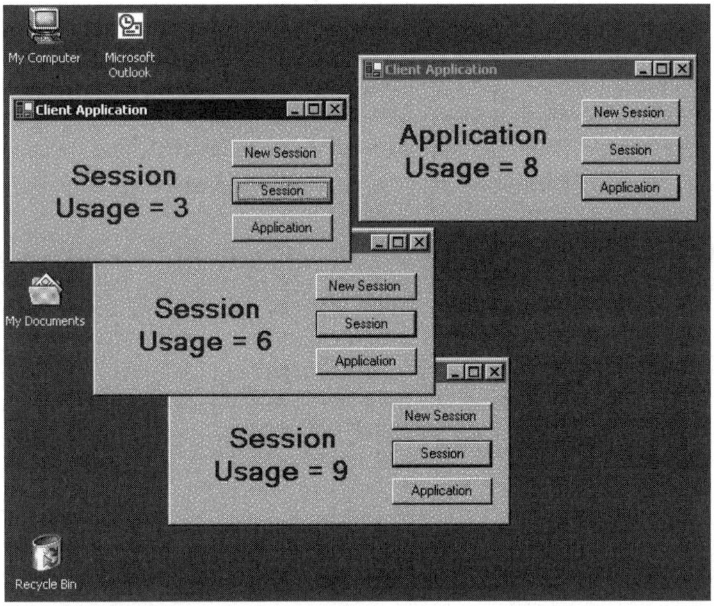

As you can see, each instance of the application will have its own user session. The `Application` object, however, is shared across all the applications. Each time the `Application` object is called from any client, the hit counter is incremented by 1.

Design Considerations

This section will cover additional topics about application and session state management that you may wish to take into consideration when developing your server-side Web Service or client application.

Application State

Now that we have a big-picture overview of ASP.NET's state management capabilities, let's focus on the `Application` object and learn more about its features.

The HttpApplicationState Class

Behind the `Application` object that we use to manage state in our ASP.NET application is the base class **`HttpApplicationState`**. The `HttpApplicationState` class is designed to give the developer the ability to share global information throughout an application. A single instance of an `HttpApplicationState` class is created the first time a client requests any URL resource from within a particular ASP.NET application virtual directory. A separate single instance is created for each ASP.NET application on a web server. Because of this, the `Application` object is not shared across applications. A reference to each instance is then exposed via the intrinsic `Application` object. This class exposes a key-value dictionary of objects that we can use to store both .NET Framework objects and scalar values related to multiple web requests from multiple clients. The following are the steps a typical ASP.NET web application will go through to enable `Application` state management:

- An instance of the `HttpApplicationState` class is created the first time any client requests a URL resource from within a particular ASP.NET application's virtual directory namespace. This is the case for each web application that is stored on the computer.
- Access to this per-application instance is provided through an `HttpContext` property named `Application`.
- All HTTP modules and handlers, such as an ASP.NET page, have access to an instance of the context and therefore have access to the `Application` property during a given web request.

Here is a table of the key `HttpApplicationState` class members accessible via the `Application` object.

Class Member	Description
`Add` (Method)	Adds a new object to the `HttpApplicationState` collection.
`Clear` (Method)	Removes all objects from the `HttpApplicationState` collection.
`Count` (Property)	Gets the number of objects in the `HttpApplicationState` collection.
`Remove` (Method)	Removes the named object from the `HttpApplicationState` collection.
`RemoveAll` (Method)	Removes all objects from the `HttpApplicationState` collection.
`Item` (Property)	Gets access to an object in the `HttpApplicationState` collection. This property is overloaded to allow access to an object by name or numerical index.

Application State Issues

Well designed application-level variables can be very powerful in web applications. You can do a one-time (or infrequent) loading and calculation of information and then use application state to cache it for speedy, in-memory access during later web requests.

For example, a stock market web site might fetch extensive financial stock information from a database every five minutes during the day and then cache it in application state where all subsequent lookup requests can access it. The result is a dramatic improvement in per-request performance, since incoming requests do not require cross-process, cross-computer, or database roundtrips.

You have to be aware of the `Application` object's limitations, however, to make effective use of its capabilities. Here are a few considerations you will have to think about when developing your Web Service application.

Memory Implications

Application-state variables are, in effect, global variables for a given ASP.NET application. Like client-side application developers, ASP.NET programmers should always consider the impact of storing anything as a global variable.

Consider the memory impact of storing something in application state. The memory occupied by variables stored in application state is not released until the value is either removed or replaced, unlike for an individual web page, in which all resources are torn down at the conclusion of a web request. Keeping seldom-used data retrieved from 10MB recordsets in application state permanently, for example, is not the best use of system resources.

Concurrency and Synchronization

Consider the concurrency and synchronization implications of storing and accessing a global variable within a multithreaded server environment. Multiple threads within an application can access values stored in application state simultaneously. You should always be careful to ensure that:

- If an application-scoped object is free-threaded, it contains built-in synchronization support.
- If an application-scoped object is not free-threaded, explicit synchronization methods are coded around it to avoid deadlocks, race conditions, and access violations.

For performance reasons, the built-in collections in the .NET Framework do not contain built-in synchronization support. You must explicitly use the **`Lock`** and **`Unlock`** methods provided by the **`HttpApplicationState`** class in order to avoid problems when you place them into application state.

Multiple threads within an application can simultaneously access values stored in application state. Consequently, when you create something that needs to access application-state values, you must always ensure that the application-state object is free-threaded and performs its own internal synchronization or else performs manual synchronization steps to protect against race conditions, deadlocks, and access violations. The `HttpApplicationState` class provides two methods, `Lock` and `Unlock`, that allow only one thread at a time to access application-state variables.

Calling `Lock` on the `Application` object causes ASP.NET to block attempts by code running on other worker threads to access anything in application state. These threads are unblocked only when the thread that called `Lock` calls the corresponding `Unlock` method on the `Application` object.

The following code example demonstrates the use of locking to guard against race conditions:

```
' From within a page, a handler, or Global.asax.
Application.Lock()
Application("SomeGlobalCounter") = CType(Application("SomeGlobalCounter"), _
                                   Integer) + 1
```

If you do not explicitly call `Unlock`, the .NET Framework automatically removes the lock when the request completes, when the request times out, or when an unhandled error occurs during request execution and causes the request to fail. This automatic unlocking prevents the application from deadlocking.

Application State Durability

Consider the life-cycle implications of information stored in application state. The .NET application domain or the process hosting a .NET application can be torn down and destroyed at any moment during application execution (as a result of crashes, code updates, scheduled process restarts, and so on). Because global data stored in application state is not durable, it is lost if the host containing it is destroyed. If you want state to survive these types of failures, you should store it in a database or other durable store.

Scalability

Consider the scalability implications of storing and accessing a global variable within a multithreaded server environment. Locks that protect global resources are themselves global, and code running on multiple threads accessing global resources ultimately ends up contending on these locks. This causes the operating system to block the worker threads until the lock becomes available. In high-load server environments, this blocking can cause severe thread thrashing on the system. On multiprocessor systems, it can lead to processor underutilization (since all of the threads for a processor theoretically can be stalled while waiting for a shared lock) and significant drops in overall scalability.

Application state is not shared across a web farm (in which an application is hosted by multiple servers) or a web garden (in which an application is hosted by multiple processes on the same server). Variables stored in application state in either of those scenarios are global only to the particular process in which the application is running. Each application process can have different values. Therefore, you cannot rely on application state to store unique values or update global counters, for example, in web farm and web garden scenarios.

Session State

Quite possibly the most important decision you will make when implementing session management in your Web Service application is how to store session state. Session state storage has an impact on your application's ability to scale and has a bearing on how well your system will perform. There are three general configuration settings we can look at in more detail to help you in your decision-making process. The three options are: in-process mode, StateServer mode, and SQL Server mode.

In-Process Mode

In-process mode simply means using ASP.NET session state in a similar manner to classic ASP session state. That is, session state is managed in process, and if the process is recycled, state is lost. Given the new settings that ASP.NET provides, you might wonder why you would ever use this mode. The reasoning is quite simple: performance. The performance of session state, the time it takes to read from and write to the session state dictionary, will be much faster when the memory read to and from is in process, as cross-process calls add overhead when data is marshaled back and forth or possibly read from SQL Server.

In-process mode is the default setting for ASP.NET. When this setting is used, the only other relevant session `web.config` settings used are `cookieless` and `timeout`.

In-process mode performs best because the session state memory is kept within the ASP.NET process. For web applications hosted on a single server, applications in which the user is guaranteed to be re-directed to the correct server, or when session state data is not critical, this is the mode to choose.

StateServer Mode

One of the great new features available in ASP.NET is a session state store named StateServer. StateServer is a Windows service that can be configured to run on the same machine as the Web Server or on a totally separate server. Running the service on a separate server gives our web application the ability to share session state across a web farm.

This mode is best used when performance is important but you can't guarantee which server a user will request an application from. By using StateServer, which operates out-of-process, you get the performance of reading from memory and the reliability of a separate process that manages the state for all servers.

SQL Server Mode

The SQL Server mode option is similar to that of the Windows StateServer mode, except that the information persists to SQL Server rather than being stored in memory.

To use SQL Server as our session state store, we first must create the necessary tables and stored procedures that ASP.NET will look for on the identified SQL Server. Thankfully, the .NET SDK provides us with a SQL script (`InstallSqlState.sql`) to do just that. The file can be found in *`[system drive]`*`\Windows\Microsoft.NET\Framework\`*`[version]`*.

The `InstallSqlState.sql` file contains the SQL commands used to create the **ASPState** database. This script creates two tables and several stored procedures. ASP.NET uses both the tables and the procedures to store data in SQL Server.

Once the SQL Server tables have been generated, our Web Service application can make use of this session store simply by changing the configuration settings in the `web.config` file. An added benefit of using the SQL Server option is that we could cluster the SQL Servers such that if one SQL Server happened to be unavailable, another server that was replicating its data could take its place. This provides a level of reliability that was not available before in ASP.

This mode is best used when the reliability of the data is fundamental to the stability of the application, as the database can be clustered for fail-over scenarios. The performance of this operation isn't as fast as StateServer, but the tradeoff is the higher level of reliability.

Summary

Microsoft has managed to create a state management facility in ASP.NET that is leaps and bounds beyond what previous versions of ASP provided. At the same time, the seasoned programmer will be very comfortable in this new environment. The familiar `Application` and `Session` objects are still there and work in a very similar manner to previous versions.

As we have seen in this chapter, ASP.NET session state is a very much improved version of the ASP `Session` object. The new capability of session state that is not bound to the ASP.NET process means that developers can begin to use session state in server farm environments without worrying about whether the client is coming through a proxy server. Additionally, with the cookieless state functionality, it is even easier to use session state and guarantee that all clients can take advantage of the session state feature.

Because Web Services make use of the ASP.NET infrastructure, they too can take advantage of the available state management features. State is optional and is turned off by default. The reason for this is that a typical Web Service may not require this feature. Enabling the feature, however, is very easy to do, and it won't take much for a developer to start developing stateful Web Service applications. Here is a rundown of what we have seen in this chapter:

- State management in ASP.NET
- Implementing a stateful Web Service
- The `Application` object in ASP.NET
- The `Session` object
- Session state configuration

PROFESSIONAL
ASP.NET
WEB
SERVICES

11

Transactions with Web Services

A transaction is simply a group of operations that succeeds or fails as a single unit of work. A developer uses a transaction to maintain reliable database integrity. For instance, if you are running a credit card transaction, you want to credit the store and debit the cardholder. If the transaction to debit the cardholder fails, you will want to roll back the crediting of the store and pass an error to the credit card machine.

Though this is a rather simplistic example, this is a very significant requirement for a system architect. Having to keep track of the success or failure of a process is just part of building a data-driven application. When we are making many related changes to a database, or updating several databases at once, we will want to ensure that all of the changes are correctly executed. If any of the changes fail, we will want to restore the original state of the database tables.

There are two issues we have to handle when providing transactions as part of Web Services. Firstly, we need to be able to control a transaction as part of a Web Service that we are providing. Since we have control of the network layer within the ASP.NET application providing the service, we can employ COM+, as we'll see. Secondly, however, we have to look at encapsulating transactions into applications that consume Web Services. Here we have no control of the network layer. We'll discuss the Distributed Transaction Coordination problem later in the chapter.

So, in this chapter, we will cover:

- Providing a Web Service that is in itself transactional
- Consuming Web Services in a transactional environment

Providing a Transactional Web Service

Let's jump right in and get our feet wet. Our client, a doctor's office, wants to update a public web site with the doctor's availability. The design is simple: provide a form that lists the doctors in the database and the available status listings, then allow the user to set the availability of a given doctor. The table we'll use to display the availability of the doctors is not important right now, so we'll skip it. Our form looks something like

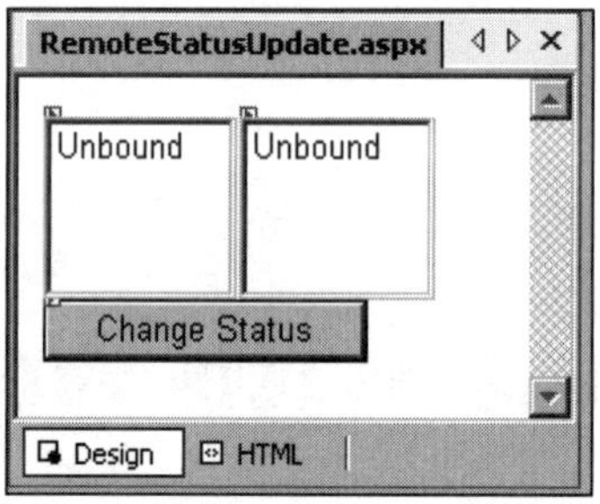

This, of course, doesn't have to be done with a Web Service: we could simply put the whole form on the same server as the remote database and change the settings there, but it wouldn't do for our example. Also, this will be expanded further when we go to update the example for consuming services. So, for now we'll say that they want to expose this logic to a number of offices to consume as they wish.

Creating the Database

We start out with the now familiar routine of setting up the service. First, we'll build a SQL Server database in SQL Server that looks like this, called `RemoteStatus`:

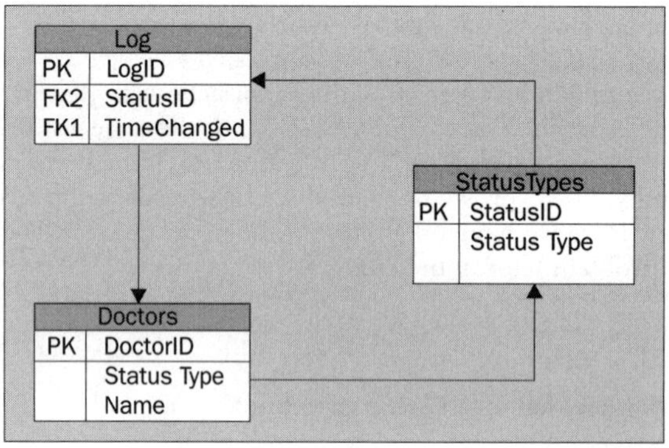

Creating the Tables

We need to insert some sample data in `Doctors` and `StatusTypes`. The log is empty.

You can find the SQL scripts to create and populate the database in the code download.

Doctors

DoctorID	StatusID	Name
1	1	Bill
2	1	Kim
3	1	Dave

StatusTypes

StatusID	StatusType
1	Available
2	Not Available

As you can see, we have the added complexity of a log (in the form of the log table) to deal with. That is our transactional challenge. We update the doctor, then the log. If the doctor fails to update because of business rules, for instance, then we want the whole transaction rolled back. This is known as a two-phase commit. If either of the database calls fails, we need to abort the whole transaction.

This concept fits in nicely with several development problems. As we mentioned above, providing two related banking services without a transaction could be damaging to your bank balance. Even the act of collecting information can sometimes benefit from a transaction. Sometimes it may be better to abort a function call than to return incomplete data. Finally, transactions help an architect to define logical units of work in an application by making functional code more clear.

The .NET Framework provides several ways to do this. Over the course of this chapter we'll look at all of them, but we'll focus on the ASP.NET support for automatic transactions. Automatic participation in transactions is an added benefit of the object orientation of ASP.NET – where ASP.NET pages can inherit some of the more advanced functionality of COM+. This is by far the easiest way and has the added benefit of fitting nicely with the topic of this book.

Essentially, we want the consumer to be able to pass in a `DoctorID` and a `StatusID`, then update the `Doctors` table with this information. Behind the scenes, we want to pass in the `DoctorID`, `StatusID`, and the current time for the log file. If either fails, we want a rollback – pretty straightforward, really.

Obviously, if we were to do this for real we would have to provide a mechanism for the consumer to get the `DoctorID` and the `StatusID`, since there is currently no way for a generic consumer to know what those values could be. For this example, we are going to hard-code that to a local version of the database.

In order to better show the transaction options, we'll write two private methods. One of these methods will update the `Logs` table, the other will update the `Doctors` table. Our new `WebMethod` will accept the `DoctorID` and the `StatusID`, and run the two subs.

First, let's finish setting up our project. You'll probably need to start Distributed Transaction Coordinator on your SQL Server (if it isn't already running) – you can find it under **Support Services** in Enterprise Manager.

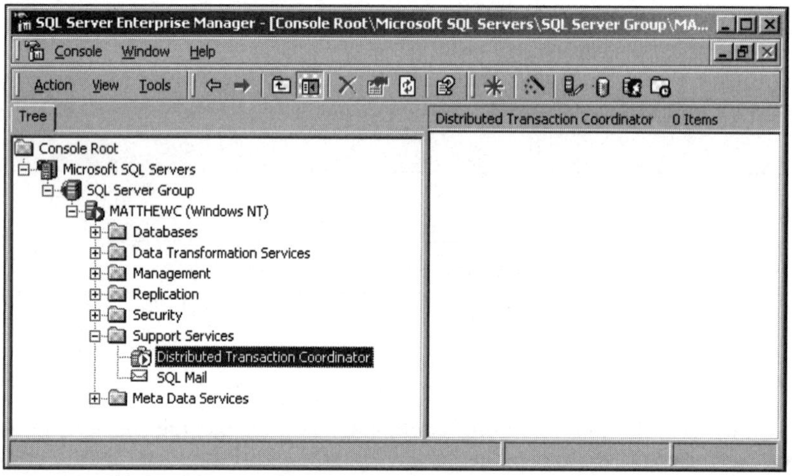

Now we've completed the database needs, we'll set up the project in Visual Studio .NET (or we can also use the code that we have provided in the `RemoteUpdate` folder of the code download for this chapter).

1. Create a new VB.NET Web Service project at http://localhost/PWS/Ch11/RemoteUpdate.

2. Import the `System.EnterpriseServices` and `System.Data.SqlClient` namespaces, and add a reference to the `System.EnterpriseServices.dll` assembly.

Now we'll proceed to set up the transactional support.

Inheriting Support from the WebMethodAttribute

Throughout the .NET documentation, Microsoft recommends that you inherit from `WebMethodAttribute` as part of your ASP.NET Web Services, but notes that it is not a required reference – it is inherited by default. `WebMethodAttribute` gives you a number of powerful features that are not always necessary, including:

- `BufferResponse` – gives you the ability to buffer the Web Service response.
- `CacheDuration` – gets and sets the length of time the response is held in the cache.
- `Description` – an easy way to set the description in the WSDL file returned by `?wsdl` in the URL. It is used by the default page IIS shows for Web Services, and UDDI.

- `EnableSession` – turns on and off the Session State support for the method.
- `MessageName` – more easy access to the WSDL, setting the name used in the SOAP header.
- `TransactionOption` – turns on automatic transaction support.

So, we have finally found what we are looking for – the `TransactionOption`. What's great about this is the "automatic" part. Transaction support in Windows (or any other system) is a complicated task, requiring Just-In-Time activation, synchronous method handling, and several other service component features handled by COM+. Since we don't have an actual DLL file here, how do we support transactions? Automatically – thanks to the `WebMethodAttribute`.

As part of our `<WebMethod()>` statement, then, we'll include the `TransactionOption` attribute, like so:

```
<WebMethod(TransactionOption := TransactionOption.RequiresNew)>
```

With this, all of the features we need are enabled automatically for us, added to the configuration of the Web Service in the compiled MSIL. Even more, there are all of the COM+ style types of transactional options, including:

- `Disabled` – executes the Web Service without a transaction
- `NotSupported` – executes the Web Service without a transaction

(These two are the same because the `TransactionOption` values are inherited from the COM+ `EnterpriseServices`, which has more comprehensive transactional support.)

- `Supported` – participates in a transaction, but does not create a new transaction when invoked.
- `Required` – works the same as `RequiresNew`, since Web Services can't create a new transaction. We'll cover this in the next section.
- `RequiresNew` – the important one – fires up a new transaction when invoked.

So, you can see that these look a lot like the attributes in COM+ that tell a consumer how an object is to be treated in a transaction. Strangely, that isn't really what these attributes are used for in the `WebMethod` statement. In this environment, the `TransactionOption` attribute tells the `WebMethod` how it should treat those calls within itself – more or less the opposite of the way COM+ works.

This works exactly how you would imagine it would. If an exception is thrown by any of the code in the `WebMethod`, the transaction is automatically aborted. Its exceptions are handled by a "`try...catch`" block, then the transaction is automatically committed unless explicitly aborted by the `SetAbort` method. We can access `SetAbort` from the `ContextUtil` object, which is in the `System.EnterpriseServices` namespace. We'll go over that a little later.

Our StatusUpdate WebMethod

So, we will start with the necessary header information in the VB.NET code.

```
Imports System.Web.Services
Imports System.Data.SqlClient
Imports System.EnterpriseServices

Namespace RemoteUpdate

  Public Class RemoteStatusTool
    Inherits System.Web.Services.WebService
```

As we mentioned above, we need to import `System.Data.SqlClient` and `System.EnterpriseServices` for the data access and the transaction support, respectively, and add a reference to the `System.EnterpriseServices.dll` assembly. We'll set up a new namespace at `RemoteUpdate`, call our class `RemoteStatusUpdate`, and have the class inherit from the `WebService` class so that we have the `TransactionOption` and other attributes of `WebMethod`.

Next, we'll write our two private `Update` subroutines, which will be the implementation for our transaction test:

```
Private Sub UpdateDoctor(DoctorID As Integer, StatusID As Integer)
  Dim RemoteUpdateConnection As SqlConnection
  Dim UpdateCommand As SqlCommand
  Dim SqlString As String
  'DateTime UpdateTime;
  SqlString = "UPDATE Doctors SET StatusID = " & StatusID _
             & " WHERE DoctorID = " & DoctorID

  'Connect to the DB
  RemoteUpdateConnection = New _
          SqlConnection("Server=localhost;database=RemoteStatus;uid=sa;pwd=;")
  RemoteUpdateConnection.Open()
  'change the doctor status
  UpdateCommand = New SqlCommand(SqlString, RemoteUpdateConnection)
  UpdateCommand.ExecuteNonQuery()
  RemoteUpdateConnection.Close()
End Sub
```

```
Private Sub InsertLog(DoctorID As Integer, StatusID As Integer)
  'Get our objects
  Dim RemoteUpdateConnection As SqlConnection
  Dim InsertCommand As SqlCommand
  Dim SqlString As String
  Dim UpdateTime As DateTime

  'Get time for the log
  UpdateTime = DateTime.Now
  SqlString = "INSERT Log (StatusID, DoctorID, TimeChanged) VALUES ("  _
          & StatusID & ", " & DoctorID & ", '" & UpdateTime & "' )"
```

```
    'Connect to the database
    RemoteUpdateConnection = New _
          SqlConnection("Server=localhost;database=RemoteStatus;uid=sa;pwd=;")
    RemoteUpdateConnection.Open()
    'Insert the log entry
    InsertCommand = New SqlCommand(SqlString, RemoteUpdateConnection)
    InsertCommand.ExecuteNonQuery()
    RemoteUpdateConnection.Close()
  End Sub
```

Both of these methods do similar work in the database. After getting the necessary objects to speak to SQL Server, they get a connection to the server (obviously you would want to make sure that the code above reflected your actual settings). After opening the connection, we run the SQL statement in the string variable against the database using `ExecuteNonQuery`, so that the method call doesn't try to return anything from the command. This code isn't how you would want to write a highly scalable enterprise application, but it shows the process in a fairly transparent fashion.

Now we need to set up our web method:

```
  <WebMethod(TransactionOption := TransactionOption.RequiresNew)> _
  Public Sub UpdateStatus(DoctorID As Integer, StatusID As Integer)
     UpdateDoctor(DoctorID, StatusID)
     InsertLog(DoctorID, StatusID)
  End Sub
```

As we discussed above, we have used the `TransactionOption` attribute of the `WebService` and set it to `RequiresNew` – really the only useful value of this attribute as it stands. Since the attribute defaults to `Disabled`, and that is the only other useful option, we needn't worry much about the other values.

This method accepts the `DoctorID` and `StatusID` from the consumer, only to pass them on to the subroutines being called within the transaction. Thanks to the `TransactionOption` attribute, if one of the methods throws an exception, the entire transaction is scrapped and no data is changed.

The Output of Our Service

If you go to your browser to view the service, it looks and acts exactly like any other Web Service, as we see below.

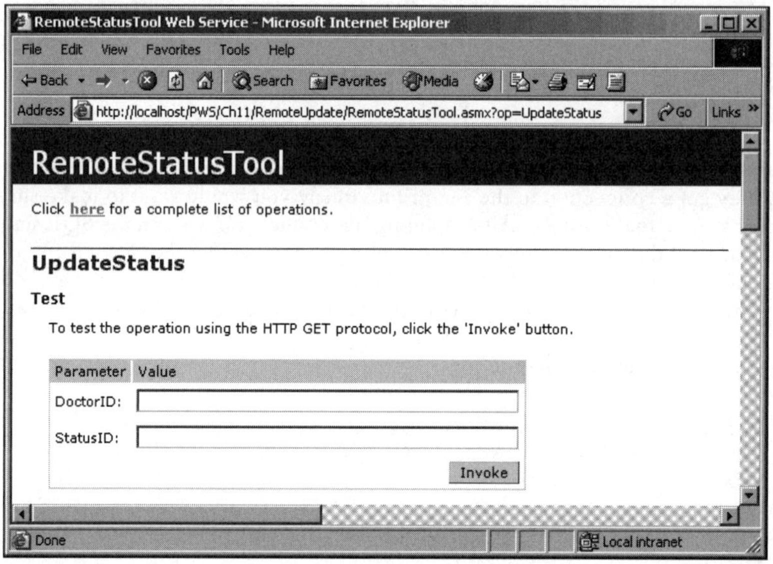

This flows with the whole Microsoft transactional systems model like we see in Fitch and Mather, in which transactions are just something handled by the Distributed Transaction Coordination and the consumers don't need to worry about the implementation. In fact, we really didn't have to worry about much of anything here in the way of special coding. This is by design.

When Microsoft first started to create enterprise services in 1996 with NT 3.51 and SQL Server 5.5, they wrapped the complex transactions of the two-phase commit in a SQL Service called the Distributed Transaction Coordinator. This handled transactions at the stored procedure level and made writing the related COM objects rather complex. The two-phase commit is a very complex operation as it is, as shown here:

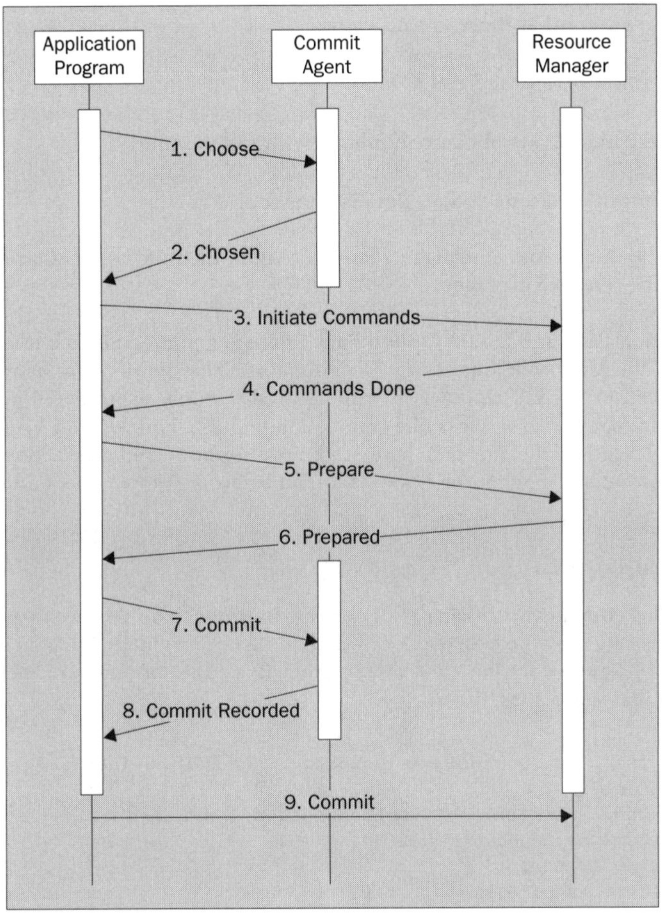

The transaction protocol has two distinct phases – the "Prepare" phase and the "Commit" phase. The application program chooses a controlling agent – the Commit Agent. The Commit Agent can be one of the participating resource managers, like COM+, or another resource manager. Here is a look at the steps they go through.

1. The condition of each resource manager is evaluated
2. Acknowledgment from COM+, in our case
3. The methods each manager will handle are initiated
4. Acknowledgment that they are initiated
5. The application checks to make sure all managers will successfully complete their function – sort of a "dry run"

6. Acknowledgment that there are no errors

7. That condition is reported to COM+

8. Acknowledgment that we can commence with the commit

9. The commit is then sent and all data is changed

If any of the participating resource managers fail to commit, then the application must abort the transaction in all the resource managers.

As part of the Option Pack in NT 4.0's Option Pack, there is a point-and-click interface for the OLE-based DTC called the Microsoft Transaction Coordinator. These services are knows as Microsoft Transaction Services, or MTS. This powerful tool allowed not only the transaction support of DTC, but also other important enterprise services like connection pooling. Finally, with Windows 2000, COM+ was introduced, adding Just-In-Time activation and more sophisticated transaction support. The .NET Enterprise Services we are using in this example are an Interop wrapper around those existing COM+ services.

Does It Really Work?

Let's see if all of this complex processing really works. In order to do this, we need to throw an error in one of the methods called by the `WebMethod`. We'll do this by manually introducing an error using the `Exception` object. Right before the `InsertCommand.ExecuteNonQuery()` method, we add a `Throw()` method that sends a test error.

```
Private Sub InsertLog(DoctorID As Integer, StatusID As Integer)
  'Get our objects
  Dim RemoteUpdateConnection As SqlConnection
  Dim InsertCommand As SqlCommand
  Dim SqlString As String
  Dim UpdateTime As DateTime

  'Get time for the log
  UpdateTime = DateTime.Now
  SqlString = "INSERT Log (StatusID, DoctorID, TimeChanged) VALUES (" _
            & StatusID & ", " & DoctorID & ", '" & UpdateTime & "' )"

  'Connect to the database
  RemoteUpdateConnection = New _
        SqlConnection("Server=localhost;database=RemoteStatus;uid=sa;pwd=;")
  RemoteUpdateConnection.Open()
  'Insert the log entry
  InsertCommand = New SqlCommand(SqlString, RemoteUpdateConnection)
  Try
    Finally
    Throw New Exception("This is the test error")
  End Try
  InsertCommand.ExecuteNonQuery()
  RemoteUpdateConnection.Close()
End Sub
```

Now if we run the method from the test interface by changing the status of one of the doctors manually, we get something like this:

```
System.Web.HttpException: Exception of type System.Web.HttpException was thrown. -
--> System.Reflection.TargetInvocationException: Exception has been thrown by the
target of an invocation. ---> System.Exception: This is the test error
   at RemoteUpdate.RemoteStatusTool.UpdateStatus(Int32 DoctorID, Int32 StatusID)
in c:\inetpub\wwwroot\remoteupdate\remotestatustool.asmx.cs:line 66
   at System.Reflection.RuntimeMethodInfo.InternalInvoke(Object obj, BindingFlags
invokeAttr, Binder binder, Object[] parameters, CultureInfo culture, Boolean
isBinderDefault, Assembly caller, Boolean verifyAccess)
   at System.Reflection.RuntimeMethodInfo.InternalInvoke(Object obj, BindingFlags
invokeAttr, Binder binder, Object[] parameters, CultureInfo culture, Boolean
verifyAccess)
   at System.Reflection.RuntimeMethodInfo.Invoke(Object obj, BindingFlags
invokeAttr, Binder binder, Object[] parameters, CultureInfo culture)
   at System.Reflection.MethodBase.Invoke(Object obj, Object[] parameters)
   at System.Web.Services.Protocols.LogicalMethodInfo.Invoke(Object target,
Object[] values)
   at System.Web.Services.Protocols.WebServiceHandler.Invoke()
   at System.Web.Util.TransactedInvocation.ExecuteTransactedCode()
   at System.Web.Util.Transactions.InvokeTransacted(TransactedCallback callback,
TransactionOption mode, Boolean& transactionAborted)
   at System.Web.Util.Transactions.InvokeTransacted(TransactedCallback callback,
TransactionOption mode)
   at System.Web.Services.Protocols.WebServiceHandler.InvokeTransacted()
   at System.Web.Services.Protocols.WebServiceHandler.CoreProcessRequest()
```

We don't need to see the majority of the error, but the bold parts are important. We can see in the first line that the `HttpException` (what .NET throws when there is a problem with a Web Service) returns the code in our `Exception` statement. In the third line, the `Commit` phase attempts to run, but we run a rollback via `TransactionAborted` in the fourth line. We can see the callback of the `UpdateDoctor` subroutine in the fourth and fifth line of the error.

So it works. If we look at the data, there was no line added to the log, and the doctor in question was not changed. What's more, we didn't really write any transaction code to do this – but that isn't specific to .NET. COM+ provides automatic transactions as part of the Microsoft Management Console by allowing the system administrator to set the transaction mode of each object on the actual COM object itself as it is viewed in the console.

Using EnterpriseServices To Roll Your Own

In MTS we were required to manually set, complete, or abort transactions in our COM code. In COM+, we still had this option by instantiating the `ObjectContext` object of the COM+ Services Library and using the transaction methods of that class. In .NET, these methods are handled by COM+ Enterprise Services.

In the above code we imported `System.EnterpriseServices` so when we code the `TransactionOption` the IntelliSense works. If you are writing your ASP.NET code by hand, you don't need to know this, but Visual Studio .NET gives you the little wavy underline that says there is no `TransactionOption` attribute. IIS knows what it is, so we would be OK.

What if we wanted to catch our errors? Some errors are good for business logic purposes. If we are using structured error handling, which we should be doing, we are better off setting the transaction modes manually when we can, so that we can handle all of the errors we know could exist. With `System.EnterpriseServices`, this becomes a task similar to the original COM coding. Since ASP.NET is so much better integrated with the API, we have much more control at the IIS level, and thus within ASP.NET.

`System.EnterpriseServices`, as we mentioned before, is the namespace that provides much of the functionality of COM+, only now it is much more programmatically controlled. The namespace includes several classes that replicate COM+:

- `ApplicationAccessControlAttribute` – sets the security settings for the library or server container holding the object. Works just like the first step in the **Add New COM+ Object** wizard.
- `ApplicationActivationAttribute` – handles the creation property of the assembly, creator or system controlled.
- `ContextUtil` – this is the method in question, the replacement for `ObjectContext`.
- `InterfaceQueueingAttribute` – enables MSMQ, which is going to be important for widely distributed transactions.
- `JustInTimeActivationAttribute` – turns Just-In-Time Activation (JITA) on and off. This is handled automatically in the example above.
- `ObjectPoolingAttribute` – as one would imagine, this handles Object Pooling, another feature of COM+.
- `SecurityRoleAttribute` – the old MTS roles in a tidy object-oriented package, used for role-based security.

All the old friends are there, just in different clothes. Not only do we have access to the important parts of manual transaction processing, we have all of the other important features of COM+. The planning for this toolset isn't quite finished, but check out the MSDN documentation for a complete listing of tools in this powerful namespace.

The `ContextUtil` object is especially important to our cause, as it replaces the `ObjectContext` object we used in Visual Basic 6. Along with a number of application-level attributes, which are largely inherited by various web-savvy namespaces, these methods are allowed:

- `EnableCommit` – turn on object consistency
- `DisableCommit` – turn off object consistency
- `GetNamedProperty` – return a named property of the context
- `IsCallerInRole` – determines if the caller is in the specified role
- `SetAbort` – rolls back the methods encased by the transaction
- `SetComplete` – allows the transaction to complete when asked by the DTC

Putting It To Use

Managing our own transactions works just like in Visual Basic 6 – only now we can handle it with ASP.NET and any other .NET language code-behind. In VB6 we referenced the COM+ Services Library in the class. Now, to set up the `ContextUtil` object, we need to have a design that supports our manual transactions. We'll use structured error handling to essentially replicate the automatic error handling we created above – just for example purposes.

To do this, we encase the method calls in a "`try...catch`" block, with the `SetAbort` method of the `ContextUtil` as the code run on the error condition. For this example, we'll catch the imaginary `NoStatusException`, set up elsewhere in our code. We'll leave writing the exception as an exercise for the reader.

```
<WebMethod(TransactionOption := TransactionOption.RequiresNew)> _
Public Sub UpdateStatus(DoctorID As Integer, StatusID As Integer)
   Try
      ContextUtil.EnableCommit()
      UpdateDoctor(DoctorID, StatusID)
      InsertLog(DoctorID, StatusID)
      ContextUtil.SetComplete()
   Catch e As Exception
      ContextUtil.SetAbort()
      'We could put logic here to determine
      'how the rollback occurs
      Throw e
   End Try
End Sub

Class NoStatusException
   'Some code in here
End Class
```

What this allows us to do is trap known user errors, like empty text fields that should be zeros, and insert a zero, then commit the transaction. Though this isn't always what we want to do, it is an effective way to manage transactions in ASP.NET in general, and Web Services in particular.

Consuming Transactional Web Services

There are really two topics here. The first is consuming transactional Web Services, which, it turns out, works just like consuming any other kind of Web Service. We'll take a look at that, as well as the implications.

The second is consuming Web Services in a transactional way. This is something of a problem, as we discussed in the introduction. According to the Microsoft documentation:

> *Web Service methods can only participate as the root object in a transaction, due to the stateless nature of the HTTP protocol. Web Service methods can invoke COM objects that participate in the same transaction as the Web Service method, if the COM object is marked to run within a transaction in the* Component Services *administrative tool. If a Web Service method, with a* `TransactionOption` *property of* `Required` *or* `RequiresNew`*, invokes another Web Service method with a* `TransactionOption` *property of* `Required` *or* `RequiresNew`*, each Web Service method participates in their own transaction, because a Web Service method can only act as the root object in a transaction.*

What this says, is "if you plan to build an application using a Web Service in a transactional context with local methods, forget it." So, according to Microsoft, it doesn't work. We'll look at why, and some possible workarounds, later in the chapter.

Consuming Our StatusUpdate WebMethod

To begin, let's write a little ASP.NET file that consumes our Web method from before. This should be a quick form, just to test the transactions. Then we have a base to try a few other options. First, set up the project:

- Make a replica database on your SQL Server called `LocalStatus` and copy the contents of the `RemoteStatus` database into it via Data Transformation Services. (Again the scripts to create and populate this database can be found in the code download.)
- Create an ASP.NET application called `LocalStatus` at http://localhost/PWS/Ch11/LocalStatus.
- Add a Web Reference to the Web Service created in the previous section: http://localhost/PWS/Ch11/RemoteStatus/RemoteStatusTool.asmx.
- Drop the ASP.NET code below into your solution. This is `WebForm1.aspx` in the code download.

We'll start by referencing the tools we'll need to consume our Web Service. Your namespace may be slightly different based on your local machine name and specifics in naming your project. We need the data tools to fill the `Doctor` and `Status` list boxes later.

```
<%@ Page Language="VB" Debug="true" %>
<%@ Import Namespace="System" %>
<%@ Import Namespace="System.Data" %>
<%@ Import Namespace="System.Data.SqlClient" %>
```

Next, we'll add the code for the page load event. When the page loads, without a post-back, we want it to fill the list boxes we have below in the HTML section. Again, we have used fairly simple `SqlClient` code to do this for example purposes.

```
<HTML>
  <script language="VB" runat="server">

  Private Sub Page_Load(Sender As Object, E As System.EventArgs)
    Dim LocalUpdateConnection As SqlConnection
    Dim DoctorsCommand As SqlCommand
    Dim StatusCommand As SqlCommand
    Dim DoctorsReader As SqlDataReader
    Dim StatusReader As SqlDataReader
    Dim DoctorsSQL As String
    Dim StatusSQL As String

    If Not Page.IsPostBack Then
      DoctorsSQL = "SELECT DoctorID, Name FROM Doctors"
      StatusSQL = "SELECT StatusID, StatusType FROM StatusTypes"
```

```
    'Connect to the database
    LocalUpdateConnection = New
      SqlConnection("Server=localhost;database=LocalStatus;uid=sa;pwd=;")
    LocalUpdateConnection.Open()

    DoctorsCommand = New SqlCommand(DoctorsSQL, LocalUpdateConnection)
    DoctorsReader = DoctorsCommand.ExecuteReader()

    'Get the information from the page into the dataconnection
    DoctorsList.DataSource = DoctorsReader
    DoctorsList.DataTextField = "Name"
    DoctorsList.DataValueField = "DoctorID"
    DoctorsList.DataBind()

    DoctorsReader.Close()

    StatusCommand = New SqlCommand(StatusSQL, LocalUpdateConnection)
    StatusReader = StatusCommand.ExecuteReader()


    StatusList.DataSource = StatusReader
    StatusList.DataTextField = "StatusType"
    StatusList.DataValueField = "StatusID"
    StatusList.DataBind()

    StatusReader.Close()
  End If
End Sub
```

Another subprocedure we'll add is the `UpdateStatus` sub that will run when the user clicks the button. This will reference and run the Web Service we added to the Web References folder.

```
Sub UpdateStatus(sender As Object, e As EventArgs)
  a.Text = DoctorsList.SelectedItem.Value.ToString()
  Dim RemoteUpdate As New LocalStatus.localhost.RemoteStatusTool
  RemoteUpdate.UpdateStatus(DoctorsList.SelectedItem.Value, _
                            StatusList.SelectedItem.Value)
End Sub
```

Finally, we want to add our HTML code at the bottom. This creates the server controls for the list boxes, and the button, and specifies the code to run for the `OnClick` event.

```
<HEAD>
  <title></title>
</HEAD>
  <body>

    <form id="StatusForm" method="post" runat="server">
      <asp:ListBox id="DoctorsList" runat="server" />
      <asp:ListBox id="StatusList" runat="server" />
      <br />
```

```
        <asp:TextBox ID="a" Runat="server" />
        <br />
        <asp:Button id="Search"
                    runat="server"
                    OnClick="UpdateStatus"
                    Text="Change Status" />
      </form>
    </body>
  </HTML>
```

Now we have finished our ASP.NET file, and can take a look using the browser:

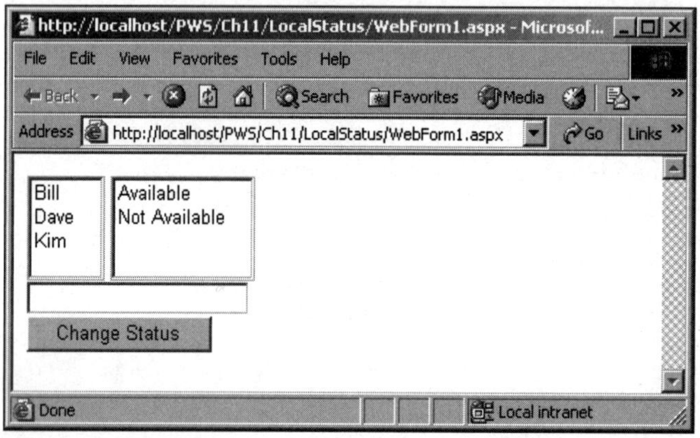

When you click the Change Status button, you get a blank page in return, but if you check the remote database you'll see that the status of the doctor you selected has changed, hopefully. This proves that a Web Service can be run remotely as the root of a transaction and successfully commit. While this is good news, and certainly a significant contribution to transactional processing in general, we have yet to move to the most interesting part.

Transactions Calling Web Services

The ability to call a Web Service in the context of a transaction is, according to Microsoft, not possible. It will just take a few minutes to change our example above to run a consuming transaction. Let's see what actually happens when we give it a try.

First, we need to add some code to update the `LocalStatus` database. To do this, add a private subprocedure that mimics the changes made by the `UpdateDoctors` sub in the Web Service code-behind.

```
Sub UpdateDoctor( DoctorID As Integer, StatusID As Integer)
  Dim RemoteUpdateConnection As SqlConnection
  Dim UpdateCommand As SqlCommand
  Dim SqlString As String
  SqlString = "UPDATE Doctors SET StatusID = " & StatusID _
            & " WHERE DoctorID = " & DoctorID
  RemoteUpdateConnection = New _
```

```
            SqlConnection("Server=localhost;database=LocalStatus;uid=sa;pwd=;")
    RemoteUpdateConnection.Open()
    UpdateCommand = New SqlCommand(SqlString, RemoteUpdateConnection)
    UpdateCommand.ExecuteNonQuery()
    RemoteUpdateConnection.Close()
  End Sub
```

Then, we need to add the method call below to the button `OnClick` event, and wrap the two method calls in a transaction using automatic transaction participation. If this works, it will provide a two-phase commit or abort if the calls both succeed or if one fails, respectively.

```
  Sub UpdateStatus(sender As Object, e As EventArgs)
    a.Text = DoctorsList.SelectedIndex.ToString()
    Dim RemoteUpdate As New LocalStatus.localhost.RemoteStatusTool

    UpdateDoctor(DoctorsList.SelectedItem.Value, StatusList.SelectedItem.Value)

    RemoteUpdate.UpdateStatus(DoctorsList.SelectedItem.Value, _
                              StatusList.SelectedItem.Value)
  End Sub
```

The highlighted code is the reference to our new method. Now all we have to do is add automatic transaction participation to the ASP.NET page – one line added into the page declaration statements.

```
  <%@ Page Language="VB" Debug="true" Transaction="Required" %>
```

Then, we are ready to run. Remember to comment out the error code we added to the Web Service, if you haven't already; we'll open it up soon enough. Running this code produces the same results as above without the transaction. Remember, we are forcing two transactions here – one at the Web Service local level, and one at the ASP.NET level, with the local method and the Web Service included.

So what's the big deal? The big deal is that the Web Service is not participating in the transaction. Throw some error (stop the database for example) and look at the stack trace. There is no top-level transaction occurring. Why? It's because we are using a Web Service as something other than the root of a transaction. The .NET Framework will not let this happen! So, compared to DCOM, we have uncovered a significant weakness.

Why Is This a Problem?

Transactions depend on a set of logical properties called ACID. The term ACID conveys the role transactions play in mission-critical applications. A term used in the earliest documents about transaction concept, ACID stands for **atomicity**, **consistency**, **isolation**, and **durability**. These ensure the kind of environment leading to the predictable behavior of code, reinforcing the role of transactions as all-or-none propositions that reduce the management load when there are many variables.

Atomicity defines a transaction as a unit of work in which a series of operations occur between the `BEGIN TRANSACTION` and `END TRANSACTION` statements of an application. A transaction executes exactly once and is atomic – all the work is done or none of it is. Operations associated with a transaction usually share a common intent and are interdependent. By performing only a subset of these operations, the system could compromise the overall intent of the transaction. Atomicity eliminates the chance of processing a subset of operations.

A transaction is a unit of integrity because it preserves the **consistency** of data, transforming one consistent state of data into another consistent state of data. Consistency requires that data bound by a transaction is essentially preserved. Some of the responsibility for this belongs to the architect, who must make sure that all known integrity constraints are enforced by the application. For example, in developing an application that transfers money, you should avoid arbitrarily moving decimal points during the transfer.

A transaction is also a unit of **isolation** – allowing concurrent transactions to behave as though each were the only transaction running in the system. Isolation requires that each transaction appear to be the only transaction manipulating the data store, even though other transactions may be running at the same time. A transaction should never see the intermediate stages of another transaction.

Transactions attain the highest level of isolation when they are serializable. At this level, the results obtained from a set of concurrent transactions are identical to the results obtained by running each transaction serially. As a high degree of isolation can limit the number of concurrent transactions, some applications reduce the isolation level in exchange for better throughput.

A transaction is also a unit of recovery. If a transaction succeeds, the system guarantees that its updates will persist, even if the computer crashes immediately after the commit. Specialized logging allows the system's restart procedure to complete unfinished operations, making the transaction **durable**.

How Does This All Apply To Web Services?

By definition, Web Services don't meet the standards of ACID. They are loosely coupled, which goes against the principles of durability. Also, they are uncontrolled, which runs the risk of altering the consistency of processing.

Microsoft transaction processors, specifically DTC, depend on knowledge of the underlying network layer to control the durability of a transaction. Since all network traffic on a Microsoft network is in constant communication with the operating system, distributed transactions report the durability of the network to the caller. DTC uses this information to determine if a rollback is necessary. If a network call has failed, DTC knows it and acts accordingly.

The consistency issue is a bit more ethereal. Though we have the WSDL to define the interface of a remote service, little of the underlying logic is accessible to the DTC. This is mostly due to the fact that COM+ has not caught up to the rest of the .NET world (we call this .NOT) and it doesn't speak WSDL. Therefore, we cannot be sure, as architects, that the data will be handled in the consistent manner prescribed by ACID. To use the above example, we don't really know if the decimal point is being moved or not.

So for those primary reasons, we cannot include a Web Service in a serviced ASP.NET page without it running in its own transaction. This is a significant weakness of Web Services in general – not just of the Microsoft implementation.

What Can We Do About This?

A good question, and a serious topic of debate among those who are making the decisions. All of the solutions are of the roll-your-own type at this time, however. We'll look at some of them here, at least in theory.

The XLang Specification

An XLang service description extends the WDSL of a Web Service by describing the behavioral aspects of the service. XLang specifies an operation, a single unit of a business transaction, as the root of a business scenario, and describes the ways this operation fits within the scope of the scenario. For instance, here is the XLang description of a stock trade, the operation sequence being the focus of the service description.

```
<xlang:behavior>
  <xlang:body>
    <xlang:sequence>
      <xlang:action operation="AskLastTradePrice"
                    port="pGetRequest" activation="true"/>
      <xlang:action operation="SendLastTradePrice"
                    port="pSendResponse"/>
    </xlang:sequence>
  </xlang:body>
</xlang:behavior>
```

This service description sits within the `Service` section of the WSDL file. It describes a very simple behavior, in which the sequence in which two asynchronous operations occur in a single trade price query interaction is defined. This straightforward example assists greatly in the consistency of the service, since the consuming application now knows in what order the pieces of logic within the service are to be executed. Since communication of the logic of Web Services is not inherent in the WSDL specification, XLang goes a long way towards providing the technology needed for true transactional systems with Web Services.

XLang is a Microsoft specification that has been opened to public commentary. The author, Satish Thatte, has made the specification available at http://www.gotdotnet.com/team/xml_wsspecs/xlang-c/default.htm.

BPML

The Business Process Management Language is an abstracted execution model for the modeling of business processes, similar to how XML is the abstracted description model for business data. Described initially by a large number of business process concerns, BPML was made public in March of 2001. BPML processes can be described as a specific business process modeling language layered on top of the extensible BPML XML Schema. BPML represents business processes as the interleaving of control flow, data flow, and event flow, while adding orthogonal design capabilities for business rules, security roles, and transaction contexts.

Essentially, the Business Process Management Initiative is attempting to describe the programmers' responsibility to atomicity in business process behavior – thus again taking us one step closer to the Holy Grail of transaction environments – ACID. The BPML employs a message-based model in which all participants in the process interact through the exchange of messages, and the process defines the manner in which messages flow between participants, as well as the information conveyed in each message. This technology could and can be used in private implementations of transactional messaging protocols like BizTalk. More information about BPML can be found at http://www.bpmi.org.

ebXML

Where BPML provides the private implementation of transactional business process messaging, ebXML is recommending the public implementation of this important service. ebXML is a powerful force, even being enlisted by RosettaNet as the standard of choice for message delivery.

ebXML is a modular suite of specifications that enables enterprises of any size and in any geographical location to conduct business over the Internet. Using ebXML, companies now have a standard method to exchange business messages, conduct trading relationships, communicate data in common terms and define and register business processes. It utilizes XML in a similar fashion as does XLang to specify message delivery. Though it is less specific to defining transactions, it is still potentially a powerful protocol in the e-commerce world of business message delivery. Read more about ebXML at http://www.ebXML.org.

The BizTalk Framework

Microsoft has created a platform-specific set of tools in the BizTalk Framework that use the essential features of Web Services – SOAP headers with BizTalk-only entries and XML bodies – to transport messages between servers of like technology and rigid standards. Though this is slightly beyond the scope of this book, it is a consideration when considering the need for transactions in distributed procedure calls.

BizTalk uses three Microsoft-only standards – the BizTalk Document, BizTags, and the BizTalk Message – to provide an interdependent messaging standard for the Microsoft world of networks. While technically platform-independent, BizTalk clearly is designed to bring slightly simplified document transfer to Microsoft shops that wish to escape the world of EDI. This it undeniably does very well. Though not a real replacement for a Web Service – nor a claimant to that title – BizTalk is a real consideration when attempting to produce document-handling applications that have need of the two-phase commit.

But What Can We Really Do About This?

These advanced frameworks and protocols could be the road to the future, but until they are embraced by our clients and other solution providers, they do us little good. While it is nice to know they exist, that knowledge still leaves us wondering how to actually implement these cross-service transactions.

We mentioned above that not everything is a Web Service. In many cases, if you are architecting a large application, one of the many other distributed architectures will do the job for you. Sometimes, it is better just to rebuild logic, even though it seems that exposing methods via Web Services is the answer. In some cross-platform situations, CORBA, RMI or DCOM – each with their own transaction processing – is the best solution. But the question remains – what is the real .NET solution?

A simple answer is .NET Remoting. As a replacement for DCOM, Remoting is a strong contender for the distributed architecture of an application. In .NET Remoting, objects are passed from one application to another in a binary bitstream, thus ending the potential for network-level confusion on the part of the client or consumer. Since you can directly touch the passed object, similar to Java's Jini protocol, the transaction can be consummated against a known object in most circumstances.

We won't get into a technical discussion of Remoting here, since this is a Web Services book, but if interested, you should check out *Microsoft .NET Remoting: A Technical Overview* by Piet Obermeyer and Jonathan Hawkins on the MSDN Library. All of the sample code is in C# and the document is an excellent introduction to the concepts presented by the Remoting tools in .NET. For a VB.NET specific look at Remoting, see Chapter 20 of "*Professional VB.NET 2nd Edition*" (Wrox Press, ISBN 1-86100-716-7)

Summary

We have discovered that providing a Web Service with transactional commitment is quite simple in the ASP.NET scenario, and can even be controlled MTS-like with the new `ContextUtil` object. Now we have no excuse not to architect transactional support into the Web Services we provide.

Consuming Web Services under the .NET Framework proved to be another hurdle altogether. Although a small number of new protocols exists to ease the ACID support of Web Services, none of them are quite mature enough to fit within the tightly architected Framework, and consuming services in a transactional manner is not yet supported. While this leaves us with some pretty basic limitations, new protocols like the BizTalk framework and XLang promise to bring some hope in the form of a usable distributed transaction effort.

We all, as developers, know the power of transactional systems. While Web Services are not the principal means for the creation of scalable and reliable n-tier systems, they do hold a remarkable potential to change the way businesses do business and computers do computing. The addition of a two-phase commitment system like automatic transactions for Web Services, as provided by .NET, has the potential to take Web Services that one step closer to Programming Nirvana.

Professional
ASP.NET
Web
Services

12

Data Caching

"**Your competitor is on the next page!**" should be the slogan that every web application developer, vendor or content provider should follow in the Internet arena. If we don't provide the service at the speed that the customer is expecting, then someone else will, and we'll lose business.

Whenever we're planning or building an application or a Web Service the first thing that should come to mind is "How can we increase performance and make this Web Service scalable?" There are many ways we can do this – one way is **caching**.

Caching is an important technique for building highly available and scalable Web sites. A Web Service's performance can be significantly boosted by using caching techniques, such as caching in-memory frequently used data or data structures that are expensive to create – instead of reconstructing the data at every request from a relatively slow data source such as a database or a legacy system.

Below is a breakdown of what we'll cover in this chapter:

- **Output Caching** – we'll start with a basic output caching example and we'll see how it can improve performance. We'll also see the pitfalls of this technique.
- **Data Caching** – we'll see how to use the `Cache` object and how to use it in Web Services to cache arbitrary objects such as a `DataSet`.
- **Dependency Caching** – we will also see how to take advantage of dependency caching using file dependency, key dependency, and time-based dependency.
- **Callback** – when an item is removed from cache storage, the .NET runtime can fire an event back to us and say this item has been removed from the cache. We'll learn about the callback events in detail.

Let's get started with an overview of caching.

Caching Overview

Caching is a very broad term in the world of the Internet. Caching happens everywhere on the Internet, from your browser to the proxy server to web caching servers, and so on. All this caching happens on the Internet to improve the performance of web sites/applications and to give the best possible experience to the end users.

What is a Cache?

A cache is a buffer that holds the data frequently used by the applications in a faster consumable containers such as OS memory, files, databases, and so on. For example, if an application depends on an external data source and it consumes data from the external data source whenever the application is used, then it is wise to cache the external data internally, either in memory, or in a file, or in a local database.

The memory-based caching technique is the fastest and most widely used by the applications to improve performance and this technique is 100% supported by the .NET Framework. The memory-based cache is an in-memory data store that can store temporary objects such as a file, database query result, or any arbitrary object, with or without an expiry policy. The expiry policy could be time-bound or data value-based or file change-based. Accessing an in-memory data store is always faster (probably in the order of hundreds or even thousands of times faster based on the hardware and software configuration of the server) than accessing the database from a database server or a file from network storage or from a file server.

Pros and Cons of Caching

Of course, there are advantages and disadvantages of caching.

Pros

- No need to reprocess the same request or the database query again and again to produce the same result.
- Faster response time, close to that of a static page (since the `Cache` holds the processed data).
- Reduces the network traffic between the Web Service and the database server or file server.
- Reduces the workload on the database server or file server.

Cons

- The first time caching happens, the application will take a little more time to respond.
- Caching will not work on personalization-based applications. For example, if the cached data is based on the user then there is no sense in caching the data for a specific user.
- If the nature of the caching data changes rapidly then the caching will not make sense in that case. Most of the time the application will try to cache the data and the clients will receive inconsistent data. This could create a bottleneck in the application.
- More powerful hardware and more memory on the server are needed.
- Finding the best possible caching policy to cache the output of the Web Service or arbitrary objects using the `Cache` object is difficult.

Output Caching

Output caching is a caching technique that caches the entire page output (either an ASP.NET page or a Web Service) for a specified time period. Web Services support output caching by using an attribute (`CacheDuration`) of the `WebMethod` declaration.

For a heavy traffic Web Service, automatic time-based caching makes perfect sense. Even setting a caching interval as low as five minutes could give a big performance benefit to the Web Service. Let's say we have 20 requests per minute. Without caching, this would result in 100 Web Service results generated in a five-minute period. With caching, we only generate the Web Service once, and the next 99 requests will be served from the cache.

Let's see an example for Web Service output caching. Fire up your favorite text editor and type the following code, or alternatively download the code for this chapter from http://www.wrox.com, and open up `OutputCache1.asmx`:

```
<%@ WebService Language="VB" Class="OutputCache1" %>
Imports System.Web.Services

Public Class OutputCache1
  Inherits WebService


    '*
    '* Set output caching time for 60 seconds
    '*
    <WebMethod(CacheDuration := 60)> _
    Public Function GetServerDateTime() As String
      Return "Current Date/Time = " + System.DateTime.Now.ToString()
    End Function
End Class
```

Next, save this file, naming it `OutputCache1.asmx`, in a virtual directory. This example creates a class named `OutputCache1` with a single method: `GetServerDateTime`. The `GetServerDateTime` method returns the current date and time at the server.

Testing Our Web Service

Point Internet Explorer at the `OutputCache1.asmx` file on your web server:

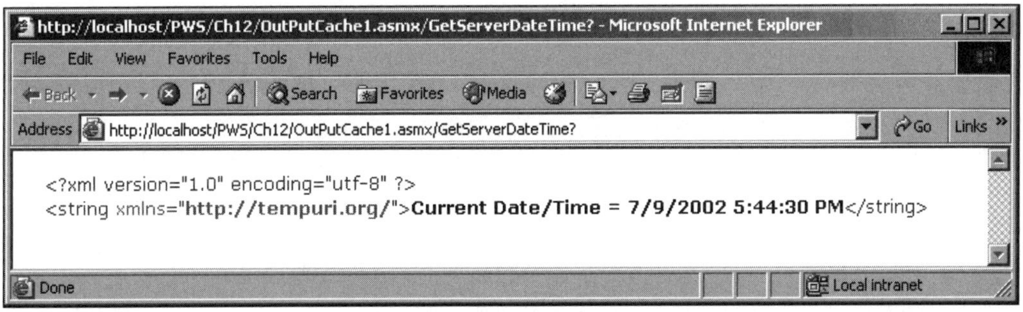

If we click the refresh button a few times we'll continue to see the same date and time returned from the server for 60 seconds. After that the output cache will be discarded and a new cache will be built on a request to the Web Service.

Let's look at the code closely. We've created a simple Web Service with the class name as `OutputCache1`, which inherits from the `WebService` class. Then we have a standard `WebMethod` that doesn't take any parameters and returns the current date and time at the server as a string.

```
<WebMethod(CacheDuration := 60)> _
```

We've used the `CacheDuration` attribute of the `WebMethod` to set the output cache time as 60 seconds.

ASP.NET supports a similar kind of output caching using the `OutputCache` directive. However, ASP.NET provides broader support with attributes such as `VaryByParam`, `VaryByHeader`, `VaryByControl`, and `VaryByCustom` for output caching. Web Services don't support these attributes and by default, Web Services output caching reacts to the `VaryByParam="*"` attribute. That is, vary by all parameters.

Let's see an example of this. Let's assume that we're exposing a traffic report Web Service, which takes the highway number (such as I90, I94) and the direction (East, West) of travel to provide the traffic information. Our traffic Web Service relies on an external source – suppose this external source provides the traffic data every three minutes. If this is the case, then it won't make any sense to query the data from the data source for every request. Hence, we can cache the output of the Web Service for three minutes. This will save a lot of querying and processing time for the Web Service, reducing the stress on the server and improving the output performance of the Web Service.

Here is the code for the Web Service, `Traffic1.asmx`:

```
<%@ WebService Language="VB" Class="Traffic" %>

Imports System.Web.Services

Public Class TrafficInfo
   Public HighWayNumber As String
   Public DirectionOfTravel As String
   Public TrafficInformation As String
   Public LastUpdated As String
End Class

Public Class Traffic
  Inherits WebService

  '*
  '* Set output caching time for 180 seconds
  '*
  <WebMethod(CacheDuration := 180)> _
  Public Function GetTrafficInfo(sHighWayNum As String, _
                                 sDirection As String) As TrafficInfo

    'Create a string array to return the
    'traffic information
    Dim objTrInfo As New TrafficInfo()
    'Assign the Highway number and the
    'direction of travel to the object
    objTrInfo.HighWayNumber = sHighWayNum
    objTrInfo.DirectionOfTravel = sDirection
    objTrInfo.LastUpdated = System.DateTime.Now.ToString()
    '*
```

```
    '* Let's hardcode a few US Highways near Chicago
    '*
    Select Case sHighWayNum
      Case "I90" 'For Interstate Highway 90
        If sDirection = "East" Then
          objTrInfo.TrafficInformation = "Kennedy inbound from O'hare " _
                                       & "Airport to the Loop - 42 minutes"
        Else
          objTrInfo.TrafficInformation = "Kennedy outbound from the Loop " _
                                       & "to O'hare Airport - 27 minutes"
        End If
      Case "I94" 'For Interstate Highway 94
        If sDirection = "North" Then
          objTrInfo.TrafficInformation = "Edens outbound from the Loop " _
                                       & "to Deerfield Rd - 41 minutes"
        Else
          objTrInfo.TrafficInformation = "Edens inbound from Deerfield Rd. " _
                                        & "to the Loop - 63 minutes"
        End If
      Case Else 'For other Highways
        objTrInfo.TrafficInformation = "No information available at " _
                                     & "this time."
    End Select

    'Return the TrafficInfo object
    Return objTrInfo
  End Function
End Class
</script>
```

Let's see how the Web Service looks in IE:

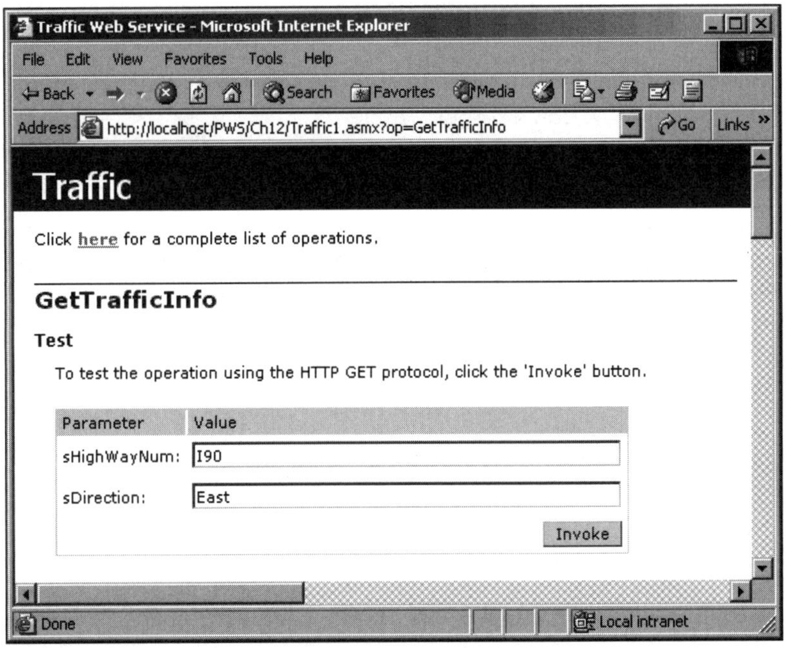

Enter the highway number as "I90" and direction as "East" and click the Invoke button. You'll see the XML output from the Web Service with a timestamp:

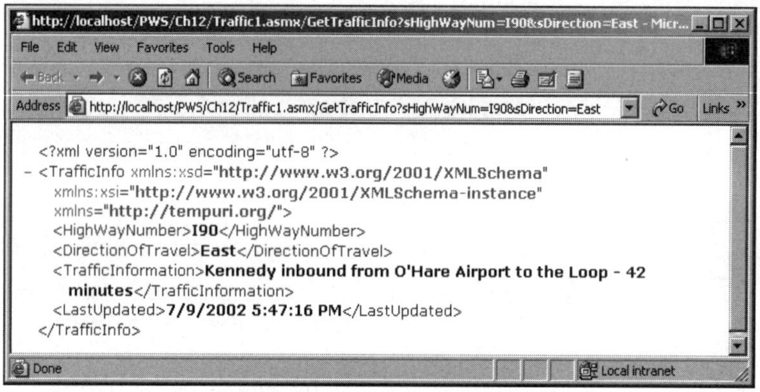

Run the Web Service for another combination like "I90" and "West":

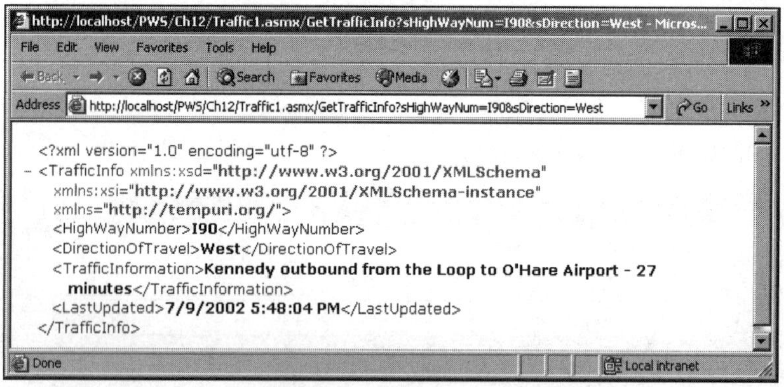

If we look at the `<LastUpdated>` attribute of the Web Service, each parameter change will have a different timestamp unless they are accessed at the same time. This is because each `WebMethod` parameter change stores something different in the cache.

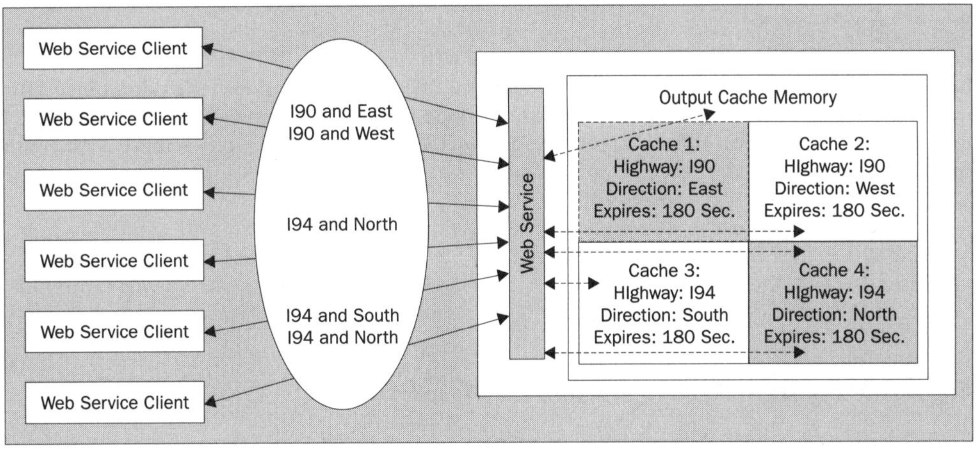

In the above figure, the Web Service is getting five calls with four different argument combinations. If we look at the output cache memory we have four different outputs stored in cache based on the four different combinations of the Web Service arguments. Each of these output cache storages will be cached for 180 seconds. Within the three-minute caching period, if a new request comes with the same Web Service argument combination, then the output will be returned from the cache. If that particular argument combination didn't have an output cache, then the Web Service request will be processed and the result will be sent back to the client. At the same time, the generated Web Service output will be cached for three minutes in the output cache memory.

When using output caching in a web farm environment, the output cache only applies to the server where it was created. This cache will not affect the cache state of the other servers on your web farm.

Potential Pitfalls of Output Caching

Since the output cache is based on the variation of incoming arguments to the `WebMethod`, you should be very careful when planning such implementations. Let's say your Web Service argument values can vary from 1000 to 10000. You'll end up creating between 1000 and 10000 cache storages of your Web Service output based on the argument variations, and this could be a performance bottleneck for the Web Service. You should also note that when using in-memory caching the server needs lots and lots of memory.

So before planning for output caching implementation, find out how many number of parameter variations are possible for the Web Services and find out how many cache items will be created based on that. If you think the server hardware can handle the number of cache items, then the output caching Web Service implementation will be OK. But this raises a new problem.

For example, say our Web Service is based on the `ItemCode` parameter and we have item codes from `Itm1` to `Itm10000` in the database. If the Web Service receives the item codes – whether they are in the database or not – it will create an output cache container for the item code. A Web Service client could bring the Web Service down by sending different types of item codes to the `WebMethod`, and end up consuming all the memory in the server. Ultimately this could become something like a **denial of service attack** for the Web Service. There is no way to control this kind of attack. The best way to handle this, if the Web Service is a secured Web Service, is by denying access to the web client, if you know the IP address of the client. For more information about security read Chapters 13 and 14.

Data Caching

Output caching is declarative, in the sense that we just declare the output caching duration and the Web Services takes care of caching output of the Web Service for the different variations of the input parameters. It also takes care of the expiration and recreation of the cache item – there is no coding here and we can't manipulate the caching via code.

On the other hand, data caching is explicit and purely manageable from the code. The code controls what kind of data gets cached into the cache memory pool. Data caching provides more control over caching such as how the cache will be created, where it will be stored, and when it will expire. Our code can remove the cache item from the memory when needed.

Using the Application Object for Caching

Like ASP.NET applications, Web Services can have access to both the `Application` and `Session` objects.

The `Application` object is global to the web application, (in the web farm scenario it is global to the web application on the current server) and every piece of code in the application has access to it. On the other hand the `Session` variable can only be accessed by the code if the `WebMethod` enables the `SessionState` attribute.

Those of us with a background in ASP can remember the use of "`Application`" and "`Session`" objects as cache containers to store frequently used data in our ASP applications. In the same way, we can use the `Application` object to cache some frequently used data for Web Services.

We can also use the `Session` object to cache some user-specific data. The `Session` object can only be used if the Web Service uses personalization for the Web Services and session state is enabled. Otherwise we'll end up caching the same duplicate data for each and every user for the Web Service. For more information about the session state, read Chapter 10, *Managing State.*

> *In ASP, we couldn't store objects written in VB6 in the application scope due to the threading (apartment model multithreading) and the serialization/marshalling limitations imposed by VB6. The only objects that were eligible to be stored in the application scope were free threaded or "Both" threaded objects. With VB.NET all the components are by default free threaded and we can use these components in the application scope without any performance problems.*

Application-scope variables can be used to store both non-structured (or scalar) data, such as a number or a string, and structured data (as an object reference) such as an XML document. Let's see an example of this. Let's say we want to write a Web Service that exposes the entire range of product categories back to our clients. Our clients will call this Web Service to get the updated range of product categories for their web sites. We're going to expose a "`GetProductCategories`" `WebMethod` and this will read the famous Northwind SQL Server database and return all the categories back to the client in an ADO.NET `DataSet`.

Here is the code for `ApplicationExample1.asmx`:

```
<%@ WebService Language="VB" Class="ApplicationExample1" %>

Imports System
Imports System.Data
Imports System.Data.SqlClient
Imports System.Web.Services

Public Class ApplicationExample1
   Inherits WebService

   '*
   '* Store some data in the application object
   '*
   <WebMethod()> _
   Public Function GetProductCategories() As DataSet
      'If the application variable is not set then
      'call the SetApplicationData() function to
      'add the Category DataSet to the
      'application variable
      If Application("CategoriesDataSet") Is Nothing Then
         SetApplicationData()
      End If

      'Return the DataSet back to the client
      Return CType(Application("CategoriesDataSet"), DataSet)
   End Function 'GetProductCategories

   Private Function SetApplicationData() As Boolean
      'Build the Database connection string
      Dim ConnStr As String = "server=localhost;uid=sa;pwd=;database=Northwind"

      'Create a new connection object
      Dim SQLConn As New SqlConnection(ConnStr)

      'Create a new SQL Data Adapter object
      Dim SQLAdp As New SqlDataAdapter("SELECT CategoryID, CategoryName, " _
                              & "Description FROM Categories", SQLConn)

      'Create a new Dataset object
      Dim SQLDS As New DataSet()

      'Fill the Dataset object using the SQL Data Adapter object
      SQLAdp.Fill(SQLDS, "Category")

      'Lock the application
      Application.Lock()

      'Store the DataSet in the Application memory
```

```
        Application("CategoriesDataSet") = SQLDS

        'UnLock the application
        Application.UnLock()

        'return True back to the calling function
        Return True
    End Function
End Class
```

In the WebMethod, we're checking if the Application object holds a valid DataSet object in the CategoriesDataSet variable. If not, we're calling the SetApplicationData method to add the data to the application variable.

```
        If Application("CategoriesDataSet") Is Nothing Then
            SetApplicationData()
        End If
```

In the SetApplicationData method we're opening a connection to the SQL Server and creating a SqlDataAdapter object to read all the categories from the Categories table in the Northwind database.

```
        Dim ConnStr As String = "server=localhost;uid=sa;pwd=;database=Northwind"
        'Create a new connection object
        Dim SQLConn As New SqlConnection(ConnStr)
        'Create a new SQL Data Adapter object
        Dim SQLAdp As New SqlDataAdapter("SELECT CategoryID, CategoryName, " _
                                & "Description FROM Categories", SQLConn)
```

We then declare a new DataSet object and fill it with the results from the SqlDataAdapter object. Then we lock the application, assigning the DataSet object to the Application object and unlocking the Application object. Since the application variables are global and each line of code in the application has access to these variables, there is a chance that more than one client request could try to modify the same application variable at the same time. This would raise the concurrency issue, and so to avoid it we're using the lock and unlock statements. We then return a True flag back to the GetProductCategories method.

```
        'Create a new Dataset object
        Dim SQLDS As New DataSet()

        'Fill the Dataset object using the SQL Data Adapter object
        SQLAdp.Fill(SQLDS, "Category")

        'UnLock the application
        Application.Lock()

        'Store the DataSet in the Application memory
        Application("CategoriesDataSet") = SQLDS

        'Lock the application
        Application.UnLock()

        'return True back to the calling function
        Return True
```

Now let's build a proxy for the above Web Service and deploy it in the `bin` folder. See Chapter 3 for more details on building a Web Service Proxy class. The following file, `ApplicationExample1Build.bat`, can be found in the `bin` folder of the code download and should be run from the command line. You may need to alter the path to the WSDL file according to where you have installed the code on your server. Please note that the line breaks in the following commands are only for the sake of readability:

```
WSDL /l:VB /n:AppExpNamespace /out:ApplicationExample1.VB ↴
http://localhost/PWS/Ch12/ApplicationExample1.asmx?WSDL

VBC /r:system.dll /r:System.Web.dll /r:System.Xml.dll /r:System.Web.Services.dll ↴
/r:System.Data.dll /t:library /out:ApplicationExample1.dll ApplicationExample1.VB
```

Finally, let's build a web client for the Web Service and access it. The following code is `ApplicationExample1Client.aspx` in the download:

```
<%@ Page Language="VB" Debug="true" %>
<%@ Import Namespace="AppExpNamespace" %>
<%@ Import Namespace="System.Data" %>
<%@ Import Namespace="System.Data.SqlClient" %>
<html>
<script language="VB" runat="server">

  Sub Page_Load(src As Object, e As EventArgs)
    Dim objWS As New AppExpNamespace.ApplicationExample1()
    Try
      Dim objDS As DataSet = objWS.GetProductCategories()
      AppCacheDG.DataSource = objDS.Tables("Category").DefaultView
      AppCacheDG.DataBind()
    Catch Ex As Exception
      Msg.Text = Ex.ToString()
    End Try
  End Sub

</script>
<body style="font: 10pt verdana">
  <h3>DataSet Cached on Application Object</h3>
  <form runat="server">
      <asp:DataGrid id="AppCacheDG" runat="server"
        BackColor="#FFFFFF"
        BorderColor="black"
        ShowFooter="False"
        CellPadding=3
        CellSpacing="0"
        Font-Name="Verdana"
        Font-Size="8pt"
        HeaderStyle-BackColor="Gray"
        EnableViewState="false">
        <HeaderStyle ForeColor="#FFFFFF"/>
        <AlternatingItemStyle BackColor="Silver"/>
      </asp:DataGrid>
      <br/><asp:Label id="Msg" runat="server" />
    </form>
</body>
</html>
```

If we navigate to this file in our browser we should see the following output:

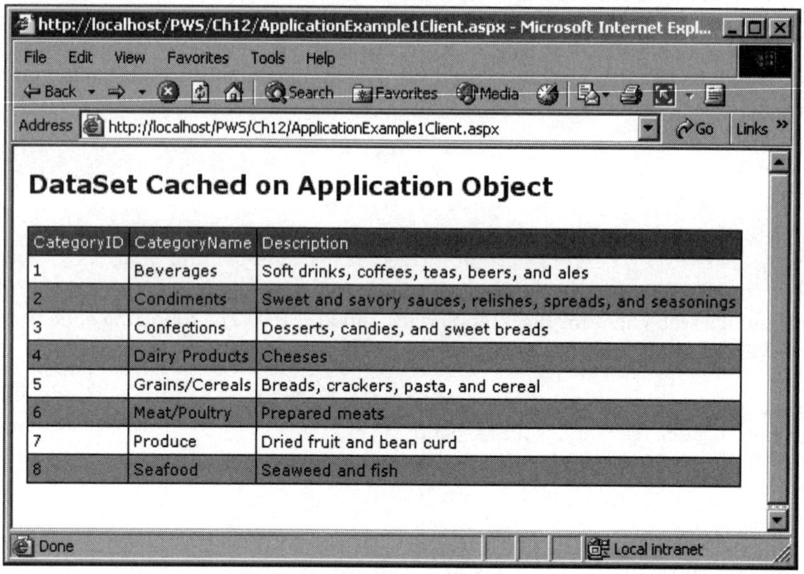

Everything works fine so far. However, the categories stored in the database table could change, and with the current implementation of the Web Service, there is no way of knowing if any of the categories in the database have changed recently. One way of doing this is to create a time-based expiration for the application cache and to refresh the application cache after the time has expired. For example, we can refresh the category's application variable every ten minutes to make sure the categories we are outputting reflect the change in the categories table.

To create a time-based expiration scheme, we have to add one more application variable and check the variable every time we access the `WebMethod` as in the following code, `ApplicationExample2.asmx`:

```
<%@ WebService Language="VB" Class="ApplicationExample2" %>

Imports System
Imports System.Data
Imports System.Data.SqlClient
Imports System.Web.Services

Public Class ApplicationExample2
  Inherits WebService

  '*
  '* Store some data in the application object
  '*
  <WebMethod> _
  Public Function GetProductCategories() As DataSet
    'If the application variable is not set then
    'call the GetProductCategories() function to
    'add the Category DataSet to the
    'application variable
    If Application("CategoriesDataSet") Is Nothing Then
```

```
        SetApplicationData()
      Else
        'If the datetime stored in the application variable + 10 minutes
        'is greater than the current server time then refresh the DataSet
        'store in the application object.
        If DateTime.Compare(CType(Application("TimeStamp"),DateTime).AddMinutes(10) _
                  , DateTime.Now()) < 0 Then
          SetApplicationData()
        End If
      End If

      'Return the DataSet back to the client
      Return CType(Application("CategoriesDataSet") , DataSet)
    End Function

    Private Function SetApplicationData() as boolean
      'Build the Database connection string
      Dim ConnStr as String = "server=localhost;uid=sa;pwd=;database=Northwind"

      'Create a new connection object
      Dim SQLConn as new SqlConnection(ConnStr)

      'Create a new SQL Data Adapter object
      Dim SQLAdp as new SqlDataAdapter("SELECT CategoryID, CategoryName, " _
                              & "Description FROM Categories", SQLConn)

      'Create a new Dataset object
      Dim SQLDS as new DataSet()

      'Fill the Dataset object using the SQL Data Adapter object
      SQLAdp.Fill(SQLDS, "Category")

      'Lock the application
      Application.Lock()

      'Store the DataSet in the Application memory
      Application("CategoriesDataSet") = SQLDS

      'Store the timestamp of the application
      Application("TimeStamp") = DateTime.Now()

      'UnLock the application
      Application.UnLock()

      'return true back to the calling function
      Return True
    End Function
  End Class
```

In this code example, we've added one more application variable called `TimeStamp` that stores the timestamp value of the cache time in the `SetApplicationData` method.

```
//Store the timestamp of the application
Application("TimeStamp") = DateTime.Now()
```

We've added one more condition in the WebMethod, which checks if the timestamp stored in the database, plus ten minutes, is greater than the current time. If the time is greater, then calling the SetApplicationData method will refresh the DataSet stored in the Application object. If we build an ASP.NET client for the Web Service as we did before and view it in the browser, we can see that we get exactly the same output:

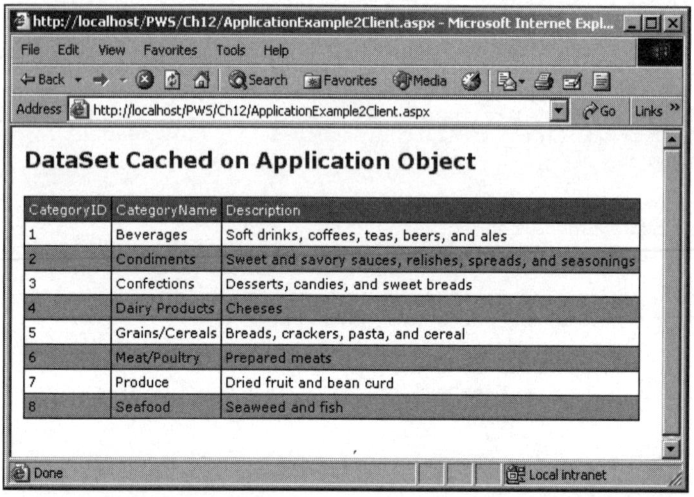

Everything is fine so far. Now let's open the Northwind database and insert a new row into the Categories table using SQL Server Enterprise Manager, with "Frozen Food" as the CategoryName and "Frozen food items" as the Description. If we now refresh the ASP.NET web client after ten minutes we will see the newly inserted category in the DataGrid.

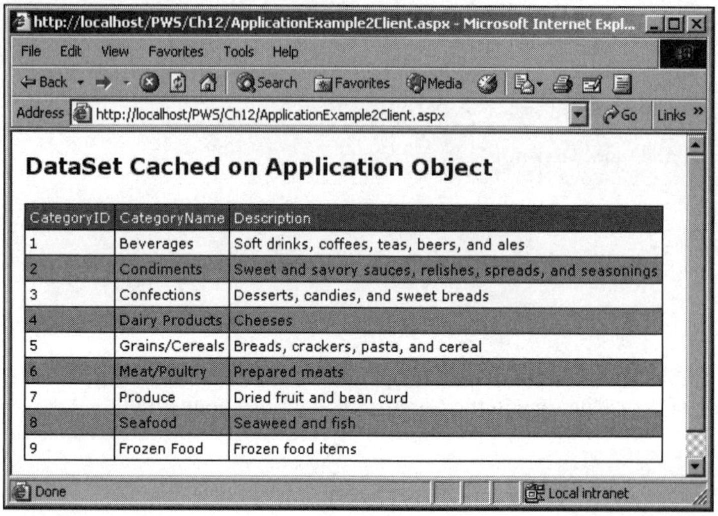

This time-based checking ensures that we can only view refreshed data every ten minutes. There is, however, a pitfall to the above approach. If, say, the `Categories` table changes within the ten minutes and our Web Service serves 300 requests without refreshing the data then all 300 requests will receive inconsistent data.

Using the Cache Object for Caching

The .NET Framework provides a `Cache` class in the `System.Web.Caching` namespace. An instance of the `Cache` class is created per application domain and the `Cache` class instance is available to the Web Service via the `Context` property of the `WebService` class. The `Cache` object provides easy-to-use methods to cache expensive data using key/value pairs and to retrieve it later using the key.

The `Cache` object is functionally equivalent to the `Application` object. However, the `Cache` object provides much more flexibility in manipulating the cached data.

- The `Cache` object provides options to expire the cached content based on a timeframe. The expiration time can be an absolute time such as a specific date/time combination or a sliding expiration, such as adding a specified number of minutes, hours or days to the current `DateTime` and expiring the content based on the timeframe. When a request comes in between the time the item is cached and the time it expires, then the sliding timeframe will be reset again. This is also possible with the `Application` object, but we have to write some code to validate the timestamp. On the other hand, the `Cache` object provides built-in support for timeframe-based cache expiration.
- The `Cache` object provides options to expire the cached content based on a dependency such as a file or key combination. For example, if your Web Service depends on an XML file data feed and you want to refresh all the subsequent Web Service requests immediately after the XML file is changed, then file-based dependency caching is the way to go. If, however, you want to change the caching based on the key supplied to the Web Service, then key-based dependency caching is the way to go.
- The `Cache` object also allows us to set priorities to cached items, and, based on the priority of the cached item, that item will stay in or be removed from the memory in the event of there being insufficient memory on the server.
- The `Cache` object automatically removes unused cached items from the memory.
- The `Cache` object also allows us to set a callback function when an item is removed from the cache memory for any reason.

Caching With the Cache Object

In its simplest form, we can use the `Cache` object as we used the `Application` object previously. We just call the `Cache` object's constructor with a key name and set the key to the value that we want to cache. For example, if we modify the previous application cache code, we get the following, `CacheExample1.asmx`:

> *Before seeing an example, let's discuss the `Context` property of the `WebService` class. The `Context` property provides access to the `HttpContext` class. We need to use the `Context` property to access the `Cache` object, since we can't directly create an object type of the `Cache` class, and an instance of the `Cache` class is created for each application domain.*

```
<%@ WebService Language="VB" Class="CacheExample1" %>

Imports System
Imports System.Data
Imports System.Data.SqlClient
Imports System.Web.Services
Imports System.Web.Caching

Public Class CacheExample1
  Inherits WebService

  '*
  '* Store some data in the application object
  '*
  <WebMethod> _
  Public Function GetProductCategories() As DataSet
    'If the Cache variable is not set then call the SetCacheData()
    'function to add the Category DataSet to the Cache variable
    If Context.Cache("CategoriesDataSet") Is Nothing then
      SetCacheData()
    End If

    'Return the DataSet back to the client
    Return CType(Context.Cache("CategoriesDataSet") , DataSet)
  End Function

  Private Function SetCacheData() as boolean
    'Build the Database connection string
    Dim ConnStr as String = "server=localhost;uid=sa;pwd=;database=Northwind"

    'Create a new connection object
    Dim SQLConn as new SqlConnection(ConnStr)

    'Create a new SQL Data Adapter object
    Dim SQLAdp as new SqlDataAdapter("SELECT CategoryID, CategoryName, " _
                              & "Description FROM Categories", SQLConn)

    'Create a new Dataset object
    Dim SQLDS as new DataSet()

    'Fill the Dataset object using the SQL Data Adapter object
    SQLAdp.Fill(SQLDS, "Category")

    'Store the DataSet in the Cache object
    Context.Cache("CategoriesDataSet") = SQLDS

    'return true back to the caller
    Return True
  End Function
End Class
```

As you can see, the changes we've made are only very simple. We've changed the class name (`CacheExample1`) to reflect what we're doing. We've changed the method name from `SetApplicationData` to `SetCacheData`. Then we're adding the dataset `SQLDS` using the `Context.Cache` with the key `CategoriesDataSet`.

```
//Store the DataSet in the Cache object
Context.Cache("CategoriesDataSet") = SQLDS
```

You will also notice that we're not using the lock and unlock methods when we're writing to the `Cache` object. This is because the `Cache` object handles the locks internally. If more than one thread tries to write to the same `Cache` object then the first process will win and acquire the lock.

Reading Cached Items in the Cache Object

The `Cache` object itself provides a collection to read all the items in the cached objects. This will be useful if you want to see what is in the cache. Let's write a simple Web Service that lists what is in the `Cache` object's memory pool, `CacheExample1a.asmx`:

```
<%@ WebService Language="VB" Class="CacheExample1a" %>

Imports System
Imports System.Collections
Imports System.Web.Caching
Imports System.Web.Services

Public Class CacheExample1a
  Inherits WebService

  '*
  '* Get the list of all cached items.
  '*
  <WebMethod> _
  Public Function GetCacheList(blnShowSystem as Boolean) As ArrayList
    'ArrayList variable to read all the Cache items
    Dim AryLst As new ArrayList()
    Dim StrKey As String

    'Object variable to read each element in the cache object
    Dim objCheItem as Object

    Try
      'Loop through the Cache collection
      For Each objCheItem In Context.Cache
        'If Show System Cache Object
        If blnShowSystem = True then
          AryLst.Add(objCheItem.Key)
        Else
          'Get the Cache Key
          StrKey = objCheItem.Key.ToString()
```

```
          'Ignore all the cache items with key as "System."
          if (Not StrKey.StartsWith("System")) And (Not _
              StrKey.StartsWith("ISAPIWorkerRequest")) Then
            AryLst.Add(StrKey)
          End If
        End If
      Next
    Catch Ex As Exception
      AryLst.Add(Ex.ToString())
    End Try
    'Return the ArrayList back to the client
    Return CType(AryLst, ArrayList)
  End Function
End Class
```

We have here a very simple Web Service that exposes a single `WebMethod` `GetCacheList`. The `GetCacheList` `WebMethod` returns an `ArrayList` with all the cache keys in it. The ASP.NET runtime uses the `Cache` object to cache ASP.NET-specific information, so we're giving an option for the clients to filter the System Cache items using the Boolean argument `blnShowSystem` variable. The System Cache items usually start with `"System."` or `"ISAPIWorkerRequest."` and we're excluding such entries when the `blnShowSystem` variable is set to `false`.

Here is how the output of the Web Service looks when we input each of the two arguments in turn. First, `False`:

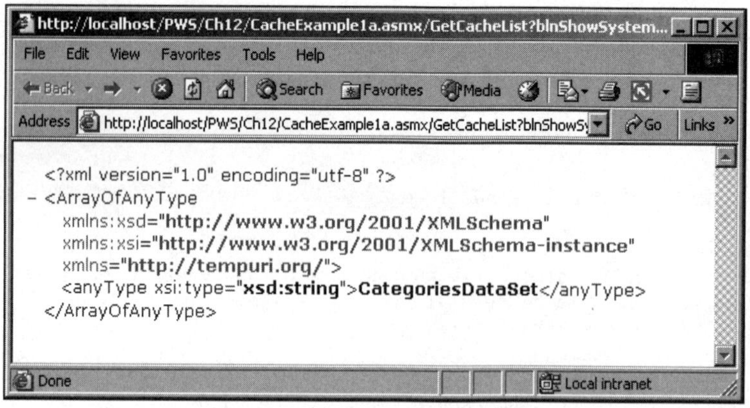

and then True:

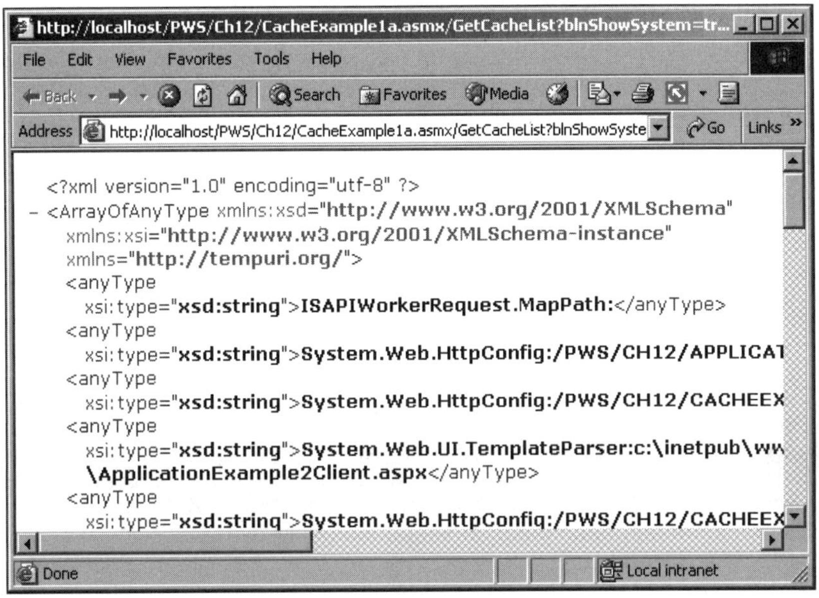

Time-Based Cache Expiration

The Cache object exposes Add and Insert methods to add items to the Cache object. The Add method is available in one flavor, while the Insert method is overridden multiple times, but both do the same thing. The Cache object provides two ways to implement time-based cache expiration: **absolute** expiration and **sliding** expiration. Absolute expiration expires the cache content (the object associated with the key is removed from the cache) on a specific date and time. Sliding expiration expires the cache content a specified number of minutes, hours, or days after the time of the last request.

We have already implemented time-based caching with the Application object. In order to achieve this functionality we wrote code to timestamp the cache and we checked the cached time for every request. With the Cache object, time-based cache expiration is very easy. Here we'll use one of the overrides of the Insert method for caching:

Syntax

```
Context.Cache.Insert(Key, Value, Dependencies, Absolute Expiration, _
                        Sliding Expiration)
```

The first two arguments, Key and Value, are the usual key/value pairs to cache the content. Don't worry about the third parameter, Dependencies, right now; we'll cover it later in this chapter. The fourth and the fifth arguments of the Insert method provide the time-based caching facility.

Absolute Expiration

Let's see a simple example for this, `CacheExample2.asmx`:

```
<%@ WebService Language="VB" Class="CacheExample2" %>

Imports System
Imports System.Data
Imports System.Data.SqlClient
Imports System.Web.Services
Imports System.Web.Caching

Public Class CacheExample2
  Inherits WebService

  '*
  '* Store the DataSet in the Cache object
  '*
  <WebMethod> _
  Public Function GetProductCategories() As DataSet
    'If the Cache variable is not set then call the SetCacheData()
    'function to add the Category DataSet to the Cache variable
    If Context.Cache("CategoriesDataSet") Is Nothing Then
      SetCacheData()
    End If

    'Return the DataSet back to the client
    Return CType(Context.Cache("CategoriesDataSet") , DataSet)
  End Function

  Private Function SetCacheData() as boolean
    'Build the Database connection string
    Dim ConnStr as String = "server=localhost;uid=sa;pwd=;database=Northwind"

    'Create a new connection object
    Dim SQLConn as new SqlConnection(ConnStr)

    'Create a new SQL Data Adapter object
    Dim SQLAdp as new SqlDataAdapter("SELECT CategoryID, CategoryName, " _
                                     & "Description FROM Categories", SQLConn)

    'Create a new Dataset object
    Dim SQLDS as new DataSet()

    'Fill the Dataset object using the SQL Data Adapter object
    SQLAdp.Fill(SQLDS, "Category")

    'Store the DataSet in the Cache object for 10 minutes
    Context.Cache.Insert("CategoriesDataSet", SQLDS, Nothing, _
                         DateTime.Now.AddMinutes(10), TimeSpan.Zero)

    'return true back to the caller
    Return True
  End Function
End Class
```

In this code example we're just changing the class name and the way we're adding the dataset to the Cache object. The key and value pair remains the same. We're passing Nothing to the third argument, Dependencies, since this cache is not dependent on anything other than time. For the fourth argument, we're adding ten minutes to the current date time and passing it. This will make sure that the cache expires in ten minutes from the current time. The fifth argument is set to zero (the last parameter is expected as a TimeSpan object) meaning we're not using any sliding expiration for this cache. We can also set NoSlidingExpiration instead of Zero for the last parameter.

```
'Store the DataSet in the Cache object for 10 minutes
Context.Cache.Insert("CategoriesDataSet", SQLDS, Nothing, _
                     DateTime.Now.AddMinutes(10), TimeSpan.Zero)
```

So the cache will expire ten minutes after it is inserted into the Cache object.

Sliding Expiration

Sliding expiration is useful if you want to cache the content as long as there is demand for it – for example, a summary of the current score for a sports Web Service. When we are using sliding expiration, the expiration time for the cached item will be reset to the specified time each time it is requested. For example, if we've specified a sliding expiration of ten minutes and there is a request for the cached item at the ninth minute, then the item will be cached for another ten minutes from the time it was last accessed. We have converted the above example to use sliding expiration, see CachingExample3.asmx in the download.

In this code example we've just changed the class name and used the sliding expiration technique to expire the data inserted in the Cache object. To disable absolute expiration we're passing the Cache.NoAbsoluteExpiration field of the Cache class. Then for the sliding expiration argument we're specifying the time span as ten minutes:

```
'Store the DataSet in the Cache object for 10 minutes
Context.Cache.Insert("CategoriesDataSet", SQLDS, Nothing, _
                     Cache.NoAbsoluteExpiration, TimeSpan.FromMinutes(10))
```

When we use the Cache.NoAbsoluteExpiration argument, the maximum possible DateTime value of 12/31/9999 11:59:59 PM will be used, which is equivalent to DateTime.MaxValue.

Dependency-Based Cache Expiration

Dependency caching is very good if the cached content depends on an external resource such as an OS file or a cache item or time. Let's take the traffic Web Service example that we've seen previously. If the traffic Web Service depends on an XML file feed that we get from the traffic information provider every three minutes then we may want to refresh the cache in the Web Service as soon as we've received a new file. In this kind of scenario, file-based dependency caching is very useful.

Let's see an example for file-based dependency caching. Here we have an abridged version of the XML file we are going to use, `TrafficFeed.xml`.

```
<?xml version="1.0"?>
<TravelTimes>
  <TravelInfo>
    <Highway>Kennedy</Highway>
    <Direction>East</Direction>
    <From>O'Hare Airport</From>
    <To>Loop</To>
    <TravelTime>62 (mins)</TravelTime>
  </TravelInfo>

  ...

  <TravelInfo>
    <Highway>Edens</Highway>
    <Direction>North</Direction>
    <From>Deerfield Rd</From>
    <To>Loop</To>
    <TravelTime>73 (mins)</TravelTime>
  </TravelInfo>
 </TravelTimes>
```

Now we need a Web Service that consumes the `TrafficFeed.xml` file. This is `CacheExample4.asmx` in the download:

```
<%@ WebService Language="VB" Class="CacheExample4" %>

Imports System
Imports System.Data
Imports System.Web.Services
Imports System.Web.Caching

Public Class CacheExample4
  Inherits WebService
  '*
  '* Store the Traffic information in the Cache object
  '*
  <WebMethod> _
  Public Function GetTrafficInfo() As DataSet
    'If the Cache variable is not set then call the SetTrafficInfo()
    'function to add the Traffic Info to the Cache variable
    If Context.Cache("TrafficInfo") Is Nothing then
      SetTrafficInfo()
    End If

    'Return the DataSet back to the client
    Return CType(Context.Cache("TrafficInfo") , DataSet)
  End Function

  Private Function SetTrafficInfo() as boolean
    'Create a new DataSet object
    Dim objTrafficDS As New DataSet
```

```
    'Read the XML file into the DataSet object using the ReadXml method
    objTrafficDS.ReadXml(Server.MapPath("TrafficFeed.xml"))

    'Create a new dependency object
    Dim objDep As New CacheDependency(Server.MapPath("TrafficFeed.xml"))

    'Store the DataSet in the Cache object which depends
    'on the TrafficFeed.xml file
    Context.Cache.Insert("TrafficInfo", objTrafficDS, objDep)

    'return true back to the caller
    Return True
  End Function
End Class
```

In this example we've used a different implementation of the `Insert` method of the `Cache` object. In the `SetTrafficInfo` method, we're declaring a new `DataSet` object and we're filling the dataset with the data from the XML file (`TrafficFeed.xml`).

```
'Create a new DataSet object
Dim objTrafficDS As New DataSet

'Read the XML file into the DataSet object using the ReadXml method
objTrafficDS.ReadXml(Server.MapPath("TrafficFeed.xml"))
```

Then we're creating an instance of the `CacheDependency` class and passing the XML file path to its constructor.

```
'Create a new dependency object
Dim objDep As New CacheDependency(Server.MapPath("TrafficFeed.xml"))
```

We're using the `Insert` method of the `Cache` object to insert the `DataSet` with the XML dependency object.

```
Context.Cache.Insert("TrafficInfo", objTrafficDS, objDep)
```

As before, we need to build a proxy class for the Web Service, compile it as a DLL and place it in the `bin` folder. There is a batch file in the `bin` subfolder, `CacheExample4Build.bat`, to accomplish this. Again, you may need to alter the path to the Web Service according to where you have installed it on your server.

Next, we need to build a simple ASP.NET client, `CacheExample4Client.aspx`, and access the Web Service.

```
<%@ Page Language="VB" Debug="true" %>
<%@ Import Namespace="CacheExp4Namespace" %>
<%@ Import Namespace="System.Data" %>
<%@ Import Namespace="System.Data.SqlClient" %>
<html>
```

```
<title>Caching Client</title>
<script language="VB" runat="server">

  Protected Sub Page_Load(Src As Object, E As EventArgs)
    Dim objWS As CacheExp4Namespace.CacheExample4 = _
                                  New CacheExp4Namespace.CacheExample4()

    Try
      Dim objDS As DataSet = objWS.GetTrafficInfo()
      AppCacheDG.DataSource = objDS.Tables(0).DefaultView
      AppCacheDG.DataBind()
    Catch Ex as Exception
      Msg.Text = Ex.ToString()
    End Try
  End Sub

</script>
<body style="font: 10pt verdana">
  <h3>DataSet Cached on Cache Object</h3>
  <form runat="server">
      <asp:DataGrid id="AppCacheDG" runat="server"
        BackColor="#FFFFFF"
        BorderColor="black"
        ShowFooter="False"
        CellPadding=3
        CellSpacing="0"
        Font-Name="Verdana"
        Font-Size="8pt"
        HeaderStyle-BackColor="Gray"
        EnableViewState="false">
        <HeaderStyle ForeColor="#FFFFFF"/>
      <AlternatingItemStyle BackColor="Silver"/>
      </asp:DataGrid>
      <br/><asp:Label id="Msg" runat="server" />
    </form>
</body>
</html>
```

Here is how the output of the Web Service looks:

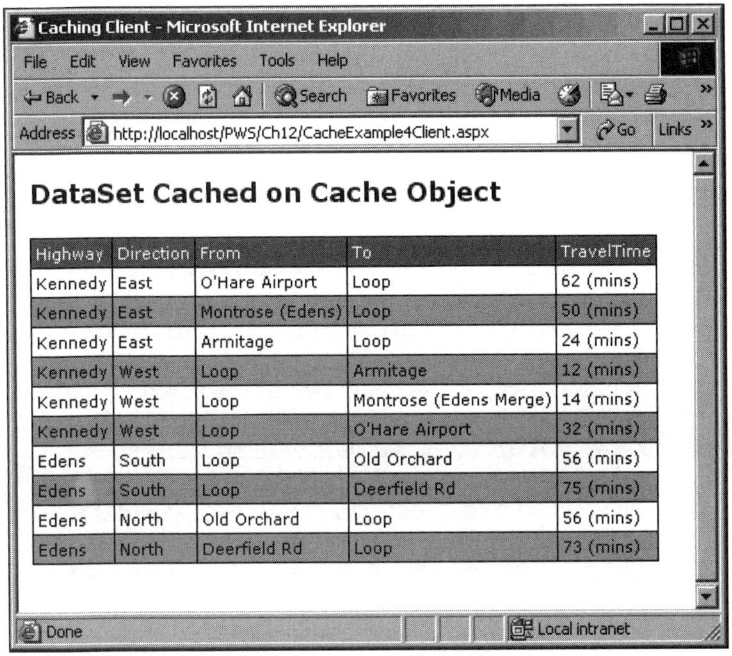

Let's open the `TrafficFeed.XML` file and change the travel time of the last record from 73 minutes to 35 minutes.

```
<TravelInfo>
    <Highway>Edens</Highway>
    <Direction>North</Direction>
    <From>Deerfield Rd</From>
    <To>Loop</To>
    <TravelTime>35 (mins)</TravelTime>
  </TravelInfo>
</TravelTimes>
```

Now refresh the Web Service client.

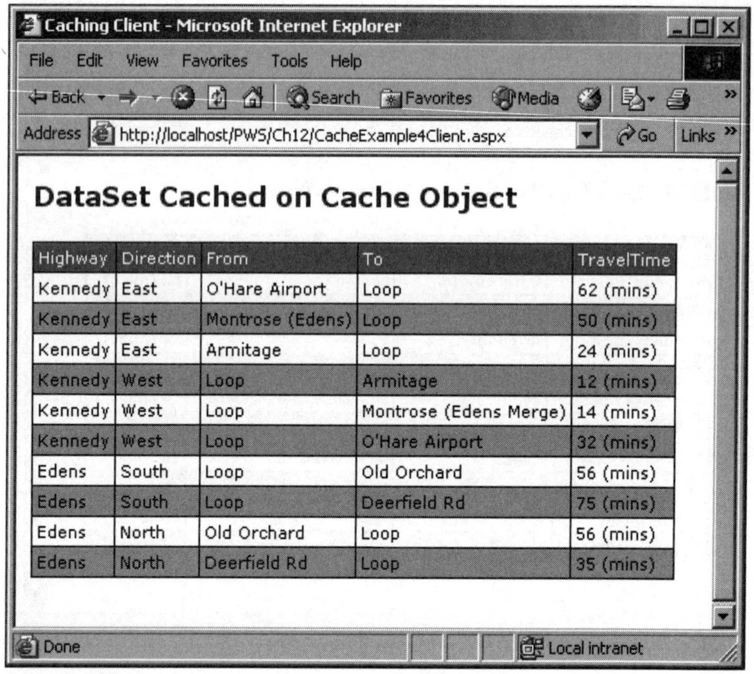

DataSet Cached on Cache Object

Highway	Direction	From	To	TravelTime
Kennedy	East	O'Hare Airport	Loop	62 (mins)
Kennedy	East	Montrose (Edens)	Loop	50 (mins)
Kennedy	East	Armitage	Loop	24 (mins)
Kennedy	West	Loop	Armitage	12 (mins)
Kennedy	West	Loop	Montrose (Edens Merge)	14 (mins)
Kennedy	West	Loop	O'Hare Airport	32 (mins)
Edens	South	Loop	Old Orchard	56 (mins)
Edens	South	Loop	Deerfield Rd	75 (mins)
Edens	North	Old Orchard	Loop	56 (mins)
Edens	North	Deerfield Rd	Loop	35 (mins)

In the previous traffic Web Service example, we used the output cache to cache the output of the Web Service for three minutes. There are a few pitfalls of using output caching in this example, which is based on an XML file. In the output caching example, we cached the output for three minutes regardless of whether the data in the XML file has changed or not. If the traffic data in the Web Service did change during the three minutes it is cached, the users who initiate requests during those three minutes will not see the updated traffic information until the output cache is expired and a new output cache has been created. However, if we use file-based dependency caching then our users will always get up-to-date traffic information and don't have to worry about refreshing the Web Service every now and then to make sure they have the latest information.

Directory Dependency Cache

Cache objects also support a directory-level cache dependency. We can change the above example to depend on a directory-level cache dependency instead of on a file.

```
'Create a new dependency object
Dim objDep As New CacheDependency(Server.MapPath("."))
```

Multiple Files Dependency Cache

The `Cache` object also allows the use of multiple file-based dependency caching. If we're caching information based on more than one file, then multiple dependency caching is the perfect fit in this scenario.

Let's expand our previous example to use multiple files dependency caching. Let's expose one more `WebMethod` from the same Web Service for weather information that depends on the `WeatherFeed.XML` file. Let's assume the traffic feed data will also change whenever the weather feed data arrives. Now we have two dependency files for the `TrafficInfo` cache item and the cache should be refreshed if either one of the XML files changes. Here is an abridged version of the weather information XML file, `WeatherFeed.XML`.

```
<?xml version="1.0" ?>
<WeatherInfo>
  <WeekDay>
    <Day>Sunday</Day>
    <MaxTemp>81 F</MaxTemp>
    <MinTemp>63 F</MinTemp>
    <Weather>A secondary surge of cooler air arrives on brisk northeast winds.
Abundant sunshine prevails.</Weather>
  </WeekDay>

  ...

  <WeekDay>
    <Day>Saturday</Day>
    <MaxTemp>80 F</MaxTemp>
    <MinTemp>60 F</MinTemp>
    <Weather>Bright sunshine and comfortable humidities start a pleasant
weekend.</Weather>
  </WeekDay>
</WeatherInfo>
```

Now we create the Web Service to consume the XML files, `CacheExample5.asmx`.

```
<%@ WebService Language="VB" Class="CacheExample5" %>

Imports System
Imports System.Data
Imports System.Web.Services
Imports System.Web.Caching

Public Class CacheExample5
  Inherits WebService
  '*
  '* Store the Traffic information in the Cache object
  '*
  <WebMethod> _
  Public Function GetTrafficInfo() As DataSet
    'If the Cache variable is not set then call the SetTrafficInfo()
    'function to add the Traffic Info to the Cache variable
    If Context.Cache("TrafficInfo") Is Nothing then
      SetTrafficInfo()
    End If

    'Return the DataSet back to the client
    Return CType(Context.Cache("TrafficInfo") , DataSet)
  End Function
```

```
'*
'* Store the Weather Information in the Cache object
'*
<WebMethod> _
Public Function GetWeatherInfo() As DataSet
  'If the Cache variable is not set then call the SetWeatherInfo()
  'function to add the Weather Info to the Cache variable
  If Context.Cache("WeatherInfo") Is Nothing then
    SetWeatherInfo()
  End If

  'Return the DataSet back to the client
  Return CType(Context.Cache("WeatherInfo") , DataSet)
End Function

Private Function SetTrafficInfo() as Boolean

  'Create a string array and load the two XML
  'file paths into it.
  Dim strFilesArray(1) as String
  strFilesArray(0) = Server.MapPath("TrafficFeed.xml")
  strFilesArray(1) = Server.MapPath("WeatherFeed.xml")

  'Create a new DataSet object
  Dim objTrafficDS As New DataSet

  'Read the Traffic XML file into the DataSet object
  'using the ReadXml method
  objTrafficDS.ReadXml(Server.MapPath("TrafficFeed.xml"))

  'Create a new dependency object
  Dim objDep As New CacheDependency(strFilesArray)

  'Store the DataSet in the Cache object
  Context.Cache.Insert("TrafficInfo", objTrafficDS, objDep)

  'return true back to the caller
  Return True
End Function

Private Function SetWeatherInfo() as boolean
  'Create a new DataSet object
  Dim objDS As New DataSet

  'Read the XML file into the DataSet object using the ReadXml method
  objDS.ReadXml(Server.MapPath("WeatherFeed.xml"))

  'Create a new dependency object using the XML file path
  Dim objDep As New CacheDependency(Server.MapPath("WeatherFeed.xml"))

  'Store the DataSet in the Cache object which depends on the WeatherFeed.xml file
  Context.Cache.Insert("WeatherInfo", objDS, objDep)
```

```
      'return true back to the caller
      Return True
    End Function
  End Class
```

This code is very similar to the previous example, but we've changed the class name (`CacheExample5`) of the Web Service and added a new `WebMethod` (`GetWeatherInfo`) and a private method (`SetWeatherInfo`).

We've also changed the `SetTrafficInfo` method to depend on more than one file. In the `SetTrafficInfo` method we've created a string array with two elements and we've stored the XML files paths in the array elements:

```
'Create a string array and load the two XML
'file paths into it.
Dim strFilesArray(1) as String
strFilesArray(0) = Server.MapPath("TrafficFeed.xml")
strFilesArray(1) = Server.MapPath("WeatherFeed.xml")
```

The `DataSet` object is created in the same way as before and we read the XML file into the `DataSet` using the `ReadXml` method. Then we pass the string array to the `CacheDependency` object's constructor.

```
    'Create a new dependency object
    Dim objDep As New CacheDependency(strFilesArray)
```

This dependency object will make the cache depend on the two XML files listed in the string array. Then we've inserted the `DataSet` into the cache object as usual.

We now create a proxy for the Web Service using the batch file `CacheExample5Build.bat` in the `bin` folder as before. Now we can create a client to consume the Web Service, `CacheExample5Client.aspx`:

```
<%@ Page Language="VB" Debug="True" %>
<%@ Import Namespace="CacheExp5Namespace" %>
<%@ Import Namespace="System.Data" %>
<%@ Import Namespace="System.Data.SqlClient" %>
<html>
<script language="VB" runat="server">
  Protected Sub Page_Load(Src As Object, E As EventArgs)
    Dim objWS As CacheExp5Namespace.CacheExample5 = _
                 New CacheExp5Namespace.CacheExample5()
    Try
      Dim objDS As DataSet = objWS.GetTrafficInfo
      AppCacheDG.DataSource = objDS.Tables(0).DefaultView
      AppCacheDG.DataBind()

      Dim objDS1 As DataSet = objWS.GetWeatherInfo
      AppCacheDG1.DataSource = objDS1.Tables(0).DefaultView
      AppCacheDG1.DataBind()
    Catch Ex As Exception
```

```
        Msg.Text = Ex.ToString()
      End Try
    End Sub
  </script>
  <body style="font: 10pt verdana">
  <form runat="server" ID="Form1">
    <font size="2"><b>Traffic Information</b></font>
    <hr color="#000000"/>
    <asp:DataGrid id="AppCacheDG" runat="server" BackColor="#FFFFFF"
                  BorderColor="black" ShowFooter="False" CellPadding="3"
                  CellSpacing="0" Font-Name="Verdana" Font-Size="8pt"
                  HeaderStyle-BackColor="Gray" EnableViewState="false">
      <HeaderStyle ForeColor="#FFFFFF" />
      <AlternatingItemStyle BackColor="Silver" />
    </asp:DataGrid>
    <br/>
    <font size="2"><b>Weather Forecast</b></font>
    <hr color="#000000"/>
    <asp:DataGrid id="AppCacheDG1" runat="server" BackColor="#FFFFFF"
                  BorderColor="black" ShowFooter="False" CellPadding="3"
                  CellSpacing="0" Font-Name="Verdana" Font-Size="8pt"
                  HeaderStyle-BackColor="Gray" EnableViewState="false">
      <HeaderStyle ForeColor="#FFFFFF" />
      <AlternatingItemStyle BackColor="Silver" />
    </asp:DataGrid>
    <br/>
    <asp:Label id="Msg" runat="server" />
  </form>
  </body>
  </html>
```

We've added two `DataGrid` objects and we're populating the first `DataGrid` with the traffic information and the second with weather information.

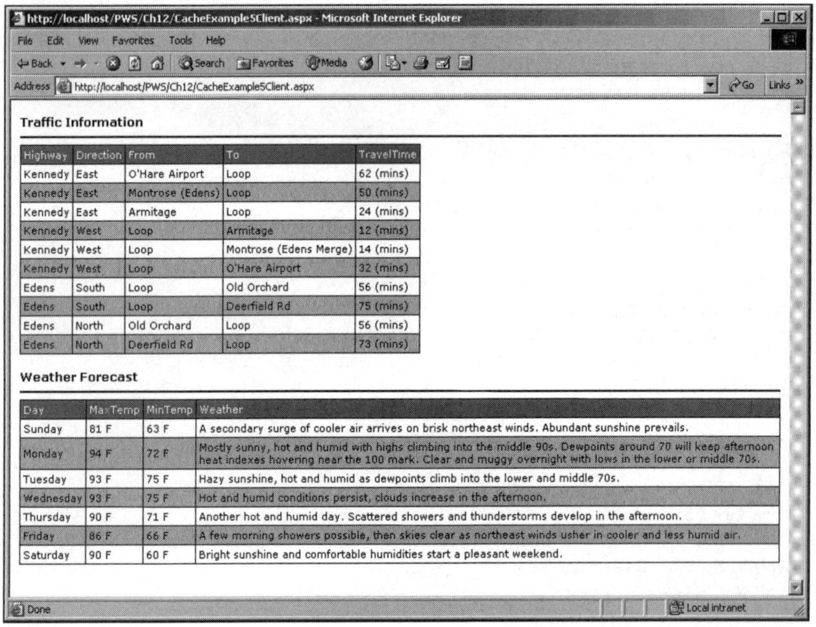

Highway	Direction	From	To	TravelTime
Kennedy	East	O'Hare Airport	Loop	62 (mins)
Kennedy	East	Montrose (Edens)	Loop	50 (mins)
Kennedy	East	Armitage	Loop	24 (mins)
Kennedy	West	Loop	Armitage	12 (mins)
Kennedy	West	Loop	Montrose (Edens Merge)	14 (mins)
Kennedy	West	Loop	O'Hare Airport	32 (mins)
Edens	South	Loop	Old Orchard	56 (mins)
Edens	South	Loop	Deerfield Rd	75 (mins)
Edens	North	Old Orchard	Loop	56 (mins)
Edens	North	Deerfield Rd	Loop	73 (mins)

Day	MaxTemp	MinTemp	Weather
Sunday	81 F	63 F	A secondary surge of cooler air arrives on brisk northeast winds. Abundant sunshine prevails.
Monday	94 F	72 F	Mostly sunny, hot and humid with highs climbing into the middle 90s. Dewpoints around 70 will keep afternoon heat indexes hovering near the 100 mark. Clear and muggy overnight with lows in the lower or middle 70s.
Tuesday	93 F	75 F	Hazy sunshine, hot and humid as dewpoints climb into the lower and middle 70s.
Wednesday	93 F	75 F	Hot and humid conditions persist, clouds increase in the afternoon.
Thursday	90 F	71 F	Another hot and humid day. Scattered showers and thunderstorms develop in the afternoon.
Friday	86 F	66 F	A few morning showers possible, then skies clear as northeast winds usher in cooler and less humid air.
Saturday	90 F	60 F	Bright sunshine and comfortable humidities start a pleasant weekend.

If we change anything in the `TrafficFeed.xml` file, the `TrafficInfo` cache item will expire and our code will rebuild the cache again. If we change the `WeatherFeed.xml` file then both the cache items will expire and our code will rebuild them.

File-Based and Time-Based Dependency Cache

We can also use both the time-based dependency and the file-based dependency at the same time. The time-based dependency expiration can be either absolute expiration or sliding expiration. Just change the `Cache.Insert` code in the previous example to add absolute time based expiration (`CacheExample6.asmx` in the download):

```
' Make the cache object depend on both the TrafficFeed.xml,
' WeatherFeed.xml, and time. The cache will be refreshed whenever any
' of the XML files change or every 10 minutes.
Context.Cache.Insert("CategoriesDataSet", objTrafficDS, objDep, _
                     DateTime.Now.AddMinutes(10), TimeSpan.Zero)
```

Key-Based Dependency Caching

The `Cache` object also supports a key-based dependency, meaning that one cache item can depend on another cache item, and when the first cache item changes, the second cache item will expire. For example, we could expose a financial information Web Service that could have two web methods to send financial data and financial news. Let's say our Web Service depends on an external source for the data feed and the external source provides the financial data and news in two separate XML files. We may want to cache both the XML files and we may want the financial news XML file cache to depend on the financial data XML cache. This will make sure that whenever we're refreshing the financial data cache item we'll also refresh the financial news cache item. Here are how abridged versions of the financial data (`FinData.xml`) and financial news (`FinNews.xml`) data feed XML files look:

FinData.xml

```
<?xml version="1.0" ?>
<FinancialData>
  <Exchange>
    <Name>NYSE</Name>
    <AdvancingIssues>1,532</AdvancingIssues>
    <DecliningIssues>1,181</DecliningIssues>
    <UnchangedIssues>261</UnchangedIssues>
    <TotalIssues>2,974</TotalIssues>
    <NewHighs>89</NewHighs>
    <NewLows>20</NewLows>
    <UpVolume>186,857,856</UpVolume>
    <DownVolume>130,259,632</DownVolume>
    <UnchangedVolume>14,090,040</UnchangedVolume>
    <TotalVolume>N/A</TotalVolume>
  </Exchange>

  ...

  <Exchange>
    <Name>Bulletin Board</Name>
    <AdvancingIssues>329</AdvancingIssues>
    <DecliningIssues>440</DecliningIssues>
    <UnchangedIssues>324</UnchangedIssues>
    <TotalIssues>1,093</TotalIssues>
    <NewHighs>13</NewHighs>
```

```
    <NewLows>27</NewLows>
    <UpVolume>79,504,000</UpVolume>
    <DownVolume>120,649,296</DownVolume>
    <UnchangedVolume>8,917,700</UnchangedVolume>
    <TotalVolume>N/A</TotalVolume>
  </Exchange>
</FinancialData>
```

FinNews.xml

```
<?xml version="1.0"?>
<FinancialNews>
  <HourlyNews>
    <Time>08:00 AM</Time>
    <News>The tone in pre-market trading remains firmly negative with the S&amp;P
futures currently 7.10 points below fair value while the Nasdaq 100 futures are
15.50 points below fair value. This is, however, a slight improvement from earlier
levels. The Cisco downside guidance, lack of visibility, and expectation for a
more challenging environment in Europe and Asia have weighed. A subsequent
downgrade in
 the European telecom sector by Merrill Lynch and a sizeable warning for Emulex
(taking other storage stocks lower) have also pressured.</News>
  </HourlyNews>

  ...

  <HourlyNews>
    <Time>10.00 AM</Time>
    <News>The Dow is still holding onto a negative bias but the Nasdaq has inched
back into positive territory as the headline culprits behind the early session
weakness (CSCO, EMLX) have staged solid recoveries of their early session lows.
The networking and storage stocks have pushed higher with these stocks and
continued strength is being seen among the semiconductor/comm IC stocks. The
Nasdaq has held again near the 2010/2000 support range once again and given the
extent of the recent four-day slump, is certainly due for some type of short-term
upswing. Volume continues at a modest pace with market internals now mixed. DOT
+0.6%, XOI +0.3%, SOX +1.3%, NYSE Adv/Dec 1376/1173, Nasdaq Adv/Dec
1426/1482</News>
  </HourlyNews>
</FinancialNews>
```

Let's build the financial Web Service, `CacheExample7.asmx`:

```
<%@ WebService Language="VB" Class="CacheExample7" %>

Imports System
Imports System.Data
Imports System.Web.Services
Imports System.Web.Caching

Public Class CacheExample7
  Inherits WebService
  '*
  '* Store the Financial information in the Cache object
  '*
  <WebMethod> _
  Public Function GetFinancialData() As DataSet
```

```
    'If the Cache variable is not set then call the SetFinancialInfo()
    'function to add the financial data to the Cache variable
    If Context.Cache("FinancialData") Is Nothing Then
      SetFinancialInfo()
    End If

    'Return the DataSet back to the client
    Return CType(Context.Cache("FinancialData") , DataSet)
  End Function

  '*
  '* Store the Financial News in the Cache object
  '*
  <WebMethod> _
  Public Function GetFinancialNews() As DataSet
    'If the Cache variable is not set then call the SetFinancialInfo()
    'function to add the Financial News in the Cache variable.
    'Check the cache variable "FinancialData" rather than "FinNews"
    'since the FinNews cache item depends on the FinancialData cache item.
    If Context.Cache("FinancialData") Is Nothing Then
      SetFinancialInfo()
    End If

    'Return the DataSet back to the client
    Return CType(Context.Cache("FinNews") , DataSet)
  End Function

  Private Function SetFinancialInfo() As Boolean
    'Create a Dataset to store the financial Data
    Dim objFinData as New DataSet()

    'Read the Financial Data into the Dataset
    objFinData.ReadXml(Server.MapPath("FinData.xml"))

    'Create a Cache item to store the financial Data. This cache
    'entry will establish the dependency relstionship.
    Context.Cache.Insert("FinancialData", objFinData, _
                         New CacheDependency(Server.MapPath("FinData.xml")))

    'Create a cache item to store the financial news
    'dependencies XML file. We're storing the Cache
    'Key of the Financial Data in the string array
    'to establish the key-based dependency
    Dim StrDepKey(0) As String

    StrDepKey(0) = "FinancialData"

    Dim objFinNews As New DataSet()

    objFinNews.ReadXml(Server.MapPath("FinNews.xml"))

    ' Cache the XML document
    Context.Cache.Insert("FinNews", objFinNews, _
                         New CacheDependency(Nothing, StrDepKey))
```

```
        'return true back to the caller
        Return True
      End Function
    End Class
```

We've created a Web Service with two WebMethods – GetFinancialData and GetFinancialNews. The WebMethods depend on the XML files fed by an external source. The private method SetFinancialInfo creates the cache for the Web Service. The SetFinancialInfo method creates the key-based cache dependency. We declare a DataSet object and read the FinData.Xml file into it. Then, we insert the DataSet into the Cache object:

```
Dim objFinData as New DataSet()

'Read the Financial Data into the Dataset
objFinData.ReadXml(Server.MapPath("FinData.xml"))
```

Then we create a string array and assign the key of the financial data cache (FinancialData) into the string array. In the previous examples we've assigned the XML file names into the string array to create the file-based dependency. Instead of assigning the XML file name, we're assigning the cache key name into the string array and this will create the key-based dependency.

```
'Create a cache item to store the financial news
'dependencies XML file. We're storing the Cache
'Key of the Financial Data in the string array
'to establish the key based dependency
Dim StrDepKey(0) As String

StrDepKey(0) = "FinancialData"
```

Next we create a DataSet and read the FinNews.xml file into it. Then we insert the DataSet into the Cache object and specify the FinancialData cache item as a dependency.

```
' Cache the XML document
Context.Cache.Insert("FinNews", objFinNews, _
                     New CacheDependency(Nothing, StrDepKey))
```

We're creating a new dependency object and passing Nothing and the string array to the constructor. The dependency class constructor supports three overloads. The first overload accepts a filename as a string, the second overload accepts a string array of filenames, and the third overload accepts two string arrays – the first is a list of filenames and the second is a list of cache keys.

We're using the third overload to make the FinNews cache item depend on the FinancialData cache item. If we build the proxy as usual and fire up our browser with the client, CacheExample7Client.aspx, then we get the following output:

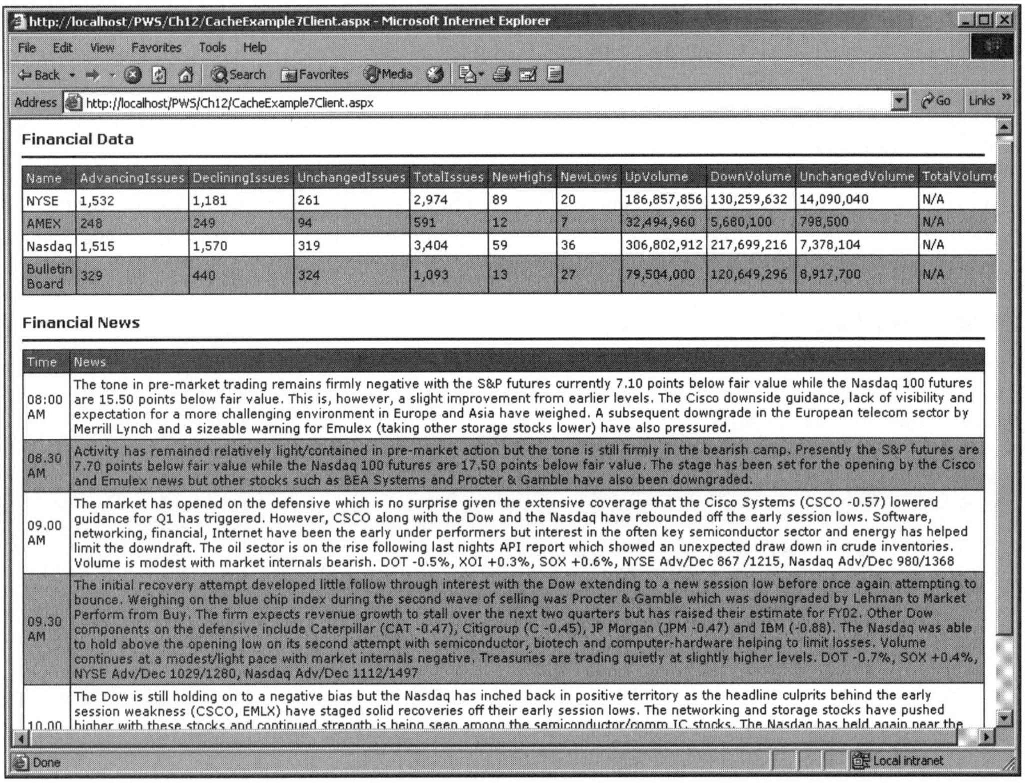

Manually Removing Items from the Cache Object

A cached item can be removed from the `Cache` object manually using the `Remove` method of the `Cache` object. The `Remove` method accepts a key as the parameter and removes the cached item from the `Cache` object. For example, if we want to remove the cached item `CategoriesDataSet`, then we use the following:

```
'Remove the item CategoriesDataSet from the Cache
Context.Cache.Remove("CategoriesDataSet")
```

Automatic Cache Expiration

Cached items can also be removed automatically from the `Cache` object for several reasons:

- **Reached the expiration time** – when the cached item reaches the expiration time set by the absolute expiration or sliding expiration then the item will be removed from the cache object's memory pool.
- **Dependency change** – when the dependency resource (such as an XML file or a cache key) assigned to the cached item changes then the item will be removed from the memory pool.

- **Underused** – when the cached item is underused (when the cache item is not utilized frequently when compared with others) or unused by the Web Service, the cache item will be removed from the memory automatically.
- **Server is low on memory** – when the server is running low on memory the cached item can be removed from the `Cache` object.

When the cache items are removed from the `Cache` object, they follow the cache item priority. The namespace `System.Web.Caching` exposes an enumeration, `CacheItemPriority`, to support assigning and reading the priority of the cache item.

Cache Item Priority

When the web server that hosts the Web Service is running low on memory, it'll try to purge the cached items to reclaim memory. When the purge process occurs, the cache items will be removed from the cache based on their `CacheItemPriority` setting.

The `CacheItemPriority` enumeration has the following values.

Enumeration Member Name	Description
`Default`	When we don't assign any priority to the cache item on insertion, the default is used and the value for the cache item priority is `Normal`.
`High`	The cache items with `High` priority will be less likely to be deleted from the cache memory pool.
`AboveNormal`	The cache items with `AboveNormal` priority will be less likely to be deleted before deleting the `Normal` priority items.
`Normal`	The cache items with `Normal` priority will be deleted after the `BelowNormal` and `Low` priority items.
`BelowNormal`	The cache items with `BelowNormal` priority will be deleted after the `Low` priority items.
`Low`	The cache items with `Low` priority will be the first ones to be deleted to free system memory.
`NotRemovable`	The cache items with `NotRemoveable` priority will not be deleted from the cache object to reclaim system memory.

The following figure shows the cache object memory pool:

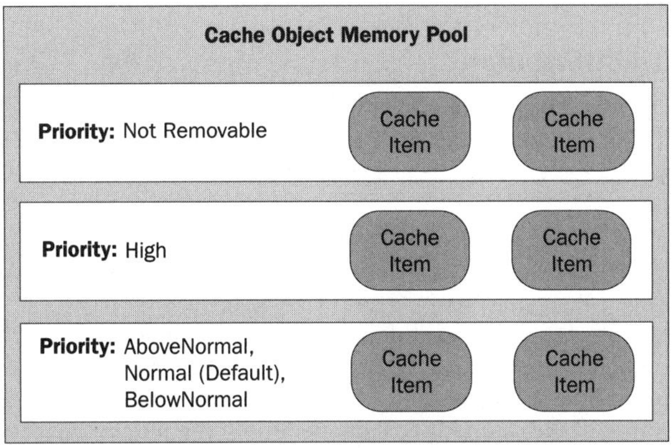

Let's see how we can set the priority of the cache items. We can use one of the overloads of the `Insert` method of the `Cache` object to insert the `CacheItemPriority`. The following file is CacheExample8.asmx in the code download:

```
<%@ WebService Language="VB" Class="CacheExample8" %>

Imports System
Imports System.Web.Services
Imports System.Web.Caching

Public Class CacheExample8
  Inherits WebService
  <WebMethod> _
  Public Function SetCachePriority() As String
    If Context.Cache("PriData") Is Nothing Then
      Context.Cache.Insert("PriData", "Cached Priority Data", Nothing, _
                           DateTime.Now.AddMinutes(10), TimeSpan.Zero, _
                           CacheItemPriority.Low, Nothing)
    End If

    Return Context.Cache("PriData")
  End Function
End Class
```

We're using the `Insert` method of the `Cache` object to insert the data and we're using absolute time-based expiration without any dependency. We're also setting the `CacheItemPriority` as `Low`. This means the cached item can be removed from the cache memory pool if it is not used frequently.

```
Context.Cache.Insert("PriData", "Cached Priority Data", Nothing, _
                     DateTime.Now.AddMinutes(10), TimeSpan.Zero, _
                     CacheItemPriority.Low, Nothing)
```

We set Nothing for the last parameter to disable the cache item callback functionality when the item is removed from the Cache object.

Using Callback Functionality

When an item in the Cache object is removed, the Cache object can notify the Web Service by raising an event back. This callback functionality is implemented through the CacheItemRemovedCallback delegate available in the System.Web.Caching namespace.

```
Public Delegate Sub CacheItemRemovedCallback(key As String, value As Object, _
                                    reason As CacheItemRemovedReason)
```

The CacheItemRemovedCallback event delegate exposes three parameters. The first two parameters inform the application about which cache key was removed from the Cache object and the value the cached item was holding. The third parameter holds the reason why the cached item was removed from the memory as a member of the CacheItemRemovedReason enumeration. The following table shows the CacheItemRemovedReason enumeration values:

Enumeration Member Name	Description
Removed	When we use the Remove method to manually remove an item from the cache or use the Insert method to insert a new value to an existing cache item this reason will be used.
Expired	When the cache item expires this reason will be used.
DependencyChanged	When the dependency object changes this reason will be used.
Underused	When the cached item is under used or unused or the system removed it from the memory to reclaim memory then this reason will be used.

Callback event functionality can be extremely useful. For example, we might want to log all the cached items that are removed so that we can later figure out if too many cached items are being removed due to the Underused reason, so we know that either our caching practice is ineffective or our server is running low on memory and may need upgrading.

We can even use the callback event to recreate the cache if it's not removed because of the Underused reason. If it is Underused then it could be due to the server running low on memory or that there are no subscribers for this cache item. If Underused is not the reason, then we can recreate the cache item in the callback event so that it will be read by the next Web Service request, rather than it being recreated in the next Web Service request, thus avoiding the slow response time we would get if we had to recreate it.

Let's see an example for this. We'll create a simple Web Service, CacheExample9.asmx, which will cache a string "Cached for Callback removal" in the key CallBack. In the callback event we'll recreate the cache with the reason why the cache item was removed from the memory and the timestamp.

```
<%@ WebService Language="VB" Class="CacheExample9" %>

Imports System
Imports System.Web.Services
Imports System.Web.Caching

Public Class CacheExample9
  Inherits WebService
  'Declare a Shared Callback handler
  Private Shared OnCacheItemRemove As CacheItemRemovedCallback = Nothing

  'Callback event handler
  Public Sub CacheItemRemovedCallback(strCacheKey As String, _
                                      objCacheObject As Object, _
                                      RemovalReason As CacheItemRemovedReason)
    'String value for recreated Cache
    Dim strCacheValue as String = "Cached item removed due to the reason = " _
                                 & RemovalReason.ToString() _
                                 & ". Recreated at " & DateTime.Now.ToString()

    'Recreate the Cache item again with the timestamp
    Context.Cache.Insert("CallBack", strCacheValue, Nothing, _
                         DateTime.Now.AddMinutes(1), TimeSpan.Zero, _
                         CacheItemPriority.Default, OnCacheItemRemove)
  End Sub

  <WebMethod> _
  Public Function ImplementCacheCallBack() As String

    OnCacheItemRemove = New _
          CacheItemRemovedCallback(AddressOf Me.CacheItemRemovedCallback)

    If Context.Cache("CallBack") Is Nothing Then
      'Create the cache object with out any dependency,
      'with one minute absolute expiration
      'with no sliding expiration
      'with default value for CacheItemPriority and
      'CacheItemPriorityDecay and on the event of the cache
      'object removal call the event handler OnCacheItemRemove
      Context.Cache.Insert("CallBack", "Cached for Callback removal", Nothing, _
                           DateTime.Now.AddMinutes(1), TimeSpan.Zero, _
                           CacheItemPriority.Default, Me.OnCacheItemRemove)
    End If

    Return Context.Cache("CallBack")
  End Function
End Class
```

We now have a simple Web Service that implements one `WebMethod` (`ImplementCacheCallBack`) and one public event handling method (`CacheItemRemovedCallback`). We have declared a class-level private `static` (`shared` in VB.NET) variable of type `CacheItemRemovedCallback` and we've initialized it with `null` (`Nothing` in VB.NET).

```
'Declare a Shared Callback handler
Private Shared OnCacheItemRemove As CacheItemRemovedCallback = Nothing
```

Then we've declared a public event handler, `CacheItemRemovedCallback`.

```
'Callback event handler
Public Sub CacheItemRemovedCallback(strCacheKey As String, _
                                    objCacheObject As Object, _
                                    RemovalReason As CacheItemRemovedReason)
```

Inside the event handler we're recreating the `Cache` object with the reason for the cache removal and the timestamp.

```
'String value for recreated Cache
Dim strCacheValue as String = "Cached item removed due to the reason = " _
                            & RemovalReason.ToString() _
                            & ". Recreated at " & DateTime.Now.ToString()

'Recreate the Cache item again with the timestamp
Context.Cache.Insert("CallBack", strCacheValue, Nothing, _
                     DateTime.Now.AddMinutes(1), TimeSpan.Zero, _
                     CacheItemPriority.Default, OnCacheItemRemove)
```

In the `WebMethod` we assign a new object of the type of the event handler (`CacheItemRemovedCallback`) that we've created and pass the address of the event handler to the constructor using the `AddressOf` operator.

```
OnCacheItemRemove = New _
          CacheItemRemovedCallback(AddressOf Me.CacheItemRemovedCallback)
```

Then we check if the `Cache` object is missing. If the object is missing then we add the item to the `Cache` object using the `CallBack` event variable as a parameter.

```
If Context.Cache("CallBack") Is Nothing Then
  Context.Cache.Insert("CallBack", "Cached for Callback removal", Nothing, _
                       DateTime.Now.AddMinutes(1), TimeSpan.Zero, _
                       CacheItemPriority.Default, Me.OnCacheItemRemove)
End If
```

The first time the Web Service is executed the `WebMethod` will create the cache item:

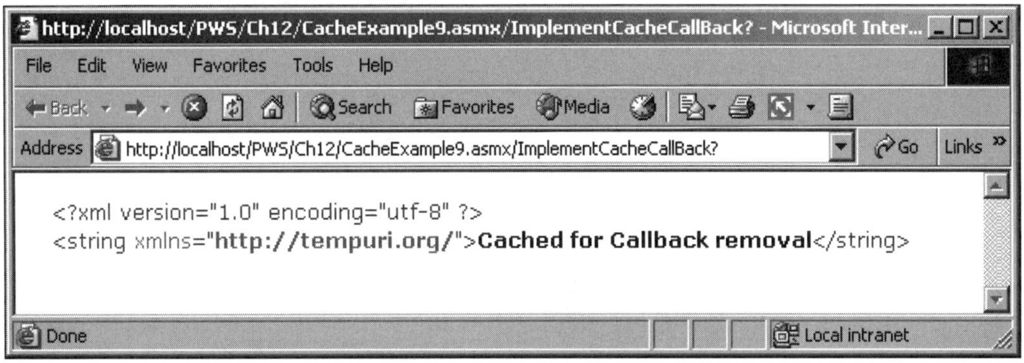

When the cache expires, due to the time or any other reason, the cache item will be recreated by the `CacheItemRemovedCallback` event handler:

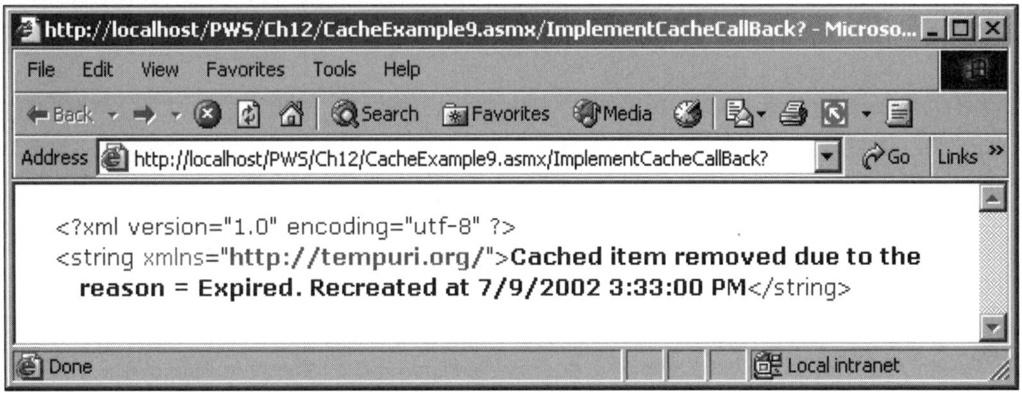

Caching Performance Counters

The `Cache` object exposes a few performance counters that can be monitored using the Windows Performance Monitor utility. This utility can be opened in Windows 2000 by doing the following steps: select Start | Run and type perfmon.exe. Select System Monitor, right-click in the right-hand pane and choose Add Counters. All the caching performance counters are available under the ASP.NET Applications category.

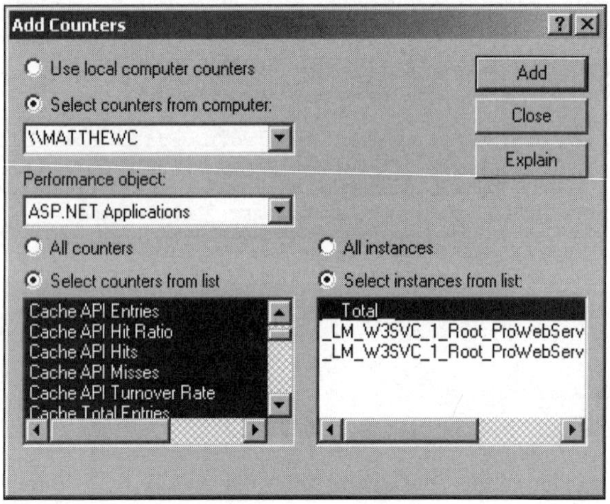

There are two different sets of performance counters, one for the `Cache` object and the other for output caching. Here is a list of available performance counters:

Performance Counters For Cache Object

Counter Name	Description
Cache Total Entries	Total number of entries stored in the `Cache` object including internal objects cached by the .NET Framework and application-specific objects.
Cache Total Hits	Total number of requests served from the `Cache` object.
Cache Total Misses	Total number of failed cache requests per application.
Cache Total Hit Ratio	The ratio of requests served and missed from the `Cache` object
Cache Total Turnover Rate	The number of inserts and removals from the `Cache` object per second.
Cache API Entries	The total number of entries in the application cache.
Cache API Hits	The total number of hits to the `Cache` object when using the Cache APIs.
Cache API Misses	Total number of failed cache requests when using the Cache APIs per application.
Cache API Hit Ratio	The ratio of requests served and missed from the `Cache` object when using the Cache APIs.
Cache API Turnover Rate	The number of inserts and removals from the `Cache` object per second when using the Cache API's.

Performance Counters For Output Cache

Counter Name	Description
Output Cache Entries	The total number of entries in the output cache memory pool.
Output Cache Hits	Total number of requests served from the output cache.
Output Cache Misses	The number of requests that failed when accessing the output cache per application.
Output Cache Hit Ratio	The ratio of total requests served from the output cache.
Output Cache Turnover Rate	The number of inserts and removals from the output cache per second. This is very useful to determine how effective our output cache scheme is. If the turnover is large, then the cache is not being used effectively.

If we select all the cache and output cache counters in the Add Counters window and click on Add, then we get this simple view of the cache counters in the Performance Monitor:

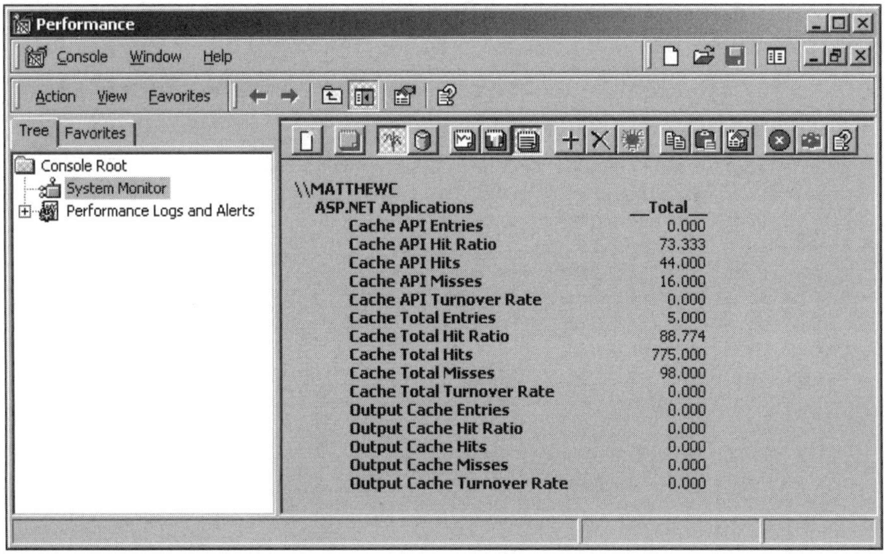

We can also read these performance counters from any .NET application, including a Web Service. The .NET Framework exposes a few classes in the `System.Diagnostics` namespace to read the performance counters.

We're going to build a simple Web Service that uses the `PerformanceCounter` class in the `System.Diagnostics` namespace to read the cache-specific performance counter values for the instance "`__Total__`" and we'll return the value in an array of objects. Here is the code, `CachePerformanceCounter.asmx`:

```
<%@ WebService Language="VB" Class="CachePerformanceCounter" %>

Imports System
Imports System.Web.Services
Imports System.Diagnostics

Public Class CachePerfCntr
  Public CounterName  As String
  Public CounterValue As String
End Class


Public Class CachePerformanceCounter
  Inherits WebService
  '*
  '* Get the Performance counter information for the Cache object
  '*
  <WebMethod> _
  Public Function GetCachePerformanceCounters() As CachePerfCntr()
    'Declare an Object array type of CachePerfCntr
    Dim objProf(10) As CachePerfCntr

    'Declare an object type of PerformanceCounter
    Dim objPC as new PerformanceCounter

    Try
      'Set the Category type as 'ASP.NET Applications'
      objPC.CategoryName = "ASP.NET Applications"

      'Get Performance counter information
      'for Cache Total Entries
      objPC.CounterName = "Cache Total Entries"
      objPC.InstanceName = "__Total__"
      objProf(0) = new CachePerfCntr
      objProf(0).CounterName = "Cache Total Entries"
      objProf(0).CounterValue = objPC.NextValue.ToString()

      objPC.CounterName = "Cache Total Hits"
      objPC.InstanceName = "__Total__"
      objProf(1) = new CachePerfCntr
      objProf(1).CounterName = "Cache Total Hits"
      objProf(1).CounterValue = objPC.NextValue.ToString()

      objPC.CounterName = "Cache Total Misses"
```

```
      objPC.InstanceName = "__Total__"
      objProf(2) = new CachePerfCntr
      objProf(2).CounterName = "Cache Total Misses"
      objProf(2).CounterValue = objPC.NextValue.ToString()
      objPC.CounterName = "Cache Total Hit Ratio"
      objPC.InstanceName = "__Total__"
      objProf(3) = new CachePerfCntr
      objProf(3).CounterName = "Cache Total Hit Ratio"
      objProf(3).CounterValue = objPC.NextValue.ToString()

      objPC.CounterName = "Cache Total Turnover Rate"
      objPC.InstanceName = "__Total__"
      objProf(4) = new CachePerfCntr
      objProf(4).CounterName = "Cache Total Turnover Rate"
      objProf(4).CounterValue = objPC.NextValue.ToString()

      objPC.CounterName = "Cache API Entries"
      objPC.InstanceName = "__Total__"
      objProf(5) = new CachePerfCntr
      objProf(5).CounterName = "Cache API Entries"
      objProf(5).CounterValue = objPC.NextValue.ToString()

      objPC.CounterName = "Cache API Hits"
      objPC.InstanceName = "__Total__"
      objProf(6) = new CachePerfCntr
      objProf(6).CounterName = "Cache API Hits"
      objProf(6).CounterValue = objPC.NextValue.ToString()

      objPC.CounterName = "Cache API Misses"
      objPC.InstanceName = "__Total__"
      objProf(7) = new CachePerfCntr
      objProf(7).CounterName = "Cache API Misses"
      objProf(7).CounterValue = objPC.NextValue.ToString()

      objPC.CounterName = "Cache API Hit Ratio"
      objPC.InstanceName = "__Total__"
      objProf(8) = new CachePerfCntr
      objProf(8).CounterName = "Cache API Hit Ratio"
      objProf(8).CounterValue = objPC.NextValue.ToString()

      objPC.CounterName = "Cache API Turnover Rate"
      objPC.InstanceName = "__Total__"
      objProf(9) = new CachePerfCntr
      objProf(9).CounterName = "Cache API Turnover Rate"
      objProf(9).CounterValue = objPC.NextValue.ToString()
    Catch Ex as Exception
      'Handle the error
    End Try

    Return objProf
  End Function
End Class
```

We declare a custom class with two properties, `CounterName` and `CounterValue`:

```
Public Class CachePerfCntr
  Public CounterName  As String
  Public CounterValue As String
End Class
```

Inside the `WebMethod` we declare an array of ten objects of the type `CachePerfCntr`. Then we create a new object of type `PerformanceCounter`.

```
'Declare an Object array type of CachePerfCntr
Dim objProf(10) As CachePerfCntr

'Declare an object type of PerformanceCounter
Dim objPC as new PerformanceCounter
```

Next we use the `CategoryName` property of the `PerformanceCounter` counter object name to use the counters from the "`ASP.NET Applications`" category. We then read all the cache counters one by one and assign the values to the array of objects.

```
'Set the Category type as 'ASP.NET Applications'
objPC.CategoryName = "ASP.NET Applications"

'Get Performance counter information
'for Cache Total Entries
objPC.CounterName = "Cache Total Entries"
objPC.InstanceName = "__Total__"
objProf(0) = new CachePerfCntr
objProf(0).CounterName = "Cache Total Entries"
objProf(0).CounterValue = objPC.NextValue.ToString()
```

At the end we return the object array back to the client. The following screenshot shows the output of the Web Service:

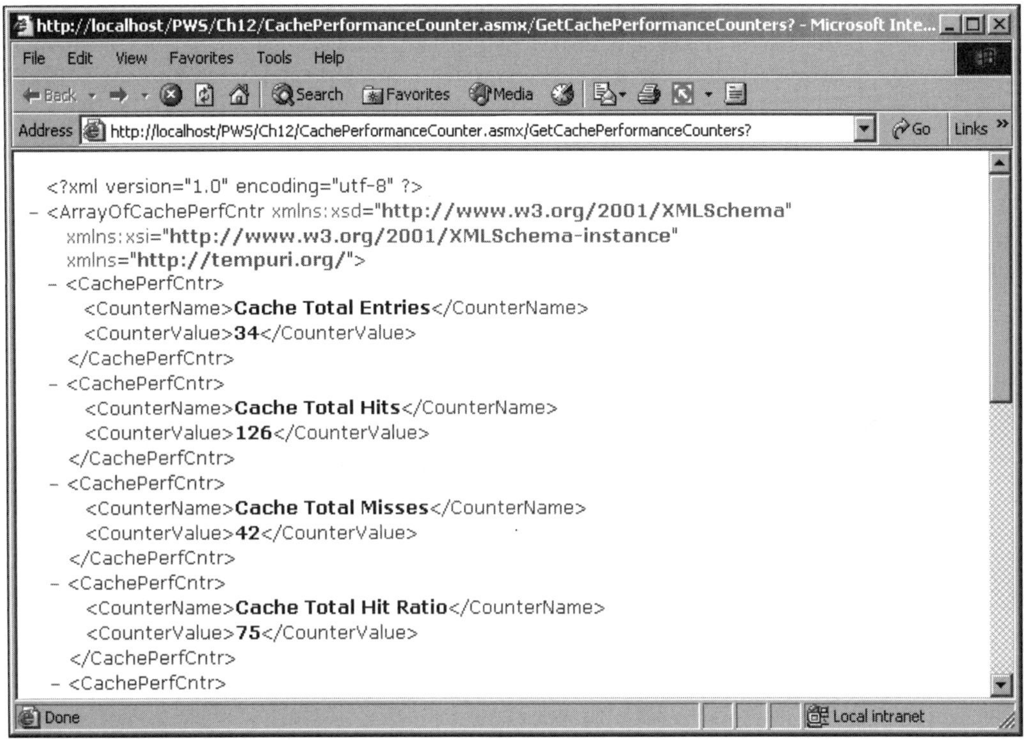

Summary

As we have learned in this chapter, when it comes to caching we have three options:

- Output caching
- The `Application` object
- The `Cache` object

When using output caching, the entire output of the Web Service will be cached for the specific timespan as defined by the Web Service. With the `Application` and `Cache` objects, we can pretty much cache anything, from simple data types such as integers and strings to complex data types such as an array of objects, a `DataSet`, and so on.

The `Cache` object supports multiple types of expiration, ranging from absolute expiration, sliding expiration, file- or directory-based dependency expiration, to key-based expiration, which is not supported by the `Application` object. We can either use the time-based expiration options or dependency expiration options or a combination of both with the `Cache` object.

The Cache object supports manual and automatic removal of cached items, and optionally they can also raise an event back and inform the application, about the removal of the cached item. The removal of an item from the Cache object is based on its CacheItemPriority setting.

Additionally, cache objects expose a number of performance counters that can be used to determine the effectiveness of the cache scheme used. These performance counters can be read from the Windows Performance Monitor application or from any .NET application, including from Web Services.

Professional
ASP.NET
Web
Services

13

Authentication

As soon as you start to gather information about designing a Web Service, you must ask yourself: "who do I want to see this?" The chances are that unless you actively protect your Web Service resources, they'll be available to anyone with a connection to the Internet. When it comes to Web-based applications such as Web Services, security plays a major role in implementing these applications. In the client/server application world, where most of the clients and the server are in the same private network and the network is secure, no one can get into the network from the outside world. Unlike a client/server application, Web applications are deployed in public networks and thus pose a security risk where servers can be broken into and information stolen, such as details from a customer database, customers' credit card information, and so on. It is therefore very important to secure our Web Service (regardless of whether it's internal or external) from hackers, and others who we don't want to have access to this kind of sensitive information.

Why do we want to secure the Web Service? Well, there are three main reasons:

- **Protecting our Web Service from unauthorized usage** – we want to make sure we'll only allow users who have subscribed to the Web Service to consume it.
- **Protecting the data** – we want to protect the users' data stored in the database from the prying eyes. This gives more confidence to the users who use our service.
- **Protecting the transmission** – we want to protect the data transmitted between the users and our server, to protect the valuable users' data and their privacy.

When we're securing the Web Service, we also get these additional benefits:

- **Personalizing the Web Service for the given user** – we want to minimize the data received from the user to identify them and provide the data they require through the personalized settings that he or she has already entered. For example, if our Web Service provides general news and weather information to the user, then we can give appropriate local news and weather information to the user, if we know who the user is.
- **Keeping track of usage** – if the Web Service that you are exposing is based on usage count licensing – meaning the user will be billed based on the usage count on the site – you may want to keep track of how many times the given user has accessed the Web Service.

In this chapter, we'll learn all about security and how to secure our Web Services. Web Services are just like ASP.NET applications and they have access to all the ASP.NET security methods and SOAP authentication techniques. In this chapter, we'll learn about the following topics:

- Windows Authentication Methods
- Forms Authentication
- Impersonation
- URL Authorization

What Is Security?

Security is a process that guards private property from the public world and gives access to the private property by verifying proper identification. The identification can be a simple username and password, or digital identity such as a client certificate or smart cards.

When we're dealing with security, there are a few entities to remember. They are:

- **Credentials** – credentials is usually a Username/Password pair that is entered or sent by the client. We can also count client certificate and smart cards as credentials.
- **Authentication** – authentication is a process that acts on behalf of the user or client, which accepts the credentials from the user and verifies them against single or multiple authorities.
- **Authority** – the authority is usually a verification entity such as a Windows NT user account database or a custom database schema defined by the application where the credentials can be verified.
- **Authorization** – authorization is a process that verifies whether this person has access to the resource that they are trying to access.
- **Privacy** – privacy is a process that makes sure the information that we're transmitting can't be seen or interpreted by anyone other than the original user and the intended recipient.
- **Non-repudiation** – non-repudiation is a technique that provides a foolproof way to securely encrypt and decrypt the data, and prevent non-repudiation of the original data from the encrypted data by unauthorized hands.

Web Service Security Architecture

The security architecture of a Web Service is somewhat different from that of an ASP.NET application. Typically in an ASP.NET application scenario, there will be one security setting and session management between the ASP.NET client and the server. In the Web Service scenario, it is applications that consume Web Services rather than humans directly. Thus, security and session management considerations should be between applications for Web Services. Consider the following figure:

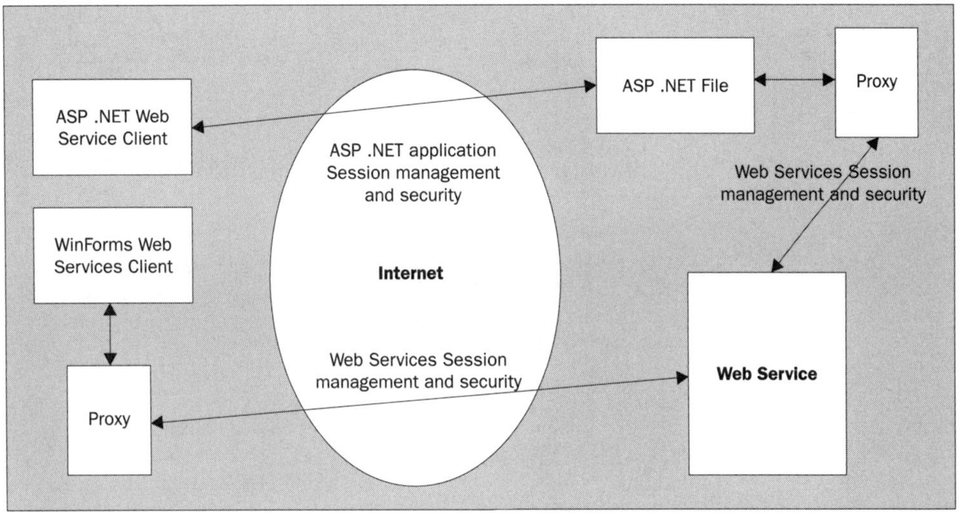

In the Web Service scenario, the server-side ASP.NET page will consume a Web Service and the result will be sent back to the client. In this case, we have to maintain two sets of security settings and session management. The first one is between the ASP.NET application and the client and the next one is between the ASP.NET application and the Web Service. Consider the following example:

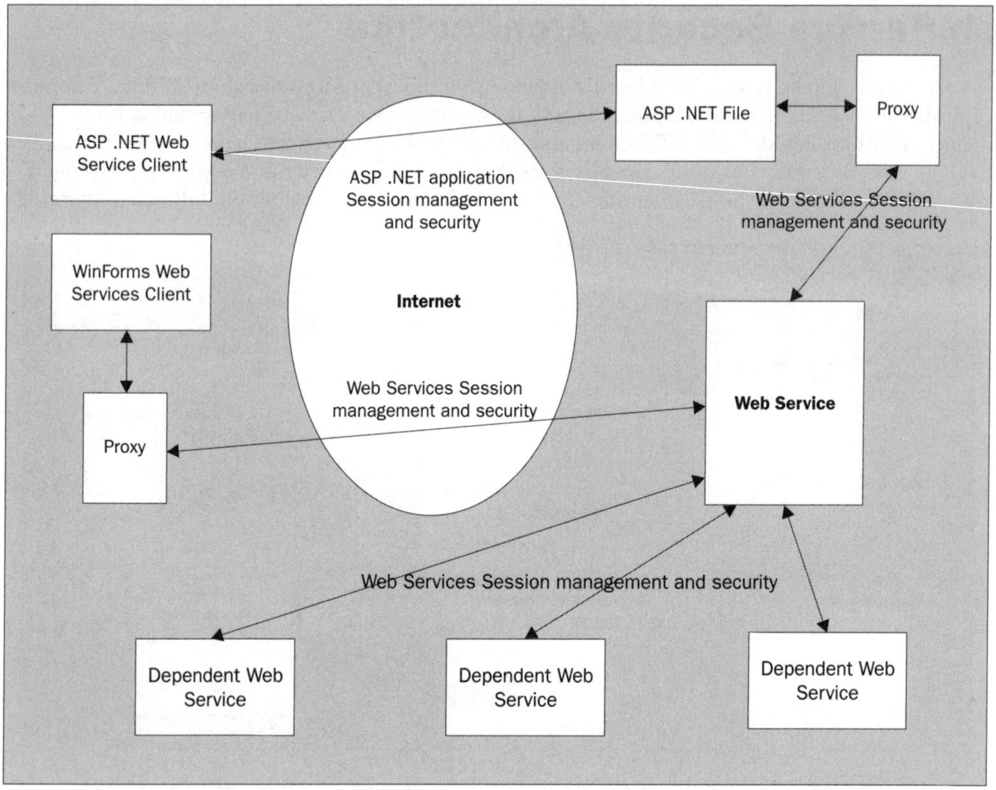

If the Web Service we're consuming using the proxy is dependent on other Web Services, then the source Web Service has to maintain the session management and security settings for the other Web Services that it is consuming.

Security Options Available with Web Services

Web Services support a number of security settings for our ASP.NET applications. They are:

- Basic Authentication with or without SSL
- Digest Authentication
- Integrated Windows Authentication
- Client Certificate Authentication
- Forms Authentication with or without SSL
- Custom Authentication and Authorization

The Basic, Digest, and Integrated Windows Authentication methods are provided as a service to Web Services by IIS (Internet Information Server). The .NET Framework classes provide the Form authentication and further Passport authentication and SOAP techniques. ASP.NET and Web Services handle the authentication by using the authentication providers (authentication providers are code modules which have the necessary code to authenticate a user based on their credentials). The current release of ASP.NET is shipped with a Windows authentication provider, Passport authentication provider, and Forms authentication providers.

ASP.NET Authentication Architecture

Before we go any further, let's understand the architecture of ASP.NET security. The following figure shows the architecture of an ASP.NET application:

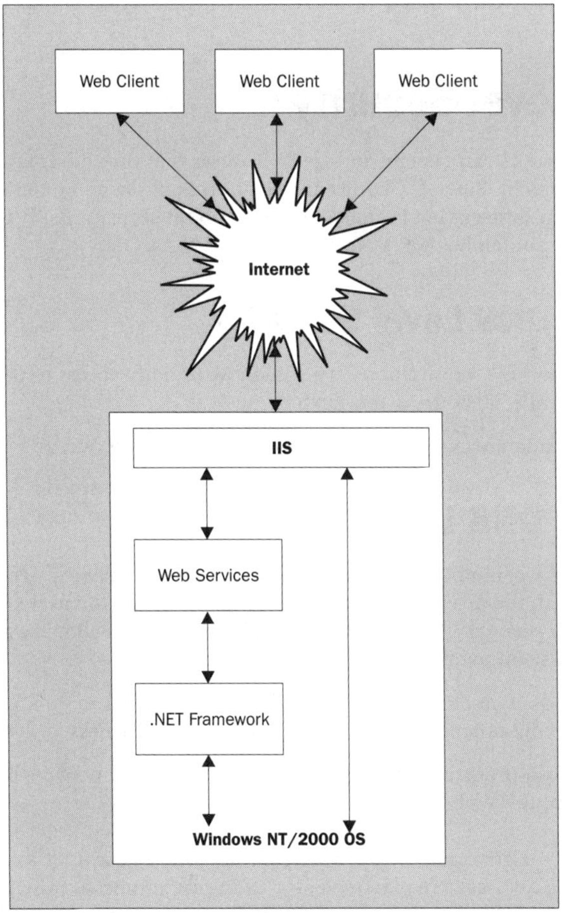

When a request comes from a web client to the Web Service, it will first reach the web server (IIS) as shown above. If the Allow Anonymous option is checked in the IIS Microsoft Management Console (MMC) then no authentication will occur at the server side. If the web application requires any authentication such as Basic, Digest, or Integrated Windows, then IIS will pop up a dialog box to collect the username and password from the user.

If we're passing the username, password and domain information using the Web Service proxy then the dialog box will not be shown.

If authentication is successful, then IIS will pass the web request to the Web Service. If authentication fails then IIS will throw a HTTP status 401: Access Denied error message to the client. When we use the Basic, Digest or Integrated Windows authentication methods, IIS assumes that the credentials provided by the web client are mapped to a Windows user account. If the Web Service requires Form or Passport authentication then IIS will pass on the request to the Web Service. The Web Service will then authorize or deny the client based on the credentials presented by the client.

IP and DNS Level Security

Web Service administrators can take advantage of features that provide Internet protocol (IP) address validation to secure content. Since IIS knows the IP address of the computer requesting the Web Service, IIS can use this information to make decisions about security. TCP/IP restrictions are processed before any attempt for authentication is made.

Pros of IP and DNS Level Security

- Using the IP **and** DNS restrictions, we can allow or deny access to the Web Service based on a single, or multiple, IP address and DNS names.
- This authentication occurs before any other authentication occurs.

Cons of IP and DNS Level Security

- If the clients are behind a proxy server or a firewall then all we'll see is that the connection is originating from the proxy server or the firewall, not from the user's computer. This means we could only see a single IP address for a set of clients. This will make restriction based on an IP address virtually impossible.
- If we're using domain name-based restrictions, then IIS has to do a DNS lookup to find the IP address, and if the process fails the client will be denied access to the Web Service.
- The DNS lookup process is time-consuming and this could become a bottleneck for the performance of the Web Service.

Using TCP/IP restrictions gives us a way to single out a group of users, or a single user, who should have access to our Web Service. We may have, for example, an intranet site that should only be accessible from a group of IP addresses. As a first line of security, we can configure IIS to reject all requests that don't fit the IP address criteria. We can grant or deny access for the following criteria:

- Any Web Service client connecting from a single IP address
- Any Web Service client connecting from a range of IP addresses (including subnet mask)
- Any Web Service client connecting from a single host name
- Any computer connecting from a particular domain name (like www.wrox.com)

Implementing IP and DNS Security

Implementing IP and DNS name-based security is very simple. Open up the IIS management console, go to the virtual directory or the web site that you want to secure, right-click on it and select the Properties option. Go to the "Directory Security" tab in the new dialog box and click the "Edit..." button in the "IP address and domain name restrictions" frame. With the "IP Address and Domain name restrictions" dialog box we can grant or deny access:

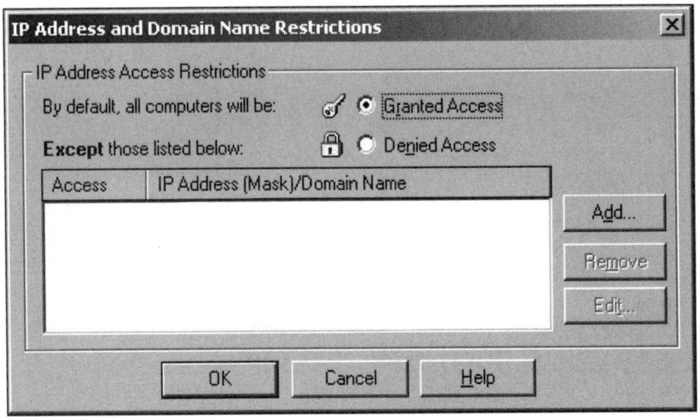

Windows Security

Before implementing Windows security for ASP.NET applications, it's important to understand Windows Operating System security. Security is unavoidable on the Windows OS. Anything that we do in Windows is going to involve some kind of security check. For example, if we want to create a text file or delete a Word document we need permission for that. Mostly we don't notice any security problems with Windows because we are logging in as an administrator, and the administrator has no permission restrictions.

The heart of Windows security revolves around a Windows user account, and user groups or roles (a group in Windows, or role in ASP.NET, is a logical name for a set of users grouped together, or rights such as Read, Execute, Write, etc.). In Windows, all user information is stored in a central place called the Windows User Account Database. This database can be stored in the local computer or it can be on a server where it will be called a Domain server or Primary Domain Controller (PDC).

The Domain server is the central place to which all the computers in a network will be connected. For the examples in this chapter, the domain name is "Sruthi". The following figure shows a simple Windows architecture for the domain Sruthi.

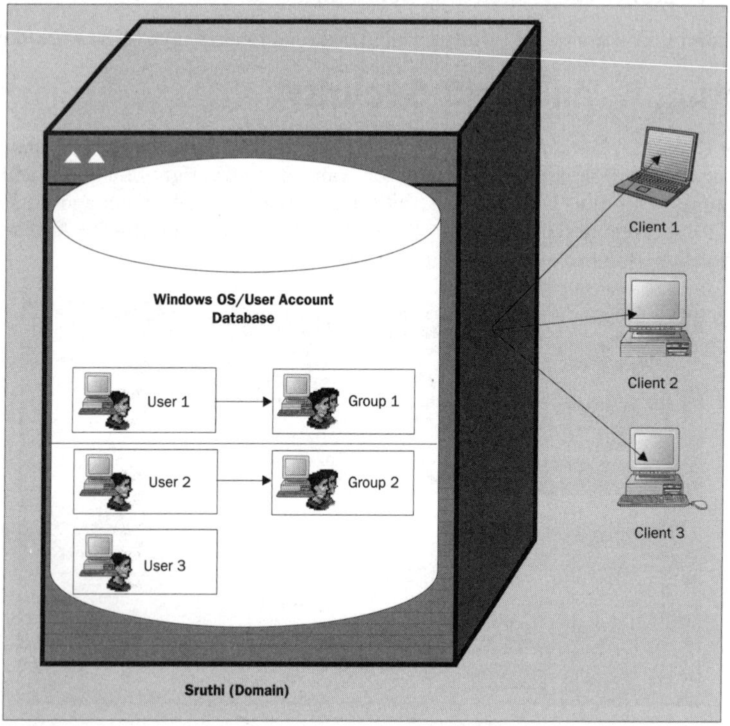

In the Sruthi domain, there are three users (User, 1, 2, and 3) and two groups (Group 1 and 2). User 1 belongs to the group 1 and user 2 belongs to group 2. User 3 is not a part of any group. These are three different clients trying to connect to the domain Sruthi.

When you install IIS, it creates a user account called iusr_machinename. *For example if your computer name is Sruthi, then you'll see a user account in the name of* iusr_Sruthi. *IIS uses this account to give anonymous access to web resources.*

Access Control Lists (ACL)

An access control list (ACL) is a table that tells a computer's operating system which access rights each user has to a particular system object, such as a file directory or individual file. An ACL is a list of Access Control Entries (ACE) and each ACE will contain the file system object ID and permissions related to the file system object. The ACL has an entry for each system user with access privileges. The most common privileges include the ability to read a file (or all the files in a directory), to write to the file or files, and to execute the file (if it is an executable file, or program). The list is implemented differently by each operating system based on the file system it is using. The NTFS file system supports the ACLs and the FAT or FAT32 file system doesn't support it.

We can view the ACL information for a file or a directory by viewing the `Properties` page of the file or folder.

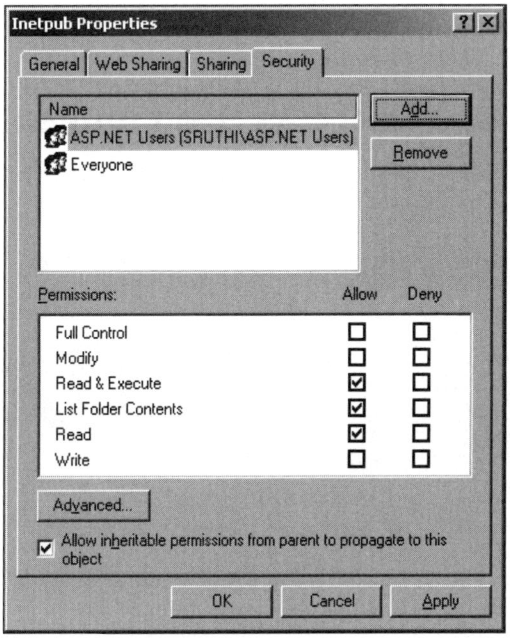

ACLs provide an excellent way to restrict the privileges of the user. In a secured application, a logged-in user's intention is to access the application. So all that is needed is the `Read` privilege. If we give more options to the user, he can misuse his privilege and tamper with the system. If he had `Full Control` privilege then he could do anything, including deleting files. This is obviously not desirable.

What is Next?

So far, we've seen some basic architectural information regarding general security concepts including Windows OS security features, IP- **and** DNS-based security, and more. In the following sections, we'll take more of a practical approach and see how to implement the security to the Web Services. Let's start this process by looking at how to read who is logged into the Web Service.

Reading User Information

The `User` object (exposed using the `Context` property of the Web Service) can be used to read information on a logged-in user. The `User` object exposes the `Identity` property. The `Identity` property exposes the `Name` and `AuthenticationType` properties to get information about the current logged-in user and the type of authentication. For example, the following code will display the current username and the type of authentication used:

```
<WebMethod()> _
Public Function WhoAmI() As String
   Return "You are: " & Context.User.Identity.Name & " and you are using " _
         & Context.User.Identity.AuthenticationType + " authentication type. "
End Function
```

Checking Whether a User Has Been Authenticated

The `User.Identity` property exposes an `IsAuthenticated` property. This property returns `True` or `False` depending on whether the user is authenticated or not.

```
If Context.User.Identity.IsAuthenticated = True Then
   ' Authenticated
Else
   ' Not authenticated
End If
```

Roles

A role is a common name for a set of permissions allowing such things as reading a file, creating a file, and so on, and one or more users belong to a role. It can be created based on a specific functionality or task that they do or it can be generic. For example, we can group the employees of an organization based on their job profiles like: "Directors", "Managers", "Administrators", and so on. Alternatively, we could group them based on the department they are working in like "Finance", "Human Resources", etc.

The Windows OS has a number of built-in roles such as "Administrator", "Power Users", "Users", "Authenticated Users", and so on. We can also define custom roles with Windows.

Roles make it easier to manage users with the same privileges. Let's say that your Web Service has three different flavors, like basic, premium, and gold, and you have users in each of the above flavors of the Web Service. Therefore, managing the privileges of the user will be very simple if we create three different roles (basic, premium, and gold), and assign a user to any of the roles. From our code, we can hide or show the information based on their privileges.

How To Use Roles

The Windows user account supports roles (although they are called groups in Windows). When we're using any of the Windows Authentication methods, we can use the Windows NT/2000/XP roles from our code. These roles can be predefined internal roles of the Windows operating system, or custom-defined application- or organization-specific roles.

The `User` object exposes an `IsInRole` method, which allows us to verify Windows groups from our code. Let's see some examples of this. We'll create a Web Service that will check to see if the user is part of a built-in Windows Operating System role. For your convenience, the code for this example can be found in the `Roles` folder of the code download. Map the folder as a virtual directory in IIS, then assign Basic or Integrated Windows Authentication to the virtual directory. This example will use the following `web.config` file:

```
<configuration>
  <system.web>
    <authentication mode="Windows" />
  </system.web>
</configuration>
```

Now, let's create a Web Service with the class name `Roles`, and a `WebMethod` name `GetRoles`. This is `Roles.asmx` in the `Roles` folder.

```
<%@ WebService Language="VB" Class="Roles" %>

Import System.Web.Services

Public Class Roles
   Inherits WebService

   Private Function ReadRoles() As String
      Dim strRoles As String = ""

      'Custom Application specific Role
      If Context.User.IsInRole("SRUTHI\WebServiceUsers") Then
         strRoles = " 'Web Service Users'"
      End If
      'Built in Windows OS roles
      If Context.User.IsInRole("BUILTIN\Administrators") Then
         strRoles += ", 'Administrators'"
      End If
      If Context.User.IsInRole("BUILTIN\Power Users") Then
         strRoles += ", 'Power Users'"
      End If
      If Context.User.IsInRole("BUILTIN\Users") Then
         strRoles += ", 'Users'."
      Else
         strRoles += "You are not part of any role."
      End If
      Return strRoles
   End Function 'ReadRoles


   <WebMethod()> _
   Public Function GetRoles() As String
      Return "Hello " & Context.User.Identity.Name & ". You are consuming '" _
               & Context.User.Identity.AuthenticationType _
               & "' authentication and you are part of following roles (" _
               & ReadRoles() & ")"
   End Function
End Class
```

We define a private method in the `Roles` class to read the information about the roles. We're using the `IsInRole` method of the `User` object to see if the given user is a member of a role and we're using the three predefined Windows OS roles and an application-specific custom role (`WebServiceUsers`) in our code. Notice that when we're using the Windows built-in roles, we're using the `BUILTIN` keyword in the `IsInRole` method, and when we're using the custom role, we're using the domain name. Here is how the output looks:

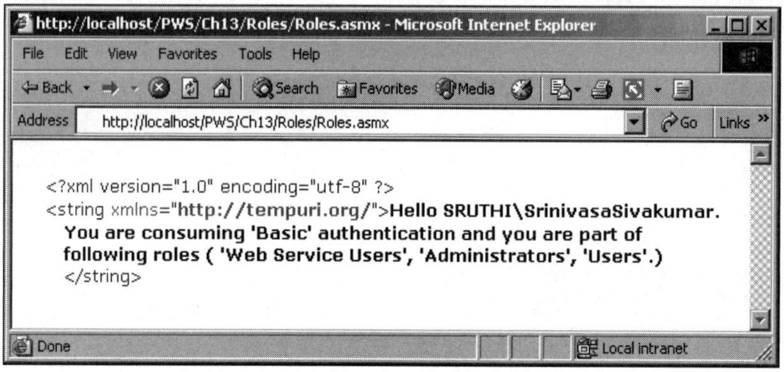

Basic Authentication

When basic authentication is used, IIS will ask the web browser to collect credentials from the user if we're accessing the Web Service without a proxy. Then the web browser will pop up a dialog box to collect a username and password from the user. If we're accessing the Web Service using a proxy and we have provided the credentials, the dialog box will not be shown. In this case, the collected information will be sent back to the server as encoded text. Encoding is not a strong encryption and anyone can read the username and password information over the wire and hack into the Web Service. Consider the following HTTP header example:

```
GET /www.Wrox.com/MyInfo.asmx
HOST: www.Wrox.com
HTTP/1.0
Connection: Keep-Alive
Authorization: Basic QWRTAW5pa3RyYYY
Accept: image/gif, image/x-bitmap, image/jpg, image/pjpg,
```

In the above example, we're accessing the MyInfo Web Service from www.wrox.com. In the HTTP header, the word `Basic` says that we're using basic authentication and the junk text next to the word `Basic` is the Base-64 encoded version of the username/password pair. The domain name, username and the password are encoded in "`BASIC: Domain\Username:Password`" format and transmitted with the `Authorization` HTTP header.

The encoded username/password information is sent to the IIS server. Then the server will compare the username/password against the Windows NT/2000/XP user account database. If the submitted credentials match the Windows NT/2000/XP user account database then IIS will send the requested Web Service result back to the client. Otherwise IIS will send "HTTP status 401 – Access Denied" back to the client.

Pros of Basic Authentication

- Easy to implement and almost all Web Servers support it, including IIS
- No development required – a few mouse clicks inside the IIS MMC will implement basic authentication
- Supported by almost all browsers
- Supported by all proxies and firewalls

Cons of Basic Authentication

- Username and password is sent in unencoded format (clear text)
- Username and password is passed with every request
- Can't be used against a custom authority such as a database

Why and When

Basic authentication is a part of HTTP 1.0 protocol and most of the browsers, proxies and firewalls support this authentication method. In spite of the wide support, basic authentication still sends the username and password in clear text format. Moreover, basic authentication is also very fast when compared with other authentication methods. Therefore, this brings security concerns to the Web Service. If your Web Service is dealing with any highly sensitive data, like online banking or stock trading, you should not use basic authentication.

We can fix this problem when we combine basic authentication with SSL. We'll see more details about this later.

Implementing Basic Authentication

Implementing basic authentication is very simple. We have to set up basic authentication for the Web Service from the IIS Microsoft Management Console (MMC). Then we create a `Web.config` file to reflect the authentication procedure that we're using. That's it.

Let's create a simple Web Service that says "hello" to whoever logs in to the Web Service. For your convenience, you can find the following code in the code download. This is the `SayHello.Asmx` file, which you can find in the `BasicAuthServer` folder.

```
<%@ WebService Language="VB" Class="Hello" %>

Imports System.Web.Services
```

```
Public Class Hello
  Inherits WebService

  <WebMethod()> _
  Public Function SayHello() As String
     Return "Hello " & Context.User.Identity.Name & ". You are consuming '" _
               & Context.User.Identity.AuthenticationType & "' authentication."
  End Function 'SayHello
End Class 'Hello
```

Let's create a `Web.Config` file to use Windows authentication.

```
<configuration>
  <system.web>
    <authentication mode="Windows" />
  </system.web>
</configuration>
```

Let's map the current folder as an IIS Virtual folder. Now let's create a proxy for the Web Service with the following batch file, `SayHelloBuild.bat`. Please note that you may have to edit this file and change the path to the WSDL file, depending on where you install the code for this example on your system:

```
WSDL /l:VB /n:SayHelloNS /out:SayHello.vb http://localhost/PWS/ SayHello.asmx?WSDL

VBC /r:system.dll  /r:System.Web.dll /r:System.Xml.dll /r:System.Web.Services.dll
/t:library /out:SayHello.dll SayHello.vb
```

Place the `SayHello.dll` into the `bin` folder when it has been created. Now we need a simple ASP.NET client, `BasicAuthClient.aspx`, to access the `SayHello` Web Service.

```
<%@ Import Namespace="System.Net" %>
<%@ Import Namespace="SayHelloNS" %>
<html>
<head>
<title>Basic Authentication Web Client</title>
<style type="text/css">
  body {font-face:verdana; font-size:10pt; font-weight:normal}
</style>
</head>
<script language="VB" runat="server">

Public Sub Page_Load(sender As Object, E As EventArgs)
  Try
    Dim objWebSvc As New SayHelloNS.Hello()
    objWebSvc.Credentials = New NetworkCredential("MyUserName", _
                                          "MyPassword", "MyDomain")
    lblResult.Text = objWebSvc.SayHello()
  Catch Ex As Exception
    lblResult.Text = Ex.ToString()
  End Try
End Sub
</script>
<body>
<h3>Basic Authentication - Web Service Client</h3>
<form runat="server">
<b>Result:</b><br /> <asp:Label id="lblResult" runat="server"/>
</form>
```

```
</body>
</html>
```

In the Page_Load event, we pass the Windows 2000 username, password, and the domain name to the Web Service's proxy object using the NetworkCredential class (available in the System.Net namespace). This will avoid the messy pop-up dialog box from the browser that collects user information.

Before trying this example, be sure to change the username, password, and domain on the BasicAuthClient.aspx file.

Now we have to set up basic authentication for the Web Service. Go to the IIS MMC, expand the web sites tree, and find our virtual directory. Select the SayHello.asmx file, and right-click on it. Select the Properties option from the shortcut menu. You'll see a new dialog box. Go to the File Security tab and click the Edit button in the Anonymous Access and Authentication Control section. In the Authentication Methods dialog box, deselect the Anonymous access and Integrated Windows authentication checkboxes and check the Basic authentication (password is sent in clear text) checkbox and click Yes to continue. Then click the Edit... button and enter your domain name.

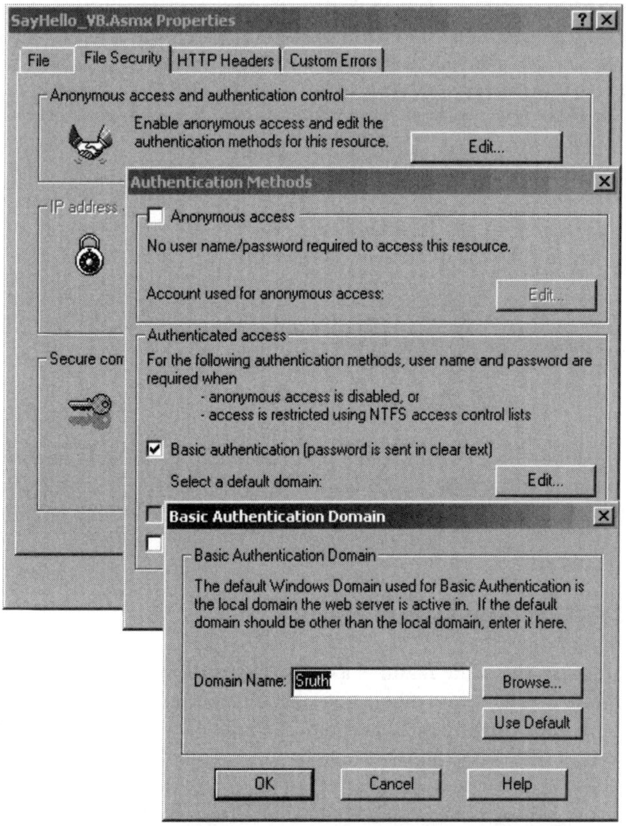

Click OK in each dialog box to finish basic authentication setup. Now when we run the ASP.NET Web Service client, we will see something like the following in our browser window:

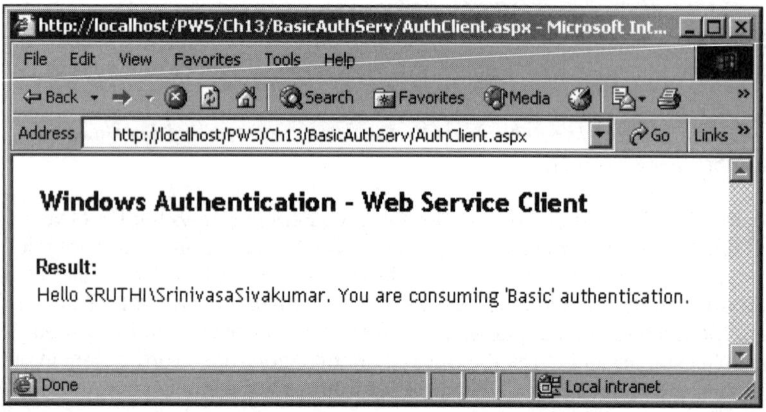

> **Do remember to set up basic authentication in IIS *after* creating the proxy DLL. If you try to create the proxy DLL file after setting up basic authentication you will get an "HTTP 401.2 – Unauthorized" error.**

The `Page_Load` event creates an object of the type of the Web Service from the proxy. Then it creates a new `NetworkCredential` object, passes the username, password, and domain name to the constructor, and assigns the `NetworkCredential` object to the `Credentials` property of the Web Service object. Then we call the `SayHello` method of the Web Service object.

```
Dim objWebSvc As New SayHelloNS.Hello()
objWebSvc.Credentials = New NetworkCredential("MyUserName", _
                                              "MyPassword", "MyDomain")
lblResult.Text = objWebSvc.SayHello()
```

When this method is called, the `Credentials` property will pass the information to IIS and IIS will compare the supplied credentials against the user account database. If the supplied credentials match, then IIS will forward the request to the Web Service and the Web Service will return the data.

Digest Authentication

Digest authentication offers the same features as basic authentication, but transmits the credentials in a different way. The authentication credentials pass through a one-way process referred to as **hashing**. The result of hashing cannot feasibly be decrypted. Additional information is added to the password before hashing so that no one can capture the password hash and reuse it. This is a clear advantage over basic authentication, because the password cannot be intercepted and used by an unauthorized person.

Hashing is a set of mathematical calculations (algorithms) that can be used to encrypt and decrypt data safely. The MD5 (Message Digest 5) and SHA1 (Secure Hash Algorithm 1) are two well-known one-way hashing algorithms. When using one-way hashing algorithms the value can't be rehashed back to the original value.

Pros of Digest Authentication

- Easy to implement, like basic authentication. We've already seen how easy it is to implement basic authentication for our Web Service.
- Supported by all proxies and firewalls.
- Username/password is never sent as clear text.

Cons of Digest Authentication

- Only supported by Windows 2000/IIS 5 and above, not available with IIS 4. If you are using the Windows NT operating system then you can't use this authentication method.
- Only supported by web browsers such as Internet Explorer 4.0 and above and Netscape 4.0 and above.
- The Windows Server OS should be using the Active Directory (AD) to store all the Windows user account database information or the server should have access to the Active Directory to look up the user account information.
- Can't be used against a custom authority such as a database. When we use digest authentication, the credentials will be always compared against the Windows user account database stored in an Active Directory – we can't compare the credentials against a custom authority such as a text file or a database.

Why and When

Digest authentication is a part of the HTTP 1.1 protocol and W3C, which addresses the problem faced in the basic authentication. This is a safer authentication option when compared with basic authentication. Since digest authentication uses Active Directory, it is a more scalable solution. We can use this authentication method for slightly more secured applications, such as e-mail accounts or calendar applications, etc.

Implementing Digest Authentication

To implement digest authentication we need to install Active Directory where IIS is installed, or have access to an Active Directory Server. If you have all that is required for digest authentication then you can follow the same steps we followed for basic authentication and instead of checking the Basic authentication (password is sent in clear text) checkbox, simply check the Digest authentication for Windows domain servers checkbox. The same code that we used for basic authentication will work for this too, including the `Web.config` and the Web Service client and server code.

If you are interested in how to set up Digest authentication, check out the Microsoft Support Knowledge Base article at http://support.microsoft.com/support/kb/articles/Q222/0/28.asp *for more information.*

For more information about Digest authentication, see the specification RFC 2069 at http://www.ietf.org/rfc/rfc2069.txt.

Integrated Windows Authentication

Integrated Windows authentication (previously known as NTLM or Windows Challenge/Response authentication) is similar to digest authentication but uses more sophisticated hashing. The beauty of Integrated Windows authentication is that the username and password are not sent over the network. Integrated Windows authentication supports both the Kerberos V5 authentication protocol and the challenge/response protocol. If Active Directory Services is installed on the server and the browser is compatible with the Kerberos V5 authentication protocol, both the Kerberos V5 protocol and the challenge/response protocol are used – otherwise only the challenge/response protocol is used.

When we request a web site that consumes Integrated Windows authentication, the web server will send a random number back to our client. Then, the client will send the username, domain name, and a token back to the server. The token contains the password encrypted with the random number. Then, the Web server will send the username, domain, and token to the Domain Controller. The Domain Controller will verify the validity of the credentials and send a response back to IIS.

Pros of Using Integrated Windows Authentication

- Easy to implement and supported by IIS. We've already seen how easy it is to implement basic authentication for our Web Service.
- No development required. All we have to do is a couple of mouse clicks here and there and Integrated Windows authentication is ready to use.
- Password is never sent over the network. The password will be transmitted from the client IIS to the PDC as a hash value, so the privacy of the password is guaranteed.

Cons of Using Integrated Windows Authentication

- Only supported by Internet Explorer Version 2.0 and above. Other browsers such as Netscape and Opera don't support Integrated Windows authentication.
- Integrated Windows authentication doesn't work with proxy servers.
- Additional TCP ports need to be opened in the firewall to use Integrated Windows authentication. (Every protocol uses a port to operate. For example, port 80 is used by the HTTP protocol.)
- Can't be used against a custom authority such as a database. When we use basic authentication the credentials will always be compared against the Windows user account database, thus we can't compare the credentials against a custom authority such as a text file or a database.

Why and When

Integrated Windows authentication is Microsoft's extension to the HTTP protocol and is only supported by IIS and IE. Integrated Windows authentication is used in the intranet scenario in today's web applications, since it is only supported by IE – other browsers like Netscape don't support this authentication method. Moreover, each corporation has a standard for browsers and if IE happens to be the standard, then there is no problem in using this authentication method.

However, Web Services are different. Since the Integrated Windows authentication happens at the server side, there is no browser involved in this authentication. Therefore, it is safe to use the Integrated Windows authentication with Web Services. Nevertheless, be aware of the additional TCP ports that need to be opened for this authentication. Many companies may hesitate to open these ports, since they can pose a potential security breach to their internal network.

Implementing Integrated Windows Authentication

To implement integrated Windows authentication we can follow the same steps we followed for basic authentication and instead of checking the Basic authentication (password is sent in clear text) check box, we check the Integrated Windows authentication checkbox. The same code that we tried for basic authentication should work for this too, including the `Web.config` and the Web Service client and server code.

Forms Authentication

If your Web Service is going to be used by a large number of users, and if you are concerned about scalability and security, then Forms authentication is for you. Forms authentication allows you to authenticate the user against any custom authority such as a database or an **Active Directory**. Forms authentication is fully customizable, provides built-in features to manage cookies, and takes care of all the complexities involved with encrypting, decrypting, validating, as well as such things as transferring the user to a login page if the user is not authorized, and so on.

When we request a web site that consumes Forms authentication, the web server will pass the request to the ASP.NET runtime. The ASP.NET runtime will check if the web request contains a valid cookie as specified in the `web.config` file. If the cookie exists in the web request, then the ASP.NET runtime will pass the request to the Web Service page. If the cookie doesn't exist, then the ASP.NET runtime will pass the web request to the login page defined in the `web.config` file.

Pros of Using Forms Authentication

- **Easy to implement** – all we have to do is define the `web.config` file and build the authenticating mechanism using a database or Active Directory, for example.
- **No development required** – the ASP.NET runtime takes care of all the details of managing the cookie.
- **Custom authorities supported** – can be used against a custom authority such as a database or Active Directory.

Cons of Using Forms Authentication

- **Cookie needed** – Forms authentication uses cookies to authenticate users and the code will fail if the client does not support cookies.
- **More memory and processing power** – Forms authentication requires more memory and processing power since it is dealing with external authorities such as a database or Active Directory.

Why and When

Forms authentication is a very popular authentication method in today's sites, including Amazon.com and Yahoo.com. Forms authentication brings the flexibility of validating the credentials against any authority such as a database or Active Directory or a simple XML file. Based on your requirements, you can choose the authority and you can scale the Web Service. Therefore, we can use this authentication method with all our applications. If you want more security, then consider SSL with these authentication options. The only pitfall to this approach is that the client needs to accept cookies, and if the client has turned off cookies then the authentication will fail.

Implementing Forms Authentication

Forms-based authentication is founded on cookies. When a user logs into our ASP.NET application using Forms authentication, ASP.NET will issue an authentication cookie that will be sent back and forth between the server and client during the web requests. If the authentication cookie type is persistent, then a copy of the authentication cookie will be stored on the user's hard drive and whenever they visit the ASP.NET Web Service, they can be pre-authenticated again based on it. If the authentication cookie type is non-persistent, then the authentication cookie will be destroyed at the end of the browser or client's session. In this case, when they visit the ASP.NET Web Service again, we can't pre-authenticate the user, and they have to provide their credentials all over again.

For example, if you visit the www.ASPToday.com or www.CSharpToday.com sites, they use persistent cookies. Once you've checked the "Remember my password" checkbox before clicking the "Login" button, the server will place a persistent cookie on the computer and you never have to present your credentials when visiting ASPToday.com or CSharpToday.com site from the same computer. This gives you the freedom of visiting the sites without presenting the credentials repeatedly. There is also a pitfall to this method. If someone else has access to your computer then they will also be able to visit the sites without presenting the credentials with your identity. Therefore, the rule of thumb is, if the information stored in the site is sensitive, then don't place a persistent cookie.

When using Forms authentication, ASP.NET will redirect the request to the login page defined in the `web.config` file. This will be a problem for Web Services, since the client will be requesting a SOAP response from the Web Service. To fix this problem we have to specify the login page (`SayHello.asmx`) to be the same as the Web Service page:

```
<configuration>
  <system.web>
    <authentication mode="Forms">
      <forms name=".WebSvcDemo" loginUrl="SayHello.asmx"
```

```
                protection="All" timeout="60" path="/" />
        </authentication>
      </system.web>
    </configuration>
```

All we have done here is make the login page the same as the Web Services page (SayHello.asmx), so that this will not redirect the unauthorized user to a different login page. The following table describes the possible values for the forms tag:

Tag Attribute	Description
name	Name of the authentication cookie. If you are hosting more than one ASP.NET application from your web server, make sure you give different names to each of the authentication cookies that you're using.
loginurl	The login page where unauthenticated users should be redirected. This loginurl can be on the same server, or a different one. If the loginurl is on a different server then both the servers should use the same decryptionKey parameter in the machineKey tag.
protection	This is used to protect the authentication cookie. The protection tag has four possible values (All, Encryption, Validation, None). When you set the value to All, both the validation (the cookie will be validated against the original content placed in the cookie before transmitting to the client) and encryption (cookie will be encrypted using the Triple-DES or 3DES algorithm, before transmitting to the client, and the cookie will be decrypted after receiving from the client) will be performed against the authentication cookie to protect it from prying eyes. For validation and decryption, the values specified in the validationKey and decryptionKey parameters of the machineKey tag will be used. The value All is the default, and suggested, value for this parameter. When you set the value as None, the cookie will be transferred between the client and the server as plain text and you can turn off encryption and validation with the machineKey tag. When you set the value as Encryption, the cookie will be decrypted as per the value specified in the decryptionKey of the machineKey tag and the content of the cookie will not be validated. When you set the value as Validation, the cookie will be validated when received from the client as per the value specified in the validationKey of the machineKey tag, and the content of the cookie will not be encrypted and decrypted. It is always a good idea to use 'All' as the value for the protection tag, since it uses all the goodies available to protect the authentication cookie.
timeout	The timeout value for the cookie to expire since the last request was made. The default value is 30 minutes.

The next problem is when the client submits the credentials: we don't want to transfer the client back to a different page, and we want to set the authentication cookie at the same time. We're going to solve the problem by using the `SetAuthCookie` method of the `FormsAuthentication` class. The `SetAuthCookie` method takes two parameters: the first one is the username and the second is a Boolean value to place a persistent or non-persistent cookie. Let's create a Web Service, again called `SayHello.asmx`, but this time in the `FormsAuthServer` folder, to use Forms authentication.

```
<%@ WebService Language="VB" Class="Hello" %>
Imports System.Web.Services
Imports System.Web.Security

Public Class Hello
  Inherits WebService
  Private CN_NeedToLogin As String = "WS1001"

  <WebMethod()> _
  Public Function SayHello() As String
    If Context.User.Identity.IsAuthenticated = True Then
      Return "Hello " & Context.User.Identity.Name & ". You are consuming '" _
             & Context.User.Identity.AuthenticationType & "' authentication."
    Else
      Return CN_NeedToLogin
    End If
  End Function 'SayHello

  <WebMethod()> _
  Public Function Login(sUsername As String, sPwd As String) As Boolean
    If sUsername = "SrinivasaSivakumar" And sPwd = "MyPass" Then
      FormsAuthentication.SetAuthCookie(sUsername, True)
      Return True
    Else
      Return False
    End If
  End Function


  <WebMethod()> _
  Public Function Logout() As String
      If Context.User.Identity.IsAuthenticated = True Then
         FormsAuthentication.SignOut()
         Return "OK"
      Else
         Return "You've not logged in."
      End If
   End Function
End Class
```

We've created a Web Service with three web methods to log in, say hello, and log out of the Web Service. In the login method, we verify the credentials supplied with `SrinivasaSivakumar` and `MyPass`, and if they match then we set the authentication cookie. If they don't match then we just send `false` back. The authentication cookie that we're setting is persistent, and if the client didn't call the `Logout` method, then the cookie would stay on the client's hard drive and the client would be re-authenticated when he called the `SayHello` method.

If the user directly calls the `SayHello` method, then we check to see if the user has already logged in, and if not we return the constant `CN_NeedToLogin` back to the client. Here is the "Login" view.

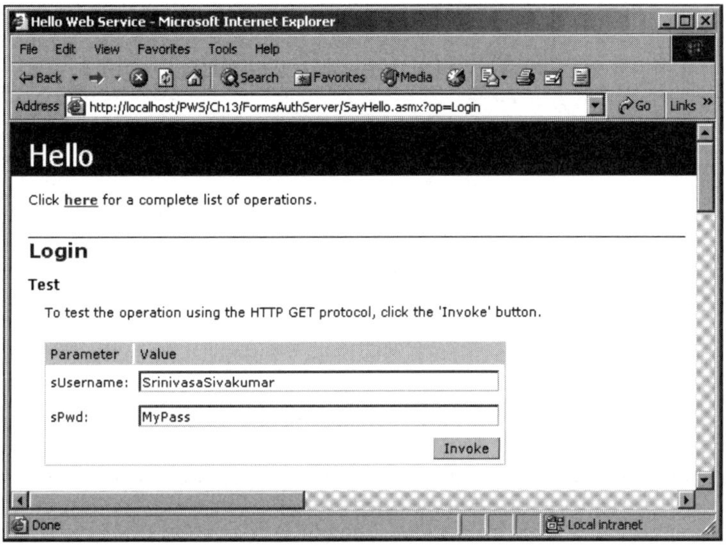

Here is the result of our login:

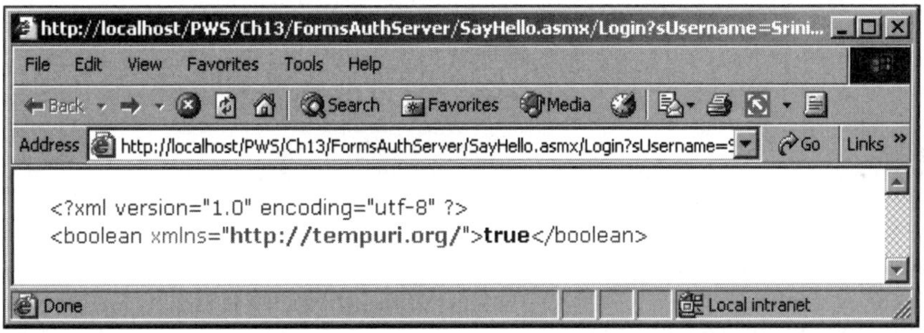

Here is the "`SayHello`" method call view:

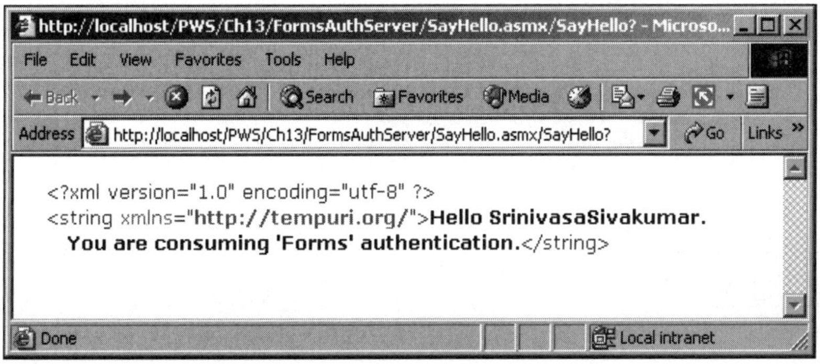

In this example, we have hard-coded the username and the password. We can also store the credentials in the web.config file and authenticate the users against it. You can find the code for this example in the FormsAuthServer1 folder in the code download:

```
<configuration>
  <system.web>
    <authentication mode="Forms">
      <forms name=".WebSvcDemo" loginUrl="SayHello_CS.asmx"
             protection="All" timeout="60" path="/">
        <credentials passwordFormat="Clear">
          <user name="SrinivasaSivakumar" password="MyPass" />
        </credentials>
      </forms>
    </authentication>
    <authorization>
      <deny users="?" />
    </authorization>
  </system.web>
</configuration>
```

Here we have added a username and a password to the web.config file using the credentials tag. We can modify the Login method a little bit to check against the web.config file to authenticate. For that, we're going to use the Authenticate method of the FormsAuthentication class.

```
<WebMethod()> _
Public Function Login(sUsername As String, sPwd As String) As Boolean
  If FormsAuthentication.Authenticate(sUsername, sPwd) Then
    FormsAuthentication.SetAuthCookie(sUsername, True)
    Return True
  Else
    Return False
  End If
End Function
```

In this example, we have stored the passwords in the web.config file as clear text. We can also store the passwords in one-way hash formats, SHA1 and MD5, as supported by the credentials tag. You can find the code for this example in the FormsAuthServer2 folder of the code download:

```
<configuration>
  <system.web>
    <authentication mode="Forms">
      <forms name=".WebSvcDemo" loginUrl="SayHello_CS.asmx"
             protection="All" timeout="60" path="/">
        <credentials passwordFormat="SHA1">
          <user name="SrinivasaSivakumar"
                password="E9363073B4EC360E68C7642823CAFC559402E76C"
          />
        </credentials>
      </forms>
    </authentication>
    <authorization>
      <deny users="?" />
    </authorization>
  </system.web>
</configuration>
```

We have changed the `passwordFormat` attribute of the `credentials` tag to "`SHA1`" and we have stored the hashed password in the `password` attribute of the `user` tag. We can use the `HashPasswordForStoringInConfigFile` method of the `FormsAuthentication` class to generate the hashed password to store in the `web.config` file.

For high-performance, highly scalable web sites, we need a database or an Active Directory to authenticate the users against. To see a sample of this, we're going to create a SQL Server 2000 database with the name `WebServicesAuthDB` and we're going to add a single table called `Tbl_MA_Users`. This table will have four columns `Username`, `Pwd`, `Firstname`, and `Lastname`, and we've inserted a single record with the following values. For your convenience, there is a SQL script, `WebServicesAuthDB.sql`, which will create the database, and in the `FormsAuthServer3` folder of the code download you can find the rest of the code for this example:

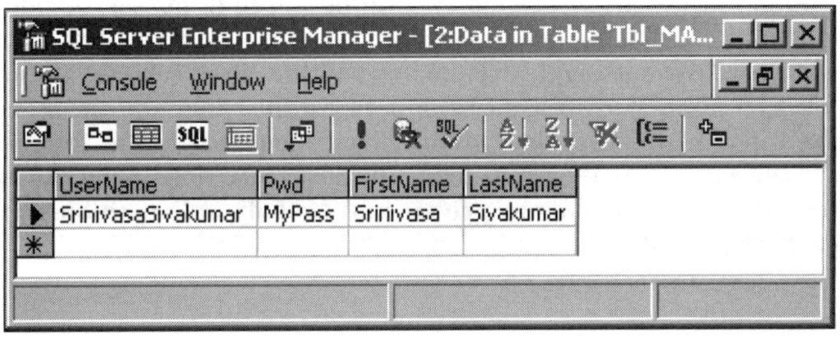

We are simply going to change the login method to authenticate the user from the database rather than hard-coding the username and password as we have done previously:

```
<WebMethod()> _
Public Function Login(sUsername As String, sPwd As String) As Boolean
  Dim dbConn As New SqlConnection("server=localhost;uid=sa;pwd=;" _
                              & "database=WebServicesAuthDB;")
  'Open the connection
  dbConn.Open()

  'Create a SQL Command object
  Dim SQLCmd As New SqlCommand("SELECT Pwd FROM Tbl_MA_Users WHERE UserName " _
                           & "= '" & sUsername & "'", dbConn)

  'Create a datareader object
  Dim SQLDr As SqlDataReader=SQLCmd.ExecuteReader(CommandBehavior.CloseConnection)

  'Get the first row and check the password.
  If SQLDr.Read() Then
     If SQLDr("Pwd").ToString() = sPwd Then
      FormsAuthentication.SetAuthCookie(sUsername, True)
      Return True
    Else
      Return False
    End If
  Else
    Return False
  End If
  //Close the DataReader
  SQLDr.Close
End Function
```

Note that this `Login` WebMethod is still an HTTP call and potentially anyone can read the username and password over the wire. We can easily fix this problem using SSL, as we'll see next.

Secured Socket Layer (SSL)

The Secure Socket Layer 3.0 and Transport Layer Security (TLS) 1.0 protocols (commonly referred to as SSL) are the de facto standard for secure communication over the Web. Using SSL, data that's passed between server and browser is encrypted using Public Key Infrastructure (PKI) techniques.

Public Key Infrastructure encryption/decryption is based on pairs of keys – that is, a private key and public keys. The private key will be stored in the server side (in the SSL scenario) and the public key will be available at the client side. The server sends data in the encrypted form using its private key and the client receives the data and decrypts it using its public key. If someone inbetween the client and the server gets the data, he or she will not be able to decrypt it without the public key of the encrypted private key. In the same way, the client sends the encrypted data using the public key and the server will decrypt it using its private key. Nobody in the middle can decrypt the data without the private key.

In that way, no one intercepting TCP/IP packets over the Internet can interpret the transmitted content. To use SSL in a commercial web site we must first obtain a SSL certificate from a Certification Authority (CA) such as **VeriSign** or **Thawte**.

Both VeriSign and Thawte issue trial SSL certificates for test purposes. Try the following links to get a test certificate:

https://www.verisign.com/products/site/index.html

http://www.thawte.com/getinfo/products/server/contents.html

Getting a SSL certificate is a two-phase process. First, we have to generate a Certificate Signing Request (CSR) from IIS. When we create a CSR using IIS, it will create a certificate-signing request in a file, and a private key. The generated CSR should be sent to the Certification Authority to get an SSL certificate. For more information about implementing SSL read the following articles:

Generating a CSR for Your Web Server Certificate:

http://www.verisign.com/support/csr/microsoft/v04.html (For IIS4)

http://www.verisign.com/support/csr/microsoft/v05.html (For IIS5)

Installing a SSL Certificate on IIS:

http://www.verisign.com/support/install/microsoft/v40.html#global (For IIS4)

http://www.verisign.com/support/tlc/class3_install_docs/microsoft/iis5g.html (For IIS5)

In the Secure Socket Layer (SSL) 3.0 and Transport Layer Security (TLS) 1.0 protocols, public key certificates and embedded trust points in browsers are the key cornerstones. Client/server applications use the TLS "handshake" protocol to authenticate each other and to negotiate an encryption algorithm and cryptographic keys before an application starts transmitting data. The handshake protocol uses public key cryptography, such as RSA or DSS, to authenticate and transmit data. Once a channel is authenticated, TLS uses symmetric cryptography, such as DES or RC4, to encrypt the application data for transmission over the private or public network. Message transmission includes a message integrity check, using a keyed message authentication code (MAC), computed by applying a secure hash function (such as SHA or MD5).

When a user connects to a web site using SSL, they download the server SSL certificate obtained from a CA. The server certificate on the server holds an attribute about the issuing authority. The issuing authority should match with one of the root certificates already installed on the user's computer by IE or Navigator. When you install IE or Navigator, a number of trusted root certificates will be installed into your computer as part of the installation. When the server certificate is downloaded to the client's computer, it'll be matched against a root certificate already present in the client's computer. If the server certificate is from a valid CA and it is trustworthy, then secure communication will begin between the server and the client. If the server certificate is not trustworthy then the browser will prompt a message box and inform the user about the untrustworthiness of the server certificate. From the message, the user may wish to continue browsing the site or leave the site.

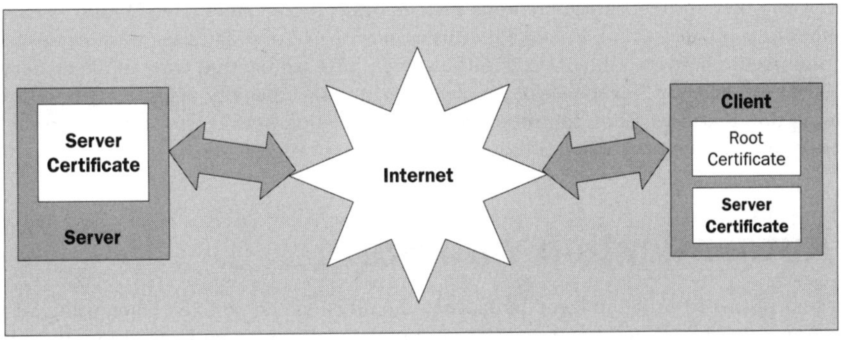

Pros of SSL

- **Server Identification** – when a user wants to use a highly sensitive Web Service that deals with his or her personal data such as medical records or 401K retirement benefit information, the user may or may not trust the online site unless the Web Service has been verified and certified by an independent third-party security company. This should give the customer the confidence they need to use the Web Service.

- **Data Integrity** – data integrity is assured when transmitting between client and the server using SSL.

- **Confidentiality** – when data is transmitted over an unprotected network, SSL gives the data privacy by assuring the transmitted data can only be read by the specific client.

Cons of SSL

- **Performance** – performance will be the one consideration that we have to be aware of when we're planning an SSL implementation. When SSL is used, the whole channel between the client and the server is secured and the data is transmitted in the encrypted format. Therefore the client and server have to process an encrypt and a decrypt operation for each web request and this will affect performance.
- **Need to open SSL port** – by default SSL works on port number 443, and if the user is behind a firewall, then port 443 needs to be opened for the HTTPS traffic.
- **HTTP to HTTPS** – SSL uses the HTTPS protocol and if the user is trying to access the secured resource using HTTP instead of HTTPS, then the user will receive the "HTTP 403.4 – Forbidden: SSL required" error message. We can fix this by writing a custom ASP.NET file that transfers the user from HTTP to HTTPS and install it as the replacement on the IIS server for the 403.4 error, or we can add the "customErrors" tag in the `web.config` file. However, these options are very cumbersome.
- **Extra Cost** – we need to spend some extra money to buy the SSL certificates and to renew the certificates when they expire.

Why and When

SSL is an excellent way to protect communication between the server and the client. SSL can be combined with other authentication methods such as basic, digest, Integrated Windows authentication, Forms authentication, and so on, to make it more secure. 100% of today's secure sites use SSL to protect their communication between the client and the server. SSL can be used with any Web Service that needs bulletproof security. Nevertheless, we pay a performance penalty when using SSL. Since SSL uses strong encryption and decryption to protect the communication between the server and the client, this is slow. So, make sure you switch on SSL where it is really needed.

Basic Authentication with SSL

The clear text password problem faced by basic authentication can be fixed when using basic authentication with SSL. When SSL is used in conjunction with basic authentication, the whole channel is secured and no one can read the username and password as it is passed between the client and the server. Once you've received an SSL certificate from a valid CA such as VeriSign or Thawte, and installed the certificate, then setting up basic authentication for a web site or virtual directory is very simple, as we'll now see.

Go to the IIS MMC and expand the tree to reach the desired virtual directory or web site. In our example, we'll set up SSL for the previous basic authentication virtual directory, `BasicAuthServer`. Right-click on the virtual directory or web site, select the Properties option and go to the Directory Security tab. In the Secure Communications frame, you'll see two enabled command buttons, "View Certificate..." and "Edit..."

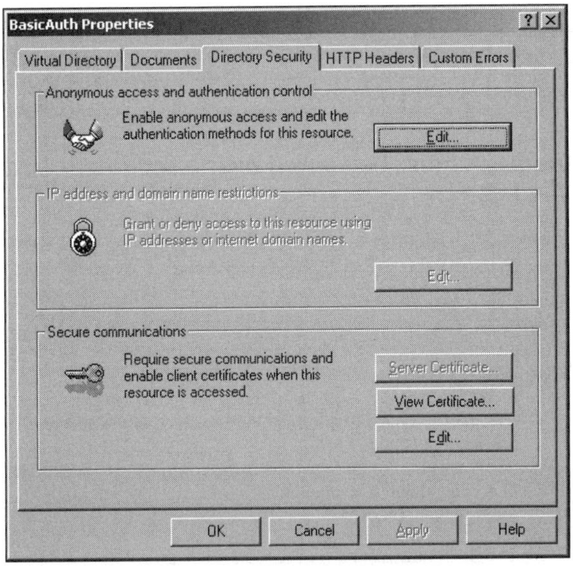

Click the "Edit..." button. You'll see the "Secure Communications" dialog box. Check the "Require secure channel (SSL)" checkbox.

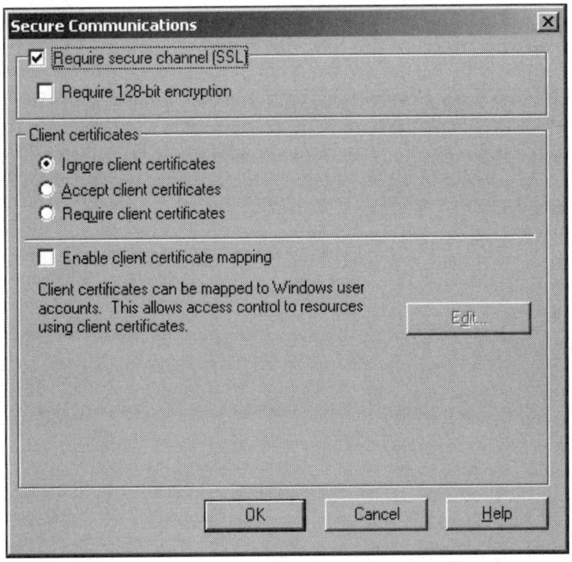

If the SSL certificate you have received from the CA is a 128-bit certificate then you can check the "Require 128-bit encryption" checkbox. Click the OK button on the open dialog boxes to finish setting up SSL. Now all our client applications will require the use of SSL (HTTPS is a secured HTTP protocol and it'll be used when SSL is required by the server) to access the `BasicAuth` virtual directory.

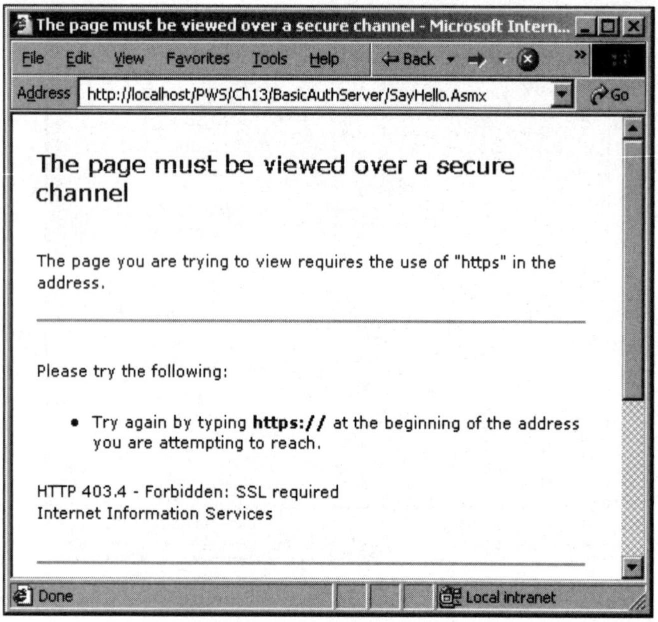

If you've installed a test certificate from VeriSign or Thawte and you try to access the basic authentication examples, substituting https for http in the path, you'll see a warning dialog box from the browser about the untrustworthiness of the SSL certificate:

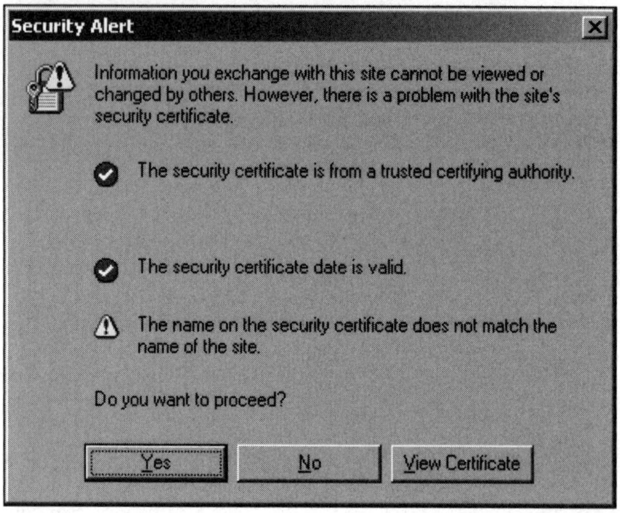

Click Yes to continue using the secure channel or View Certificate, as shown in the screenshot. We're seeing this message because the SSL certificate was generated with a different site name (sruthi) and we're accessing the SSL certificate using localhost.

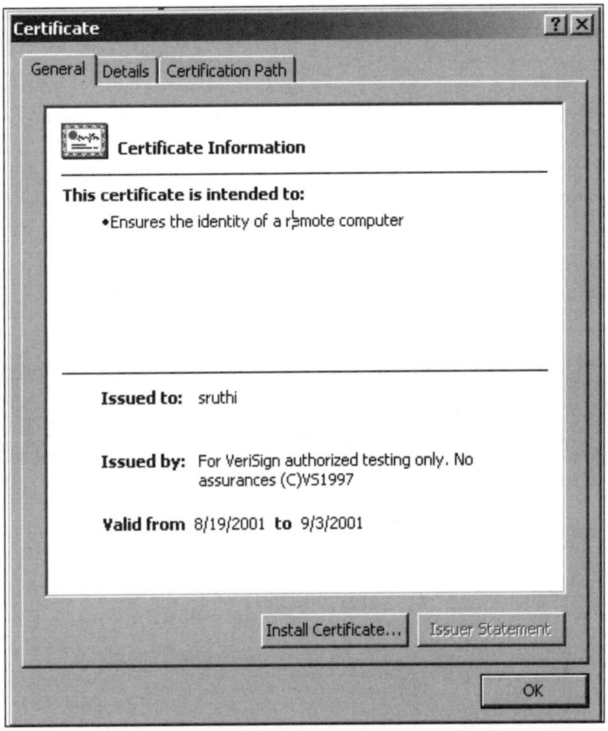

Since we're using a secured channel, we have to recompile the proxy DLL to use HTTPS instead of HTTP. For this we have to change the batch file that we used to build the proxy DLL:

```
WSDL /l:VB /n:SayHelloNS /out:SayHello.VB
https://localhost/PWS/Ch13/basicauthserver/SayHello.asmx?WSDL

VBC /r:system.dll  /r:System.Web.dll /r:System.Xml.dll /r:System.Web.Services.dll
/t:library /out:SayHello.dll SayHello.VB
```

We have simply changed the WSDL file reference to build a new proxy class source. This is the only change that we need to make to use the SSL version of the Web Service.

Remember to remove the check next to basic authentication and check the anonymous box in IIS before creating the new proxy DLL, and then to reapply basic authentication after building the proxy DLL.

Client Certificates Authentication

Server Certificates are to identify the trustworthiness of the server, and Client Certificates to identify a client to the server. A CA issues both client and server certificates after verifying their identity. When the client is requesting a web resource, it can also send Client Certificates along with the request. The server can then determine who the client is and authorize or deny them.

You can purchase a Client Certificate from VeriSign or Thawte. Thawte issues Client Certificates free of charge with your e-mail address and without your name in the subject line (the subject line will include the name as "Thawte Freemail Member" instead of your name, as shown below). After confirming your identity using a notary in your area, your name will be shown in the client certificate. On the other hand, VeriSign gives a 60-day evaluation Client Certificate for test purposes with your name on it.

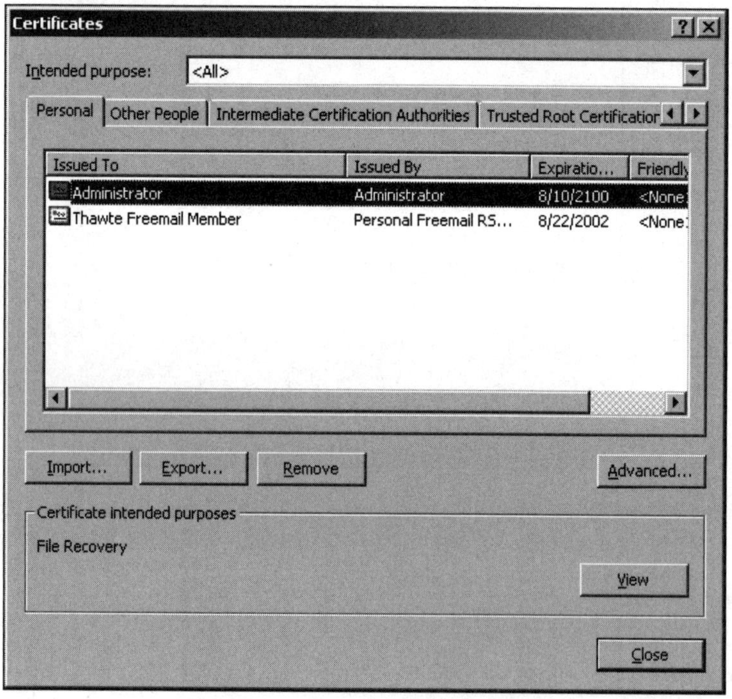

You can obtain Client Certificates at the following sites:

http://www.verisign.com/client/enrollment/index.html

http://www.thawte.com/getinfo/products/personal/contents.html

Client Certificates are usually installed on web clients such as browsers and e-mail clients. You can view all the Client Certificates installed in IE if you select Tools | Internet Options... and in the new dialog box go to the Content tab:

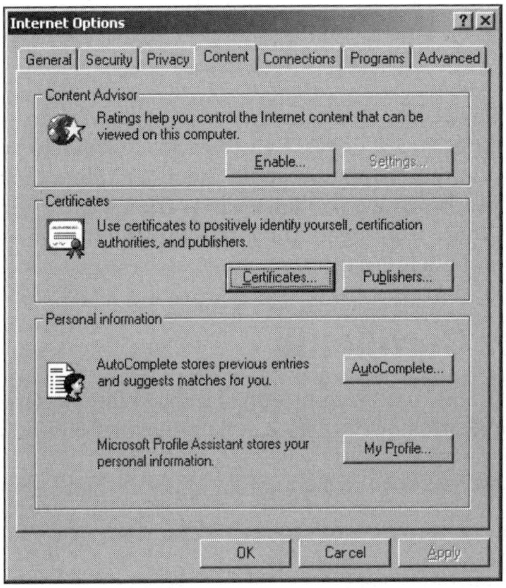

Click the Certificates... button. As you can see, the example browser has two Client Certificates installed in IE6:

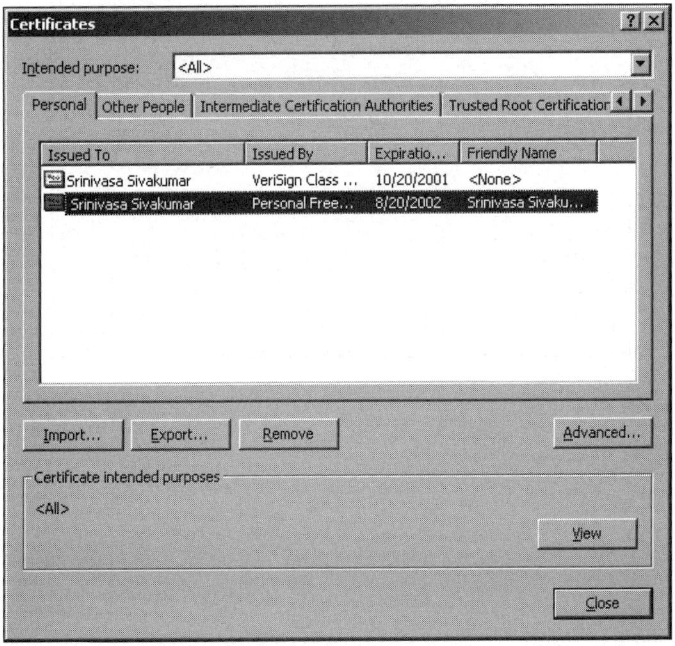

Why and When

Client Certificates are a step forward in securing applications. The Client Certificates are always used with SSL and we can always trust Client Certificates issued by a valid CA, since the CA verifies the identity of the user before issuing it. Client Certificates add one more layer to the security of our applications.

Sometimes we can't trust the user with just the username and password pair. If we really want to identify the user and trust him, then Client Certificates are the way to go. Each Client Certificate has a subject line that contains more information about them, including their name, e-mail address, and so on. We can extract the user's name or e-mail address from the certificate and authenticate him based on that. In this case, there is no need to log into the application with a username and password. All we need to have is a valid client certificate.

Configuring Client Certificate

Client Certificate configuration is part of SSL configuration. When we are configuring SSL, we select either the Accept client certificates or Require client certificates option button.

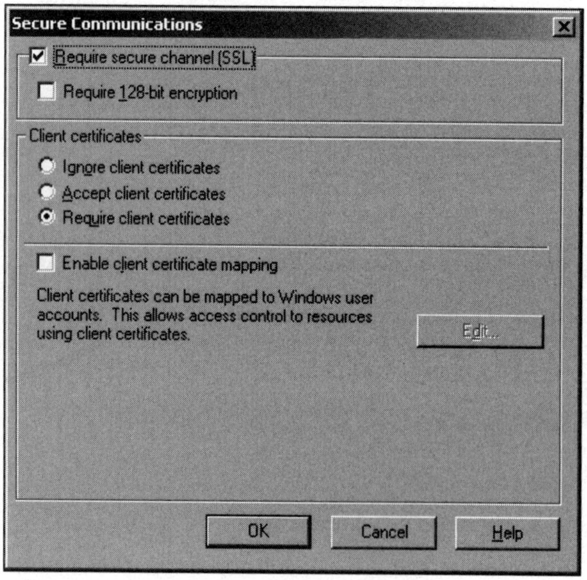

If we select Accept client certificates, the client certificates are not mandatory, and if there is a client certificate available at the client side it'll be transmitted to the server. When you select the Require client certificates option, the client certificate is necessary when a web request is issued to the server. If there is no client certificate included as part of the request, then IIS will deny access to the client and will throw a "HTTP 403.7 – Forbidden" error.

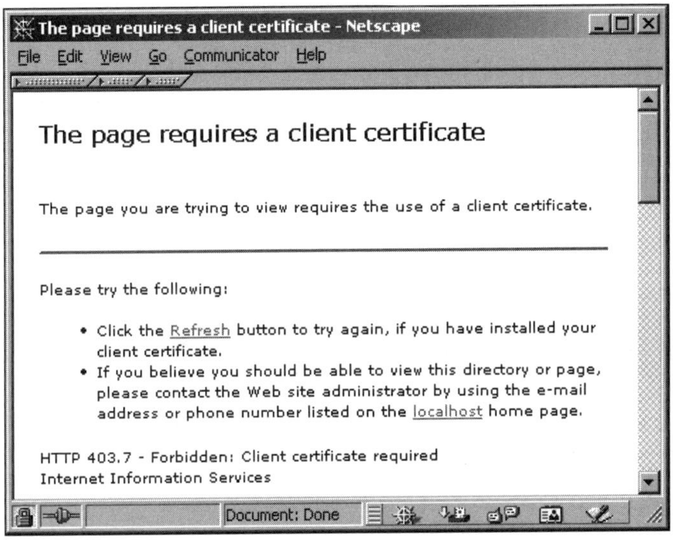

Steps to Follow in Client Certificate Authentication

- Require Client Certificate – when a web request is sent from the client to the server, the server will check if the client is sending a client certificate. If the client certificate is not a part of the web request then access to the web resource will be declined.
- Perform public key and digital signature match – if the web request includes a client certificate then the server will check if the public key found in the client certificate matches the digital signature.
- Is it valid today? – if the user has a client certificate then the server will check the client certificate's valid from and to dates with the server's date to make sure the client certificate is valid today.
- From a valid CA – the server will check if the client certificate is from a valid issuer such as VeriSign or Thawte.
- Validate the digital signature – finally the server will validate the digital signature with the public key of the CA.

If all the above steps were successful then the request will be forwarded to the `WebMethod` in the `.asmx` file.

How To Read the Content of a Client Certificate

The `ClientCertificate` property of the `Request` object can be used to obtain information about the submitted client certificate. Let's see a simple example. We're going to expose a Web Service, `GetClientCertificateInfo.asmx` in the `ClientCertificate` folder of the code download, that will return information about the submitted client certificate.

```
<%@ WebService Language="VB" Class="GetClientCertificateInfo " %>

Imports System
Imports System.Web.Services
Imports System.Web.Security

Public Class ClientCertificateInfo
  Public Issuer As String
  Public IsValid As Boolean
  Public KeySize As Integer
  Public Subject As String
  Public SerialNumber As String
  Public Cookie As String
  Public SecretKeySize As Integer
  Public ValidFrom As DateTime
  Public ValidUntil As DateTime
End Class

Public Class GetClientCertificateInfo
  Inherits WebService

  <WebMethod()> _
  Public Function GetInfo() As ClientCertificateInfo
    Dim objCrti As New ClientCertificateInfo()

    objCrti.Issuer = Context.Request.ClientCertificate.Issuer
    objCrti.IsValid = Context.Request.ClientCertificate.IsValid
    objCrti.KeySize = Context.Request.ClientCertificate.KeySize
    objCrti.Subject = Context.Request.ClientCertificate.Subject
    objCrti.SerialNumber = Context.Request.ClientCertificate.SerialNumber
    objCrti.Cookie = Context.Request.ClientCertificate.Cookie
    objCrti.SecretKeySize = Context.Request.ClientCertificate.SecretKeySize
    objCrti.ValidFrom = Context.Request.ClientCertificate.ValidFrom
    objCrti.ValidUntil = Context.Request.ClientCertificate.ValidUntil

    Return objCrti
  End Function
End Class
```

We have created a Web Service with the class name `GetClientCertificateInfo` and we have exposed a `WebMethod` with the name `GetInfo`. The `GetInfo` `WebMethod` returns an object type of `ClientCertificateInfo`. The `WebMethod` simply reads the client certificate information from the `Request` object and assigns it to the `objCrti` object.

Since the client certificate is already stored in IE when we access the Web Service, IE will automatically send the client certificate to the Web Service and the information about the certificate will be read by the Web Service. Here is how the output looks:

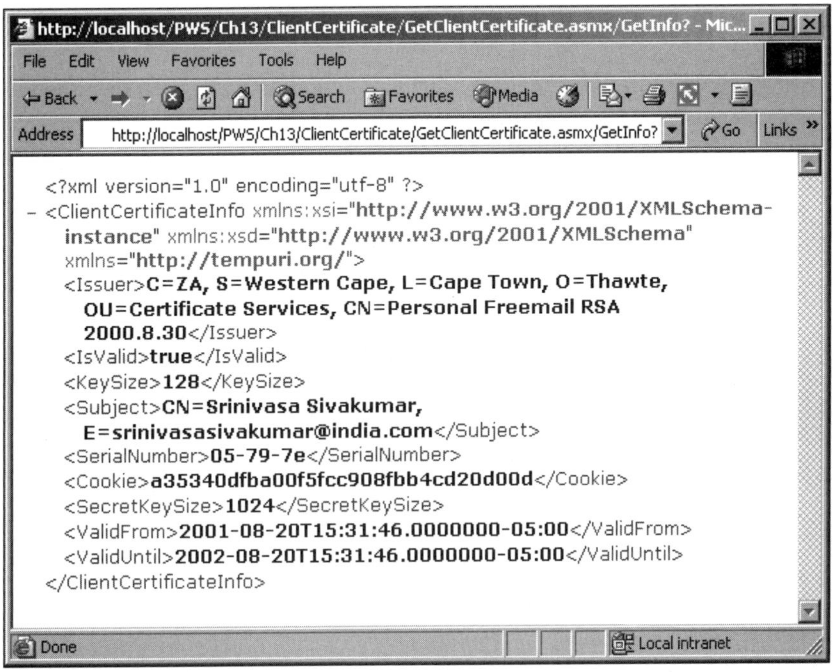

How Do We Authenticate a User?

The subject property of the client certificate will provide information about the user. For example, the example client certificate has a subject of "CN=Srinivasa Sivakumar, E=srinivasasivakumar@india.com". We can extract the username and the e-mail address from the subject and authenticate the user against a database or Active Directory or any other user store. Here is a simple example:

```
<%@ WebService Language="VB" Class="Hello" %>

Imports System
Imports System.Web.Services
Imports System.Web.Security

Public Class Hello
  Inherits WebService

  Private CN_InvalidUserName As String = "WS1010"

  <WebMethod()> _
```

```
Public Function SayHello() As String
  Dim strUserName As String = Context.Request.ClientCertificate.Subject

  '*****************************************************************
  '* 1. Extract the name from the client certificate
  '*****************************************************************
  Try
    '* Make sure there are no commas in the Subject line. If
    '* there is a comma then get the index of it
    Dim i As Integer = strUserName.Indexof(",")

    If i > 0 Then
    '* The user name excluding the CN= attribute. You'll
    '* get something like 'Srinivasa Sivakumar' as the output
      strUserName = strUserName.Substring(strUserName.Indexof("CN=") + 3, i - 3)
    Else
    'The user name found
      strUserName = strUserName.Substring(strUserName.Indexof("CN="))
    End If

    'Authenticate the user
    If CheckTheUser(strUserName) := True Then
      Return "Hello " And strUserName And "!!!"
    Else
      Return CN_InvalidUserName
    End If
  Catch Ex As Exception
    Return Ex.ToString() '
  End Try
End Function


Private Function CheckTheUser(strSubject As String) As Boolean
  'Can also be checked against a DB
  If strSubject = "Srinivasa Sivakumar" Then
    Return True
  Else
    Return False
  End If
End Function
End Class
```

In the `WebMethod` we have extracted the username from the subject line of the client certificate and we've passed the username to the `CheckTheUser` method. Then we have hard-coded the username check and if the user is "Srinivasa Sivakumar" then we say hello to him. Otherwise we return the error code "`WS1010`", that is `CN_InvalidUserName` (Username not found).

Let's test the code to make sure it works fine:

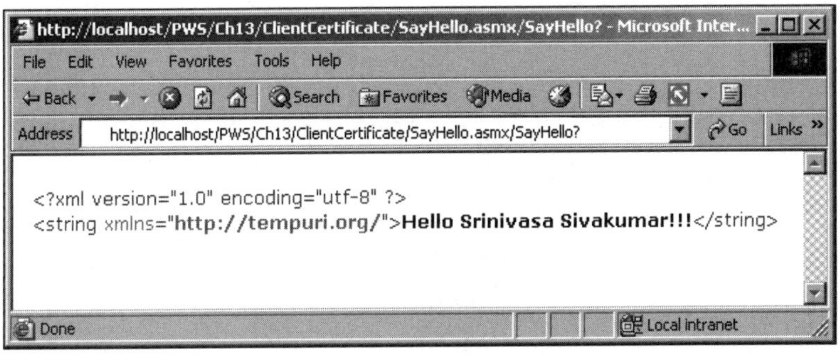

Let's now build a proxy DLL for the Web Service with the `SayHello_CS_Build.bat` batch file, and access the Web Service using SOAP.

```
WSDL /l:VB /n:SayHelloNS /out:SayHello.VB
http://localhost/PWS/Ch13/ClientCertificate/SayHello.asmx?WSDL

VBC /r:system.dll /r:System.Web.dll /r:System.Xml.dll↵
/r:System.Web.Services.dll /t:library /out:SayHello.dll SayHello.VB
```

Now place the `SayHello.DLL` file in the `bin` folder.

Exposing the Client Certificate To the Proxy

If we're using the Client Certificates from IE to login to the application or Web Service, IE will take care of sending the Client Certificates and all the details about this. Since we're accessing the Web Service using a proxy DLL, there is no way our proxy DLL will know where the Client Certificates are. Therefore, we have to export the Client Certificates into a file and place it somewhere the proxy DLL can use it.

Let's create an ASP.NET web client for the Web Service. Before that, we have to expose the client certificate to the proxy DLL so it can use the client certificate when it tries to access the Web Service. To expose the client certificate to the proxy, go to the certificate dialog box in IE as we did before through the Internet Options menu. Select a client certificate that you want to export and click the Export... button. You'll see the Certificate Export Wizard and click Next on the wizard screen.

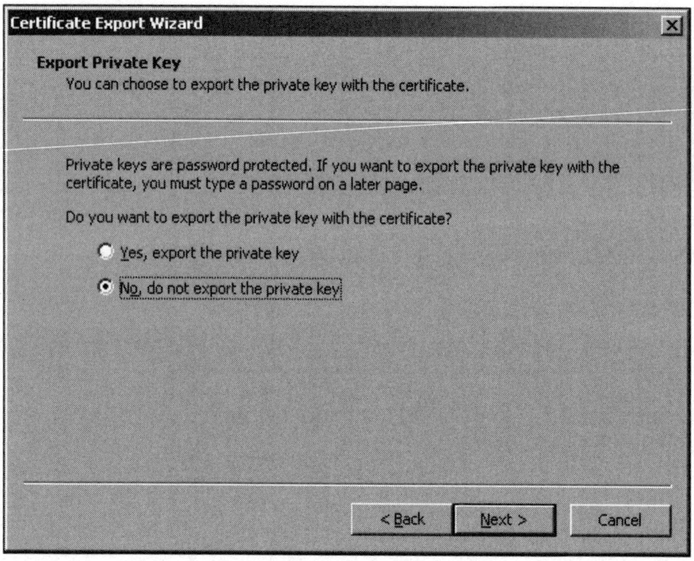

In the next wizard screen, select the No, do not export the private key option and click Next.

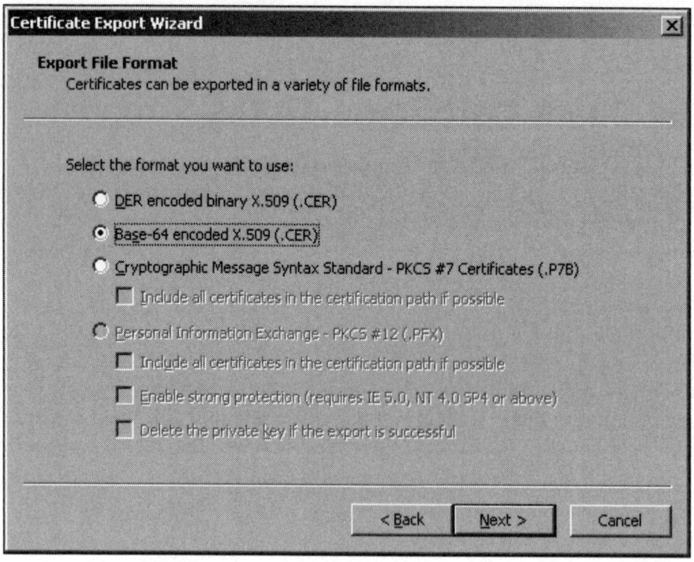

Select the Base-64 encoded X.509 (.CER) option and click Next. You'll be prompted to enter a file name. Give a file name like `ClientCerti.cer` or `MyCertificate.cer` and click Next. You'll see a summary screen:

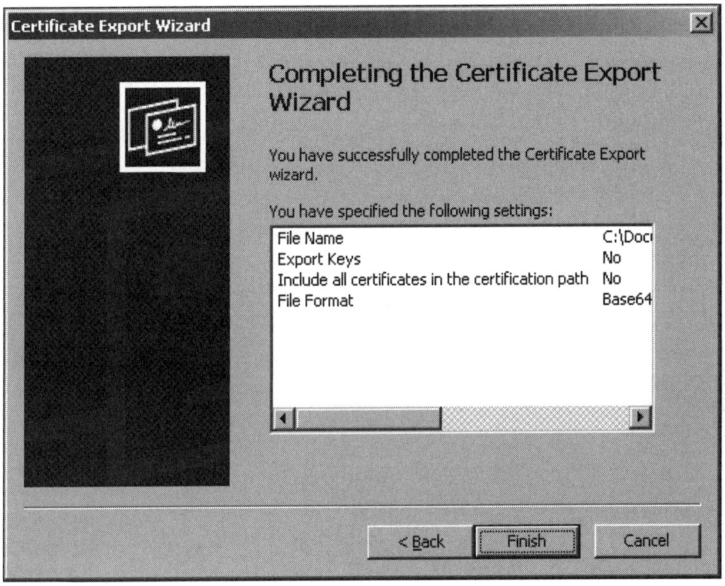

Click the Finish button. The client certificate will be exported to a file. Let's place the exported certificate file (.CER) in the ASP.NET client's folder.

Let's create an ASP.NET client to access the Web Service using the client certificate. For your convenience, this file is included in the code download. It is `SayHelloClient.aspx` in the `ClientCertificate` folder.

```
<%@ Import Namespace="System.Security.Cryptography.X509Certificates" %>
<%@ Import Namespace="SayHelloNS" %>
<html>
<head>
<title>Client Certificate Authentication Web Client</title>
<style type="text/css">
    body {font-face:verdana; font-size:10pt; font-weight:normal}
</style>
</head>
<script language="VB" runat="server">

Public Sub Page_Load(sender As Object, E As EventArgs)
  Try
    'An object type of the Web Service
    Dim objWebSvc As New SayHelloNS.Hello()

    'Read the client certificate from the file
    'into the object variable of the type X509Certificate
```

```
    Dim objClientCerti As X509Certificate = _
        X509Certificate.CreateFromCertFile(Server.MapPath("ClientCerti.cer"))


    'Add the client certificate to the
    'Web Service object
    objWebSvc.ClientCertificates.Add(objClientCerti)

    'Call the SayHello Method
    lblResult.Text = objWebSvc.SayHello()
  Catch Ex As Exception
    lblResult.Text = Ex.ToString()
  End Try
End Sub
</script>
<body>
<h3>Client Certificate Authentication - Web Service Client</h3>
<form runat="server">
<b>Result:</b><br /> <asp:Label id="lblResult" runat="server"/>
</form>
</body>
</html>
```

Client Certificate Authentication Using Windows Account Mapping

Client certificates can be mapped to a Windows user account. This process makes the authentication process easy. The mapping can be one-to-one or many-to-one. A one-to-one mapping maps a single client certificate to a single Windows user account, and a many-to-one mapping maps multiple client certificates to a single Windows user account using a criterion. The one-to-one mapping is best if a single user is going to use the Web Service. If multiple users from a corporation are going to use the Web Service, then the many-to-one mapping is useful and we can assign the same rights to all the users in the corporation.

The drawback to the many-to-one mapping is that we can't personalize the Web Service on an individual basis.

The client certificate with Windows user account mapping solves the authentication problem, since the client certificate will be automatically read by IIS and logs the user in with a Windows identity. This is a good option if you are using any of the Windows authentication methods with SSL and client certificates, and you don't want to take care of the details of authenticating the user with client certificates.

We can use the IIS MMC to do the configuration. Start the IIS MMC, find the virtual directory where you want to use client certificates, and go to the client certificate configuration dialog box as before:

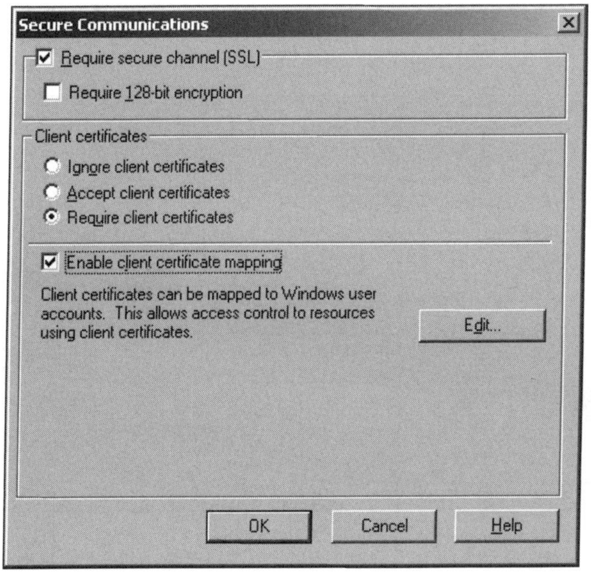

Click the Enable client certificate mapping checkbox and click on the Edit... button.

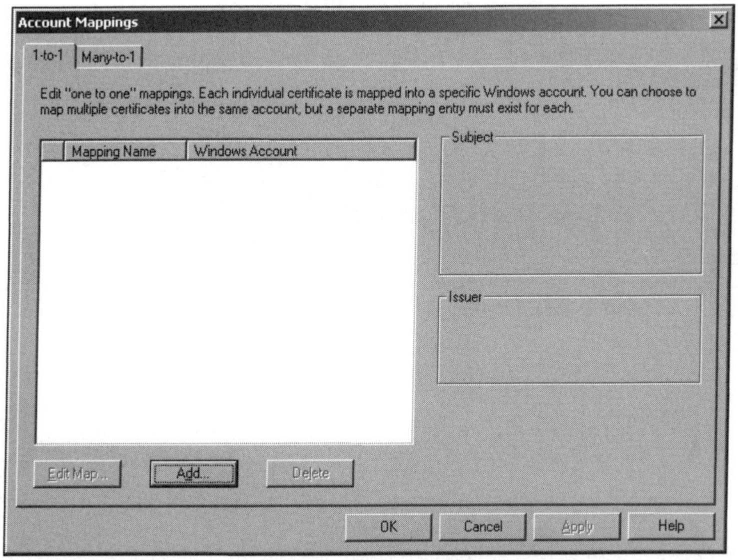

Click the Add button, select the exported client certificate file and click the OK button.

The client certificate should be exported by selecting the Base-64 encoded X.509 (.CER) file format.

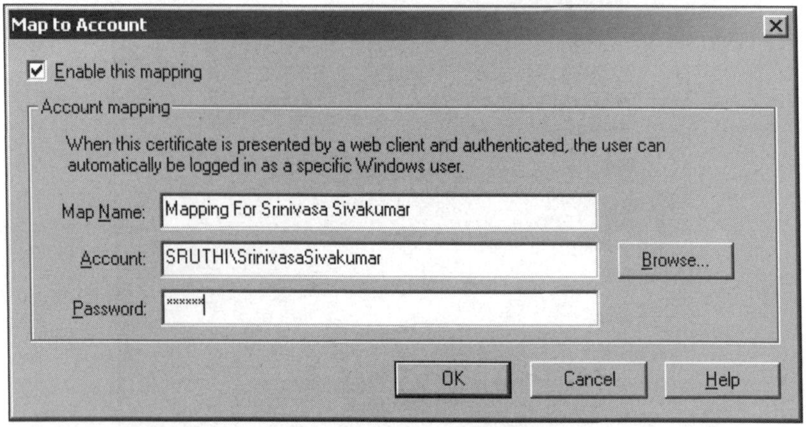

In the new dialog box, give a descriptive name for the mapping, select the Windows user account, type a password into the dialog and click the OK button. You can see the mapping on the screen now. On the right side of the screen, you can see the issuing authority and the subject name in the client certificate.

The descriptive name you type should be unique for each entry.

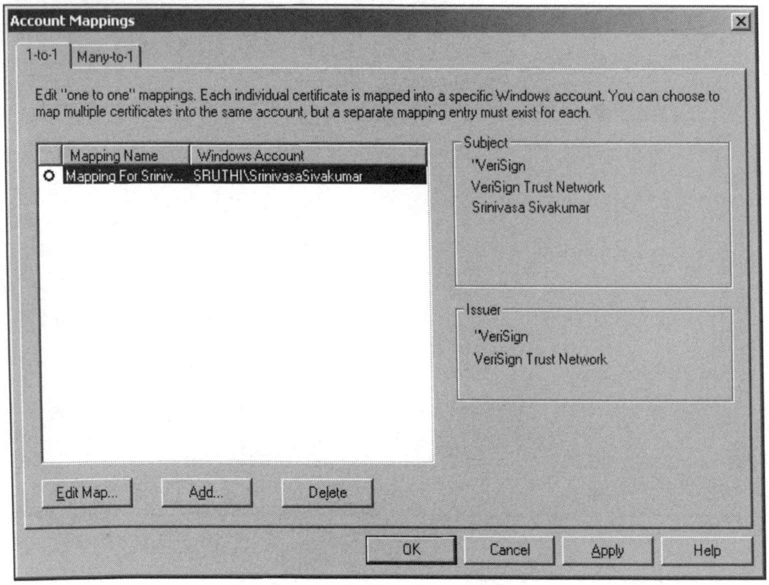

Click the OK button to finish mapping the client certificate to a Windows user account. Let's create a simple Web Service to say hello to the logged-in user. You can find this file, `SayHello.asmx`, in the `ClientCertificate-WindowsAuth` folder of the code download.

```
<%@ WebService Language="VB" Class="Hello" %>

Imports System.Web.Services
Imports System.Web.Security

Public Class Hello
  Inherits WebService

 Private CN_NeedToLogin As String = "WS1001"

  <WebMethod()> _
  Public Function SayHello() As String
    If Context.User.Identity.IsAuthenticated = True Then
      Return "Hello " & Context.User.Identity.Name & ". You are consuming '" _
           & Context.User.Identity.AuthenticationType & "' authentication."
    Else
      Return CN_NeedToLogin
    End If
   End Function
End Class
```

Here is how the output looks:

Many-To-One Mapping

Many to one mappings can be used when the Web Services users are from a primary entity and all of them have a common identity on their Client Certificate. Let's say all the users from "Wrox Press" have client certificates with the company name on it and if they want to access a 401K Web Service, then it's easy for the Web Services admin to map all the "Wrox Press" employees to a single Windows user account and assign privileges to it including ACL. This makes the admin person's life easier.

Many to one mapping can be based on an exact match on the subject line of the client certificate, or wild card-based mapping. Go to the client certificate mapping dialog box as before, go to the Many-to-1 tab, and click the Add… button.

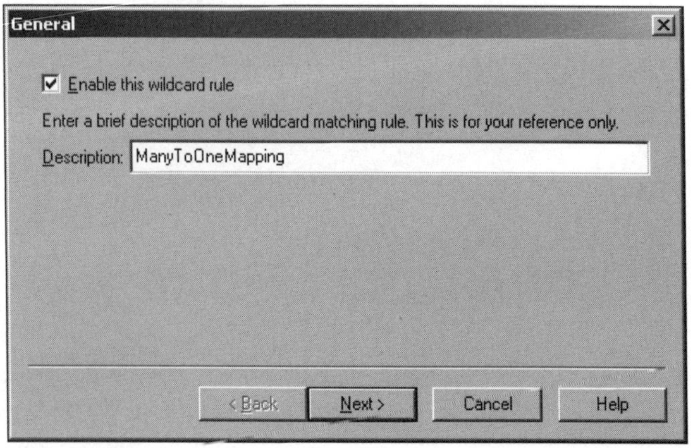

Give a descriptive name for the mapping and click the Next > button. In the next screen, click the New… button.

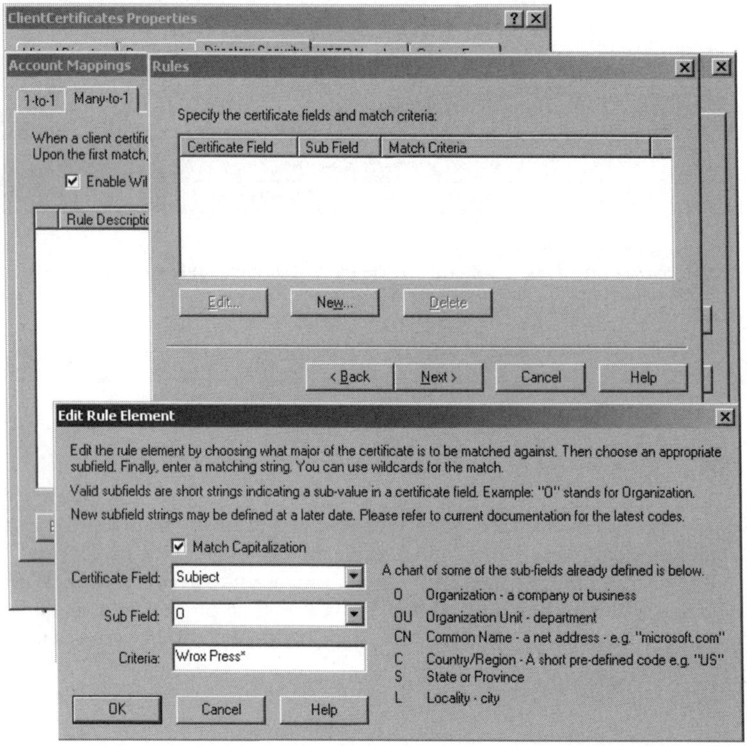

Select Subject from the Certificate Field dropdown box, and select O from the Sub Field. Then type the criteria as Wrox Press* and click the OK button. This will filter all the users with a client certificate subject line as "O=Wrox Press Inc." or "O=Wrox Press Ltd.". We can also use the OU field in the subject line to filter the users based on their department. Click Next, select the Windows user account, type the password, and click the Finish button.

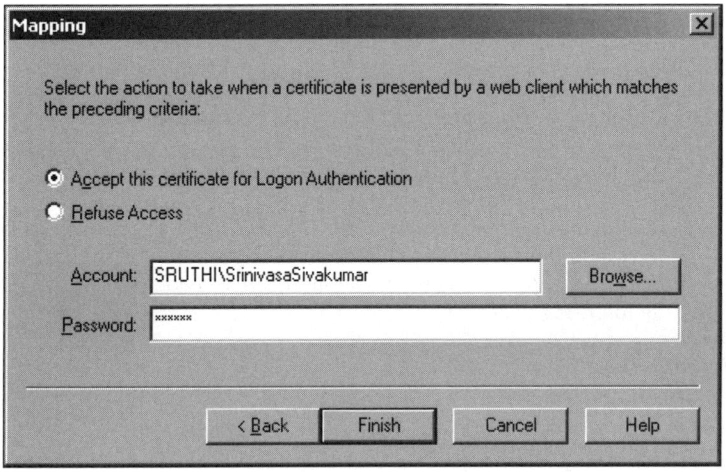

We can also use this screen to deny access to clients that have the same criteria.

This many-to-one mapping will make sure whoever has a client certificate with the subject line text as "O=Wrox Press Inc.", "O=Wrox Press Ltd.", etc., will be running under the Windows user account "`SRUTHI\SrinivasaSivakumar`".

Impersonation

In beta release of the .NET Framework, all the ASP.NET applications and Web Services were running under the powerful system identity ("`NT AUTHORITY\SYSTEM`") even if users were logged in as anonymous users or with a valid Windows username. This has been changed in the final release version of the .NET Framework, and now all ASP.NET applications and Web Services runs under a special account **ASPNET**. This Windows account is created when we install the .NET Framework, and the password for this account is maintained by Microsoft. The **ASPNET** account has very limited privileges compared with the previous system account. For example, the **ASPNET** account can only write performance counter data and can't read such data. If the ASP.NET application or Web Service needs to read performance counter data or create performance counter categories then the ASPNET account needs more privileges such as **Administrator** or **Power User**.

This unique requirement is a good candidate for impersonation. Impersonation is a process that allows the code to run under a different identity to that of the currently logged-in user. The `impersonate` attribute of the `identity` tag in a configuration file allows us to do this. By default the `impersonate` attribute is set to `False`, so the code runs on the **ASPNET** identity.

WindowsPrincipal Object

When any of the Windows authentication methods (basic, digest, and Integrated Windows Authentication) are used, Web Services attach a WindowsPrincipal object (from the System.Security.Principal namespace) to the request. This object contains a WindowsPrincipal class that exposes an Identity property and an IsInRole method that allows you to check Windows user/group membership information.

The only difference between the WindowsPrincipal and User objects is that the User object's properties represent the user who logged in and the WindowsPrincipal members represent the system user account under which the code is running. The WindowsIdentity class represents the current Windows user account that the system is using to run the code.

Let's see a simple example for this. We'll create a Web Service that will say hello to the logged-in user and it'll also say under whom the current account is running. Make the Impersonation folder into a virtual directory in IIS, and assign Basic authentication to it. The Impersonation folder contains a web.config with the following code:

```
<configuration>
  <system.web>
    <authentication mode="Windows"/>
    <!-- This is the Default value -->
    <identity impersonate="false" />
  </system.web>
</configuration>
```

Now, let's look at our Web Service, SayHello.asmx, in the Impersonation folder.

```
<%@ WebService Language="VB" Class="Hello" %>

Imports System.Web.Services
Imports System.Security.Principal

Public Class Hello
  Inherits WebService

  Public<WebMethod()> _
  Function SayHello() As String
    'Create a new Windows Principal object
    Dim objWinPrn As New WindowsPrincipal(WindowsIdentity.GetCurrent())

    Return "Hello " & Context.User.Identity.Name & ". You are consuming '" _
         & Context.User.Identity.AuthenticationType + "' authentication. " _
         & "This Web Service is running under the Windows user account '" _
         & objWinPrn.Identity.Name + "' and is consuming '" _
         & objWinPrn.Identity.AuthenticationType + "' authentication. "
  End Function
End Class
```

We create an object of type `WindowsPrincipal` and pass `WindowsIdentity.GetCurrent` to the constructor of the `WindowsPrincipal` class. The `WindowsIdentity.GetCurrent` method retrieves the username that is used by the system to run the code. In the `Return` statement, we access the username and the authentication type from the `WindowsPrincipal` object. Here is what the output looks like:

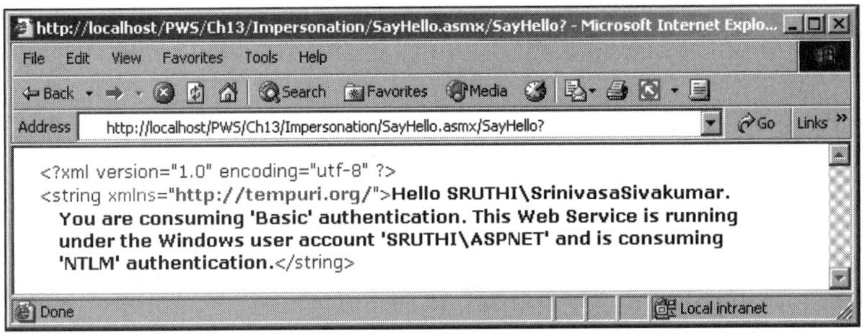
http://localhost/PWS/Ch13/Impersonation/SayHello.asmx/SayHello? - Microsoft Internet Explo...
File Edit View Favorites Tools Help
Back Search Favorites Media
Address http://localhost/PWS/Ch13/Impersonation/SayHello.asmx/SayHello?
Go Links
<?xml version="1.0" encoding="utf-8" ?>
<string xmlns="http://tempuri.org/">Hello SRUTHI\SrinivasaSivakumar. You are consuming 'Basic' authentication. This Web Service is running under the Windows user account 'SRUTHI\ASPNET' and is consuming 'NTLM' authentication.</string>
Done
Local intranet

You can clearly see that the currently logged-in user is "Srinivasa Sivakumar" and he is consuming "Basic" authentication. However, the Web Service is running under the name "ASPNET" and using "NTLM" authentication.

Let's Impersonate

There are two ways we can impersonate the application. The first way is just to set the `impersonate` attribute of the `identity` tag to `true` in the `web.config` file. When you do this, the Web Service will run on the identity of the user who logged in:

```
<configuration>
  <system.web>
    <authentication mode="Windows"/>
    <identity impersonate="true" />
  </system.web>
</configuration>
```

Here is what the output looks like:

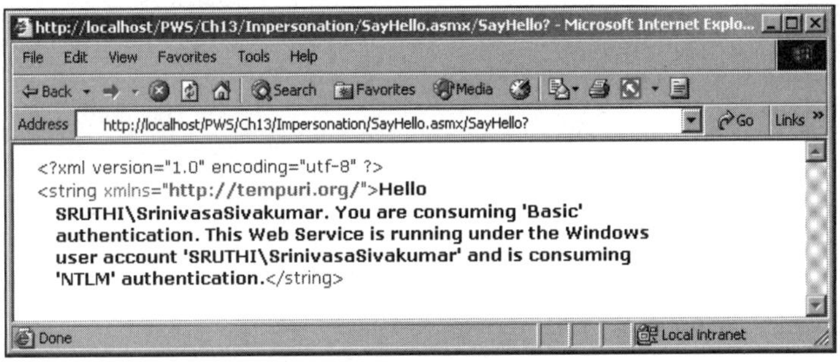
http://localhost/PWS/Ch13/Impersonation/SayHello.asmx/SayHello? - Microsoft Internet Explo...
File Edit View Favorites Tools Help
Back Search Favorites Media
Address http://localhost/PWS/Ch13/Impersonation/SayHello.asmx/SayHello?
Go Links
<?xml version="1.0" encoding="utf-8" ?>
<string xmlns="http://tempuri.org/">Hello SRUTHI\SrinivasaSivakumar. You are consuming 'Basic' authentication. This Web Service is running under the Windows user account 'SRUTHI\SrinivasaSivakumar' and is consuming 'NTLM' authentication.</string>
Done
Local intranet

If the virtual directory is using anonymous access then the output will look like this:

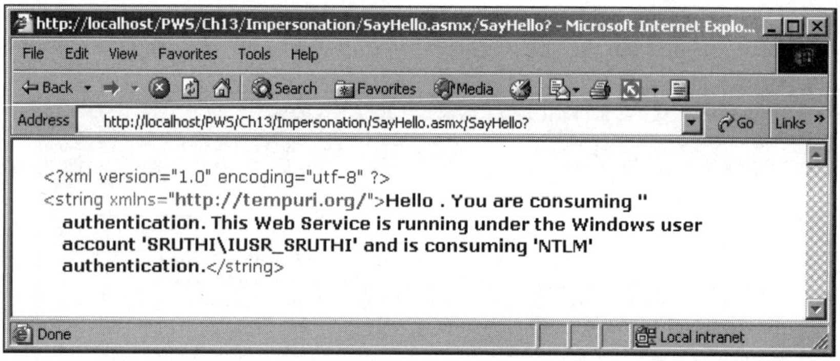
http://localhost/PWS/Ch13/Impersonation/SayHello.asmx/SayHello? - Microsoft Internet Explo...
File Edit View Favorites Tools Help
Back Search Favorites Media
Address http://localhost/PWS/Ch13/Impersonation/SayHello.asmx/SayHello?
Go Links
<?xml version="1.0" encoding="utf-8" ?>
<string xmlns="http://tempuri.org/">Hello . You are consuming '' authentication. This Web Service is running under the Windows user account 'SRUTHI\IUSR_SRUTHI' and is consuming 'NTLM' authentication.</string>
Done
Local intranet

The next option is to impersonate the Web Service with a different username. For example, you may have defined an ACL for a user and you want to impersonate the Web Service with that particular username. We can do that too. Just change the `identity` tag in the `web.config` file:

```
<configuration>
  <system.web>
    <authentication mode="Windows"/>
    <identity impersonate="true" userName="Admin" password="MyPass" />
  </system.web>
</configuration>
```

However, this process can do more than just specify the username and password in the `<identity>` tag. The ASP.NET process should run under the System account, and we can use the `<processModel>` section of the `userName` and password attributes in the machine configuration file to do this (the `machine.config` file is in the `\config` subdirectory of the installation root). The default values for the `userName` and password attributes are `Machine` and `AutoGenerate` respectively, and these values tell ASP.NET to use the built-in ASPNET account, and to use a cryptographically strong random password stored in the Local Security Authority for that account. To configure the process to run under the System account, use the following in the `machine.config` file:

```
<processModel  userName="System" password="AutoGenerate" .../>
```

In addition, if a user account needs to impersonate it needs the "Act as part of the operating system" special privilege. We can assign this privilege by using the Local Security Settings tool that can be found in the Start | Programs | Administrative Tools menu.

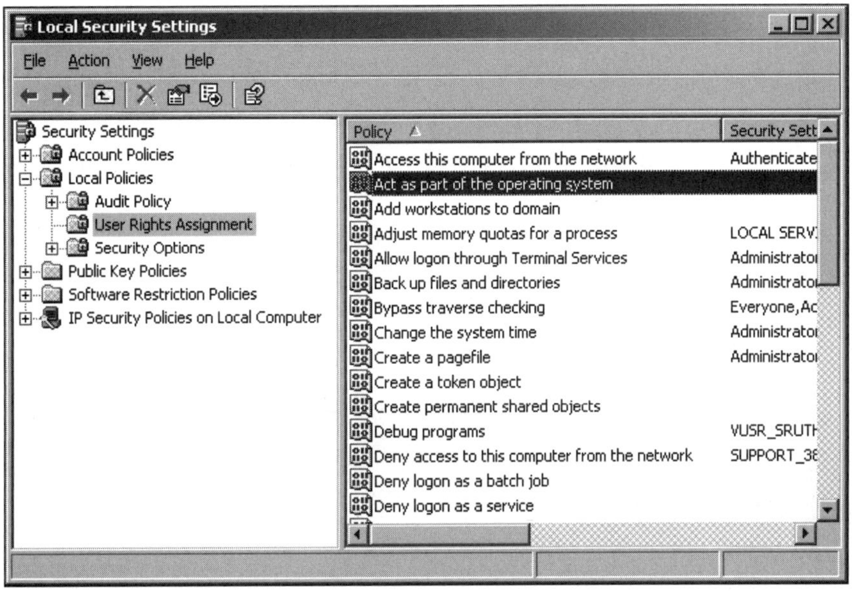

In the Local Security Settings tool, navigate to the User Rights Assignment leaf of the Local Policies folder and double click on the Act as part of the operating system item. Now click the Add... button to add the ASPNET account to the list. Click OK and save the changes. After this, restart IIS. This will assign the "Act as part of the operating system privilege" to the ASPNET account providing enough privileges to impersonate.

These changes make the impersonating account more powerful. So, use this option with caution.

Now let's run the impersonation code that we've used previously and you'll see the ASP.NET application runs under the new impersonating user (`SRUTHI/Admin`) regardless of the kind of authentication that the ASP.NET application is using and who has logged into the application. Here is what the output looks like:

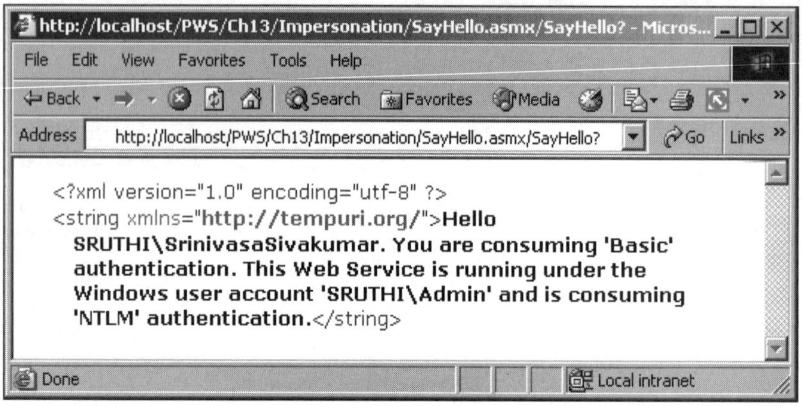
http://localhost/PWS/Ch13/Impersonation/SayHello.asmx/SayHello? - Micros...
File Edit View Favorites Tools Help
Back Search Favorites Media
Address http://localhost/PWS/Ch13/Impersonation/SayHello.asmx/SayHello? Go Links
<?xml version="1.0" encoding="utf-8" ?>
<string xmlns="http://tempuri.org/">Hello SRUTHI\SrinivasaSivakumar. You are consuming 'Basic' authentication. This Web Service is running under the Windows user account 'SRUTHI\Admin' and is consuming 'NTLM' authentication.</string>
Done
Local intranet

URL Authorization

URL Authorization is a service provided by the `UrlAuthorizationModule` class to control access to resources such as `.asmx`, `.aspx` files. It is very useful if you want to allow or deny certain pages in your ASP.NET Web Service to selected people, or roles. For example, you may want to restrict a Financial Web Service to users with the `Financial` role assigned to their profile and deny access to others. This can be achieved very easily with URL Authorization.

URL Authorization can be configured in the `web.config` file with the `<allow>` and `<deny>` tags. The `<allow>` and `<deny>` tags support the `users`, `roles`, and `verb` attributes. We can add multiple users and groups by separating them with commas.

> **There are two special characters – asterisk/star (*), and question mark (?) – supported by the `UrlAuthorizationModule`. The asterisk (*) stands for all users, and the question mark (?) stands for anonymous users.**

For example, we can allow the user "`SrinivasaSivakumar`" and the role "`Financial`" access to our Web Service and deny all anonymous users from using our Web Service:

```
<configuration>
  <system.web>
    <authorization>
      <!--Allow the user SrinivasaSivakumar -->
      <allow users="SrinivasaSivakumar" />
      <!--Allow the roles Financial -->
      <allow roles="Financial" />
      <!--Deny all anonymous users -->
      <deny users="?" />
    </authorization>
  </system.web>
</configuration>
```

We can also allow and deny access based on the HTTP `verb`. For example if you want to restrict people from using the HTTP `POST` method to access the Web Service then just add a `deny` tag to the `web.config` file with the verb as `POST` and users as `*`. This will deny everyone from using HTTP `POST` to access the Web Service.

```
<configuration>
  <system.web>
    <authorization>
      <!-- Deny HTTP Post for all the users -->
      <deny verb="POST" users="*" />
    </authorization>
  </system.web>
</configuration>
```

We can also restrict URL Authorization for a single file or directory. For example, the following code restricts access to `FinancialWebService.asmx`.

```
<configuration>
  <location path="FinancialWebService.Asmx">
    <system.web>
      <authorization>
        <!--Allow the user SrinivasaSivakumar -->
        <allow users="SrinivasaSivakumar" />
        <!--Allow the roles Financial -->
        <allow roles="Financial" />
        <!--Deny all the anonymous users -->
        <deny users="?" />
      </authorization>
    </system.web>
  </location>
</configuration>
```

The ASP.NET application doesn't verify the path that we've specified in the `path` attribute. If the given path is invalid then ASP.NET will not apply the security setting.

Summary

As we learned in this chapter, Web Services security architecture is based on application-to-application communication rather than application-to-user communication. Web Services can be secured using various methods. In this chapter, we discussed the following:

- **IP and DNS security** – how to filter users using the IP and DNS security. This includes how to grant or deny access to clients with the IP or DNS name.
- **Windows authentication methods** – we saw how to implement Windows authentication methods such as basic, digest and Integrated Windows Authentication. We've also seen when and why we should use these authentication methods, and their pros and cons.
- **Forms authentication method** – we discussed the Forms authentication method and how to use it, including when, why and its pros and const.
- **Basic authentication with SSL** – we looked at how to make basic authentication more secure using SSL.

- **Client Certificate authentication** – we saw how to read a client certificate and how to authenticate a user using Client Certificates.
- **Client Certificates and Windows user account** – we looked at how to map single or multiple Client Certificate(s) onto a Windows user account, with a one-to-one or many-to-one mapping.
- **Impersonation** –we saw what impersonation is, how to use it, and how to view it using the `WindowsPrincipal` object.
- **URL Authorization** – finally, we saw what URL Authorization is, and how to protect the Web Service using this method.

Professional
ASP.NET
Web
Services

14

SOAP Security

Simple Object Access Protocol (SOAP) is a high-level protocol that can work on top of any low-level protocols such as HTTP, SMTP, and so on. The authentication techniques that we discussed in the previous chapter will only work with the HTTP protocol. If we are accessing Web Services using the SMTP protocol to send and receive SOAP messages then we can't use the above techniques. To overcome this limitation, we can use some custom SOAP techniques to authenticate a user. We have already seen some custom SOAP techniques in Chapter 6. In this chapter we will concentrate on using these techniques for authentication purposes.

We'll learn the following techniques from this chapter:

- **SOAP Header** – how to use the SOAP Header to authenticate users
- **Custom Authentication and Authorization** – how to use Custom Authentication and Authorization techniques using the HTTP Modules
- **Tracing SOAP Messages** – how to trace SOAP messages using the SOAP Extensions
- **Encrypting and Decrypting SOAP Messages** – how to encrypt and decrypt the data passed in the SOAP message body

Let's not waste any more time and jump into the chapter to see the existing world of SOAP.

SOAP Envelope

Before going any further, let's stop for a second and recap some information about the structure of the SOAP message. We have already had a detailed discussion about the SOAP protocol in Chapter 5, so we won't repeat it all here, but we'll just have a quick recap. Every SOAP message contains a SOAP envelope and within the envelope there is a header and a body:

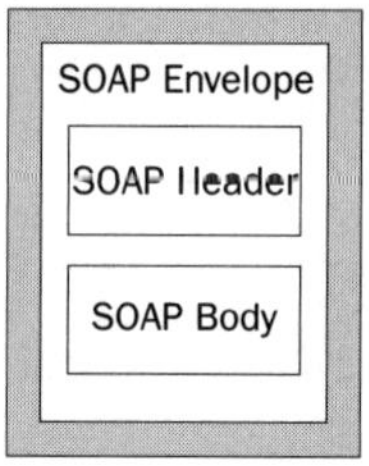

The SOAP protocol is extendable and we can add application-specific information to it. For example, we can add application-specific information to the SOAP header and transport it between the client and the Web Service.

> *The extensions will only work with SOAP and can't be used with HTTP GET or POST. We can use HTTP as a carrier for SOAP messages though, and then use the extensions.*

When we create a proxy object and access a Web Service using the SOAP protocol it will create a SOAP envelope and pass the values to the Web Service:

```
<?xml version="1.0" encoding="utf-8"?>
<soap:Envelope xmlns:xsi="http://www.w3.org/2001/XMLSchema-instance"
               xmlns:xsd="http://www.w3.org/2001/XMLSchema"
               xmlns:soap="http://schemas.xmlsoap.org/soap/envelope/">
  <soap:Body>
    <SayHello xmlns="http://tempuri.org/" />
  </soap:Body>
</soap:Envelope>
```

When we return a value from the Web Service, it will arrive back as a SOAP envelope.

Custom SOAP Header

We can add custom values to the SOAP header for the purposes of the application. For example, if we add a username and password variables to the SOAP header, then the SOAP envelope will look like this:

```
<?xml version="1.0" encoding="utf-8"?>
<soap:Envelope xmlns:xsi="http://www.w3.org/2001/XMLSchema-instance"
               xmlns:xsd="http://www.w3.org/2001/XMLSchema"
               xmlns:soap="http://schemas.xmlsoap.org/soap/envelope/">
  <soap:Header>
    <SOAPHeaderAuth xmlns="http://tempuri.org/">
      <UserName>SrinivasaSivakumar</UserName>
      <Password>MyPass</Password>
    </SOAPHeaderAuth>
  </soap:Header>
```

```
  <soap:Body>
    <SayHello xmlns="http://tempuri.org/" />
  </soap:Body>
</soap:Envelope>
```

To use the SOAP header in the Web Service, we have to implement our own class that inherits from the `SoapHeader` class (available in the `System.Web.Services.Protocols` namespace). Let's see a simple example for this, `SayHello.asmx` in the `SoapAuth1` folder of the code download for this chapter:

```
<%@ WebService Language="VB" Class="Hello" %>

Imports System.Web.Services
Imports System.Web.Services.Protocols

'A Simple SOAP Header extension class
Public Class SOAPHeaderAuth
  Inherits SoapHeader
  Public UserName as String
  Public Password as String
End Class

Public class Hello
  Inherits WebService
  'Public instance of the SOAP Header extension
  Public objSoapHeaderAuth as SOAPHeaderAuth

  Const CN_InvalidUserNameOrPassword as String = "WS1001"

  <WebMethod, SoapHeader("objSoapHeaderAuth", _
            Direction := SoapHeaderDirection.InOut, Required := true)> _
  Public Function SayHello() as String
    If Authenticate(objSoapHeaderAuth.Username, objSoapHeaderAuth.Password) Then
      Return "Hello " & objSoapHeaderAuth.Username & " and your password is " _
          & objSoapHeaderAuth.Password
    Else
      Return CN_InvalidUserNameOrPassword
    End if
  End Function

  Function Authenticate(sUser as String, sPwd as String) As Boolean
    If sUser = "SrinivasaSivakumar" And sPwd = "MyPass" Then
      Return True
    Else
      Return False
    End If
  End Function
End Class
```

First we include the System.Web.Services.Protocols namespace to get access to the SoapHeader class. Then we define a new class (SOAPHeaderAuth) with two public members (UserName and Password) that inherit from the SoapHeader base class:

```
Imports System.Web.Services.Protocols

Public Class SOAPHeaderAuth
  Inherits SoapHeader
  Public UserName as String
  Public Password as String
End Class
```

After this, we create a class-level public instance of the class type SOAPHeaderAuth and we pass the variable into the SoapHeader constructor in the WebMethod declaration. We also specified the SOAP header direction as in and out and SOAP header as being required. This will modify the default SOAP header and add the custom values to the SOAP header and make the SOAP header bi-directional and required. Then we've defined a constant to return to the user if the authentication fails:

```
Public objSoapHeaderAuth as SOAPHeaderAuth

Const CN_InvalidUserNameOrPassword as String = "WS1001"

<WebMethod, SoapHeader("objSoapHeaderAuth", _
            Direction := SoapHeaderDirection.InOut, Required := true)> _
```

In the SayHello method body, we're passing the username and the password to the Authenticate method. In the Authenticate method, if the username is "SrinivasaSivakumar" and the password is "MyPass" then we're returning True, otherwise we're returning False. If we get a True back from the Authenticate method then we're returning the username and the password back to the client. Otherwise we're returning the CN_InvalidUserNameOrPassword constant back:

```
  Public Function SayHello() as String
    If Authenticate(objSoapHeaderAuth.Username, objSoapHeaderAuth.Password) Then
      Return "Hello " & objSoapHeaderAuth.Username & " and your password is " _
            & objSoapHeaderAuth.Password
    Else
      Return CN_InvalidUserNameOrPassword
    End if
  End Function

  Function Authenticate(sUser as String, sPwd as String) As Boolean
    If sUser = "SrinivasaSivakumar" And sPwd = "MyPass" Then
      Return True
    Else
      Return False
    End If
  End Function
End Class
```

If we look at the WSDL file generated for the Web Service we notice that `SOAPHeaderAuth` has been added to the SOAP header with all the public members:

```
<s:element name="SOAPHeaderAuth" type="s0:SOAPHeaderAuth" />
<s:complexType name="SOAPHeaderAuth">
  <s:sequence>
    <s:element minOccurs="1"
               maxOccurs="1"
               name="UserName"
               nillable="true"
               type="s:string" />
    <s:element minOccurs="1"
               maxOccurs="1"
               name="Password"
               nillable="true"
               type="s:string" />
  </s:sequence>
</s:complexType>
```

To use the SOAP header extensions we need to access the Web Service through the SOAP protocol. And to do that, we need to create a proxy object. We will use the `SayHelloBuild.bat` batch file in the `SOAPAuth1` folder to do this:

```
WSDL /l:VB /n:SayHelloNS /out:SayHello.VB
http://localhost/PWS/Ch14/soapauth1/SayHello.Asmx?WSDL

VBC /r:system.dll  /r:System.Web.dll /r:System.Xml.dll
/r:System.Web.Services.dll /t:library /out:SayHello.dll SayHello.VB
```

Let's place the `SayHello` DLL in the `bin` folder and build an ASP.NET client for the Web Service, `SOAPAuthClient.aspx`:

```
<%@ Import Namespace="SayHelloNS" %>
<html>
<head>
<title>SOAP Authentication Web Client</title>
<style type="text/css">
     body {font-face:verdana; font-size:10pt; font-weight:normal}
</style>
</head>
<script language="VB" runat="server">
Sub Page_Load(s as Object, E as EventArgs)
  Try
    Dim objWebSvc As New SayHelloNS.Hello()
    Dim objSoapHeader As New SOAPHeaderAuth()

    'Set the Username and Password
    objSoapHeader.UserName = "SrinivasaSivakumar1"
    objSoapHeader.Password = "MyPass"

    'Pass the custom SOAP header object
    objWebSvc.SOAPHeaderAuthValue = objSoapHeader

    lblResult.Text = objWebSvc.SayHello()
```

```
    Catch Ex As Exception
      lblResult.Text = Ex.ToString()
    End Try
  End Sub
  </script>
  <body>
  <h3>SOAP Authentication - Web Service Client</h3>
  <form runat="server">
  <b>Result:</b><br /> <asp:Label id="lblResult" runat="server"/>
  </form>
  </body>
  </html>
```

We create an object that represents the Web Service (`objWebSvc`) and the custom SOAP Header (`objSoapHeader`). Then, we add the username and password to the SOAP Header object:

```
Dim objWebSvc As New SayHelloNS.Hello()
Dim objSoapHeader As New SOAPHeaderAuth()

'Set the Username and Password
objSoapHeader.UserName = "SrinivasaSivakumar1"
objSoapHeader.Password = "MyPass"
```

Next, we assign the SOAP header object to the public property of the Web Services class and call the `WebMethod`:

```
'Pass the custom SOAP header object
objWebSvc.SOAPHeaderAuthValue = objSoapHeader

lblResult.Text = objWebSvc.SayHello()
```

The `SOAPHeaderAuthValue` property in the above code represents the custom SOAP Header class value. To access the SOAP Header value, we append `Value` to the header class name.

As we stated, our `WebMethod` is essentially the same as before, except that we are returning a typed `DataSet` called `SupplierDataSet1`, which is of type `SupplierDataSet`. Where did the `SupplierDataSet` type come from you ask? Ah, this is the voodoo magic that happened when we generated the `DataSet` from our `SupplierDataAdapter`. As was briefly mentioned before, when we use the Component Designer, Visual Studio .NET does all the grunt work and creates the necessary files for our typed `DataSet`. The `SupplierDataSet` class is just one of them.

SupplierDataSet.vb

If you open Solution Explorer and click the Show All Files icon, then expand SupplierDataSet.xsd, you will notice the `SupplierDataSet.vb` file that Visual Studio was able to create for us. This class uses the `System.Runtime.Serialization` namespace which is used to serialize and deserialize objects. What this does for us is create a typed `DataSet` class based on the XML schema we created to allow us to access the `DataSet` objects in a more object-oriented manner. This will become clearer after we create the Web Service client.

Testing CompanyService

Before building the client, let's do a quick test to make sure CompanyService works properly. Open the Solution Explorer and right-click on CompanyService.asmx and select Set As Start Page. Now click the Debug menu item and select Start Without Debugging. This will bring up the Web Service description page in Internet Explorer. Click on the GetSupplierList hyperlink, then click the Invoke button. This will bring up the XML that will be returned to the caller when the `GetSupplierList` web method is called. If you scroll down you should see something like this:

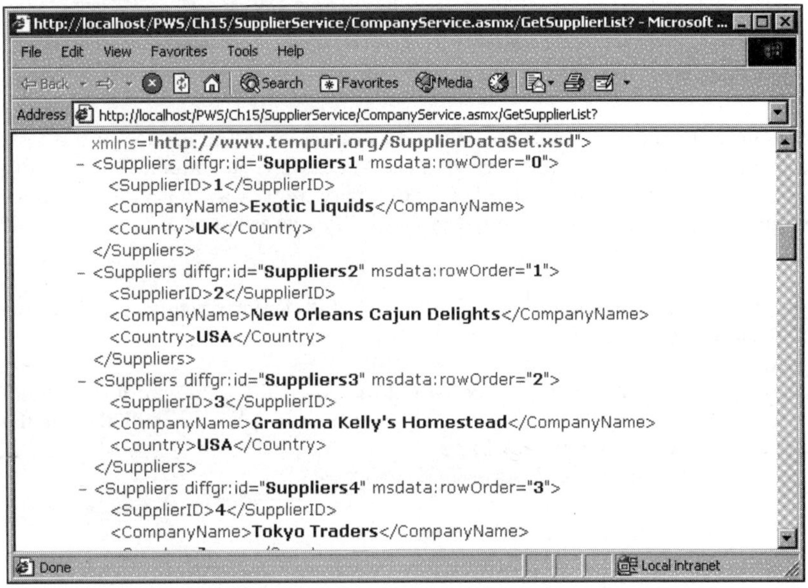

Now that we know everything is working as planned, we can move on to creating the Web Service client.

Creating the Web Service Client for CompanyService

Instead of creating a new client for this service, let's build on our previous one, ProductSupply. Open the Designer for index.aspx.

First we are going to add a Label control to our page (I placed mine just above the DataGrid) to help us demonstrate the difference between an untyped DataSet and a typed DataSet. Right-click on the Label object and select Properties. Change the (ID) from Label1 to UntypedData. Also, remove Label from the Text property. Now, switch to the code-behind page. We are going to add a bit more to our existing code:

```
Private Sub Page_Load(ByVal sender As System.Object, _
                      ByVal e As System.EventArgs) Handles MyBase.Load
  If Not Page.IsPostBack Then
    ' Create a new ProductService object
    Dim ps As ProductService = New WebService.ProductService ()
    Dim ds = ps.GetPavlovaProduct()

    ' Bind data to DataGrid
    ProductDataSet.DataSource = ds.Tables(0).DefaultView
    ProductDataSet.DataBind()
    'Demonstrate how to access a particular item in an untyped DataSet
    Dim ProductName As String = ds.Tables(0).Rows(4)("ProductName").ToString()
    UntypedData.Text = ProductName
  End If
End Sub
```

Here, we demonstrate how you would access the data in the DataSet located in the first table, in the fifth row (remember all arrays are zero-based) of the ProductName column. Then we display the data using a Label server control. Obviously, this is not a very pretty way to access data, but because we are accessing an untyped DataSet, which only exposes its objects as collections, we are really left with no other choice.

Before testing this in a browser we need to refresh the Web Reference: right-click Web Service and select Update Web Reference.

Now you can comfortably run index.aspx. As before, you will see the ProductDataSet DataGrid populated with the DataSet returned by GetPavlovaProduct, but you will also see the Label server control populated with the text, Outback Lager.

Open index.aspx in design mode again so we can add a couple more objects. First add another Label server control to the page just below the ProductDataSet DataGrid. View the Label's properties, change the (ID) to **TypedData**, and remove **Label** from the **Text** property. Now drag a DataGrid server control onto the page just below the TypedData Label. View its properties and change the (ID) to **SupplierGrid**. The designer should look something like the screenshot on the right.

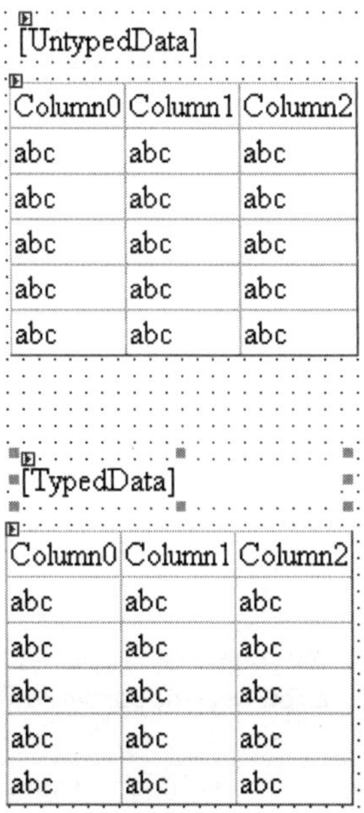

The next step is to add another **Web Reference** to our project. In the Solution Explorer, right-click **Web References** and select **Add Web Reference**. In the following **Address** field we must supply the URL to our Web Service description page, which will look something like this: **http://localhost/PWS/Ch15/SupplierService/CompanyService.asmx**. Before going any further, let's change the default Web Service name **localhost** to the more meaningful **CompanyWebService**. If you now expand **CompanyWebService** in the Solution Explorer, you'll see that in addition to the .DISCO and .WSDL files, the SupplierDataSet schema has also been created. As we now know, this is one of the key players for our typed DataSet.

Open the code-behind file index.aspx.vb and add the following namespace alias:

```
Imports ProductSupply.CompanyWebService
```

Now we want to add the code that creates an instance of the CompanyWebService, fills our typed DataSet via our GetSupplierList web method, and binds it to our SupplierGrid. Again, we will add this to our existing code as shown below:

```
Private Sub Page_Load(ByVal sender As System.Object, _
                      ByVal e As System.EventArgs) Handles MyBase.Load
  ' Create a new ProductService object
  If Not Page.IsPostBack Then
    Dim ps As ProductService = New WebService.ProductService ()
    Dim ds = ps.GetPavlovaProduct()

    ' Bind data to DataGrid
    ProductDataSet.DataSource = ds.Tables(0).DefaultView
    ProductDataSet.DataBind()
    'Demonstrate how to access a particular item in an untyped DataSet
```

```
        Dim ProductName As String = ds.Tables(0).Rows(4)("ProductName").ToString()
        UntypedData.Text = ProductName

        ' TYPED DATASET EXAMPLE
        ' Create a new Company Service object
        Dim cs As CompanyService = New CompanyWebService.CompanyService()
        Dim supplierDS As CompanyWebService.SupplierDataSet = cs.GetSupplierList()

        ' Bind data to DataGrid
        SupplierGrid.DataSource = supplierDS.Suppliers.DefaultView
        SupplierGrid.DataBind()

        ' Demonstrate how to access a particular item in a typed DataSet
        Dim CompanyName As String = supplierDS.Suppliers(4).CompanyName
        TypedData.Text = CompanyName
      End If
    End Sub
```

As you probably have already noticed, this is very similar to our first web client code, but does contain a few very important differences. Let's look at the first difference:

```
' Untyped DataSet
Dim ds = ps.GetPavlovaProduct()

' Typed DataSet
Dim supplierDS As CompanyWebService.SupplierDataSet = cs.GetSupplierList()
```

In our first example, we simply created an untyped `DataSet` that was populated from the `GetPavlovaProduct` web method. However, in our second example we created a type called `SupplierDataSet`, which is a class that inherits from the base class `System.Data.DataSet`. You may remember from our discussion above that we talked about the `SupplierDataSet` class and the `SupplierDataSet` schema being generated by our `SupplierDataAdapter`. Where this really comes into play is when we want to programmatically access specific data in the `DataSet`. Which brings us to our next difference:

```
' Demonstrate how to access a particular item in an untyped DataSet
Dim ProductName As String = ds.Tables(0).Rows(4)("ProductName").ToString()
UntypedData.Text = ProductName

' Demonstrate how to access a particular item in a typed DataSet
Dim CompanyName As String = supplierDS.Suppliers(4).CompanyName
TypedData.Text = CompanyName
```

Here we can see that with a typed `DataSet` we can use object-oriented programming methodologies to access particular data, instead of accessing data as collections. We'll come back to this soon, but first let's run our example to see what we get. Select **Debug | Start Without Debugging**.

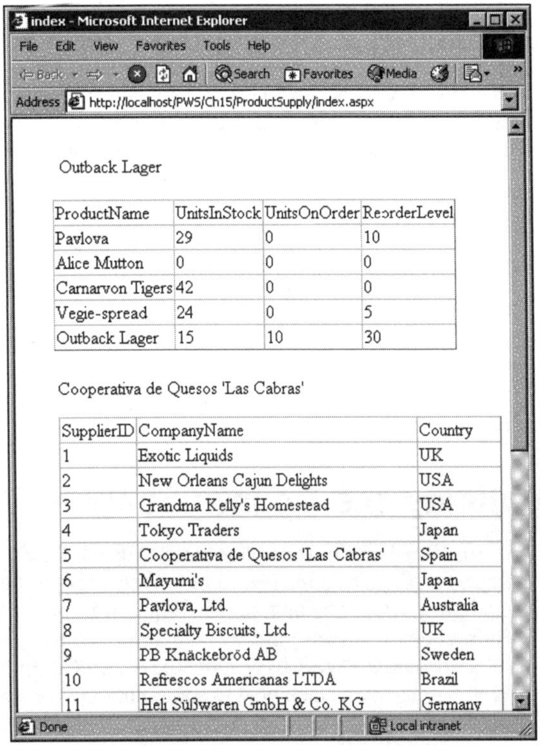

In this case, it makes no difference to the user whether the developer used an untyped `DataSet` or a typed `DataSet`; the data still gets displayed. Where it does make a difference is to the developer if they wanted to modify the data that gets displayed.

Let's open `index.aspx.vb` again and try another example. This time we are going to say, "Hey, Mr. Fancy-Schmancy Typed `DataSet`, we want the company name for the company with a SupplierID equal to six." Since .NET doesn't have built-in coding by speech recognition quite yet, here's what we have to do:

```
' Demonstrate how to access a particular item in a typed DataSet
'Dim CompanyName As String = supplierDS.Suppliers(4).CompanyName
Dim CompanyName As String = supplierDS.Suppliers.FindBySupplierID(6).CompanyName
TypedData.Text = CompanyName
```

We commented out our first `CompanyName` string and replaced it with another one. Because we have a typed `DataSet` that contains a unique key, `SupplierID`, the `SupplierDataSet` class created a nice little method for us called `FindBySupplierID`. This method takes one parameter: the integer `SupplierID`, and returns a data row to us, or more specifically a `SupplierDataSet.SuppliersRow`. Each `SuppliersRow` has several methods and properties, one property being `CompanyName`.

While we're beginning to see the power of the typed `DataSet`, we have really just scratched the surface. Don't worry though, we'll touch on this again in our next example.

Creating a Nested Web Service

No matter where you go these days, no one is happy with things the way they are. You go out to eat with a group of friends and at least one of them can't order straight off the menu. "Yeah, can you leave the onions and peppers off my curry, please?" Anyway, as Web Services become more prevalent in the real world there are bound to be times that the Web Service that you are looking at returns more data than you need. Enter nested Web Services. Or as Microsoft has coined the term: **Federated Services**.

In this example, we are going to use one of our previous services, CompanyService. As you'll remember, this service returns a typed `DataSet` containing all the suppliers in the Northwind database. It returned the `SupplierID`, `CompanyName`, and `Country`. While that may be useful for some, we're going to pretend that we only want certain suppliers from a certain country. Instead of creating a `DataSet` that returns suppliers from a particular country, we are going to give the caller the option of selecting which country they want. This will give us an opportunity to show off some more features of a typed `DataSet`.

Building the CountrySupplier Web Service

Open Visual Studio and create a new VB.NET ASP.NET Web Service called NestedWebService. Delete `Service1.asmx` and create a new Web Service called `CompanyByCountry.asmx`. Right-click on CompanyByCountry.asmx in the Solution Explorer and select Set As Start Page. Now add the Web Reference to `CompanyService` that we created earlier, and which is located at: http://localhost/PWS/Ch15/SupplierService/CompanyService.asmx. As before, we will rename the default Web Service name localhost to something more meaningful: CompanyWebService. Add the following namespace alias to the Web Service:

```
Imports NestedWebService.CompanyWebService
```

As mentioned above, this time we are going to allow the Web Service caller to pass the method a parameter. We want to know which company list they want based on the country column. If this parameter was simply the string `CountryName` we would run into problems, because developers would be bound to pass an invalid string which would result in a blank `DataSet`, or worse yet, an error. In other words a consumer could pass a string value of `Mattyville`, which is a valid string parameter, but we all know is not a valid country. To eliminate this problem we are going to add a `Country` data type to our Web Service with the following code:

```
<WebService(Namespace:="http://www.wrox.com/")> _
Public Class CompanyByCountry
  Inherits System.Web.Services.WebService

  Public Enum Country
    Australia
    Brazil
    Canada
    Japan
    Spain
    Sweden
    UK
    USA
  End Enum
```

Now when a developer consumes our service they have to pass in one of our country values. If they are using Visual Studio .NET or any other editor that provides IntelliSense, then they will be able to easily select one of these country values. We'll look at this in just a minute.

Notice that we only included a partial list of valid countries for this example. Obviously, if this was a Web Service we were going to expose to the world, we would want to include all valid countries.

Next we add a web method called `GetSuppliersByCountry` that first gets a `SupplierDataSet` from the `CompanyService`, and then iterates through all the rows, adding all the matching ones to a new `SupplierDataSet` that will be returned to the `GetSuppliersByCountry` caller:

```
<WebMethod()> _
Public Function GetSuppliersByCountry(ByVal countryName As Country) _
                                   As CompanyWebService.SupplierDataSet

  Dim cService As CompanyWebService.CompanyService = New _
                                     CompanyWebService.CompanyService()
  Dim sDS As CompanyWebService.SupplierDataSet = cService.GetSupplierList()

  ' Create a new SupplierDataSet to hold
  ' just the data we want
  Dim newDS As SupplierDataSet = New CompanyWebService.SupplierDataSet()

  ' Iterate through each SupplierDataSet row
  Dim sRow As SupplierDataSet.SuppliersRow
  For Each sRow In sDS.Suppliers

    ' Check to see if the company is from the country we are after
    If (sRow.Country = countryName.ToString()) Then
      ' Add the row to our new dataset if it is from the right country
      newDS.Suppliers.AddSuppliersRow(sRow.CompanyName, sRow.Country)
    End If
  Next
  Return newDS
End Function
```

Again, because we are using a typed `DataSet` here, our life is made much easier because it provides us with built-in functionality that we would not get with an untyped `DataSet`. For example, in the above code, the `Suppliers` typed `DataSet` provides us a method called `AddSuppliersRow`.

Time to test our Web Service. Select **Debug | Start Without Debugging**. When we test our Web Service we must supply a parameter value for `countryName`. Notice though that we do not have a list of options, but have to type a known value. Our `Country` data type won't come into play until we build the client.

After you click the Invoke button, you will see the XML returned by our service. It looks very similar to our `CompanyService` except it only contains the companies that are from the USA. So to recap, what we have done here is take an existing service, CompanyService, that returns all the suppliers, and built a nested service, or federated service, called CompanyByCountry that returns a subset of the CompanyService data. In our case, all the suppliers that are from a particular country.

A Client for the CompanyByCountry Service

We have already built a few Web Service clients in this chapter, so it isn't necessary to go into great detail again. However, I will point out how our `Country` data type comes into play and how it makes it much easier for someone to call our service. Let's look at the code:

```
' Create a new Company
Dim nestedService As CompanyByCountry = New NestedWebService.CompanyByCountry()

' Set Country value
Dim countryName As Country = Country.Canada

Dim nsDS As NestedWebService.SupplierDataSet = _
                                nestedService.GetSuppliersByCountry(countryName)
NestedGrid.DataSource = nsDS.Suppliers.DefaultView
NestedGrid.DataBind()
```

Essentially, it is the same as our previous examples, but this time we had to create a `Country` data type variable and give it a value. This in turn is passed as a parameter in the `GetSuppliersByCountry` method. What isn't apparent here is that when you create the `countryName` variable you will see the following help from Visual Studio's IntelliSense:

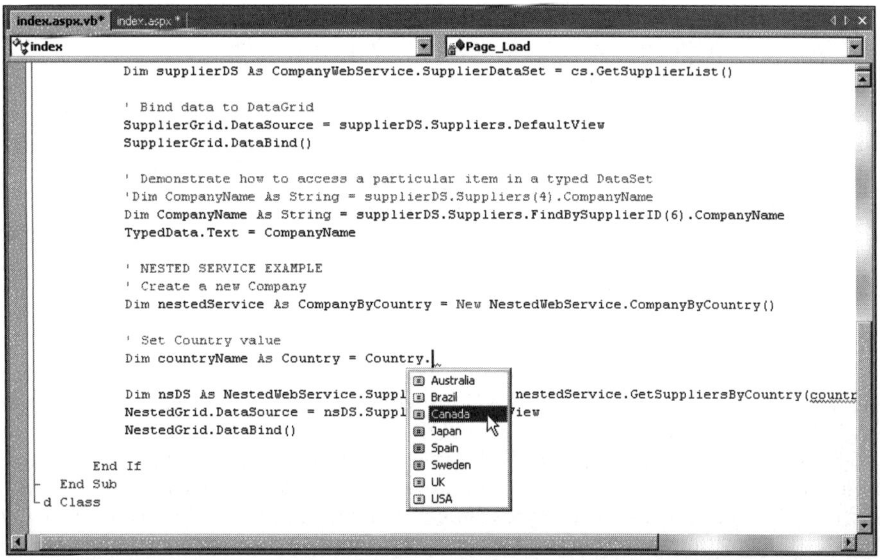

As you can see, by creating the `Country` data type we have made it a snap for callers to provide a valid value for the `countryName` parameter of `GetSuppliersByCountry`.

Though it would be a difficult task to simplify our special order requests at a local restaurant, we have demonstrated here that it is possible to modify an existing Web Service to better meet our needs and our customer's needs.

Exposing XML

Let's take a minute to step back and examine another business-to-business example. It's not always necessary to have a Web Service connect to a database each time it is called. For one, this could cause unnecessary traffic to your database. For example, if you have a database that, for one reason or another, does not allow systems to connect to it directly to access information, it would be possible to export that data to some format, enter XML, and have the service grab the necessary information from that file, thus easing the load to your database server. To demonstrate this scenario we're going to create a console application that can be scheduled to run every night. This application will query a database, grab the data, and export it to an XML file that we'll consume through a Web Service. Note that creating the XML file could also be done by creating a Windows Service or even easier yet, a stored procedure.

Creating the CreateXmlFile Console Application

Create a new Visual Basic Console Application called CreateXmlFile in Visual Studio .NET. You know the drill: delete the default file, `Class1.vb` and create a new class called `ProductList.vb`. In the Solution Explorer open `ProductList.vb` and add the following namespaces:

```
Imports System
Imports System.Data
Imports System.Data.SqlClient
```

All right, just a bit more prep work. We can delete the method that was generated for us, `ProductList`, and add `Main`. `ProductList.vb` should look like this:

```
Imports System
Imports System.Data
Imports System.Data.SqlClient

Module ProductList
  Sub Main()

  End Sub
End Module
```

Whew, time for the good stuff, and trust me, I think you're going to like how we're going to create this XML file. First, we're going to connect to the Northwind database as we have in the previous examples. However, this time we're going to use an inline SQL statement instead of creating a stored procedure. I would highly suggest using a stored procedure for any production application, though. Once we have connected to the database we will again fill a `DataSet` with the `SqlDataAdapter` method `Fill`. For the grand finale, we will use a very handy `DataSet` method, `WriteXML`. That's all we have to do to create our XML file with data from a database. Let's look at the actual code now:

```
Module ProductList
  ' Local connectionString variable
  Private Const connectionString As String = "uid=sa;pwd=;initial " _
                                  & "catalog=Northwind;data source=localhost"
  Sub Main()
    Dim query As String = "SELECT Products.ProductName, " _
                          & "Suppliers.CompanyName FROM Products, " _
                          & "Suppliers WHERE Products.SupplierID = " _
                          & "Suppliers.SupplierID ORDER BY Products.ProductName"
    Dim myConnection As SqlConnection = New SqlConnection(connectionString)
    Dim myCommand As SqlDataAdapter = New SqlDataAdapter(query, myConnection)

    Dim ds As DataSet = New DataSet()
    myCommand.Fill(ds, "Titles")

    ds.WriteXml("c:\ProductList.xml")
  End Sub
End Module
```

How did we do? Time to find out, I guess. Execute the application, **Debug | Start**, then check for `ProductList.xml` in the root of your `C:` drive; it should look something like this:

```
<?xml version="1.0" standalone="yes"?>
<NewDataSet>
  <Titles>
    <ProductName>Alice Mutton</ProductName>
    <CompanyName>Pavlova, Ltd.</CompanyName>
  </Titles>
  <Titles>
```

```
      <ProductName>Aniseed Syrup</ProductName>
      <CompanyName>Exotic Liquids</CompanyName>
    </Titles>
    <Titles>
      <ProductName>Boston Crab Meat</ProductName>
      <CompanyName>New England Seafood Cannery</CompanyName>

  ...

    <Titles>
      <ProductName>Zaanse koeken</ProductName>
      <CompanyName>Zaanse Snoepfabriek</CompanyName>
    </Titles>
  </NewDataSet>
```

All right, if you weren't impressed with that, then maybe I can impress you with how we create the web method that grabs this XML data.

Creating the GetProductList Web Method

Just to recap; we have created a console application that will be scheduled to run nightly that grabs data from our database and sticks it into an XML file. Now it is time to create a new web method to our existing ProductService Web Service.

Open the SupplierService project containing `ProductService.asmx` in Visual Studio .NET. With only 6 lines of actual code we will expose our XML file, `ProductList.xml`, to the world through our ProductService service. Add the following code to `ProductService.asmx.vb` (I added it below our other web method, `GetPavlovaProduct`):

```
<WebMethod()> _
Public Function GetProductList() As DataSet

  Dim ds As New DataSet()
  ds.ReadXml("c:\ProductList.xml")

  Return ds
End Function
```

And that's all we have to do to expose our XML file to the world! Don't believe me? We better check, Debug | Start Without Debugging. In the Internet Explorer browser click GetProductList, then click the Invoke button. You will see the XML data that will be passed to the caller. Call me weird, but I'd rather look at data in an HTML table than an XML document, so let's make the necessary changes (there's only two) to our web page to display the data returned by `GetProductList`.

Open the ProductSupply project in Visual Studio. The first thing we need to do is refresh our WebService Web Service proxy. Open the Solution Explorer, double-click Web References, right-click the WebService icon, and select Update Web Reference. Now open the code-behind file for `index.aspx` and comment out the following line of code:

```
Dim ds = ps.GetPavlovaProduct()
```

and replace it with this line:

```
Dim ds = ps.GetProductList()
```

Now we're ready to test again, Debug | Start Without Debugging:

ProductName	CompanyName
Alice Mutton	Pavlova, Ltd.
Aniseed Syrup	Exotic Liquids
Boston Crab Meat	New England Seafood Cannery
Camembert Pierrot	Gai pâturage
Carnarvon Tigers	Pavlova, Ltd.
Chai	Exotic Liquids

This concludes our XML example. You may have noticed that neither the console application nor the web method contained any error handling code. This was omitted for brevity, but I would highly recommend adding some sort of error handling before putting something like this in a production environment.

Exposing Active Directory

Active Directory is yet another possible data source for Web Services. However, one thing we need to be careful of when exposing Active Directory as a Web Service is security (covered in Chapter 13). Not that other data is not worthy of security, just that we may want to be extra careful in this case. At the same time, there can be instances where providing this sort of data as a Web Service could be very useful. Let's take a look at a few examples:

- **Contact information**. It may be beneficial for you to expose member data from a particular group. Information like e-mail address, phone number, and so on.
- **User Monitoring**. Expose user information like: logon name, number of times logged on, number of bad password attempts, last logon date, and so on.
- **Admin tool**. Create several web methods to allow administrators to add, modify and delete users.

Obviously, there are many other such examples.

As we have gone over quite a few exercises in this chapter already, we won't cover this example step by step. However, a full example can be downloaded with the rest of the book's source code. We'll also assume some level of understanding of Active Directory and won't drill down into all the "whys", as that is beyond the scope of this book.

The `System.DirectoryServices` namespace exposes Active Directory to us. It contains many classes, but for simplicity we will just look at one: the `DirectoryEntry` class that allows us to access specific Active Directory data for reading, modifying, or even adding. For example, if we wanted to access the Active Directory Users we would write something like:

```
Dim dirEntry As New DirectoryEntry("LDAP://CN=Users,DC=adsd,DC=ebohling,DC=com")
```

The MusicListeners Web Service

What our Web Service will do is return a typed DataSet of all the members of a particular group, MusicListeners. Plus, it will contain information about each member such as account name, e-mail address, username, and so on. To give you a point of reference, a screenshot of all the members in the MusicListeners group is below:

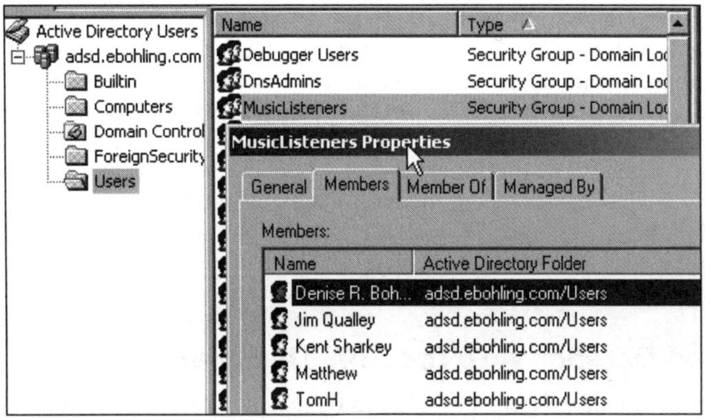

So, let's now take a look at the code we need to use to access these members and some of their information:

```
Private Function GetData(ByVal ADobject As String, _
                         ByVal PropertyName As String) As String
  Dim strValue As String = "none"
  Dim UserAccount As DirectoryEntry = New _
                         DirectoryEntry("LDAP:'" + ADobject.ToString())

  ' Get Property Value
  If (UserAccount.Properties(PropertyName).Count > 0) Then
    strValue = UserAccount.Properties(PropertyName)(0).ToString()
  End If
  Return strValue
End Function

<WebMethod()> _
Public Function GetMusicListeners() As MLUsers

  Dim dirEntry As DirectoryEntry = New _
   DirectoryEntry("LDAP://CN=MusicListeners,CN=Users,DC=adsd,DC=ebohling,DC=com")

  Dim objValue As Object
  For Each objValue In dirEntry.Properties("member")

    Dim Account As String = GetData(objValue.ToString(), "cn")
    Dim Email As String = GetData(objValue.ToString(), "mail")
    Dim LogonName As String = GetData(objValue.ToString(), "sAMAccountName")
```

```
        Dim LogonCount As String = GetData(objValue.ToString(), "logonCount")
        Dim Created As String = GetData(objValue.ToString(), "whenCreated")
        Dim Changed As String = GetData(objValue.ToString(), "whenChanged")

                ' Add data to data row
        userDS.Users.AddUsersRow(Account, Email, LogonName, LogonCount, Created)
      Next
      Return userDS
    End Function
```

The unfortunate thing, which you may have already noticed, is that the data we access in Active Directory is in the form of collections, which makes it less elegant than if it were truly object-oriented, but we can still work with it. What we have done here is first to get the `Directory` entry for the MusicListeners group. We then iterate through all of its members using `dirEntry.Properties("member")`. To save a lot of typing and to make our code more streamlined we have created a private wrapper method that takes our member path, `objValue.ToString`, and property name, and returns the appropriate value. Again, not very elegant, but the best we can do in this situation. After we have gathered all the information we want for a particular member, we add the data to our typed `DataSet userDS`. Though it is not obvious here, we used the XML Designer to create `MLUser.xsd`, so we could return a typed `DataSet` to the caller. The XML Designer was used in this case because we did not have direct access to the data source.

Creating a Typed DataSet with the XML Designer

Since we used the Component Designer earlier in the chapter, let's take a moment to look at how we create a typed `DataSet` using the XML Designer. This time we will need to add a `DataSet` to our project by following the steps. First, right-click on the project ADService | Add | Add New Item... Then select Data Set in the list and call it MLUsers.xsd. Then open the Toolbox and drag an `element` object from the XML Schema tab. You should now see the following on your screen:

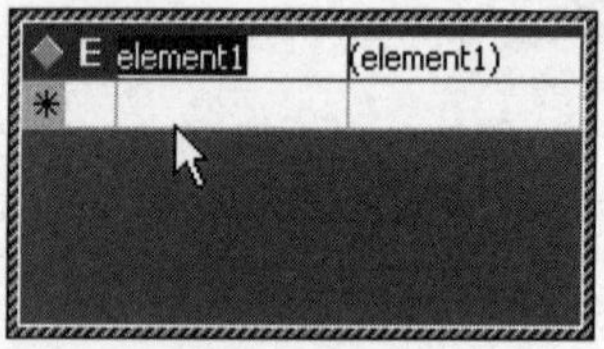

Again, we are using the XML Designer instead of the Component Designer because we cannot automatically create the XSD file from a data source, so we will create it ourselves. First change element1 to Users. Then we will add the following string elements: `AccountName`, `Email`, `LogonName`, `LogonCount`, `Created`, giving us the following:

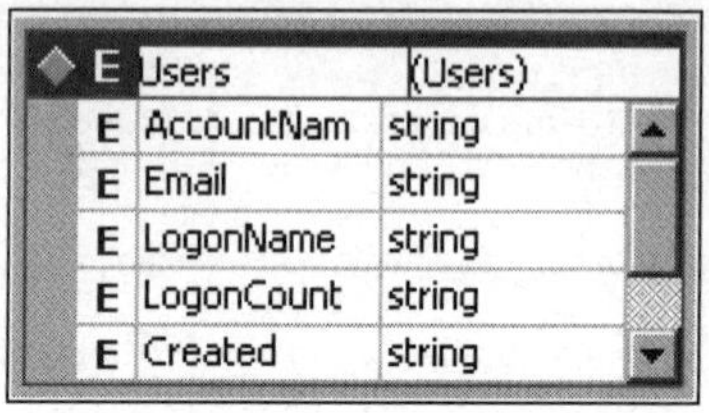

Now, simply save the file. This action will automatically create our `MLUsers` class, `MLUsers.vb`. That's all there is to it.

For our final step, after we have gone through each member of the MusicListeners group, we return the `userDS DataSet`.

Though we won't cover it here, you should now be able to create a client of your choice to consume this Web Service. Again, a sample client has been provided in the book's source code.

Summary

ASP.NET Web Services have provided the developer community with a fairly straightforward and efficient way to expose many data sources. Everything from ADO.NET to Active Directory can be exposed to create read-only or writeable data. The advantages we gain by exposing these data sources as Web Services include:

- The ability to access information from other operating systems
- The permission for access across firewalls
- The ability for developers to reuse code very easily
- The limitation of database connections to servers
- The empowerment of business to embrace new business models that were previously very hard or impossible to achieve

Though we only covered a small portion of the abilities in each of our data sources, this chapter has given you a starting point from which you can explore the richness of using data with Web Services.

PROFESSIONAL
ASP.NET
WEB
SERVICES

16

Web Services in Your Business

Web Services have the potential to replay history as a microcosm of the Internet. They have many similarities to the Internet: new protocols like SOAP, doing the same thing but in a different way, lots of hype, industry support. They have a few differences: obviously being a fish in the fishbowl is one of them. Yet, history is the best teacher, and it serves us well here.

We aren't looking back to the beginnings of the Internet for our lesson. We need only go to the mid-nineties. That time when the first entrepreneur went to a banker and laid down a great pitch for a business. This business had no real motive or profit expectation, yet it used the Internet, so it was deemed good. This was the beginning of what we called the "Tech Bubble".

The upside of the Internet being such a force in business was that it is a fantastic technology that is easy to use. The problems came in when investors and customers realized two things. First, just because the Internet is great doesn't make the business using it great. Second, since it is easy to use, everyone and their brother are using it if they know what they're doing, or even if they don't.

From this example alone, we can see that Web Services could follow the same path. Businesses can use SOAP because it is great technology and it is easy to use, although this will never make a bad business plan better, or a difficult solution easier. Yet that same ease of use could easily propel reams of worthless and potentially damaging Web Services into the Internet.

Our goal here is to prevent that. Lesson one: Web Services are not a hammer for every programming nail. We have hammered home that concept (excuse the pun) since the beginning of the book, and it is still a focus. The key to building good business solutions with Web Services is knowing when to use them, when not to use them, and how they fit into business enterprise solutions. We've learned about design and development, now we need to discuss implementation.

> **Remember the old adage – "Business drives technology, technology does not drive business."**

Just like with the Internet, Web Services are a powerful weapon against business problems that have communication as their primary focus. To build strong solutions, we must start with the problem, not the technology. So, we will start here with some business problems that need to be solved. These are the kinds of problems that Web Services have already solved well in the last 18 months.

Now that we have a starting place for knowing when to use Web Services, we need to fit them into the larger scope. Specifically, we need to keep out of trouble, and then reap the rewards. So, we'll go over legal issues, then getting paid – more or less the opposite sides of the same coin.

Once the problems have been solved and the issues have been ironed out, we have finished Web Services. We'll then take a look at business examples of Web Services. Finally, we'll take a look at talking to company principals about Web Services, with some ideas for language and examples that may help you to get the point across to managers who need these solutions, but don't know it yet.

In summary, here is what we are going to cover in this chapter:

- Business problems that need solutions
- Legal issues with Web Services
- Getting paid for your efforts
- A few business case studies
- Talking to your boss about Web Services

Business Problems That Need Solutions

The core of Information Technology is using available information effectively to get a job done. The expanse of industries using computers to handle this store of information today is somewhat overwhelming. Something is common among them, though. All of them are using the technology to solve their problems – to get something done faster, cheaper, easier, better. Then, when one of these new processes has a problem – solve that too. Generally, computers are tools used to smooth the road ahead, just as machines were a hundred years ago.

As mentioned above, Web Services solve specific kinds of problems, just as the Internet did for savvy businesses in 1996. When Netscape coined the term "intranet", many industrious Internet specialists (author included) were using the web to do just that, and were glad for something to call it! Web Services are similar – hundreds of home-grown solutions at varying degrees of success are out there, and now a standardizing force has come along to help with the interoperation.

Why did we work to get intranets running in the mid 1990s? Simply put – to get information there faster and more accurately. We had a problem to solve, and we solved it – long before there was a name for it. Then, after there was a name, the technology was used to solve problems that just didn't exist. Web Services can fall into the same trap – they can be used to solve problems that just don't exist.

There is, fortunately, a roadmap; three fairly well understood problems that Web Services solve well. The first of these is the intranet solution – internal communication between disparate applications inside your company's network. The second is the extranet solution – exposing business logic to partners and customers in a controlled fashion. Finally, the third solution is the Internet solution, or sales of a universally needed service to the masses. It must be mentioned that Web Services are a piece of this puzzle, not the whole solution, but they can be an important piece indeed.

One more note before we get into the meat of this topic. The strict attitude presented here should not discourage anyone from creating a new, unforeseen use for a Web Service. Let the ideas here act as a focal point for your creative problem solving, not as a ceiling to prevent you from looking upward.

Internal To Your Business

Web Services provide an interesting tool in the tool belt of the average enterprise architect. Firstly, they provide a mechanism to standardize logic throughout the organization. Secondly, they provide a solution to the problem of interoperability between various platforms in use inside the enterprise. Both of these non-traditional uses for Web Services provide a good introduction to SOAP for your organization, and an easy sale to the management. Let's look at each in turn.

Standardized Logic

When working in the role of an enterprise architect, one of the most difficult problems to face is that of best practices. A structured development environment can have as many rules and life cycle plans as possible, and the code is still at the mercy of the attitude of the reviewers at code review time.

Many project managers and architects solve this dilemma with standard code, in raw or compiled format. For instance, a common practice is to create a standard DLL that is used for data access. It includes a standard method for the creation of a data connection object, for the creation of a recordset from a table, and so on. Another example is standard error handling in the form of an included ASP file.

The problem with this is portability. Keeping all of the projects up to date with the standard code is very hard. MDAC versions change in the middle of a project; or half of your enterprise may be using ASP 2 and half may be using ASP 3, for example. The code needs to be constantly redistributed to meet the needs of your organization. While this isn't impossible by any means, it is remarkably inconvenient. Another problem, specifically for ASP and other uncompiled code, is that of changes by the developers. It's a common problem, and tough to catch in code reviews.

Web Services provide a simple and straightforward way to provide controlled access to standardized code that can be used throughout an organization in many cases. An enterprise-level machine, similar to an Exchange server, can be used to provide internal access to exposed logic for these standardized tasks, like error handling of database access.

Interoperability Between Platforms

Microsoft didn't create Web Services, and though .NET plays very well with SOAP, it is an open platform. IBM, Sun, Fujitsu, and many other big players are offering functionality to support XML Web Services on their platforms. This can be a massive benefit to IT shops with divergent platforms. For more on the design considerations for this topic, see the *Design* section in Chapter 8.

Interoperability is a major problem for IT managers. When HTML made an appearance on the intranet front around 1996, developers started creating user interfaces that were platform-agnostic. With Web Services, we can create business logic that is platform-agnostic. If the corporate database is huge, and an AS400 is used to store customer data, Web Services can be developed to access the data then touched by any of the platforms discussed above – any that support SOAP. This platform interoperability will make a significant impact on the future deployment plans of many organizations.

External To Partners

XML has long been thought of as the new language of business data. A role that Electronic Data Interchange (EDI) has held for many years, business data exchanges are a sure bet when looking for a way to streamline your business. A decrease in the cost of each business document goes a long way towards an increase in the bottom line.

For years, companies have held a lock on the secure networks used to transfer EDI files from partner to partner. The creation of XML was seen as a beginning to the end of the lock. But something remains to be done. The secure networks that transfer the documents are still necessary, still locked up. This is because the EDI companies have found ways to increase the value of their document transfer service by creating small bits of logic on either side to interface, for instance, with the invoicing or shipping system. Enter Web Services. With a secure channel, the SOAP protocol now provides everything the EDI VAN does:

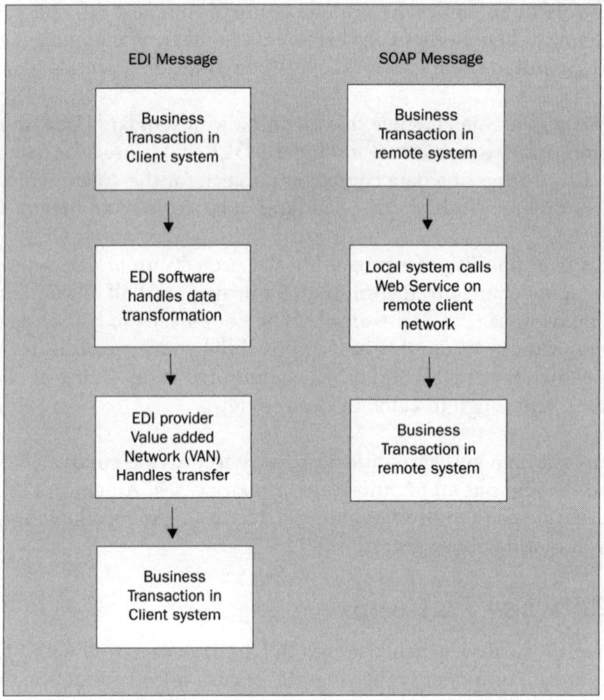

As shown in the above diagram, the XML system has fewer steps and doesn't require a third party. Here are some key things to note about the comparison:

- Security – with SSL, 128-bit security is possible for use in protecting the document transfer.
- XML Document – XML is the anointed successor to EDI, and SOAP is designed to carry an XML payload.
- Exposed business logic – the last piece of the puzzle. Since Web Services by nature expose business logic, the final lock on the EDI market is broken.
- Industry standards – though the data dictionary still needs to be standardized, the standardization of XML will go a long way toward global acceptance in this world marketplace we live in.

Microsoft's Foot in the Door

BizTalk is Microsoft's shot at using SOAP and XML to take a bite out of the EDI market. Touted as a business class message passing system, BizTalk is a good tool for Microsoft-based organizations that need EDI-like services.

The problem? It's a shot in the dark. There are several differing standards for business document transfer, and at least with EDI you were sure that your partners could read your format correctly, with no programming. Read more about BizTalk in Chapter 17.

Making it Happen

So why isn't BizTalk, along with XLang, ebXML, Rosettanet, and all the others, taking over with their XML-based message passing? It's because EDI has a massive hold on a tremendous number of markets.

The background of EDI presses back into the late 1970s. Organizations just beginning to use computers for business traffic realized that a standard of some type would be necessary in order to streamline the tremendous amounts of paperwork generated by our growing economy, especially within the federal government. The standard needed to provide four things:

- Hardware independence
- Clarity
- Reduction in data re entry
- Transaction support

In 1979 the American National Standards Institute (ANSI) gave the X12 standard its stamp of approval and created an Accredited Standards Committee to oversee the delivery of the standard. The International Standards Organization, working with the European nations, eventually settled on a standard called EDIFACT in 1987. Although these two standards are generally not interoperable, both have continued in joint development since that time.

Both of these standards do the same thing – provide the data schema for tens of thousands of business documents in scores of industries. Both of these standards have the backing of a major standards organization. Both of these standards have years of history. Our extranet plans – well, they have none of these.

So What Can We Really Do?

Realistically, we can't replace EDI tomorrow. There is too much investment and history, and many of these companies won't change from one protocol to another to create a standard. What we can do is take a page from EDI's book. The problems that EDI solved in the 70s are here today still for many companies, and XML Web Services will have a place in solving them.

Let's look at a problem that I am solving right now. A major distributor of computer equipment provides an interface to its online catalog for value added resellers to use in a number of different ways. Among other options, they can customize a hosted store, or download the catalog nightly to their own server. Then the VAR can sell directly from the distributor catalog with their markup, and provide their own interface.

This is a pretty standard scenario in a number of different markets, and can be expanded to many different arrangements as well. But what if it were implemented as an EDI-like Web Service? The distributor could open several methods for partner use, replicating a shopping-cart-like functionality. This would have to include requests for lists of product, and finalizing a transaction. The partner could implement the actual session-level stuff. It would look something like this:

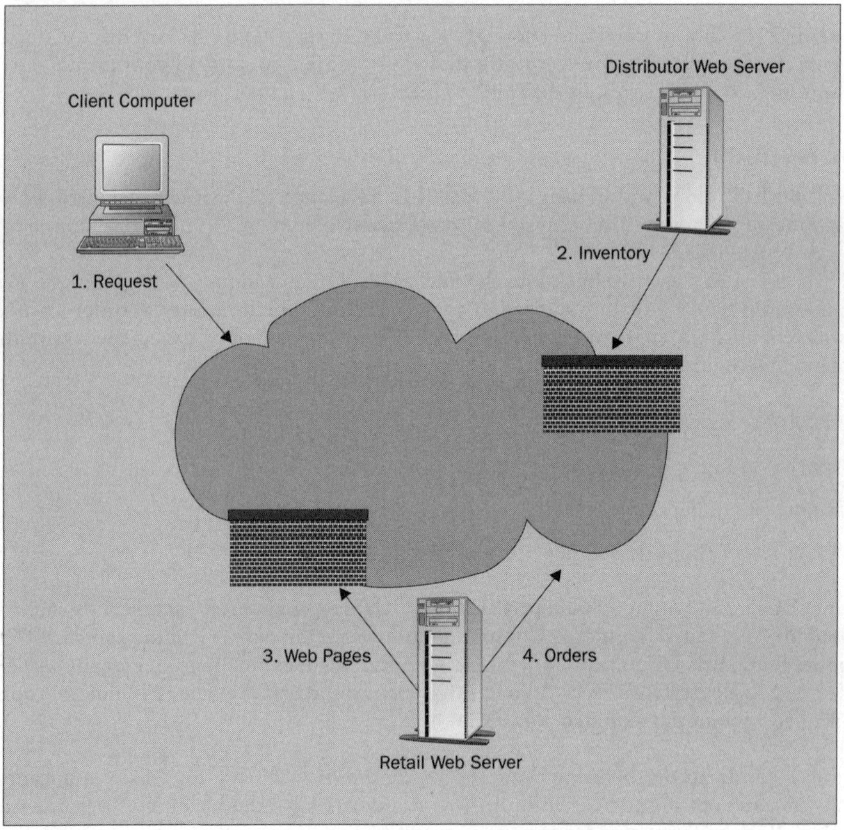

The client makes a request that is handled by our retail web server. The code behind that web server makes a Web Service call to the distributor web server, getting inventory information that supports the client request and returns it to the client in the form of a web page. Then, when the order is completed, it is sent to the distributor with a second service, completing the sale.

Solutions like these will come closer to reality as bandwidth gets more stable, but there are a number of systems that run just this way, only worse, using older technologies – right now. So this is a better solution, in many ways, than the retail web server generating an EDI purchase order and wiring it to the distributor. In addition, the SOAP messages via Web Services are scalable and extensible for future technologies and business problems.

Other Extranet Uses

Hopefully this has started your mind working. There is a quantity of EDI-like logic that can be implemented between partners, even those who don't share the same technology. How about a simple messaging application, for instance? It could simply be something that can be reused, which accepts messages in a known format for distribution within an organization. This has a myriad of uses within the financial and IT sectors of partnering companies.

Even more directly, how about allowing your partner companies to expose some of your logic directly on their web sites? For example, if you make widgets and have a Widget Support application that accepts plain text queries from clients on your page, how about exposing that as a Web Service? Your retailers could expose the application with little trouble, and support for your widgets would be even easier to use.

All of this fits into the "Business to Business" mold that was cast before the mighty crash of 2000. The truth is that if you are internal to the situation and considering some software to help hook your business to your partners you may be able to create your own using Web Services and save some cash – this is one of the few things that really is easier than it looks!

External to Customers

There are so many opportunities to sell these tools to the outside world that we couldn't possibly talk about all of them – or even a segment – here. Maybe Wrox will do a book just on ASP.NET Web Services That Are External To Customers or something. In discussion with my interviewees for this book, we looked at hundreds of opportunities already out there as test-types of services, including:

- Microsoft Passport
- .NET My Services
- Subscription software systems
- Chat Services
- Credit Card Services
- Pay Pal-like financial services
- Mailing list management
- Registration services
- Conversion services (financial or otherwise)

- Shipping calculations
- 'Frequent Surfer' services
- Stock services
- Translators (Even VB.NET to C#!)
- Air travel weather
- Network Management
- Anonymous Remailers
- Tip of the Day server
- News Headlines

The list goes on and on. We have finally encountered the world of Software as a Service, just as Bill Gates envisioned in "Business @ the Speed Of Thought", and as several before him sketched. In fact, Microsoft is really banking on this, with their Passport and Registration Web Services. They are actually changing their very successful business model to work with an envisioned New World of business technology.

Smart Services?

A good example of this is the Smart Tags Microsoft is building into Windows and Office XP. A Smart Tag is a string with some type of information attached to it. A knowledge worker can leverage the intelligence of applications that support Smart Tags to provide what a human knows intuitively–that is, the ability to recognize a particular string as type "person's name" and to respond with a list of possible actions. From that list the user can select an appropriate action. The actions include sending an e-mail message to, to scheduling a meeting with, and getting the telephone number or accessing personal records of the said person.

By defining a common interface for annotating data within documents, and by providing a standard architecture for associating actions with this annotated data, developers can supply logic and a set of consistent actions for data. One analogy is that Smart Tags make tasks "object-oriented," rather than "application-oriented".

Though the Smart Tags in themselves are a pretty neat technology, imagine these tags as a logical user interface to Web Services. Even just a corporate custom dictionary that checks the spelling of corporate products could make a huge difference in the way employees use office technology.

It goes further than that, though. A great example is in the Smart Tag SDK Documentation. Microsoft suggests a Smart Tag distributed by a bookstore, which references their book library every time a user reads a book title, author or other reference in an e-mail or web page. Aside from the fact that some of us would find that annoying, imagine that some would really like the ability to just use WidgetBooks.com to take a look at a book when their buddy references it in an e-mail. Plus, WidgetBooks.com would sell a lot more books because of this.

Microsoft has provided the Smart Tag API Version 1 for use with Visual Basic 6 and Visual C++, but since the Smart Tag supports an XML list for its recognizers and actions, we could easily implement them as .NET Web Services. Plus, it is likely that it won't be long before there is .NET Smart Tag API .

A Smart Tag **recognizer** is a piece of code that adds type information to a piece of text sent to it. For example, a recognizer for our WidgetBooks.com would label "Wrox Press" as type `BookPublisher`. At the technical level, using the current API, recognizers are implemented as automation servers, implementing the `IDispatch` function. This is no longer necessary in .NET since classes are self-describing, and Web Services are no different.

Smart Tag **actions** are user-invoked "verbs" that are associated with data of a particular type. In our example, "List books by this publisher" might be an action that is implemented by a given piece of recognized text.

Now let's be clear, Office XP – the prime focus for Smart Tags right now – doesn't support .NET. That doesn't mean an enterprising company couldn't create an entire catalog of Smart Tags that are run from their public web server as Web Services.

Legal Issues

Like most technologies, Web Services can be easily mishandled. Just as publish-it-yourself web pages caused a ton of copyright violations, Web Services have a host of problems of their own. On the copyright angle, we have the whole Screen Scraping technology, designed to make it easier to expose information from static web pages as Web Services. At the contractual level, there are a number of security and Quality of Service concerns that make the issue of revenue-generating services a little harder. Like most issues of this type, however, good planning will get past the problems.

Screen Scraping and Intellectual Property

Screen scraping is parsing information from a static file, such as an HTML file, and exposing the information as a Web Service. This is a fantastic technology if you own the HTML file in question. If your competitor owns it, that's another matter. I am neither a lawyer, nor do I play one on TV. There is, however, a legal way and an illegal way to screen scrape. If you have an application that is presenting information using ASP or another server-side scripting technology, scraping this information from a known format may be easier than rewriting the back-end application. A Web Service can make this information available even back to the hosting application, for a small sacrifice of performance. An illegal example of this is looking up a stock quote on CNNFN and selling access to the quote as part of your service. Pretty clear distinction.

Avoiding legal trouble here is fairly easy – restrain yourself from using someone else's information. In a project I recently looked at, the client had a rather restrictive Point Of Sale system that created text reports formatted for printing, but didn't provide a CSV-formatted version of this information. I suggested an ASP.NET Web Service that would expose the information in the repost using a private method that parsed the known format of the text report:

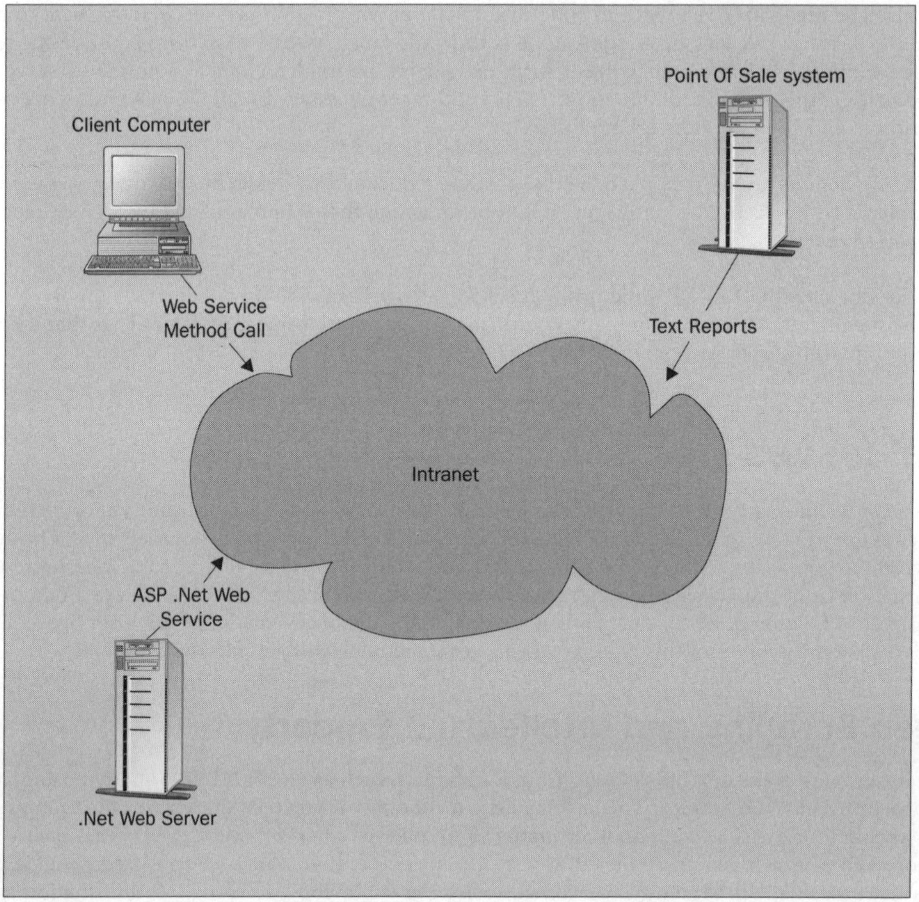

Screen scraping has a problem other than legal issues: a change in report format breaks your application, thus your service. If you have control of the starting point, though, this is not an issue – another reason for staying away from using other people's information. HTML does help with this, though. If you are in an environment that is using Office 2000 or XP to publish documents to an intranet, it is easy to use screen scraping to get to this information programmatically using the easily parsed HTML format.

Security

Another legal consideration is the guarantee of security from you to the users of the service. Security considerations were covered in Chapters 13 and 14, where we discussed different techniques including:

- Encryption
- Client Certificates
- Windows Authentication

- Basic Authentication
- SOAP-based header security
- Digital Signatures

The fact is, even 128-bit public key encryption can be broken in time. How does one guarantee security under those circumstances? The same way you guarantee the security of your shopping cart software.

- Authenticate users
- Encrypt traffic
- Monitor usage
- Use exception reporting
- Maintain physical security
- Take care of it if it breaks

Authentication of users seems to be the simplest of considerations, but it is being overlooked in too many circumstances. If you start the SOAP request in SSL, you can even pass the username and password as part of the remote method invocation.

While this is moving along, check your logs. 80% of encroachment can be caught through watching the exceptions recorded by IIS or your service. If someone is trying to break in, they will likely have to try a few times before they get it right. Make sure you are ready when that happens. Several products currently available over the counter (such as Ipswitch WhatsUp Gold) will watch log files and warn the administrator via pager or e-mail when there is a problem.

Finally, be prepared to make reparation when something does go wrong. Assume the worst, and then build that into your business plan. Fortunately, the banks are much more Internet-friendly than they once were and will cover losses to crackers under some circumstances – especially when your security is up to par. However, be ready for the worst, and then hope it doesn't happen.

QOS

Quality of Service, or QOS, is a general term that applies to any kind of product that provides a lasting benefit to a user. In the software world, it represents everything from availability to scalability to performance to mean time between failures. With regards to Web Services, QOS generally breaks down into these areas:

- Accuracy
- Availability
- Stability

While each of these will be taken in turn, the package is a major consideration as well. Generally, be careful what you guarantee. By a recent statistic, Schwab loses a million dollars a minute when there is a glitch in its trading system. Consider carefully what kind of service quality you are going to offer and stick to it.

Accuracy

This is pretty straightforward. Like any other method, you should return accurate information with your Web Service. Just because it is a slick new technology doesn't let you out of testing, testing, and more testing. In your Quality of Service statement, mention the likelihood of a problem with the information being returned. Take into account the source of your information. Test over a large span of time and try to compile statistics. You'll be surprised to find that you aren't 100% accurate most of the time.

Availability

This is a sticky point. Since the availability of your service depends on so many things, you have to be careful how you approach the availability statement. Consider all of the points of failure between you and the client:

- Your internal LAN
- Your Internet connection
- Your firewall
- Your ISP
- The client ISP
- The client firewall
- The client Internet connection
- The client LAN

If you are producing a service with a requirement for high availability, consider redundancy. Providing Quality of Service for a Web Service is just like providing Quality of Service for a web site, and has similar benefits. Being able to state with certainty that your service will be available is a major sales point. Consider the following steps for preventing network-related downtime:

- Host from two locations
- Provide Network Load Balancing for your IIS Servers, and clustering for your SQL Servers
- If you are a single location, bring in connectivity from two ISPs
- Ensure stability and security of the physical environment
- Avoid single points of failure, like network and RAID cards

Stability

Stability in Web Services basically comes down to error handling. You have to consider the possibility of crashing your IIS server, and of crashing the consuming application. Crashing IIS 5.0 is not likely, because ASP applications are well encapsulated. Using Windows Scripting Host (WSH), in fact, you can even set IIS to restart if locked in an endless loop or crashed. The more significant concern is damaging a client application. Logging of errors for later exception handling is another good move.

Client-use stability is simple if a good, understandable error handling routine is established. Make sure that there is a generic handler, no matter what method you choose. Finally, make sure your documentation clearly states how to implement traps for known errors on the consumer's side. This will prevent the "he said, she said" arguments when the client has problems.

Getting Paid

Whether selling to customers or providing value-added services to partners, we'll want to get paid for our Web Service. Payment for small bits of processing has been a problem since CompuServe and Prodigy started selling small services and documents online in the Eighties. There isn't a good way to do it, because credit card companies – the primary currency on the Internet – charge a percentage with a floor for each transaction. If Visa wants 1.9 % with a minimum of forty cents for every transaction, it doesn't take much out of our profit for the average $200 COM component. But for a single-use Web Service at fifty cents, it eats a massive hole in the bottom line.

A key point in developing a business model for payment for Web Services is defining your customer. In most cases the customer for a service is the end user – the one who reaps the benefit from using the service. In the case of Web Services, though, the customer is often the developer who is providing his or her own service or software to the public. This makes for some interesting twists in design for your service, as discussed in Chapter 8, and it also provides for some non-traditional payment systems.

Generally, to get paid for your service you'll want to know who is using it. That will be the first on your task list no matter what. From there you have a couple of options, which we'll cover here.

Accepting Authentication

Authentication itself was covered as part of the chapter on security, Chapter 13. Generally speaking, the consumer passes in a user ID and password, and we check it against our database of users. Users, in this case, can be the service consumers, or the end users. If they are paying for the service, this is where we charge them.

But how to charge? The simplest method, like the model adopted by the NorthernLight search engine, is to keep an account full on behalf of the user, essentially aggregating several future uses of the service into one credit card transaction. NorthernLight gives your account $10 in "free" money when you set up your account. After you use that up in $1.50 white paper purchases, they bill your card for another $10. This is a simple model that translates nicely to Web Services.

For instance, when the user uses the service, include a private method call as part of the exposed method that debits the set amount from their account. You'll need to use ASP.NET transactions for this – covered in Chapter 11. When the account gets to a specified level, use a SQL trigger to debit their card on file for another payment of the larger set amount.

The problem with this is tracking accounts for users. Even with this simple model, there will be problems. How long do you store user information? If they haven't used it in five years, do you credit their card? What if it is gone? If their card fails, and they use the service, do you throw an error? All tough questions, with no simple answers. This may be more trouble than most developers are interested in taking on for the creation of a Web Service.

Outright Purchase

When we create a COM component for public use, we sell it through a broker like Component Source. Will this work for Web Services? As it turns out, it really doesn't.

First, Web Services don't really work the same way as COM components. They are, as the name implies, a service. Selling them like a product is outside the logical model. Let's look at the technology there. If you were to physically sell the code behind the service, you are essentially selling a .NET Component (DLL file) just as if you were selling a COM component. Exposing it as a Web Service would be at the owner's expense and on their system. This is acceptable, of course, but outside the scope of the concept of Web Services.

Second, Web Services open up a new and exciting model to those of us who sell software. With a subscription-based model, clients won't have to buy a ton of software only to use a pound of it. Plus, we have a fantastic new revenue stream, gaining continuous income from a product that would normally be a one-shot payment.

Micropayments

As mentioned above, micropayments are a technology sought after since the beginnings of public access networks. We also talked about how the credit card companies often charge a fee for each transaction, and that percentage fee has a floor of some number of cents – if you have a transaction of only a dollar for instance, a 75-cent credit card charge will put quite a dent in your profit.

A micropayment is a low-friction electronic commerce system that allows for quality transactions and ease of use for the consumer. The W3C took on the frightful task of writing a standard for micropayments and gave up – largely because the definition of micropayment is so diverse from user to user.

For our purposes, micropayments are any small transaction that puts money in our pocket. They need to be able to handle as many transactions as there are users of our service, at a reasonable cost. We can manage this two ways – through a third-party service, or through our own.

Third-Party Micropayment Services

There are a host of third-party services, each with their own format, charges, protocol, and amount of flexibility. This is rather outside the scope of this book, but we'll mention some that worked with the W3C during their review of the micropayment standard.

- Cartio Micropayments
- Clickshare
- CyberCash: CyberCoin
- DigiCash
- Enition
- Internet Dollar
- Jalda
- Millicent by Compaq
- NewGenPay MicroPayments
- OpenMarket
- Pay2See
- Trivnet
- The Ultimus Solution
- Wave Systems Corp
- PayFlowPro by Verisign

Implementing one of these solutions works essentially in the same way as mentioned in the *Accepting Authentication* section above, except we will be communicating with an outside network to register the user. Another option in this would be the use of a Web Service-specific broker, like SalCentral, who will even take the authentication off our hands. Either of these would be a good solution for a quick, simple way to get a body of clients using our service, and paying for the privilege.

Rolling Our Own Micropayment Service

This is a potential service in itself. If you compare the requirements of a micropayment service and the benefits of a Web Service, you find unerring matches throughout.

- A light, quick protocol
- Multi-platform support
- Secure
- Ubiquitous

The only problem is the distributed transaction issue – as things stand we can't include a Web Service as part of a transaction, which would likely be a requirement. If we could get past that, through XLang or another protocol, a new breed of services could be born.

Can we convince credit card companies to allow us to do this cheaply? Right now, transaction fees will eat it alive, but there is still hope. Alternatively, you could use the NorthernLight model above, and batch smaller transactions into larger ones for the sake of the banks. A host of opportunities abound.

Still, as we'll see, aggregation through subscription seems to be the best model. The micropayment strategy on the Internet is not mature enough yet for a production system, and rolling your own – while a fantastic business idea – probably won't be high up on most developers' task lists when trying to get something else done.

Subscriptions

Sometimes technology works better when it is simple. Subscriptions are the way cable companies, newspapers, and Six Flags have made their money for as long as money has been spent on such things. Pay one fee to get into the park, and all the rides – as many as you can ride – are free. This is undoubtedly the quickest, simplest and most effective way to get paid for your Web Service.

As part of your authentication information, you should have a user table, either in Active Directory, or in the SQL Server database. Along with the authorization information, an effective date is all you need to make the subscription system work.

Information	Type
Username	`VarChar(20)`
Password	`VarChar(12)`
Effective date	`DateTime`

A little code in our authentication method that checks the date, and a little code in our payment module that changes the date when the user pays for the subscription, are all we need to support the system. The only difficulty here is determining the charge, which is heavily dependent on the business model. As part of beta testing, we should track average usage, and assure that our subscription charges meet our costs given a certain number of subscribers. This is especially true if we are paying for our content.

The first argument against the use of a subscription system is that it doesn't have much of a history of working on the Internet. Many content providers attempting to make money charging subscription fees have failed or gone to advertising supported models. For our case, however, this is not so much of an issue. Remember that the consumer of our product – the one paying the fees – is a programmer, or a company using our service to provide some value-added service to another. Companies have a much higher incidence of supporting subscription-supported content than do consumers.

Favorites Service Model

The MSDN Architecture team took a tack on the payment issue that may shed light on Microsoft's future model as a corporation as a whole. They have implemented a licensing model, allowing developers to license the Favorites service as if it were content. A license is an agreement between a customer and a Web Service provider regarding use of the Web Service. Since they have defined "customer" as the developer, not the end user, the developer becomes a licensee of their Favorites service.

Because the Favorites service also offers a login module for the end user, they have a more complex system than our simple subscription model above. They are genuinely setting up companies as licensees, and when the user logs into the licensee, they are also logging into the service. This is not the usual model, but since they are offering to track each user's favorites, it must be part of the service.

Their licensing system works in this way. As you might imagine, it added a significant amount of complexity to the rather simple service. When a SOAP request comes into the Web Service, a login method contacts the Login DLL. This component checks the licensee against the data structure for licensees – similar to our subscriptions above – then passes the request on to the Favorites service. In addition to this, there is a public and internal HTTP web site that allows for users to update their license information, or a phone center to update the license on the customer's behalf.

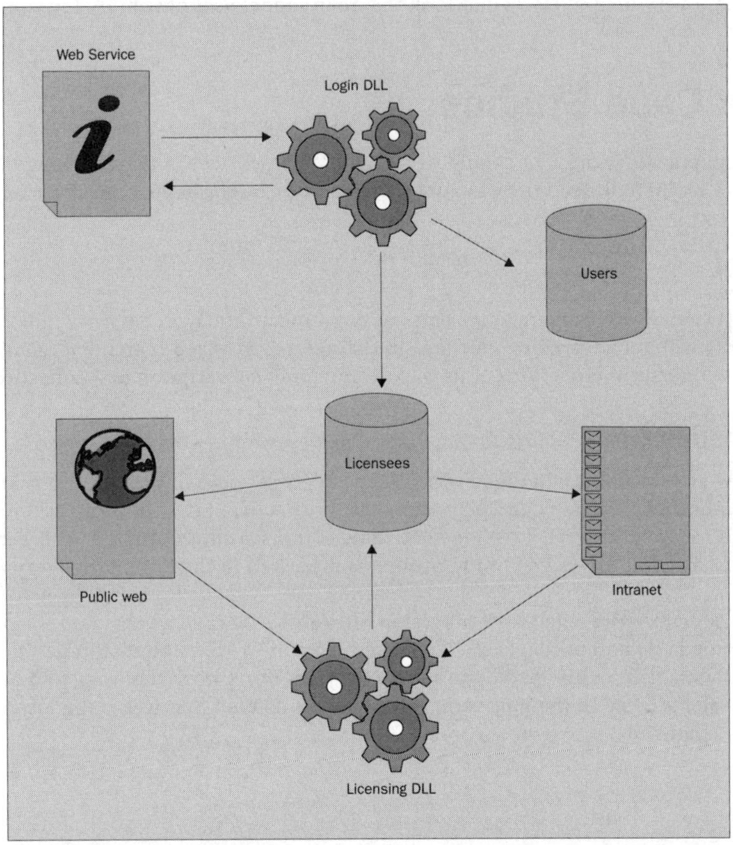

This model is a very good example of a service that needs to communicate with a body of consumers of the service along with the end users.

A Final Thought On Payment

We've looked at a number of potential solutions for payment, including:

- Simple authentication and billing
- Outright purchase
- Micropayments
- Subscriptions
- Licensing

What we didn't cover is the simplest method – free services. The Internet was bred on free services, and Web Services shouldn't overlook that in their effort to become commonplace. What better way to show off what your software can do than to offer a limited access to the product through a Web Service? By doing this you can track users, gather a mailing list, test new functionality, get feedback, and make your sales department very happy. Don't overlook the open model as a possibility for your services.

Business Case Studies

Many organizations are using – or should be using – Web Services in their existing business model. Here we take a moment to see how what others have done might impact our decision making process.

SalCentral

SalCentral is a centralized brokerage for helping consumers find Web Services. They provide Web Service creators with an advertising mechanism that offers advanced search and quality assurance. SalCentral also offers a Web Service of its own: centralized subscription and collection of fees.

Business Challenge

SalCentral saw an opportunity in the new market of Web Services to provide a service of its own, supporting application designers and programmers. With a firm grasp of "Software As A Service", and the distributed nature of the World Wide Web, SalCentral set out to provide Web Service creators with a brokerage service that solves two of the problems discussed in the book: discovery and getting paid.

Software components – the client/server version of Web Services – are easy to sell and distribute. Since they are downloadable and packageable, they can be burnt to CDs and distributed to existing retailers, or given to retailers with online paradigms. Web Services don't work that way, and one of the more significant problems faced in the long-term development of Web Services is the location of services floating in the ether.

Traditional software is also easier to get paid for. Since it is packageable and rarely carefully licensed, programmers most often follow the outright purchase model discussed earlier in the chapter. Web Services, with their use-as-needed business paradigm, are more suited to a subscription model. There are few existing services available for independent developers to collect for use of their services, leaving them to build a system into each service.

Solution

In a single site, SalCentral provides solutions to both of these pressing problems. As part of their Authorize function, they provide an authentication and subscription service. As part of their listing service, they provide a potent search facility. In fact, they are planning on providing a peer-to-peer information service soon, which will improve their search functionality even more.

SalCentral's search functionality uses the documentation features of WSDL to provide almost perfect searching of Web Services. Their simple registration feature makes good use of the SOAP protocol in similar ways to UDDI – a protocol they plan to soon support. Collecting some generic data about the producing company completes their straightforward and efficient data collection procedure, and searching on the variety of information is fast and accurate. This is a good use of the WSDL format, and shows a good understanding of the information available.

Web Services will make a mark servicing Web Services, and SalCentral shows this with their Authorize services. Essentially, they have built their own SOAP subscription model, and a producer of a Web Service can easily plug it into their own system to assure that users are paying fees for the use of the service. In addition to the arguments a Web Service normally accepts, the author need only add a username and password and pass them to the Authorize service at SalCentral. This is a fantastic example of a technology supporting itself, and we should all take note of the efficiency of its use.

Benefits

SalCentral has a broad-reaching set of benefits:

- It benefits programmers everywhere by providing an easy-to-use set of tools to discover and subscribe to powerful Web Services developed by individuals and corporations alike.
- It benefits Web Service developers by providing a marketing and payment system almost impossible to achieve individually.
- It benefits the Web Service movement at large by showing how the system is supposed to work, and quieting at least two critic claims – that Web Services are hard to find, and harder to get paid for.

The Search for Extraterrestrial Intelligence (SETI) At Home

SETI wins the award for the "Most Likely Candidate For Using A Web Service That Isn't Actually Using One". This fantastic distributed client/server application – and others like it – can make good use of Web Services to slip their information through corporate firewalls without complex proxy protocols.

Business Challenge

The challenge for applications like SETI and United Devices' MetaProcessor is to function normally in this world of high security. Using non-standard ports, these programs have complicated setup schemes and often simply fail to work in secure environments. Today's system administrators, ever wary of crackers, lock down ports used by peer-to-peer and distributed applications because the network hardware has no pre-existing filters for the information. Providing access to these higher numbered ports is a security risk.

Solution

Web Services, running on the standard ports 40 and 443, provide an excellent mechanism for these products to run free of security concerns. In cases like MetaProcessor, where the information may be sensitive in itself, use of SSL port 443 and 128-bit encryption provides the security needed without setting off alarms at the network layer.

Benefits

Since many of these programs were conceived before the creation of the SOAP protocol, many versions are not using this technology, but they should. Web Services have a place inside existing applications too – a utilization that must not be overlooked. In our design cycle, we must remember that we all have a secure, open protocol for having our traditional applications communicate with the "mother ship".

Microsoft Passport

Microsoft decided to roll its own subscription service, rather than use SalCentral. Passport is the cornerstone to the .NET My Services platform, providing three services, Single Sign In Service (SSIS), Passport Express Purchase (PXP), and Kids Passport.

Business Challenge

As part of the software-as-a-service (SAAS) challenge, Microsoft produced the HailStorm initiative, subsequently rechristened .NET My Services. .NET My Services is a set of XML Web Services designed to integrate the oft-disjointed 'silos' of information managed by most of us who use technology to manage our day-to-day existence. Microsoft's challenge to implement .NET My Services was the same we face in the development of our Web Services – authentication, legal issues, and getting paid.

Solution

Passport is their solution – a globalized set of Web Services designed to funnel all users of the .NET My Services products and sites that use them through a common authentication mechanism. Microsoft has solved three problems with three subspecies of Passport:

- Single Sign In Services
- Passport Express Purchase
- Kids Passport

With Single Sign In, Microsoft has solved the authentication problems for not only .NET My Services, but also for those who choose to integrate .NET My Services into their web applications. SSIS provides some basic information to the provider, allowing it to customize the site for that user without having to maintain a large store of user information.

Express Purchase provides essentially the same service, but with more information collected from the end user and exposed to the consumer. Like the earlier Microsoft Wallet, PXP collects credit card information and has user authentication methods built in for shopping functionality. This flexible Web Service will be used by sites like Buy.com for purchasers of goods, and consumers of .NET My Services products to pay for information storage and retrieval.

Finally, Microsoft took on a few legal challenges with Kids Passport. Many states are producing strict laws as to what information can be collected from children. Microsoft has provided Kids Passport to allow children to experience the benefits of a customized Internet experience without having to subject themselves to giving their private information to everyone who asks.

Benefits

The Passport set of Web Services is again far reaching in its benefits. Microsoft has created a new paradigm, giving SAAS a path to reality without choking life from the protocols supporting it.

- Consumers benefit by having a more customized and centralized Internet experience.
- Web Service programmers get their services paid for, and have access to .NET My Services silos.
- Site designers don't have to maintain expensive client access lists for their domain.

Using These Sketches

Take a minute after you have read this section and look at the web for Web Services in use, or applications using Web Services. Use the three-point outline (Business Challenge, Solution, and Benefits) we used above to sketch out the features and benefits. Is this something you can use in your business? Is there something to learn? Does someone have a really new idea somewhere? Does it make you really think about your organization and how Web Services can help? Focusing on the successes of others will assist you in our next topic, talking to the boss.

Talking To Company Principals About Web Services

We have now discussed most of the business issues in place with Web Services. The final area of focus is developing a methodology to discuss this complex subject with non-technical stakeholders. Most of us have been in the position of having to talk to our boss about the pros and cons of a technology, or to a client about why spending the money to upgrade is a good idea. The concepts are the same; the message is different. Here are a few pointers to help clarify Web Services to the masses.

Features and Benefits – Not Protocol and Code

Business stakeholders are interested in the bottom line. There is no doubt that SOAP is a fantastic technology, and it is going to become an industry standard very quickly. The fact is, most business owners are not interested in that. Some are, but most are interested in the non-technical aspects of Web Services.

- They solve the communication problems between systems from different manufacturers
- System manufacturers currently in our IT shop support them already

- They are inexpensive to produce and maintain high Return on Investment
- They play well with Microsoft products, but are not a Microsoft technology
- There is a proven track record of recovering communication costs
- Communication is improved without sacrificing security
- Web Services fit into the existing Internet strategy

Web Services are a communication protocol, and they should be sold as such. If we stick to the communication benefits of SOAP, we will make a clearer presentation to end users. In fact, we often shouldn't even mention XML in most conversations, because there is such a sense of regimented thinking around that over-used buzzword. Web Services just help machines talk better. That's the take-home.

Leave the Ego On the Doorstep

Despite assurances in the above section, Web Services are a relatively unproven technology. Getting on the collective IT high horse and guaranteeing that Web Services will solve all the company's problems might not end well. As technology experts, we are recommending a stretch into a new technology because of the features and benefits mentioned above. Betting our reputation on a new technology is not the path to fame and riches. Risk planning takes effect here, even if your organization doesn't follow a software development cycle. Things can go wrong with any technology, and they are much more likely to go wrong with new technology.

Suggest to the boss that the organization implement some type of software risk management (SRM). SRM is a three-cog process that includes:

- Identification and analysis of potential risks
- Mitigation and control of downstream problems
- An Early Warning System that the risks are causing specific problems

Several organizations are dedicated to assisting software companies with SRM, not least the Software Engineering Institute (SEI). Acknowledging that there are risks associated with a new technology and planning to deal with them will allay some fears of management, and make continuing discussions much easier.

Make a Plan; Write It Down

Often, experienced software developers don't feel that they have the time to properly document the software development process for a project. Be aware that doing just that can save hours of discussion and argument in design meetings with decision makers. Just three documents will make everyone's life so much simpler:

- Project definition – describe what you are trying to do in one page. I even try to do it in 101 words; I call it a "MicroDesign".
- Project Specification – actually lay out how you are going to do the project.
    - Project Overview
    - Business Case

  - ❑ Recommendations
  - ❑ Cost – Benefit Analysis
  - ❑ Risk Analysis
  - ❑ Assumptions, dependencies and constraints
  - ❑ Stakeholders
  - ❑ Deliverables
- ❑ Test Plan – how we are going to go about making sure the application actually works like we said it would.

Couch the Discussion in Terms the Client Knows

"Web Services are like ..." well, OK, part of the reason Web Services are such an important technology is that they aren't much like anything else. But if we can find a few technologies that Web Services do resemble, we'll be in a better place.

Web Services are like DCOM. Microsoft's original distributed method call technology allows for the invocation of an object by a remote computer. If an organization is using distributed technology already, you're on your way. The only changes being made are moving to a standards-based format from a proprietary format, and the transportation of text-based information rather than binary.

Web Services are like peer-to-peer. If a non-technological person uses MS Messenger, then that person is familiar with peer-to-peer. Remember Microsoft and AOL arguing over merging their IM technology? This helps our case – if these tools used Web Services for their P2P protocol, there would be no argument.

Web Services are like Gentran (or BizTalk, or RosettaNet). That may be a stretch, but it is a closer match than some may think. EDI and XML are very similar, and Web Services and Gentran both pass XML around for system use. The parallels that can be drawn there lead us to many interesting uses of Web Services.

The point is that if we find technology within the organization that Web Services could potentially replace, in a standard, simple way, our job is that much easier. At their root, Web Services are nothing more than a standard way to run code on a remote computer. Find the existing system – preferably a problematic one – that does this already, and the entrance to the conversation about Web Services has been found.

Focus On the Need and the Solution

Earlier in the chapter we discussed a serious problem faced by the Internet. The technology became a buzzword, and was used when other technologies might have been better. If in thought and action every IT manager focuses on the need and the solution rather than the technology behind the solution, this problem will be averted in the arena of Web Services.

As IT specialists, we try to be solution providers, not solution seekers. Looking for a technology that solves a problem is so difficult because we are so often misled by marketing and a misinformed press. If we focus on the need at hand, and the solutions a technology brings to the table, it is less likely we will be drawn off track. Presenting that line of reasoning in our conversations will make the job of talking about Web Services to company principals that much easier.

Summary

This "in your business" chapter started with business problems that need to be solved, and ended with discussing them with the boss. In the meantime, we covered legal issues, including intellectual property, security, and quality of service. We also looked at payment for Web Services and determined that a subscription or licensing system is the best bet, until micropayments makes some headway as a standard. Finally we looked at some existing services and service candidates.

Our desire in writing this book is to assist the developer in the trenches with not only being able to implement Web Services with ASP.NET, but also to implement them well, and for the right reasons. To that end, we discussed the need for planning before talking, and the potential pitfalls of Web Services. We also went over the things that Web Services do well, and what they don't. It is our wish that this will spark some new ideas and debate, and help to make Web Services the technology of the hour, at least.

Professional ASP.NET Web Services
Professional ASP.NET
Web Services
Professional ASP.NET
Web Services
Professional ASP.NET
Web Services
Professional ASP.NET
Web Services
Professional ASP.NET
Web Services
Professional ASP.NET
Web Services
Professional ASP.NET
Web Services
Professional ASP.NET
Web Services
Professional ASP.NET
Web Services
Professional ASP.NET
Web Services
Professional ASP.NET
Web Services
Professional ASP.NET
Web Services
Professional ASP.NET
Web Services
Professional ASP.NET
Web Services
Professional ASP.NET
Web Services
Professional ASP.NET
Web Services
Professional ASP.NET
Web Services
Professional ASP.NET
Web Services
Professional ASP.NET
Web Services
Professional ASP.NET
Web Services
Professional ASP.NET
Web Services
Professional ASP.NET
Web Services
Professional ASP.NET
Web Services
Professional ASP.NET

17

Case Study – BizTalk

In this case study, we will take a look at Microsoft's BizTalk Server 2000. BizTalk is not a part of the .NET Framework, but it is one of the building blocks of the .NET platform. We will work through a great case study to see how BizTalk can be leveraged and the powerful role it can play in a Web Services architecture.

This chapter looks at:

- A brief overview of BizTalk Server 2000
- How to use BizTalk Server 2000 to aggregate Web Services

It is not intended to fully explain and explore BizTalk Server 2000, as that would be a complete book in itself (and in fact it is; see *Professional BizTalkr*, ISBN 1-86100-329-3). This chapter assumes some familiarity with BizTalk, and the aforementioned publication is an excellent way to get that familiarity.

In addition, the Web Services used in this case study have been kept simple so as not to detract from the focus of the chapter: the aggregation of .NET Web Services using BizTalk Server. Examples of more complex Web Services can be found in other chapters throughout this book.

BizTalk in a Nutshell

BizTalk is a two-pronged initiative from Microsoft. It consists of:

- BizTalk Framework specification
- BizTalk Server 2000 product

While it is not the goal of this chapter to be a definitive guide to BizTalk, we will briefly discuss the various components of the BizTalk initiative in order to provide you with a basic grounding. For more detailed information on BizTalk, please refer to Wrox's *Professional BizTalk* (ISBN 1-86100-329-3).

BizTalk Framework

The BizTalk Framework (version 2.0 was current at the time this was written) defines a SOAP-compliant message envelope. It adds value to the current SOAP specification (version 1.1, although there is a version 1.2 working draft) by focusing on business-related details such as idempotent delivery, guaranteed delivery via receipt request, finite document lifetime and more.

The BizTalk Server is capable of routing any XML document, not just BizTalk Framework-compliant documents. Although BizTalk Server 2000 works internally with XML documents, it can easily import EDI documents such as X12 or UN/EDIFACT, or flat files, allowing us to do custom transformations on the way in. Rather than shunning existing EDI initiatives, BizTalk Server embraces them, which makes it easy to use the BizTalk Server as a routing and processing controller for EDI documents.

BizTalk Server uses BizTalk Framework-compliant documents to provide "reliable messaging". It can also be used as a wrapper for non-XML messages.

Our BizTalk implementation will use standard XML documents as the input and output of the business process. We will not be using BizTalk Framework-compliant documents in our implementation.

BizTalk Server 2000

BizTalk Server 2000 is an extremely ambitious product, and is a key piece of Microsoft's .NET initiative. Microsoft's vision is to provide a product that addresses all facets of the interoperability puzzle, including inter-application and inter-enterprise interoperability. Most players in this space started with products focused either on B2B integration, or on Enterprise Application Integration, and then added on the other capability. This yields results that are often not optimally integrated. BizTalk, on the other hand, tightly integrates these capabilities.

The key premise behind BizTalk is to remove integration code from the applications, and instead to perform integration by configuring data flow and acting on the data. This approach yields loosely-coupled applications that are better suited to modern business requirements, and more resilient to the inevitable changes that will occur. BizTalk Server moves us away from creating extensive tightly-coupled application integration layers, towards a world of integration done via configuration.

For the benefit of readers completely unfamiliar with BizTalk Server 2000, it includes the following tools:

Tool	Description
BizTalk Editor	Edits the schema that defines a document (an XML document in most cases, but not necessarily)
BizTalk Mapper	Establishes transformation relationships between two documents
BizTalk Messaging Manager	Creates and maintains BizTalk entities (ports, channels, and so on)
BizTalk Orchestration Designer	Visual modeling tool based on Visio for defining a business process and its implementation
BizTalk Server Administrator	Tool for cross-server system-level maintenance of BizTalk Servers
Document Tracking	Web-based interface to the tracking database

As mentioned, this chapter will not attempt to be a comprehensive guide to the entire product, nor is it intended to serve as a tutorial. Instead, we will focus on how BizTalk Server 2000 can be used in conjunction with .NET Web Services.

Application Overview

The source code for this application is included with the downloads. The installation has been simplified with the use of setup scripts. Please see the accompanying `README.TXT` *file for instructions.*

We will be creating a BizTalk Orchestration schedule that will do the following:

- Retrieve an order from Message Queuing
- Call a Web Service to pre-authorize a credit card
- If the pre-authorization fails, move the order to a "Suspended" Message Queuing queue
- If the pre-authorization succeeds, call a Web Service at a fulfillment partner site to ship the order
- Call a Web Service to charge the credit card
- If the customer provided an e-mail address, call a Web Service that sends a shipment confirmation e-mail
- Place the completed order on a "Completed" Message Queuing queue

These workflow steps are shown below, graphically represented by the BizTalk Orchestration designer:

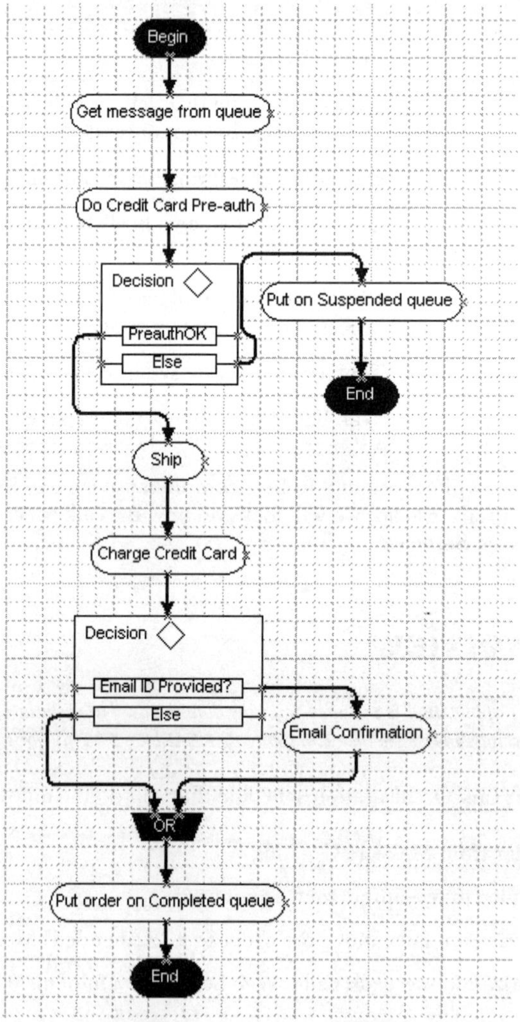

The above diagram should be fairly self-explanatory. It includes shapes for the following tasks:

Task	Description
Begin	The filled-in "Begin" shape is the starting point for the Orchestration schedule.
Oval task shapes	The white ovals (for example "Get message from queue") are tasks in the business process.

Task	Description
Decision	The square decision shape is a branching point identical to a programmatic "If" statement.
Or	The filled-in "Or" shape denotes two branches of the business process merging together. We will look at this more closely later in the chapter.
End	The filled-in "End" shape in this case marks an end point for the business process and is also used to mark the end of a looping construct, as we will see later in this chapter.

We will use BizTalk Server 2000's Orchestration Designer to model the business process, and it will be managed automatically for us by BizTalk's Orchestration engine: the XLANG Scheduler. However, before we move on to the workflow, we will start by defining the various pieces it will require.

Defining the Messages

There are two levels of message definition in BizTalk Server:

- Creating a document specification in the BizTalk Editor
- Registering it in the BizTalk Messaging Manager

Document definition in the Messaging Manager adds an entry to the repository of available documents, and basically tells BizTalk Messaging that the document exists. We will need to do this in order to set up our messaging channel (the pipe through which our message will flow).

For our purposes, we will have a single message that travels through the business process. The fulfillment partner will modify the message by populating the shipping reference element as the document passes through them.

We will use the BizTalk Editor to create the document specification. The BizTalk Editor is an editing tool that allows you to define message characteristics such as the grammar and vocabulary of an XML message, cardinality and allowable data ranges. The output of the editor is an XML schema document. The BizTalk editor also supports importing from well-formed XML documents, DTDs, and existing XML schemas.

Two bonus features of the BizTalk Editor are that it allows for the creation of an instance document and validation of a specific instance. Creating an instance document means creating an XML document that conforms to the schema you've created, populated with dummy data. This saves the developer some of the tedium of creating test data. Validating a specific instance document against a schema allows the developer to check the system inputs to ensure that the message origin point is creating messages properly.

In order to declare the documents as being available to the BizTalk Messaging Manager, we will have to tell it which specification they conform with, making specification definition our logical starting point.

For our implementation, we've opted to use Message Queuing (formerly known as MSMQ) as a coupling mechanism to other applications. A loose coupling between applications like this has some key advantages, notably scalability and reliability. If our "front-end" web site gets heavily used, we could scale up to any number of web servers, and have them all place messages on the same queue. This means that the front end (from our viewpoint) could be scaled without having any impact on architecture. We would also gain reliability: should the power supply on the BizTalk Server computer catch fire, orders would continue to accumulate on the server hosting the queue, and once the BizTalk Server is resurrected, the backlog of orders will be cleared automatically.

The following screenshot shows several messages in the BizTalk Messaging Manager. The one we will be using throughout our example is WroxBTSWS:

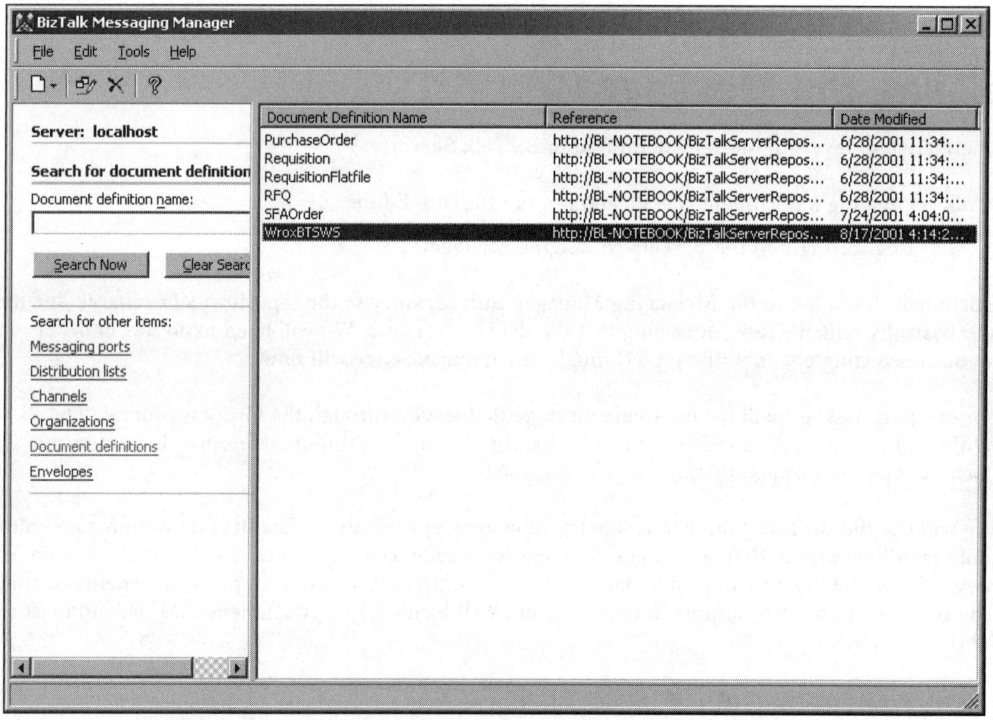

After discussions with the e-commerce architects who are creating the system that will deposit messages on the message queue, we know that they will be sending us an order that will look like this (`WroxBTSWS_Instance.xml` in the code download):

```
<?xml version="1.0"?>
<Order Reference="ORD87443">
  <Customer>
    <ContactInfo>
```

```
        <FirstName>Melissa</FirstName>
        <LastName>Stevenson</LastName>
        <HomePhone>619-123-4567</HomePhone>
        <WorkPhone>858-123-4567</WorkPhone>
        <Email>bloesgen@stellcom.com</Email>
      </ContactInfo>
      <ShipTo>
        <Address1>17 Miriam Way</Address1>
        <Address2>Suite 1705</Address2>
        <City>La Costga</City>
        <State>CA</State>
        <ZipCode>92009</ZipCode>
      </ShipTo>
      <BillTo>
        <Address1>17 Miriam Way</Address1>
        <Address2>Suite 1705</Address2>
        <City>La Costga</City>
        <State>CA</State>
        <ZipCode>92009</ZipCode>
      </BillTo>
      <Billing>
        <CardNumber>8111-1111-1111</CardNumber>
        <Expires>09/04</Expires>
      </Billing>
    </Customer>
    <OrderItems>
      <Item>
        <ProductID>4500IPAQ</ProductID>
        <Quantity>1</Quantity>
        <Price>450.00</Price>
      </Item>
      <Item>
        <ProductID>123CASE</ProductID>
        <Price>28.00</Price>
      </Item>
    </OrderItems>
    <OrderTotal>478.00</OrderTotal>
    <Shipping>
      <ShipDate>02/02/2002</ShipDate>
      <ShipReference>TR-143M98</ShipReference>
    </Shipping>
  </Order>
```

We can import this document directly into the BizTalk Editor. This is a time-saving step that will create the structure of the XML document. When you import a document into the BizTalk Editor (using the **Tools | Import** menu option), you will not have any information about cardinality or data types. You can use the editor after importing to add these important schema elements. After we import the message, this is what it looks like in the BizTalk Editor:

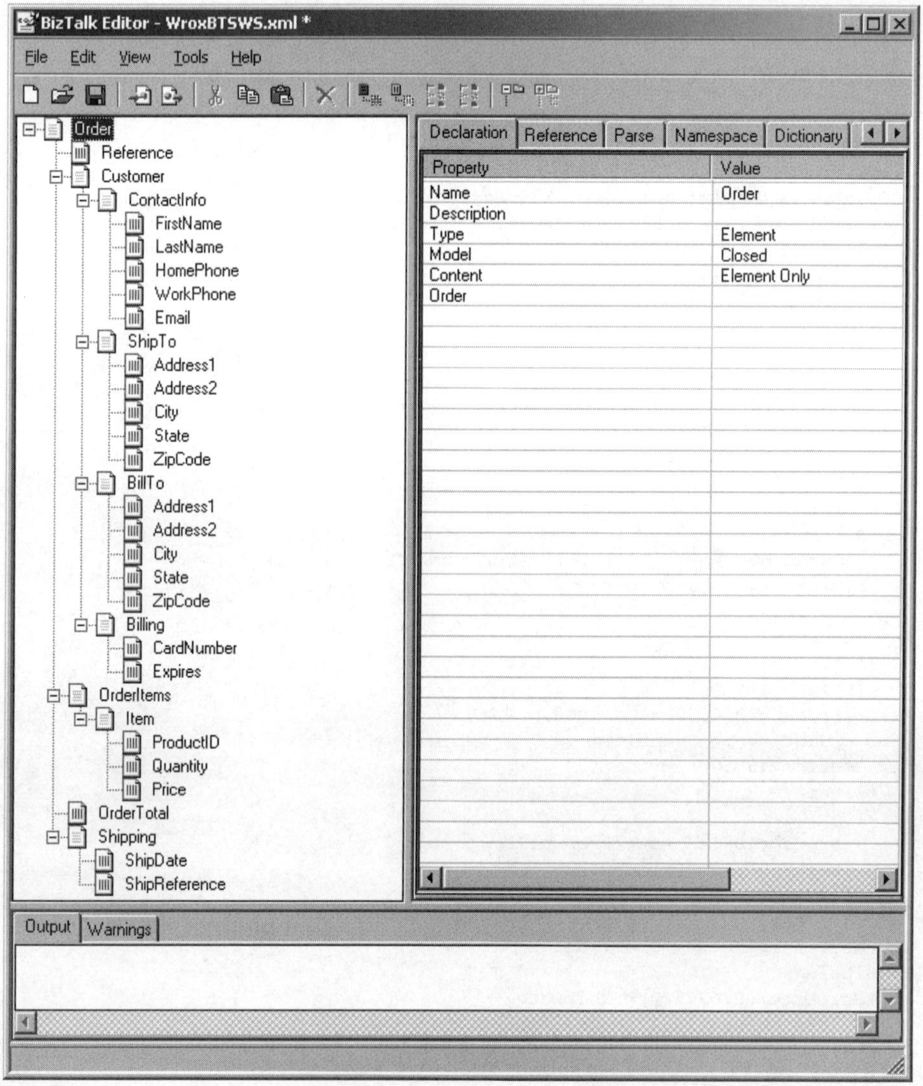

The left-hand pane of the editor shows a tree structure representing the schema. A database-oriented record/field nomenclature is used, which may strike you as odd if you are coming from an XML background. However, this starts to make sense when you consider that BizTalk Messaging is about moving documents, and that those documents could start life as a non-XML entity, for example, a flat file. The XML terminology of "elements" and "attributes" does not make sense when applied to a flat file, although the records/fields semantics still make sense. The difference between records (with horizontal lines across the icon) and fields (vertical lines down the icon) is that records can contain fields, allowing the creation of hierarchical documents. When you import a document into the BizTalk Editor, it will automatically create a field for an element in your XML document that does not contain any child nodes.

The BizTalk Editor does not impose any design constraints; we can structure our documents any way we want, and we are free to use either attribute-normal or element-normal constructs. A dropdown allows us to convert a "field" to be either an element or an attribute.

Mapping Messages

In the nascent days of XML (and some would argue that we're still there!), converting between different document definitions meant doing so by code either by applying an XSL transformation, or programmatically.

BizTalk Server 2000 introduces the BizTalk Mapper, a graphical solution to the mapping problem. With the BizTalk Mapper, you load source and destination document definitions, and then establish a relationship between them by dragging lines between the data entities that travel from the source to the destination. The output of the BizTalk Mapper is still an XSLT (see the output window), but defining the relationships in a GUI environment is far more productive than doing so in XSLT.

We will not be using the Mapper in our example, but it is worth mentioning, as it is an important part of BizTalk Server 2000 messaging. As messages move through a message "channel", we can convert them from one type of XML document to another, or from other document types to XML.

The following is a screenshot showing a message being mapped to a file of similar, but essentially different structure:

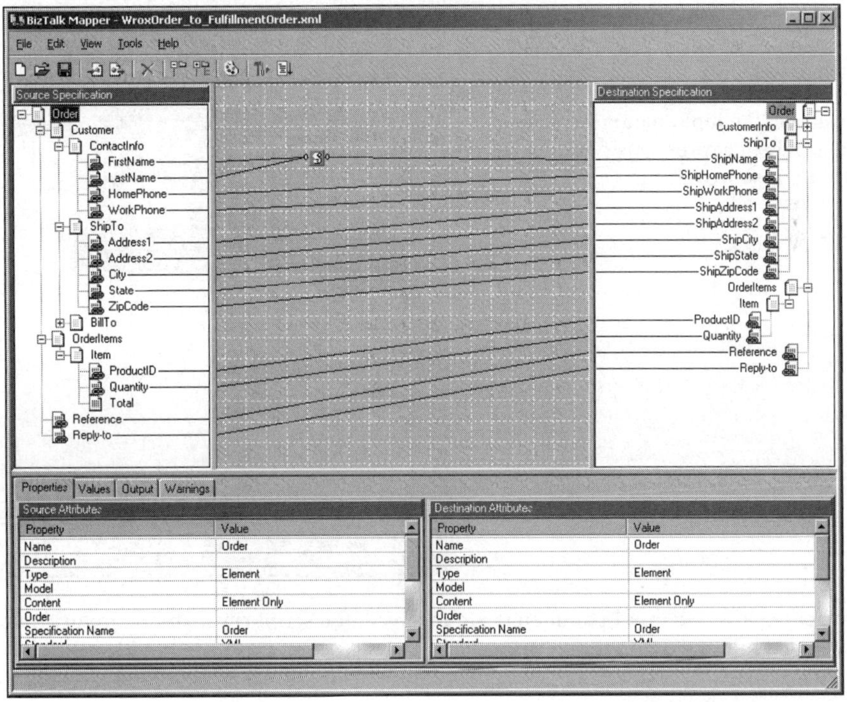

You'll notice from looking at the map that most of the relationships are one-to-one: a line directly connects an entity in our source document with a corresponding entity in the destination document (note that in our case some of the names are different).

An exception to this is the fact that our source specification has a `FirstName` and `LastName` element, with connection lines that converge to a box in the middle of the map before a single line connects that box with `ShipName` in the destination specification. As you may have suspected, there is a transformation occurring. The box is a "functoid", which is an intermediate step that can be introduced into the mapping process.

The BizTalk Mapper includes a large selection of functoids for common tasks such as string manipulation, financial and scientific functions, custom script, and even database access (very powerful, but watch performance considerations with these last two!). In our case, we have used a custom script functoid to concatenate the first name, a blank space, and the last name. The following screenshot shows the property dialogs for this functoid:

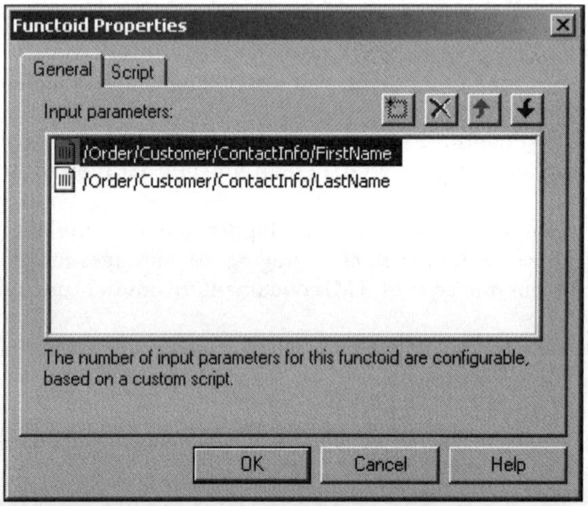

As you can see, the input parameters are specified as XPath expressions pointing to elements in our source document

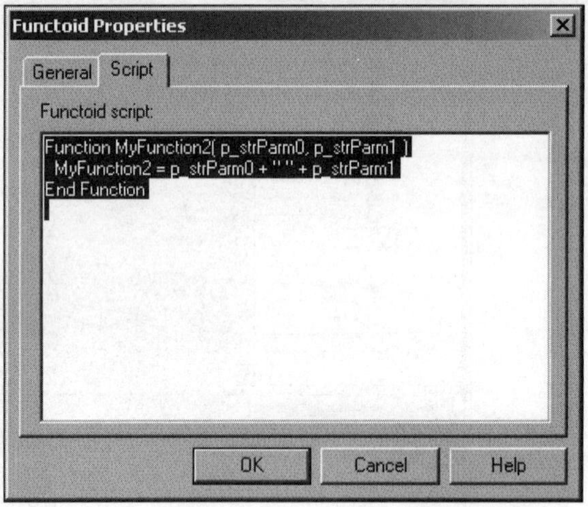

On the script tag, the two input parameters are received, the script runs, and the return value of the script is inserted into the destination element.

BizTalk uses a WebDAV repository to store both document specifications created by the BizTalk Editor and the maps created by the BizTalk Mapper. This allows for centralized access through HTTP and a web interface, and allows access without needing to expose a file share. This is a level of indirection that would make it possible for the WebDAV repository to be relocated without affecting any of the developers or applications that depend on it.

Messaging Ports

There are two types of ports in BizTalk, BizTalk Messaging Ports and the ports used by BizTalk Orchestration. This seems to be a major cause of confusion to newcomers to BizTalk, until they realize that they are two separate and unrelated things.

BizTalk Orchestration ports will be discussed in greater detail when we create our schedule, but they are essentially a "bridge" between the design and the implementation of a business process.

In this section, we are only concerned about BizTalk Messaging Ports, which are one type of entry point to BizTalk messaging. A Messaging Port binds a specific organization or application with up to two transports (primary and backup, such as HTTP and SMTP).

For our use, we will only need one Messaging port, which is the port involved in the activation of our Orchestration schedule.

As with other parts of BizTalk, everything is driven by wizards both in the original creation of the entity and in any subsequent editing operations. The most important of those dialogs from the BizTalk Messaging Manager is shown here:

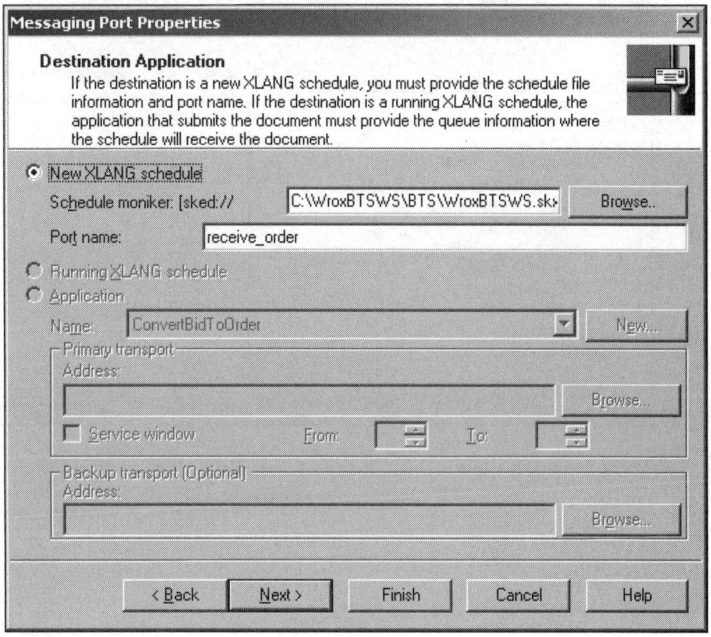

Note that this is a messaging port to a new XLANG schedule. The Port Name referred to above is the port inside the Orchestration schedule.

Defining the Channel

A BizTalk channel is a grouping mechanism that combines a source (application or organization) with a target (application or organization) and specifies things like mapping, document specifications, and auditing.

In our application, we only have one channel; the one associated with the port described above that is used to activate our Orchestration schedule. If you look at the Orchestration schedule, you'll see lots of implementation shapes, but only the activation step involves a channel. The Web Service calls are done through a COM shape, and the output goes to Message Queuing queues, the location of which we explicitly specify.

Starting It All Off...

Up to this point, we have seen most of the BizTalk Messaging pieces that will compose our business process, but there is one important piece missing, which is the initiation of the entire process.

To do this, we will create a BizTalk receive function. The function will monitor the message queue, and when an order appears on our inbound queue, it will launch a new instance of the Orchestration process.

The receive function "WroxBTSWS" is shown below in the BizTalk Server Administration tool:

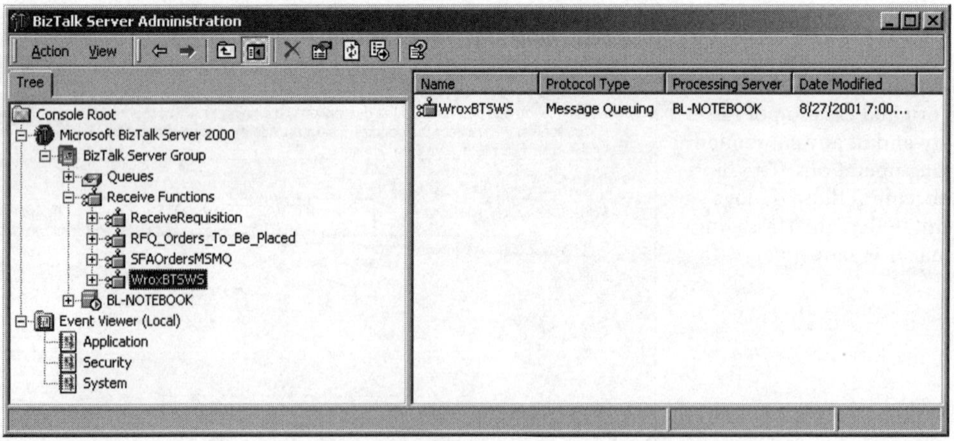

Let's step through the various screens to see how this receive function is set up.

The first screen, which you get to by right-clicking on the receive function name and choosing "Properties", is where we specify the name and access information:

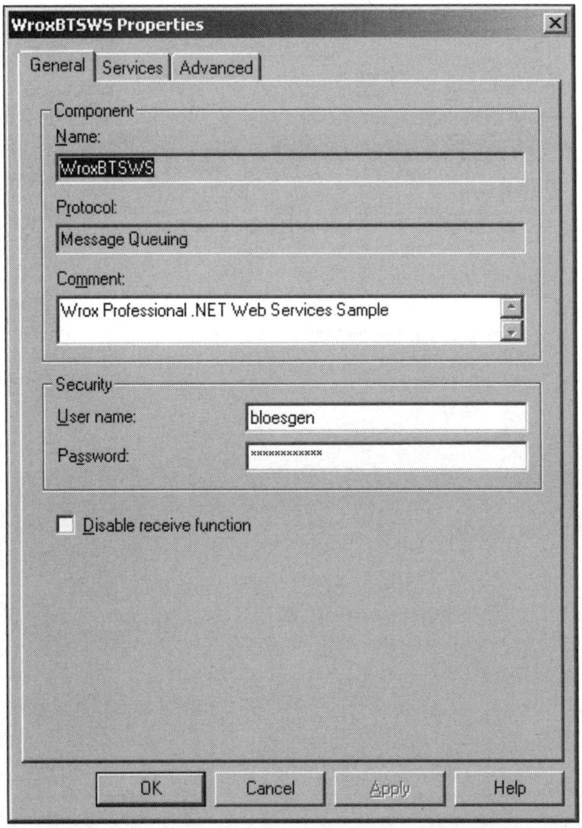

We need to ensure that the user ID information we specify has sufficient rights to gain access to the location (in our case, a queue in Message Queuing) that is being polled. Note also that receiving can be turned off by checking the Disable receive function checkbox, giving us a single point to control the availability of an entry point into a channel.

For this example, we are polling a message queue. You can also create polling functions for file receipt. In that case, a folder can be monitored, and when a file appears in that folder (by file copy or FTP), it can be passed into a channel. It is important to note that a receive function does not waste CPU cycles by constantly polling a folder. Instead, it receives an operating system event when a file is placed in the folder.

The Services tab is where we specify which computer the receive function should run on, and the name of the receive function:

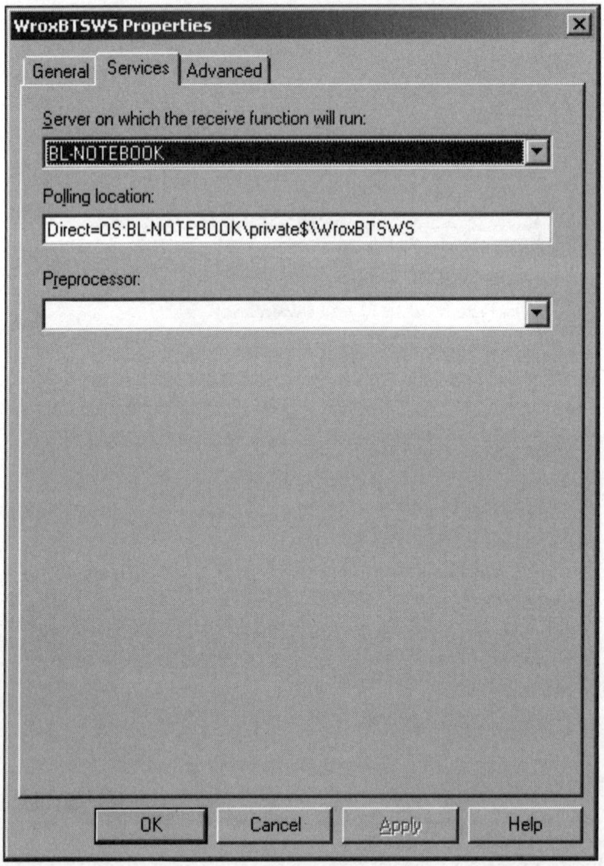

Finally, the Advanced tab is where we specify which channel we want to run when a message is received from our polling location (in this case it is the message queue specified as the Polling location on the Services tab):

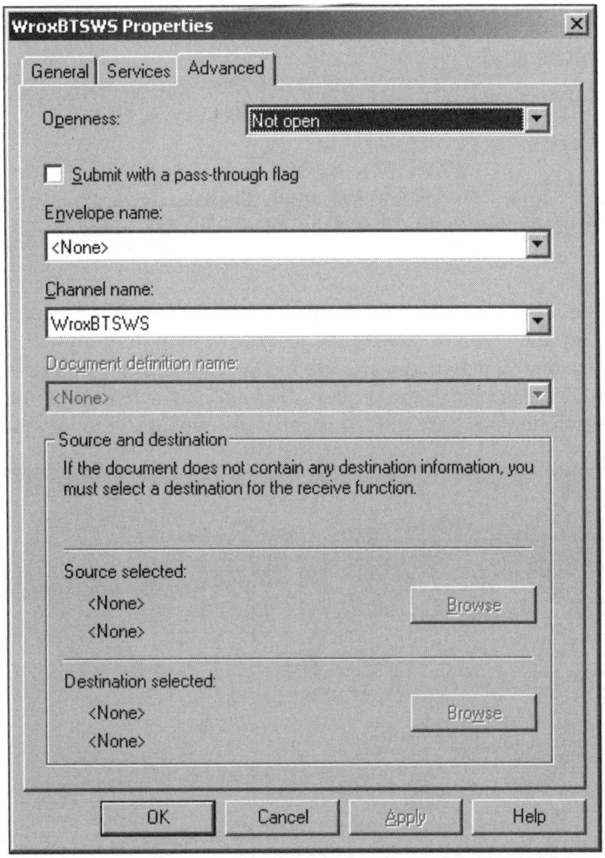

The channel we are using here is called WroxBTSWS. As we're not providing a comprehensive look at BizTalk here, only relevant fields will be explained, where not self-explanatory.

Now let's move on to the actual Orchestration schedule.

Drawing the Orchestration Schedule

We have now defined all the infrastructure pieces that are required to support our schedule. The next step is to draw and implement the schedule itself.

When you first start the BizTalk Orchestration Designer, you'll notice it seems to be split down the middle. The reasoning behind this is that the business analyst and end user work together to model the business process in the left-hand pane, and then the developer connects the implementation pieces in the right-hand pane. In BizTalk Server 2000, tasks are implemented by one of the following means (see the shapes in the right-hand margin):

- A COM component
- A script component
- Message queuing
- BizTalk Messaging

The file we will be working with is `WroxBTSWS.SKV`. There is a compilation process, which will produce a file called `WroxBTSWS.SKX`. This is the XLANG XML file that will be used by the XLANG scheduler to actually "run" our orchestration.

The tool palettes to the left and right of the design surfaces reflect these roles. The left-hand palette has flow control shapes that allow you to control the workflow, including branching, joining, decisions, and looping. The shapes on the right-hand palette are for the creation of orchestration "ports". Ports in this context are the rectangles that bridge the process diagram on the left and the implementation on the right. It is important to note that these ports bear no relationship to the Messaging Ports we saw earlier.

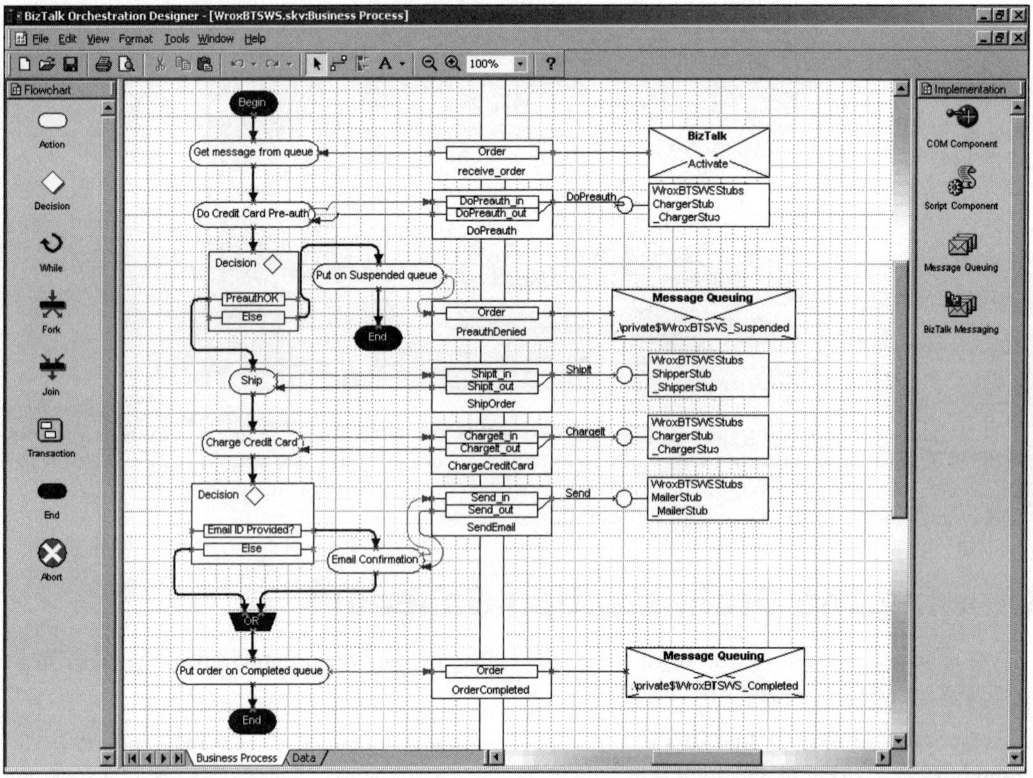

Note that the work surface has two tabs: Business Process and Data. The business process tab shows the flow of execution. The data tab shows the actual message flow. We will need to work on both of these tabs in order to implement our workflow.

Let's examine this schedule moving sequentially from the top down through the tasks.

Our entry point to this workflow is through the receive function. It will be polling the message queue, and when an order appears, it will take the order and send it through the WroxBTSWS BizTalk Messaging channel that we designated in the receive function properties. This channel in turn is associated with the BizTalk Messaging port we created, which is where we start this new instance of the schedule from.

"Get message from queue" Task

The first task following the Begin shape is the Get message from queue task shown on the left-hand design surface. The Orchestration port (straddling the double line) receive_order is our entry point from the BizTalk Messaging channel that our receive function sends the order through.

All of the elements shown in the Orchestration Designer were created by running wizards, and they can subsequently be edited using the same wizards.

Double-clicking on the line to the right of the receive_order port invokes the Biztalk Messaging Binding Wizard. The first two steps in the wizard specify that the name of this port is receive_order, and that it is a receive port. The next step is crucial, as this is where we specify that this port creates a new instance of the schedule:

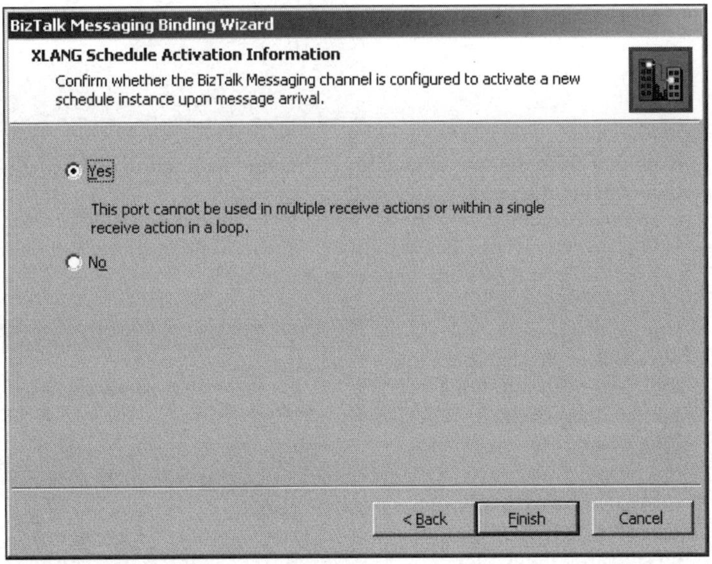

Clicking on the line to the left of the receive_order port invokes the Communication Wizard that will tie the message we received to our Orchestration schedule. This dialog box is the same as will be shown for the first screen of the Communications Wizard, regardless of the port implementation:

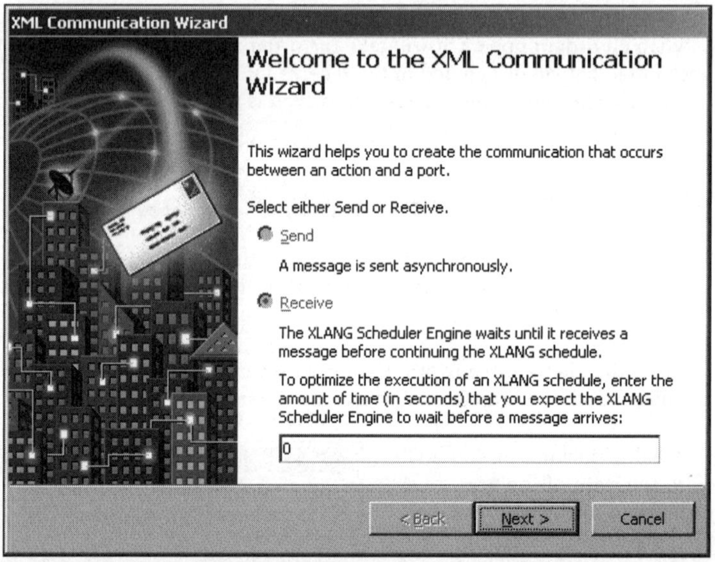

Note the "time to wait" field. This is the field that tells the XLANG Scheduler how long the schedule should remain in memory prior to being persisted to disk. In this case, the question is irrelevant as this is an activation step, and the schedule instance did not exist prior to the message being received. This field is extremely significant in the case where the task may be waiting for a response from a business partner, or is part of some long-running process.

The next screen in the wizard is where we specify the name we want to use on the data page (which we'll look at later) to represent the message we are receiving. Referring to the schedule, you'll notice that Order is the name that appears inside the small rectangle inside the receive_order port. The label in the small rectangle tells us at a glance the name of the message flowing through a port:

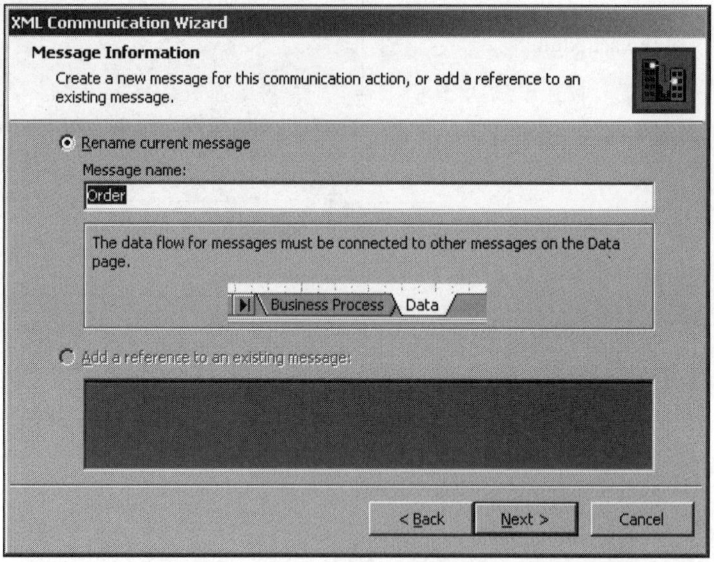

The XML Translation Information step (not shown) specifies that we are receiving an XML message (rather than a string, which could be an EDI message or some other structured or delimited string).

The next screen is where we define the message type. BizTalk Messaging uses this to identify the message removed from the queue. This would be used to identify documents in the event that you had multiple documents being placed in the same queue:

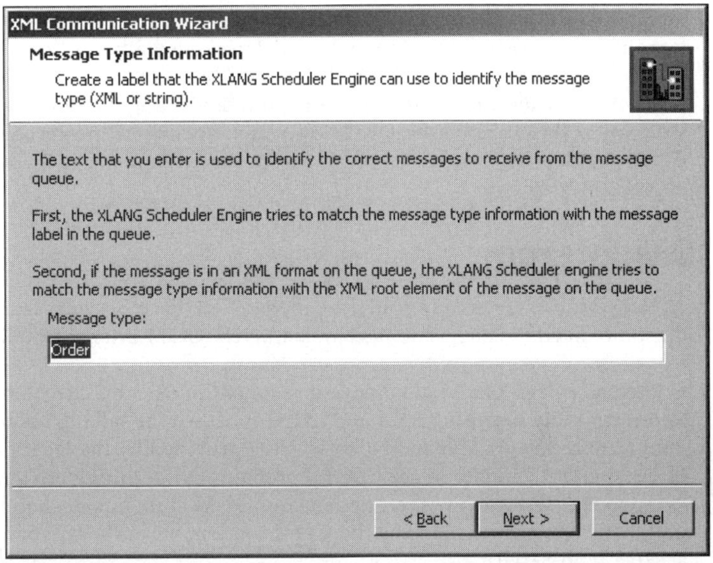

The screen following this is where we provide message specification information. In this case, we are validating the received documents in order to ensure that they conform to this specification. If we accepted input only from internal applications where the documents were programmatically created, applications that we can trust to send sensible data, we may opt not to have validation performed:

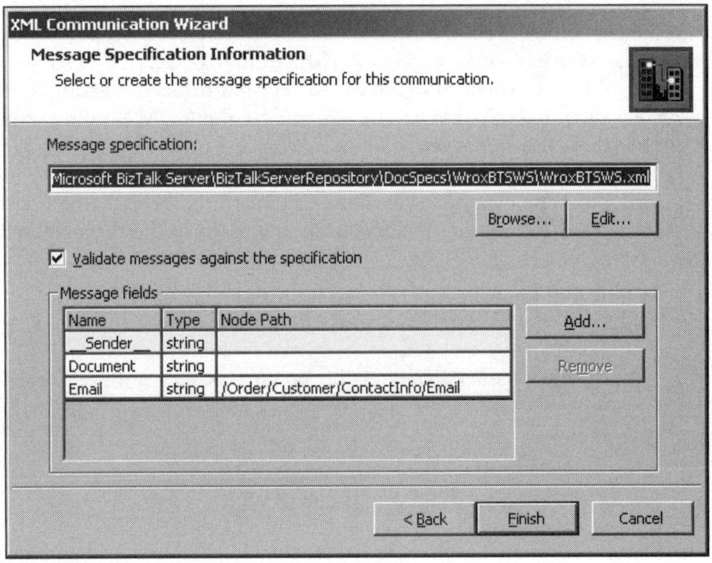

Note the Add button. BizTalk is all about XML, but you don't need to know XML in order to use it. In some places, such as this, XML is just an implementation detail. The Document message field shown represents the entirety of our inbound XML message. At the schedule level, we don't know anything about the content of the message, we are just passing it around as a monolithic chunk of data. However, later in the schedule we will be making a decision whether to send an e-mail or not based on whether or not an e-mail ID has been provided. The Add button allows us to reach into the document and surface parts of it by using an XPath expression and navigating the document structure. We know the document structure at this stage because we know which document specification the document conforms to. The Email field has been surfaced, and is shown here as a message field with the corresponding XPath expression beside it.

COM Interop

At long last, we are getting ready to invoke .NET Web Services from BizTalk Orchestration. Before we do so, we need to take a sideways look at .NET COM interoperability.

In the real world, there is a massive investment in existing COM objects. When people talk about interoperability between COM and .NET, most will be talking about new .NET components and applications that are able to invoke services provided by the legacy COM components. The BizTalk Orchestration Designer in BizTalk 1.0 predates .NET, and doesn't understand Web Services or .NET components. It does, however, understand COM components, and includes a COM-binding wizard. So, our challenge becomes making the COM binding wizard aware of something that we can use to invoke a .NET Web Service.

We have two choices; we can create a COM object using VB6 or our favorite development tool that uses the SOAP Toolkit Version 2.0 SP2 to invoke a .NET Web Service (due to WSDL issues it was not compatible with versions of the SOAP Toolkit prior to Version 2 Service Pack 2). Alternatively, we can write a class in .NET that will be callable by the COM binding wizard. Being forward thinkers, we choose the .NET approach.

In order to keep everything as simple as possible, we will create a separate namespace (`WroxBTSWSStubs`) that includes stub interfaces to the three Web Services we will call.

Let's look at a portion of one of the stubs in order to understand what is required from an interoperability perspective:

```
Imports System.Runtime.InteropServices
Imports System.IO

<ComVisible(True), ClassInterfaceAttribute(ClassInterfaceType.AutoDual), _
 GuidAttribute("537F23E9-BBD4-45ea-920F-41C617AE449C")> _
Public Class ChargerStub
  ...
End Class
```

Specifying a `ClassInterfaceType` of `AutoDual` is required in order for the class to expose an interface that is COM-callable. The interface will have the same name as the class, prefixed with an underscore.

We have explicitly assigned a GUID (generated for us by the tool in Visual Studio .NET). Although this step is not explicitly required, it was done in order to ensure binary consistency across multiple machines and to ease debugging.

A step that is not shown here in code is accomplished through the GUI. Using the Solution Explorer, edit the namespace properties and ensure that Register for COM Interop in the Configuration | Build properties of the WroxBTSWS project is checked.

One last point worth mentioning about COM interoperability, although we don't use it in our example, is the ComVisible attribute. Once we've followed the steps above, our class will be visible to COM, but we can use this attribute to make specific methods, classes or attributes hidden COM.

Once the `WroxBTSWSStubs` namespace has been built and properly registered on the target machine, our .NET stubs will be visible to COM.

"Do Credit Card Preauth" Task

The first action that occurs in our orchestration schedule is a credit card pre-authorization.

If you look to the right-hand implementation side of this task, you will see a COM shape. In this implementation, we take the order we removed from the queue and pass it to our .NET stub, which will in turn invoke a .NET Web Service.

The first two screens of the COM Component Binding wizard allow us to name the port and to specify that we want static instantiation of our COM component (let the XLANG Scheduler instantiate it). Next, we get to the Class Information page:

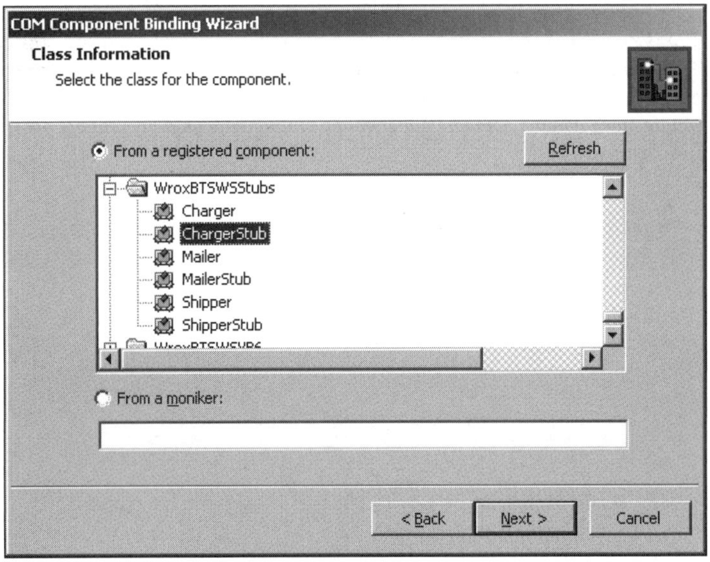

The next screen (not included here) shows us the interface we've exposed from our class, in this case _ChargerStub.

The screen after this shows us a list of available public methods (including the default methods exposed by all .NET objects). This is where we specify which methods we will be able to call from our schedule:

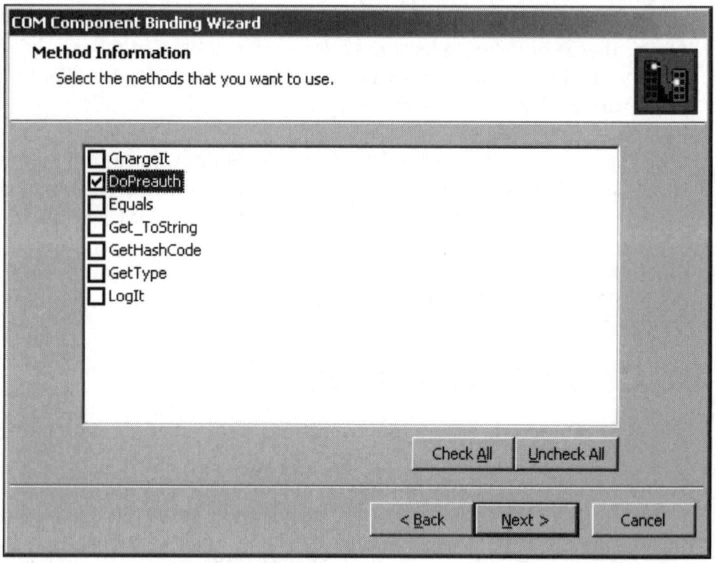

In this case, we only specify the `DoPreauth` method. Alternatively, we could have specified both the `DoPreauth` and `ChargeIt` (which we will use later) methods, but we will expose these methods separately in order to keep the schedule visually cleaner and easier to follow.

The final wizard screen (not shown) allows us to set advanced properties. In this case, we just accept the default values.

Up until this point, in examining the workflow, we have only seen a flow of actions. We haven't really seen how data flows through the different tasks. The Data page of the Orchestration Designer is where we control the actual data flow:

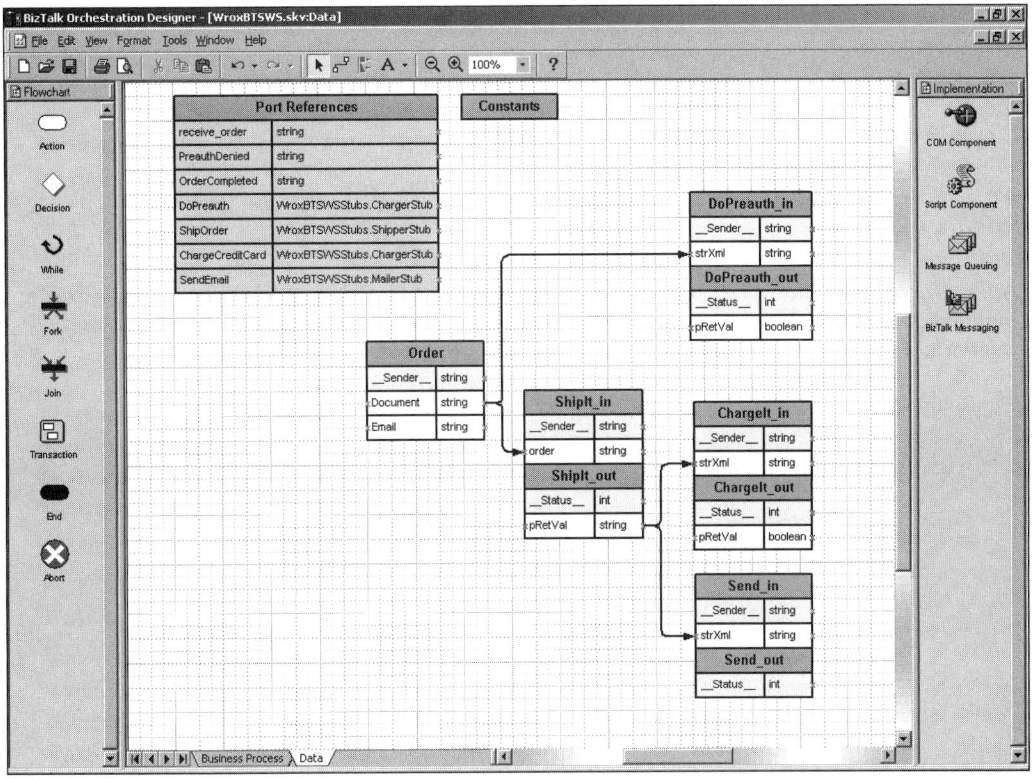

This page shows the different messages used in our schedule and establishes the relationships between them. Also notice the "Port References" box. This list contains one entry for each of the Orchestration Ports we have defined in our workflow.

For now, we are working with the `DoPreauth` port. Note the arrow going from Document in the Order message to the `strXML` parameter of our `DoPreauth_in` method call. This means that we take the Order we removed from the queue and pass it through as a parameter to our stub.

Now that we know what's being passed to the `DoPreauth` method of our `ChargerStub` class, the next step is to take a look at what it does with it:

```
Public Function DoPreauth(ByVal strXml As String) As Boolean
  Dim xmldoc As New System.Xml.XmlDocument()
  xmldoc.LoadXml(strXml)
  xmldoc.Save(Console.Out)
  Dim name As String = _
xmldoc.SelectSingleNode("Order/Customer/ContactInfo/FirstName").InnerText _
+ " " + xmldoc.SelectSingleNode("Order/Customer/ContactInfo/LastName").InnerText
  Dim cardnum As String = _
```

```
              xmldoc.SelectSingleNode("Order/Customer/Billing/CardNumber").InnerText
    Dim expiration As String = _
                 xmldoc.SelectSingleNode("Order/Customer/Billing/Expires").InnerText
    Dim amount As Decimal = _
       Convert.ToDecimal(xmldoc.SelectSingleNode("Order/OrderTotal").InnerText)

#If Debug Then
   LogIt("Preauth was called...")
#End If

    Dim Charger As New ChargerHost.Charger()
    Return Charger.DoPreauth(name, cardnum, expiration, amount)
  End Function
```

As you can see, the stub is relatively straightforward: we load the passed XML document, extract required information from it, and invoke the Web Service specified by the `ChargerHost` web reference. This reference would have been created as usual, using the Solution Explorer.

Continuing to follow the message flow, the next stop would be the service itself:

```
Imports System.Web.Services

<WebService(Namespace:="http://stellcom.com/webservices/")> _
Public Class Charger
  Inherits System.Web.Services.WebService

...

  <WebMethod()> Public Function ChargeIt(ByVal name As String, _
                                         ByVal cardnum As String, _
                                         ByVal expiration As String, _
                                         ByVal amount As Decimal) As Boolean
    Return True
  End Function

  <WebMethod()> Public Function DoPreauth(ByVal name As String, _
                                          ByVal cardnum As String, _
                                          ByVal expiration As String, _
                                          ByVal amount As Decimal) As Boolean
    Return True
  End Function

End Class
```

As you can see, any pre-authorization attempts are blindly accepted. In the real world, of course, at this point you would call a third-party service such as CyberCash or PayFlowPro to do the authorizations, but this step has been simplified for the sake of the case study. The return value of `True` would percolate back up to the original method call from the Orchestration schedule, where it would eventually become the `pRetVal` Boolean referred to in the data page for the `DoPreauth_out` message.

Next, let's run the wizard on the left-hand design side of the implementation port. This is the first screen we see:

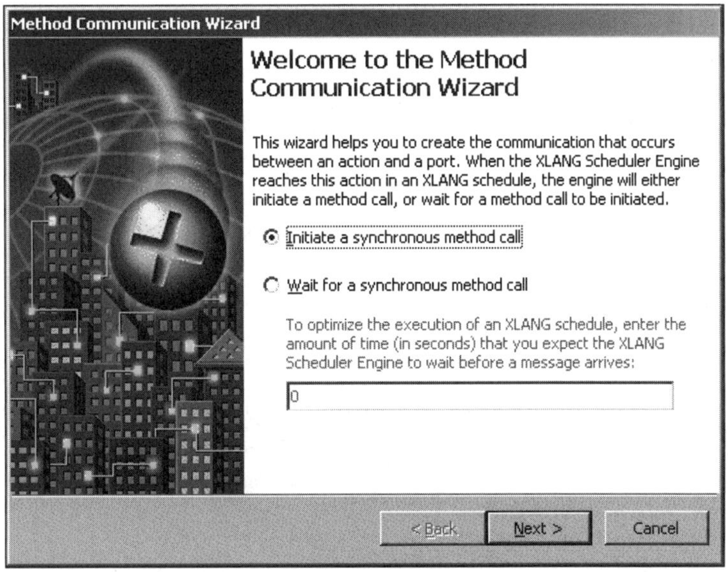

In this case, we are specifying that we want to initiate a method call.

This next screen in the wizard lists all of the available methods (one in this case) and allows us to select the method we want to call from a drop-down list (this is only relevant if we specified more than one method when we ran the COM-binding wizard). Inputs and outputs are also shown:

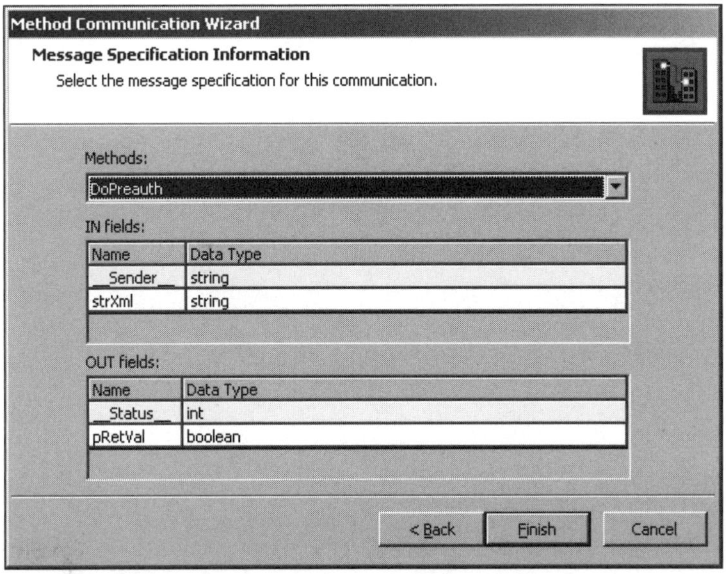

After we have made this method call, our task is complete, and we have the result generated by the Web Service on the Boolean `pRetVal`.

"PreauthOK" Task

In our business scenario, if the credit card preauthorization failed, then we would not want to process the order. In order to implement this, we have an Orchestration decision: either continue on in the flow, or branch and place the order on an outbound "suspended order" queue where some other system would pick it up and act upon it.

The following wizard screen shows how a rule is implemented in BizTalk Orchestration:

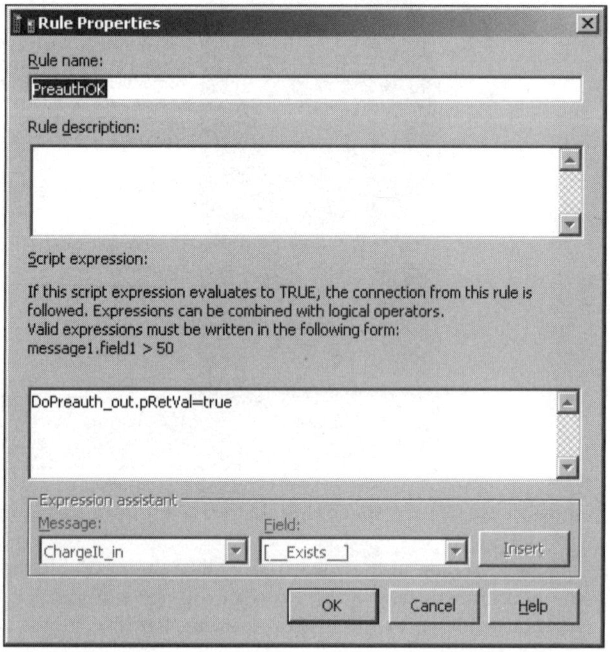

The result of evaluating this script decision determines the direction message flow will take leaving the decision point.

If preauthorization fails, BizTalk will follow the else branch and perform the Put on Suspended Queue task. The relevant screen of the Message Queuing wizard is:

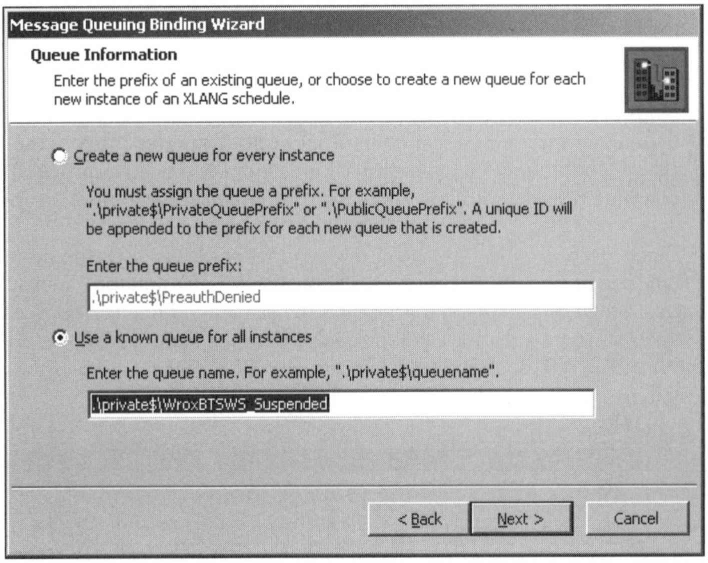

Messages in Message Queuing have a label associated with them. As the XLANG Scheduler will be putting this message on the queue, it needs to know which label to associate with the message:

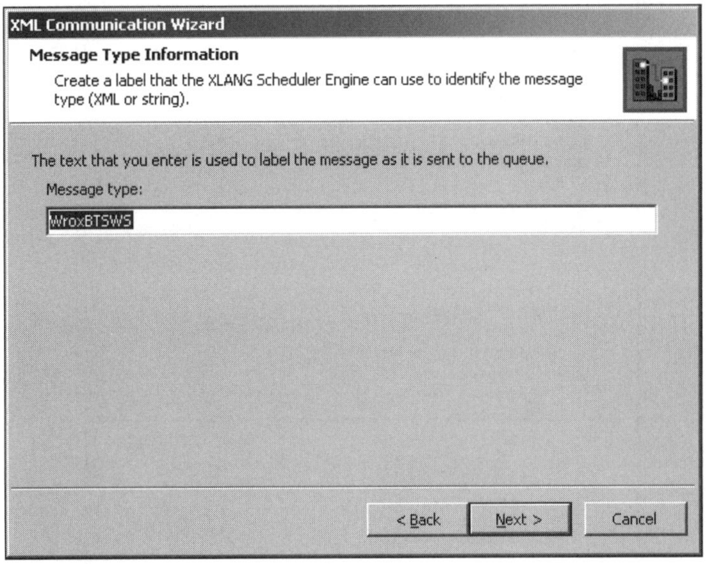

Once we've put the message on the suspended queue, we branch to the End shape, which terminates this instance of the orchestration schedule.

Ending

The other steps in the schedule follow the model presented on these preceding pages. We call a service to ship the order, another to actually charge the credit card and, if we have an email ID, yet another to send a confirming email.

Note that if we do send an e-mail, then the message flow has forked (the fork branch taken being dependent on if we have an e-mail ID or not). We need to join the two paths together by using the Join shape. Join shapes can be a Boolean AND join (we need approval by two people in order for flow to continue past the join), or Boolean OR (if either person approves then flow can continue).

Once the two paths have been rejoined, we proceed on to the next step in the schedule flow, which is to take the order and place it on a "WroxBTSWS_completed" queue. This is done in exactly the same way that we placed suspended orders on the suspended queue. If you change the return result of the DoPreauth web service call to False then the message will be placed on the WroxBTSWS_suspended queue instead. The following shows the three queues used in this case study (all are prefixed with WroxBTSWS):

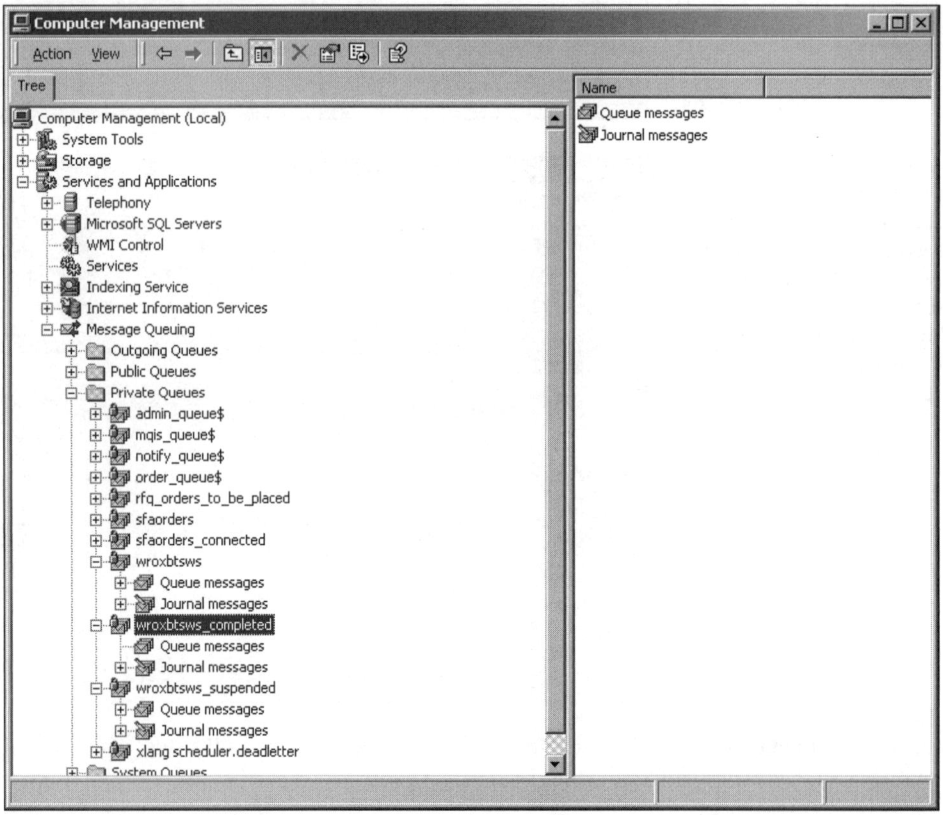

The final shape in the orchestration schedule is the "End" shape, which terminates this instance of the orchestration schedule.

Summary

In this case study, we have seen how Microsoft's BizTalk 2000 Server can be used to automate a business process by orchestrating .NET Web Services. We looked at:

- Using message queues to loosely couple this application with external systems
- Using the BizTalk Editor to create document specifications
- Using BizTalk Orchestration to manage the transmission and reception of documents between ourselves and a trading partner.

The sample code is configured for everything to run on one machine; however, you can see how easy it would be to point at external services, such as using a third-party credit card service or fulfillment service.

The workflow used was a straightforward serial flow, with no transactions or looping. However, we have shown enough of how BizTalk Server works that you now understand some of the power it brings to your development arsenal, and why BizTalk Server is an important pillar in the .NET strategy.

PROFESSIONAL
ASP.NET
WEB
SERVICES

18

Case Study – Passport-Style Authentication Service

Throughout the preceding chapters, we've looked at the main concepts involved in implementing and consuming ASP.NET Web Services with the Microsoft .NET Framework.

In this case study, we are going to look at how to use ASP.NET to create a centralized Web Service to offer authentication and profiling services across platforms in the enterprise. We will proceed step by step through the process of building and consuming the ASP.NET Web Service. In this way the chapter will provide insight into how we can use ASP.NET, XML, SOAP, and HTTP to provide cross-platform services on the web.

The basic concepts and issues we'll look at in this chapter are as follows:

- How to design and code an ASP.NET Web Service
- How to build the proxy
- How to secure the service
- How to deploy the Web Service
- How to test the Web Service

Overview of the Web Service

Corporations today face the challenge of administering and supporting several application-specific directories. A directory is a database of usernames, passwords, and profile information of every user on the network. It is used to manage user accounts and permissions. When sent a username, it returns the attributes of that individual, which may include a telephone number as well as an e-mail address. An application directory can include any user data store such as NT/Active Directory, Lotus Notes databases, MS Exchange directories, phone lists, other RDBMSs, lookup tables, text files, and so on. These directories can number up to several hundred and possibly even thousands at the world's largest corporations. As each new directory goes online, the costs to develop, administer, and support them continues to spiral upward and out of control. Each of these data stores can contain unique user credentials that are required for access to the application. Combine this with having to remember a PIN for voice-mail, another PIN for the ATM, and yet another PIN for online banking (which are also user directories) and it is not hard to see why many of us have resorted to writing passwords on Post-Its in order to remember them.

Web Services can help corporations better utilize and secure information within their own companies by enabling them to link disparate information systems in a standard way. One of the key factors in linking these disparate systems is providing a standard way of authenticating users against a common credential store. The value of a single credential store can then be further enhanced by storing and making other user-specific information such as their gender, location, language, and so on, available to many systems within the enterprise. This data can then be reused to make access to information easier as well as targeting information to users based on the data.

Microsoft Passport goes a long way towards solving this problem on the Internet. However, the privacy issues associated with the Internet make it difficult for today's corporations to make use of this service. The corporate enterprise needs a similar solution that can be managed in-house, in other words "Microsoft Passport in a box". Since Microsoft has not made public any plans to release such a product, corporations will need to develop this service internally.

Currently, Microsoft Active Directory is being used by many companies to reduce the number of credentials that users are required to remember on a daily basis. The wide support of Active Directory and the integration of Windows Authentication by Independent Software Vendors has provided seamless transitions between many third-party applications and has further reduced the number of credentials that users must remember. Enterprises running Active Directory can use the Lightweight Directory Access Protocol (LDAP, described below) provider and ASP.NET Web Services to provide cross-platform access to information stored in the Active Directory. This has the effect of simplifying a user's experience by limiting the number of IDs and passwords they are required to remember, and further limits the number of times they are required to authenticate during a normal day.

Not all companies have implemented Active Directory. Some corporations have decided to continue supporting their existing Windows NT 4.0 account domains and hold off on the implementation. Yet others have decided to forego Active Directory for Netscape IPlanet, Novell eDirectory, or another directory product. Some companies have decided that the best of course of action is to implement MetaDirectory services to integrate existing directories and decrease the proliferation of new directories. A MetaDirectory is a directory that contains information about other directories. It functions as a master directory gleaning information from all the other directories. The directory services mentioned above are all accessible via an LDAP interface.

The LDAP (Lightweight Directory Access Protocol) v3.0 specification provides a standard protocol used to access a directory listing. Many software products including web browsers, e-mail programs, and line-of-business applications are now providing an LDAP interface to enable the use of an existing LDAP-compliant directory service. LDAP is a sibling protocol to HTTP and FTP and uses the ldap:// prefix in its URL. It is expected that LDAP will provide a common method for searching e-mail addresses on the Internet, eventually leading to global White Pages.

LDAP is a simplified version of the DAP protocol, which is used to gain access to X.500 directories. It is easier to code the query in LDAP than in DAP, but LDAP is less comprehensive.

In this case study, we will bring several of these ideas together by building and consuming a Web Service that provides cross-platform authentication services. We will expose a centralized LDAP directory that is currently providing authentication services for a single platform and make it available to applications, web sites, and services across the enterprise.

Web Service Setup

Before we examine the various aspects of this project, we're going to take this section to detail the software requirements and the necessary steps to get the Web Service set up and running.

Software Requirements

The following software is required:

- Microsoft Windows 2000 Server
- Microsoft Windows 2000 Service Pack 2
- Microsoft Windows 2000 Support Tools
- Visual Studio .NET

Post-Software Installation Configuration

Our case study uses Active Directory to provide data services. Active Directory was not chosen for any specific reason other than it provides us with an LDAP v3.0-compliant directory service. Any other LDAP v3.0-compliant directory could be substituted with relatively minor changes to the code to adjust for changes in the schema.

In the next few steps, we'll create and configure the Active Directory that will be used for the directory. We won't go into the steps involved in implementing an enterprise-ready Active Directory, as that is way beyond the scope of this case study.

Create the Active Directory

1. Install Windows 2000 Server or Advanced Server and apply Service pack 2.

2. Select Start | Run and enter dcpromo in the Open: box then click OK.

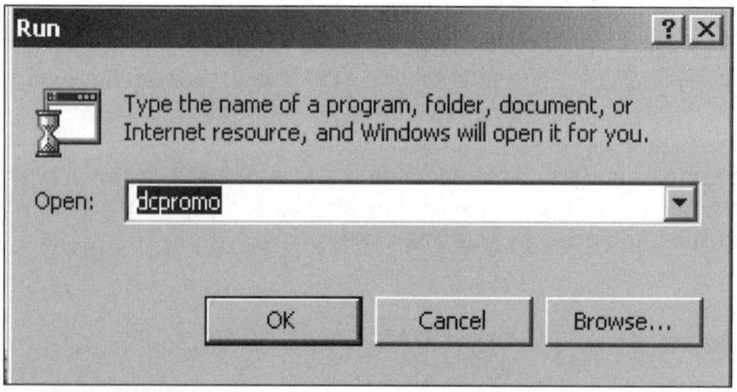

3. The Active Directory Wizard is launched. Click Next.

4. Click Domain controller for a new domain. Click Next.

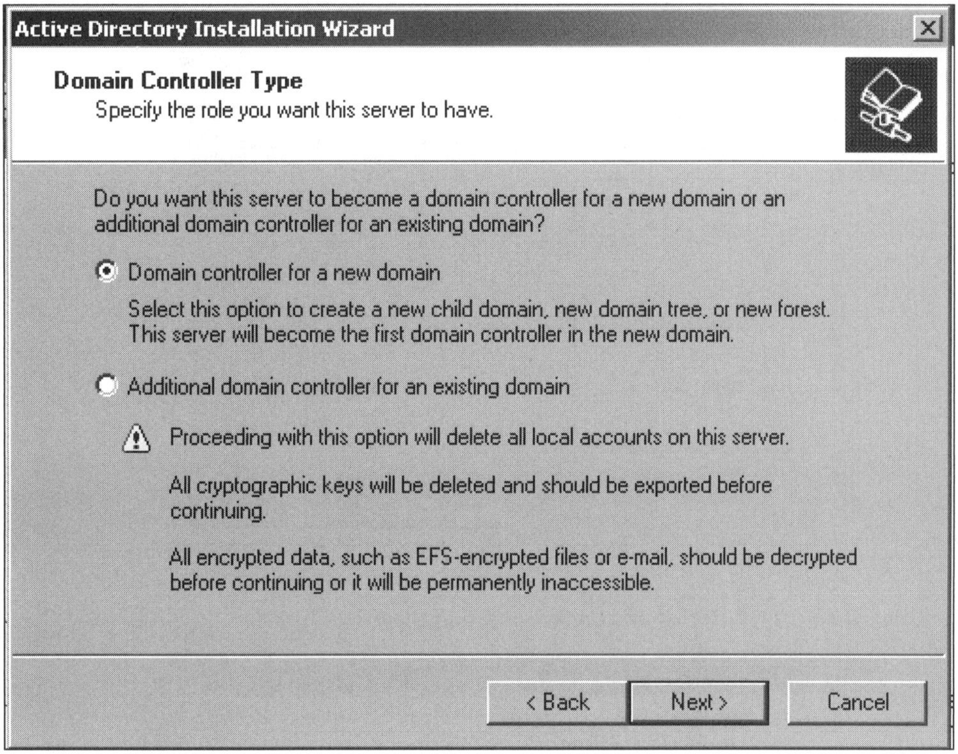

5. Click Create a new domain tree, and then click Next.

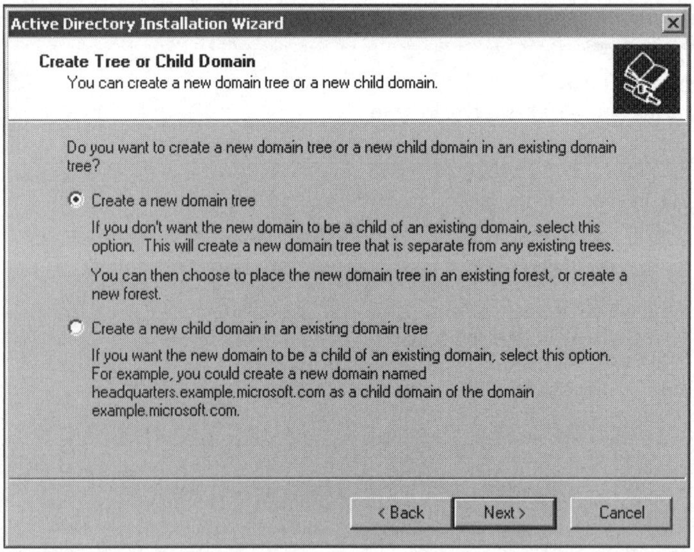

6. Click Create a new forest of domain trees, and then click Next.

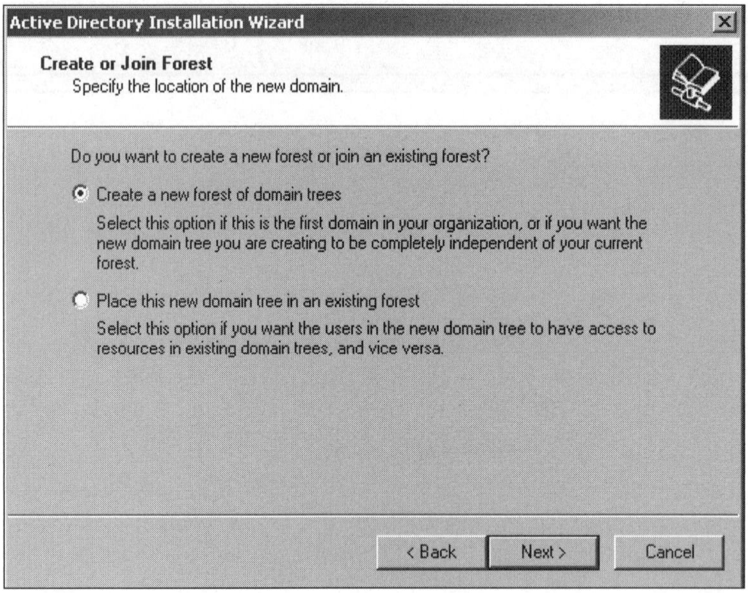

7. Specify myAD.com as the full DNS name for the new Active Directory. Click Next.

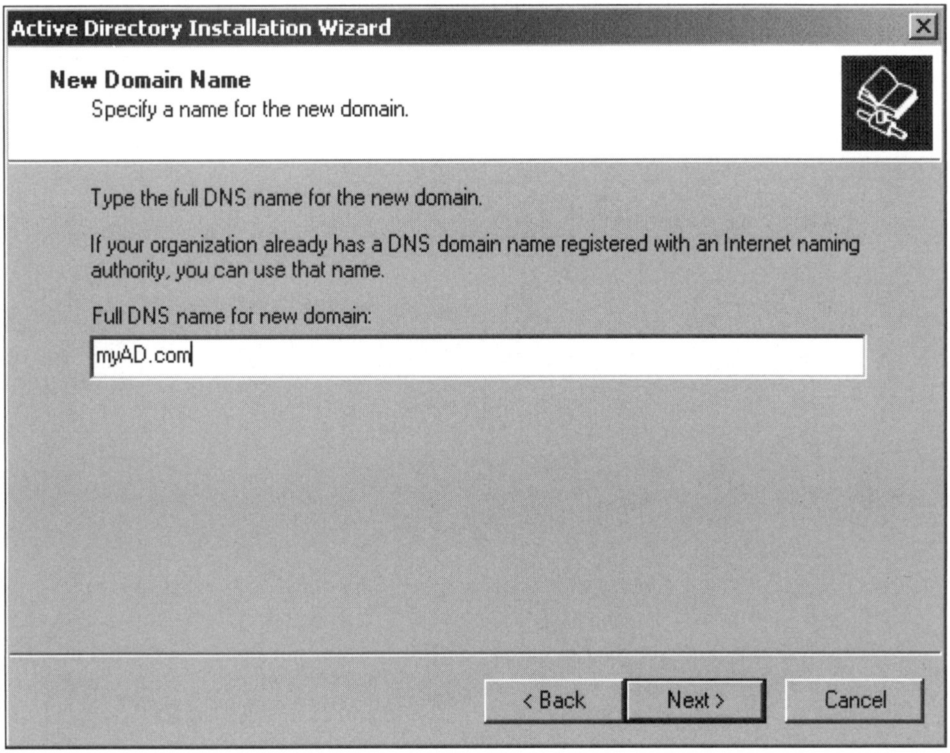

8. Accept the default domain NetBIOS name. Click Next.

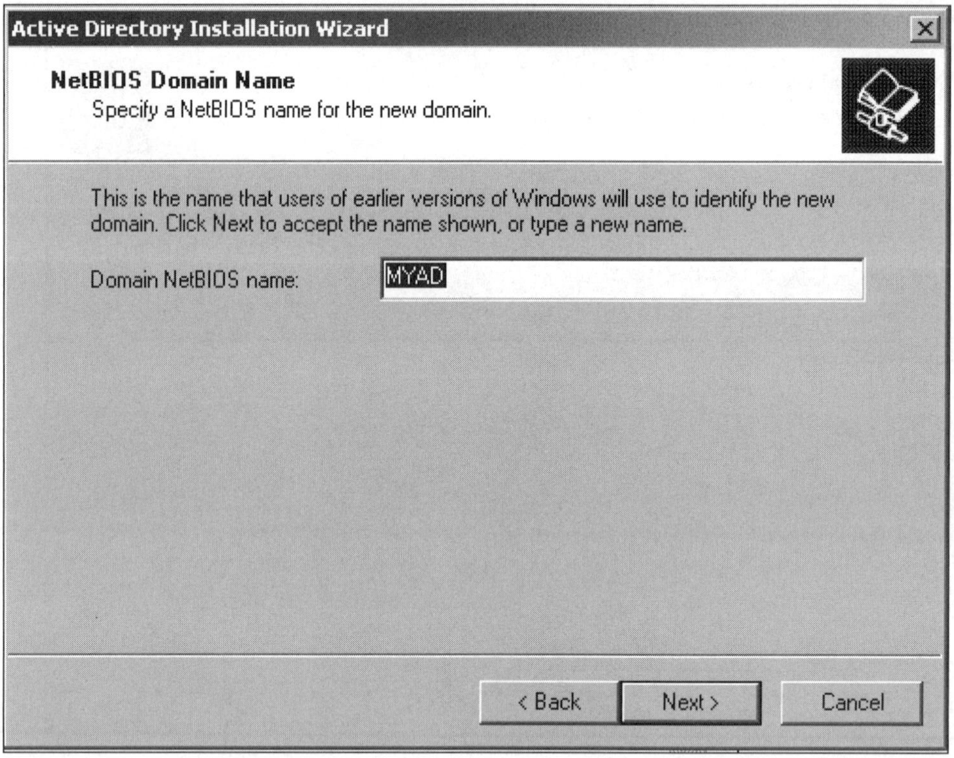

9. Set the database and log file location to the default setting of the `c:\winnt\ntds` folder, and then click Next.

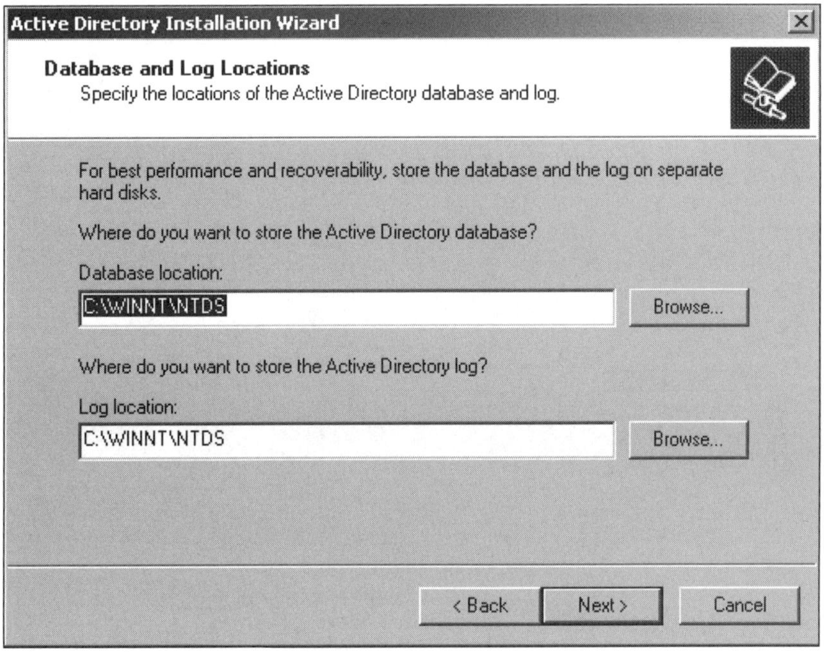

10. Set the Sysvol folder location to the default setting of the c:\winnt\sysvol folder, and then click Next.

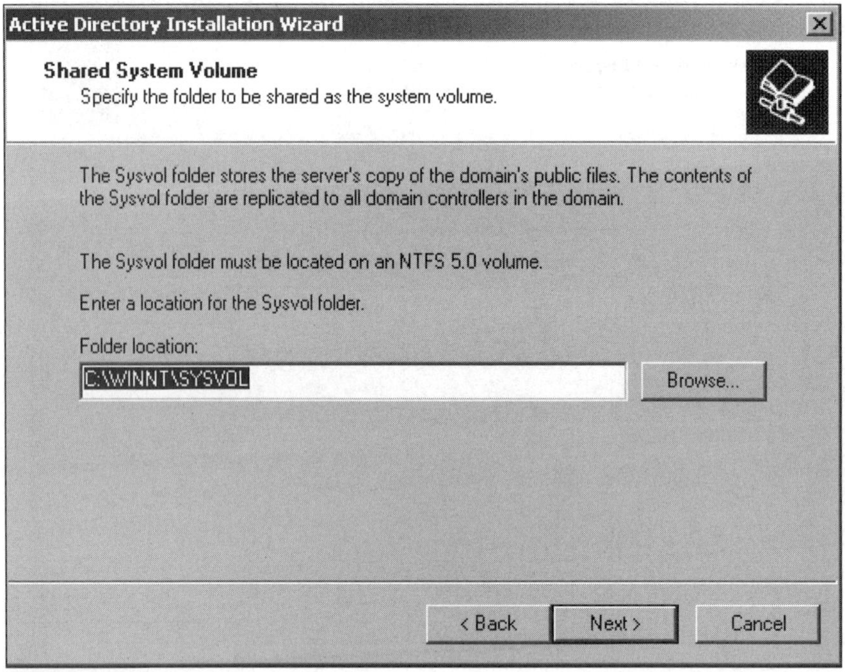

11. The installation process will notify you that it can't communicate with the DNS server that handles myAD.com and requests that you install a new DNS server now. Click OK.

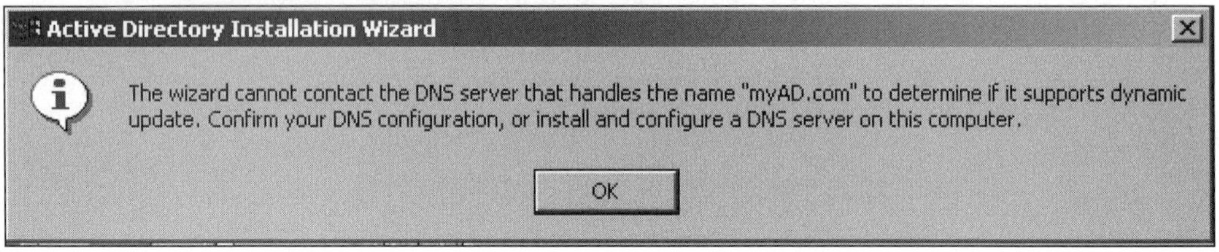

12. Click Yes, install and Configure DNS... and then click Next.

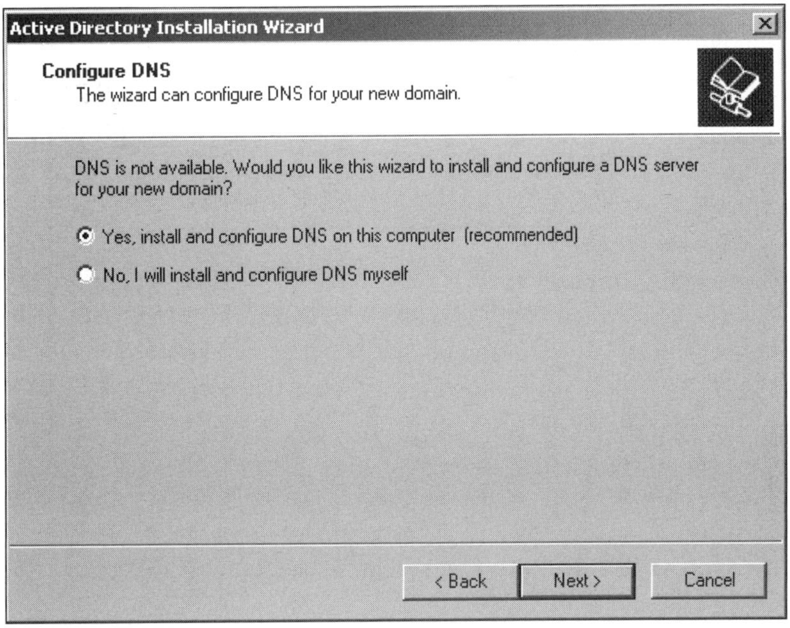

13. Click Permissions compatible only with Windows 2000 servers, and then click Next.

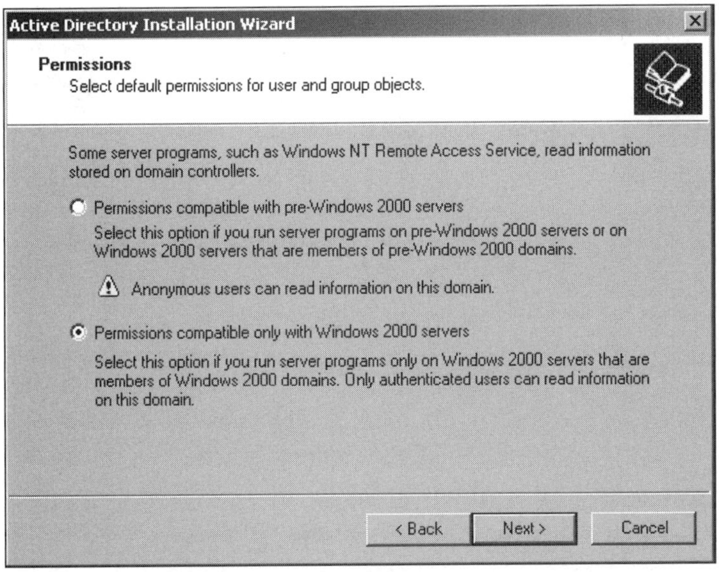

14. Set the password for the "Directory Services Restore Mode Administrator" to `password`. Click **Next**.

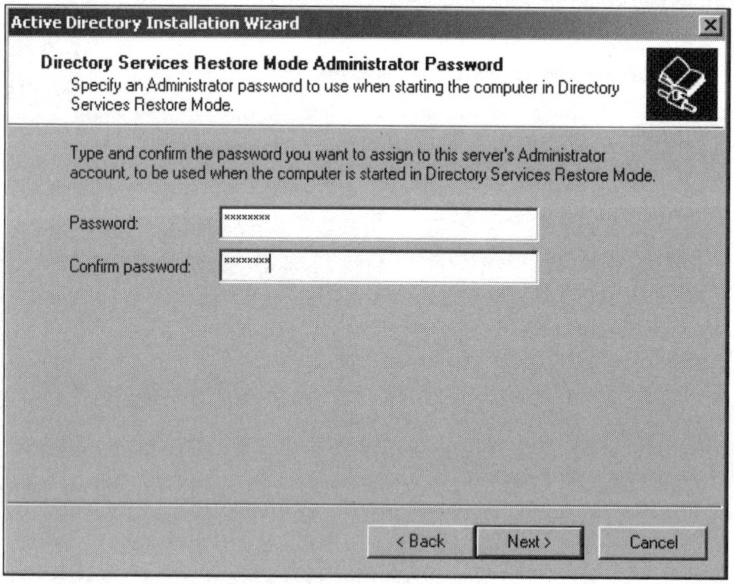

15. Next, you are prompted to review and confirm the options we selected. Do this, and then click **Next**.

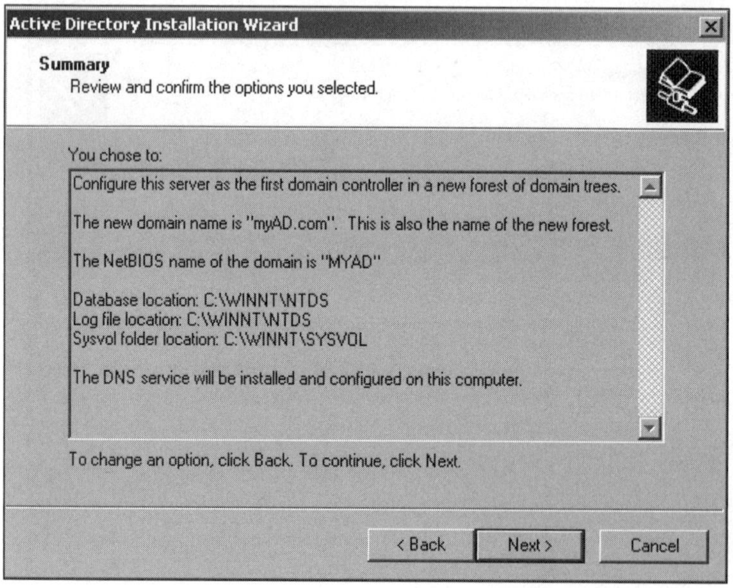

16. The Configuring Active Directory progress screen appears:

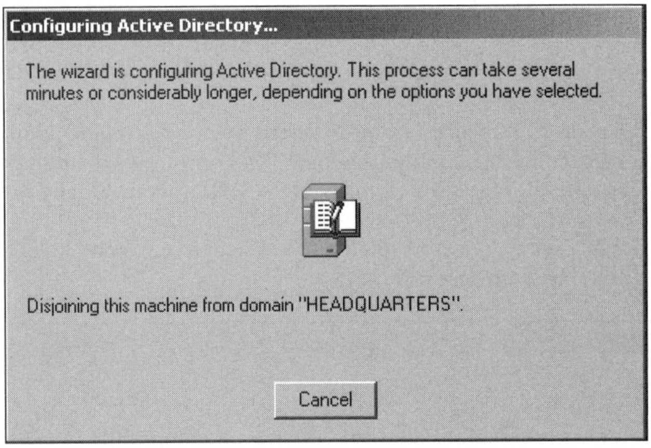

17. When the installation is complete, the Completing the Active Directory Installation Wizard screen will appear. Click Finish.

18. When you are prompted, restart the computer.

It is very important to this case study that your Active Directory and DNS installation is installed and configured correctly. After the computer restarts, Open the DNS console (**Start | Programs | Administrative Tools | DNS**) and confirm that the DNS service location records for the new domain controller have been created. Click the server name, click **Forward Lookup Zones**, and expand the **myad.com** domain. Verify that the `_msdcs`, `_sites`, `_tcp`, and `_udp` folders are present. These folders and the service location records are crucial to Active Directory and Windows 2000 operations.

If the folders and service location records are not present open a command prompt and run **`ipconfig /registerdns`** to re-register the machine in the local DNS server. Next stop and restart the NetLogon service to force the registration of the SRV records in the DNS server. Finally restart the machine.

If Active Directory and DNS have been installed and configured correctly your DNS administrative console should appear like the next screenshot:

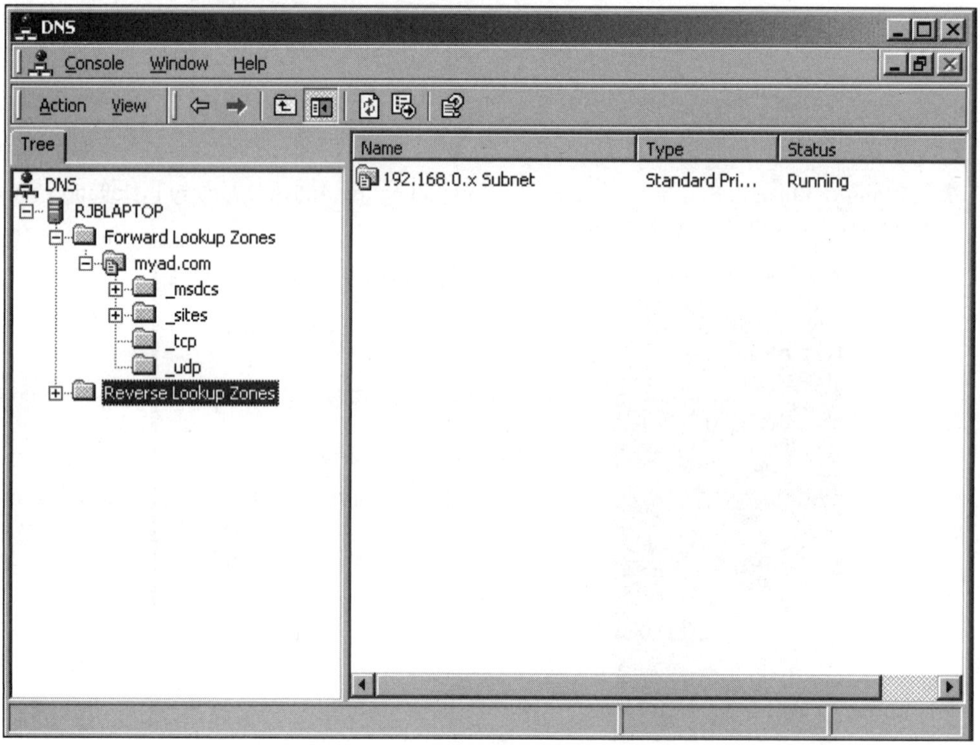

To test your DNS configuration run `nslookup` at the command prompt.

```
Nslookup <machine_name>.myAD.com

Nslookup <ip_address>
```

You should see something like the following results if it is configured correctly:

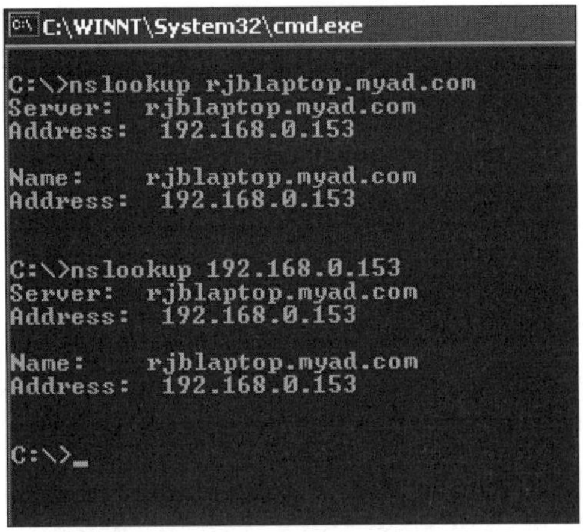

Adding Users to the myAd.com Active Directory Domain

Open the Active Directory Users and Computers administrative console from Start | Programs | Administrative Tools and take a look at the Active Directory domain that we created. You can see in the screenshot below that Active Directory includes a Users organizational unit (OU). Inside the users OU are our users.

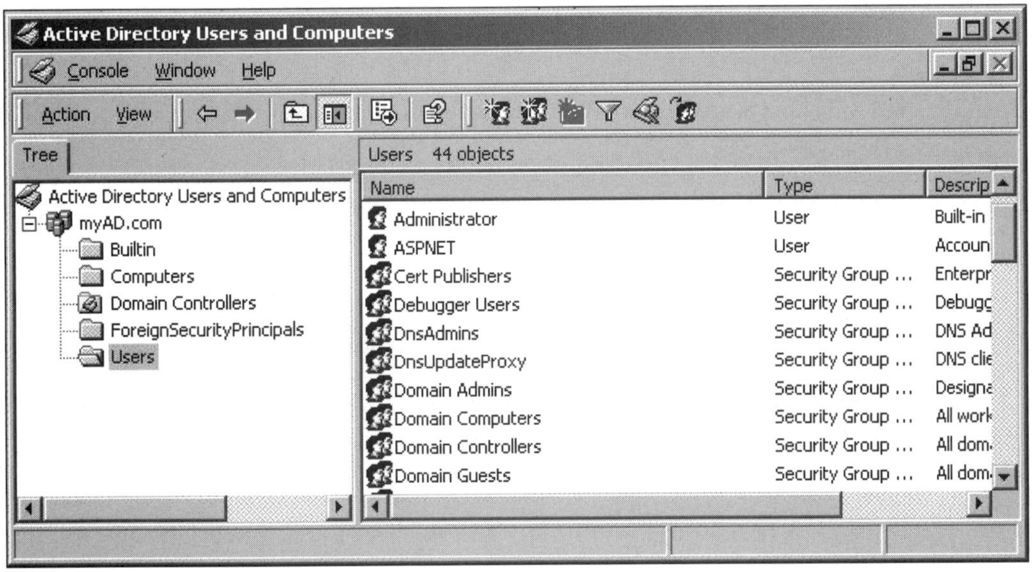

From here we could manage all the user properties stored in Active Directory. The Users OU is where we will be storing all user data that we create in our directory. We'll take a closer look at this later when we start registering new members.

Setting Up the Web Service

To set up the Web Service, open the Internet Services Manager from the Administrative Tools folder on the Start menu. Create a new virtual directory called AuthWebService by right-clicking on the default site and selecting New | Virtual Directory from the context menu that appears.

Complete the information requested by the wizard that appears, mapping it to the `AuthWebService` directory from the files that you downloaded.

The configuration of the Web Service is now complete. You can test the configuration by entering the URL http://localhost/authwebservice/authservice.asmx. You should see the Web Service description page appear:

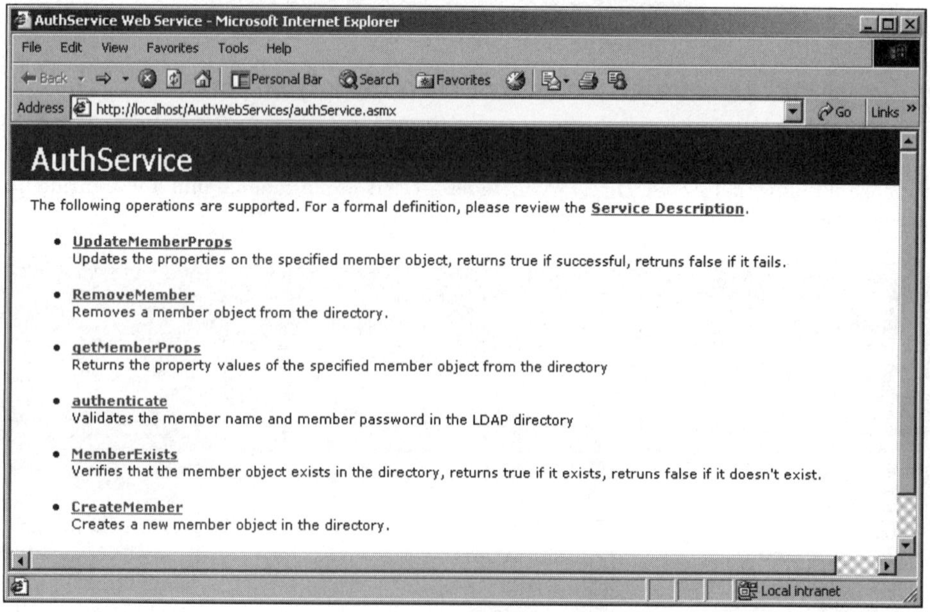

That's it. The service has been successfully configured. Let's move on now and discuss the architecture of our Web Service.

Passport-Style Authentication Service Architecture

The Passport style Authentication Web Service is built upon a Microsoft Windows 2000 Server Platform with Microsoft Internet Information Services 5.0. It uses standard n-tier application design principles to ensure the service can be scaled to meet the needs of even the largest enterprise:

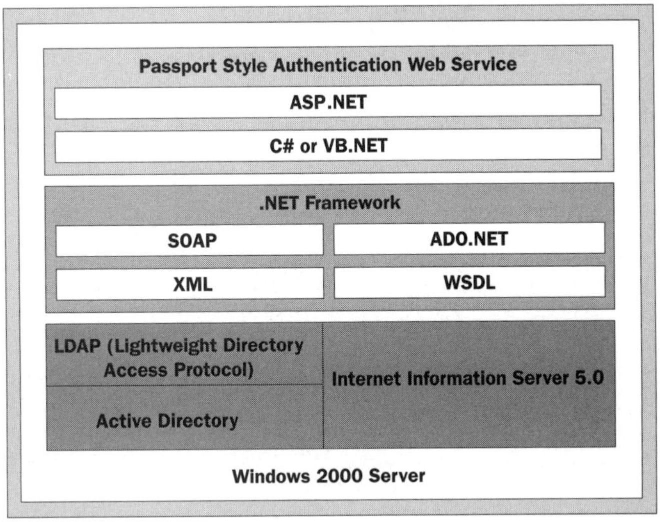

The Microsoft .NET Framework is used to provide support for SOAP over HTTP. The presentation tier consists of an ASP.NET interface supported by a collection of .NET assemblies. These communicate with an LDAP layer for access to the Active Directory service.

Application Overview

In the following section we will discuss:

- How the Passport-Style Authentication Web Service works
- How consumer sites implement the service
- How members register for the service
- How members sign in and out of the service

How the Passport-Style Authentication Web Service Works

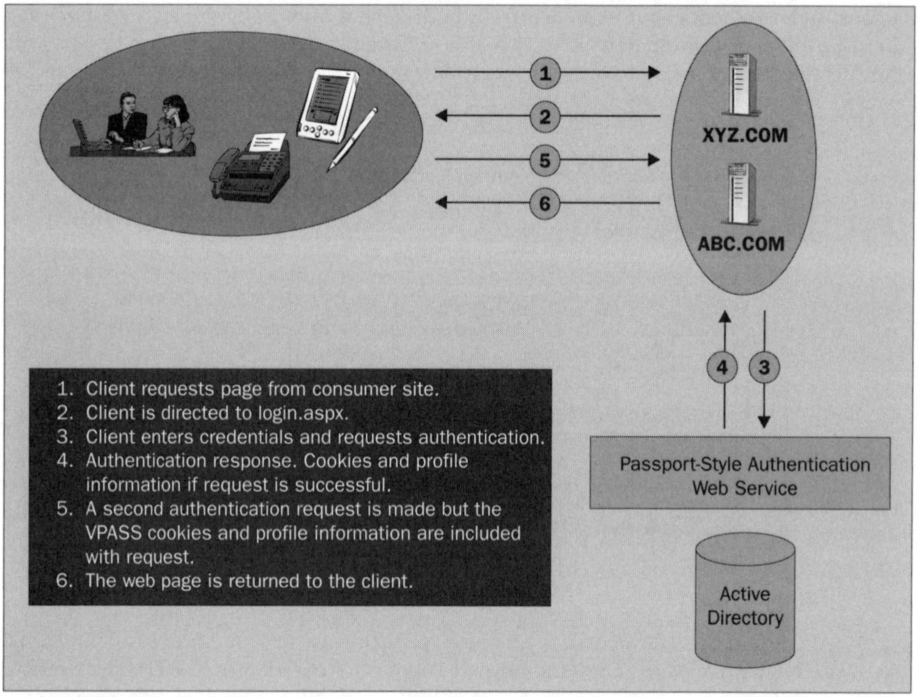
XYZ.COM
ABC.COM
1
2
5
6
4
3
1. Client requests page from consumer site.
2. Client is directed to login.aspx.
3. Client enters credentials and requests authentication.
4. Authentication response. Cookies and profile information if request is successful.
5. A second authentication request is made but the VPASS cookies and profile information are included with request.
6. The web page is returned to the client.
Passport-Style Authentication Web Service
Active Directory

Take a look at the flow of communication in the diagram above. When a consumer site of the Web Service needs to identify a visitor, the site inspects the HTTP query string for an encrypted authentication ticket. The encrypted authentication ticket is a globally unique 32-bit identifier (GUID) and a timestamp that are encrypted and returned to the consumer site along with the profile information. If the encrypted ticket is not in the HTTP query string the site visitor is redirected to the `login.aspx`. If the visitor is a member of the Web Service, they will enter their member name and password. If the Web Service successfully authenticates the member, an authentication ticket and the member profile information is encrypted and placed as parameters in the HTTP query string. The consumer site decrypts the information, manages authentication and profile access, caches the user's authentication and profile information in cookies on the user's browser, and silently recertifies the cookies as the user moves from page to page at the site. The site may use information in the profile cookie to personalize the user's experience in some way.

When a user signs into the Web Service, the user ID and password are transmitted over the network to the Web Service login server using the Secure Sockets Layer (SSL) protocol. The Web Service sends the user's authentication and profile information, which includes the encrypted authentication ticket, to the consumer site using Triple DES encryption.

How Consumer Sites Implement the Service

The .NET Framework allows clients from different platforms to interoperate with the Web Service. It does this by using the SOAP protocol. Any client that can format SOAP can communicate with the Web Service.

How Members Register for the Service

New members register for the service when a consumer site redirects them to the sign-in page, `login.aspx`. If the user does not have an existing account, they can create one by selecting **Register Me**. This redirects the user to the new member registration page (`register.aspx`), which prompts the new user to enter the information required to create their account and profile.

The Passport Style Authentication Web Service will create the new account and assign a globally unique 32-bit identifier (GUID). This identifier will be encrypted along with a timestamp and sent to consumer sites as the authentication ticket.

How Members Sign In and Out of the Service

Members sign in to the Web Service when they attempt to access a participating site. If the consumer site does not detect an authentication ticket on the client, the client will be redirected to the consumer site hosting the sign-in page (`login.aspx`). Users can sign out from the Web Service by selecting the **logoff** button hosted by the consumer site, which redirects users to the Web Service logoff page (`Logoff.aspx`). The logoff page automatically signs the user out of the Web Service.

Scalability

As we have seen, the Passport Style Authentication Web Service adopts an n-tier architecture that is divided into presentation, business logic, and data layers. More specifically, the Web Service is divided into layers consisting of ASP.NET pages that provide the user interface (`login.aspx`, `register.aspx`, and `logoff.aspx`), and a .NET assembly (proxy), which is used to encapsulate the business logic and make all calls to the Web Service. In turn, the Web Service itself consists of an `.asmx` that calls a code-behind to communicate with the directory through the LDAP tier. Therefore, the Web Service can be scaled using traditional scaling techniques. This is to say that it can be spread across multiple machines, as the following diagram demonstrates:

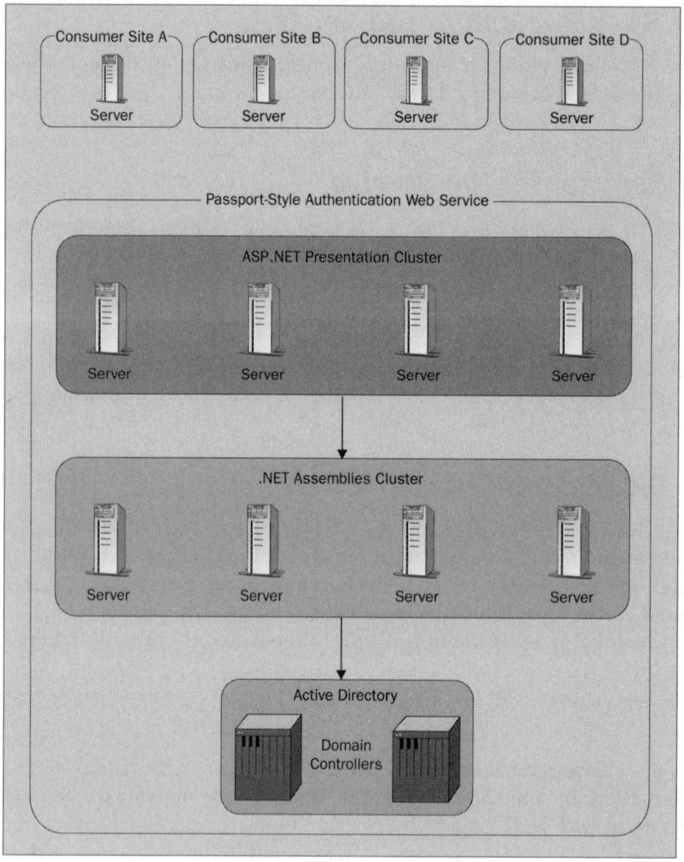

Running the Web Service on multiple servers that are working together to meet client requests is a very effective way of increasing reliability.

All state is stored client-side through the use of cookies or on the query string. When the Passport-Style Authentication Web Service authenticates a user, authentication ticket and profile information is encrypted and stored in a string that is sent back to the consumer site. The participating site has the option to continue to pass the information in the query string throughout the site or cache it to a client cookie.

Security

Let's define what we mean by a secure Web Service. There are many aspects to security – for example, authentication, authorization, auditing, data privacy, data integrity, availability, and non-repudiation.

Authentication is the process of verifying that someone (or something) is who they claim to be. The someone or something is known as a **principal**. Authentication requires evidence, or **credentials**. For example, a client application could present a password as its credentials. If the client application presents the correct credentials, it is assumed to be who it claims to be. In our example, we have the Unique Identifier (GUID) that our Web Service assigns the user at registration. This is a unique 32-bit identifier sent (encrypted) to client sites as the authentication ticket when a user signs in.

For more information on securing Web Services see Chapter 14.

Directory Services and LDAP

Directory services are designed to provide quick access to information over the network. They are optimized to provide many reads and infrequent writes. A directory service uses a naming structure to identify and organize objects that represent information stored in the directory. It is a hierarchical database, but the specifics of its schema are less relevant than the protocol used to define how a client can access the data the directory contains.

LDAP defines the way clients should access data on the server, but it does not specify how the data should be stored internally. LDAP offers excellent access to other directory services and has been implemented as a front end to many data stores. Many of the major directory vendors have revised or are revising their products to incorporate, and take advantage of, LDAP.

As mentioned earlier, our Web Service is driven by a directory service and LDAP. Our directory will store the user authentication credentials and additional user profiling data that can be used for site personalization. Even though we've chosen to implement the LDAP and directory service from Windows 2000 in our case study, LDAP provides the flexibility to swap out the directory and replace it with another directory with minimal changes to the Web Service.

The logical, hierarchical organization of the directory is known as the Directory Information Tree (DIT). The DIT for our directory contains a root organization (O) and six organizational units (OU). Each item displayed under the root organization in the tree is an organizational unit and is capable of containing more organizational units or objects. For our case study, all users of the service will be stored in the Users OU.

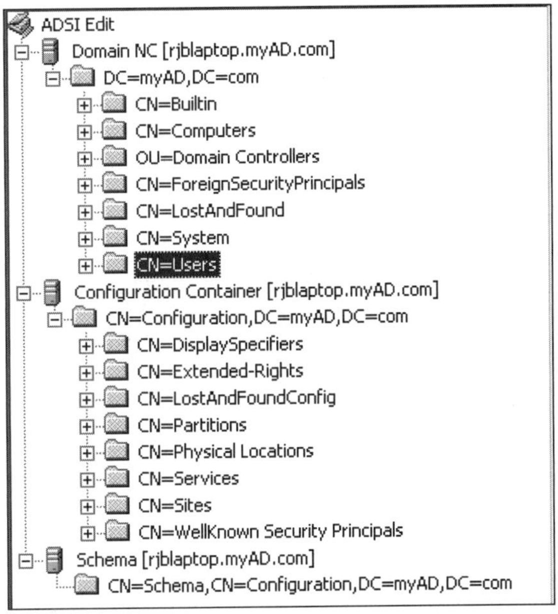

If you installed the Windows 2000 support tools from the support folder of the Windows 2000 installation media as suggested earlier, open the ADSI Edit tool now (Start | Programs | Windows 2000 Support Tools | Tools | ADSI Edit). ADSI Edit is a great low-level editing tool for navigating and editing the Active Directory. ADSI Edit gives us access to everything stored in the Active Directory including the configuration and schema. One of the things that I really like about ADSI Edit is that it displays the Distinguished Name for each object in the directory. This will come in very handy later when we need to start building paths to connect to objects in our directory. A word of advice here: be careful. It is very easy to make a little change using ADSI Edit that can turn into a big nightmare.

Let's use ADSI Edit to take a slightly closer look at our directory tree above.

Active Directory Domain

The top level organizational container shown in my directory is called `Domain NC [rjblaptop.myAD.com]`. This container represents our Active Directory domain. Windows 2000 uses Active Directory domains as security boundaries. Objects within an Active Directory domain are stored in hierarchical order and can be referenced through code using their Distinguished Name. The Distinguished Name for our Active Directory Domain is `DC=myAD,DC=com`. It contains all the data in our directory.

Configuration Container

Active Directory stores configuration information about itself within the configuration container. Information about Physical Locations, Services, Sites, etc. is stored within this container.

Schema

Every object stored within our Active Directory is an instance of a class that is defined in the schema container. The schema is broken down into the `classSchema` and `attributeSchema`. The `classSchema` defines the types of objects stored in our directory, as well as the mandatory and optional attributes of an object. Some examples of a `classSchema` include computer, site, and user. The `attributeSchema` defines what an attribute of an object looks like. Examples include `common-name`, `e-mail-address`, `given-name`, `surname` and `user-password`.

Let's look at the `User` class and its mandatory and optional attributes. Navigate down the schema tree in ADSI Edit to `CN=Schema,CN=Configuration,DC=myAD,DC=com` and click. In the right-hand window of ADSI Edit locate the `User` class (CN=User), right-click and select Properties from the context menu. The `User` class properties dialog box appears. If you select Mandatory in the properties to view box, the properties required for creating an object of the `User` class are displayed. This will be important for us later when we write our web methods in our Web Service to register new users.

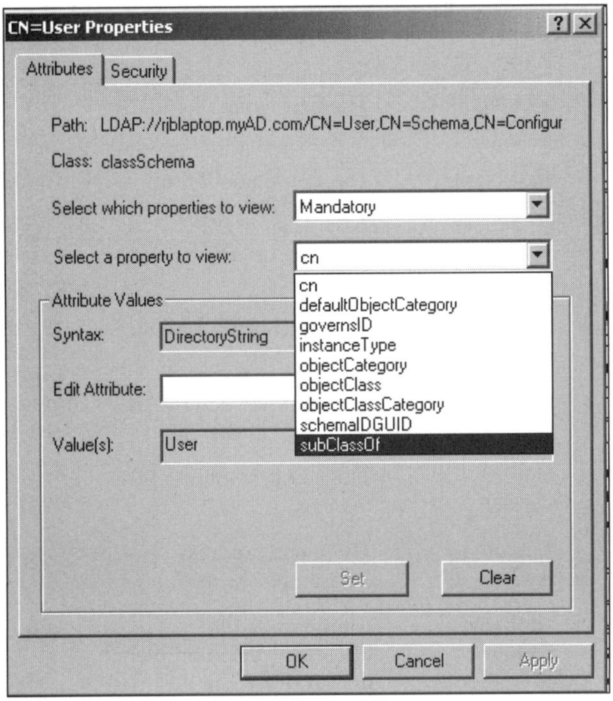

The `User` class is actually a subclass of the `organizationPerson`. This can be seen be viewing the `subClassOf` property of the `User` class. `User` derives many of its properties from `organizationPerson`. Likewise, `organizationPerson` is a subclass of the `Person` class and therefore derives many of its properties from the `Person` class. Finally, the `Person` class is derived from the root class `Top`.

The `User` class defines all the user objects created by the Passport-Style Authentication Web Service. Outlined in the next table are the properties of the `User` class that are important for our Web Service. Many of these properties are derived from a parent class. This can also be seen in the table.

Common Name	Display Name	Description	Derived from	Required
`cn`	Common name	The identifier of the registered user that will be used by the user to sign in.	`Top`	*
`user-password`	User Password	The password entered by the user.	`Person`	

Table continued on following page

Common Name	Display Name	Description	Derived from	Required
givenName	First Name	The first name of the user.	organizationalPerson	
sn	Last Name	The last name of the user.	Person	
l	User City	The city entered by the user.	organizationalPerson	
st	User State	The state entered by the user.	organizationalPerson	
postalCode	Zip Code	The zip code entered by the user.	organizationalPerson	
c	Country-name	The country entered by the user.	organizationalPerson	
mail	E-mail Address	The e-mail address entered by the user.	organizationalPerson	
objectGUID	Globally Unique Identifier	A unique 32-bit identifier generated by the service when the user is registered.	Top	*
telephoneNumber	Telephone Number	The telephone number entered by the user.	Person	

Objects and Assemblies

The `AuthService` class of our ASP.NET Web Service has been written using Visual Basic .NET. The class contains six web methods that provide the Web Service with the core business logic and directory access code. We will review this class and its web methods in detail here, and discuss the `System.DirectoryServices` namespace, which supports the class in accessing our directory service.

AuthService Business Object – authservice.asmx

The `AuthService` class provides the web methods for accessing our directory service to read, update, and remove user data from the Active Directory service. The class contains the following six web methods:

- `Authenticate` – validates the member name and member password in the directory
- `getMemberProps` – returns the property values of the member object to the consumer site
- `MemberExists` – verifies the member object exists in the directory
- `UpdateMemberProps` – updates the property values of the specified member object

- `CreateMember` – creates a new member object in the directory
- `RemoveMember` – removes the specified member object from the directory

Let's go ahead and look at the class. Open the file named `authservice.asmx` from the code you downloaded for this chapter. We begin by declaring the `WebService` directive, along with the language, code behind, and class attributes on the first line.

```
<%@ WebService Language="VB" Codebehind="AuthService.asmx.vb"
               Class="AuthWebService.AuthService" %>
```

Because we have decided that our web service will be using a code-behind file, this is the only code that will appear in the `authservice.asmx` file. The remainder of our code will be written in `AuthService.asmx.vb`, the code-behind file.

The first thing we need to do in the code-behind file for our Web Service is to declare the namespaces that it will require.

```
Imports System
Imports System.Web.Services
Imports System.Web.Security
Imports System.DirectoryServices
Imports System.Configuration
```

This is pretty basic stuff so far, but let's just briefly look at each namespace to emphasize the significance of it to this project (feel free to skip the rest of this section if it is not relevant to you – we will review the specific classes of the namespaces when we discuss the web methods within our object and explain why each is required in more detail below):

- `System` – the classes that define commonly-used value and reference data types, events and event handlers, interfaces, attributes, and processing exceptions.
- `System.DirectoryServices` – the classes in this namespace provide access to directory services via the Active Directory Service Providers. These providers include IIS, NTDS, LDAP, and Novell Netware. We will be using the LDAP provider to connect to our directory service and will make extensive use of the `DirectoryEntry` and `DirectorySearcher` classes.
- `System.Web` – this namespace provides the basic classes for exchanging information between the Web Service and its clients. We will make use of `HTTPRequest` to receive information from forms and `HTTPResponse` to send information back to our clients.
- `System.Web.Services` – this namespace provides the hooks to enable us to build and use our Web Services. It makes specific classes available to us that are required for building Web Services such as the `WebService` directive mentioned above, and the `WebMethod` directive described below. ASP.NET Web Services require us to include a reference to this namespace and use the attributes within the namespace to enable consumer sites to call our methods.
- `System.Web.Security` – this namespace provides the user authentication modules used in Web Services. Specifically, we will be looking at the `FormsAuthenticationModule` and its members.
- `System.Configuration` – this namespace provides classes and interfaces that allow you to programmatically access .NET Framework configuration settings and handle errors in configuration files (`.config` files).

The next section of code calls the WebService attribute to set up our namespace and give our Web Service a description.

Technically, the WebService attribute class is optional, and not required by our Web Service. However, its members provide functionality that will be required by practically every published Web Service. By default, a Web Service receives a Namespace property of http://tempuri.org. By including the Namespace property as part of our WebService attribute we can change the default namespace to a more permanent name, such as our company's Internet domain name.

We could also include the Description property of the WebService attribute. This property allows us to provide a description of our Web Service to potential consumers. To include the Description property, we would modify the code as follows:

```
<WebService(Description := "Provides user authentication and profiling.", _
            Namespace:="http://www.wrox.com/authwebservice")> _
```

The next line of code exposes our AuthService class and inherits from the WebService base class:

```
Public Class AuthService
  Inherits System.Web.Services.WebService
```

WebMethods

Now we can get into the core infrastructure of our Web Service. In this section we will review each of our web methods that can be called from the web via the SOAP protocol. These web methods are the ones we will rely on to do the work for our Web Service. Let's take a look at the steps required to build the authenticate method first.

authenticate

The authenticate method provides the key authentication services behind our Web Service. It enables our consumer sites to pass in two parameters, strMemberName, which is the unique user identifier chosen by the member when they registered with the service, and strMemberPassword, which is the password also chosen by the member when they registered for the service. The function returns True when the strMemberName and strMemberPassword variables are successfully validated against the directory service and False if the validation attempt fails.

The next line of code in our object declares the WebMethod attribute and includes the Description property. Inline with the WebMethod attribute we declare the authenticate method:

```
<WebMethod(Description:="Validates the member name and member " _
                      & "password in the LDAP directory")> _
  Public Function authenticate(ByVal strMemberName As String, _
                               ByVal strMemberPassword As String)
```

The next few of lines of code establish the variables we will be using and their associated data types:

```
    Dim sPath As String
    Dim sLDAPpath As String          'Delare a var for the root LDAP path
    Dim strMemberPath As String      'Declare a var for the full path to the user
```

```
Dim sUsersContainerPath As String 'Declare a var for the full path to the
                                  'users container
Dim ADserver As String            'Declare a var to hold the IP address of
                                  'the Active Directory Server
```

Next we establish a variable and build the physical directory path to the OU where our user objects are stored in our directory. It's important to note here that we're also including the Active Directory Service Interface `LDAP://` as part of the physical path. We have chosen to hard-code the path to the OU as part of the function. However, if we wanted to increase the flexibility of the code and simplify potential issues when migrating from one directory service to another, we could modify the code very easily to pass the provider and OU path into the function as additional variables.

The first variable that we set the value for is the location of the Active Directory Server that we will use for authentication. `ConfigurationSettings.AppSettings` is used to extract the value from the `AppSettings` element of the `Configuration` container in our `web.config` file. We'll look at the `web.config` file in more detail later on. The remaining variables are used as build paths to objects in the Active Directory based on values passed into the method.

```
ADserver = ConfigurationSettings.AppSettings("ActiveDirectoryServer")
sUsersContainerPath = "CN=Users,DC=headquarters,DC=rjbtech,DC=com"
sLDAPpath = "LDAP://" & ADserver
strMemberPath = "CN=" & strMemberName & _
                ",CN=Users,DC=headquarters,DC=rjbtech,DC=com"
```

We are now ready to begin our `Try ... Catch` block. This statement specifies a block of code that is always executed and enables us to catch errors that occur during the execution of that code block:

```
Try      'Begin our try/catch block
```

Underneath the opening `Try`, we can create a new instance of the `DirectoryEntry` object, which we get from the `System.DirectoryServices` namespace that we imported earlier, and use our new instance to bind to the physical path defined in the previous line. We attempt to bind to the directory with the user ID and password passed to us by the consumer site.

Once we are bound to the directory, we create a new instance of the `DirectorySearcher` object which allows us to query the bound OU. Then we initialize an instance of the `SearchResult` object to store the results of our query. We use the `Filter` property and the `FindAll` method of the `DirectorySearcher` object to locate the specific member object we need in the OU and store the `SearchResult`:

```
Dim oEntry As New System.DirectoryServices.DirectoryEntry(sLDAPpath, _
       strMemberPath, strMemberPassword, AuthenticationTypes.ServerBind)
Dim oEntrySearch As New System.DirectoryServices.DirectorySearcher(oEntry)
Dim oEntrySearchResult As System.DirectoryServices.SearchResult
oEntrySearch.Filter = "CN=" & strMemberName & ""
For Each oEntrySearchResult In oEntrySearch.FindAll()
  sPath = oEntrySearchResult.GetDirectoryEntry.Path
Next
```

If the directory bind is successful, we access the `FormsAuthentication` module and call its `SetAuthCookie` method to create an authentication ticket and return it in the cookie collection of the outbound response:

```
         FormsAuthentication.SetAuthCookie(strMemberName, True)
         Return True
      Catch
         Return False
      End Try

   End Function
```

If all has gone well up to this point, the function returns a Boolean value of `True` to the consumer site. If the username and password submitted to the function by the consumer site do not match the value stored in our directory our attempt to bind to the directory will fail and we return a Boolean value of `False`.

Throughout the remaining methods we won't repeat the same level of detail that we went through discussing the `authenticate` method. In other words, we will skip over blocks of code that are the same as the ones we've already discussed and focus on what is new about each function.

MemberExists

The `MemberExists` function is very simple. The method is used to verify that the member object exists in our directory service before calling one of our other methods. Using the method will help prevent errors when making changes to the member object.

The key operation of the `MemberExists` method is implemented using the `Exists` method of the `DirectoryEntry` object. The `Exists` method enables us to search our directory for the specified member to see if the entry exists. It returns `True` if the member object exists at the specified path and `False` if not. The code is as follows:

```
   <WebMethod(Description:="Verifies that the member object exists in the " _
                      & "directory, returns true if it exists, returns " _
                      & "false if it doesn't exist.")> _
   Public Function MemberExists(ByVal strMemberName As String)

      Dim strpath As String
      'Declare a var to hold the IP address of the Active Directory Server
      Dim ADserver As String
      'Delare a var for the root LDAP path
      Dim sLDAPpath As String
      'Declare a var for the full path to the users container
      Dim sUsersContainerPath As String
      'Declare a var for the full path to the user
      Dim strMemberPath As String

      ADserver = ConfigurationSettings.AppSettings("ActiveDirectoryServer")
      sLDAPpath = "LDAP://" & ADserver
      sUsersContainerPath = "CN=Users,DC=headquarters,DC=rjbtech,DC=com"
      strMemberPath = "CN=" & strMemberName & "," & sUsersContainerPath
      strpath = sLDAPpath & "/" & strMemberPath
```

```
    Try
      System.DirectoryServices.DirectoryEntry.Exists(strpath)
      Return True
    Catch
      Return False
    End Try
  End Function
```

getMemberProps

The `getMemberProps` web method returns the values of the properties of the specific member passed into the method as an array. The array returned to the consumer sites could be used to dynamically personalize content or streamline an online purchase process.

The method itself is very similar to the `authenticate` method: we establish the variables, build the path to the OU, create instances of the necessary objects that enable our code to search for the member and then use the `Invoke` method to read the property values of the member object:

```
<WebMethod(Description:="Returns the property values of the specified " _
                      & "member object from the directory")> _
Public Function getMemberProps(ByVal strMemberName As String)
  Dim sFirstName As String
  Dim sLastName As String
  Dim sPath As String
  Dim sGuid As String
  Dim sCountryName As String
  Dim sEmailAddress As String
  Dim sZip As String
  Dim sCity As String
  Dim sState As String
  Dim strpath As String = "LDAP://myADserver/CN=Users,DC=myAD,DC=com"
  Dim ADMIN As String = "CN=Administrator,CN=Users,DC=myAD,DC=com"
  Dim ADMINPASS As String = "password"

  Try
    Dim oEntry As New System.DirectoryServices.DirectoryEntry(strpath, _
      ADMIN, ADMINPASS, System.DirectoryServices.AuthenticationTypes.ServerBind)
    Dim oEntrySearch As New System.DirectoryServices.DirectorySearcher(oEntry)
    Dim oEntrySearchResult As System.DirectoryServices.SearchResult
    oEntrySearch.Filter = ("cn=" & strMemberName & "")
    For Each oEntrySearchResult In oEntrySearch.FindAll()
      sPath = oEntrySearchResult.GetDirectoryEntry.Path
    Next
    oEntry.Close()
    oEntry.Path = sPath
    If strMemberName <> "" Then
      sGuid = oEntry.Guid.ToString()
      sLastName = oEntry.Invoke("GET", "sn")
      sFirstName = oEntry.Invoke("GET", "givenName")
      sCountryName = oEntry.Invoke("GET", "c")
      sEmailAddress = oEntry.Invoke("GET", "mail")
      sZip = oEntry.Invoke("GET", "postalCode")
      sCity = oEntry.Invoke("GET", "l")
```

```
        sState = oEntry.Invoke("GET", "st")
        oEntry.Close()
        Return "FirstName=" & sFirstName & "&LastName=" & sLastName & "&Guid=" _
               & sGuid & "&CountryName=" & sCountryName & "&EmailAddress=" _
               & sEmailAddress & "&Zip=" & sZip & "&City=" & sCity & "&State=" _
               & sState
      Else
        Return False
        Exit Function
      End If
    Catch
      Return False
    End Try
  End Function
```

UpdateMemberProps

The `UpdateMemberProps` web method provides our object with the capability to modify the properties of the specified user object. It is important to take note of two primary differences from the method we reviewed above. The `Properties` property of our `DirectoryEntry` object enables us to update the values of the properties set on the user object. The updated properties are held in the local cache at this point. To enter them into the directory and perform the actual update on the member object we must call the `CommitChanges` method. Uncommitted changes are lost forever. Here is the code:

```
  <WebMethod(Description:="Updates the properties on the specified member " _
                      & "object, returns true if successful, returns false " _
                      & "if it fails.")> _
  Public Function UpdateMemberProps(ByVal strMemberName As String, _
                                    ByVal strMemberPassword As String, _
                                    ByVal strMemberFirstName As String, _
                                    ByVal strMemberLastName As String, _
                                    ByVal strMemberEmailAddress As String, _
                                    ByVal strMemberCity As String, _
                                    ByVal strMemberState As String, _
                                    ByVal strMemberPostalZipCode As String, _
                                    ByVal strMemberCountry As String)

    Dim err As Object
    Dim strpath As String = "LDAP://rjb-compaq-500/CN=" & strMemberName & _
                            ",CN=Users,DC=headquarters,DC=rjbtech,DC=com"
    Dim ADMIN As String = _
                    "CN=Administrator,CN=Users,DC=headquarters,DC=rjbtech,DC=com"
    Dim ADMINPASS As String = "dogtail"
    Dim oEntry As New System.DirectoryServices.DirectoryEntry(strpath, ADMIN, _
             ADMINPASS, System.DirectoryServices.AuthenticationTypes.ServerBind)

    Try
      If oEntry.Properties.Contains("givenName") Then
        oEntry.Properties("givenName")(0) = strMemberFirstName
      Else
        oEntry.Properties("givenName").Add(strMemberFirstName)
      End If
```

```
    If oEntry.Properties.Contains("strMemberLastName") Then
      oEntry.Properties("sn")(0) = strMemberLastName
    Else
      oEntry.Properties("sn").Add(strMemberLastName)
    End If

    If oEntry.Properties.Contains("mail") Then
      oEntry.Properties("mail")(0) = strMemberEmailAddress
    Else
      oEntry.Properties("mail").Add(strMemberEmailAddress)
    End If

    If oEntry.Properties.Contains("l") Then
      oEntry.Properties("l")(0) = strMemberCity
    Else
      oEntry.Properties("l").Add(strMemberCity)
    End If

    If oEntry.Properties.Contains("st") Then
      oEntry.Properties("st")(0) = strMemberState
    Else
      oEntry.Properties("st").Add(strMemberState)
    End If

    If oEntry.Properties.Contains("postalCode") Then
      oEntry.Properties("postalCode")(0) = strMemberPostalZipCode
    Else
      oEntry.Properties("postalCode").Add(strMemberPostalZipCode)
    End If

    If oEntry.Properties.Contains("c") Then
      oEntry.Properties("c")(0) = strMemberCountry
    Else
      oEntry.Properties("c").Add(strMemberCountry)
    End If

    oEntry.CommitChanges()
    Return True
  Catch
    Return False
  End Try
End Function
```

CreateMember

The `CreateMember` web method provides the capability to create new member objects within the member's OU. As with the methods we've previously discussed, we begin by establishing the variables, building the path to the member's OU, and creating an instance of the directory entry object:

```
<WebMethod(Description:="Creates a new member object in the directory.")> _
Public Function CreateMember(ByVal strMemberName As String, _
                             ByVal strMemberPassword As String) As String

  Dim strpath As String = "LDAP://myADServer/CN=Users,DC=myAD,DC=com"
```

```
    Dim ADMIN As String = "CN=Administrator,CN=Users,DC=myAD,DC=com"
    Dim ADMINPASS As String = "password"
    Dim oEntry As New System.DirectoryServices.DirectoryEntry(strpath, ADMIN, _
              ADMINPASS, System.DirectoryServices.AuthenticationTypes.ServerBind)
    Dim oCollection As System.DirectoryServices.DirectoryEntries
    Dim oMember As DirectoryServices.DirectoryEntry
```

However, in the next line of code we deviate from the previous methods and we create an instance of the `DirectoryEntries` object, which we will use later to obtain the child entries of our member's `DirectoryEntry`. After this we establish a variable as a `DirectoryEntry` to store our new member object:

We are now ready to retrieve a collection of all child member objects under the members OU. We accomplish this by using the `Children` property of the `DirectoryEntry` object. Once we have obtained the collection of child entries, we call the `Add` method of the `DirectoryEntries` object to create a new entry in the member's OU. The `Add` method requires us to pass in two parameters, the name of the new entry as a string and the name of the schema used for the new entry as a string:

```
    Try
      oCollection = oEntry.Children()
      oMember = oCollection.Add("cn=" & strMemberName, "user")
      oMember.Properties("sAMAccountName").Value = strMemberName
      oMember.Properties("userPrincipalName").Value = strMemberName
      oMember.Properties("userpassword").Value = strMemberPassword
      oMember.CommitChanges()
      Return "True"
    Catch
      Return False
    End Try
  End Function
```

Lastly, we call `CommitChanges` to enter the new entry into the directory. If all went well and the new member was successfully added to the directory, the method returns `True`. If the operation failed, we return `False`.

RemoveMember

The `RemoveMember` web method follows the same format as the previous methods. The only real difference is the use of the `DirectoryEntries` object's `Remove` method. We get our `DirectoryEntry` by creating `oMember` as the member object we want to delete.

```
  <WebMethod(Description:="Removes a member object from the directory.")> _
  Public Function RemoveMember(ByVal strMemberName As String)
    Try
      Dim strpath As String = "LDAP://myADServer/cn=users,dc=myAD,dc=com"
      Dim ADMIN As String = "CN=Administrator,CN=Users,DC=myAD,DC=com"
      Dim ADMINPASS As String = "password"
      Dim oEntry As New System.DirectoryServices.DirectoryEntry(strpath, ADMIN, _
                ADMINPASS, System.DirectoryServices.AuthenticationTypes.ServerBind)
      Dim oCollection As System.DirectoryServices.DirectoryEntries
      Dim oMember As DirectoryServices.DirectoryEntry
```

```
        oCollection = oEntry.Children
        oMember = oCollection.Find("cn=" + strMemberName)
        oCollection.Remove(oMember)
        Return True
      Catch
        Return False
      End Try
    End Function
```

Using the Web Service

In order to use the Web Service, we must know what classes and methods are available and understand how to use them. As we have seen throughout this book, ASP.NET provides a Web Service Help page that provides exactly that information for us. We can access the page by using our browser to create an HTTP GET request to call the Web Service on our local machine by pointing our browser at http://localhost/authwebservice/authservice.asmx. ASP.NET generates a page that shows us that the Web Service provides a class named `AuthService` and six public methods that we can call:

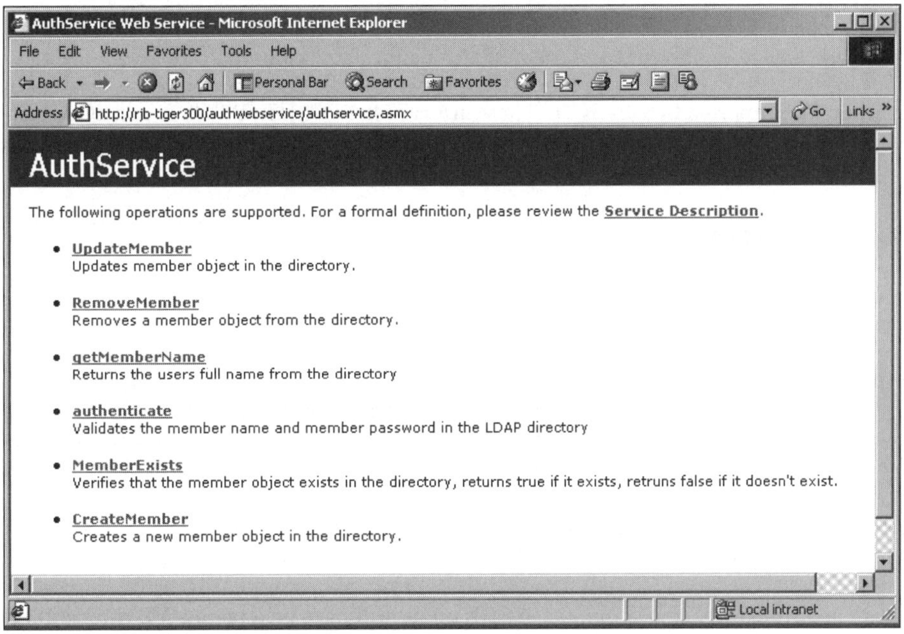

The Web Service also has a service description page, which takes you to the WSDL file. This page can be accessed by clicking on the Service Description link as shown in the screenshot above or it can be accessed directly by entering the following URL into the web browser: http://localhost/authwebservice/authservice.asmx?WSDL.

Testing the Service

The first step we will look at is how we can test the Web Service and more specifically the `authenticate` method. By directing our browser to http://localhost/authwebservice/authservice.asmx?op=authenticate or clicking the link on the above page for the authenticate method we can manually test the Web Service. We can use the HTML form provided to pass two string values to the `authenticate` method. Let's enter a member name and member password and click `Invoke` now so we can take a closer look at the results.

The screenshot below shows the XML results from the `authenticate` method call. By examining the document we can determine that the method returns a Boolean value `true` if the authentication was successful and `false` if authentication failed:

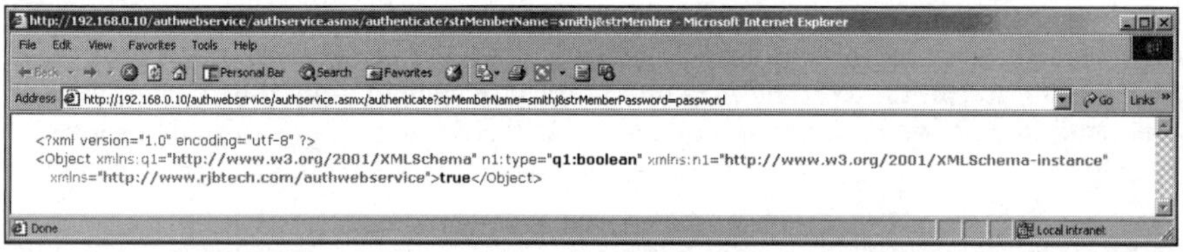

The Help page for the `authenticate` method also defines how communication with the web takes place. For our `authenticate` method, for example, we can see that the service supports all three of the default protocols supported by ASP.NET. These are HTTP GET, HTTP POST, and SOAP. For now, we will use HTTP GET to test our Web Service. Later on in the chapter, we will look at how to create a proxy that uses SOAP as the default protocol.

Creating the Proxy

To access our Web Service, we need to build a proxy that will allow consumer sites to communicate directly with the Web Service.

To create the proxy, we will use the command-line utility that generates code for Web Service clients and ASP.NET Web Services from WSDL contract files. The utility is `WSDL.exe` and it requires us to use several different switches in addition to some optional switches that are also available. To simplify the use of the utility, we have created a batch file called `build.bat` that contains the following code:

```
wsdl http://localhost/authwebservice/authservice.asmx?WSDL /l:VB ↵
/n: AuthWebService /o:authwebservice.vb
```

If there are no errors when this is run, the WSDL utility will have generated a VB source file for us named `authwebservice.vb` that we can use to compile a DLL.

Authwebservice Assembly

The source code for the authservice assembly is contained in the file authwebservice.vb. We can use the VB.NET compiler to compile the source code and create our proxy DLL. Once again, we have placed the command into a batch file in order to prevent typing errors. This time we will call the file make.bat. With this, the VB.NET compiler creates a library assembly. Let's go ahead and execute our batch file. Once the VB.NET compiler has completed processing the source file and creating our assembly, we can copy it to the /bin directory of our web application.

Web.Config

The web.config file of our Web Service is very straightforward. It simply provides support for our Active Directory by allowing us to store its location in the <appSettings> element within the configuration container.

```
<configuration>
  <appSettings>
    <add key="UseActiveDirectory" value="true"/>
    <add key="ActiveDirectoryServer" value="myADServer"/>
  </appSettings>
<configuration/>
```

Application Interfaces

When a consumer site wants to call our web page, they will need to create a series of web page user interfaces. Let's take a look at how a site might build an .aspx page to call our Web Service.

To call our Web Service consumer sites will need to create an .aspx similar to the one below, login.aspx. This page creates a simple form to input the member's name and their password and uses the Import directive to reference the namespace of our Web Service. In this case the namespace is AuthWebService.

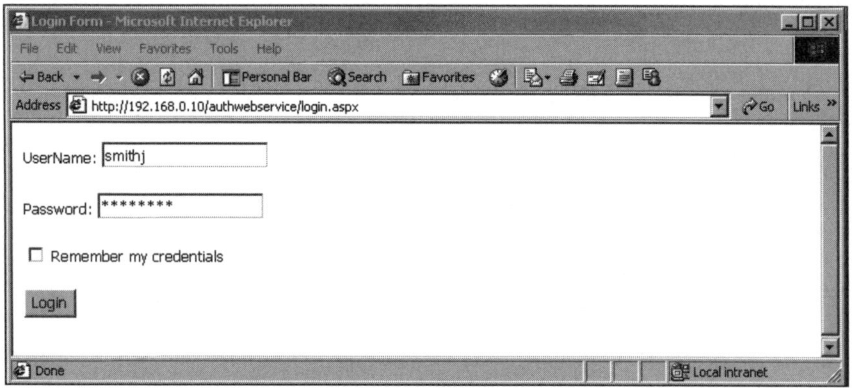

In the `Validate` sub we make use of our proxy to access the Web Service to authenticate the client. Our `Validate` sub is executed when our **Login** button is clicked. Once our script has been executed we establish our variables and collect the values of the arguments passed into our sub from the form. We then set a flag, `bIsAuthenticated`, to indicate if authentication has been successful. Initially, we'll set the flag to `False` and only change it to `True` if our user has been successfully authenticated.

Now that our script setup is out of the way we can proceed to create a new instance of our proxy object. We are ready to call the `authenticate` method of the Web Service and pass in the values given to us by the client. If the client is successfully validated against the Web Service, it will return a value of `True`, and because our Web Service supports forms authentication, we will also receive an authentication ticket back as part of the cookie collection. We can then change the value of our flag from `False` to `True`:

```
<%@Page Language="VB" Debug="true" %>
<%@Import Namespace="AuthWebService"%>

<html>
  <head>
  <title>Login Form</title>
  </head>
  <body>
  <FORM name=".ASPXAUTH" action="login.aspx" method="post" runat="server">
  UserName: <input id="txtUsr" type="text" runat="server" />
  <p />
  Password: <input id="txtPwd" type="password" runat="server" />
  <p />
  <ASP:CheckBox id="chkPersist" runat="server" />
  Remember my credentials
  <p />
  <input type="submit" value="Login" OnServerClick="Validate" runat="server" />
  <p />
  <div id="outMessage" runat="server" />
  </FORM>
  </body>
</html>
<script language="VB" runat="server">
  Public Sub Validate(sender As Object, e As EventArgs)
    Dim strMemberName As String = txtUsr.Value
    Dim strMemberPassword As String = txtPwd.Value
    Dim lblResult As Boolean
    'Set flag to indicate if authentication is successful
    Dim bIsAuthenticated As Boolean = False
    Try
      'create a new  object
      Dim AWS As New AuthService()
      lblResult = AWS.authenticate(strMemberName,strMemberPassword)
      If lblResult = True Then
        bIsAuthenticated = True
      End If
    Catch oErr As Exception
      outMessage.InnerHtml = "Invalid credentials please re-enter.<BR />" _
                           & oErr.Message & "<br />" & oErr.Source
```

```
      Exit Sub
    End Try
  End Sub
</script>
```

Register.aspx

The Web Service provides a registration page that can be used by consumer sites on a corporate intranet to register new members in the directory service using the Web Service proxy. The registration page implements two methods of our proxy (`createMember` and `updateMemberProps`) to create a new member. Consuming sites can pass values into these methods via the proxy and registration page and store them in a centralized location. These values can then be used by other consumer sites to target content to visitors.

The code for the registration page is as shown:

```
<%@ Page Language="vb" Debug="true"%>
<%@ Import Namespace="AuthWebService"%>

<html>
<head>
<title>Registration Form</title>
</head>
<body>
<FORM name=".ASPXAUTH" action="register.aspx" method="post" runat="server">
<table>
  <tr>
    <td>UserName:</td>
    <td><input id="txtUsr" type="text" runat="server" NAME="txtUsr" /></td>
  </tr>
  <tr>
    <td>Password:</td>
    <td><input id="txtPwd" type="password" runat="server" NAME="txtPwd" /></td>
  </tr>
  <tr>
    <td>First Name:</td>
    <td>
  <input id="txtFirstName" type="text" runat="server" NAME="txtFirstName" />
  </td>
  </tr>
  <tr>
    <td>Last Name:</td>
    <td><input id="txtLastName" type="text" runat="server" NAME="txtLastName" />
    </td>
  </tr>
  <tr>
    <td>Email Address:</td>
    <td>
      <input id="txtEmailAddress" type="text" runat="server"
             NAME="txtEmailAddress" />
  </td>
  </tr>
```

```
    <tr>
      <td>City:</td>
      <td><input id="txtCity" type="text" runat="server" NAME="txtCity" /></td>
    </tr>
    <tr>
      <td>State:</td>
      <td><input id="txtState" type="text" runat="server" NAME="txtState" /></td>
    </tr>
    <tr>
      <td>Postal Zip Code:</td>
      <td>
        <input id="txtPostalZipCode" type="text" runat="server"
               NAME="txtPostalZipCode" />
      </td>
    </tr>
    <tr>
      <td>Country:</td>
      <td><input id="txtCountry" type="text" runat="server" NAME="txtCountry"
/></td>
    </tr>
    <tr>
      <td></td>
      <td>
        <input type="submit" value="CreateUser" OnServerClick="Register"
               runat="server" />
      </td>
    </tr>
    <tr>
      <td></td>
      <td><div id="outMessage" runat="server" /></td>
    </tr>
    <tr>
      <td></td>
      <td><div id="lblResult" runat="server" /></td>
    </tr>
  </table>
  </FORM>
  </body>
  </html>
```

The page starts out by importing a reference to our Web Service proxy. Then we include a series of input controls on the body of the page to collect values from new visitors.

In the code below, we create a sub called `Register` to accept the value pairs from our form:

```
<script language="VB" runat="server">
  Public Sub Register(sender As Object, e As EventArgs)
    Dim strMemberName As String = txtUsr.Value
    Dim strMemberPassword As String = txtPwd.Value
    Dim strMemberFirstName As String = txtFirstName.Value
    Dim strMemberLastName As String = txtLastName.Value
    Dim strMemberEmailAddress As String = txtEmailAddress.Value
```

```
    Dim strMemberCity As String = txtCity.Value
    Dim strMemberState As String = txtState.Value
    Dim strMemberPostalZipCode As String = txtPostalZipCode.Value
    Dim strMemberCountry As String = txtCountry.Value
    Dim lblResult As String
  Try
    'create a new  object
    Dim AWS As New AuthService()
    lblResult = AWS.CreateMember(strMemberName,strMemberPassword)
    If lblResult = True Then
      lblResult = AWS.UpdateMemberProps(strMemberName, _
                strMemberPassword, strMemberFirstName, strMemberLastName, _
                strMemberEmailAddress, strMemberCity, strMemberState, _
                strMemberPostalZipCode, strMemberCountry)
    End If
  Catch oErr As Exception
    outMessage.InnerHtml = "Error creating or updating user.<BR />" _
                         & oErr.Message & "<br />" & oErr.Source
    Exit Sub
  End Try
  lblResult = "User successfully created!<BR />"
End Sub
</script>
```

Here, we establish some variables and set them to values posted to our form page. We need to create a new instance of our Web Service proxy object next and call the `createMember` method. If the method is successful and the new member object is created, we can proceed to update the properties of the member object with the additional values entered by the member. We close our `Try` ... `Catch` statement, add some code to inform us if an exception is detected, and finally close our sub.

displayme.aspx

The Web Service provides profiling services to its consumer sites by collating the most commonly requested information from users in one location. This centralized profiling service enables consumer sites to streamline their processes to make completing transactions easier and more efficient for both the consumer site and the member.

To demonstrate how the service provides this information we will build a page called `displayme.aspx`, which very simply retrieves member profile data from the Web Service for an authenticated member. In order to get access to the methods of our web proxy, the first thing we need to do is import the namespace `AuthWebService`. We'll add `<div>` tags to the body of the file and use these tags to display the information we retrieved about the member from the Web Service:

```
<%@ Page Language="VB" Debug="true"%>
<%@ Import Namespace="AuthWebService"%>
<html>
  <head>
    <title>Login Form</title>
  </head>
  <body>
    <div id="FirstName" runat="server" />
    <BR>
```

```
      <div id="LastName" runat="server" />
      <BR>
      <div id="Guid" runat="server" />
      <br>
      <div id="CountryName" runat="server" />
      <br>
      <div id="EmailAddress" runat="server" />
      <br>
      <div id="Zip" runat="server" />
      <br>
      <div id="City" runat="server" />
      <br>
      <div id="State" runat="server" />
      <br>
      <div id="outMessage" runat="server" />
      <br>
    </body>
  </html>
```

Next we add a new sub called Page_Load to displayme.aspx, which will automatically be called when the page loads. Now we can go ahead and establish a few variables for use within our Page_Load sub. For the purposes of the demonstration, we'll hardwire the strMemberName parameter of the Web Service to the user smithj from our directory service. The getMemberProps web method of our Web Service is the one we'll use to access the member's profile information. This method will return a single string containing the values.

```
<script language="VB" runat="server">
  Public Sub Page_Load(sender As Object, e As EventArgs)

    Dim strMemberName As String = "smithj"
    Dim lblResult As String
    Dim sResult

    Try
      'create a new  object
      Dim AWS As New AuthService()
      lblResult = AWS.getMemberProps(strMemberName)
      sResult = Split(lblResult,"&")
      FirstName.InnerHTML = SResult(0)
      LastName.InnerHTML = SResult(1)
      Guid.InnerHTML = SResult(2)
      CountryName.InnerHTML = SResult(3)
      EmailAddress.InnerHTML = SResult(4)
      Zip.InnerHTML = SResult(5)
      City.InnerHTML = SResult(6)
      State.InnerHTML = SResult(7)
    Catch oErr As Exception
      outMessage.InnerHtml = "Error accessing directory.<BR />" _
                           & oErr.Message & "<br />" & oErr.Source
      Exit Sub
    End Try
  End Sub
</script>
```

Once we have begun our Page_Load sub, you can see from the code above that we then create a new instance of our AuthService class. This proxy class that we created contains all the web-callable methods of our service. In the next line, we call the getMemberProps method and pass in the strMemberName variable that we set earlier. If all goes well the function will return a single concatenated string containing all the profile values stored by the service.

We chose to return the values from the method as a single string rather than multiple name value pairs to help offset the potential performance and availability issues of Web Services running on the Internet. It's important to limit the number of requests a consumer site has to make of the service. Since our Web Service is designed to run as an internal Web Service on a corporate intranet, the number of requests and the efficiency of each request become less critical with LAN speeds now reaching into the gigabits per second. One potential modification that we could make to the Web Service to increase efficiency would be to immediately return the profile information when the member is successfully authenticated instead of returning `True` from the `authenticate` web method.

You can see in the code that our string actually contains eight distinct profile values. We assign these values and set the content of the controls we placed in the body of our page using the `InnerHTML` property. Finally, we do some cleanup and end our sub.

The page generated by all this looks like this:

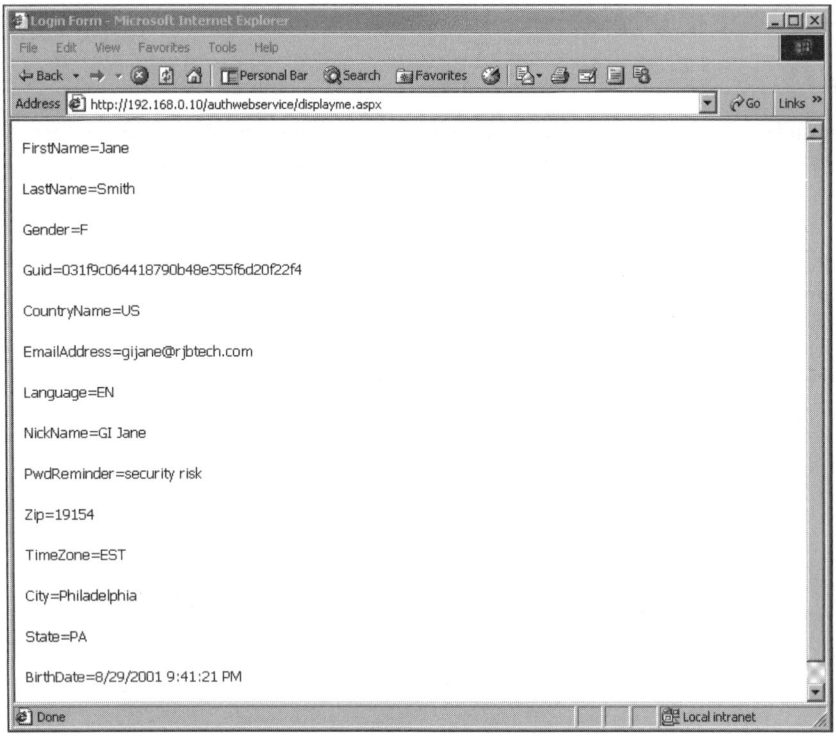

Logoff.aspx

When a user wants to end their session, it's important that we delete all cookies. We can accomplish this by calling the `SignOut` method of the forms authentication object. The `SignOut` method removes the authentication ticket from the cookie that was issued to the user.

```
<%@ Page Language="vb" Debug="true" %>
<script language="VB" runat="server">
  Sub Page_Load()
    'destroy the users authentication cookie
    FormsAuthentication.SignOut()
    'and redirect them to the login page
    Response.Clear()
    Response.Write ("LogOff Complete!")
  End Sub
</Script>
```

Summary

In this case study we've shown how ASP.NET Web Services can provide a simple authentication and profiling service to an intranet-based application. More specifically, we have:

- Looked at the creation of the service and its web proxy.
- Built some ASP.NET pages to illustrate how consumer sites would implement the service as part of their site.
- Used the `DirectoryServices` namespace to access Active Directory.

PROFESSIONAL
ASP.NET
WEB
SERVICES

19

Case Study – Distributed Processing

Distributed processing is the principle of taking a large processing "job" and breaking it down into many tiny pieces. A separate computer then processes one or more of those pieces, returning the results to a central server when it's complete. So, rather than investing in a single, powerful computer to process data, you can use a collection of less powerful, yet less expensive computers to do the same job.

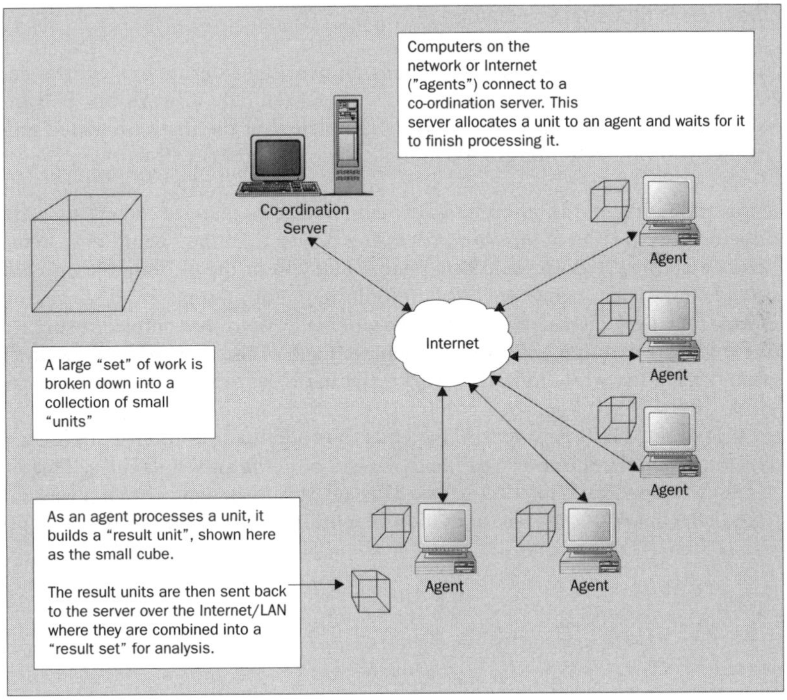

Computers on the network or Internet ("agents") connect to a co-ordination server. This server allocates a unit to an agent and waits for it to finish processing it.
Co-ordination Server
Agent
Agent
Agent
Internet
A large "set" of work is broken down into a collection of small "units"
As an agent processes a unit, it builds a "result unit", shown here as the small cube.
The result units are then sent back to the server over the Internet/LAN where they are combined into a "result set" for analysis.
Agent
Agent

The idea behind distributed processing is not new, but the Internet has made distributed processing on a massive scale possible. The idea behind each of these projects is that you donate processor capacity on your own computer.

Here are three distributed processing projects that you can get involved in.

- **SETI@Home**, or the "Search for Extraterrestrial Intelligence at Home" is one of a collection of projects involved in the larger "SETI" initiative. The central principle is that radio telescopes around the world analyze a vast quantity of data looking for telltale signs that one of the signals was sent by intelligent life from outside our own solar system. Like most Internet-centric distributed computing projects, you can download an agent from http://setiathome.ssl.berkeley.edu/ to get involved.
- **distributed.net** is an organization looking to find volunteers interested in cryptographic and mathematical research. You can find them at http://www.distributed.net/.
- **Intel-United Devices Cancer Research Project** is a project operated in cooperation between Intel, United Devices, the National Foundation for Cancer Research, and the Department of Chemistry at the University of Oxford. They are looking for volunteers to help analyze interaction between modules and proteins with an aim to finding a way to prevent the cancer from spreading inside a patient. You can learn more about this project here: http://members.ud.com/projects/cancer/.

When the computer has some spare capacity, it goes off over the Internet to a central coordination server where it downloads a work unit containing an amount of data to work on. This processing task may take a few minutes, several hours, or weeks to complete, but the interconnected nature of the Internet means that you can have hundreds of thousands of computers all working on a single project.

In the case of something like the Intel-United Devices Cancer Research Project, the organizations involved find themselves in control of more processing power than they could ever actually "own" themselves, because all they're doing is asking people like you or me to donate computing time to the project. What tends to happen is that we'll donate "idle" computing time. In this way, our computer works for the project or projects we're interested in whenever we're not actively using it. In my office here, I have three servers and one main work machine. Each of the servers runs the Intel-United Devices program constantly, while my main work machine is set to run the program at night.

This is a screenshot of the THINK program, which is the code that the Intel-United Devices distributed application uses to crunch the numbers that analyzes the proteins and molecules. This program runs inside of an agent developed by United Devices. This agent is designed in such a way that United Devices can task the agent with different activities depending on their and their users' preferences.

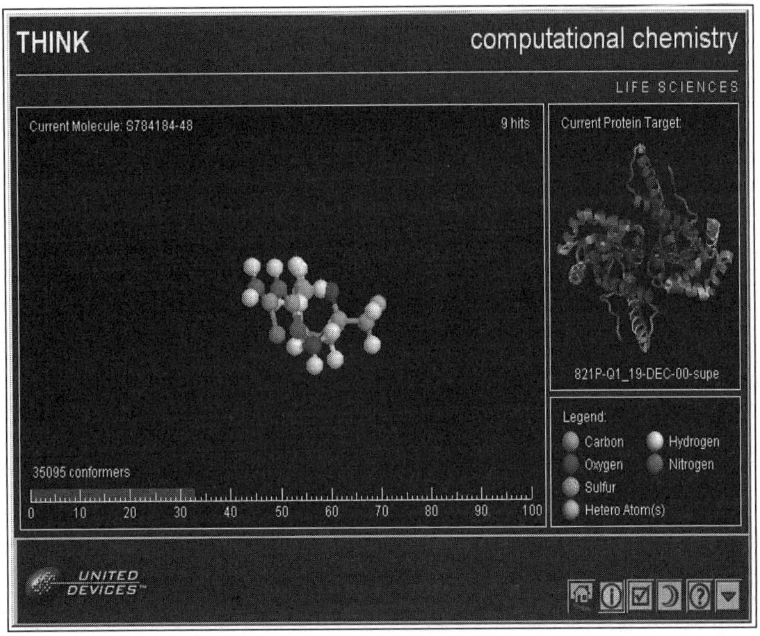

The complexity in building a distributed application tends to be in "coordination" activities, that is, the activities involved in sending work to the agent and receiving results from the agents. The three projects we've seen here predate the existence of Web Services, but Web Services and other features of .NET make building software that handles these essential distributed processing coordination activities very easy. In this case study, we're going to be taking a look at building our own applications.

Even if your organization doesn't directly benefit from analyzing complex chemical interactions with the aim of designing a new drug, there are still legitimate uses for distributed processing in commercial environments.

The example we're going to be working through here is developing an application that analyzes server log activity. Imagine you have a large server farm and need to analyze the logs from each of the servers in the farm. This could be a large job that would take a single powerful computer a long time to do. Alternatively, it could be a large job that would take the computers on your company LAN less time, but perhaps more importantly leverages your existing investment in computing hardware.

"WorkSets" and "WorkUnits"

In this case study, we're not going to build too much code. Instead, we're going to concentrate on building a solution. This means you'll need to download some prepared utilities from the Wrox site at http://www.wrox.com. For example, rather than expecting you to have a large server farm that generates gigabytes of log files each month, we'll use a utility to generate fake ones that we can use with the application.

As we saw in the diagram before, we're going to use a server running an ASP.NET Web Service as a coordination server. The agents running on the LAN or Internet will be able to connect to this Web Service to get work and report results. This whole thing will back onto a SQL Server database, and depending on what you have, this can either be a full copy of SQL Server 7, SQL Server 2000, or MSDE.

We already know that we're going to employ lots of computers on our LAN or on the Internet to do our work. The software running on each of these computers will be known as an "agent".

The system we build here will be "extensible". By that I mean that although we're going to build it now to analyze server logs, you'll be able to create new .NET classes that enable it to do other activities. We'll call each of these classes a "module".

The large job we have to do will be known as a "work set". For example, the 250MB of log data collected over a week will be known as a "work set".

Each of the smaller jobs that the work set is split into will be known as a "work unit". An agent will request a work unit, do some processing on it, and return a "result unit". Eventually, these result units will be combined into a larger "result set".

For testing purposes we're going to build our agent application in such a way that we can start multiple agents from the same desktop. This will let us make sure that the system we build works properly under load without having to go away and install .NET and the agent on computers around our LAN.

OK, so let's look at the database structure. We're going to see screenshots of the table definition together with some sample data, but you won't have this yet. We'll be building the database in a little while.

The "Agents" Table

This table contains a list of the registered agents. Each agent will have a name (this doesn't have to be unique) and will also maintain a register of the work unit that it's supposed to be working on.

Column Name	Data Type	Length	Allow Nulls
AgentId	int	4	
Name	varchar	64	
Created	datetime	8	
LastRequest	datetime	8	✓
CurrentWorkUnitId	int	4	✓
WorkUnitExpires	datetime	8	✓

AgentId	Name	Created	LastRequest	CurrentWorkUnitId	WorkUnitExpires
59	Chimaera	22/08/2001 15:15:57	22/08/2001 15:46:04	1471	23/08/2001 15:46:04

The "Modules" Table

This table contains a list of the modules available for processing. At the moment there's only one – `Distributed.LogAnalyzer` – the .NET class that will be used for analyzing Web server logs.

	Column Name	Data Type	Length	Allow Nulls
🔑	ModuleId	int	4	
	Name	varchar	256	
	Score	int	4	
▶				

	ModuleId	Name	Score
	1	Distributed.LogAnalyzer	1000
▶			

The "WorkSets" Table

This table contains a list of the work sets that are currently being processed by the agents. Each work set is related to a module. You'll also see that the table keeps track of how many work units are being processed.

	Column Name	Data Type	Length	Allow Nulls
🔑	WorkSetId	int	4	
	ModuleId	int	4	
	Path	varchar	255	
	TotalWorkUnits	int	4	
	WorkUnitsProcessed	int	4	
▶				

	WorkSetId	ModuleId	Path	TotalWorkUnits	WorkUnitsProcesse
	13	5	c:\Wrox WorkSets\13	614	614
▶					

The "WorkUnits" Table

This table contains a list of the work units that are currently owned by each work set. You'll notice that each one contains a filename containing the raw data, a status code, and the ID of an agent. (We'll cover all of this later.)

	Column Name	Data Type	Length	Allow Nulls
🔑	WorkUnitId	int	4	
	WorkSetId	int	4	
	Filename	varchar	255	
	Length	int	4	
	Status	tinyint	1	
	AgentId	int	4	✓
▶				

WorkUnitId	WorkSetId	Filename	Length	Status	AgentId
1467	11	c:\WorkSet\Words\e4db9928-1b91-4b24-98fc-bb6f71b58978.unit	721	1	59
1468	11	c:\WorkSet\Words\e534f5dd-9c1e-4077-9259-21a1d2599126.unit	712	2	<NULL>
1469	11	c:\WorkSet\Words\035e9084-d26b-45c3-8471-965d27f0d7c6.unit	729	2	<NULL>
1470	11	c:\WorkSet\Words\907cd8e2-57bc-4c9b-b1d2-5a42a84c36b5.unit	715	2	<NULL>
1471	11	c:\WorkSet\Words\72c69ecf-b1dc-4783-a392-244a7409283b.unit	705	2	<NULL>
1472	11	c:\WorkSet\Words\7a058f54-feac-4e31-8bbb-7b56dd602fdd.unit	724	2	<NULL>
1473	11	c:\WorkSet\Words\4ca45798-41e5-4aca-8dd4-50f16a691808.unit	722	0	<NULL>
1474	11	c:\WorkSet\Words\172c2e81-a935-4441-a388-c1ae31b0dc69.unit	727	0	<NULL>

The Logic

The tricky part of building a distributed processing solution is working out which agent should do what, and when.

The first thing to consider is when the agent will actually run. If your users are trying to work with the computer, it might not be such a smart idea to have the agent using up all the processing power chewing through data. So, you might want to configure agents to run only at night, or when the screensaver is on. (This issue is partially mitigated by the fact we'll be running the agent on a very low priority thread – more later.) It's likely that you'll have the agent running all the time, but that the agent will only be "awake" at certain times.

The second thing to consider is which work unit the agent will be working on. Two things will determine this – the capability of the agent and the availability of work.

The capability of the agent is down to the modules that are installed. Imagine we have modules `Distributed.LogAnalyzer` and `Distributed.WordCounter` known to the coordination server. For the sake of this application, we're going to assume that modules have to be physically installed on the agent. If the agent doesn't have `Distributed.WordCounter` installed, the agent will obviously not be able to work on a work set that uses this module. (This is to keep things simple in this example. As modules are stored in assemblies, the agent could download the assembly from a web server, install it and have access to the extended functionality.) Therefore, whenever an agent asks the coordination server for work, we'll have to provide a list of the modules that are installed on the computer.

When the agent asks the coordination server for work, the server will look through the available work sets in order from the oldest to the newest, providing that the agent has the module installed that the work set requires. (The premise being that older work sets have to be completed before new work sets can be started. If an old work set is no longer required, it should be deleted from the database. The database is transitory – there's no need to archive old, unanalyzed work data.)

Once a work set has been determined, the next available, unprocessed work unit will be chosen for the work set. If there are no more unprocessed work units, the first **expired** work unit will be chosen.

When work units are allocated, they are given an expiry time. If the agent does not return the unit within that given time, it's fair game for another agent that needs work. The principle here is that if the agent doesn't return the results for some reason, that work unit has to be done by someone else.

As each work unit is completed, the agent will return a matching result unit. This is where, conceptually, things get a little tricky. Simply, it's logical to assume that each result unit stands alone – in other words looking at the data in a result unit will yield some meaningful information. By and large this is not the case. Just as the work set itself stands as an individual unit, typically only the *complete* result set will yield the results that explain the entire work set.

Here's an example. If we have 250MB of server logs and split it into 25KB chunks, what we're looking for is a list of instances where a given page appears. However, by looking at the result unit for that 25KB chunk, we'll only know how many times a given page appears in that **work unit**. To understand how many times a given page appears in the entire work set, we have to look at the entire **result set**.

Building the Database

To follow along with this exercise, you're going to need a SQL Server database: either a full SQL Server 7/2000 database or a MSDE database.

Create a new database called Distributed. In the download package that accompanies this case study you'll find a file called `Distributed.bak`, which is a SQL Server database backup file which you can restore to your version of SQL Server, or you can run the `Distributed.sql` script.

Creating Sample Data

As we mentioned before, we're going to be using a utility to create fake server logs for use with this application. You can find the files for this utility in the `Dummy Server Log Builder` folder of the code download package.

Run the Dummy Server Log Builder utility. It will prompt you for a database connection string, and in particular remember to change the name of the server ("Data source") from localhost to whatever yours is called if you need to:

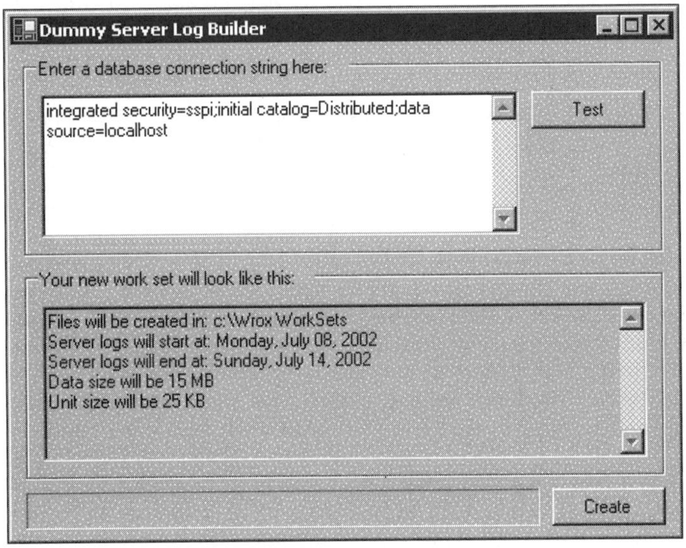

Make sure the database connection works by pressing the Test button. When you're happy, click Create. After a few moments, you'll see a message similar to this. The number at the end of the path (shown here as 28) will very likely be different on your machine:

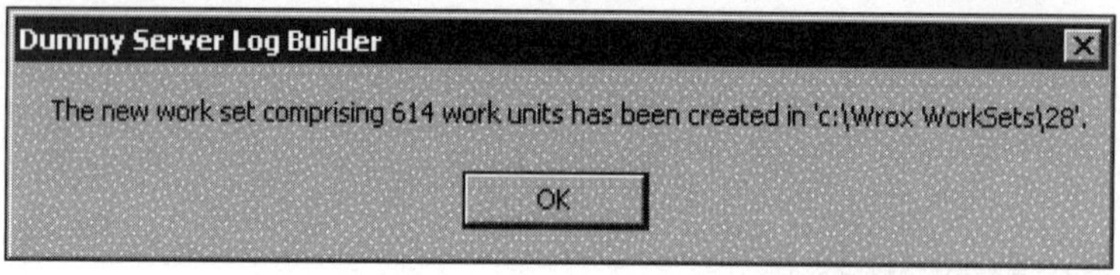

Using Windows Explorer, open the folder referenced in the message box. It will contain several hundred 25KB (or thereabouts) files. Open one of the files with Notepad and you'll notice a bundle of lines, each one looking similar to this. (I've had to break mine into two lines to suit the book format, but if you look at the file using Notepad make sure word wrapping is switched off by using the option on the Format menu.)

```
2002-07-19 12:27:02 128.106.153.150 GET ↵
                /coffee.aspx Microsoft-Visual-Studio.NET/7.00.9254 200
```

The server log format that we're simulating matches the W3C Extended Log File format. IIS uses this format by default. Each line in the log file represents a request from a browser. Using the logging options in IIS we can control the information that appears against each entry. Specifically, the utility uses this format:

- Date – the date at which the request was received.
- Time – the time at which the request was received.
- IP address – the IP address of the browser, proxy or firewall that made the request. (Those of you who understand the mechanics of TCP/IP may note that the utility sometimes doesn't generate valid IPs.)
- Method – the type of request. (The utility always uses GET as the method.)
- URI stem – the resource that was requested from the server. (The utility uses one of a possible twelve ASP.NET pages. On real server logs, you'll see pictures and other resource types here as well as pages.)
- Agent – the user agent that made the request.
- Status – the status of the request. (200 means "OK". The utility only generates 200 codes.)

In a real-world implementation of the system we're going to see here, we'd expect to have a cluster of computers in a server farm and each of those computers would generate their own log. Let's say we have ten computers in the farm and on an average day, each one of those computers creates a 500MB server log. In total, that's 5GB of logs per day, or 35GB per week. That kind of size is worth distributing using the techniques we're going to see here. The 15MB work set that our utility creates is just for fun!

IIS can be set to create a new log file each day, so at the end of the week you'd fire off a utility that created a new work set, as shown here. (You can follow along with your own database, as the utility will have populated this with data. Again, your results will be *similar*, so the IDs and the TotalWorkUnits may well not match these.)

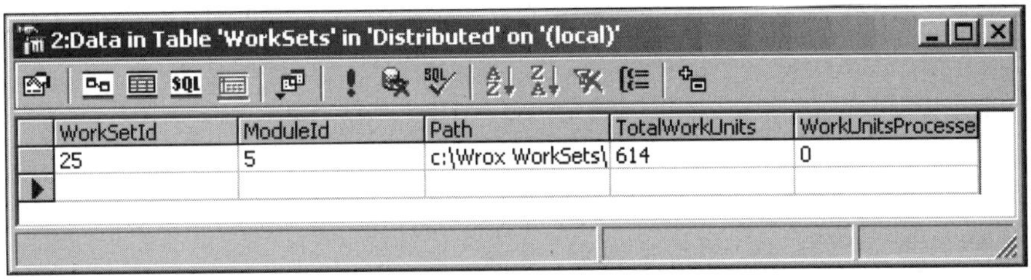

WorkSetId	ModuleId	Path	TotalWorkUnits	WorkUnitsProcesse
25	5	c:\Wrox WorkSets\	614	0

The work set needs a folder on disk in which to save the work units. (We could store this in the database, but for this example we're going to use disk files.) We go through each of the logs in turn and generate new work units. We've picked 25KB as the size of a work unit. Each work unit is saved on disk (as we've already seen) and also saved in the database.

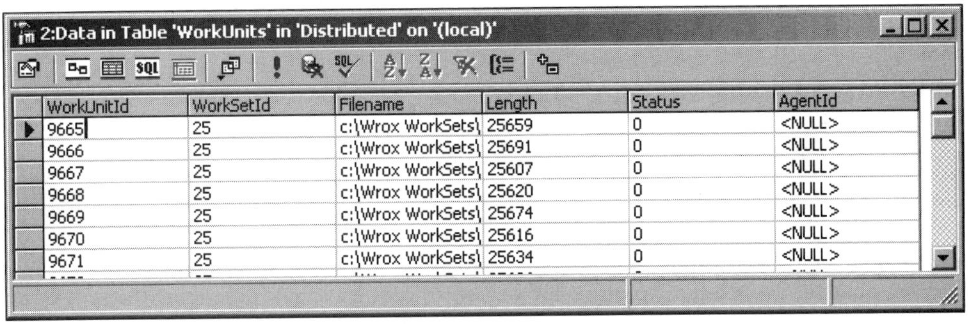

WorkUnitId	WorkSetId	Filename	Length	Status	AgentId
9665	25	c:\Wrox WorkSets\	25659	0	<NULL>
9666	25	c:\Wrox WorkSets\	25691	0	<NULL>
9667	25	c:\Wrox WorkSets\	25607	0	<NULL>
9668	25	c:\Wrox WorkSets\	25620	0	<NULL>
9669	25	c:\Wrox WorkSets\	25674	0	<NULL>
9670	25	c:\Wrox WorkSets\	25616	0	<NULL>
9671	25	c:\Wrox WorkSets\	25634	0	<NULL>

In the WorkUnits table, a Status value of 0 means "unprocessed", 1 means "being processed", and 2 means "completed". The work set is deemed complete when the Status column for every work unit is set to 2.

Once we get to that point, we can start distributed processing across the agents. Each agent will request a work unit. We'll give it one back and wait for it to return results.

The Work

So what work does the agent have to do? Well, we want the agent to go through the work unit and create a list of the number of times a given page is requested each day. It will format the information as XML, and it will look similar to this:

```
<Results>
  <Day>
  <Year>2002</Year>
  <Month>7</Month>
  <Day>22</Day>
  <Pages>
    <Page>
    <Name>/coffee.aspx</Name>
    <Hits>27</Hits>
    </Page>
    <Page>
```

```
      <Name>/default.aspx</Name>
      <Hits>105</Hits>
      </Page>
    </Pages>
    </Day>
    <Day>
    <Year>2002</Year>
    <Month>7</Month>
    <Day>21</Day>
    <Pages>
      <Page>
      <Name>/coffee.aspx</Name>
      <Hits>99</Hits>
      </Page>
      <Page>
      <Name>/default.aspx</Name>
      <Hits>667</Hits>
      </Page>
    </Pages>
    </Day>
</Results>
```

As we mentioned before, a result unit only becomes useful when it's aggregated into a larger result set. However, once the set is complete we should be able to create a report describing the activity per page per day.

Building the Service

The first part of the problem we should look at is building the service. This is going to be an ASP.NET Web Service that I'm sure by now you're familiar with, so we'll jump right in.

First off, create a new **Visual Basic | ASP.NET Web Service** project. Call it **DistributedCoordinator** and set it to use **localhost** as the server.

Using Solution Explorer, delete the default `Service1.asmx` page. Create a new Web Service page called `Coordinator.asmx`, by right-clicking on the project and selecting **Add | Add Web Service**. Again using Solution Explorer, right-click on the new page and select **Set as Start Page**.

The first thing we should do is change the namespace used for the SOAP envelopes from **http://www.tempuri.org/** to something else. Open the code editor for `Coordinator.asmx` and add this attribute to the class definition:

```
<WebService(Namespace:="http://www.wrox.com/distributed/")> _
Public Class Coordinator
    Inherits System.Web.Services.WebService
```

Also, add these namespace import declarations:

```
Imports System.Web.Services
Imports System.Data.SqlClient
Imports System.IO
Imports System.Threading
```

To communicate with the database server, we need a connection string. Add this member:

```
' members...
Private Shared _statusLock As New ReaderWriterLock()
Public DbString As String = "uid=distributed;pwd=distributed; " _
                    & "initial catalog=Distributed; data source=localhost"
```

Remember, you'll need to change the database name and server name so that the connection string will work on your configuration, in particular the user ID and password.

In this project, we're going to make heavy use of stored procedures. Here's the first one called `RegisterAgent`, which we'll use in our `CallRegisterAgent` method below:

```
CREATE PROCEDURE RegisterAgent
(
  @name varchar(64)
)
 AS
  insert into agents (name) values (@name)
  return @@identity
```

Add this method to `Coordinator.asmx.vb`:

```
Protected Function CallRegisterAgent(ByVal connection As SqlConnection, _
                                     ByVal name As String) As Int32

   ' create a command...
   Dim command As New SqlCommand("RegisterAgent", connection)
   command.CommandType = CommandType.StoredProcedure

   ' params...
   Dim nameParam As SqlParameter
   nameParam = command.Parameters.Add("@name", SqlDbType.VarChar, 64)
   nameParam.Value = name

   ' add a return param...
   Dim returnValueParam As SqlParameter
   returnValueParam = command.Parameters.Add("@returnValue", SqlDbType.Int)
   returnValueParam.Direction = ParameterDirection.ReturnValue

   ' execute...
   command.ExecuteNonQuery()

   ' cleanup...
   command.Dispose()
```

```
    ' return...
    Return returnValueParam.Value

  End Function

  Protected Function CallRegisterAgent(ByVal dbString As String, _
                                       ByVal name As String) As Int32
    Dim connection As New SqlConnection(dbString)
    connection.Open()
    Dim results As Int32 = CallRegisterAgent(connection, name)
    connection.Close()
    Return results
  End Function
```

Now, add this new web method:

```
  ' RegisterAgent - register an agent...
  <WebMethod()> Public Function RegisterAgent(ByVal name As String) As Integer

    ' register the agent...
    Return CallRegisterAgent(DbString, name)

  End Function
```

Run the project and use the test interface to call the `RegisterAgent` method. Enter any name you like. When the method has returned, look in the **Agents** table and you'll see your new agent:

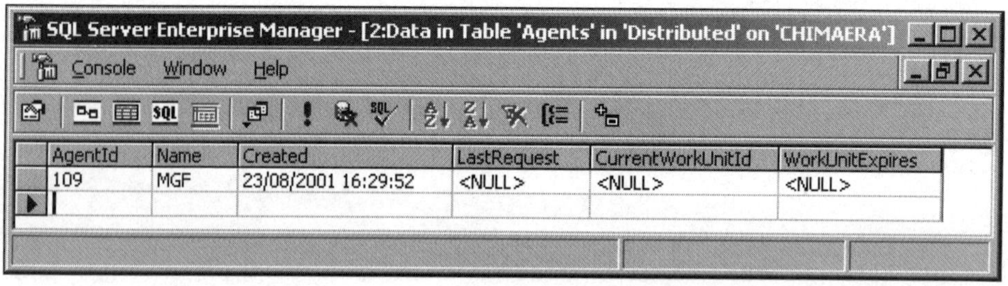

Building the Agent

Although we're far from finished at the server side, let's turn our attention to building the agent.

As we mentioned before, the agent will be a multipurpose executable that will run on the client continually and, on occasion, ask the Web Service for some work to do. The agent will follow these steps:

- If the agent has not been registered, complete registration.
- The agent requests a work unit. The agent is given a work unit ID and the name of the module that it should use for processing.
- The agent separately requests the data that makes up the work unit. (In our case, that's the file containing the server log fragment.) The coordination server marks the unit as "in progress".

- The agent processes the unit.
- The agent sends the result unit back to the coordination server. The coordination server marks the unit as "done".
- The agent requests another work unit, and so on.

The reason why we make a separate request to get the data back is because in a lot of cases SOAP will not be the most appropriate transport medium for passing work units and result units back and forth. Let's look at why this is now.

In this system, the bottleneck is when the client has to talk to the server. Ideally, we don't want agents constantly talking to the service, as if we have thousands of agents each needing information from the server every couple of seconds, we're going to lose the advantage that distributed processing gives us – we'll need to invest in a huge, powerful server to coordinate the agents' activities.

The bigger the work unit, the longer the agent has to work on it and therefore there will be more time between agent requests on the server. Unless your work unit is a few bytes long, but those few bytes dictate a great deal of work (for example "evaluate pi to infinity"), you're in a place where the bigger the work unit, the more work that has to be done by the client before the results can be returned. For example, if it takes two seconds to process a 25KB work unit and four seconds to process a 50KB work unit, we can assume that a 1MB work unit will take a little under one-and-a-half minutes. If each client has to wait 90 seconds between requests rather than two seconds, the requests should be more spread out and the load on the server should be reduced.

However, because SOAP is optimized for method calls not data transfer, moving 1MB SOAP packets about might not be the most appropriate course of action. Ideally, we would have made this application so that the work units were transferred via FTP, but the FTP support in .NET at the time of writing is so dire that we decided to illustrate the technique using SOAP throughout. Nevertheless, the need to switch SOAP out with another transfer mechanism led us to have the "request work unit" and "get work unit data" as separate steps.

Creating the Project

In this section, we're going to build one **client** that can manage several **agents**. Each agent will be implemented in a class called `AgentView`. The view will show a log of activity for each agent, together with the agent's name and a status bar.

Open a new instance of Visual Studio and create a new Visual Basic | Windows Application project. Call it Agent. The purpose of all this is to have the agent running in a separate solution to the server.

We want to create a form that follows a design classic – we want a tree control on the left-hand side of the form and when different items are selected on the tree we want the right-hand side of the form to show us specifics about that item. Follow these instructions carefully.

When Form1 appears, add a new `Panel` control to the left-hand side. Set its Dock property to `Left`. Don't worry about the Name property.

Inside the panel, add a `TreeView` control so that it occupies almost all of the available space. Set its Name property to `treeviewAgents`. Set its Anchor property to `Top`, `Bottom`, `Left`, `Right`. Set its HideSelection property to `False`.

Now add a `Splitter` control to the form. It should appear to the right of the panel. Make it about ten pixels wide.

Next, add another `Panel` control to the form on the right-hand side of the `Splitter` control. Set its **Name** property to `panelView` and its **Dock** property to `Fill`.

You'll now have something like this. If you run the project you'll be able to grab hold of the splitter to change the width of the tree control.

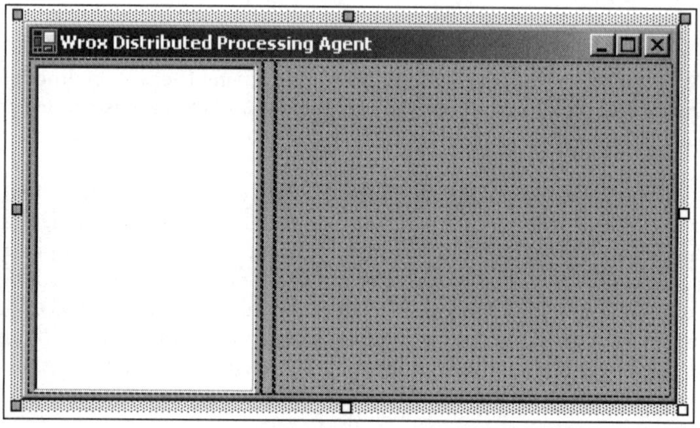

Creating "AgentView"

Using Solution Explorer, create a new User Control. Call it `AgentView`.

When the Designer appears, add these controls:

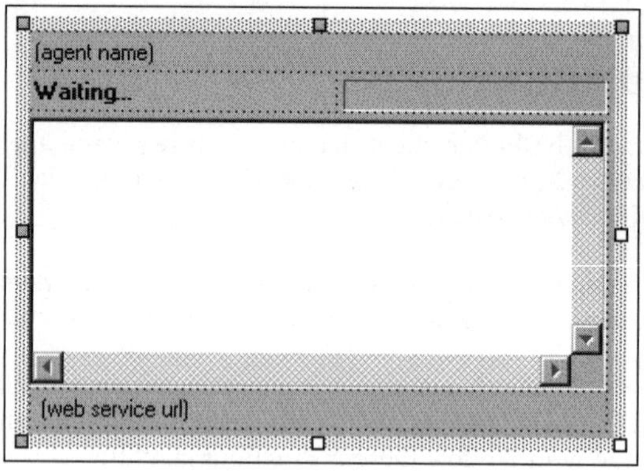

Set these properties:

Control	Property	Value
First label:	Name	labelAgentName
	Text	(agent name)
	Anchor	Top, Left, Right
Second label:	Name	labelStatus
	Text	Waiting...
	Anchor	Top, Left, Right
	Font	Bold: True
Progress bar:	Name	barStatus
	Anchor	Top, Right
Text box:	Name	textLog
	Multiline	True
	WordWrap	False
	ScrollBars	Both
	Anchor	Top, Bottom, Left, Right
	Text	Clear this property
Third label:	Name	labelWebServiceUrl
	Text	(Web Service url)
	Anchor	Bottom, Left, Right

Next, add a new class to the project called `Configuration`. `Configuration` objects will be used to tell each `AgentView` who they are and what they're supposed to be doing. When the name of the agent is set by a method called `SetAgentDetails` of `AgentView` that we're yet to build, we'll load a new `Configuration` object from disk by using `System.Xml.Serialization.XmlSerializer`. Add this code to `Configuration`:

```
Imports System.IO
Imports System.Xml.Serialization

Public Class Configuration

  ' members...
  Public AgentId As Integer
  <XmlIgnore()> Public Filename As String
```

We need a shared method on `Configuration` called `Load`. This will take a filename and attempt to deserialize a `Configuration` object from the file that it references. If no configuration can be loaded (either because the file doesn't exist or some deserialization problem occurs), we'll create a new blank `Configuration` object and return that to the caller.

```
' Load - load a configuration file...
Public Shared Function Load(ByVal filename As String) As Configuration

  ' try and load the file...
  Dim newConfig As Configuration
  Dim stream As FileStream
  Try

    ' open the file...
    stream = New FileStream(filename, FileMode.Open)

    ' create a serializer...
    Dim serializer As New XmlSerializer(GetType(Configuration))
    newConfig = serializer.Deserialize(stream)

  Catch
  Finally

    ' close the file...
    If Not stream Is Nothing Then
      stream.Close()
    End If

  End Try

  ' do we have one?
  If newConfig Is Nothing Then
    newConfig = New Configuration()
  End If

  ' store the filename...
  newConfig.Filename = filename

  ' return what we got...
  Return newConfig

End Function
```

When we create an `AgentView` object, we'll supply them with a name and an instance number starting at `1`. This will prompt the agent to load the configuration file and start working.

Open the code editor for `AgentView` and add these members:

```
Imports System.IO

Public Class AgentView
  Inherits System.Windows.Forms.UserControl
```

```
' members...
Private _agentName As String
Private _agentInstance As Integer
Private _configuration As Configuration
```

Next, add these properties:

```
' Configuration property...
Public ReadOnly Property Configuration() As Configuration
  Get
    Return _configuration
  End Get
End Property

' AgentName property...
Public ReadOnly Property AgentName() As String
  Get
    Return _agentName
  End Get
End Property

' AgentInstance property...
Public ReadOnly Property AgentInstance() As Integer
  Get
    Return _agentInstance
  End Get
End Property
```

We also need a method that will be used to get the name and instance of the agent and also prompt the configuration to be loaded. Add this code:

```
' SetAgentDetails - set the details for the agent...
Public Sub SetAgentDetails(ByVal agentName As String, _
                           ByVal agentInstance As Integer)

  ' set the details...
  _agentName = agentName
  _agentInstance = agentInstance

  ' formulate a filename...
  Dim filename As String
  filename = Form1.DataPath & "\" & _agentName & "." _
           & _agentInstance & ".config"

  ' load the configuration...
  _configuration = Configuration.Load(filename)

End Sub
```

You'll notice there that `DataPath` has not been defined as a property of `Form1`. Open the code editor for `Form1`. First of all, add this namespace import declaration and the `_dataPath` member:

```
Imports System.IO

Public Class Form1
```

```
Inherits System.Windows.Forms.Form

' members...
Private Shared _dataPath As String
```

Then, add this property:

```
' DataPath property...
Public Shared ReadOnly Property DataPath() As String
  Get

    ' do we have one?
    If _dataPath = "" Then

      ' get the executable path...
      Dim fileInfo As New FileInfo(Application.ExecutablePath)

      ' get a new folder by going down the tree and up one...
      _dataPath = fileInfo.Directory.Parent.FullName & "\Data"

      ' create the new folder...
      Dim folderInfo As New DirectoryInfo(_dataPath)
      If folderInfo.Exists = False Then folderInfo.Create()

      End If

      ' return it...
      Return _dataPath

    End Get
End Property
```

What we want to do with `DataPath` is, if our application is running from this executable:

`c:\Wrox WorkSet\Agent\bin\Agent.exe`

...then we want configuration files to be stored in this folder:

`c:\Wrox WorkSet\Agent\Data`

The property also checks to make sure that the folder exists and, if it doesn't, creates it.

Before we move on, add this overridden implementation of `ToString` to `AgentView`:

```
' ToString...
Public Overrides Function ToString() As String
  Return AgentName & "." & AgentInstance
End Function
```

Creating AgentViewCollection

As ultimately we're going to be working with more than one agent view, we need to be able to hold a list of them in a collection. We'll do this by creating a new class called `AgentViewCollection` and inheriting from `System.Collections.CollectionBase`. We'll then provide strongly-typed implementations of `Add`, `Remove`, and `Item`. This is a .NET "best practice" that makes it easier to manage lists of `AgentView` objects.

First of all, add a new class called AgentViewCollection. Add this code to make it inherit from CollectionBase:

```
Public Class AgentViewCollection
   Inherits CollectionBase
```

Then, add these two methods and this indexer:

```
  ' Add - add a view...
  Public Sub Add(ByVal view As AgentView)
    List.Add(view)
  End Sub

  ' Remove - remove a view...
  Public Sub Remove(ByVal view As AgentView)
    List.Remove(view)
  End Sub

  ' Item property...
  Default Public Property Item(ByVal index As Integer) As AgentView
    Get
      Return list.Item(index)
    End Get
    Set(ByVal Value As AgentView)
      list.Item(index) = Value
    End Set
  End Property

End Class
```

That's all! Now we have a strongly-typed collection that we can use to hold a list of agent view objects.

Creating Agents

Now we need a way to create agents. What we'll do is add a top-level item to the tree control and give this the intelligence to create agents. (The motivation for doing this will become clear when we come to create a number of agents.)

Add a new class called AgentListNode. Add this code to make it inherit from System.Windows.Forms.TreeNode:

```
Public Class AgentListNode
   Inherits TreeNode
```

We'll also need another class that inherits from System.Windows.Forms.TreeNode that will reference a specific AgentView instance. Create a new class called AgentNode and add this code:

```
Public Class AgentNode
   Inherits TreeNode

   ' members...
   Public AgentView As AgentView
```

```
    ' New...
    Public Sub New(ByVal agentName As String, ByVal agentInstance As Integer)

      ' create a new view...
      Me.AgentView = New AgentView()
      Me.AgentView.SetAgentDetails(agentName, agentInstance)

      ' set our text...
      Me.Text = AgentView.ToString()

    End Sub

  End Class
```

As you can see here, whenever we create a new instance of an `AgentNode`, we'll provide a name and an instance to the constructor. The constructor will then create a new `AgentView` object and call `SetAgentDetails`, passing in the name and the instance of the agent.

The `AgentListNode` class will be responsible by creating new `AgentNode` objects and by proxy creating new `AgentView` objects. This will be done through two versions of an `Add` method, which we'll now implement. In an ideal world, we want to be able to add a specific number of agents with a single call, hence the second version of `Add`. The first version simply calls the second version with a parameter of `1`.

First of all, add this version of `Add` to `AgentListNode`:

```
    ' Add - add a new agentnode...
    Public Sub Add()
      Add(1)
    End Sub
```

Then, add this method:

```
    Public Sub Add(ByVal numAgentsToAdd As Integer)

      ' loop...
      Dim index As Integer
      For index = 1 To numAgentsToAdd

        ' choose the name and the instance...
        Dim agentName As String = Me.Text
        Dim agentInstance As Integer = Me.Nodes.Count

        ' create a new agent node...
        Dim newNode As New AgentNode(agentName, agentInstance)

        ' add the node...
        Me.Nodes.Add(newNode)

      Next

      ' make sure we are expanded...
      Me.Expand()
    End Sub
```

The alternative version of Add takes an integer that dictates how many new instances to create. The first few times we run this application we'll use 1.

The name of the new agent is based on the name of this node itself. The instance is based on the total number of nodes already added to the list of child nodes that AgentListNode knows about. In the first instance, this will be 0, then 1, and so on. Once the node is created, and therefore the AgentView has been created in the constructor of AgentNode, we add the node to the list of child nodes. Finally we make sure that we are expanded.

Now, open the code editor for Form1. Add this member:

```
Imports System.IO

Public Class Form1
  Inherits System.Windows.Forms.Form

  ' members...
  Private Shared _dataPath As String
  Private _agentListNode As AgentListNode
```

Then, add this code to the constructor for the form.

```
  Private Sub Form1_Load(ByVal sender As System.Object, _
                         ByVal e As System.EventArgs) Handles MyBase.Load

    ' create a new agents node...
    _agentListNode = New AgentListNode()

    ' set the name...
    _agentListNode.Text = "Chimaera"

    ' add the node...
    treeviewAgents.Nodes.Add(_agentListNode)

    ' create a single agent...
    _agentListNode.Add()

  End Sub
```

Try running the project now and you should see that a single agent called Chimaera.0 is created. You can use whatever name you like here, but I've used Chimaera.

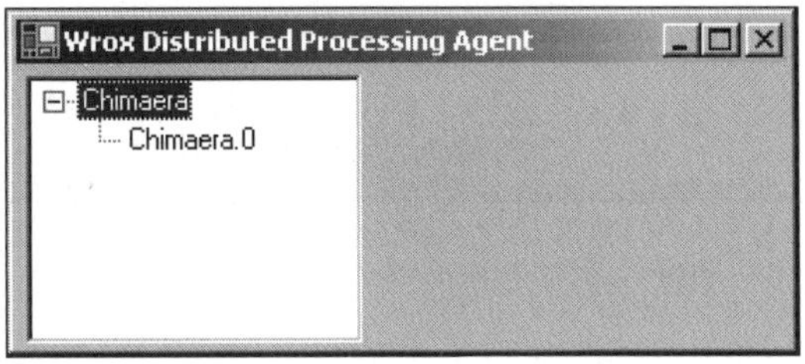

Showing the AgentView

That goes to prove a lot, but we can't actually see the agent view. To fix this we need to listen for selection changes on the tree control and display the control in the right-hand panel on the form.

If the program is running, close it. Open the Designer for `Form1` and double-click on the tree control. This will usefully create an event handler for `AfterSelect`, which is exactly what we want. As part of the arguments for this event we'll be given a `TreeNode` object that represents the new selection. All we have to do is cast this to an `AgentNode` object and use the `AgentView` member of that object to extract the corresponding view. We can then add this view to the controls list of the panel on the right-hand side to display the agent. Add this code:

```
Private Sub treeviewAgents_AfterSelect(ByVal sender As System.Object, _
                     ByVal e As System.Windows.Forms.TreeViewEventArgs) _
                     Handles treeviewAgents.AfterSelect

  ' clear the current control...
  panelView.Controls.Clear()

  ' have we selected an agent view?
  Try
    Dim agentNode As AgentNode = CType(e.Node, AgentNode)

    ' ok, we have, so add it...
    panelView.Controls.Add(agentNode.AgentView)
    agentNode.AgentView.Dock = DockStyle.Fill

  Catch
  End Try

End Sub
```

Now run the project and you'll be able to display the view by clicking on Chimaera.0:

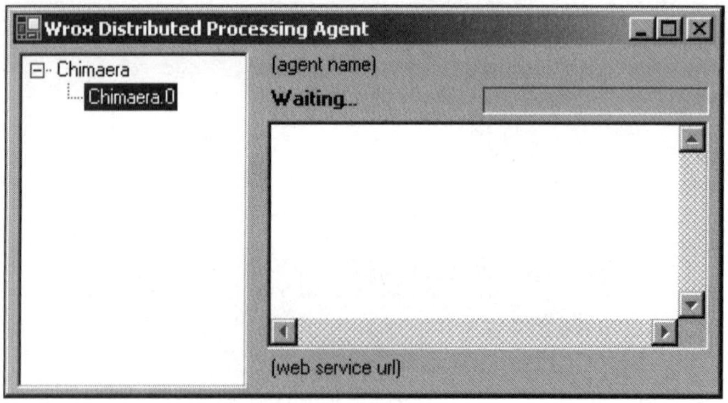

Of course, we haven't written any code to update the view, so we'll do that now.

If the program is running, close it and open the code editor for `AgentView`. Find the `SetAgentDetails` method and add this code:

```
' SetAgentDetails - set the details for the agent...
Public Sub SetAgentDetails(ByVal agentName As String, _
                           ByVal agentInstance As Integer)

  ' set the details...
  _agentName = agentName
  _agentInstance = agentInstance

  ' formulate a filename...
  Dim filename As String
  filename = Form1.DataPath & "\" & _agentName & "." _
             & _agentInstance & ".config"

  ' load the configuration...
  _configuration = Configuration.Load(filename)

  ' update the display...
  labelAgentName.Text = Me.ToString
  labelWebServiceUrl.Text = Form1.WebServiceUrl

End Sub
```

Next, open the code editor for `Form1` and add this member:

```
' members...
Private Shared _dataPath As String
Private _agentListNode As AgentListNode
Public Shared WebServiceUrl As String = _
         "http://localhost/PWS/Ch19/DistributedCoordinator/Coordinator.asmx"
```

Run the project now and the agent name and URL of the Web Service should be displayed.

Registering the Agent

We're now at a point where we can ask `AgentView` to start work. All of the work that the agent has to perform will be done in a separate thread. We'll use the classes defined in `System.Threading` to do this.

First of all, open the code editor for `AgentView` and add this namespace import declaration:

```
Imports System.IO
Imports System.Threading
```

Next, add these members:

```
Public Class AgentView
  Inherits System.Windows.Forms.UserControl

  ' members...
  Private _agentName As String
  Private _agentInstance As Integer
  Private _configuration As Configuration
  Private _thread As Thread
  Private _isCancelled As Boolean
```

To start the thread, we'll add a `SpinUp` method. (`ThreadEntryPoint` is undefined at the moment – we'll build it in a little while.)

```
' SpinUp - start the thread...
Public Sub SpinUp()

  ' running?
  If _thread Is Nothing Then

    ' create the thread and start it...
    _thread = New Thread(AddressOf Me.ThreadEntryPoint)
    _thread.Start()

  Else
    Throw New Exception("Thread is already running")
  End If

End Sub
```

We'll also need a corresponding `SpinDown` method.

```
' SpinDown - stop the thread...
Public Sub SpinDown()

  ' running?
  If Not _thread Is Nothing Then

    ' abort, join and reset...
    _thread.Abort()
    _thread.Join()
    _thread = Nothing

  End If

End Sub
```

Whenever the agent has anything to report to the user, it will use a property we need to build called `Status`. This will change the value displayed by `labelStatus` and also add a line of text to `textLog`. Add this property to `AgentView`:

```
' Status - report status...
Public Property Status() As String Implements Distributed.IAgent.Status
  Get
    Return labelStatus.Text
  End Get
  Set(ByVal Value As String)

    ' set the text...
    labelStatus.Text = Value

    ' update the log...
    If Value <> "" Then
      textLog.Text = Date.Now.ToLongTimeString() & ": " _
```

```
                            & Value & ControlChars.CrLf & textLog.Text
      End If

    End Set
  End Property
```

You've probably guessed that we'll need a reference to the Web Service sooner or later, so we'll do this now. Using Solution Explorer, add a Web Reference to the project that points to the `Coordinator.asmx` Web Service that we built previously. When the reference has been added, rename it from localhost (or whatever your server name is) to Coordination.

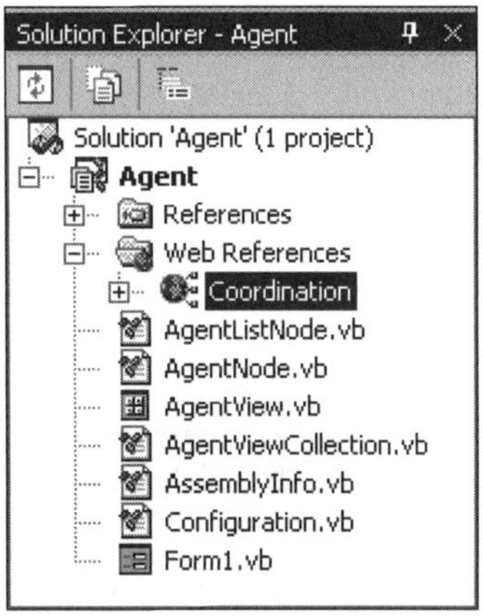

Finally we can build the `ThreadEntryPoint` method. This method will coordinate all of the work of the agent, but specifically we want to be able to call into the Web Service's `RegisterAgent` method if we detect that we don't have an agent ID. We'll build in the remainder of the functionality later. Add this method to `AgentView`:

```
   ' ThreadEntryPoint - start work...
   Private Sub ThreadEntryPoint()

      ' tell the user...
      Status = "Thread started"

      ' connect to the service...
      Dim service As New Coordination.Coordinator()

      ' set the url for the service...
      service.Url = Form1.WebServiceUrl

      ' do we have an agent ID?
      If Configuration.AgentId = 0 Then

         ' tell the user...
         Status = "Registering agent '" & Me.ToString() & "'..."

         ' get the id...
         Configuration.AgentId = service.RegisterAgent(Me.ToString())

      End If
```

```
        ' tell the user...
        Status = "Agent has an ID of " & Configuration.AgentId

        ' tell the user...
        Status = "Thread finished"

    End Sub
```

At the moment, we haven't called the `SpinUp` method so the agent will not be called. Add this code to the existing `SetAgentDetails` method:

```
    ' SetAgentDetails - set the details for the agent...
    Public Sub SetAgentDetails(ByVal agentName As String, _
                               ByVal agentInstance As Integer)

        ' set the details...
        _agentName = agentName
        _agentInstance = agentInstance

        ' formulate a filename...
        Dim filename As String
        filename = Form1.DataPath & "\" & _agentName _
                   & "." & _agentInstance & ".config"

        ' load the configuration...
        _configuration = Configuration.Load(filename)

        ' update the display...
        labelAgentName.Text = Me.ToString
        labelWebServiceUrl.Text = Form1.WebServiceUrl

        ' spin up...
        SpinUp()

    End Sub
```

Run the project and you should find that the agent registers itself:

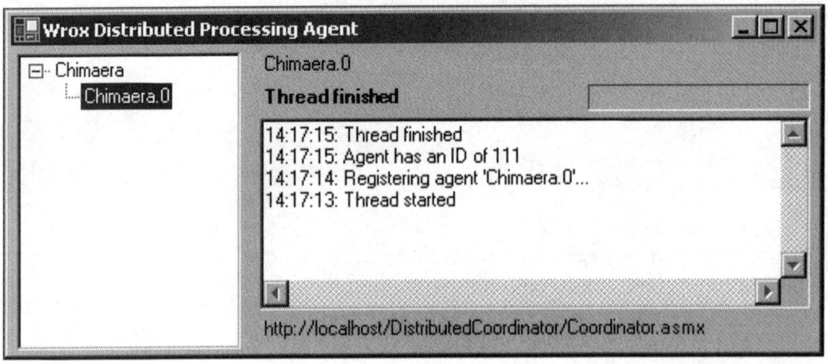

If you peek into the **Agents** table, you'll see an entry for the new agent.

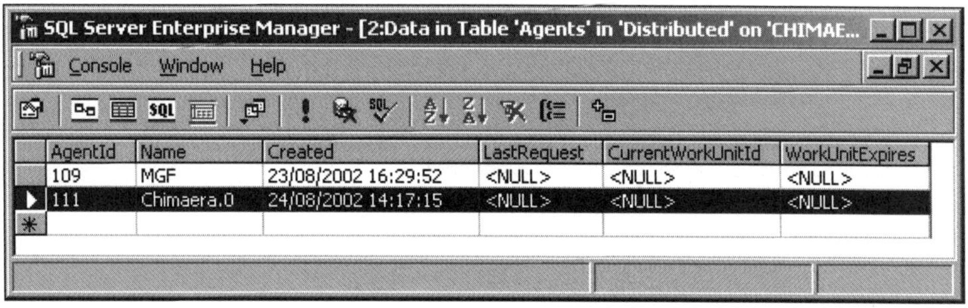

Saving the Agent ID

If you run the client again, you'll notice that another agent gets added to the database.

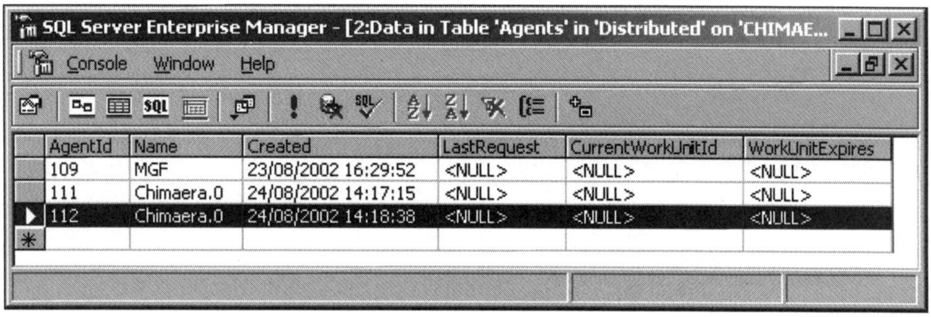

This isn't ideal as there's no reason why we need to create a new agent each time the agent runs. We can solve this by saving the `Configuration` object for the agent.

When we loaded the `Configuration` object using the shared `Load` method, we stored the filename in the `Filename` public member. All we have to do is build a `Save` method that uses `XmlSerializer` to serialize an instance of the object to that file.

Open the code editor for `Configuration` and add this method:

```
' Save - save the configuration file...
Public Sub Save()

   ' delete the old version...
   Dim info As New FileInfo(Filename)
   If info.Exists = True Then info.Delete()

   ' save it...
   Dim stream As New FileStream(Filename, FileMode.Create)
   Dim serializer As New XmlSerializer(Me.GetType())
   serializer.Serialize(stream, Me)
   stream.Close()

End Sub
```

Now open AgentView and add this call to the ThreadEntryPoint function:

```
Private Sub ThreadEntryPoint()

  ' tell the user...
  Status = "Thread started"

  ' connect to the service...
  Dim service As New Coordination.Coordinator()

  ' set the url for the service...
  service.Url = Form1.WebServiceUrl

  ' do we have an agent ID?
  If Configuration.AgentId = 0 Then

    ' tell the user...
    Status = "Registering agent '" & Me.ToString() & "'..."

    ' get the id...
    Configuration.AgentId = service.RegisterAgent(Me.ToString())

    ' save...
    Configuration.Save()

   End If

   ' tell the user...
   Status = "Agent has an ID of " & Configuration.AgentId

   ' tell the user...
  Status = "Thread finished"

End Sub
```

Run the project and a new agent will be registered. However, if you look in the Data folder (remember, this is a sibling of the bin folder that Visual Studio creates the project executables in), you'll see a .config file matching the agent name.

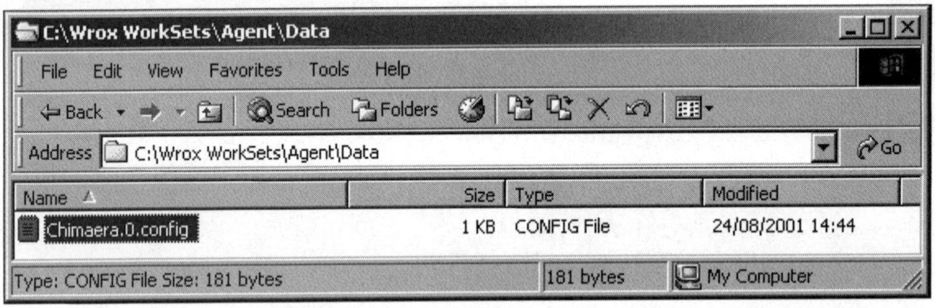

Now run the agent again and you should find that the agent will use the old agent ID and not re-register itself. At this point we'll have some invalid data in the database – feel free to remove the orphaned agents if you want, but there's no harm in leaving them.

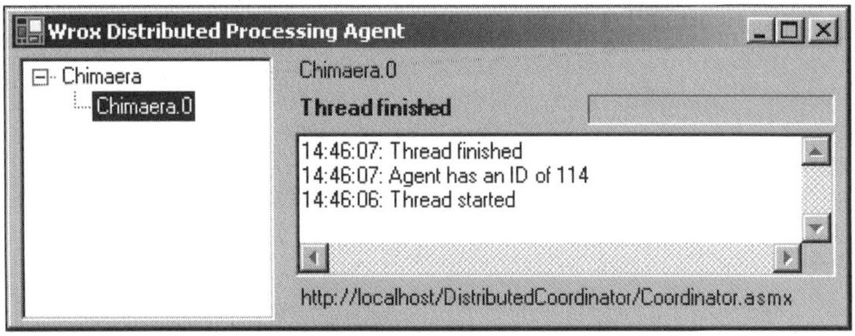

Creating Distributed.LogAnalyzer

If you look in the `Modules` table, you'll notice that we've referred to a class called `Distributed.LogAnalyzer`.

ModuleId	Name	Score
5	Distributed.LogAnalyzer	1000

This is the class that will process the work unit once it's been downloaded and we need to build this class now. However, there's a slight wrinkle.

As we mentioned before we want our client application to be able to handle more than one distributed processing task. Even though in this exercise we're building the system exclusively to analyze server log fragments, we might later on want to use the system to perform a different kind of processing.

Each of the modules will be derived from a class we'll build in a separate class library. This class will be called `ProcModule`. (Short for "`ProcessingModule`". This is a great example of programmer laziness – "`ProcessingModule`" takes so long to type!) These modules will communicate with the `AgentView` through an interface called `IAgent`, also defined in the new class library.

From the Visual Studio menu, select File | Add Project | New Project. Create a new Visual Basic | Class Library project and call it Distributed.

When the project has been created, delete `Class1` and create a new class called `ProcModule`. (Deleting and creating a new class tends to be less work than renaming an existing class.) Add this code to the new class:

```
Public MustInherit Class ProcModule

  ' ProcessWorkUnit - called when the proc needs to do something...
  Public MustOverride Sub ProcessWorkUnit(ByVal agent As IAgent)

End Class
```

Then, create a new class called `IAgent` also in the `Distributed` project. Change the class definition to an interface definition and add this code:

```
Public Interface IAgent

  ' ui calls...
  Property Status() As String
  Property BarMinimum() As Integer
  Property BarMaximum() As Integer
  Property BarValue() As Integer
  Sub IncrementBar()

  ' work calls...
  ReadOnly Property AgentId() As Integer
  ReadOnly Property AgentName() As String
  ReadOnly Property WorkSetId() As Integer
  ReadOnly Property WorkUnitId() As Integer
  ReadOnly Property WorkUnitFilename() As String
  ReadOnly Property ResultUnitFilename() As String

End Interface
```

To access these classes from within the `Agent` project, you'll need to add a reference to the `Distributed` project. Using Solution Explorer, right-click on the `References` object underneath the **Agent** project and select **Add Reference**. Change to the **Projects** tab, highlight **Distributed**, click **Select** and add a reference to the `Distributed` project.

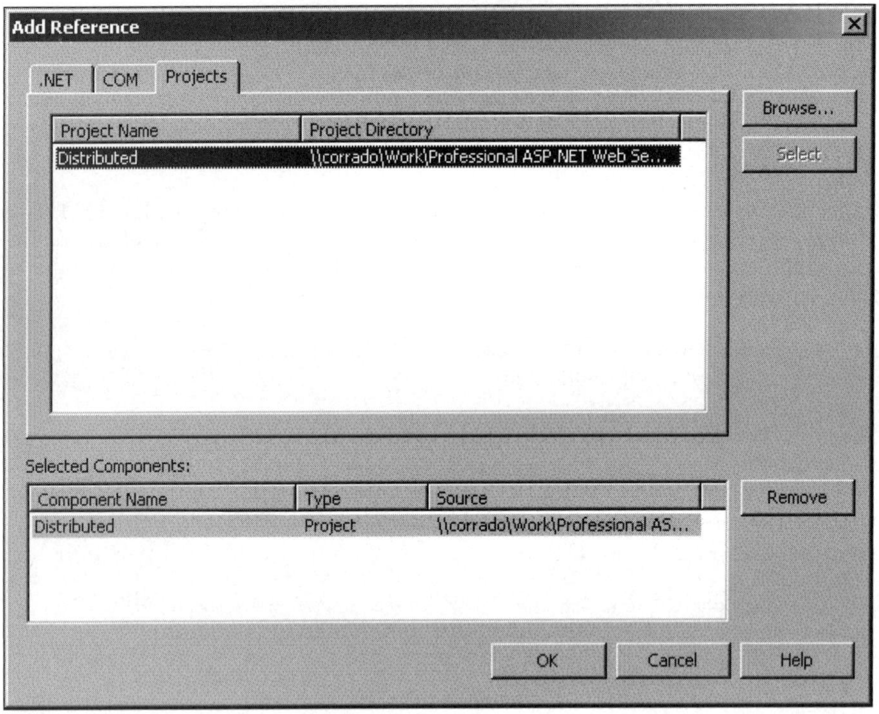

`IAgent` provides a number of methods and properties that allow the module to communicate with the agent that created it. Open the code editor for `AgentView` and add a reference to the `Distributed` project.

```
Imports System.Threading
Imports System.IO
Imports Distributed
```

Also, make the class implement `IAgent`.

```
Public Class AgentView
  Inherits System.Windows.Forms.UserControl
  Implements IAgent
```

The `Status` and `AgentName` properties defined in `IAgent` technically already have an implementation within `AgentView`. We need to wire the existing `Status` property into the `IAgent` implementation. Find the `Status` property and add the `Implements` call, like this:

```
  ' AgentName property...
  Public ReadOnly Property AgentName() As String _
                                  Implements Distributed.IAgent.AgentName
    Get
      Return _agentName
    End Get
  End Property
```

Add this method to defer the `AgentId` property to the matching property of the `Configuration` object:

```
  Public ReadOnly Property AgentId() As Integer _
                                    Implements Distributed.IAgent.AgentId
    Get
      Return Configuration.AgentId
    End Get
  End Property
```

The three properties and one method related to the progress bar simply defer their values to the `barStatus` control:

```
  Public Property BarMaximum() As Integer _
                              Implements Distributed.IAgent.BarMaximum
    Get
      Return barStatus.Maximum
    End Get
    Set(ByVal Value As Integer)
      barStatus.Maximum = Value
    End Set
  End Property

  Public Property BarMinimum() As Integer _
                             Implements Distributed.IAgent.BarMinimum
    Get
      Return barStatus.Minimum
    End Get
    Set(ByVal Value As Integer)
      barStatus.Minimum = Value
    End Set
  End Property
```

```
    Public Property BarValue() As Integer Implements Distributed.IAgent.BarValue
      Get
        Return barStatus.Value
      End Get
      Set(ByVal Value As Integer)
        barStatus.Value = Value
      End Set
      End Property

    Public Sub IncrementBar() Implements Distributed.IAgent.IncrementBar
      BarValue += 1
    End Sub
```

The remaining four properties refer to the actual work unit that the module is destined to process. We'll need private members for these, which will be filled when we ask the coordination server for the work.

```
    ' members...
    Private _agentName As String
    Private _agentInstance As Integer
    Private _configuration As Configuration
    Private _thread As Thread
    Private _isCancelled As Boolean
    Private _workSetId As Integer
    Private _workUnitId As Integer
    Private _workUnitFilename As String
    Private _resultUnitFilename As String
```

Then we need to return these values:

```
    Public ReadOnly Property WorkSetId() As Integer _
                                   Implements Distributed.IAgent.WorkSetId
      Get
        Return _workSetId
      End Get
    End Property

    Public ReadOnly Property WorkUnitId() As Integer _
                                   Implements Distributed.IAgent.WorkUnitId
      Get
        Return _workUnitId
      End Get
    End Property

    Public ReadOnly Property WorkUnitFilename() As String _
                               Implements Distributed.IAgent.WorkUnitFilename
      Get
        Return _workUnitFilename
      End Get
    End Property

    Public ReadOnly Property ResultUnitFilename() As String _
                             Implements Distributed.IAgent.ResultUnitFilename
      Get
        Return _resultUnitFilename
      End Get
    End Property
```

Creating "Distributed.LogAnalyzer"

Using Solution Explorer, create a new class called `LogAnalyzer` in the `Distributed` project. This new class will have a full name of `Distributed.LogAnalyzer`, which fits in with the name we're trying to get.

When the code editor for the new class appears, add this code:

```
Public Class LogAnalyzer
  Inherits ProcModule

  Public Overrides Sub ProcessWorkUnit(ByVal agent As Distributed.IAgent)

    ' tell the user...
    agent.Status = "Processor started"

    ' we'll write code here later on...

    ' tell the user...
    agent.Status = "Processor finished"

  End Sub

End Class
```

When the client starts, it will scan all of the assemblies installed in the directory it's installed in looking for types that are derived from `Distributed.ProcModule`. Once it finds one, it will create an instance of it and add it to a collection for later use by the agent code. For this to work, we need to get both the `Agent` and `Distributed` projects to compile into the same folder on our disk.

Using Solution Explorer, right-click on the `Agent` project and select `Properties`. Using the list on the left, expand Configuration Properties and select Build. Set the Output Path to c:\Wrox WorkSets\Agent\bin. (You don't have to use this folder, but if you use a different one, remember to use the folder used here when you change the same Output Path property for the `Distributed` project.)

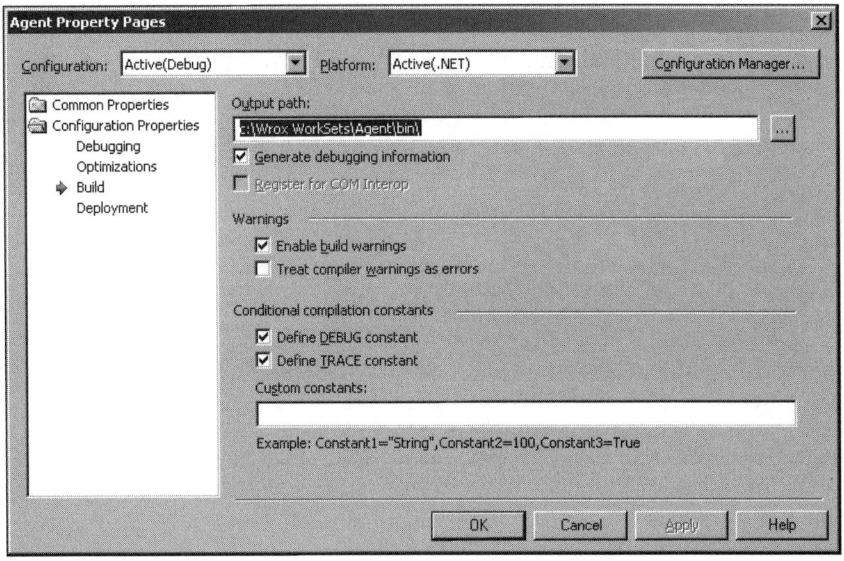

Now, click OK and open the same dialog for the `Distributed` project. Change the Output Path value to the same folder name.

Click OK. The projects should build as normal, but if you look in the output folder you'll find both assemblies.

Finding ProcModules

Now we need to provide a way for the client to scan through the assemblies installed in the folder and for the client to hold a collection of appropriate objects in a collection.

In the `Distributed` project, create a new class called `ProcModuleCollection`. Inherit this class from `CollectionBase` and add the standard `Add`, `Remove`, and `Item` members.

```
Public Class ProcModuleCollection
  Inherits CollectionBase

  ' Add - add a module...
  Public Sub Add(ByVal procModule As ProcModule)
    list.Add(procModule)
  End Sub

  ' Remove - remove a module...
  Public Sub Remove(ByVal procModule As ProcModule)
    list.Remove(procModule)
  End Sub

  ' Item...
  Default Public Property Item(ByVal index As Integer) As ProcModule
    Get
      Return list.Item(index)
    End Get
    Set(ByVal Value As ProcModule)
      list.Item(index) = Value
    End Set
  End Property
```

The classes that we need to scan assemblies and read metadata are included in the `System.Reflection` namespace. We'll also need `System.IO`. Add these namespace import declarations:

```
Imports System.IO
Imports System.Reflection
```

To scan the folder, we'll need two methods. The first, `ScanFolder`, accepts a folder as input and looks through each of the files looking for DLL files. The second, `ScanAssembly`, accepts the path of an assembly as input and looks through each of the types defined therein for ones derived from `ProcModule`.

The implementation of `ScanFolder` is quite straightforward and uses the `System.IO.DirectoryInfo` and `System.IO.FolderInfo` classes to look for all of the files in the given folder. Any files with an extension of `.dll` are loaded using the shared `LoadFrom` method of `System.Runtime.Assembly` and passed over to `ScanAssembly` for further processing.

```
' ScanFolder - look through a folder for assemblies...
Public Sub ScanFolder(ByVal folderName As String)

  ' get the folder...
  Dim folder As New DirectoryInfo(folderName)

  ' go through each file...
  Dim file As FileInfo
  For Each file In folder.GetFiles()

    ' do we have a dll?
    If String.Compare(file.Extension, ".dll", True) = 0 Then

      ' load the assembly...
      Dim testAssembly As [Assembly]
      Try

        testAssembly = [Assembly].LoadFrom(file.FullName)

        ' try it...
        ScanAssembly(testAssembly)
      Catch ex As Exception
        MsgBox("The assembly '" & file.FullName _
            & "' could not be loaded: " & ex.Message)
      End Try
    End If
  Next
End Sub
```

Once we have an assembly, we can use `GetTypes` to return a collection of `System.Type` objects, each one representing a class in the assembly. The `BaseType` property of `System.Type` tells us what type the class is derived from. As our processor class might be derived from another class derived from `ProcModule`, we have to walk up the `BaseType` tree. If we find a type that appears to derive from `ProcModule`, we create an instance of it and add it to the collection.

```
' ScanAssembly - look through the types in the assembly...
Public Sub ScanAssembly(ByVal testAssembly As [Assembly])

  ' loop the types...
  Dim type As Type
```

```
    For Each type In testAssembly.GetTypes()

      ' is it derived?
      Dim valid As Boolean = False
      Dim baseType As Type = type.BaseType
      Do While Not baseType Is Nothing

      ' match?
      If baseType Is GetType(ProcModule) Then
        valid = True
        Exit Do
      End If

      ' next...
      baseType = baseType.BaseType

      Loop

     ' is this type valid?
     If valid = True Then
       Try
         Dim instance As ProcModule
         instance = Activator.CreateInstance(type)
         ' add it...
         Add(instance)
       Catch ex As Exception
         MsgBox("The class '" & type.FullName & "' in " _
              & testAssembly.FullName & " could not be loaded: " & ex.Message)
       End Try
     End If
   Next
 End Sub
```

This scanning process has to happen once whenever the client is first started. Likewise, `Form1` will hold a `ProcModuleCollection` object as a shared field for all of the `AgentView` classes to use. Add this member to `Form1`:

```
' members...
Private Shared _dataPath As String
Private _agentListNode As AgentListNode
Public Shared WebServiceUrl As String = _
           "http://localhost/PWS/Ch19/DistributedCoordinator/Coordinator.asmx"
Public Shared Modules As New Distributed.ProcModuleCollection()
```

Next, add this code to the constructor for Form1:

```
Private Sub Form1_Load(ByVal sender As System.Object, _
                       ByVal e As System.EventArgs) Handles MyBase.Load

  ' scan the modules...
  Dim fileInfo As New FileInfo(Application.ExecutablePath)
  Modules.ScanFolder(fileInfo.DirectoryName)
```

```
    MessageBox.Show(Modules.Count.ToString())

    ' create a new agents node...
    _agentListNode = New AgentListNode()

    ' set the name...
    _agentListNode.Text = "Chimaera"

    ' add the node...
    treeviewAgents.Nodes.Add(_agentListNode)

    ' create a single agent...
    _agentListNode.Add()

  End Sub
```

Run the project and you'll see a basic debugging message box stating the number of `ProcModule` objects contained in the `Modules` collection.

Close the client and remove the line of code that displays the message box – we'll assume that the loaded module is indeed `Distributed.LogAnalyzer`.

Requesting a Work Unit

We can now move on to the task of getting an agent to request a work unit. To do this, we need to pass a list of the modules that we know about to the coordination Web Service. The service will look at the work sets that are still being processed and find out which ones the agent is capable of doing. When the service finds a work unit, it will return a structure containing the work unit ID, the work set ID, and the name of the module. When we ask the service for a work unit we'll also pass in the ID of the agent.

The algorithm we're going to follow when requesting work units will look like this:

- Older work units will be assumed to have precedence. As we're using identity fields in the `WorkSet` table, we'll assume that the lower the ID, the older the work set. Therefore, by selecting work sets in ascending ID order, we'll get them in age order. We'll also assume that a work set is unfinished when the `WorkUnitsCompleted` value is less than `TotalWorkUnits`.
- For each work set we'll check the module ID. If the agent doesn't support the module, we'll move on to the next one.
- If the agent does support the module, we'll go through the work units for the module, again in ascending ID order. We'll look for ones with a `Status` code of `0`, "unprocessed" in other words. If we find one, we allocate the work unit to the agent.
- If we don't find one, we look for work units with a `Status` code of `1` that have expired. If we find one, we'll allocate that work unit to the agent.

- If there are no work units remaining, we'll assume that no work is outstanding on that work set and we'll try and find another work set.
- If no work units can be found, we'll assume there's nothing for the agent to do. In our implementation the agent will stop at this point, but in a production environment you'd most likely want to get the agent to wait for a period of time before trying again.

Implementing RequestWorkUnit

Open the `DistributedCoordinator` Web Service project, and using Solution Explorer create a new class called `WorkRequest`. Replace the default class definition with this code that defines a structure.

```
Public Structure WorkRequest

  ' members...
  Public WorkSetId As Integer
  Public WorkUnitId As Integer
  Public ModuleName As String

End Structure
```

Add these methods to `Coordinator.asmx.vb`:

```
  Protected Function CallGetAllModules(ByVal connection As SqlConnection) _
                                                                As DataSet

    ' create a command...
    Dim command As New SqlCommand("GetAllModules", connection)
    command.CommandType = CommandType.StoredProcedure

    ' extract the dataset...
    Dim adapter As New SqlDataAdapter(command)
    Dim dataSet As New DataSet()
    adapter.Fill(dataSet)
    adapter.Dispose()

    ' cleanup...
    command.Dispose()

    ' return...
    Return dataSet

  End Function
```

```
  Protected Function CallGetIncompleteWorkSets(ByVal connection As _
                                              SqlConnection) As DataSet

    ' create a command...
    Dim command As New SqlCommand("GetIncompleteWorkSets", connection)
    command.CommandType = CommandType.StoredProcedure

    ' extract the dataset...
    Dim adapter As New SqlDataAdapter(command)
```

```
    Dim dataSet As New DataSet()
    adapter.Fill(dataSet)
    adapter.Dispose()

    ' cleanup...
    command.Dispose()

    ' return...
    Return dataSet

  End Function
```

```
  Protected Function CallGetNextWorkUnitForWorkSet(ByVal connection As _
                          SqlConnection, ByVal workSetId As Int32) As Int32

    ' create a command...
    Dim command As New SqlCommand("GetNextWorkUnitForWorkSet", connection)
    command.CommandType = CommandType.StoredProcedure

    ' params...
    Dim workSetIdParam As SqlParameter
    workSetIdParam = command.Parameters.Add("@workSetId", SqlDbType.Int)
    workSetIdParam.Value = workSetId

    ' add a return param...
    Dim returnValueParam As SqlParameter
    returnValueParam = command.Parameters.Add("@returnValue", SqlDbType.Int)
    returnValueParam.Direction = ParameterDirection.ReturnValue

    ' execute...
    command.ExecuteNonQuery()

    ' cleanup...
    command.Dispose()

    ' return...
    Return returnValueParam.Value

  End Function
```

```
  Protected Sub CallAssignWorkUnit(ByVal connection As SqlConnection, _
                                   ByVal agentId As Int32, _
                                   ByVal workUnitId As Int32)

    ' create a command...
    Dim command As New SqlCommand("AssignWorkUnit", connection)
    command.CommandType = CommandType.StoredProcedure

    ' params...
    Dim agentIdParam As SqlParameter
    agentIdParam = command.Parameters.Add("@agentId", SqlDbType.Int)
    agentIdParam.Value = agentId
```

```
    Dim workUnitIdParam As SqlParameter
    workUnitIdParam = command.Parameters.Add("@workUnitId", SqlDbType.Int)
    workUnitIdParam.Value = workUnitId

    ' execute...
    command.ExecuteNonQuery()

    ' cleanup...
    command.Dispose()

  End Sub
```

The `GetAllModules` stored procedure looks like this:

```
CREATE PROCEDURE GetAllModules AS
  SELECT ModuleId, Name FROM Modules ORDER BY name
```

No problems there – all we're doing is selecting the contents of the `Modules` table.

The `GetIncompleteWorkSets` stored procedure looks like this:

```
CREATE PROCEDURE GetIncompleteWorkSets
AS
  SELECT WorkSetId FROM worksets WHERE workunitsprocessed < totalworkunits
  ORDER BY worksetid
```

This stored procedure selects out the IDs of all the work sets where `WorkUnitsProcessed` is less than `TotalWorkUnits`. The IDs are returned in order so that the older work sets are processed before the newer work sets.

The `GetNextWorkUnitForWorkSet` stored procedure looks like this:

```
CREATE PROCEDURE GetNextWorkUnitForWorkSet
(
  @workSetId int
)
 AS

  /* try and select the next available with a status of 0 */
  DECLARE @workUnitId int
  SELECT top 1 @workUnitId=WorkUnitId FROM WorkUnits
  WHERE worksetid=@worksetid AND status=0 ORDER BY workunitid asc

  /* did we get anything? */
  IF @@rowcount = 0
  BEGIN

  /* get an expired one... */
  SELECT @workunitid=workunitid FROM workunits WHERE agentid IN (
    SELECT top 1 agents.agentid FROM agents
    INNER JOIN workunits ON agents.currentworkunitid =
```

```
      workunits.workunitid
    WHERE getdate() > workunitexpires AND worksetid=@worksetid
    ) ORDER BY workunitid

  END

  /* return the id... */
  RETURN @workunitid
```

This is a relatively complex stored procedure, but most of the magic that allocates work units to agents happens here. First of all, the first work unit with a status of 0 is found. If there isn't one, (they've all been processed ("2") or they're being processed ("1")) then we find the next work unit from an agent that's expired. We're not too worried about what happens when an agent returns work that's been allocated to another agent – we'll handle this later.

Finally, `AssignWorkUnit` looks like this:

```
CREATE PROCEDURE AssignWorkUnit
(
  @agentId int,
  @workUnitId int = -1
)
AS
  /* is the agent already marked as doing a unit? */
  DECLARE @currentUnit int
  SELECT @currentunit=currentworkunitid FROM agents WHERE agentid=@agentid
  IF @currentunit <> 0
  BEGIN
  UPDATE workunits SET agentid=null, status=0
      WHERE workunitid=@currentunit
  END

  /* update agents... */
  UPDATE agents SET lastrequest=getdate(),
    currentworkunitid=@workunitid,
    workunitexpires=getdate()+1 WHERE agentid=@agentid

  /* update workunits... */
  UPDATE workunits SET status=1, agentid=@agentid WHERE workunitid=@workunitid
```

What we're doing first of all is looking to see if the agent is already assigned a work unit. If the agent is assigned a unit, we can assume that if it's asking again it needs to put the old work unit back into the pool. This will happen if the agent is closed while it is processing a work unit.

We then update Agents to store the agent's new work unit ID and pick an expiry time. We're choosing an expiry time 24 hours after allocation. (Hence the `+1`.)

We then update `WorkUnits`, changing the `Status` to `1` and assigning the agent ID.

Now that we've created methods for handling those four stored procedures, we'll look at the method. Create this method header in `Coordinator.asmx.vb`:

```
<WebMethod()> Public Function RequestWorkUnit(ByVal agentId As Integer, _
                                   ByVal moduleNames() As String) As WorkRequest
```

We need to store the request in a new `WorkRequest` structure.

```
    ' set up the call...
    Dim request As WorkRequest
```

We then load all of the modules from the database. There should only be a few, so there's no problem in loading them here – although you might want to consider caching this list.

```
    ' load all of the modules...
    Dim modules As DataSet = CallGetAllModules(connection)
```

We then select out all of the incomplete work sets and loop through them, one by one.

```
    ' load all of the incomplete worksets...
    Dim incompleteWorkSets As DataSet = CallGetIncompleteWorkSets(connection)

    ' go through the work sets one by one...
    Dim workSetRow As DataRow
    For Each workSetRow In incompleteWorkSets.Tables(0).Rows
```

As a parameter to this method, we've been given an array containing the names of all of the modules that the client understands in `moduleNames`. What we have to do is, per work set, look at the module ID. We then look through the IDs stored in the `modules DataSet` looking for one that matches the module of the work set that we're currently looking at. If we find a match there, we look through `moduleNames` to make sure that the name of the module exists in the array; hence the client understands the module.

```
      ' do we have the module...
      Dim moduleToUse As String
      Dim moduleRow As DataRow
      For Each moduleRow In modules.Tables(0).Rows

        ' is this the one we want?
        If workSetRow("ModuleId") = moduleRow("ModuleId") Then

          ' does the name exist in the array...
          Dim moduleName As String
          For Each moduleName In moduleNames
            If String.Compare(moduleName, moduleRow("Name"), True) = 0 Then

              ' the agent does have the module!
              moduleToUse = moduleName
              Exit For

            End If
          Next

          ' stop...
          Exit For
```

```
    End If

        Next
```

If the client is able to process the work unit, we ask the database to return a work unit.

```
        ' does the agent have the module?
        If moduleToUse <> "" Then
          ' try and get a work unit...
          Dim workUnitId As Integer = CallGetNextWorkUnitForWorkSet(connection, _
                                                       workSetRow("WorkSetId"))
```

If we get one, then great! We can populate `request` and assign the work unit to the agent. Importantly, we use `Exit For` to drop out of the loop that's scanning through all of the incomplete work sets. That way, if there were no work units available for this work set, we'd automatically drop through and try working with the next incomplete work set.

```
          If workUnitId <> 0 Then

            ' ok, we now need a work unit for that module...
            request.WorkSetId = workSetRow("WorkSetId")
            request.WorkUnitId = workUnitId
            request.ModuleName = moduleToUse

            ' now, assign this work unit to this agent...
            CallAssignWorkUnit(connection, agentId, request.WorkUnitId)

            ' stop looking...
            Exit For

          End If
```

Finally, we return the request. If `WorkUnitId` is `0`, the agent should assume that there's nothing for it to do, otherwise it should create an instance of the required module and start work.

```
        ' return the request...
        Return request

    End Function
```

To make these new methods available to our agent, rebuild the DistributedCoordinator project.

Calling RequestWorkUnit

To call `RequestWorkUnit`, we need to tweak our `ProcModuleCollection` object so that it's capable of returning an array of strings – each item in the array representing one of the classes inherits from `ProcModule` that the client knows about.

Flip back to the `Distributed` project and add this method to `ProcModuleCollection`:

```
' GetNames - return an array of names...
Public Function GetNames() As String()

  ' create a new array...
  Dim names(Me.Count - 1) As String

  ' loop...
  Dim procModule As ProcModule, index As Integer
  For Each procModule In Me.InnerList
    names(index) = procModule.ToString()
    index += 1
  Next

  ' return it...
  Return names

End Function
```

Using Solution Explorer, right-click on the `Coordination` Web Service under the `Agent` project and select **Update Web Reference**. This will allow you to call the server's `RequestWorkUnit` method.

Open the code editor for `AgentView` and find the `ThreadEntryPoint` method. Add this code that will call `RequestWorkUnit` on the server.

```
' ThreadEntryPoint - start work...
Private Sub ThreadEntryPoint()

  ' tell the user...
  Status = "Thread started"

  ' connect to the service...
  Dim service As New Coordination.Coordinator()
  ' set the url for the service...
  service.Url = Form1.WebServiceUrl

  ' do we have an agent ID?
  If Configuration.AgentId = 0 Then

    ' tell the user...
    Status = "Registering agent '" & Me.ToString() & "'..."
    ' get the id...
    Configuration.AgentId = service.RegisterAgent(Me.ToString())

    ' save...
    Configuration.Save()

  End If

  ' tell the user...
  Status = "Agent has an ID of " & Configuration.AgentId

  ' request a work unit...
  Dim request As Coordination.WorkRequest
  request = service.RequestWorkUnit(Configuration.AgentId, _
                                    Form1.Modules.GetNames())

  ' did we get one?
  If request.WorkUnitId <> 0 Then
```

```
      ' tell the user...
      Status = "Processing work unit " & request.WorkUnitId _
            & " with module " & request.ModuleName
    Else
      ' tell the user...
      Status = "The agent was given nothing to do."

    End If

  ' tell the user...
    Status = "Thread finished"

  End Sub
```

Run the project. If you look at the view for Chimaera.0, you'll notice that we were given a work unit:

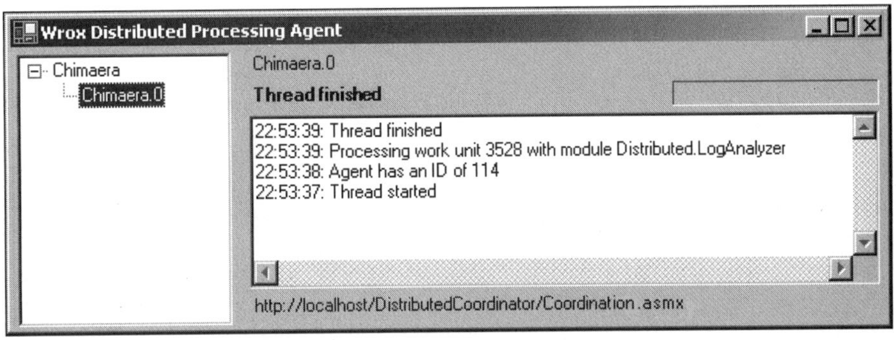

Look in the `WorkUnits` table and you'll notice that the unit has been assigned to an agent:

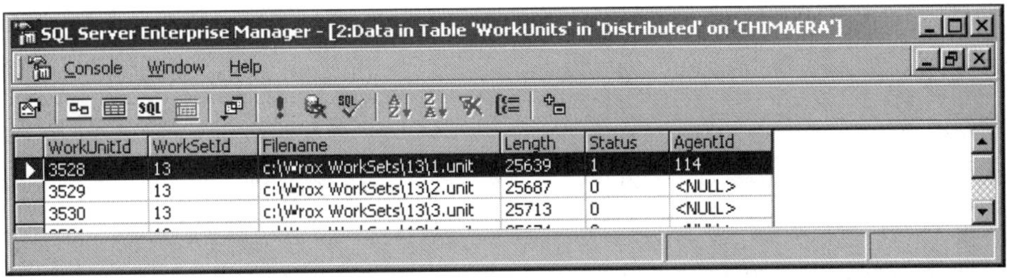

The `Agents` table also reports the activity of the agent:

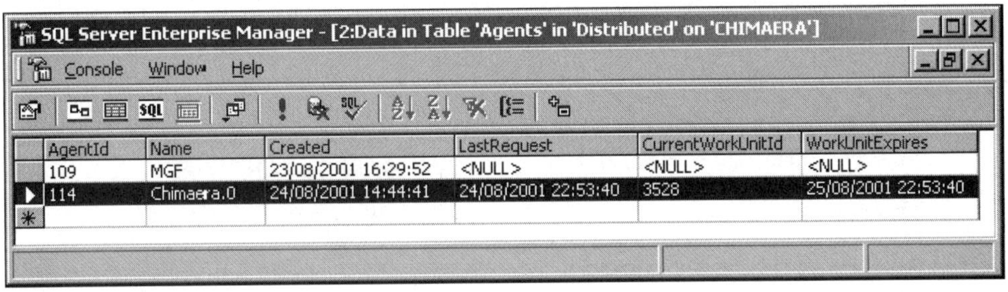

Finally, you'll see that the `WorkSets` table indicates that one of the units is out being processed:

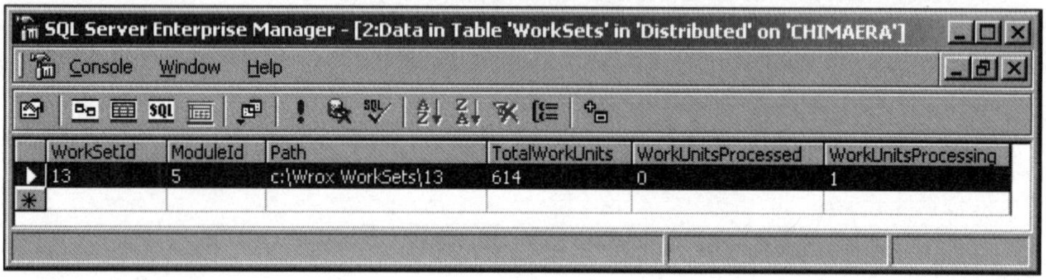

Processing the Work

Although we can allocate a work unit to an agent, we haven't yet provided a way to download the data behind the work unit from the server. We'll create a new method called `GetWorkData` for the agent.

> **If we decide to use FTP to transfer work and result data between client and server, it's this method that we'd need to replace.**

Add these methods to `Coordinator.asmx.vb`:

```
Protected Function CallGetAgentForWorkUnit(ByVal connection As SqlConnection, _
                                           ByVal workUnitId As Int32) As Int32

  ' create a command...
  Dim command As New SqlCommand("GetAgentForWorkUnit", connection)
  command.CommandType = CommandType.StoredProcedure

  ' params...
  Dim workUnitIdParam As SqlParameter
  workUnitIdParam = command.Parameters.Add("@workUnitId", SqlDbType.Int)
  workUnitIdParam.Value = workUnitId

  ' add a return param...
  Dim returnValueParam As SqlParameter
  returnValueParam = command.Parameters.Add("@returnValue", SqlDbType.Int)
  returnValueParam.Direction = ParameterDirection.ReturnValue

  ' execute...
  command.ExecuteNonQuery()

  ' cleanup...
  command.Dispose()

  ' return...
  Return returnValueParam.Value

End Function
```

```
Protected Function CallGetFilenameForWorkUnit(ByVal connection As _
                         SqlConnection, ByVal workUnitId As Int32) As String

  ' create a command...
  Dim command As New SqlCommand("GetFilenameForWorkUnit", connection)
  command.CommandType = CommandType.StoredProcedure

  ' params...
  Dim workUnitIdParam As SqlParameter
  workUnitIdParam = command.Parameters.Add("@workUnitId", SqlDbType.Int)
  workUnitIdParam.Value = workUnitId
  Dim filenameParam As SqlParameter
  filenameParam = command.Parameters.Add("@filename", SqlDbType.VarChar, 255)
  filenameParam.Direction = ParameterDirection.Output

  ' execute...
  command.ExecuteNonQuery()

  ' cleanup...
  command.Dispose()

  ' return...
  Return filenameParam.Value

End Function
```

The code for the `GetAgentForWorkUnit` stored procedure looks like this:

```
CREATE PROCEDURE GetAgentForWorkUnit
(
  @workUnitId int
)
AS
  DECLARE @agentid int
  SELECT @agentid=agentid FROM workunits WHERE workunitid=@workunitid
  RETURN @agentid
```

The code for the `GetFilenameForWorkUnit` stored procedure looks like this:

```
CREATE PROCEDURE GetFilenameForWorkUnit
(
  @workUnitId int,
  @filename varchar(255) out
)
AS
  SELECT @filename=filename FROM workunits WHERE workunitid=@workunitid
```

Now, add this new method to `Coordinator.asmx.vb`:

```
<WebMethod()> Public Function GetWorkData(ByVal agentId As Integer, _
                              ByVal workUnitId As Integer) As String

  ' connect...
```

```
    Dim connection As New SqlConnection(DbString)
    connection.Open()

    ' does the agent own the work unit?
    Dim assignedAgentId As Integer = CallGetAgentForWorkUnit(DbString, workUnitId)

    ' match?
    Dim data As String
    If assignedAgentId = agentId Then

      ' get the filename
      Dim filename As String = CallGetFilenameForWorkUnit(connection, workUnitId)

      ' read it all...
      Dim stream As New FileStream(filename, FileMode.Open)
      Dim reader As New StreamReader(stream)
      data = reader.ReadToEnd()
      reader.Close()
      stream.Close()

    Else

      ' throw an exception...
      connection.Close()
      Throw New Exception("Agent is not allocated this work unit")

    End If

    ' close...
    connection.Close()

    ' return the data...
    Return data

  End Function
```

Build the project. You can test this new method by running the project and selecting the `GetWorkData` method from the list.

You'll notice in this method that we've asked for both an agent ID and a work unit ID. This is a simple security measure to deter would-be crackers from attempting to download the entire work set by repeatedly calling this method providing incremental work unit IDs. This is an essential precaution when working with Web Services – make sure that you only return data that the client is allowed to have.

Open the `Agent` project and using Solution Explorer, right-click the `Coordination` Web Service and select Update Web Reference. `GetWorkData` will now become available.

Next, find the `ThreadEntryPoint` method in `AgentView` and add this code. (I've omitted some code for brevity.)

```
    ' request a work unit...
    Dim request As Coordination.WorkRequest
    request = service.RequestWorkUnit(Configuration.AgentId, _
                                      Form1.Modules.GetNames())
```

```
' did we get one?
If request.WorkUnitId <> 0 Then

  ' tell the user...
  Status = "Processing work unit " & request.WorkUnitId & " with module " _
          & request.ModuleName

  ' we need to download the work from the server...
  Dim data As String = service.GetWorkData(Configuration.AgentId, _
                                           request.WorkUnitId)

  ' get filenames...
  _workUnitFilename = Form1.DataPath & "\" & Me.ToString & "." _
                     & request.WorkUnitId & ".unit"
  _resultUnitFilename = Form1.DataPath & "\" & Me.ToString & "." _
                     & request.WorkUnitId & ".result"

  ' create the file...
  Dim info As New FileInfo(_workUnitFilename)
  If info.Exists = True Then info.Delete()
    Dim stream As New FileStream(_workUnitFilename, FileMode.Create)
    Dim writer As New StreamWriter(stream)
    writer.Write(data)
    writer.Close()
    stream.Close()
    Status = "Work data saved to: " & _workUnitFilename
    Status = "Results will be saved to: " & _resultUnitFilename

    ' find the module...
    Dim procModule As ProcModule = Form1.Modules.Find(request.ModuleName)
    If Not procModule Is Nothing Then

      ' call it...
      procModule.ProcessWorkUnit(Me)

    End If
  Else

    ' tell the user...
    Status = "The agent was given nothing to do."
```

The first thing we're doing there is making up two filenames. These will be based on the format `AgentName.WorkUnitId.unit` and `AgentName.WorkUnitId.result`. Once we have the filenames, we create a new `.unit` file and save the data.

The `Find` method on `ProcModuleCollection` is yet to be built, but you can probably guess here that it is used to look through the modules for ones with a given name. When it finds it, it calls `ProcessWorkUnit` passing over a reference to the current `AgentView` instance. As `AgentView` implements `IAgent`, the processor will be able to talk back to the client.

Before we can run the project we need to add that `Find` method. Open the code editor for `ProcModuleCollection` and add this code:

```
' Find - find a module with the given name...
Public Function Find(ByVal searchFor As String) As ProcModule

  ' loop...
  Dim procModule As ProcModule
  For Each procModule In Me.InnerList
    If String.Compare(procModule.ToString, searchFor, True) = 0 Then
      Return procModule
    End If
  Next

End Function
```

Run the project and the log will report that a new work unit has been allocated and that the processor has been called. (Remember, the Processor finished and Processor started messages are sent from within the processor. We did this when we first created `LogAnalyzer`.)

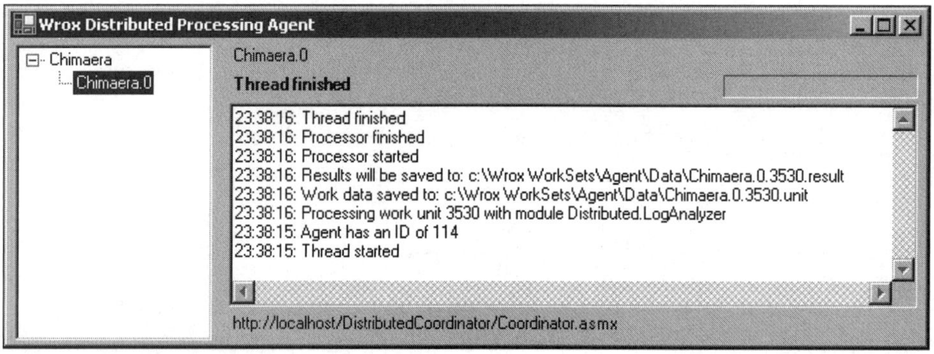

In addition, if you look in the `Data` folder, you'll see the `.unit` file. Its contents will match the equivalent data file held on the server – although in this case the server is the same computer! Now that we have downloaded the data, we're ready to process it and return the results.

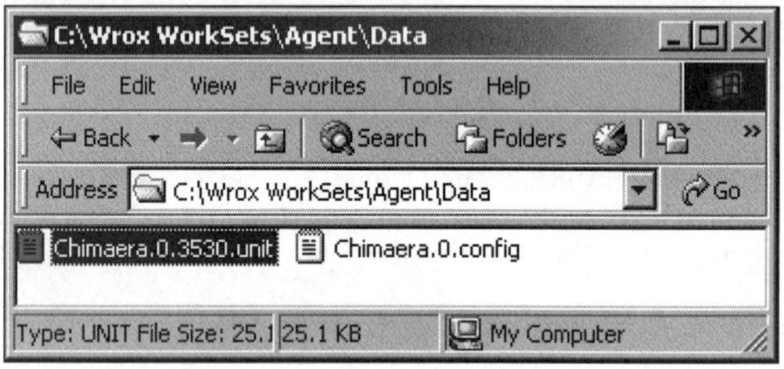

Returning Result Units

To process the results, we need to load the data contained within the `.unit` file and create a new `.result` file. We'll need to add some code to `LogAnalyzer`, which we can find in the client-side Distributed project.

What we're trying to do is get `LogAnalyzer` to produce an XML file that fits this format:

```
<Results>
  <Day>
  <Year>2002</Year>
  <Month>8</Month>
  <Day>22</Day>
  <Pages>
    <Page>
    <Name>/coffee.aspx</Name>
    <Hits>27</Hits>
    </Page>
    <Page>
    <Name>/default.aspx</Name>
    <Hits>105</Hits>
    </Page>
  </Pages>
  </Day>
  <Day>
  <Year>2002</Year>
  <Month>8</Month>
  <Day>21</Day>
  <Pages>
    <Page>
    <Name>/coffee.aspx</Name>
    <Hits>99</Hits>
    </Page>
    <Page>
    <Name>/default.aspx</Name>
    <Hits>667</Hits>
    </Page>
  </Pages>
  </Day>
</Results>
```

One easy way to do this is to build two classes that represent the day (`Day`) and the page (`Page`) and an additional two classes that hold a collection of `Day` objects and `Page` objects. If we play our cards right, we can use `System.Xml.Serialization.XmlSerializer` to take these objects that we build and spit out XML that we can save into our `.result` file.

First off, let's create our `Page` class. Create a new class in the **Distributed** project and add this code:

```
Public Class Page

  ' members...
  Public Name As String
  Public Hits As Integer

  ' Constructor...
  Public Sub New()
  End Sub

  Public Sub New(ByVal name As String)
```

```
    Me.Name = Name
  End Sub

End Class
```

Now, create a new class called Day and add this code:

```
<Serializable()> Public Class Day

  ' members...
  Public Year As Integer
  Public Month As Integer
  Public Day As Integer
  Public Pages As New PageCollection()

  ' Constructor...
  Public Sub New()
  End Sub

  Public Sub New(ByVal newDate As Date)
    Me.New(newDate.Year, newDate.Month, newDate.Day)
  End Sub

  Public Sub New(ByVal newYear As Integer, ByVal newMonth As Integer, _
                 ByVal newDay As Integer)
    Me.Year = newYear
    Me.Month = newMonth
    Me.Day = newDay
  End Sub

End Class
```

To hold a collection of Page objects, we'll create a new PageCollection class and inherit it from System.Collections.CollectionBase. Create a new class and add this code:

```
Public Class PageCollection
  Inherits CollectionBase

  ' Add...
  Public Sub Add(ByVal newPage As Page)
    list.Add(newPage)
  End Sub

  ' Indexer...
  Default Public Property Item(ByVal index As Integer) As Page
    Get
      Return list.Item(index)
    End Get
    Set(ByVal Value As Page)
      list.Item(index) = Value
    End Set
  End Property
```

```
' Find - find a page...
  Public Function Find(ByVal name As String) As Page

    ' loop...
    Dim page As Page
    For Each page In InnerList
      If String.Compare(page.Name, name, True) = 0 Then
        Return page
      End If
    Next

  End Function

End Class
```

When we process the `.unit` file, we'll need to find a `Page` object matching a particular name. The `Find` method provides that functionality.

We also need a class to hold a collection of `Day` objects. Because the top-level tag in our XML file should be called `Results`, rather than calling our new collection class `DayCollection` as .NET guidelines suggest, we'll call it `Results`. That way when `XmlSerializer` spits out our XML, the top-level tag will be called `Results` and not `DayCollection`.

```
Imports System.IO
Imports System.Xml.Serialization

Public Class Results
  Inherits CollectionBase

  ' Add...
  Public Sub Add(ByVal newDay As Day)
    list.Add(newDay)
  End Sub

  ' Indexer...
  Default Public Property Item(ByVal index As Integer) As Day
    Get
      Return list.Item(index)
    End Get
    Set(ByVal Value As Day)
      list.Item(index) = Value
    End Set
  End Property
```

This class will also need a `Find` method:

```
  ' Find - find a day...
  Public Function Find(ByVal findDate As Date) As Day
    Return Find(findDate.Year, findDate.Month, findDate.Day)
  End Function
```

```
Public Function Find(ByVal findYear As Integer, _
                     ByVal findMonth As Integer, ByVal findDay As Integer)

  ' loop...
  Dim day As Day
  For Each day In InnerList

    ' compare...
    If day.Year = findYear And day.Month = findMonth And day.Day = findDay Then
      Return day
    End If

  Next

End Function
```

It will also need a Save method that uses XmlSerializer:

```
' Save - save the results to a file...
Public Sub Save(ByVal filename As String)

  ' create the file...
  Dim stream As New FileStream(filename, FileMode.Create)

  ' serialize it...
  Try
    Dim serializer As New XmlSerializer(Me.GetType())
    serializer.Serialize(stream, Me)
  Catch ex As Exception
    Do While Not ex.InnerException Is Nothing
      ex = ex.InnerException
    Loop
    MsgBox(ex.Message)
  End Try

  ' close...
  stream.Close()

End Sub
```

Now we can process the file. Open the code editor for LogAnalyzer and add this namespace import declaration for System.IO to the top of the listing:

```
Imports System.IO
```

We'll add some code to the ProcessWorkUnit method that we started earlier, specifically to add useful code instead of the "We'll add code here later" comment.

```
Public Overrides Sub ProcessWorkUnit(ByVal agent As Distributed.IAgent)

  ' tell the user...
  agent.Status = "Processor started"
```

Firstly, we'll open up the `.unit` file and store each line separately in an array. We'll then loop through the array in the second phase. We could process the file in a single loop, but this method provides us with the number of entries in the file and allows us to display a progress bar tracking the process.

```
    ' load up the file...
    agent.Status = "Loading work unit from file..."
    Dim stream As New FileStream(agent.WorkUnitFilename, FileMode.Open)
    Dim reader As New StreamReader(stream)

    ' read each line in turn and hold it in an array...
    Dim entries As New ArrayList()
    Dim entry As String
    Do While True

      ' get the string...
      entry = reader.ReadLine
      If entry Is Nothing Then
        Exit Do
      End If

      ' add it...
      entries.Add(entry)

    Loop

    ' close the file...
    reader.Close()
    stream.Close()
```

We're going to store the results in a new `Results` object:

```
    ' create a new results object...
    Dim results As New Results()
```

We can now walk through each line. We configure the progress bar that we can access through `IAgent` with the minimum, maximum and current values.

```
    ' now we can process each line...
    agent.Status = "Processing " & entries.Count & " entries..."
    agent.BarMinimum = 0
    agent.BarMaximum = entries.Count
    agent.BarValue = 0
    For Each entry In entries
```

Each line represents a request for a resource from the web server. Each part of that request is separated with a space, so we use `Split` to create an array of fields from the entry.

```
      ' split it into fields...
      Dim fields() As String = entry.Split(" ")
```

The date is always in `yyyy-mm-dd` format, so breaking it up is quite easy. We can create a new `System.DateTime` object from the values we get.

```
' work out the data...
Dim theYear As Integer = fields(0).Substring(0, 4)
Dim theMonth As Integer = fields(0).Substring(5, 2)
Dim theDay As Integer = fields(0).Substring(8, 2)
Dim entryDate As DateTime = New DateTime(theYear, theMonth, theDay)
```

The other field we need is the page that was requested. This is held in the fifth element of the array.

```
' get the other info...
Dim entryPage As String = fields(4)
```

We then ask the `results` collection to find a `Day` object for the date that we're working with. If we don't have one, we create a new one and add it to the collection.

```
' find the date...
Dim day As Day = results.Find(entryDate)
If day Is Nothing Then
  day = New Day(entryDate)
  results.Add(day)
End If
```

Once we have a `Day` we can do the same trick – we use the `Pages` property to access a `PageCollection` collection and then attempt to find an existing `Page` object that represents the page. (In our `Find` method we've done a case-insensitive search for the name. On Windows, files are case-insensitive so `hello.DAT` is the same as `HeLLo.dAt`. This is not the case on UNIX systems; so if you're adapting this to work on that platform, **don't** do a case-insensitive comparison!)

```
' find the page...
Dim page As Page = day.Pages.Find(entryPage)
If page Is Nothing Then
  page = New Page(entryPage)
  day.Pages.Add(page)
End If
```

Eventually we'll have a `Page` object that belongs to the correct `Day` object. We increase the hits.

```
' increment the hit...
page.Hits += 1
```

We then move the progress bar...

```
' next...
agent.IncrementBar()
System.Threading.Thread.Sleep(100)
```

Finally, we wait for 1/10th of a second. This is to slow down the process so we can see what's going on when debugging! Obviously in a production system we wouldn't want to do this.

```
' fake longer work...
System.Threading.Thread.Sleep(100)
```

Finally we can save the results.

```
        Next

        ' save...
        results.Save(agent.ResultUnitFilename)

        ' tell the user...
        agent.Status = "Processor finished"

    End Sub
```

Run the project. The agent will process the work unit and you'll find the `.result` file in the `c:\Wrox WorkSets\Agent\Data` folder.

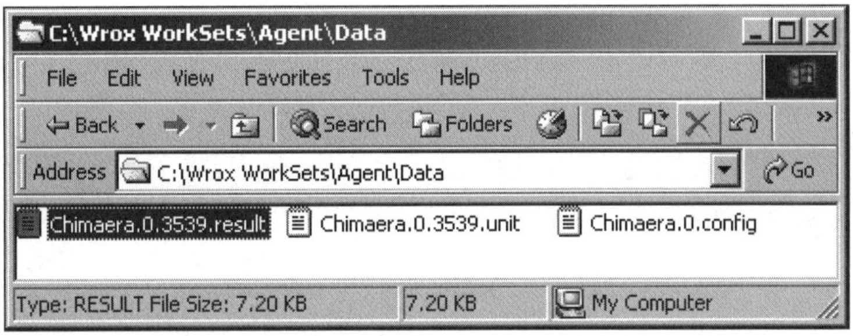

Open the file using Internet Explorer and you'll see some XML that matches the format defined before. (Ignore the `xmlns:xsi` attribute on the `Results` tag. It's something `XmlSerializer` needs, but not something that should bother us.)

```
<?xml version="1.0"?>
<Results xmlns:xsi="http://www.w3.org/2001/XMLSchema-instance"
         xmlns:xsd="http://www.w3.org/2001/XMLSchema">
  <Day>
  <Year>2001</Year>
  <Month>8</Month>
  <Day>17</Day>
  <Pages>
    <Page>
    <Name>/error.aspx</Name>
    <Hits>4</Hits>
    </Page>
    <Page>
    <Name>/coffee.aspx</Name>
    <Hits>5</Hits>
    </Page>
    <Page>
    <Name>/services.aspx</Name>
    <Hits>3</Hits>
    </Page>
    ...
```

Returning Results

Processing the results on the server is just half the battle. We need to pass the results back from the client to the server if we want to analyze the data!

We'll rely on the `AgentView` itself to pass the data back. After calling `ProcessWorkUnit`, it will look to see if the new `.result` file has been created and, if it has, it will read the contents and then call another method on the Web Service to pass the data back.

First of all, we need to add the method to the Web Service. Open the `DistributedCoordinator` project.

The `SetWorkData` method is pretty similar to `GetWorkData`. As before, the first thing we do is check the assigned agent ID against the agent ID that's giving back the result data. This time, however, we don't want to throw an exception if the IDs do not match, as we'll assume that what's happened is the work unit has been assigned to another client because the original client took too long sending the results.

```
<WebMethod()> Public Sub SetWorkData(ByVal agentId As Integer, _
                                     ByVal workUnitId As Integer, _
                                     ByVal data As String)

  ' connect...
  Dim connection As New SqlConnection(DbString)
  connection.Open()

  ' does the agent match?
  Dim assignedAgentId As Integer = CallGetAgentForWorkUnit(connection, _
                                                          workUnitId)
    If assignedAgentId = agentId Then
```

If we're OK, we get the filename back for the work unit and replace the `.unit` extension with a `.result` extension.

```
        ' get the filename...
        Dim filename As String = CallGetFilenameForWorkUnit(connection, _
                                                         workUnitId)
        filename = filename.Replace(".unit", ".result")
```

Next we create a new file and save the contents of data passed through the `data` parameter into that file.

```
        ' save it...
        Dim stream As New FileStream(filename, FileMode.Create)
        Dim writer As New StreamWriter(stream)
        writer.Write(data)
        writer.Close()
        stream.Close()
```

Finally we need to complete the `MarkWorkUnitAsCompleted` stored procedure.

```
        ' mark it as done...
        CallMarkWorkUnitAsCompleted(connection, workUnitId)
```

```
        End If
        ' close...
        connection.Close()

    End Sub
```

Build the project now, but before we go back to the client let's take a look at the SQL source for `MarkWorkUnitAsCompleted`.

```
CREATE PROCEDURE MarkWorkUnitAsCompleted
(
  @workUnitId int
)
AS
  /* reset the work unit... */
  UPDATE workunits SET agentid=null, status=2 WHERE workunitid=@workunitid

  /* reset the agent(s)... */
  UPDATE agents SET currentworkunitid=null, workunitexpires=null
    WHERE currentworkunitid=@workunitid
```

The procedure is pretty straightforward. The first thing we do is update `WorkUnits` so that the current work unit is marked as completed and the agent ID removed. Finally we update `Agents` to "disconnect" any agents that are registered as working with the work unit ID.

Here's the code to access it:

```
  Protected Sub CallMarkWorkUnitAsCompleted(ByVal connection As SqlConnection, _
                                            ByVal workUnitId As Int32)
    ' create a command...
    Dim command As New SqlCommand("MarkWorkUnitAsCompleted", connection)
    command.CommandType = CommandType.StoredProcedure

    ' params...
    Dim workUnitIdParam As SqlParameter
    workUnitIdParam = command.Parameters.Add("@workUnitId", SqlDbType.Int)
    workUnitIdParam.Value = workUnitId

    ' execute...
    command.ExecuteNonQuery()

    ' cleanup...
    command.Dispose()

  End Sub
```

Let's turn our attention to the client. Firstly, using Solution Explorer update the `Coordination` web reference. This will make the `SetWorkData` available to us.

Find the `ThreadEntryPoint` method on `AgentView`. Make this change to the code: (we've omitted quite a lot of the code for brevity).

```
    ' create the file...
    Dim info As New FileInfo(_workUnitFilename)
    If info.Exists = True Then info.Delete()
      Dim stream As New FileStream(_workUnitFilename, FileMode.Create)
      Dim writer As New StreamWriter(stream)
      writer.Write(data)
      writer.Close()
      stream.Close()
      Status = "Work data saved to: " & _workUnitFilename
      Status = "Results will be saved to: " & _resultUnitFilename

      ' find the module...
      Dim procModule As ProcModule = Form1.Modules.Find(request.ModuleName)
      If Not procModule Is Nothing Then
        ' call it...
        procModule.ProcessWorkUnit(Me)

        ' ok, open the unit...
        Dim resultInfo As New FileInfo(_resultUnitFilename)
        If resultInfo.Exists = True Then
          ' load the data...
          Status = "Preparing result unit..."
          Dim resultStream As New FileStream(_resultUnitFilename, FileMode.Open)
          Dim reader As New StreamReader(resultStream)
          Dim resultData As String = reader.ReadToEnd()
          reader.Close()
          resultStream.Close()

          ' set the unit back...
          Status = "Sending result unit back to server..."
          service.SetWorkData(Configuration.AgentId, request.WorkUnitId, resultData)

        End If
      End If
```

Now run up the client and wait for the work unit to be completed.

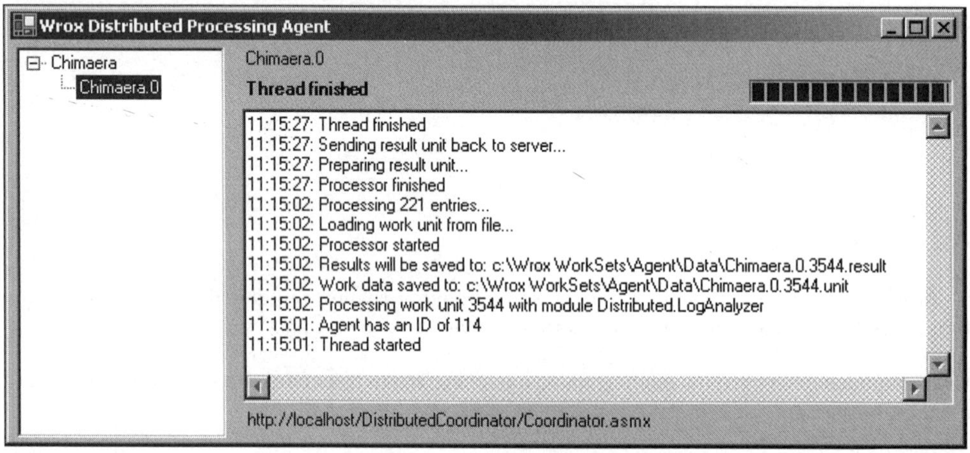

This time we need to look for the `.result` file not in the `c:\Wrox WorkSets\Agent\Data` folder, but rather in the folder assigned to the work set itself. Remember, the `.result` file will not be named after the work unit ID as it was on the client. (In the last run reported in the screenshot above, I was given a work unit with an ID of `3544`.) Instead it will be named as an ordinal of the work unit. Mine happens to be `17`. Use the Search functionality in Windows Explorer to find the `.result` file.

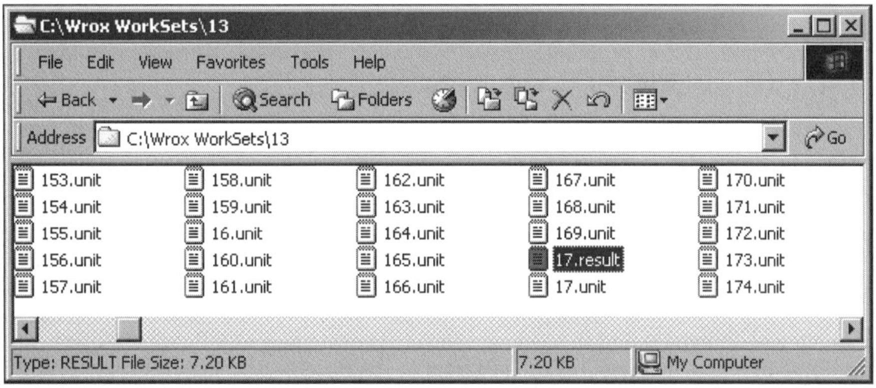

If you open the file you'll find it contains the same data as the one created by `LogAnalyzer`.

Repeating Work

At the moment, whenever we finish a work unit we stop working. Ideally, once we've finished a unit we should go back and get another one. We designed the "run once, then stop" functionality into the agent to make debugging easier, but now that it looks like we've got the basics down, we should be able to loop through many work units.

All we need to do is create an infinite loop around the `AgentView` code that requests a work unit and processes it. Find the `ThreadEntryPoint` method and add this code. (Obviously, I've omitted some code for brevity.)

```
' do we have an agent ID?
If Configuration.AgentId = 0 Then
  ' tell the user...
  Status = "Registering agent '" & Me.ToString() & "'..."

  ' get the id...
  Configuration.AgentId = service.RegisterAgent(Me.ToString())

  ' save...
  Configuration.Save()

End If

' tell the user...
Status = "Agent has an ID of " & Configuration.AgentId

' loop endlessly...
```

```
    Do While True
    ' request a work unit...
    Dim request As Coordination.WorkRequest
    request = service.RequestWorkUnit(Configuration.AgentId, _
                                      Form1.Modules.GetNames())
```

Then, towards the bottom of the code we need to end the loop. We also need to drop out of the loop if we ask for a work unit ID and get 0 back, as we can assume that either a) there's nothing for us to do any more or b) something has gone horribly wrong.

```
    ' tell the user...
    Status = "The agent was given nothing to do."
    Exit Do

  End If

  Loop
```

Run the agent now and you'll find that it works through work units ad infinitum! However, you'll notice that when you close the client window the program keeps running and the only way to stop it is to select Debug | Stop Debugging from the Visual Studio .NET menu. That's because the program will only end automatically if the startup object on the primary thread is closed **and** there are no other threads running. What we need to do is stop all of the AgentView threads when the window closes.

Spinning Down the Threads

We are already storing a list of active AgentView objects in the Nodes collection of the TreeView control. Each one is held in an AgentListNode object, so logic suggests that when our window closes we need to loop through each of these nodes and call the SpinDown method on the AgentView.

Open the code editor for Form1 and create a new handler for the Closed event. Add this code:

```
  Private Sub Form1_Closed(ByVal sender As Object, _
                        ByVal e As System.EventArgs) Handles MyBase.Closed

    ' stop the nodes...
    _agentListNode.StopAll()

  End Sub
```

Of course, there is no StopAll method at this point, so we'll need to build one. Add this code to AgentListNode:

```
  ' StopAll - stop all of the agents...
  Public Sub StopAll()

    ' loop...
    Dim node As AgentNode
    For Each node In Nodes
      node.AgentView.SpinDown()
    Next

  End Sub
```

If we loop at the `SpinDown` method in `AgentView` you'll notice that it calls `Abort` on the `System.Threading.Thread` object that we created when we first spun up the thread:

```
' SpinDown - stop the thread...
Public Sub SpinDown()

  ' running?
  If Not _thread Is Nothing Then

    ' abort, join and reset...
    _thread.Abort()
    _thread.Join()
    _thread = Nothing

  End If

End Sub
```

This is a relatively brutal method of stopping a thread that causes a `System.Threading.ThreadAbortException` to be called. As we haven't any exception handling at all at this point, we'd better do so now otherwise we'll crash when the agent has finished.

Open the code editor for `AgentView` and add this code to the start of `ThreadEntryPoint`.

```
' ThreadEntryPoint - start work...
Private Sub ThreadEntryPoint()

  ' tell the user...
  Status = "Thread started"

  Try
    ' connect to the service...
    Dim service As New Coordination.Coordinator()

    ' set the url for the service...
    service.Url = Form1.WebServiceUrl

    ' do we have an agent ID?
    If Configuration.AgentId = 0 Then
```

Then, at the bottom of the method add this code:

```
    Else

      ' tell the user...
      Status = "The agent was given nothing to do."
      Exit Do

    End If

    Loop
```

```
    Catch ex As system.Threading.ThreadAbortException
      Status = "Thread was asked to finish"

    Catch ex As Exception
      Status = "An unhandled exception occured: " & ex.Message
      ' exceptions usually due to heavy load on web site, so keep trying
      ' until we get a connection
      ThreadEntryPoint()

    End Try

    ' tell the user...
    Status = "Thread finished"

  End Sub
```

You'll notice there that we're catching two separate kinds of exception. `ThreadAbortException` will be thrown when we call the `Thread.Abort` method, so we display a status message and do nothing else. In this case, any work unit that's outstanding will be forgotten. We'll have to wait for another client to eventually pick up the work unit in order to get the results back. This is just one approach – you might want to build in a method for restarting an assigned work unit when the client is started up again.

Any other kind of exception will be indicative of a problem, such as the Web Service becoming unreachable, or something goes wrong with the files, etc. In this case we're not going to do anything clever – instead we're just going to display a message containing the exception and give up.

In a production system you'd want to look at handling these exceptions in a smarter manner. For example, if the Web Service became unreachable, you'd want to back off for a few minutes and then try again. If one of the files couldn't be opened, you'd want to ask the user to correct the problem, and so on.

But now we're at a point where although the `AgentView` continually loops through work units, if we close the agent window the client process does stop properly.

Load Testing

A distributed processing system that only has a single agent can, quite fairly, be described as useless. In this section we'll take a look at how to have a number of agents running simultaneously.

We've already built our client application so that it can automatically spin up a number of agents. This saves us from having to install the client on many computers around our network or the Internet to see if the logic of what we've done holds. Let's make our client start up 32 individual agents.

Open the code editor for `AgentListNode` and change the first version of the `Add` method so that it creates 32 agents instead of one.

```
' Add - add a new agentnode...
Public Sub Add()
  Add(32)
End Sub
```

Run the project and you'll find that 32 agents are created. However, if you look you'll notice that some of them have reported an exception.

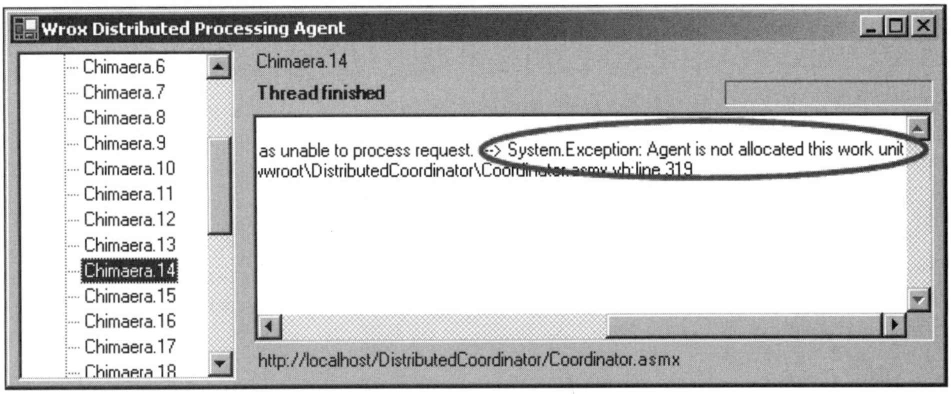

What has happened here is that two agents have effectively been allocated the same work unit. When Chimaera.14 requests the data for the work unit, the coordination service assumes that the agent is improperly trying to get the data for a unit that hasn't been allocated to it. As all of the agents start more-or-less simultaneously, there is a run on the Web Service where `RequestWorkUnit` is called by many separate incoming connections, again more-or-less simultaneously.

This causes a synchronization problem. What's happening is that an agent is coming in and being assigned a work unit. However, before that work unit is marked as "assigned" (before it has its `Status` column changed to `1`), another call to `RequestWorkUnit` has come into the server and it's looked through the available work units for ones with a status of `0` and allocated the same work unit to another client.

What we need to do is synchronize access to anything that requires access to the `Status` column. The two methods that do this are `RequestWorkUnit` and `SetWorkData`. In effect what we need to do is alter the Web Service implementation so that although the other methods will be able to handle multiple synchronous calls, these two will be handled asynchronously.

A `System.Threading.ReaderWriterLock` is what we need to use here. This will allow us to separate off portions of `RequestWorkUnit` and `SetWorkData` so that only a single thread can access it at any given moment. As each multiple simultaneous call will be handled on a separate thread, this is exactly what we need. However, as each thread creates a new instance of the `Coordinator` class itself, we need to make sure that the same instance of `ReaderWriterLock` is available to all of them by making the member shared.

Open the code editor for the `Coordinator` Web Service and add this member:

```
<WebService(Namespace:="http://www.wrox.com/distributed/")> _
Public Class Coordinator
    Inherits System.Web.Services.WebService

  ' members...
  Private Shared _statusLock As New ReaderWriterLock()
```

When using a ReaderWriterLock in this way, it's absolutely essential that every time we acquire the lock we must release the lock when we have finished. This means a call to AcquireWriterLock at the top of the method and a call to ReleaseWriterLock at the bottom. However, if an exception occurs anywhere in between, the method will return immediately and ReleaseWriterLock will not get called. The result: no thread will ever be able to access the method again causing the entire system to grind to a halt. What we need to do is catch any exceptions that occur, release the lock and then re-throw the exception again so that the client can deal with it.

Make this change to the top of RequestWorkUnit. You'll need to move the request declaration outside of the Try...Catch block.

```
<WebMethod()> Public Function RequestWorkUnit(ByVal agentId As Integer, _
                                              ByVal moduleNames() As String) _
                                              As WorkRequest

  ' set up the call...
  Dim request As WorkRequest
  Dim caughtException As Exception
  _statusLock.AcquireWriterLock(-1)

  ' try...
  Try

    ' connect to the database...
    Dim connection As New SqlConnection(DbString)
    connection.Open()

    ' load all of the modules...
    Dim modules As DataSet = CallGetAllModules(connection)
```

Then, add this code to the bottom of the method:

```
    ' close...
    connection.Close()

  Catch ex As Exception
    caughtException = ex
  End Try

  ' unlock...
  _statusLock.ReleaseWriterLock()

  ' did we get an exception?
  If Not caughtException Is Nothing Then
    Throw caughtException
  End If

  ' return the request...
  Return request

End Function
```

We need to do more or less the same thing to `SetWorkData`. Make these changes to the code:

```
<WebMethod()> Public Sub SetWorkData(ByVal agentId As Integer, _
                                     ByVal workUnitId As Integer, _
                                     ByVal data As String)

  ' set up the call...
  Dim caughtException As Exception
  _statusLock.AcquireWriterLock(-1)
  Try

    ' connect...
    Dim connection As New SqlConnection(DbString)
    connection.Open()

    ' does the agent match?
    Dim assignedAgentId As Integer = CallGetAgentForWorkUnit(connection, _
                                                             workUnitId)
    If assignedAgentId = agentId Then

      ' get the filename...
      Dim filename As String = CallGetFilenameForWorkUnit(connection, _
                                                          workUnitId)
      filename = filename.Replace(".unit", ".result")

      ' save it...
      Dim stream As New FileStream(filename, FileMode.Create)
      Dim writer As New StreamWriter(stream)
      writer.Write(data)
      writer.Close()
      stream.Close()

      ' mark it as done...
      CallMarkWorkUnitAsCompleted(connection, workUnitId)

    End If

    ' close...
    connection.Close()

  Catch ex As Exception
    caughtException = ex
  End Try

  ' unlock...
  _statusLock.ReleaseWriterLock()

  ' throw?
  If Not caughtException Is Nothing Then
    Throw caughtException
  End If

End Sub
```

Now run the agent again and you'll discover that none of the agents are reporting the "agent not assigned work unit" exception.

Testing

It's worth testing the entire process a couple of times to make sure everything works OK, and there are no unexpected surprises. If you do create a few new work sets, remove the `Threading.Thread.Sleep` call from `LogAnalyzer`. This will greatly speed up the process of running through a complete work set end-to-end and also has the advantage that the load on the Web Service is increased which gives a more realistic impression of what would happen should you have thousands of clients running on the network.

What you can see in this screenshot is four work sets in total, the first three of which have been completed.

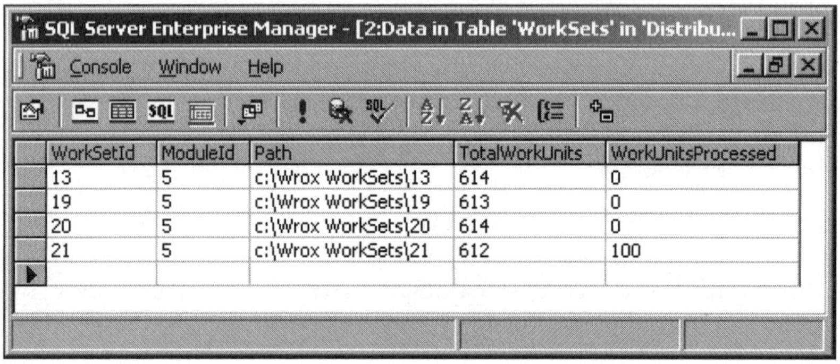

WorkSetId	ModuleId	Path	TotalWorkUnits	WorkUnitsProcessed
13	5	c:\Wrox WorkSets\13	614	0
19	5	c:\Wrox WorkSets\19	613	0
20	5	c:\Wrox WorkSets\20	614	0
21	5	c:\Wrox WorkSets\21	612	100

Analyzing Results

So far in this case study we've illustrated the key concepts involved in building a distributed application. What we have is a client application into which you can "plug in" new processing modules to support your distributed processing needs. The client we've built can also simulate many different network clients running simultaneously.

What we haven't looked at is how to analyze the results when all of the units have been processed. We won't be looking at this here because it's a fairly artificial problem.

As we mentioned before, in order to analyze the results we typically need to get all of the related information together before we can draw meaningful conclusions. We'll need to gather all of the results before we can process the data.

In some cases you'll find it useful to split the work set up into smaller work sets first. So, if you have to analyze server logs for a year, you might break the logs into separate sets, one set per month. That way if you collect all the results for May you can analyze that while you're waiting for June to come in.

Summary

In this case study we looked into:

- The world of distributed processing, specifically how to achieve the aims of distributed processing by using a Web Service.
- The fundamentals of the process and the concepts of sets and units.
- Building a database structure that could hold the state of the system while processing was going on.
- Building the agent and service together, adding functionality to each until eventually we had a fully functional client that could request those units back to the client.

We built the client in such a way that new processing modules could be plugged in order to get the system to do different things, depending on the needs of the business. We didn't look at how to process the entire result set once processing had been completed, as this was a fairly academic discussion. However, we did show how we could collect a large set of XML documents that should be fairly trivial to import into an analysis application for reporting.

Professional
ASP.NET
Web
Services

A

.NET My Services

The .NET My Services project (originally codenamed 'HailStorm') is still in its infancy, but there are signs that indicate within a few years, .NET My Services will be a powerful force for applications available over the Internet. It's the kind of technology that we will look back on in 10 years time and say to colleagues, "I was there in the early days".

During this appendix, we will cover what is already a moving target. We'll discuss some of the basic ideas behind .NET My Services, and why we need to keep a close eye on this technology. We will also examine some practical scenarios about how it can help us develop applications faster, and more robustly. Undoubtedly, some of what we discuss within this appendix will be improved upon and finalized when the completed version becomes available. However, we hope to give an objective insight into how .NET My Services could look and how they will change the way we develop in the future.

All that we can cover within this appendix is a technical insight into .NET My Services. Currently, information is simply too sketchy to document, and it is more advantageous to give a greater insight into the aim and some of the repercussions of .NET My Services. More information about .NET My Services can be found at Microsoft's site, http://www.microsoft.com/netservices/.

> *"Hailstorm is a key .NET milestone to delivery on the Microsoft mission to empower people through great software, any time, any place, and on any device." Bill Gates March 19 2001, Redmond, WA.*

Microsoft's determination in becoming the force behind Web Service development for the near future made it consider the commercial options for Web Services at a very early stage in its history.

One of the ideas to come out of the Microsoft think-tank was originally codenamed "Hailstorm", but is now known as .NET My Services. The concept of .NET My Services is to solve two basic problems with today's development practice:

- Personal information needs to be controlled by people ("user-centric"), not companies
- Individuals need information to be available to any device and any operating system

The .NET My Services project allows personal (or company) information to be held on the Internet or locally on your intranet, and to be updated and changed using a series of Web Services. This information can then be accessed from any application that supports the SOAP protocol, either by you, or by some other party that you have given authorization to, such as your local gas company, or even your Bank Manager.

Having been developed as a Web Service, .NET My Services will then also be readily available across many disparate operating system platforms, such as WAP phones, Palm OSs, Windows PCs, or even a corporate mainframe running operating systems such as Linux and Unix.

The key to this versatility is the SOAP messaging protocol and XML. For the first time, there is a basic agreement to support this protocol from many different (usually competing) software vendors, who agree that the adoption of the SOAP protocol will greatly benefit computer software development in the foreseeable future.

Microsoft has recently changed its approach to My Services, moving from the business side to the technology side. According to the "*Update to .NET My Services*" at http://www.microsoft.com/netservices/userexperiences.asp, instead of creating Microsoft-hosted services, Microsoft's interest is in building infrastructure and tools that will enable customers to run these user-centric services themselves.

The Building Blocks

.NET My Services Web Services are built around Microsoft's .NET platform and have been designed to be released in building blocks. This section will describe these building blocks and give a fuller understanding of the implications of each expected release.

.NET My Services is not solely restricted to Microsoft building blocks; because of its reliance on Web Services it has been designed to be extended by other third-party companies, though the information concerning how extensions are performed is currently quite sketchy. However, Microsoft has moved to tackle the security and privacy issues by announcing that it intends to base the next version of Passport on a technology called Kerberos and is encouraging others to do the same.

The adoption of the Kerberos security standard will mean that many different companies with their own password authentication scheme (such as AOL) would all be able to exchange information with each other because of everybody's reliance on the same basic technology. For the person in the street this would simply mean being able to log into AOL and Microsoft (and many more web sites and applications) using the same username and password.

Building Block 1 – Security

The first staged release for .NET My Services is in the guise of MS Passport, the basis of the entire security system for .NET My Services. MS Passport has in fact been around for a number of years now, and boasts a massive user base. It also has the feel-good factor of a tried and tested technology. However, the difference between the MS Passport and the .NET My Services version of MS Passport (now called .NET Passport), is that the latter can be accessed using (yes, you guessed it) a Web Service.

.NET Passport paves the way forward for functionality to be added to this basic model, as and when it becomes available. .NET Passport allows an individual to have what is termed roaming security; the ability to use a sign-in name (usually your e-mail address) and password to log in to any web site or application that uses the .NET Passport Web Service.

.NET Passport works like a wrapper around the main .NET My Services services, by allowing a user to log on and validate their access remotely using .NET My Services. Windows XP already has the ability to validate through Passport as the user logs in to their computer in the morning, similarly to how a primary domain server validates user access. This, however, is one of the first of many such applications that are expected to adopt .NET Passport for securing their application or service.

Building Block 2 – Essentials

The first of the additional feature releases will take a number of the processes we perform every day (for example, e-mailing, storing addresses, saving files), and publish them as Web Services. This release can be seen as the basic infrastructure of how .NET My Services operates.

It's important to remember that, as with all Web Services, .NET My Services is simply the functionality (business) layer provided to other client applications. The expectation is that other products such as Word, Excel, Visual Studio, and even .NET will need to be changed to incorporate Web Service technology.

Operation of .NET My Services

Let's have a look at how .NET My Services will operate using these two basic building blocks.

Currently when we use an e-mail program such as Outlook, we are able to save often-used or important addresses into the dedicated Outlook Address book for later retrieval. This information is held locally on our computer, and is not shared with other applications. The .NET My Services version of Outlook, instead of using a locally stored address book, can use .NET My Services to store our address information in a centralized storage area on the Internet, which is accessible using the SOAP messaging protocol.

Now our information is not solely restricted for use within Outlook, this information can be retrieved by any application or operating system that understands SOAP messages.

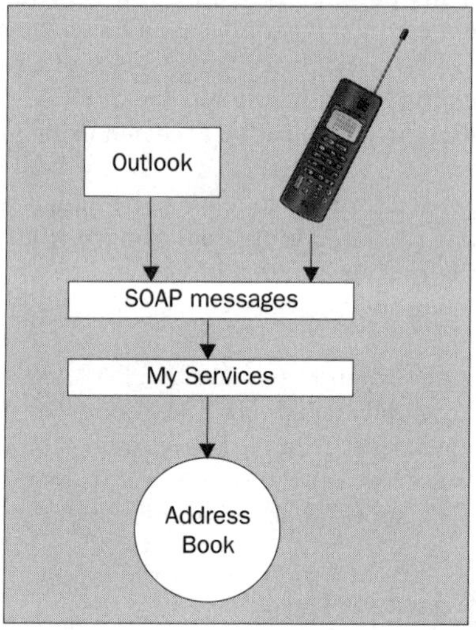

One use for this could be the ability to recall someone's phone number using a WAP mobile phone, using the same address book as our computer at work. In addition, we will be able to use the same address information whether we are abroad, or in the country where we originally created our addresses.

The expectation is that the adoption of .NET My Services will not stop with Microsoft products such as Word and Office; the intention is for .NET My Services to become an open standard, able to be incorporated within any or all development applications from many different vendors.

Once .NET My Services technology is embedded within additional applications or web sites, then the user of those applications gains the advantage of being able to store their personal (or corporate) information in .NET My Services, but use many different devices to access/update that information. There is the additional advantage of being able to share and revoke access to that information with others, placing the user firmly in control of their own personal information.

One example of authorization is that of using directory enquiries to ask for a person's phone number. The operator then tells the caller that information over the phone. However, if they had previously given directory enquiries access to their personal address book, the operator can also update the caller's personal information. So next time they use Outlook or their WAP phone, that address information has been updated and is immediately available.

This ability to make personal data available to any device is fundamental to how .NET My Services is constructed. It is also apparent that without the onset of a globally accepted standard for such Web Services and SOAP, this type of widespread compatibility would not be possible.

Below is a list of the services that are intended to be released with the Essentials building block:

Name	Description	Use
`myProfile`	Name, nickname, special dates, picture; electronic and geographic address for an identity	Personal information. `myProfile` has a synchronization feature that can update the `myContacts` information for other users.
`myContacts`	Electronic relationships/address book	Used to store contact information for others, for example entering a number on a WAP phone can make it instantly available from within Outlook on the user's PC at work. Synchronized with others' `myProfile` information.
`myCategories`	Categorization of information	Used by many services within My Service to categorize data/information into known data types or groups.
`myLocation`	Electronic and geographical location and rendezvous	The user's current location. There is also some talk about being able to pinpoint people electronically, depending on what device they are using.
`myPresence`	Online information	Contains the user's current online information. Thought to be an extension of the MSN messenger service, but described as a Web Service.
`myLists`	Generic list creation and maintenance	Uses the `myCategories` service to actually create meaningful lists of information, such as friends, families etc. This service, however, simply controls the addition, deletion, updating and retrieval of lists.
`myNotification`	Rule-based alerts and notification	Provides personalized alerts to the user.
`myInbox`	Inbox items like e-mail and voice mail, including existing mail systems	E-mail and voice mail from any device, such as WAP, PC, Mainframe, PDA.
`myCalendar`	Time and task management	Also known as scheduler. Can be updated by other companies to notify the user of events about which they may be interested.
`myDocuments`	Raw document storage	Document storage similar to files and directories.

Table continued on following page

Name	Description	Use
`myApplication Settings`	Application settings	Change an application's colors, capabilities, and options. Can mix capabilities, for example, ABC software can use options from XYZ software. Can also control basic settings such as desktop color, allowing the user to log on to different machines (in different countries) and retain desktop settings.
`myFavorite WebSites`	Favorite URLs and other Web identifiers	Keep track of favorite web sites, but recall this information for use on any device, not just Internet Explorer.
`myWallet`	Receipts, payment instruments, coupons, and other transaction records	Store credit card details and allow suppliers to debit the user's card. Automatically tracks credit card transactions.
`myDevices`	Device settings, capabilities	The devices the user wants to be able to use these services on. Also their capabilities and options.
`myServices`	Services provided for an identity	Allows the user to disable/enable access to certain .NET My Services services.

These services form the basic model for .NET My Services. However, the intention is that developers will have the ability to extend the basic .NET My Services infrastructure and list of services, allowing third-party software to be incorporated within the .NET My Services infrastructure.

Individuals will be able to update a shared and secure database containing their personal information using any of the above Web Services, therefore making sure that the information contained about them is always accurate.

Advantages and Disadvantages

We've listed below an easy-to-read summary of some of the statements that developers and customers are making about .NET My Services:

DEVELOPER – Advantages:

- Faster development timescales
- Unit testing of the .NET My Services area of an application greatly simplified
- Allows the developer to concentrate on advanced features, improving overall functionality
- Always certain of up-to-date information about a user

DEVELOPER – Disadvantages

- Reliance on the technical abilities of another company
- If .NET My Services does not succeed then there is no guarantee it will continue as a service
- Multiple My Services registries may still mean some conflicting information

CUSTOMER – Advantages

- Only need to enter information once (see disadvantages below for opposite of this)
- Personal/private information is held by a single company
- The company holding the information has licensed companies to join .NET My Services
- Control over who has access to personal information
- The information is always correct because the user can keep it up-to-date
- Information is hosted away from the user's desktop, thereby allowing disaster recovery

CUSTOMER – Disadvantages

- Not everyone will adopt .NET My Services technology; may be inconsistently used across sites
- Concerns about misuse of information
- Personal/private information is held by a single company
- Multiple databases may still mean that you have to duplicate some of your information

User-Centric Instead of Device-Centric

Today nearly all our development is based around capturing information from a user. However, in nearly all circumstances another web site or supplier has already captured that same information. We all personally have vast amounts of data held about us sitting in applications, databases, and cookies throughout the world – most of it out of date and inaccurate.

The reason that information has always been held on separate machines or databases, is that many have found it technically challenging for disparate systems to communicate with each other, for example, Windows talking to Unix or Unix to a WAP phone.

With the onset of SOAP Web Service technologies, we have broken those boundaries and now are not constrained by physical limitations of having to get the user to retype information as they progress between different web sites or applications. A user can now actually choose to bring that information with them, giving them what is effectively a global identity.

As described previously, the .NET My Services project (using Web Service technology) is based around the idea of having a central knowledge store of information, which contains information related to a user, like an Internet personal identity. Behind that identity, users can gain access to their personal information.

Microsoft has in fact taken the idea of the Internet as a country, and the user as a registered person within that country further, by issuing what they aptly name "passports" to all registered users. These passports simply contain security information to allow an individual to access their address, name, credit card details, diary, schedule, or notes.

Using this passport technology (.NET Passport), and a global identity places the user firmly in control of the information about them, with the ability to authorize or revoke access to any companies or individuals.

Who is Going to Use .NET My Services?

So far, technical details on .NET My Services have been very sketchy, and difficult to come by, so very few companies have had the opportunity to use its services, apart from the following pre-release partners who are showcasing .NET My Services on behalf of Microsoft:

- American Express
- ClickCommerce
- EBay
- Expedia
- Groove Networks

Microsoft has released the following list of products that are expected to contain .NET My Services support:

- bCentral
- MSN
- Office
- PocketPC
- Stinger
- Visual Studio
- .NET
- Windows CE
- Windows XP
- X Box
- Microsoft Reader for eBooks

Judging by the above list, and also by the number of users that will be introduced to .NET My Services, Microsoft is very, very serious about .NET My Services succeeding.

Stateful Information and .NET My Services

Cookies are a technology that created a considerable amount of controversy in the early years of the Internet, some of which continues today. Originally designed to keep stateful information to save users/customers having to type in information every time they visited a web site, it quickly became obvious that it could also be used to keep track of a customer's purchasing habits. Suppliers can then use this information to target an individual when they return to a web site, making sure that the supplier only displays what they think the user will find interesting.

Cookies are probably the single most controversial technical standard on the Internet. Not surprisingly, as users we don't like people knowing what we've bought, or where we like browsing – many see it as an invasion of privacy. In the future, we may look back at cookies fondly, as now the super-cookie is here in the form of .NET My Services.

One considerable limitation of the cookie has always been its localization; it is restricted to collecting information for a specific web site domain. In many cases, this has been a welcome limitation and many developers acknowledge that the user can at least control cookies on their local computer by simply deleting a file to remove them.

With the onset of .NET My Services, there is no longer a need for holding personal information in cookies, as stateful information can now be held within .NET My Services. This movement clearly has repercussions about user privacy.

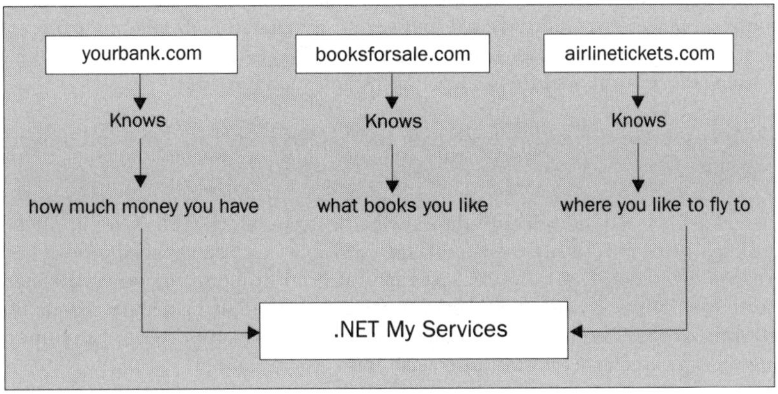

Because .NET My Services now contains information concerning **all** our browsing and purchasing habits, it could become the single most important database storage device in the world. This vast repository contains information across so many different industries that we could accurately foretell marketing trends for 100's of millions of users.

George Orwell's famous book "1984" vividly paints a picture of individuals being watched from every corner. In reality, being tracked and watched while browsing the Internet is certainly happening now. But what .NET My Services offers is greater flexibility and control, rather than the gray oppressive face of Big Brother.

Take for instance the scenario of walking down to your local **.NET My Services** shopping mall. The sales people in each shop you go into know you by name; they know what style of clothes you wear, and what your favorite colors are. Although this may seem a little spooky, realistically this could save us time, and could make shopping a more interesting proposition.

eTerrorism and .NET My Services Security

Up until now, people have been steadfast in their demand for secure information, privacy, and control. .NET My Services actually allows users to share their personal information with whom they want, but can also revoke that permission if necessary. This is a response to the misuse of personal information in the industry today, where web sites seem to believe that once they have someone's personal information, that person is fair game to be targeted in e-mail and advertising campaigns. The introduction of .NET My Services will bring the privacy debate to the forefront, and finally place users in control of their information.

.NET My Services undoubtedly brings with it a certain amount of risk. No longer will a hacker be trying to perpetrate access to a company hosting 1000's of credit card details. The risk is that .NET My Services could in fact inadvertently allow access to the personal details of a much larger number of people.

eTerrorism takes its toll on corporate and individual bank balances. Thus it's imperative that .NET My Services gets the balance between fast user response and integrated high-level user protection right the first time. Though there is a justification for expanding the .NET My Services project with new features by request from users, the security features will not allow any such freedom.

Verisign and Microsoft are currently working on the XKMS standard, a method of securing XML traffic between two points.

The XKMS standard is intended to adapt digital certificates to work with XML applications. XKMS is a similar technology (some would say the same as) to SSL but has been specially designed for XML traffic. The reason for adopting a different standard for point-to-point digital certificates is that it Microsoft wants Web Services and .NET My Services to be used using secure connections with as many different platforms as possible; however, although SOAP can be supported by any operating system, understanding digital certificates is not quite as simple.

The diagram below describes the flow of traffic from a WAP phone (doesn't understand certificates) to the .NET My Services (does understand certificates) Web Service using the XKMS security feature:

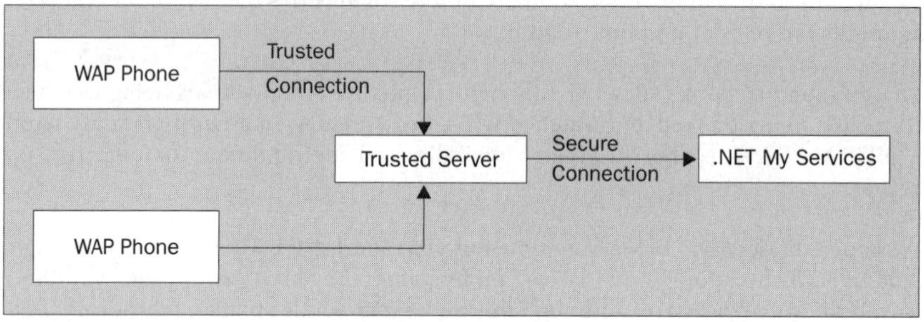

XKMS gets around the security issues of platforms that do not understand digital certificates by operating through a trusted server. In the above case, all communications between the WAP phone and the trusted server are guaranteed and already validated using the trusted server's own security technology. The trusted server simply handles all SOAP request messages to run a Web Service such as .NET My Services; making sure that the end-to-end transmission of XML traffic uses digital certificates (Kerberos authentication).

Concerns about .NET My Services

.NET My Services is already starting to drive controversy about Microsoft's intentions to control public demand and consumers' personal information. What we must all understand is that – with the onset of Web Services and the industry-changing implications of what it proposes – if Microsoft doesn't create a .NET My Services then some other corporation will. Whether we like it or not, the global strategy of creating name and address storage that millions can use is too appealing for any forward-thinking corporation and its shareholders to ignore.

Developers at first may be reluctant to incorporate someone else's technology into their own applications if they haven't yet been convinced about the technology. Microsoft has certainly got its work cut out to convince developers too, as it may appear that they are reducing the work that a consultant/contractor may be asked to do.

Nevertheless, the opportunity for developers to gain access to a substantial user base will far outweigh any concerns many of us may have, and within the next 5-10 years, we may in fact see the industry sectioned into those who do and those who don't support .NET My Services.

Security and performance will undoubtedly be key issues for developers and customers, and Microsoft's technical ability will undoubtedly be pushed like never before. Earlier this year there was an incident with MS Passport that raised concern among partners and customers. Such an incident cannot happen when you have hundreds of millions of customers all waiting to retrieve their personal information.

It all points to the fact that Microsoft must get the security and performance issues solved prior to the wave of public use that is expected to confront us all over the next few years. With a project of this size Microsoft will have one chance to get it right, before public opinion turns against the whole idea.

Summary

In this appendix we discussed:

- How .NET My Services will affect the way we develop in the future
- How the current market is positioned to accept this emerging technology
- Security features of .NET My Services
- Size of the potential market for Web Service functionality similar to .NET My Services
- Advantages and disadvantages of .NET My Services

As developers, many of us will be drawn towards developing our own versions of .NET My Services. It's a ritual we've almost all experienced with the start of a new contract, when we're desperate to start coding. But we should, in fact, consider adopting .NET My Services now – it has the potential to free us to work on more exciting developments – rather than (as some do), regarding it as an evil that will decimate the contracting market.

Once you've made a decision to use .NET My Services, it's probably going to be a decision for life, a little like choosing a programming language. Within time, it may be that we will come to see .NET My Services as an extension of our basic development language, something that we can't do without.

It could be that, as operating systems, especially Windows XP, start to use .NET My Web Services and allow millions of users to share information between home, office, and WAP phones, that customers will start to see .NET My Services as a preferred feature that some will insist upon. Public opinion has the unexpected ability to change without anybody noticing, sometimes overnight, and we must be prepared.

Professional ASP.NET Web Services
Professional ASP.NET
Web Services

B

IE6 Web Service Behaviors

First introduced with Internet Explorer 5.0, "behaviors" provide a way to attach client-side functionality to elements in a web page, using `STYLE` attributes or declarations. The major benefit of behaviors is that we can define these features separately from the actual web page, in an `.HTC` (HTML Component) file. Separating the HTC scripts from the presentation HTML simplifies sharing and managing the behavior functions. Multiple behaviors may also be applied to a single element, a big improvement over DHTML's limitations. Providing the developer with the ability to define properties, methods, and events to attach to various HTML elements makes behaviors a valuable part of the developer's toolbox.

It's important to note that behaviors currently apply to the Internet Explorer browser only.

Generally, Web Services are thought of as server-centric, meaning that integrating functionality from various services takes place before a web page is fully rendered to the client. While this is often true, it is not always the case. With Web Service behaviors, the Web Service calling and processing logic is offloaded to the client (the browser), implemented in an HTML Component.

HTML Components (.HTCs)

HTML Components (`.HTCs`) provide a powerful way to implement behaviors in simple DHTML script, using your choice of VBScript or JScript. While ActiveX controls provide similar functionality, they must be downloaded to the page separately and must be installed before use. On the other hand, HTCs are simply text, and are downloaded with the source page. Even better, HTCs give the developer the same ability to define true component characteristics, complete with properties, methods, and events, as well as providing the ability to receive notifications. For security reasons, HTCs must reside on the same server that serves the HTML that calls it.

The basic HTC file is made of up of a script that implements a specific behavior, within <PUBLIC:HTC> tags:

```
<PUBLIC:HTC>
  <PUBLIC:ATTACH EVENT="eventname" FOR="object" [ | "object" ...]
                 HANDLER="handlername" URN="URN" />
  <SCRIPT LANGUAGE="VBScript">
    ' VBScript code
  </SCRIPT>
</PUBLIC:HTC>
```

The <PUBLIC:ATTACH> HTC tag makes the connection between the HTML tag and the event for which you are defining behavior. To force a certain subroutine to execute when the source tag fires an event, the HANDLER attribute is used. A good example is changing a style when the mouse moves over the source element on the web page. We'll change its color to blue in this example (bluetext.htc).

```
<PUBLIC:HTC>
  <PUBLIC:ATTACH EVENT="onmouseover" HANDLER="Blue" />
  <SCRIPT LANGUAGE="VBScript">
    Sub Blue
      style.color = "blue"
    End Sub
  </SCRIPT>
</PUBLIC:HTC>
```

We've attached the onmouseover event in the HTML page source to the Blue VBScript subroutine in the HTC. While we could have used the FOR attribute to specifically attach the handler to a single element, by leaving the FOR attribute out, we've made this script accessible to multiple elements. The key to making it all work is to tell the browser (IE6) which behavior to use. To apply this behavior to a <P>, use this syntax:

```
<HTML>
<BODY>
<STYLE>
<!--
  @media all
  {
    .hover { behavior:url(bluetext.htc) }
  }
-->
</STYLE>
<BR><BR>
<P CLASS="hover">Hover over for blue.</P>
</BODY>
</HTML>
```

The @media rule specifies where the output is designated, with the choices being screen, print, and all. We've then attached the HTC to the hover class, then applied this class to our <P>.

Another great feature of the HTC is that it can expose properties, methods, and events, just as other components. State is also maintained, so variables can be retained between calls. Let's extend the HTC functionality to return the text to its original color when the mouse leaves the tag area. We'll be replacing our existing VBScript HTC with the following JScript (note the use of PUBLIC:COMPONENT):

```
<PUBLIC:COMPONENT>
  <PUBLIC:ATTACH event="onmouseover" handler="Blue" />
  <PUBLIC:ATTACH event="onmouseout" handler="NotBlue" />
  <SCRIPT>
    var originalColor;

    function Blue() {
      originalColor = style.color;
      style.color = "blue";
    }

    function NotBlue() {
      style.color = originalColor;
    }
  </SCRIPT>
</PUBLIC:COMPONENT>
```

When the `onmouseover` event fires, the behavior causes `Blue` to execute. The variable `originalColor` stores the color property of the event source. Upon the `onmouseout` event firing, the value in `originalColor` is placed back into the `color` property of the same event source. This simple HTC gives us plenty of room to try various style changes.

Accessing Web Services with IE5 Behaviors

Microsoft has developed an HTC that allows us to access Web Services from within a web page in IE5 and later. This script, `webservice.htc`, makes implementing this remote functionality from the client (the browser) *very* simple. The greatest advantage to calling a Web Service using the behavior HTC is data retrieval without requiring a page refresh. We won't worry ourselves with the details of this HTC, as its contents are fairly extensive, but we'll examine a few practical uses of the Web Service behavior.

The great thing about using the Web Service behavior is that we need not involve ourselves with the details of SOAP or any other elements of the data transfer. All the effort involved with parsing the XML is done behind the scenes in the browser. No page refresh or navigation occurs, keeping network activity to a minimum.

While **element behaviors** were introduced in Internet Explorer 5.5, the Web Service behavior is an **attached behavior**, providing compatibility starting with version 5.0. Attached behaviors modify the behavior of an existing page element, while element behaviors define actual custom tags that can be placed within a web page.

> **You can download `webservice.htc` and read Microsoft's documentation on Web Service behaviors at:**
>
> **http://msdn.microsoft.com/workshop/author/webservice/webservice.asp**

When we need to call a Web Service, we must ensure it is from within our own web domain (such as "wrox.com"). This can severely limit the functions we'd like to utilize, of course, since Web Services are meant to provide unbounded access to functions anywhere. I'm sure after giving it a little thought you'll understand why this security is in place: it prevents unauthorized use of other domains' Web Services.

The way around this limitation is to have the web server on our web domain request data from other web servers. Wrapping a Web Service call on our web server with another Web Service will provide us with the remote functionality we need.

Retrieving Values from GetAppSettings

A simple illustration of the use of Web Service behaviors is retrieving a string from the configuration, as the `GetAppSettings` web method (from Chapters 2 and 3) did. At the end of Chapter 3, we added a second parameter to the method called `delay`, which allows us to specify the number of milliseconds to wait before returning a result.

Building a simple web page, `getappsettings.asp` in the `AppSettings` folder of the download for this appendix, we will create a form that allows us to enter a key. When the request button is pressed, the Web Service will be called using the behavior.

```
<html>
<script language="JavaScript">
var iCallID;

function init()
{
  svcGetAppSettings.useService("http://localhost/PWS/AppB/↴
                           AppSettings/AppService.asmx?WSDL","GetAppSettings");
}

function evtAppSettings()
{
    // Error condition on this call
    if ((event.result.error) && (iCallID==event.result.id))
    {
        // Retrieve error properties
        var vCode   = event.result.errorDetail.code;
        var vString = event.result.errorDetail.string;
        var vRaw    = event.result.errorDetail.raw;

        // Would add a switch{} to handle various vCodes
    }
    // No error, confirm this is our call that is being returned
    else if ((!event.result.error) && (iCallID == event.result.id))
    {
       if (event.result.value == "") {
          // Display a default value, background of yellow
          lblResult.innerText = "No Value";
          lblResult.style.backgroundColor = "#FFFF99";
       }
       else
       {
          // Display the returned value, background of aqua
          lblResult.innerText = event.result.value;
          lblResult.style.backgroundColor = "#99FFFF";
       }
    }
    else
    {
        // This result was fired by something other than our request
    }
}
</script>
```

```
<body onload="init()">
<div id="svcGetAppSettings"
     style="display:none;behavior:url(webservice.htc)"
     onresult="evtAppSettings()"></div>
<form name="Form1" id="Form1" onsubmit="javascript:iCallID =
svcGetAppSettings.GetAppSettings.callService
                ('GetAppSettings',document.Form1.key.value, 500);return false;">
Key <input type="text" name="key" value="" size="25">
<input type="button"
       value="Get Value"
       onclick="javascript:iCallID = svcGetAppSettings.GetAppSettings.callService
                ('GetAppSettings',document.Form1.key.value, 500);">
</form>
<div id="lblResult"></div>
</body>
</html>
```

By globally declaring a call ID, we will be able to recognize the Web Service call when it returns results. This is most important when multiple calls to the same Web Service occur on a page.

```
var iCallID;
```

Our `init()` routine is called using the `onload` event. Using the `SvcGetAppSettings` <DIV> as our Web Service gateway, we tell it the location of the WSDL that defines the Web Service, as well as the name of the method to use (`GetAppSettings`). Applying the styles to the <DIV> allows us to prevent it from taking up any physical space on the page, as well as to attach it to the `webservice.htc` component. Lastly, using the `onresult` attribute, we assign the `evtAppSettings()` function to be the destination when the Web Service completes and returns a value.

```
function init()
{
  svcGetAppSettings.useService("http://localhost/PWS/AppB/↵
                         AppSettings/AppService.asmx?WSDL","GetAppSettings");
}

...

<body onload="init()">
<div id="svcGetAppSettings"
     style="display:none;behavior:url(webservice.htc)"
     onresult="evtAppSettings()"></div>
```

We have also defined a label where we will place our results when the Web Service completes:

```
<div id="lblResult"></div>
```

When the **Get Value** button is pressed, the behavior is called, placing the ID of the call into `iCallID`. Notice that we're passing the value of the `key` input field, and 500, which specifies a half-second delay.

```
<input type="button"
       value="Get Value"
       onclick="javascript:iCallID = svcGetAppSettings.GetAppSettings.callService
               ('GetAppSettings',document.Form1.key.value, 500);">
```

Once the Web Service completes, `evtAppSettings` on our web page is called. First, we check whether the ID of the result matches the one we're waiting for (`iCallID`), plus whether an error has been returned.

```
function evtAppSettings()
{
    // Error condition on this call
    if ((event.result.error) && (iCallID==event.result.id))
    {
        // Retrieve error properties
        var vCode   = event.result.errorDetail.code;
        var vString = event.result.errorDetail.string;
        var vRaw    = event.result.errorDetail.raw;

        // Would add a switch{} to handle various vCodes
    }
```

Next, if no error is returned and the ID matches `iCallID`, we process the results. If an empty value is returned, we respond with "No Value" and set the background of our receiving `<DIV>` to yellow (`#FFFF99`).

```
    // No error, confirm this is our call that is being returned
    else if ((!event.result.error) && (iCallID == event.result.id))
    {
       if (event.result.value == "") {
          // Display a default value, background of yellow
          lblResult.innerText = "No Value";
          lblResult.style.backgroundColor = "#FFFF99";
       }
       else
       {
          // Display the returned value, background of aqua
          lblResult.innerText = event.result.value;
          lblResult.style.backgroundColor = "#99FFFF";
       }
    }
```

The last case is that the call ID does not match the one returned. If this happens, we'll simply ignore it.

```
    else
    {
        // This result was fired by something other than our request
    }
}
```

Taking a look at this page in action:

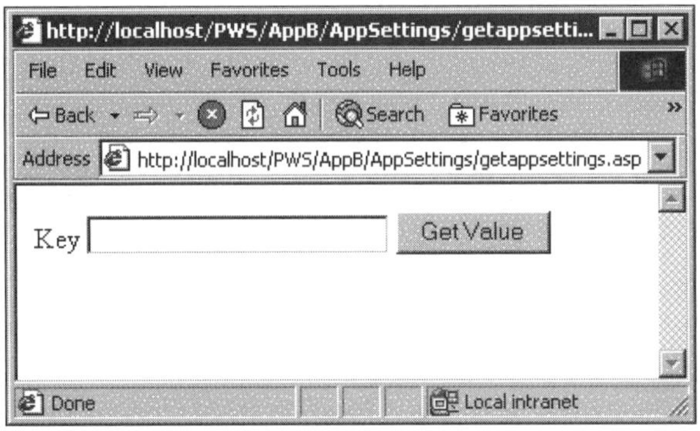

Entering "connectstring" and press the Get Value button:

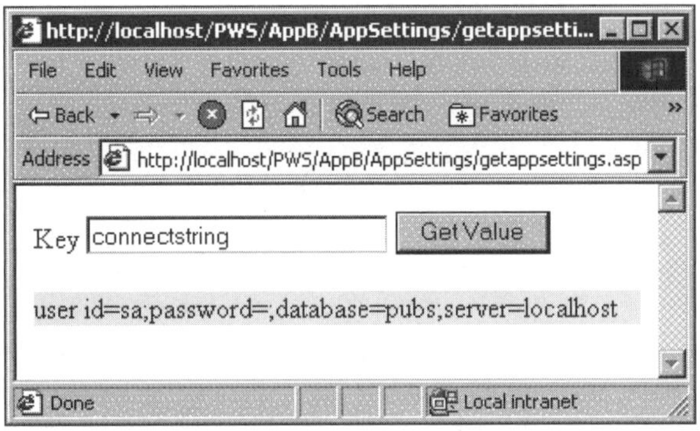

If we enter a key that doesn't exist, the results appear like this:

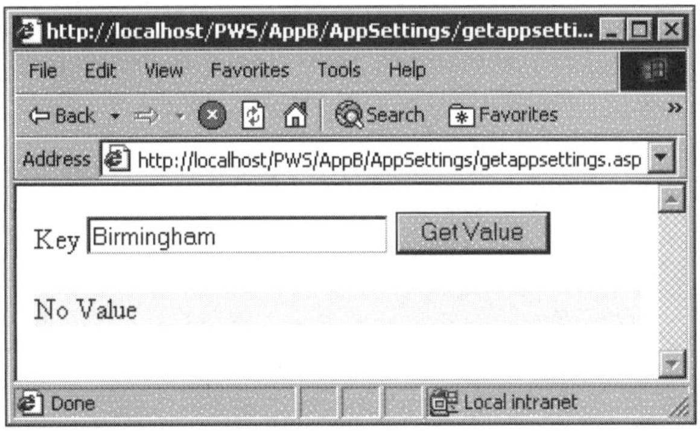

Sample Hotel Reservation Page

We can also demonstrate the use of the Web Service behavior on a page that simulates placing a hotel reservation. Keeping it simple, we'll create a short Web Service that returns whether a reservation is available or not, by saying that if the reservation is made more than thirty days in advance, it is always available. Otherwise, we'll deny the reservation. If only it worked this way in real life!

The code for our Reservation Web Service, `IsAvailable.asmx`, can be found in the `Reservation` folder of the download:

```
<WebMethod()> _
Public Function IsAvailable(ByVal dtStart As String, _
                            ByVal dtEnd As String) As String
  If Not Microsoft.VisualBasic.Information.IsDate(dtStart) Or _
           Not Microsoft.VisualBasic.Information.IsDate(dtEnd) Then
    Return "Please enter two valid dates."
  End If

  Dim Diff As Integer = DateDiff(DateInterval.Day, CDate(dtStart), _
                                 CDate(dtEnd))
  If Diff = 0 Then
    Return "ERROR: Dates are the same."
  ElseIf Diff < 0 Then
    Return "ERROR: Departure must be after the arrival."
  Else
    If DateDiff(DateInterval.Day, System.DateTime.Now(), _
              CDate(dtStart)) < 30 Then
      Return "Sorry, the hotel is booked."
    Else
      Return "Congratulations! Your room is now booked for " & Diff _
           & " night(s)."
    End If
  End If
End Function
```

After performing a few sanity checks (like checking for valid dates and correct order of arrival/departure), we hope to return a message congratulating the user for finding a room. Here's the code we use on our web page, `Hotel.htm`, which calls the Web Service behavior.

```
<html>
<script language="JavaScript">
var iCallID;
var iCallID2;

function init()
{
    DivSvcIsAvailable.useService("http://localhost/PWS/AppB/↴
                            Reservation/IsAvailable.asmx?WSDL","IsAvailable");
}

function evtIsAvailable()
{
    //if there is an error, and the call came from the call() in init()
    if((event.result.error)&&(iCallID==event.result.id))

    {
        //Pull the error information from the event.result.errorDetail properties
        window.alert(event.result.errorDetail.code);
        window.alert(event.result.errorDetail.string);
        window.alert(event.result.errorDetail.raw);
```

```
        //TODO: Add code to handle specific error codes here
    }
    //if there was no error, and the call came from the call() in init()
    else if((!event.result.error) && (iCallID == event.result.id))
    {
        lblResult.innerText = event.result.value;
        lblResult.style.backgroundColor = "#99FFFF";
    }
    else
    {
        alert("Something else fired the event!");
    }
}
  </script>
  <body onload="init()">
    <div id="DivSvcIsAvailable" style="behavior:url(webservice.htc)"
         onresult="evtIsAvailable()" style="display:none;">
    </div>
    <table width="100%" cellspacing="0" cellpadding="0" border="0">
      <tr>
        <td colspan="3" align="center">
          <img src="sunset.jpg" width="320" height="141">
        </td>
      </tr>
      <tr>
        <td width="23%">
           
        </td>
        <td width="54%">
          <form name="Form1" id="Form1">
            <table width="100%" cellspacing="0" cellpadding="0" border="1">
              <tr>
                <td width="100%">
                  <table width="100%" cellspacing="0" cellpadding="0">
                    <tr>
                      <td align="center" colspan="2">
                        <font face="arial"><i>Check Availability</i></font>
                      </td>
                    </tr>
                    <tr bgcolor="#FFFFEE">
                      <td>
                        <font face="arial">Arrival Date:</font>
                      </td>
                      <td>
                        <input type="text" name="arrival">
                      </td>
                    </tr>
                    <tr bgcolor="#FFFFDD">
                      <td>
                        <font face="arial">Departure Date:</font>
                      </td>
                      <td>
                        <input type="text" name="departure">
```

```
                        </td>
                      </tr>
                      <tr bgcolor="#FFFFCC">
                        <td align="center" colspan="2">
                          <input type="button" value="Check"
                                 onclick="javascript:iCallID=DivSvcIsAvailable.↵
                                         IsAvailable.callService('IsAvailable',↵
                                         document.Form1.arrival.value, ↵
                                         document.Form1.departure.value);"
                                 id="button1" name="button1">
                        </td>
                      </tr>
                    </table>
                  </td>
                </tr>
              </table>
            </form>
            <div align="center"
                 style="font-family:Tahoma;font-size:8pt;font-bold:True;↵
                        background-color:#FFFF99;"
                 id="lblResult">
            </div>
          </td>
          <td align="center" width="23%">
            <img src="hotel.jpg" width="162" height="171">
          </td>
        </tr>
      </table>
    </body>
    <script language="JavaScript">
    </script>
  </html>
```

After entering some sample data into our hotel page, our results will look like this:

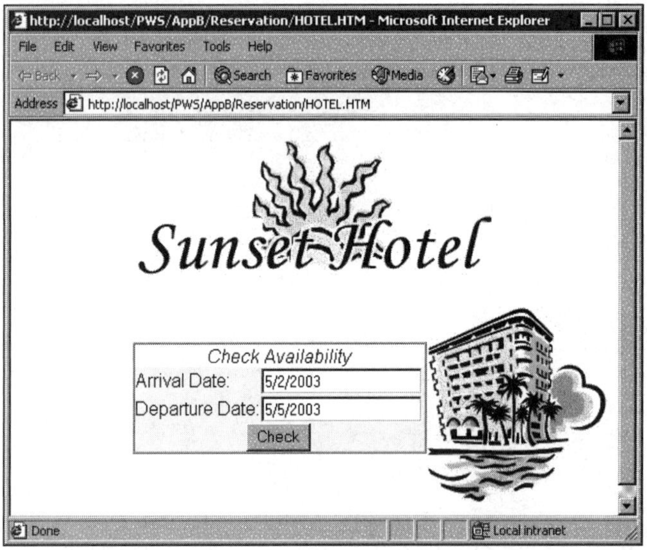

Entering dates out of order produces this result:

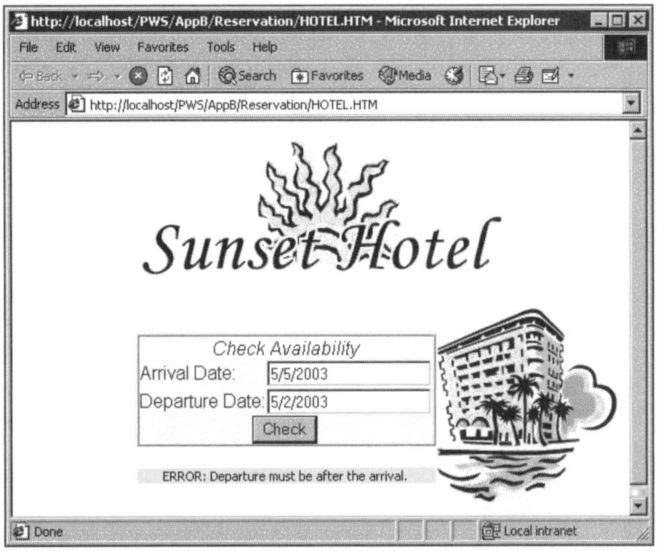

Entering dates less than 30 days from now but in the correct order also produces an error:

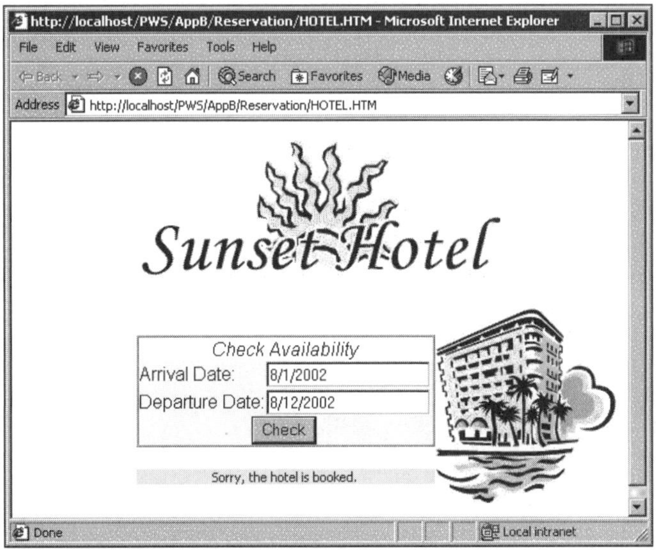

Summary

Internet Explorer 5 and later behaviors give us a way to reuse client-side code, apart from the presentation portion, in a way that is both simple and efficient, as we saw in our Sunset Hotel example. Using HTC files, behaviors are defined as components, and in our examples they attached themselves to various events that would be fired from tags to which the behavior is applied. Behaviors can range from minimal features, such as changing a font style, to extensive component definitions complete with properties and events.

The Web Service behavior, in particular, illustrates the potential of IE behaviors like nothing else. Not only can we retrieve data using this behavior, we can do all this without requiring a page refresh or other less desirable work. With the proliferation of Internet Explorer and the new-found power of client-accessible Web Services, the Web Service-integrated web pages will become increasingly prevalent.

Professional
ASP.NET
Web
Services

C

ASPToday Sample Article

ASPToday is an online solutions database for professional ASP programmers, delivering a growing collection of technical articles. Each article is written and reviewed by leading programmers to ensure that only up-to-date, relevant, and practical information is provided. This collection of unique articles makes ASPToday an invaluable tool for Just In Time solutions to everyday programming problems.

ASPToday provides you with:

- A new article every day
- A search engine based on index entries
- A growing Tips and Tricks archive
- Reference pages
- Access to over 700 archived articles
- Access to discussion forums where you can talk with fellow developers

We have included a sample article from ASPToday to illustrate the kind of content that is available on the site. A new article is published every weekday, with articles ranging from introductions to new technologies to in-depth looks at advanced techniques.

Find out more at www.asptoday.com

Using Object-Oriented Principles for Building a Web Service

By Danny Ryan, Tommy Ryan

In this article, we will show how to use traditional object-oriented principles to make your Web Services more maintainable, scalable, and reusable. We will walk you through an example of a Web Service where we apply some important object-oriented principles to create a better implementation of an application that uses Web Services. The application will show how to migrate a Web Service to a new multi-tiered architecture that uses interfaces and inheritance to implement the functionality for two system requirements.

Getting Started

Note that this article assumes that you have created a few simple Web Services. Please see the www.GotDotNet.com site if you need to get primed on Web Services. There is a section of GotDotNet that points you to resources for XML Web Services at http://www.gotdotnet.com/team/XMLWebServices/default.aspx. Also in this article, we will be using many of the object-oriented features of VB.NET.

Introduction to the Goal Server Web Service

Throughout this article, we are going to develop a couple of parts of a sample application that is used to generate goals for users via a Web Service. Let's take a look at a subset of the system requirements that we wish to implement for the first version of the Goal Server Web Service.

- System Requirement 1.1 – The system has the ability to return random daily goals via a Web Service
- System Requirement 1.2 – The system has the ability to return a goal list, based on a specified user, via a Web Service

The Data that Supports the Requirements

The Web Service for this article is built upon a simple database that stores goals for Users. The following diagram shows the tables involved and their relationships to each other.

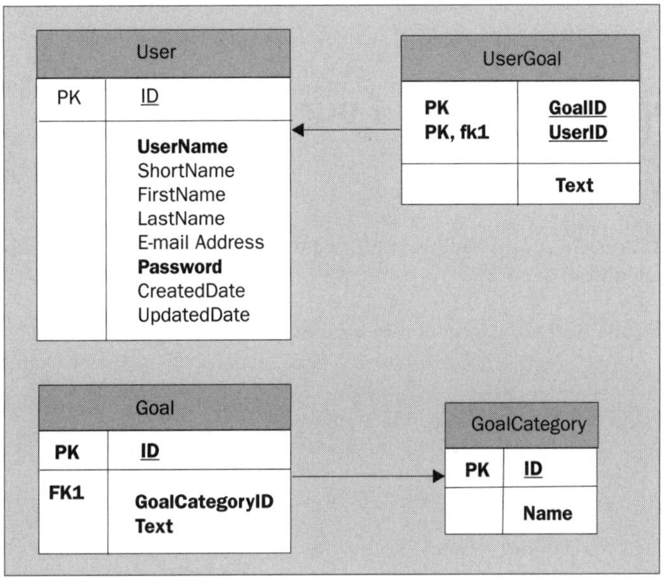

This database contains three stored procedures that the Web Services use to retrieve goals from the database. These are `getUserGoalByUserID`, `getGoalMaxID`, and `getGoalText`. The first stored procedure is for obtaining goals that a user has set, which are termed as a **UserGoal**. The second procedure is written to obtain the upper bound of a generic goal list. The last procedure is for returning the text of a specified generic goal. Generic goals are simply termed as a **Goal** in the system. Generic goals are an arbitrary list of goals stored as a starting point for users when they want to set their own goals. See the `CREATE PROCEDURE` statements below for what is in each procedure.

```
CREATE PROCEDURE getUserGoalByUserID
(@UserID int)
AS

SELECT
GoalID 'PKId', [Text]
FROM
UserGoal
WHERE
UserID= @UserID

CREATE PROCEDURE getGoalMaxID AS

SELECT
MAX(ID) AS MaxGoalID
FROM
Goal
```

```
CREATE PROCEDURE getGoalText
(@ID int)  AS

Select
[Text] from Goal
WHERE
ID = @ID
```

A Simple Implementation of our Requirements

Let's take a look at a simple realization of our requirements. With this implementation, we are going to put all of the code into the Web Service.

Looking at the `FatGoalService` Web Service, we find the `GetRandomDailyGoal` Web Method. This code implements Requirement 1.1.

Take a look at the code necessary to generate a random daily goal.

```
' Web Method that retrieves a random Daily Goal
<WebMethod()> Public Function GetRandomDailyGoal() As String
  Dim conMLG As New SqlConnection(GetConnectionString())
  Dim cmdMLG As New SqlCommand()
  Dim drGoal As SqlDataReader
  Dim intMaxGoalID As Integer
  Dim rndGoalID As New Random()
  Dim intRandomGoalID As Integer
  Dim strGoalText As String

  ' Open the database connection
  conMLG.Open()

  ' Set up the command for execution
  cmdMLG.Connection = conMLG
  cmdMLG.CommandType = CommandType.Text

  ' Run the first command to get the upper bound of the current goal list
  cmdMLG.CommandText = "EXEC getGoalMaxID"
  intMaxGoalID = cmdMLG.ExecuteScalar()

  ' With the max Goal ID, obtain a random number that can be
  ' used to retrieve a goal
  intRandomGoalID = rndGoalID.Next(1, intMaxGoalID)

  ' Now run the command again with the random ID to retrieve the Goal Text
  cmdMLG.CommandText = "EXEC getGoalText @ID=" + intRandomGoalID.ToString()
  strGoalText = cmdMLG.ExecuteScalar()

  Return strGoalText

End Function
```

Note that we are using the `Random` .NET Framework class to generate a random number with an upper bound of the goal list in the `Goal` table. Also, note that the basic architecture involved here is a Web Method calling directly to a stored procedure that returns the results.

Next, take a look at the Web Method for System Requirement 1.2, retrieving the goal list for a user.

```
' Web Method that retrieves a goal list by user id
<WebMethod()> Public Function GetGoalsByUserID(ByVal intUserID As Integer) _
                                                      As DataSet
  Dim dsGoal As DataSet = New DataSet()
  Dim conMLG As New SqlConnection(GetConnectionString())
  Dim cmdMLG As New SqlCommand()

  cmdMLG.Connection = conMLG
  cmdMLG.CommandType = CommandType.Text
  cmdMLG.CommandText = "EXEC GetUserGoalByUserID @UserID=" _
                      + intUserID.ToString()

  Dim daMLG As SqlDataAdapter = New SqlDataAdapter(cmdMLG)

  conMLG.Open()

  daMLG.Fill(dsGoal)

  conMLG.Close()

  Return dsGoal

End Function
```

Again, we find this Web Method uses the same basic architecture. Now that we've seen the code for the Web Service, let's go ahead and invoke the Web Methods. We can do this with the built-in test harness that ASP.NET provides. We can test the Web Service by directly accessing the `*.asmx` file. ASP.NET will intercept the request for this resource and display the Web Methods that are available on our Web Service.

First let's select the `GetRandomDailyGoal` method. If we submit the "Invoke" button, we will get an XML response from the `GetRandomDailyGoal` Web Method.

Here we see that a goal is generated. Hit refresh a few of times to verify that the goal returned is randomly selected.

Next, invoke the `GetGoalsByUserID`, passing in 1 for the `intUserID`. Scrolling down the XML to the `DataSet` representation we see that a goal list is generated for the user based on the User ID:

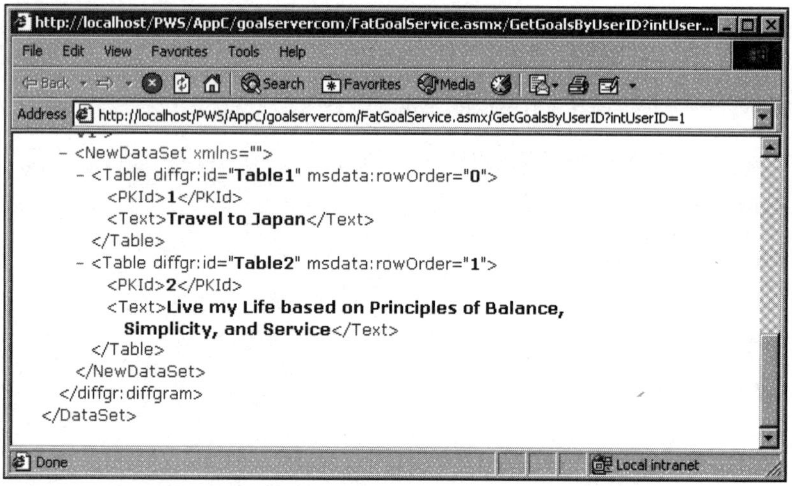

How Can We Improve This Implementation?

If this is your first Web Service, this represents at least a good morning of work (earning you at least a second cup of coffee). But, in this article, our goal is to create a Web Service that is more maintainable, scalable, and reusable. With all of the code in the Web Service, we run into a number of issues that impede these goals. These issues become even more evident as our application grows or when the requirements change.

Factors

This example is not very complex, but what we do with the improved implementation will allow us to address maintainability, scalability, and reusability for future growth and changes to the application. Let's discuss these factors and then move onto what we changed in the improved version of the application.

Maintainable

First, this code might be considered easy to maintain because it is in one file. This is fine for a simple Web Service, but as our application grows we should not have all logical layers of the application in one file. If we need to make any changes to the application, only one person at a time can do this. As this application grows, we will find that our coding will require copying and pasting of code (since we will most likely do the same type of data access code). If we find that we want to change the data access code, we will have to go and change every Web Method. This leads to inefficiencies. We could solve this by putting these shared routines into private functions inside of our Web Service. This would partially address the maintainability issue in our Web Service. We still have the issue of contention when we need multiple developers working on one file. Therefore, we need to separate these routines into logical layers (you will see this later in the article).

Disclaimer: For this sample application you could argue that we have made it more difficult to maintain. We have moved the implementation to a separate library, and now we have more layers of code to maintain. Well, that is true, and you will just have to trust us when we say that as the application grows this code separation will pay off. If you are very confident that you will not have to reuse any of the code that is in the Web Service and the code is small (like in this example), then you might find that distributing your code into several classes is not the right move. For the purpose of this article, we are assuming that your applications will grow and requirements will change.

Scalable

All of our code is contained within the same Web Services code-behind file (`FatGoalService.asmx.vb`). You might ask "What's wrong with having all your code in one Web Service?", because you know that it will be a compiled class when it is run in the CLR (Common Language Runtime). You are correct, but if we need to address bottlenecks in the code, we will have to distribute the code into separate classes that can be put in different assemblies. By extracting out the code into separate classes, we will be able to distribute the application as we wish. For example, with this architecture we could leverage the use of Component Services. This would allow us to take advantage of features such as object pooling. Also, if we have them in separate components, we can address bottlenecks in processing a request by distributing components across multiple servers.

Again, with an example of this size it might seem like more trouble than it is worth, but we are looking to set up an architecture that can grow with time.

Reusable

In the future, we may wish to create new applications that could benefit from the logic and data access that is embedded in our `FatGoalService` Web Service. By putting our code into several different classes we have the potential to reuse parts of the application. For example, the site www.mylifetimegoals.com reuses the data access components that are used by the `ThinGoalService` Web Service (the new version of the `FatGoalService` that we will show later in the article).

You probably notice from these benefits that many of the reasons why you built multi-tier applications with your Windows DNA and/or Windows .NET applications also apply to creating your Web Services. Web Services represent a new way to interface our applications and the object-oriented software development practices still apply.

Using Object-Oriented Programming Features

To respond to the challenges of creating maintainable, scalable, and reusable applications, we are going to demonstrate the central principles of object-oriented programming – abstraction, encapsulation, and inheritance.

Abstraction

Abstraction as defined by www.whatis.com is "the process of taking away or removing characteristics from something in order to reduce it to a set of essential characteristics". In the `ThinGoalService` we have abstracted a Goal Interface (we will talk more about interfaces in the "Inheritance" section) that is used for the two essential types of Goals in our Goal Server, `SystemGoal` and `UserGoal`. The abstraction of a Goal Interface allows the programmer of the Web Services (or of an ASP.NET Web Forms application) to access all goals in a uniform manner. This helps with providing consistency across the application, which will produce more maintainable applications in the long run. We do not see this benefit immediately with this application, but as our system grows we will reap the benefit.

Encapsulation

Encapsulation is the process of hiding the implementation behind an established interface (method or property signature). Encapsulation allows you to hide the complexity of what is implemented in your method or property procedure (for simplicity's sake, we will call these **operations**). With proper encapsulation, we reduce the dependencies between objects and have the ability to change implementation behind an operation without affecting the consumer of our object.

For our `ThinGoalService` implementation, each logical layer (Business, Data access, and Data layers) is encapsulated into separate classes. This helps us down the road when we want to reuse parts of the system. Also, we have included a `Resource` class. This encapsulates the common functions that we will need to provide for the application in general. The first member of this class is the `configConnectionString` property procedure. This hides the complexity of pulling the connection string from the `web.config` file. This `Resource` class will be used in this application for common functions that can be used in this application and other applications in the future (see the end of *Designing and Implementing the Data Classes, Data Access Layer, and Utility Classes* section for the code for this class).

Inheritance

When we speak of inheritance, we need to be clear on what type of inheritance we are using. The two types of inheritance are implementation and interface inheritance.

In VB6 we had interface inheritance, but not implementation inheritance. Interface inheritance allows you to inherit the interface or signature of an object, but not the code. In VB6 we could define our own interfaces with a Public Non-creatable Class (placing signatures to empty operations). This was a hack at an interface and true interfaces had to be created in IDL (a different language). Now in VB.NET the language truly supports the definitions of interfaces (see *Designing and Implementing the Goal Interface and the Business Layer* section of this article for a code example that implements an Interface). We use interface inheritance in the business layer to prepare for upcoming versions of the application where we will want to share the same interface among the various goal types.

Implementation inheritance, contrary to interface inheritance, does allow us to reuse or inherit code. This is a big benefit to VB.NET over what you can do in VB6. We will take advantage of this object-oriented feature in our data classes by inheriting the `System.Data.DataSet` .NET Framework Class.

Now let's look at the code in the Web Service that uses this new architecture.

High Level Design of Improved Architecture

For this article, we're going to simplify things a little and reuse the data, tables, and stored procedures that we used in our `FatWebService.asmx`. Here's where most of the reuse of code ends, though. From here we will take code that needs to be distributed and place it a namespace called `GoalLibrary`. `GoalServerCom` is the namespace that contains the definition of the `WebMethods` that are available for the Web Service. `GoalServerCom` depends on the `GoalLibrary` for business services and data services.

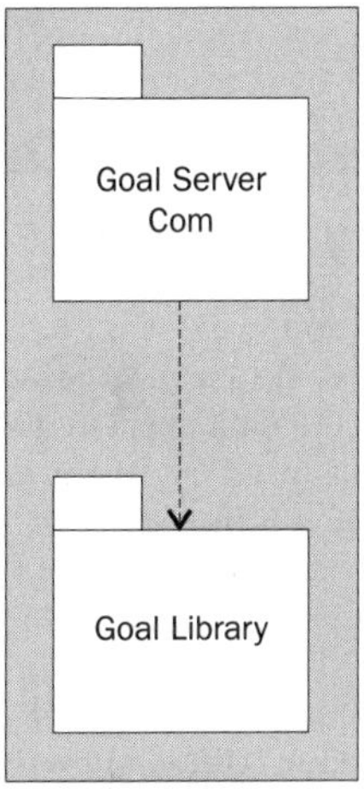

The `GoalLibrary` is structured as follows:

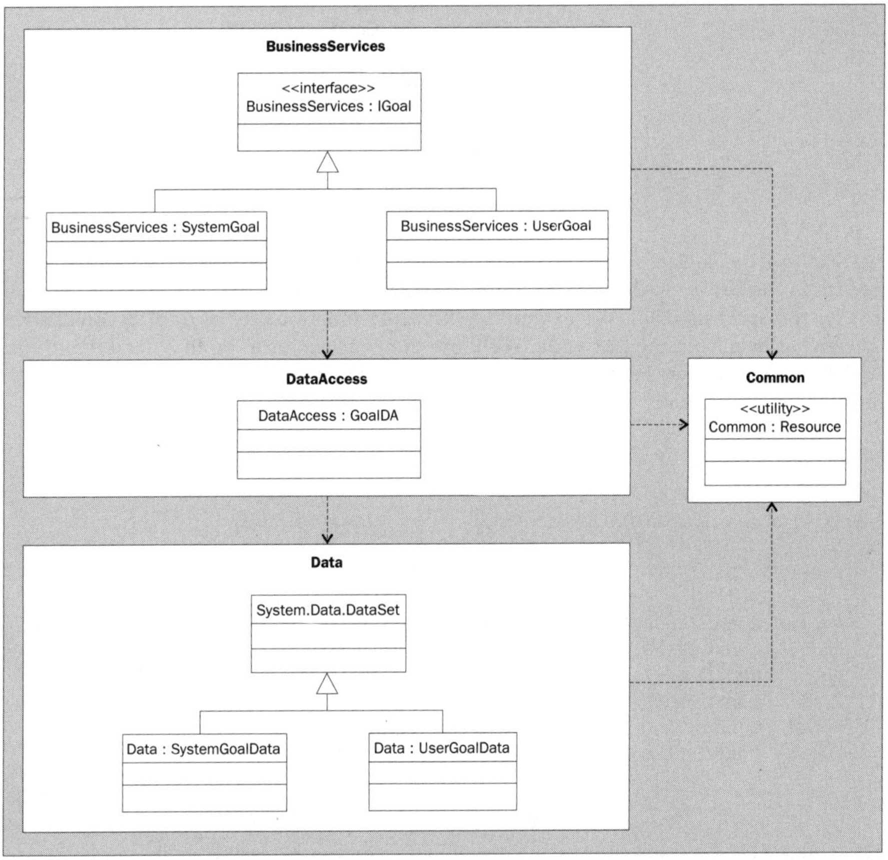

Now let's start digging into each layer.

Designing and Implementing the Data Classes, Data Access Layer, and Utility Classes

With the goal of improving our application, we'll want to take all of the data access code in our Web Service and put it into a **data access layer** (in `DataAccess.vb`). We will use this layer for retrieving and storing persistent data. Along with the data access layer, we will go ahead and create a **data class** (in `Data.vb`) to represent the System Goals (used by Requirement 1.1) and the User Goals (used by Requirement 1.2). Finally, we will create a **utility class** (in `Resource.vb`) for our application. Although this class won't be doing much initially, you can expect it to grow in the future, as your application requires shared utility functions for your components.

Let's look at what we have for the `SystemGoalData` and `UserGoalData` data classes. Since they are quite similar, let's just focus on `SystemGoalData`. Here is the class diagram for `SystemGoalData`:

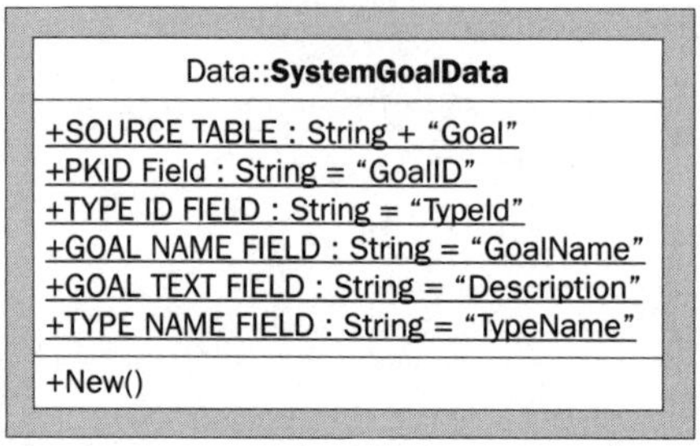

The `SystemGoalData` class will be used to represent System Goals. The class inherits `System.Data.Dataset` so that we can store structured data from the database (reusing what .NET provides for transporting data). We extend the `DataSet` functionality by adding constants that we use when retrieving data from the `DataSet`. We'll use the constructor to build a dataset and then set the class to the created dataset. Take a look at the `Data.vb` file for the `UserGoalData` data class implementation; it's basically the same.

Here's the `SystemGoalData` class's code:

```
Public Class SystemGoalData

  Inherits DataSet

  Public Const SOURCE_TABLE As String = "Goal"
  Public Const PKID_FIELD As String = "GoalID"
  Public Const TYPE_ID_FIELD As String = "TypeID"
  Public Const GOAL_NAME_FIELD As String = "GoalName"
  Public Const GOAL_TEXT_FIELD As String = "Text"
  Public Const TYPE_NAME_FIELD As String = "TypeName"


  Public Sub New()
    Dim table As DataTable = New DataTable(SOURCE_TABLE)
```

```
        With table.Columns
            .Add(PKID_FIELD, GetType(System.Int32))
            .Add(TYPE_ID_FIELD, GetType(System.Int32))
            .Add(GOAL_NAME_FIELD, GetType(System.String))
            .Add(GOAL_TEXT_FIELD, GetType(System.String))
            .Add(TYPE_NAME_FIELD, GetType(System.String))
        End With

        Me.Tables.Add(table)

    End Sub

End Class
```

Next, let's design and build the data access layer that will use these data classes. Here's what we designed for the data access layer:

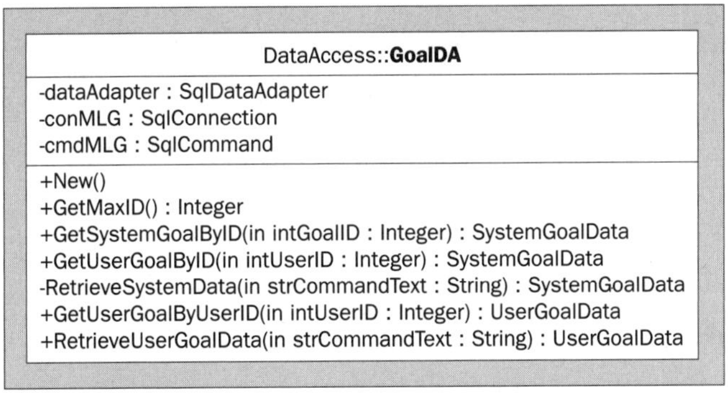

DataAccess::**GoalDA**
-dataAdapter : SqlDataAdapter
-conMLG : SqlConnection
-cmdMLG : SqlCommand
+New()
+GetMaxID() : Integer
+GetSystemGoalByID(in intGoalID : Integer) : SystemGoalData
+GetUserGoalByID(in intUserID : Integer) : SystemGoalData
-RetrieveSystemData(in strCommandText : String) : SystemGoalData
+GetUserGoalByUserID(in intUserID : Integer) : UserGoalData
+RetrieveUserGoalData(in strCommandText : String) : UserGoalData

In the data access layer, we'll share a connection (`conMLG`) and command (`cmdMLG`) that are initialized in the constructor event of the class.

Continuing to focus on Requirement 1.1, we see that we use the `GetMaxID` function for getting the highest Goal ID in the system (note that the assumption is that the Goal ID's will be contiguous from Goal ID 1 to the maximum Goal ID). This number will be used as an upper bound for generating a random goal number.

```
        Public Function GetMaxID() As Integer
        Dim intMaxGoalID As Integer

        ' Setup up the command for execution
        cmdMLG.CommandType = CommandType.Text

        ' Run the first command to get the upper bound of the current goal list
        cmdMLG.CommandText = "EXEC getGoalMaxID"

        conMLG.Open()
        intMaxGoalID = cmdMLG.ExecuteScalar()
        conMLG.Close()

        Return intMaxGoalID
    End Function
```

With Requirement 1.1, we return a random daily goal. In the data access layer, we have the exposed public function GetSystemGoalByID in the data access to return a System Goal. This method simply calls the private RetrieveSystemData function.

```
Public Function GetSystemGoalByID(ByVal intGoalID As Integer) _
                                  As SystemGoalData
  Return RetrieveSystemData("EXEC getGoalText @ID=" + intGoalID.ToString())
End Function
```

Within RetrieveSystemData, we will use our data class to get a system goal.

```
Private Function RetrieveSystemData(ByVal strCommandText As String) _
                                    As SystemGoalData

  Dim dataSystemGoal As SystemGoalData = New SystemGoalData()

  cmdMLG.CommandType = CommandType.Text
  cmdMLG.CommandText = strCommandText

  Dim daMLG As SqlDataAdapter = New SqlDataAdapter(cmdMLG)

  conMLG.Open()
  daMLG.Fill(dataSystemGoal)
  conMLG.Close()

  Return dataSystemGoal

End Function
```

Note that the return type on both the GetSystemGoalByID and RetrieveSystemData is SystemGoalData. Therefore, we will need to import the GoalLibrary.Data namespace for the data access layer.

Finally, we have to reuse that connection code we were so proud of in our FatWebService example. With our improved design, let's put it in a common utility class. Here's the code for Resource.vb:

```
Imports System.Web
Imports System.Web.Configuration
Imports System.Collections.Specialized

Namespace GoalLibrary.Common

  Public Class Resources

    Public Shared ReadOnly Property ConnectionString() As String
      Get
        ConnectionString = _
   System.Configuration.ConfigurationSettings.AppSettings("MLGConnectionString")
      End Get
    End Property

  End Class

End Namespace
```

We'll use this in our data access layer, so we can't forget to import the `GoalLibrary.Common` namespace in our data access class.

We have now designed and constructed the data, data access, and utility components. Let's continue on to the next tier and address the business layer.

Designing and Implementing the Goal Interface and the Business Layer

When building the data classes, we created a class for System Goals and for User Goals. System Goals are goals that are not associated to a specific user. If we look at the database, System Goals are stored in the Goal table. User Goals, on the other hand, are stored in the `UserGoal` table and have a one-to-many relationship with the User table.

Although the System and User Goals may be different, they do share some attributes and operations. We want the Goal interface to be reusable for both System goals and User goals. Therefore, we need to determine the attributes and operations that are common to all goal types. To keep it simple, we came up with only a couple of operations – `Add`, `Delete`, `Update`, and `GetItem`. Note that you could also implement attributes, although we won't cover that in this article.

Here is a look at the Goal Interface implementation:

```
Namespace GoalLibrary.Interfaces

  Interface IGoal
    Function Add(ByVal strGoalText As String) As Integer

    Sub Delete(ByVal intGoalID As Integer)

    Sub Update(ByVal intGoalID As Integer, ByVal strGoalText As String)

    Function GetItem(ByVal intGoalID As Integer) As DataSet

  End Interface

End Namespace
```

Now, let's continue to design the business services. We will focus on the `SystemGoal` class. Because we are implementing the `Goal` interface, we will need to include all of the operations from the interface (`Add`, `Delete`, `Update`, and `GetItem`). We know that we will need a function for getting a random goal, so we can extend the interface to include a method for this purpose (called `GetRandomGoal`).

Here we see the class diagram:

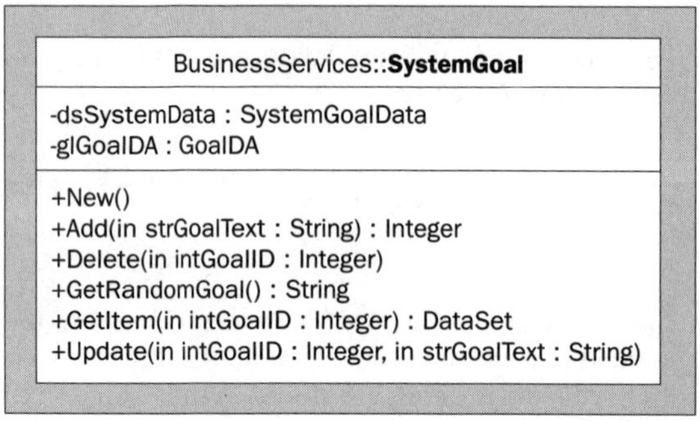

BusinessServices::SystemGoal
-dsSystemData : SystemGoalData
-glGoalDA : GoalDA
+New()
+Add(in strGoalText : String) : Integer
+Delete(in intGoalID : Integer)
+GetRandomGoal() : String
+GetItem(in intGoalID : Integer) : DataSet
+Update(in intGoalID : Integer, in strGoalText : String)

Moving forward to coding the `SystemGoal` class, we know that we will need to make sure that we have imported `GoalLibrary.Data`, `GoalLibrary.DataAccess`, `GoalLibrary.Interfaces`. Let's take a close look at the code involved in the `SystemGoal` class.

```
Public Class SystemGoal
```

To implement the `IGoal` interface, we add:

```
  Implements IGoal
```

Next, we're going to declare and instantiate some private variables for the System Goals and for retrieving the number of goals.

```
  Private dsSystemData As SystemGoalData
  Private glGoalDA As GoalDA

  Public Sub New()
    dsSystemData = New SystemGoalData()
    glGoalDA = New GoalDA()
  End Sub
```

Here's the core function for the class that returns the random goal.

```
  Public Function GetRandomGoal() As String
    ' You must first get the upper bound of the GoalID
    ' (assumption is that Goal IDs are
    ' continuous from 1 to the max value in the database.
    Dim intMaxGoalID As Integer
    Dim intRandomGoalID As Integer
    Dim randomGoalID As Random = New Random()

    intMaxGoalID = glGoalDA.GetMaxID()

    ' With the max Goal ID, obtain a random number that can be
    ' used to retrieve a goal
    intRandomGoalID = randomGoalID.Next(1, intMaxGoalID)
```

```
    dsSystemData = GetItem(intRandomGoalID)

    Return _
     dsSystemData.Tables("Table").Rows(0).Item(SystemGoalData.GOAL_TEXT_FIELD)

  End Function
```

Finally, let's add all of the functions from the `IGoal` interface.

```
  Public Function Add(ByVal strGoalText As String) As Integer _
                                                  Implements IGoal.Add
    ' Implementation goes here
  End Function

  Public Sub Delete(ByVal intGoalID As Integer) Implements IGoal.Delete
    ' Implementation goes here
  End Sub

  Public Sub Update(ByVal intGoalID As Integer, ByVal strGoalText As String) _
                                                      Implements IGoal.Update
    ' Implementation goes here
  End Sub
```

Note that the `GetItem` is the only function that we need to meet Requirements 1.1 and 1.2.

```
  Public Function GetItem(ByVal intGoalID As Integer) _
                          As System.Data.DataSet Implements IGoal.GetItem
    ' Perform validation (if necessary)

    dsSystemData = glGoalDA.GetSystemGoalByID(intGoalID)

    If Not dsSystemData Is Nothing Then
      If dsSystemData.Tables("Table").Rows.Count = 1 Then
        'see if there is really a client
        Return dsSystemData
      Else
        Throw New Exception("Random goal could not be retrieved.")
      End If
    End If

  End Function
```

Our Improved Web Service – Fifty Pounds Thinner

Here's the fun part. Now that we have moved the data, utility, and business services, our Web Service code becomes very clean. Here's the Web Service code-behind file contents:

```
Imports System.Web.Services
Imports GoalLibrary.BusinessServices
Imports GoalLibrary.Data
Imports GoalLibrary.Common
```

```
Public Class ThinGoalService
  Inherits System.Web.Services.WebService

  ' Web Method that retrieves a random Daily Goal
  <WebMethod()> Public Function GetRandomDailyGoal() As String
    Dim glSystemGoal As SystemGoal = New SystemGoal()
    Return glSystemGoal.GetRandomGoal()

  End Function

  ' Web Method that retrieves a goal list by user id
  <WebMethod()> Public Function GetGoalsByUserID(ByVal intUserID As _
                                      Integer) As DataSet
    Dim glUserGoal As UserGoal = New UserGoal()
    Dim dsGoals As UserGoalData = New UserGoalData()

    Return glUserGoal.GetList(intUserID)

  End Function

End Class
```

What Next?

Now that we have improved our Web Service, we are ready to consume the service. You can do this from a Web client, Windows Form, or perhaps even a Console Application. The process for doing this depends on the tools available to you. Visual Studio .NET makes this process quite simple, although it is not difficult to do without Visual Studio .NET. Either way, a proxy class must be created in order to consume the Web Service. Once you have the proxy class, you can declare and instantiate a variable of type Web Service like you would do when declaring and instantiating any other class.

Conclusion

In this article, we took a Web Service (appropriately named `FatGoalService`) and applied a few object-oriented techniques to improve the implementation. The `FatGoalService` was migrated to a new architecture that uses implementation and interface inheritance to satisfy the system requirements. We extracted out a data class, utility class, data access layer, and business layer to create an architecture that can grow in the future. Although these classes are all in one assembly, we can easily move our `*.vb` files that contain classes into separate assemblies (versus having to extract the code from **Fat** Web Methods).

Note that with the example as simple and small as we have in this article, the benefits of using object-oriented techniques may not be as apparent as in a large application (in fact, with a small example it may seem like more trouble than it's worth for the benefits reaped). But, again, as our application scope increases, we will reap the benefits of implementing an architecture that will grow with time.

This article is a sample of the information that is available on ASPToday. A new article is published every weekday.

For more information visit:

http://www.asptoday.com

PROFESSIONAL
ASP.NET
WEB
SERVICES
PROFESSIONAL ASP.NET
WEB SERVICES

Index

A Guide to the Index

The index is arranged hierarchically, in alphabetical order, with symbols preceding the letter A. Most second-level entries and many third-level entries also occur as first-level entries. This is to ensure that users will find the information they require however they choose to search for it.

Symbols

A

B

C

E

F

G

J

K

L

M

N

O

Q

R

S

T

U

V

W

X

Notes

Notes

Notes

Notes

Notes

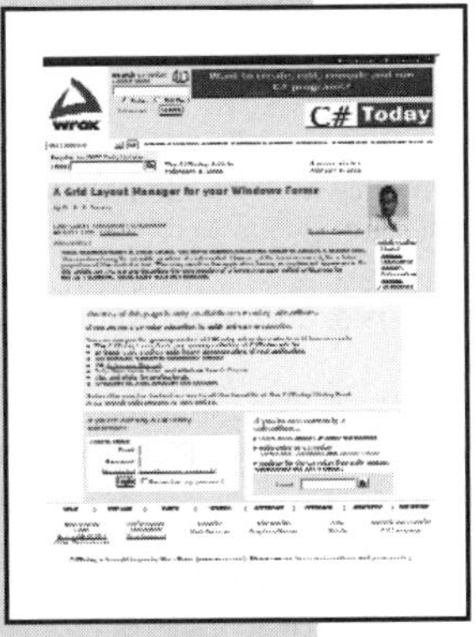

wrox **wrox**base

Got more Wrox books than you can carry around?

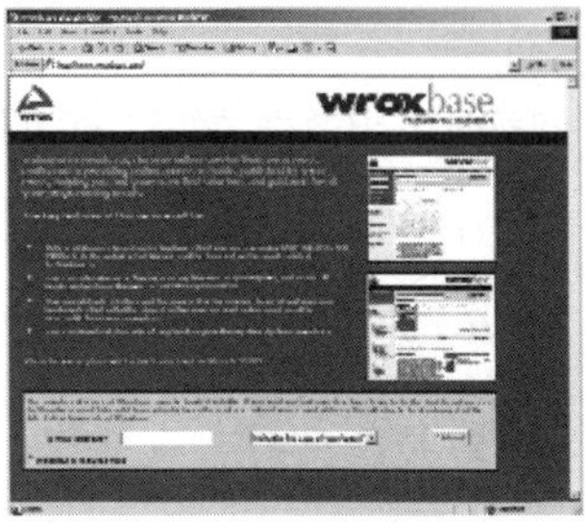

Wroxbase is the new online service from Wrox Press. Dedicated to providing online access to books published by Wrox Press, helping you and your team find solutions and guidance for all your programming needs.

The key features of this service will be:

- Different libraries based on technologies that you use everyday (ASP 3.0, XML, SQL 2000, etc.). The initial set of libraries will be focused on Microsoft-related technologies.
- You can subscribe to as few or as many libraries as you require, and access all books within those libraries as and when you need to.
- You can add notes (either just for yourself or for anyone to view) and your own bookmarks that will all be stored within your account online, and so will be accessible from any computer.
- You can download the code of any book in your library directly from Wroxbase

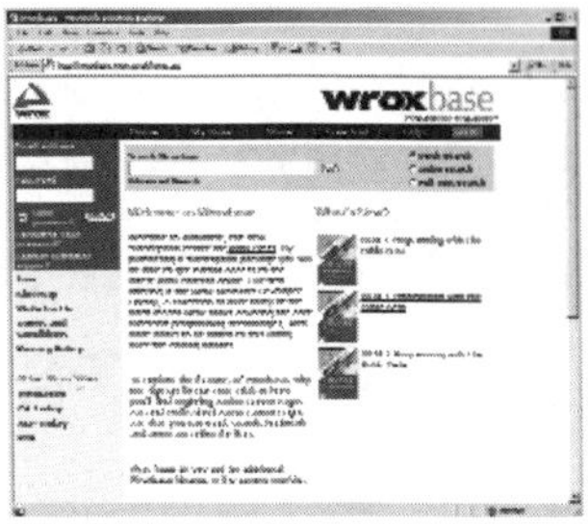

Visit the site at: www.wroxbase.com

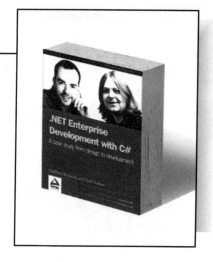